Presidential Elections, 1789–2000

CQ PRESS

A Division of Congressional Quarterly Inc.
Washington, D.C.

CQ Press

1255 22nd Street, N.W., Suite 400, Washington, D.C. 20037

Phone, 202-729-1900
Toll-free, 1-866-4CQ-PRESS (1-866-427-7737)

www.cqpress.com

Printed and bound in the United States of America

06   05   04   03   02   5   4   3   2   1

The paper used in this publication meets the minimum requirements of the American National Standard for Information Sciences—Permanence of Paper for Printed Library Materials, ANSI Z39.48-1992.

Cover illustration credits (clockwise from top right): Library of Congress; AP/Wide World Photos; AP/Wide World Photos; Reuters; White House/Bill Fitz-Patrick

Library of Congress Cataloging-in-Publication Data

in process

1-56802-790-7

Contents

Preface

The election of a president has evolved into the most dramatic political event in the United States. Every four years for more than two hundred years, the country has undergone a hectic nominating process based on rhetoric, partisan maneuvering, and character analysis as ambitious politicians vie for the nation's, and perhaps the world's, most important job.

Over the years the increase in the number of Americans eligible to participate in the choosing of the president has been one of the most striking measurements of the growth of democracy in the United States. From 1789 to 2000 there have been fifty-four presidential elections. All of these elections have been decided by the electoral college, but in the past forty-five the electors—if not the candidate—have been chosen by popular vote. After the 1870 ratification of the Fifteenth Amendment, which prohibited denying the right to vote "on account of race, color, or previous servitude," elections have been open to all races, although it took another nearly one hundred years and the Twenty-fourth Amendment against poll taxes and other voting laws to secure this right for all. The Nineteenth Amendment, ratified in 1920, opened the past twenty-two presidential elections to women voters. Since ratification in 1971, the Twenty-sixth Amendment has allowed eighteen-year-olds to vote in eight elections.

Despite the continual widening of the base of qualified voters, the last half of the twentieth century witnessed an opposing trend: a decline in electorate turnout. In 1992 more than 100 million Americans went to the polls to cast votes for president, yet that number represented only 71 percent of those registered to vote and only 55 percent of those eligible to vote. For the 1996 presidential contest only 96.2 million turned out to vote. This election was the first time since 1924 that voter turnout in a presidential race dropped below 50 percent. This decline was surprising in light of passage of the 1993 "motor-voter" law, which made voter registration easier for millions of Americans. The number increased in the 2000 contest to 105 million.

The history of presidential elections has been the subject of countless volumes, monographs, and dissertations as well as articles in academic journals. Nevertheless, it is difficult to find a single book that comprehensively and succinctly covers the basic facts and figures on the electoral college, popular vote returns, presidential primaries, nominations of major and minor party candidates, and biographical data on the candidates.

Presidential Elections 1789–2000 is a unique collection of reference material spanning the time from George Washington's first election as president in 1789 to Republican George W. Bush's election in 2000. It includes popular vote returns for president from 1824 to 1916 obtained from the Inter-University Consortium for Political and Social Research at the University of Michigan. CQ Press has updated this material with data on the presidential elections from 1920 to 2000.

The introduction provides a general overview of the changing presidential selection process and looks at the background of those leaders who have run for and have been elected president. A governorship, the vice presidency, or a U.S. Senate seat continue to be the most popular backgrounds for candidates who are launching presidential bids.

Following a chronology of presidential elections, the next section discusses the origins and development of the presidential primary, which by the 1970s had assumed preeminent importance in the presidential selection process. Overshadowing the caucus method of choosing delegates to a national convention, the primary has become the national stage where the major parties' presidential candidates are chosen.

The expanding role that the popular vote came to play in the election process is examined next. On the first Tuesday after the first Monday in November (a date established in 1845), voters go to the polls to elect the president. Although the voters are actually choosing presidential electors rather than the president, the focus of public attention is the popular vote returns.

Tables provide popular vote returns for the top four candidates for president from 1824 to 2000. These tables are presented in an easily readable format displaying the names and party affiliations of the candidates; state-by-state breakdowns of the total vote and percentage for each candidate; the total vote and winning plurality in each state; and the national totals including the national plurality of the leading popular vote candidate.

The final section of the book examines the constitutional origins and historical development of the electoral college, the uniquely American system of electing presidents. The section details complex and little-known methods used in the various states through 1832 to choose presidential electors, recounts historical anomalies in the functioning of the electoral college, and discusses reasons why a state's electoral votes frequently have been divided among several candidates. It covers the two occasions when a president was elected by the House of Representatives: Thomas Jefferson's close victory over Aaron Burr in 1800 and John Quincy Adams's election from a field of four strong candidates in 1825. It also explains procedures for counting and challenging electoral votes in Congress and de- scribes the famous 1877 Tilden-Hayes contest, which was de- cided by one electoral vote, and the 2000 Bush-Gore contest, which was decided by five electoral votes. This section con- cludes with a discussion of presidential disability and the ratifi- cation of the Twenty-fifth Amendment to the Constitution.

Electoral maps and tables display all electoral college results since 1789. Electoral vote totals for vice president from 1804 to 2000 are listed separately.

The book concludes with a biographical directory of presi- dential and vice-presidential candidates, a bibliographical list for further reading, and a comprehensive index.

Introduction

THE U.S. SYSTEM OF SELECTING a president and vice president through indirect means is perhaps more complicated than it needs to be. But it has worked with few major repairs for more than two hundred years, generally satisfying the citizenry and meeting the nation's changing needs.

The election happens every four years and permits the peaceful transfer of power or continuation of the status quo for four more years, no matter how bitter or divisive the campaign that preceded it. Indeed, the American electoral system differs from those of other nations and, for all its flaws, is the envy of many other countries. From time to time, however, pressure mounts for abolishing the electoral college system in favor of the direct popular election process used in other major democracies. After each such wave of protest, the demands for reform have gradually faded and the electoral college has survived into the twenty-first century.

Nevertheless, significant changes have taken place within the system. As the nation and the electorate have grown and technology has evolved, presidential elections have become more expensive, costing an estimated $1.2 billion in 2000. Because of the high costs, money and its abuses account for the biggest continuing blemish on the system, despite the myriad campaign finance reforms enacted since the 1970s to avoid corruption and lessen the influence of special interests.

On the more positive side, presidential nominations have become more open and representative of the voters at large. Party bosses no longer dictate the choice of nominees. Instead, the nominations are won through a hard-fought series of primary elections and party caucuses, where rank-and-file party members have an opportunity to express their preference. Once forums for determining who would head the presidential ticket, national party conventions today perform different functions, including ratification of the nominations won in the primaries.

As televised spectaculars, the conventions remain important to the parties' public relations efforts during the intense weeks before the November election. Although ratings have dropped in recent years, millions of people still watch the conventions on television and major political parties try to capture and hold as much of that audience as possible. With expert advice they have streamlined the proceedings to showcase their nominees in prime time as the countdown begins to election day. In these final campaign stages, today's nominees usually keep intact the organizations they built to help them survive the primaries. These increasingly professional organizations are made up of the candidate, his or her family, a running mate, polling and political consultants, fundraisers, media consultants, issues advisers, schedulers, advance persons, and others. Campaign strategies must be carefully managed if the candidate is to move successfully through the primary season, the nominating conventions, and the general election campaign.

Who Runs for President

Candidates for president or vice president must meet the same few constitutional requirements. They must be at least thirty-five years old and natural-born citizens who have "been fourteen Years a Resident within the United States."

Another requirement, one that affects very few people, is that the candidate must *not* have been elected president twice before. The Twenty-second Amendment, ratified in 1951, limits presidents to two four-year terms. A vice president who succeeds to the presidency and serves more than two years may be elected president only once. Franklin D. Roosevelt, whose breaking of the two-term tradition prompted the term limitation, is the only president who served more than eight years. He died in 1945 while in his fourth term.

More than half (twenty-five) of the nation's presidents have been lawyers. (A nonlawyer, George W. Bush is the forty-third president but only the forty-second person to hold the office; Grover Cleveland is counted twice because he served two separate terms.) Twenty-four presidents served in Congress. Fourteen have been vice presidents. Nineteen presidents have been territorial or state governors, including Bush, the governor of Texas 1995–2001. Most presidents have served in the military and three were career generals: Zachary Taylor, Ulysses S. Grant, and Dwight D. Eisenhower. *(See "Roads to the White House," p. 12.)*

Even for well-known public figures, the decision to seek the presidency is a difficult one. The prospective candidates must make complicated calculations about financial and time requirements. They must sort out the tangle of party and state rules and the makeup of the electorate in each state. And they must assess their own ability to attract endorsements, recruit a competent staff, and develop an "image" suitable for media presentation. They must also consider the effect a campaign will have on their families, the psychological demands of the office, and possible revelations about their personal lives that might hinder a campaign.

An example of family considerations arose in 1996 from the popularity of retired general Colin L. Powell, the first African American to head the Joint Chiefs of Staff. Although polls that year showed Powell would have been a strong contender for the Republican presidential nomination, he declined to seek it, saying he had promised his wife he would stay out of politics. Also

George W. Bush waves to a crowd of supporters after a Texas campaign rally. Bush's dominance in Republican fund-raising helped him wrap up the party's nomination by early March 2000.

in 1996, the man who won the GOP nomination, Robert J. Dole, worried that the press would disclose an affair he had while married to his first wife. In his televised debates with President Bill Clinton, who had faced a similar scandal in 1992, Dole did not raise the character issue, reportedly fearing it would open himself to the same criticism. Although Dole's affair was disclosed before the election, it received scant attention and was not a major factor in Dole's defeat.

The Exploratory Stage

The first stage in a presidential campaign is the exploratory stage, when the candidates "test the waters" for a try at the nation's highest office. Before announcing, candidates routinely establish a political action committee (PAC) to raise money and an exploratory committee to help assess the candidate's chances of challenging the competition. The exploratory advisers identify likely opponents, consider funding prospects and other preliminary factors, and, if conditions appear favorable, the committee may form the nucleus of the candidate's campaign organization.

Since 1976, when Jimmy Carter won the presidency after a two-year campaign, candidates have tended to announce their intentions well ahead of the election, in part to have time to build a strong public profile and in part because early fund raising can be crucial to a campaign. In 2000, with Clinton barred from seeking a third term, the looming White House vacancy drew a large field of Republican candidates. Among the first to form an exploratory committee in 1999 was Elizabeth Dole, wife of the 1996 GOP nominee. She decided against running, citing the difficulty of competing against George W. Bush's fund-raising powerhouse. Several other prominent Republicans challenged Bush, including Arizona senator John McCain, who won the primaries in New Hampshire and six other states. But he, like the other contenders, eventually ceded the nomination to Bush.

Dole's decision to pull out of the race one year before the election illustrates a characteristic of U.S. presidential elections: they are endurance contests. From start to finish they are much longer, for example, than the few months typically devoted to parliamentary elections in Great Britain. By Labor Day, a good two months before the November election, many American voters are tired of listening to the candidates and have already made up their minds who they are going to vote for.

The Primary and Caucus Schedule

If a candidate decides to seek a major party nomination, the next step is to enter the primaries and caucuses where Democratic and Republican Party members select delegates to their national conventions. The states and the parties have a wide variety of rules for ballot access qualifications and allocation of delegates. Candidates must follow legal requirements to qualify for state contests, and they also have to adapt their campaign strategies to each state's particular circumstances.

The filing process can be daunting. In 1988 Colorado representative Patricia Schroeder cited the complexity of state rules as a major factor in her decision not to seek the Democratic presidential nomination. Independent H. Ross Perot made it a condition of his 1992 candidacy that his supporters obtain enough signatures to get his name on the ballot in all fifty states. They succeeded.

Traditionally, the New Hampshire primary and the Iowa caucus are the first delegate-selection events, a head start that gives the two states extraordinary influence over the selection process. (For forty years beginning in 1952, no president was elected without first winning the New Hampshire primary. Clinton broke that precedent in 1992 and Bush did likewise in 2000.) Critics have complained that the system is unrepresentative because both states are predominantly rural, with largely white, Anglo-Saxon, Protestant populations. But no serious efforts have been made to change the pattern.

Democratic Party rules prevent other states from scheduling their primaries earlier than the New Hampshire and Iowa events. Republican caucuses are permitted earlier in Alaska, Hawaii, Louisiana, and Guam. For other states and territories, the primary and caucus period begins in late February or early

Table 1-1
U.S. Presidents and Vice Presidents

President and political party	Born	Died	Age at Inauguration	Native of	Elected from	Term of service	Vice president
George Washington (F)	1732	1799	57	Va.	Va.	April 30, 1789–March 4, 1793	John Adams
George Washington (F)			61			March 4, 1793–March 4, 1797	John Adams
John Adams (F)	1735	1826	61	Mass.	Mass.	March 4, 1797–March 4, 1801	Thomas Jefferson
Thomas Jefferson (DR)	1743	1826	57	Va.	Va.	March 4, 1801–March 4, 1805	Aaron Burr
Thomas Jefferson (DR)			61			March 4, 1805–March 4, 1809	George Clinton
James Madison (DR)	1751	1836	57	Va.	Va.	March 4, 1809–March 4, 1813	George Clinton
James Madison (DR)			61			March 4, 1813–March 4, 1817	Elbridge Gerry
James Monroe (DR)	1758	1831	58	Va.	Va.	March 4, 1817–March 4, 1821	Daniel D. Tompkins
James Monroe (DR)			62			March 4, 1821–March 4, 1825	Daniel D. Tompkins
John Q. Adams (DR)	1767	1848	57	Mass.	Mass.	March 4, 1825–March 4, 1829	John C. Calhoun
Andrew Jackson (D)	1767	1845	61	S.C.	Tenn.	March 4, 1829–March 4, 1833	John C. Calhoun
Andrew Jackson (D)			65			March 4, 1833–March 4, 1837	Martin Van Buren
Martin Van Buren (D)	1782	1862	54	N.Y.	N.Y.	March 4, 1837–March 4, 1841	Richard M. Johnson
W. H. Harrison (W)	1773	1841	68	Va.	Ohio	March 4, 1841–April 4, 1841	John Tyler
John Tyler (W)	1790	1862	51	Va.	Va.	April 6, 1841–March 4, 1845	
James K. Polk (D)	1795	1849	49	N.C.	Tenn.	March 4, 1845–March 4, 1849	George M. Dallas
Zachary Taylor (W)	1784	1850	64	Va.	La.	March 4, 1849–July 9, 1850	Millard Fillmore
Millard Fillmore (W)	1800	1874	50	N.Y.	N.Y.	July 10, 1850–March 4, 1853	
Franklin Pierce (D)	1804	1869	48	N.H.	N.H.	March 4, 1853–March 4, 1857	William R. King
James Buchanan (D)	1791	1868	65	Pa.	Pa.	March 4, 1857–March 4, 1861	John C. Breckinridge
Abraham Lincoln (R)	1809	1865	52	Ky.	Ill.	March 4, 1861–March 4, 1865	Hannibal Hamlin
Abraham Lincoln (R)			56			March 4, 1865–April 15, 1865	Andrew Johnson
Andrew Johnson (R)	1808	1875	56	N.C.	Tenn.	April 15, 1865–March 4, 1869	
Ulysses S. Grant (R)	1822	1885	46	Ohio	Ill.	March 4, 1869–March 4, 1873	Schuyler Colfax
Ulysses S. Grant (R)			50			March 4, 1873–March 4, 1877	Henry Wilson
Rutherford B. Hayes (R)	1822	1893	54	Ohio	Ohio	March 4, 1877–March 4, 1881	William A. Wheeler
James A. Garfield (R)	1831	1881	49	Ohio	Ohio	March 4, 1881–Sept. 19, 1881	Chester A. Arthur
Chester A. Arthur (R)	1830	1886	50	Vt.	N.Y.	Sept. 20, 1881–March 4, 1885	
Grover Cleveland (D)	1837	1908	47	N.J.	N.Y.	March 4, 1885–March 4, 1889	Thomas A. Hendricks
Benjamin Harrison (R)	1833	1901	55	Ohio	Ind.	March 4, 1889–March 4, 1893	Levi P. Morton
Grover Cleveland (D)	1837	1908	55	N.J.	N.Y.	March 4, 1893–March 4, 1897	Adlai E. Stevenson
William McKinley (R)	1843	1901	54	Ohio	Ohio	March 4, 1897–March 4, 1901	Garret A. Hobart
William McKinley (R)			58			March 4, 1901–Sept. 14, 1901	Theodore Roosevelt
Theodore Roosevelt (R)	1858	1919	42	N.Y.	N.Y.	Sept. 14, 1901–March 4, 1905	
Theodore Roosevelt (R)			46			March 4, 1905–March 4, 1909	Charles W. Fairbanks
William H. Taft (R)	1857	1930	51	Ohio	Ohio	March 4, 1909–March 4, 1913	James S. Sherman
Woodrow Wilson (D)	1856	1924	56	Va.	N.J.	March 4, 1913–March 4, 1917	Thomas R. Marshall
Woodrow Wilson (D)			60			March 4, 1917–March 4, 1921	Thomas R. Marshall
Warren G. Harding (R)	1865	1923	55	Ohio	Ohio	March 4, 1921–Aug. 2, 1923	Calvin Coolidge
Calvin Coolidge (R)	1872	1933	51	Vt.	Mass.	Aug. 3, 1923–March 4, 1925	
Calvin Coolidge (R)			52			March 4, 1925–March 4, 1929	Charles G. Dawes
Herbert Hoover (R)	1874	1964	54	Iowa	Calif.	March 4, 1929–March 4, 1933	Charles Curtis
Franklin D. Roosevelt (D)	1882	1945	51	N.Y.	N.Y.	March 4, 1933–Jan. 20, 1937	John N. Garner
Franklin D. Roosevelt (D)			55			Jan. 20, 1937–Jan. 20, 1941	John N. Garner
Franklin D. Roosevelt (D)			59			Jan. 20, 1941–Jan. 20, 1945	Henry A. Wallace
Franklin D. Roosevelt (D)			63			Jan. 20, 1945–April 12, 1945	Harry S. Truman
Harry S. Truman (D)	1884	1972	60	Mo.	Mo.	April 12, 1945–Jan. 20, 1949	
Harry S. Truman (D)			64			Jan. 20, 1949–Jan. 20, 1953	Alben W. Barkley
Dwight D. Eisenhower (R)	1890	1969	62	Texas	N.Y.	Jan. 20, 1953–Jan. 20, 1957	Richard Nixon
Dwight D. Eisenhower (R)			66		Pa.	Jan. 20, 1957–Jan. 20, 1961	Richard Nixon
John F. Kennedy (D)	1917	1963	43	Mass.	Mass.	Jan. 20, 1961–Nov. 22, 1963	Lyndon B. Johnson
Lyndon B. Johnson (D)	1908	1973	55	Texas	Texas	Nov. 22, 1963–Jan. 20, 1965	
Lyndon B. Johnson (D)			56			Jan. 20, 1965–Jan. 20, 1969	Hubert H. Humphrey
Richard Nixon (R)	1913	1994	56	Calif.	N.Y.	Jan. 20, 1969–Jan. 20, 1973	Spiro T. Agnew
Richard Nixon (R)			60		Calif.	Jan. 20, 1973–Aug. 9, 1974	Spiro T. Agnew Gerald R. Ford
Gerald R. Ford (R)	1913		61	Neb.	Mich.	Aug. 9, 1974–Jan. 20, 1977	Nelson A. Rockefeller
Jimmy Carter (D)	1924		52	Ga.	Ga.	Jan. 20, 1977–Jan. 20, 1981	Walter F. Mondale
Ronald Reagan (R)	1911		69	Ill.	Calif.	Jan. 20, 1981–Jan. 20, 1985	George Bush
Ronald Reagan (R)			73			Jan. 20, 1985–Jan. 20, 1989	George Bush
George Bush (R)	1924		64	Mass.	Texas	Jan. 20, 1989–Jan. 20, 1993	Dan Quayle
Bill Clinton (D)	1946		46	Ark.	Ark.	Jan. 20, 1993–Jan. 20, 1997	Albert Gore Jr.
Bill Clinton (D)			50			Jan. 20, 1997–Jan. 20, 2001	Albert Gore Jr.
George W. Bush (R)	1946		54	Conn.	Texas	Jan. 20, 2001–	Richard Cheney

Note: D—Democrat; DR—Democratic-Republican; F—Federalist; R—Republican; W—Whig.

March and ends in early June. The early primaries have grown in importance. Especially when the campaign does not have an obvious front-runner, the early contests single out a possible leader. After several early tests, the field of candidates shrinks. In 2000 both Republican Bush and Democrat Al Gore had secured their party's nomination by mid-March, a feat made possible by the "front loading" of primaries earlier and earlier in presidential election years.

In 2000 sixteen states held presidential primaries on Super Tuesday, March 7. Although Bush defeated McCain in most of the primaries after New Hampshire, McCain nevertheless received more than 5 million votes in the 2000 primaries—the most ever amassed by a GOP candidate who did not win the nomination. On the Democratic side, Vice President Gore's closest competitor for the nomination was former senator Bill Bradley of New Jersey, who won no primaries.

The cost of presidential campaigns is offset by grants from the federal income tax checkoff fund. Candidates who accept the grants must abide by limits on campaign spending. In the primary stage, public financing is available to candidates who raise $5,000 in matchable contributions in each of twenty states. PAC contributions are not matchable. In 2000 Bush won the Republican nomination without public funds for his primary campaign. Democrat Al Gore, however, qualified for $15.5 million in primary matching funds.

In a typical election year where, unlike 2000, the fight for delegates continues after the early primaries, the goal of the remaining candidates is to attract media attention by winning or performing better than expected in the rest of the contests. Candidates who fall behind typically withdraw. The number of delegates at stake, particularly in states that award delegates on the basis of proportional representation, begins to be important. All Democratic primaries use proportional representation. Republican primaries in some states award delegates by the winner-take-all method.

The Presidential Nomination

The primary season culminates in the two national party conventions, usually held in late July or August. At these conventions, where guests and reporters outnumber the thousands of delegates, the presidential and vice-presidential nominees are formally selected and a party platform, setting out the party's goals for the next four years, is approved. In recent elections, the convention also has become an important occasion for showcasing party unity after the sometimes divisive primary battles.

The first national convention was held in 1831, and for more than a century afterward state party leaders had the ultimate say in deciding who the presidential nominee would be. As direct primaries took hold in the twentieth century, this influence began to wane. Then in the 1970s and 1980s, the Democrats initiated a series of presidential selection reforms that opened the nominating process. The reforms were expected to result in more open conventions, but instead they led to even more primaries.

Victory in the primaries, however, does not mean the primary leader faces no opposition at the convention. Other candidates may stay in the race because they hope to benefit if the leader falters, or they may use the bloc of delegates committed to them to bargain for specific planks in the platform or to influence the selection of the vice-presidential nominee.

Before the widespread use of primaries, the conventions were more competitive and frenetic than they are today. All the candidates still in the race had substantial campaign operations at the conventions. Campaign managers and strategists kept in close contact with state delegations. Candidates deployed floor leaders and "whips" to direct voting on the convention floor and to deal with any problems that arose among state delegations. In addition, "floaters" wandered the crowded floor in search of any signs of trouble. Floor leaders, whips, and floaters often wore specially colored clothing or caps so that they could be spotted easily on the convention floor.

This spectacle, however, became a rarity. It has been decades since either major party took more than one ballot to nominate a president. But in 1996 Reform Party founder Perot faced opposition from former Colorado governor Richard D. Lamm. In a two-step procedure the party nominated Perot at the second of two conventions. In 2000 the Reform Party split into two factions that fought over the party's share of federal campaign funds. The faction headed by conservative commentator Patrick Buchanan won the money but failed to achieve the 5 percent vote needed to qualify for public funding in 2004.

The Republican and Democratic parties received $13.5 million each for their 2000 nominating conventions. The Reform Party qualified for $2.5 million.

At party conventions, nominating speeches mark the beginning of the formal selection process. These remarks are usually followed by a series of short seconding speeches, and all of the speeches are accompanied by floor demonstrations staged by delegates supporting the candidate. For many years a good deal of convention time was taken up by the nomination of favorite sons, candidates nominated by their own state's delegation. Such nominations were seldom taken seriously, and since 1972 both parties have instituted rules that have effectively stopped them.

In recent years, the balloting for the presidential nominee has been anticlimactic. More attention focuses on whom the presidential nominee will select as a running mate. Even then, much of the suspense has been removed because the leading presidential candidates may have named their running mates before the convention begins.

With the young, politically moderate, all-southern ticket of Clinton and Gore in 1992 an obvious exception, the choice of the vice-presidential candidate often has been motivated by an effort to balance the ticket geographically. For years, a balanced ticket was one that boasted an easterner and a midwesterner. More recently, the balance has shifted so that the split is more often between a northerner and a southerner. Some examples: Democrats John F. Kennedy of Massachusetts and Lyndon B. Johnson of Texas in 1960, Johnson and Hubert H. Humphrey of Minnesota in 1964, Jimmy Carter of Georgia and Walter F. Mon-

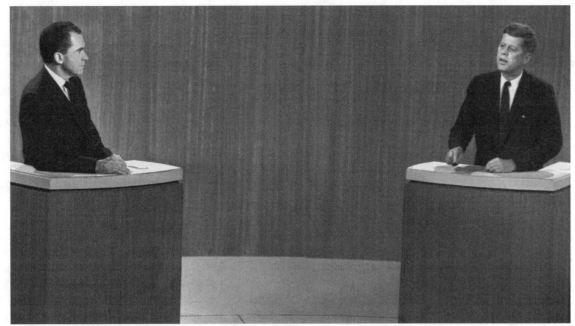

Vice President Richard Nixon debates Sen. John F. Kennedy during a live broadcast from a New York television studio October 21, 1960. Since 1976 televised debates have become a regular part of each presidential campaign.

dale of Minnesota in 1976; and Republicans Barry Goldwater of Arizona and William Miller of New York in 1964, and Bush of Texas and Richard Cheney of Wyoming in 2000.

Ideology also plays a part in the balance. A liberal presidential candidate may be paired with a more conservative running mate to attract a broader base of votes. Or the choice of the vice-presidential candidate may be used to appease party factions who are unhappy with the presidential candidate. Further, governors generally choose running mates with Washington credentials, such as senators. With the increasing number of vice presidents who go on to be president, more attention is given to the abilities of the person who is chosen, and more prominent figures are willing to accept the nomination.

The method for nominating the vice-presidential candidate mirrors the procedure for presidential nominations. The climax of the convention then occurs with the two nominees' acceptance speeches and their first appearance together, with their families, on the podium.

General Election Campaign

The traditional opening of the presidential election campaign is Labor Day, just two months before the general election on the first Tuesday after the first Monday in November. In recent years, however, candidates have been unwilling to wait until Labor Day to capitalize on their postconvention bounce in the polls. After the 1992 Democratic convention, for example, Clinton and Gore and their wives boarded buses for campaign swings through Pennsylvania and other must-win states. Their opponent, President George Bush, went from the GOP convention to Florida, which was recovering from the devastation of Hurricane Andrew. Bush won Florida's twenty-five electoral votes.

The campaign organization for the general election is usually an extension of the nomination organization, and it is separate from the national and state party organizations. Nominees normally have the prerogative of naming their party's national committee chair to help coordinate the campaign.

The national campaign committee, usually based in Washington, D.C., receives its funding from the Federal Election Commission (FEC). In exchange for federal funding, the campaign must agree not to spend more than it receives from the FEC. From 1975, when federal funding of elections began, to 2000 all major party nominees accepted the government funds for their general election campaigns. In 2000 the Bush and Gore organizations each received $67.6 million for their fall campaigns. Neither campaign, however, lived within that income. Both parties also received so-called hard money, regulated contributions given directly to candidates: $447 million for the Republicans and $270 million for the Democrats. Each party's national committee also raised about $243 million in unlimited "soft money" for party activities that indirectly supported their nominees' campaigns.

A president running for reelection has inherent advantages that may tilt the balance in the incumbent's favor. The incumbent already has the stature of the presidency and is able to influence media coverage by using official presidential actions and "pork-barrel politics" to appeal to specific constituencies. The president also benefits from the public's reluctance to reject a tested national leader for an unknown quantity.

In times of economic or foreign policy difficulties, however, the president's prominence can have negative effects on the campaign. Jimmy Carter's bid for a second term was plagued by both a sagging economy and Iran's continued holding of U.S. citizens as hostages. In 1992, after achieving record-high approval ratings for success in the Gulf War, George Bush saw his reelection hopes dashed by an economic recession, which he was slow to acknowledge and which the Democrats used to advantage with their emphasis on "it's the economy, stupid."

What They Did Before They Became President

This list gives the terms of office for each president and the public jobs each held before becoming president.

George Washington. 1759–1774, Virginia House of Burgesses; 1774–1775, delegate to Continental Congress; 1775–1783, commanding general of Continental Army; 1787, president, Constitutional Convention; 1789–1797, president.

John Adams. 1771, Massachusetts colonial legislature; 1774–1778, Continental Congress; 1778, minister to France; 1779, delegate to Massachusetts constitutional convention; 1780–1782, minister to the Netherlands; 1785–1788, minister to Great Britain; 1789–1797, vice president; 1797–1801, president.

Thomas Jefferson. 1769–1774, Virginia House of Burgesses; 1775, delegate to Continental Congress; 1775, delegate to Virginia convention; 1776, delegate to Continental Congress; 1776–1779, Virginia House of Delegates; 1779–1781, governor of Virginia; 1784–1789, envoy and minister to France; 1789–1793, secretary of state; 1797–1801, vice president; 1801–1809, president.

James Madison. 1774, Colonial Committee of Safety; 1776, delegate to Virginia convention; 1776–1777, Virginia House of Delegates; 1777, Virginia State Council; 1778, Virginia Executive Council; 1779–1783, Continental Congress; 1784–1786, Virginia House of Delegates; 1786–1788, Continental Congress; 1787, delegate to Constitutional Convention; 1789–1797, U.S. House (Va.); 1801–1809, secretary of state; 1809–1817, president.

James Monroe. 1780, Virginia House of Delegates; 1781–1783, governor's council; 1783–1786, Continental Congress; 1786, Virginia House of Delegates; 1787, delegate to Constitutional Convention; 1790–1794, U.S. Senate (Va.); 1794–1796, minister to France; 1799–1803, governor of Virginia; 1803, minister to England and France; 1804, minister to Spain; 1810, Virginia House of Delegates; 1811, governor of Virginia; 1811–1817, secretary of state; 1814–1815, secretary of war; 1817–1825, president.

John Quincy Adams. 1794–1796, minister to Netherlands; 1796–1797, minister to Portugal; 1797–1801, minister to Prussia; 1802, Massachusetts Senate; 1803–1808, U.S. Senate (Mass.); 1809–1814, minister to Russia; 1815–1817, minister to Great Britain; 1817–1825, secretary of state; 1825–1829, president.

Andrew Jackson. 1788, solicitor for western North Carolina; 1796, delegate to Tennessee constitutional convention; 1796–1797, U.S. House (Tenn.); 1797–98, U.S. Senate (Tenn.); 1798–1804, Tennessee Supreme Court; 1807, Tennessee Senate; 1812, commander, U.S. militia; 1814, general U.S. Army; 1821, governor of Florida; 1823–1825, U.S. Senate (Tenn.); 1829–1837, president.

Martin Van Buren. 1813–1820, New York Senate; 1815–1819, New York attorney general; 1821–1828, U.S. Senate; 1829, governor of New York; 1829–1831, secretary of state; 1831, minister to Great Britain; 1833–1837, vice president; 1837–1841, president.

William Henry Harrison. 1798–1799, secretary of Northwest Territory; 1799–1800, U.S. House (territorial delegate); 1801–1813, territorial governor of Indiana; 1812–1814, general, U.S. Army; 1816–1819, U.S. House (Ohio); 1819–1821, Ohio Senate; 1825–1828, U.S. Senate; 1828, minister to Colombia; 1841, president.

John Tyler. 1811–1816, Virginia House of Delegates; 1816, Virginia State Council; 1817–1821, U.S. House (Va.); 1823–1825, Virginia House of Delegates; 1825–1827, governor of Virginia; 1827–1836, U.S. Senate (Va.); 1838–1839, Virginia House of Delegates; 1841, vice president; 1841–1845, president.

James Knox Polk. 1821–1823, chief clerk, Tennessee Senate; 1823–1825, Tennessee House; 1825–1839, U.S. House (Tenn.); 1839–1841, governor of Tennessee; 1845–1849, president.

Zachary Taylor. 1808–1849, U.S. Army; 1849–1850, president.

Millard Fillmore. 1828–1831, New York Assembly; 1833–1835, U.S. House (N.Y.); 1837–1843, U.S. House (N.Y.); 1848–1849, New York controller; 1849–1850, vice president; 1850–1853, president.

Franklin Pierce. 1829–1833, New Hampshire House; 1833–1837, U.S. House (N.H.); 1837–1842, U.S. Senate (N.H.); 1850, delegate to New Hampshire constitutional convention; 1853–1857, president.

James Buchanan. 1814–1815, Pennsylvania House; 1821–1831, U.S. House (Pa.); 1832–1833, minister to Russia; 1834–1845, U.S. Senate (Pa.); 1845–1849, secretary of state; 1853–1856, minister to Great Britain; 1857–1861, president.

Abraham Lincoln. 1833, postmaster, New Salem, Illinois; 1835–1840, Illinois General Assembly; 1847–1849, U.S. House (Ill.); 1861–1865, president.

Andrew Johnson. 1828–1829, alderman, Greeneville, Tenn.; 1830–1833, mayor, Greeneville, Tenn.; 1835–1837, Tennessee House; 1839–1841, Tennessee House; 1841, Tennessee Senate; 1843–1853, U.S. House (Tenn.); 1853–1857, governor of Tennessee; 1857–1862, U.S. Senate (Tenn.); 1862–1865, military governor of Tennessee; 1865, vice president; 1865–1869, president.

Ulysses S. Grant. 1843–1854, U.S. Army; 1861–1865, general, U.S. Army; 1867–1868, secretary of war; 1869–1877, president.

Rutherford B. Hayes. 1857–1859, Cincinnati city solicitor; 1865–1867, U.S. House (Ohio); 1868–1872, governor of Ohio; 1876–1877, governor of Ohio; 1877–1881, president.

James A. Garfield. 1859, Ohio Senate; 1863–1880, U.S. House (Ohio); 1881, president.

Chester A. Arthur. 1871–1878, collector for Port of New York; 1881, vice president; 1881–1885, president.

Grover Cleveland. 1863–1865, assistant district attorney of Erie County, N.Y.; 1871–1873, sheriff of Erie County, N.Y.; 1882, mayor of Buffalo, N.Y.; 1883–1885, governor of New York; 1885–1889, president; 1893–1897, president.

Benjamin Harrison. 1864–1868, reporter of decisions, Indiana Supreme Court; 1879, member, Mississippi River Commission; 1881–1887, U.S. Senate (Ind.); 1889–1893, president.

William McKinley. 1869–1871, prosecutor, Stark County, Ohio; 1877–1883, U.S. House (Ohio); 1885–1891, U.S. House (Ohio); 1892–1896, governor of Ohio; 1897–1901, president.

Theodore Roosevelt. 1882–1884, New York State Assembly; 1889–1895, U.S. Civil Service Commission; 1895, president of New York City board of police commissioners; 1897, assistant secretary of the Navy; 1898, U.S. Army; 1899–1901, governor of New York; 1901, vice president; 1901–1909, president.

William Howard Taft. 1881–1882, assistant prosecutor, Cincinnati; 1887, assistant city solicitor, Cincinnati; 1887–1890, Cincinnati Superior Court; 1890–1892, U.S. solicitor general; 1892–1900, U.S. Circuit Court; 1900–1901, president of Philippines Commission; 1901–1904, governor general, Philippine Islands; 1904–1908, secretary of war; 1907, provisional governor of Cuba; 1909–1913, president.

Woodrow Wilson. 1911–1913, governor of New Jersey; 1913–1921, president.

Warren G. Harding. 1895, auditor of Marion County, Ohio; 1899–1903, Ohio Senate; 1904–1905, lieutenant governor of Ohio; 1915–1921, U.S. Senate (Ohio); 1921–1923, president.

Calvin Coolidge. 1899, city council of Northampton, Mass.; 1900–1901, city solicitor of Northampton, Mass.; 1903–1904, clerk of the courts, Hampshire County, Mass.; 1907–1908, Massachusetts House; 1910–1911, mayor of Northampton, Mass.; 1912–1915, Massachusetts Senate; 1916–1918, lieutenant governor of Massachusetts; 1919–1920, governor of Massachusetts; 1921–1923, vice president; 1923–1929, president.

Herbert Hoover. 1914–1915, chairman of American Committee in London; 1915–1918, chairman, Commission for the Relief of Belgium; 1917–1919, U.S. food administrator; 1919, chairman, Supreme Economic Conference in Paris; 1920, chairman, European Relief Council; 1921–1928, secretary of commerce; 1929–1933, president.

Franklin D. Roosevelt. 1911–1913, New York Senate; 1913–1920, assistant secretary of the Navy; 1929–1933, governor of New York; 1933–1945, president.

Harry S. Truman. 1926–1934, administrative judge, court of Jackson County, Missouri; 1935–1945, U.S. Senate (Mo.); 1945, vice president; 1945–1953, president.

Dwight D. Eisenhower. 1915–1948, U.S. Army; 1950–1952, commander of NATO forces in Europe; 1953–1961, president.

John F. Kennedy. 1947–1953, U.S. House (Mass.); 1953–1961, U.S. Senate (Mass.); 1961–1963, president.

Lyndon B. Johnson. 1935–1937, Texas director of National Youth Administration; 1937–1948, U.S. House (Texas); 1949–1961, U.S. Senate (Texas); 1961–1963, vice president; 1963–1969, president.

Richard M. Nixon. 1947–1951, U.S. House (Calif.); 1951–1953, U.S. Senate (Calif.); 1953–1961, vice president; 1969–1974, president.

Gerald R. Ford. 1949–1973, U.S. House (Mich.); 1973–1974, vice president; 1974–1977, president.

Jimmy Carter. 1955–1962, chairman, Sumter County (Ga.) Board of Education; 1963–1967, Georgia Senate; 1971–1975, governor of Georgia; 1977–1981, president.

Ronald Reagan. 1967–1975, governor of California; 1981–1989, president.

George Bush. 1967–1971, U.S. House (Texas); 1971–1973, ambassador to the United Nations; 1974–1975, chief of U.S. Liaison Office, Beijing, People's Republic of China; 1976–1977, director of Central Intelligence Agency; 1981–1989, vice president; 1989–1993, president.

Bill Clinton. 1977–1979, attorney general of Arkansas; 1979–1981, governor of Arkansas; 1983–1993, governor of Arkansas; 1993–2001 president.

George W. Bush. 1995–2000, governor of Texas; 2001– president.

In 2000, with the economy booming and the Treasury overflowing with surpluses, the younger George W. Bush capitalized on the Clinton administration's successes by campaigning on a platform of tax cuts and more money for popular programs such as education and national defense. Gore, by contrast, softpedaled his close association with Clinton, whose second term was tainted by his impeachment for lying under oath about his sexual relationship with White House intern Monica S. Lewinsky. Some strategists felt that Gore missed out by not taking advantage of Clinton's continued popularity and failing to claim his share of the credit for turning the economy around during the eight-year Clinton-Gore administration.

DEBATES

Now almost taken for granted, debates between presidential and vice-presidential candidates are a relatively recent phenomenon. Until the second half of the twentieth century, White House nominees did not debate. Richard Nixon and John F. Kennedy began the debate tradition on September 26, 1960, with the first of four televised meetings. When Abraham Lincoln and Stephen Douglas held their famed debates in 1858 they were Senate candidates; they did not debate as presidential candidates two years later.

There were no debates from 1960 until 1976, when President Gerald R. Ford, running behind in the polls, agreed to debate the Democratic nominee, former Georgia governor Jimmy Carter. The relatively unknown Carter gained stature in the exchange when Ford made a gaffe by saying he did not believe East European nations were under Soviet Union control. Since 1976, all major party nominees have debated on live television. Independent candidate Perot was included in the presidential debates in 1992, but he was excluded as the Reform Party nominee in 1996.

Unlike formal, academic debates, the presidential confrontations have been loosely structured, at first with a panel of journalists or audience members asking the questions. Beginning in 1992 debate sponsors began having a journalist moderator question the candidates, with the audience sometimes allowed to participate. Throughout, there have been no judges to award points and therefore no way to determine who "won" or "lost" except by public opinion polling. Media commentators make immediate assessments of winners and losers, however, and their judgments undoubtedly influence the public's opinion about which candidate "won" the debate.

With one exception, vice-presidential nominees have debated since 1976 when Ford's running mate Robert Dole faced Democrat Walter F. Mondale. There was no debate in 1980 between Vice President Mondale and the Republican nominee, George Bush. The nominees in 2000, Republican Richard Cheney and Democrat Joseph I. Lieberman, debated once.

Early in the presidential debate era, the television networks or the League of Women Voters sponsored the debates. Since 1988 they have been sponsored by the bipartisan Commission on Presidential Debates.

THE POPULAR VOTE

The United States' winner-take-all electoral college system gives presidential and vice-presidential nominees an incentive to campaign where the votes are. Because in most states the leading vote-getter wins all that state's electoral votes, the system encourages nominees to win as many populous states as possible. Nominees generally spend most of their time in closely contested states, and just enough time in "likely win" states to ensure victory. Appearances in unfavorable states are usually symbolic efforts to show that the candidate is not conceding anything.

In the electoral college, states have votes equal to their representation in Congress: two for the senators and at least one for the representatives, for a total of 538 votes. (The District of Columbia has the three votes it would have if it were a state.) Two states, Maine and Nebraska, permit splitting their electoral votes between the statewide winner and the winner in each of the congressional districts (two in Maine, three in Nebraska) but as of 2000 no such split had occurred. *(See "Electoral College," p. 12; and Chapter 5, The Electoral College.)*

Four times in U.S. history—most recently in 2000—the winner of the presidential popular vote has lost the electoral college vote. In these and other close presidential races, a shift of a few hundred votes within one or two states could have changed the result of the election. In the most notable example, George W. Bush won Florida's twenty-five electoral votes by a scant 537 votes out of more than six million popular votes cast. After the Supreme Court halted Gore's requested manual recount, those 537 votes gave Bush the bare electoral vote majority he needed to win.

The disputed Florida election brought renewed calls for abolition or reform of the electoral college system. But it also spurred demands for modernization of methods of casting, recording, and reporting of the popular vote throughout the United States. The election brought to light that 37 percent of all U.S. registered voters were still being required to use outmoded punch-card voting systems similar to those blamed for much of the difficulty in Florida. *(See box, "In Wake of 2000 "News Disaster," Pressure Mounts for Voting, Coverage Reforms," p. 10.)*

Previously, little attention had been paid nationally to voting systems. Each state or locality was free to purchase whatever type of system it wanted or could afford, although the Federal Election Commission set standards for such equipment and recommended purchase of systems that met those standards.

Campaign finance reform and efforts to make registration easier and increase voter participation received higher priority from most groups in the final decades of the twentieth century. The National Voter Registration Act of 1993, the so-called motor-voter act, which enabled people to obtain registration forms when they picked up drivers' licenses, was an example of laws that helped put millions more people on the voting rolls. Yet the changes did not necessarily translate into higher turnouts at the polls.

Actions to expand the electorate took place at both the state and federal levels. Voting qualifications varied widely because

Table 1-2
Voter Turnout in 2000 Elections

State	2000 voting age population	November 2000 registration	Percentage voting age registered	Presidential vote	Presidential Vote as Percent of Voting age population	Presidential Vote as Percent of Registered voters
Alabama	3,333,000	2,528,963	75.9%	1,666,272	50.0%	65.9%
Alaska	430,000	473,648	110.2%	285,560	66.4%	60.3%
Arizona	3,625,000	2,654,700	73.2%	1,532,016	42.3%	57.7%
Arkansas	1,929,000	1,555,809	80.7%	921,781	47.8%	59.2%
California	24,873,000	15,707,307	63.2%	10,965,856	44.1%	69.8%
Colorado	3,067,000	2,858,239	93.2%	1,741,368	56.8%	60.9%
Connecticut	2,499,000	2,031,626	81.3%	1,459,525	58.4%	71.8%
Delaware	582,000	503,672	86.5%	327,622	56.3%	65.0%
Florida	11,774,000	8,752,717	74.3%	5,963,110	50.6%	68.1%
Georgia	5,893,000	4,648,205	78.9%	2,596,645	44.1%	55.9%
Hawaii	909,000	637,349	70.1%	367,951	40.5%	57.7%
Idaho	921,000	728,085	79.1%	501,621	54.5%	68.9%
Illinois	8,983,000	7,117,449	79.2%	4,742,123	52.8%	66.6%
Indiana	4,448,000	4,000,809	89.9%	2,199,302	49.4%	55.0%
Iowa	2,165,000	1,969,199	91.0%	1,315,563	60.8%	66.8%
Kansas	1,983,000	1,623,623	81.9%	1,072,218	54.1%	66.0%
Kentucky	2,993,000	2,556,815	85.4%	1,544,187	51.6%	60.4%
Louisiana	3,255,000	2,782,929	85.5%	1,765,656	54.2%	63.4%
Maine	968,000	947,189	97.9%	651,817	67.3%	68.8%
Maryland	3,925,000	2,715,366	69.2%	2,020,480	51.5%	74.4%
Massachusetts	4,749,000	4,000,218	84.2%	2,702,984	56.9%	67.6%
Michigan	7,358,000	6,861,342	93.3%	4,232,711	56.6%	60.7%
Minnesota	3,547,000	2,801,077	79.0%	2,438,685	68.8%	87.1%
Mississippi	2,047,000			994,184	48.6%	
Missouri	4,105,000	3,676,664	89.6%	2,359,892	57.5%	64.2%
Montana	668,000	698,260	104.5%	410,997	61.5%	58.9%
Nebraska	1,234,000	1,085,272	87.9%	697,019	56.5%	64.2%
Nevada	1,390,000	878,970	63.2%	608,970	43.8%	69.3%
New Hampshire	911,000	856,519	94.0%	569,081	62.5%	66.4%
New Jersey	6,245,000	4,710,768	75.4%	3,187,226	51.0%	67.7%
New Mexico	1,263,000	928,931	73.5%	598,605	47.4%	64.4%
New York	13,805,000	11,262,816	81.6%	6,821,999	49.4%	60.6%
North Carolina	5,797,000	5,186,094	89.5%	2,911,262	50.2%	56.1%
North Dakota	477,000			288,256	60.4%	
Ohio	8,433,000	7,537,822	89.4%	4,701,998	55.8%	62.4%
Oklahoma	2,531,000	2,233,602	88.2%	1,234,229	48.8%	55.3%
Oregon	2,530,000	1,950,902	77.1%	1,533,968	60.6%	78.6%
Pennsylvania	9,155,000	7,781,997	85.0%	4,913,119	53.7%	63.1%
Rhode Island	753,000	655,107	87.0%	409,047	54.3%	62.4%
South Carolina	2,977,000	2,266,200	76.1%	1,382,717	46.4%	61.0%
South Dakota	542,000	520,881	96.1%	316,269	58.4%	60.7%
Tennessee	4,221,000	3,400,487	80.6%	2,076,181	49.2%	61.1%
Texas	14,850,000	12,365,235	83.3%	6,407,637	43.1%	51.8%
Utah	1,465,000	1,120,129	76.5%	770,754	52.6%	68.8%
Vermont	460,000	427,354	92.9%	294,308	64.0%	68.9%
Virginia	5,263,000	4,071,471	77.4%	2,739,447	52.1%	67.3%
Washington	4,368,000	3,335,714	76.4%	2,487,433	56.9%	74.6%
West Virginia	1,416,000	1,067,822	75.4%	648,124	45.8%	60.7%
Wisconsin	3,930,000			2,598,607	66.1%	
Wyoming	358,000	220,012	61.5%	218,351	61.0%	99.2%
Dist. of Col.	411,000	354,410		201,894	49.1%	57.0%
Total	205,814,000	159,049,775	77.3%	105,396,627	51.2%	66.3%

Note: Wisconsin and North Dakota do not maintain registration systems. Figures for Mississippi were unavailable. Excluding these states, the percentage of voting age population that was registered was 79.8 percent. The presidential vote as a percent of voting age population was 50.9 and as a percent of registered voters was 63.8.

Sources: Registration figures are from the Committee for the Study of the American Electorate; voting age population figures are from the U.S. Census Bureau.

In Wake of 2000 Election "News Disaster," Pressure Mounts for Voting, Coverage Reforms

The bitterly contested 2000 presidential election exposed serious flaws in how Americans cast their ballots and how the news media project and report the results. In the aftermath of the thirty-six-day Florida countdown, there was broad agreement that both systems needed overhauling.

In Congress, state legislatures, and network television boardrooms, proposals for change abounded. And if the reform fervor continued, it was likely that some improvements would be in place for the 2004 election and perhaps earlier.

Voting Systems

• **Punch Cards.** Among all the proposals, the one that seemed to command the widest agreement was phasing out the obsolescent punch cards widely used in Florida and in much of the nation. The technology, introduced in the 1960s, features the infamous *chad,* the tiny bit of paper that the voter punches out with a stylus to indicate his or her candidate choice. Failure to dislodge the chad fully (leaving it "hanging" or "dimpled") can lead to the vote's not being counted by the electronic reader.

The lack of standards for discerning the voter's intent by visual inspection of punch-card ballots was at the heart of Florida's recount problem and the U.S. Supreme Court's action in *Bush v. Gore,* which halted the spectacle of election officials holding ballots up to the light, looking for dented or incompletely detached chads. Florida counties using punch cards reported about 4 percent of six million ballots cast (240,000 ballots) were void, four times the rate of counties using optical scanning systems.

Two basically similar punch-card systems, the Votomatic and the Datavote, were still in widespread use in 2000. According to the Federal Election Commission (FEC), 37 percent of registered voters used punch-card systems, including 3.8 million in Los Angeles County, the largest U.S. voting jurisdiction.

• **Optical Scans.** The next most common voting system was the increasingly popular marksense or optical scanning device being used by 25 percent of voters. In marksense systems, the voter uses a marker to fill in an incomplete arrow or other empty block to indicate candidate choice on a ballot card. The card is then fed into a device that "reads" the card and tabulates the votes.

An advantage of optical scan over punch cards is that the cards leave a "paper trail" that can be inspected in a manual recount. Ballots spoiled by overvotes or marks outside the designated areas are rejected by the machine and deposited by precinct officials in a locked receptacle. The voter is then given a new ballot, which the machine reads and stores if the new card is properly filled out. In case of a manual recount, the voted ballot cards can be tabulated with little or no guesswork as to the voter's intent.

• **Mechanical Lever Machines.** Other than paper ballots, lever machines are the oldest type of voting system. One invented by Jacob H. Myers, a safemaker, was first officially used at Lockport, New York, in 1892, twenty-three years after Thomas A. Edison patented a similar machine. By the 1930s voting machines were being used in almost all major U.S. cities.

The machine booths typically featured a large lever that closed a privacy curtain as the voter entered. The voter pressed small levers to indicate candidate choices, or a larger lever to vote a straight party ticket. The lever that closed the curtain also opened it and returned the levers to their unvoted position and rotated counters to record the vote. When the polls closed the machines were sealed to prevent tampering in case of a recount.

At the end of the twentieth century, 21 percent of voters were still using mechanical voting machines. But they were no longer being made and computer-based systems were rapidly taking their place.

• **Paper Ballots.** Before voting machines came into widespread use, most states adopted a type of government-printed ballot introduced in Australia in 1876. It gave voters more privacy by sparing them the need to ask for a party-printed ballot. In the age of computers, 2 percent of U.S. voters still were using paper ballots, primarily in small communities. Absentee voting was also largely by paper ballot. And one state, Oregon, began conducting all elections by mail.

• **Direct Recording Electronic.** Called DRE for short, these are the newest voting systems. They display choices that the voter enters by touch-screen, button, or rotation device. A keyboard may be provided for write-in votes. The voter's choices are directly recorded in electronic memory and added to the totals for each candidate. Usage of DREs in 2000 was certain to surpass the 1996 figure of 8 percent of registered voters.

• **Mixed.** The remaining 7 percent of registered voters, according to the FEC, were in jurisdictions using combinations of old and new voting technologies.

Polls taken after the 2000 election showed broad public support for a stronger federal role in election administration. Many voters indicated they were unaware that states set most of the voting rules, even for presidential and congressional elections. A *Washington Post*-ABC News poll showed most Americans favored moving toward a national voting system, including a standard ballot design, a uniform poll-closing time, and consistent rules for manual recounts.

Many reform bills proposed funding for studies or modernization of equipment. Florida officials estimated it would cost $25 million to replace punch-card systems in twenty-four counties. In states where election officials were elected, as in Florida, reformers called for switching to bipartisan or nonpartisan appointed boards.

Although computer voting raised privacy and security concerns, prospects were bright for increased use of Internet voting systems. Arizona pioneered in this area in its 2000 Democratic primary, which gave voters a choice of using paper ballots, computer terminals, or mail-in ballots. The innovation produced a record turnout.

Three technology giants—Unisys, Dell Computer, and Microsoft—announced that they were teaming up to produce an integrated voting, registration, and reporting system. Other election equipment makers were optimistic that the 2000 election difficulties had improved the market for their products.

Media Projections

The news media's success in calling election results minutes after the polls close is based on exit polling, a relatively new technique. Through 2000, exit polls had been widely used in only five presidential elections. Until the system went spectacularly wrong in Florida in 2000, it had been remarkably accurate. But it took only that one embarrassment to force the media to reexamine themselves and promise changes to ensure the Florida mistake would not be repeated.

The reporting debacle began at 7:47 p.m. on November 7, 2000, when the networks called Al Gore the winner in Florida. About two hours later, they began retracting the call for Gore. At 2:16 a.m., some networks projected George W. Bush as the winner, which they later retracted as too close to call. *(See "The 2000 Cliffhanger: GOP Retakes the Presidency," p. 87.)*

Most of the projections were based on data from Voter News Service (VNS), a consortium formed by the Associated Press and the ABC, CBS, CNN, Fox, and NBC networks. Until 2000 VNS had only one other major error—in 1996 when for a time it projected a Democrat as the upset winner of a U.S. Senate seat in New Hampshire.

Warren Mitofsky, a former Census Bureau statistician hired by CBS, is credited with developing exit polling in the 1960s. By interviewing many thousands of citizens just after they have voted, pollsters can accurately predict election results without waiting for the official vote count. They also can gain some insight into why the voters acted as they did, along with indications of how the vote divided along lines of age, sex, race, religion, and income.

Before the formation of VNS, Jimmy Carter's decision to concede to Ronald Reagan in the 1980 presidential race at about 10:00 p.m. Eastern time on election day, while polls were still open in California, aroused controversy about exit polls and the networks' decisions to "declare" winners early. Some felt that this practice discouraged voters who had not yet cast their ballots because they thought their votes could not make a difference.

Some states subsequently tried to ban exit polls by creating so-called no-First-Amendment-zones near voting places, making it difficult if not impossible for poll-takers to identify and interview people who had just voted. But the courts ruled that First Amendment free speech and free press rights cannot be excluded from selected areas.

Congress considered similar legislation, but none was passed. In 1985 the broadcast networks pledged to Congress that they would not release exit poll results until the polls closed.

As in the 1980 case, the premature, erroneous call for Gore in Florida drew criticism because it came while people were still voting in the state's mostly Republican western panhandle, in the central time zone. Some potential voters said they stayed home after hearing Gore had "won."

What caused the wrong call? VNS managers said it was "a combination of many factors," including an unexpected increase in absentee ballots and possible underestimation of the black and Cuban votes. The later, also wrong, call for Bush was based on incorrect data from Volusia County and underestimating Palm Beach County's outstanding votes, the report said.

VNS founder Mitofsky, an election night analyst for CBS and CNN, said later he probably would have made the same call for Gore again. "Every bit of information we had was clearly pointing to a Gore call." That information was based on actual vote totals, he said, so exit polls were "not the source of the problem."

In early 2001 ABC, CBS, and NBC promised not to declare winners in any state in the future until all of its polls are closed. Members of Congress were skeptical, saying they had heard the same thing in 1985.

Fox News indicated it might not use VNS again and was exploring other polling options. CBS and NBC said they were reviewing VNS's performance. All the networks said they would make changes in their coverage, including more explanations of exit polling and how races are called.

At a congressional hearing on what columnist Ben Wattenberg called the "news disaster," he and other witnesses criticized the networks' "get it first" mentality. Wattenberg, coauthor of a CNN report on its coverage, said the networks "were competing with themselves to play beat-the-clock in a way that was ultimately truly senseless."

In an op-ed article entitled "Why Exit Polls Face Extinction," *Washington Post* polling director Richard Morin wrote that "exit polling, at least as we know it, is all but dead." He predicted that Congress would kill it because "irresponsible news organizations and self-aggrandizing" Internet journalists disregarded the networks' pledge to withhold exit poll results until the polls are closed.

Calling exit polls "the single best window we have on voting behavior," Morin mourned their possible demise. "Common sense and pleas for restraint," he said, "are no match for the anarchy of the 'Net in league with the arrogance of the media."

the U.S. Constitution (Article I, Section 2) permits the states to set their own voting standards. Early in the nation's history, the states dropped their property qualifications for voting, but some retained literacy tests as late as 1970.

On the federal level the Constitution has been amended five times to circumvent state qualifications denying the franchise to certain categories of people. The Fourteenth Amendment, ratified in 1868, directed Congress to reduce the number of representatives from any state that disfranchised adult male citizens for any reason other than commission of a crime. However, no such reduction was ever made. The Fifteenth Amendment, ratified in 1870, prohibited denial of the right to vote "on account of race, color or previous condition of servitude," and the Nineteenth Amendment in 1920 prohibited denial of that right "on account of sex." The Twenty-fourth Amendment, which came into effect in 1964, barred denial of the right to vote in any federal election "by reason of failure to pay any poll tax or other tax." Finally, in 1971 the Twenty-sixth Amendment lowered the voting age to eighteen in federal, state, and local elections.

Congress in the 1950s and 1960s enacted a series of statutes to enforce the Fifteenth Amendment's guarantee against racial discrimination in voting. A law passed in 1970 nullified state residence requirements of longer than thirty days for voting in presidential elections, suspended literacy tests for a five-year period (the suspension was made permanent in 1975), and lowered the minimum voting age to eighteen years from twenty-one, the requirement then in effect in most states. A 1970 Supreme Court ruling upheld the voting-age change for federal elections but invalidated it for state and local elections. In the same decision the Court upheld the provision on residence requirements and sustained the suspension of literacy tests with respect to both state and local elections. The Twenty-sixth Amendment was ratified six months after the Court's decision.

The right to vote in presidential elections was extended to citizens of the District of Columbia by the Twenty-third Amendment, ratified in 1961. District residents had been disfranchised from national elections except for a brief period in the 1870s when they elected a nonvoting delegate to the House of Representatives. In 1970 Congress took another step toward full suffrage for District residents by again authorizing the election of a nonvoting delegate to the House.

Through the various state or federal reforms, virtually all citizens aged eighteen or over were eligible to vote at the beginning of the twenty-first century. By 2001, following the decennial census, the U.S. Census Bureau estimated the nation's voting age population at 205.8 million. But a relatively low 105.4 million voted in the November 7, 2000, presidential election, for a turnout rate of 51.2 percent.

Because the United States does not register voters nationally, reliable figures on the number of registered voters were not available until motor-voter required states to report the numbers to the FEC. In 1996 the states reported a total of 146.2 million registered voters. Using that figure, only about 71.0 percent of voting age citizens were registered in 2000, and the turnout among registered voters was about 72.1 percent in the November election that year.

Electoral College

Even after the winner has declared victory and the loser has conceded defeat, at least two more steps must be taken before a president-elect is officially declared. The first occurs on the first Monday after the second Wednesday in December. On that day electors meet in their respective state capitals to cast their votes for president.

Each state has as many electors as it has members of Congress. Typically, slates of electors are pledged before the popular election to each of the presidential nominees. The presidential nominee who wins the state wins that state's electors. Although the Constitution does not require electors to remain faithful to their pledge of support for a particular candidate, many states have laws to that effect. Such laws, however, are generally regarded as unenforceable and likely unconstitutional. There have been several instances in which "faithless electors" did not vote for their party's nominee.

The second step occurs when the electors' ballots are opened and counted before a joint session of Congress in early January. The candidate who wins a majority of the vote is declared the president-elect and is inaugurated three weeks later on January 20. The counting of electoral votes by a joint session of Congress is normally a routine affair. But in 2001 a number of Democratic House members attempted unsuccessfully to have Florida's controversial twenty-five electoral votes for Bush thrown out.

In the rare event that no presidential candidate receives a majority of the electoral college vote, the election is thrown into the House of Representatives. If no vice-presidential candidate receives a majority of the electoral college vote, the Senate is called upon to make the selection.

Term of Office

A president's term begins with inauguration at noon on January 20 following the November election. Until the Twentieth Amendment was ratified in 1933, presidents were not inaugurated until March 4, leaving a four-month hiatus between the election and the inauguration. The briefer interval established by the so-called lame-duck amendment shortened the period in which the nation had, in effect, two presidents—the outgoing president and an incoming president-elect. Yet the amendment allowed time for an orderly transition between the old and the new administrations.

The Twentieth Amendment took effect in 1933 after President Franklin Roosevelt and Vice President John Nance Garner had been sworn in. In 1937, at the beginning of their second terms, they became the first president and vice president inaugurated on January 20.

Roads to the White House

The earliest tradition concerning the path to the presidency developed around the secretary of state, who was considered the preeminent cabinet officer and therefore the most important person in the executive branch after the president. Thomas

Jefferson was Washington's first secretary of state. Although he left the cabinet early in Washington's second term, he went on to become leader of the newly formed Democratic-Republican Party and its candidate for president in 1796, 1800, and 1804. Losing to Adams in 1796, Jefferson came back to win four years later.

In turn, James Madison, Jefferson's secretary of state for two terms, won the presidency in 1808. Madison had been a close ally of Jefferson's in the political struggles of the 1790s and served throughout Jefferson's two presidential terms as secretary of state (1801–1809). During his first term as president, Madison appointed fellow Virginian James Monroe as his secretary of state. And following in what was rapidly becoming a tradition, Monroe went on to the presidency in 1816, serving two terms (1817–1825).

Throughout Monroe's terms, the secretary of state was John Quincy Adams, son of former president John Adams. At the end of Monroe's second term, five major candidates entered the race to succeed him. Three were cabinet officers, including Adams. None of the candidates managed to acquire a majority in the electoral college, so the House of Representatives then chose Secretary of State Adams.

Adams was the last secretary of state to go directly from his cabinet post to the White House. After him, only two secretaries of state made it to the White House at all—Van Buren, who was secretary of state from 1829 to 1831 and president from 1837 to 1841, and James Buchanan, who served as secretary of state under President James K. Polk (1845–1849) and as president from 1857 to 1861.

Two other institutions died at approximately the same time as the cabinet tradition—the Virginia dynasty and "King Caucus," a derogatory term referring to the congressional party caucuses that met throughout the early 1800s to designate presidential nominees.

After the four Virginians who occupied the presidency during the first thirty-six years of the Republic—Washington, Jefferson, Madison, and Monroe—there have been no elected presidents who were born in and made their careers in Virginia. John Tyler was born there but succeeded to the presidency from the vice presidency in 1841 and was not renominated. Three other presidents were born in Virginia but made their careers elsewhere—William Henry Harrison, Zachary Taylor, and Woodrow Wilson.

During its heyday, the Washington-centered mentality of King Caucus had virtually guaranteed that cabinet officers should be among those most often nominated by the party in power. But the caucus came under attack as being undemocratic and unrepresentative and ceased to function as a presidential nominating mechanism after 1824. It was eventually replaced by the national party conventions, bodies that are not connected with Congress and that, as of the 2000 presidential election, had never met in the national capital.

MILITARY MEN

The next cycle of American politics, from the presidency of Jackson (1829–1837) to the Civil War, saw a variety of back-

Andrew Jackson (above) gained his initial fame as hero of the Battle of New Orleans. From George Washington in the late 1700s to Dwight Eisenhower in the 1950s, Americans have occasionally elevated military officers to the presidency.

grounds qualify candidates for the presidency. One of the most prevalent was the military. Jackson, who ran in 1824 (unsuccessfully), 1828, and 1832, was a general in the War of 1812, gaining near-heroic stature by his defeat of the British at the Battle of New Orleans in January 1815. Like most military officers who rose to the presidency, however, Jackson was only a part-time military man. As a politician, he had served in the U.S. House during Washington's presidency and in the Senate during John Adams's administration, as well as later under Monroe and John Quincy Adams. Only presidents Taylor, Ulysses S. Grant, and Dwight Eisenhower were career military officers.

Other candidates during this era who were or had been military officers included William Harrison, a Whig candidate in 1836 and 1840; Taylor, the Whig candidate in 1848; Winfield Scott, the 1852 Whig candidate; Franklin Pierce, the Democratic nominee in 1852; and John C. Fremont in 1856, the Republican Party's first presidential candidate. From 1824 through 1856, all but one presidential election (1844) featured a major candidate with a military background.

Like Jackson, Harrison had a mixed military and political career. A member of a distinguished Virginia family, he was the son of a signer of the Declaration of Independence. Harrison served in Congress during the John Adams administration and again under Madison, Monroe, and John Quincy Adams. In between, he battled the Indians and the British during the War of 1812.

Taylor and Scott led victorious armies in the Mexican War. Pierce also had a command in the Mexican War, although he had been primarily a politician, with service in both the House and the Senate during the 1830s and 1840s. Fremont was famous as an explorer as well as for a dashing military campaign through California during the Mexican War. Later, he was a U.S. senator from the young state of California (1850–1851).

The smoldering political conflicts of the 1840s and 1850s probably contributed to the naming of military men for the presidency. Generals usually had escaped involvement in national politics and had avoided taking stands on the issues that divided the country—slavery, expansion, the currency, and the tariff. In 1840, for example, the Whigs adopted no platform or statement of principle; they simply nominated Harrison and assumed that his personal popularity plus the resentments against Van Buren's administration would suffice for Whig victory. They were correct.

Later on, the nature of the Civil War almost automatically led at least one of the parties to choose a military officer as presidential standard-bearer every four years. To have been on the "right" side during the war—fighting to save the Union and destroy slavery—was a major political asset in the North and Midwest, where tens of thousands of war veterans were effectively organized in the Grand Army of the Republic (GAR). The GAR became part of the backbone of the Republican Party during the last third of the nineteenth century.

Consequently, it became customary for Republicans to have a Civil War officer at the head of their ticket. Except for James G. Blaine in 1884, every Republican presidential nominee from 1868 to 1900 had served as an officer in the Union Army during the Civil War. Blaine, who had spent the war years as a Maine state legislator and a member of the U.S. House, lost the election to Grover Cleveland.

Of all the late nineteenth century Republican nominees, however, only Grant, who was elected president in 1868 and 1872, was a professional military man. The others—Rutherford B. Hayes in 1876, James A. Garfield in 1880, Benjamin Harrison in 1888 and 1892, and William McKinley in 1896 and 1900—were civilians who volunteered for Civil War service. Two of them—Hayes and Garfield—were elected to the House while serving in the army. At the time of their presidential nominations. Hayes was governor of Ohio, Garfield was minority leader of the U.S. House and a senator-elect, Harrison was a former senator from Indiana, and McKinley was a former governor of Ohio.

The Democrats, who had been split over the war, had few prominent military veterans to choose from. Only twice between 1860 and 1900 did the Democrats pick a Civil War officer as their nominee. In 1864, during the war, the Democrats nominated Gen. George B. McClellan, the Union military commander who had fallen out with President Abraham Lincoln. And in 1880 Gen. Winfield Scott Hancock of Pennsylvania was the Democrats' choice.

NEW YORK AND INDIANA

From the Civil War to the midtwentieth century, several governors or former governors of New York were Democratic standard bearers. The 1868 nominee was Horatio Seymour, who had been governor there in 1853–1855 and again in 1863–1865. In 1876 the Democrats chose Samuel J. Tilden, New York's reform governor who was battling Tammany Hall. And in 1884 Cleveland, another New York reform governor, captured the Democratic nomination. He went on to become the first Democrat to win the White House in twenty-eight years. Cleveland was again the Democratic nominee in 1888 and 1892.

Besides being the most populous state, New York was a swing state in presidential politics. During the period from Reconstruction through the turn of the century, most southern states voted Democratic, although the Republicans usually carried Pennsylvania, the Midwest, and New England. A New Yorker appeared as the nominee for president or vice president of at least one of the major parties in every election from 1868 through 1892.

This general tradition was maintained through the candidacy of Thomas E. Dewey, Republican governor of New York, in 1948. Only twice between 1868 and 1948 was there no New Yorker on the national ticket of at least one of the major parties—for president or vice president. Once, in 1944, both major party presidential nominees, Democrat Franklin D. Roosevelt and Republican Dewey, were from New York.

From 1952 to 1996, however, no New Yorkers were nominated by a major party for president and only three for vice president. The latter three were Rep. William E. Miller, R, in 1964; Rep. Geraldine A. Ferraro, D, in 1984; and Rep Jack Kemp, R, in 1996. Eisenhower in 1952 and Nixon in 1968 were technically residents of New York but were generally identified with other states. President Gerald R. Ford's vice president, Nelson Rockefeller, was a former governor of New York, but he was appointed to the vice presidency. He was not asked to be on the ticket when Ford ran in 1976.

Another major swing state in the years from the Civil War through World War I was Indiana. In most elections during this period a prominent Indianan found his way onto one of the major party's national tickets. In the thirteen presidential elections between 1868 and 1916, an Indianan appeared ten times on at least one of the major parties' national tickets. However, from 1916 to 2000 only two Indianans, Wendell Willkie in 1940 and Dan Quayle in 1988 and 1992, were major party nominees.

GOVERNORS

From 1900 to 1956 Democrats tended to favor governors for the presidential nomination, whether from New York or elsewhere. Democratic governors who received their party's presidential nomination included Wilson of New Jersey in 1912, James M. Cox of Ohio in 1920, Alfred E. Smith of New York in 1928, Franklin D. Roosevelt of New York in 1932, and Adlai E. Stevenson of Illinois in 1952.

During the same period, Republican presidential nominees had a wide variety of backgrounds. There were two cabinet officers (Secretary of War William Howard Taft in 1908 and Secretary of Commerce Herbert Hoover in 1928), a Supreme Court justice (Charles Evans Hughes in 1916), a U.S. senator (Warren G. Harding in 1920), two governors (Alfred M. Landon of

Table 1-3
"Minority" Presidents

Under the U.S. electoral system, there have been eighteen presidential elections (decided by either the electoral college itself or by the House of Representatives) where the victor did not receive a majority of the popular votes cast in the election. Four of these presidents—John Quincy Adams in 1824, Rutherford B. Hayes in 1876, Benjamin Harrison in 1888, and George W. Bush in 2000—actually trailed their opponents in the popular vote.

The following table shows the percentage of the popular vote received by candidates in the eighteen elections in which a "minority" president (designated by boldface type) was elected:

Year Elected	Candidate	Percentage of Popular Vote	Candidate	Percentage of Popular Vote	Candidate	Percentage of Popular Vote	Candidate	Percentage of Popular Vote
1824	Jackson	41.34	**Adams**	30.92	Clay	12.99	Crawford	11.17
1844	**Polk**	49.54	Clay	48.08	Birney	2.30		
1848	**Taylor**	47.28	Cass	42.49	Van Buren	10.12		
1856	**Buchanan**	45.28	Fremont	33.11	Fillmore	21.53		
1860	**Lincoln**	39.82	Douglas	29.46	Breckenridge	18.09	Bell	12.61
1876	Tilden	50.97	**Hayes**	47.95	Cooper	.97		
1880	**Garfield**	48.27	Hancock	48.25	Weaver	3.32	Others	.15
1884	**Cleveland**	48.50	Blaine	48.25	Butler	1.74	St. John	1.47
1888	Cleveland	48.62	**Harrison**	47.82	Fisk	2.19	Streeter	1.29
1892	**Cleveland**	46.05	Harrison	42.96	Weaver	8.50	Others	2.25
1912	**Wilson**	41.84	T. Roosevelt	27.39	Taft	23.18	Debs	5.99
1916	**Wilson**	49.24	Hughes	46.11	Benson	3.18	Others	1.46
1948	**Truman**	49.52	Dewey	45.12	Thurmond	2.40	Wallace	2.38
1960	**Kennedy**	49.72	Nixon	49.55	Others	.72		
1968	**Nixon**	43.42	Humphrey	42.72	Wallace	13.53	Others	.33
1992	**Clinton**	43.01	G. Bush	37.45	Perot	18.91	Others	.64
1996	**Clinton**	49.24	Dole	40.71	Perot	8.40	Others	1.65
2000	Gore	48.38	**G. W. Bush**	47.87	Nader	2.74	Others	1.01

Kansas in 1936 and Dewey of New York in 1944 and 1948), a private lawyer (Willkie in 1940), and a general (Eisenhower in 1952 and 1956). Calvin Coolidge of Massachusetts, the 1924 nominee, and Theodore Roosevelt of New York, the 1904 nominee, who succeeded to the presidency from the vice presidency, had been governors of their respective states.

Curiously, the two world wars did not produce a plethora of military candidates. The only general besides Eisenhower who made a strong bid for a presidential nomination was Gen. Leonard Wood, who had commands in the Spanish-American War and World War I. Wood led on five ballots at the 1920 Republican National Convention before losing out on the tenth ballot to Harding. Otherwise only a few military men were even mentioned for the presidency in the twentieth century—most notably Gen. Douglas MacArthur in the 1940s and 1950s (he got little support at GOP conventions) and Gen. Colin Powell in the 1990s. Powell the former chairman of the armed forces joint chiefs of staff during the 1991 Persian Gulf War, received a lot of national attention in 1995 before he announced he would not seek the 1996 Republican nomination.

SENATORS AND FORMER VICE PRESIDENTS

An abrupt change took place in 1960 with the nomination of John F. Kennedy, a senator, and Nixon, a former senator and sitting vice president. It was only the second time in the twentieth century that an incumbent U.S. senator was nominated for the presidency. The first time was in 1920 when the Republicans nominated Harding from Ohio. In the nineteenth century the phenomenon also had been rare, with National-Republican Henry Clay in 1832, Democrat Lewis Cass in 1848, and Democrat Stephen A. Douglas in 1860 the only incumbent senators nominated for president by official party conventions. Republican James A. Garfield was a senator-elect at the time of his election in 1880. Beginning with Kennedy's ascension from the Senate to the White House in 1960, senators dominated presidential campaigns until 1976. During those sixteen years every major party nominee was a senator or former senator.

The nomination of Nixon, like the nomination of Kennedy, was also a sign of things to come. It was the first time since 1860 and only the third time in the history of party nominating conventions that an incumbent vice president was chosen for the presidency. Beginning in 1960 the vice presidency, like the Senate, became a presidential training ground. Vice President Hubert H. Humphrey was chosen by the Democrats for president in 1968. That same year the Republicans renominated Nixon, who went on to win the presidency eight years after being vice president.

Vice President Spiro T. Agnew was the leading contender for the 1976 Republican presidential nomination before his resignation in October 1973. In 1984 former vice president Walter F. Mondale, who had served under Jimmy Carter, emerged as the

Democratic choice for the presidential nomination. When George Bush won the presidency in 1988, after filling the second spot under Reagan for eight years, it marked the first time a sitting vice president had been elected president since Van Buren in 1836. Democratic vice president Al Gore tried to duplicate Bush's success in 2000. He won the popular vote but lost in the electoral college to Bush's son, George W. Bush.

Even defeated vice presidential nominees have been considered for the nomination—witness Henry Cabot Lodge Jr. of Massachusetts in 1964, Edmund S. Muskie of Maine in 1972, Sargent Shriver of Maryland in 1976, and Bob Dole of Kansas in 1980, 1988, and 1996, when he was the GOP nominee.

GOVERNORS AGAIN

The field of candidates for the 1980 presidential nomination continued a trend that first appeared in the 1976 campaign—the reemergence of governors as leading contenders in the nomination sweepstakes. Although there was no shortage of senators in the 1976 campaign, it was the governors who attracted the most attention. Former California governor Reagan came close to depriving incumbent Ford of the Republican presidential nomination. The Democratic nominee and eventual winner, former Georgia governor Carter, faced a dramatic last-minute challenge from the governor of California at the time, Jerry Brown. Reagan (successfully), Carter, and Brown were candidates again in 1980; Reagan was again successful in 1984.

In 1988 and 1992 the field of Democratic presidential candidates contained a near equal mix of governors and senators, but two Democratic governors established momentum early in the primaries. In 1988 Massachusetts governor Michael S. Dukakis won enough delegates by June to take the Democratic nomination, but he lost to Vice President Bush in the November general election. In 1992 Arkansas governor Clinton secured the nomination by early April and went on to defeat the incumbent Bush. Bush's son George, the Texas governor, continued the trend in 2000 by locking up the GOP nomination in March and going on to defeat the incumbent vice president, Gore.

2

Chronology of Presidential Elections

IN THE EARLY YEARS of the Republic, the American people and their leaders were ambivalent about the concept of democracy. On the one hand, Americans searched for ways to prevent the kind of tyranny they had experienced at the hand of elite rulers such as King George. On the other hand, political elites feared the instability that might result from mass participation in politics. This ambivalence was evident in the compromise for presidential selection worked out at the Constitutional Convention in 1787 and in the halting steps the nation took toward party competition.

The presidential selection process has changed significantly since George Washington was elected to his first term in 1789. The electoral college is still the center of the system, but all of the related institutions and processes are dramatically different, in part because the constitutional provisions for presidential selection are so vague.

The major features of the electoral system have developed over time as a process of trial and error. The Constitution contains no provisions for organizing political parties, nominating candidates, or campaigning for office. The Framers assumed, incorrectly, that the selection process would be a reasoned one that would transcend petty partisanship. The original provision for balloting by the electoral college was flawed and had to be superseded by the Twelfth Amendment in 1804.

Until the eighteenth century, competitive elections were rare. The nation's first legislative body, the Virginia House of Burgesses, had largely single-candidate elections until the 1700s, and later, even when the elections for state legislatures attracted more than one candidate, there was little active campaigning. It was only with the decline of homogeneous communities and the end of elite control over politics that election contests began to occur.

The very concept of the political party—a way to organize electoral coalitions—was viewed with distrust by the nation's earliest leaders. As George Washington described the dangers of parties in a letter: "A fire not to be quenched; it demands a uniform vigilance to prevent its bursting into a flame, lest instead of warming it should consume."[1] Only after the experience of factional debate in Congress, where bitter strife developed over issues such as banking, tariffs, and slavery, did the idea of parties seem necessary and capable of control.

The Emergence of the Electoral Process

The method of choosing presidential and vice-presidential candidates has moved through four distinct phases, according to political scientist Richard P. McCormick.[2] The first phase was a period marked by uncertain and hazardous rules that lasted until the Twelfth Amendment was ratified in 1804. The second phase, continuing through 1820, saw the decline of the Federalists as a national force and the dominance of the Democratic-Republicans. This phase is associated with "King Caucus"—the nomination of candidates by congressional caucuses. In the third phase, King Caucus was replaced by factional politics and unsettled rules for selecting candidates. The fourth phase—still in effect today—evolved between 1832 and 1844. It is characterized by a two-party system that nominates candidates by national conventions. In recent years, however, the conventions have been rendered obsolete by mass politics, which takes the form of mass media presentations of candidates to the public and mass participation of party members in primary elections.

WASHINGTON'S FIRST ELECTION: 1789

Establishment of the rules for democratic decision making in the United States occurred inauspiciously. The states completed their separate ratifications of the Constitution in July 1788—nearly nine months after the close of the Constitutional Convention in Philadelphia. The Continental Congress then decided that New York City would serve as the seat of government. There, on September 13, 1788, Congress passed a resolution requiring the states to appoint electors on the first Wednesday in January, the electors to assemble and vote in their respective states on the first Wednesday in February, and the new government to convene on the first Wednesday in March.

Under the Constitution, the method of choosing electors was left up to the individual state legislatures. (See "Methods of Choosing Electors," p. 159.) The requirement that all electors be chosen on the same day proved to be troublesome for the states. Some did not have time to call elections. In New York, for example, where electors were to have been chosen by the legislature, dissension between the two houses led to a stalemate and prevented the state from participating in the election.

No formal nomination of candidates took place in 1788. Nevertheless, it had been widely anticipated since the Constitutional Convention the previous year that George Washington of Virginia, the reluctant hero of the Revolutionary War, would be president. The only real question was who would be the vice president. Leaders of the Federalists, a group organized in the fall of 1787 to achieve ratification of the Constitution, ultimately decided to support John Adams of Massachusetts.

The inherent flaws of the electoral system became evident quickly. Under the Constitution, each elector was to cast two votes for president. The two votes had to be for different persons, and the two candidates could not both receive votes from a

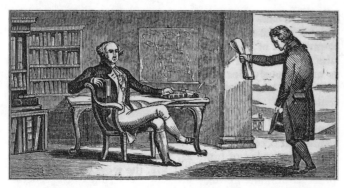

After riding his horse for a full week, Charles Thomson, secretary of the Continental Congress, arrived at Mt. Vernon on April 14, 1789, with the official news of George Washington's election as the first president of the United States.

common home state. The individual receiving the votes of a majority of the electors was to be named president, and the person receiving the second highest total was to be named vice president. Because no distinction was made between balloting for president and vice president, it was possible for more than one candidate to receive an equal number of votes, thereby throwing the election into the House of Representatives. It also was possible that a candidate for vice president—through fluke or machination—actually could end up with the most votes and become president.

The Federalist leader Alexander Hamilton recognized the danger, and his personal animosity toward Adams aggravated his concern. In response, he plotted to siphon away votes from Adams. In a letter to James Wilson of Pennsylvania, Hamilton wrote: "Everybody is aware of that defect in the constitution which renders it possible that the man intended for vice president may in fact turn up president." To prevent such a crisis, Hamilton recommended that several votes that would otherwise have gone to Adams be thrown away on other candidates: "I have proposed to friends in Connecticut to throw away 2 [votes], to others in New Jersey to throw away an equal number and I submit to you whether it would not be well to lose three or four in Pennsylvania."[3]

Hamilton's efforts were successful. Washington was unanimously elected president with sixty-nine electoral votes. Adams, however, won the vice presidency with only thirty-four electoral votes. Just two states—New Hampshire and his own Massachusetts—voted solidly for him. Because in other states Federalist leaders withheld support from Adams and sometimes worked against him, he did not receive *any* votes from Delaware, Georgia, Maryland, and South Carolina, and he received only one vote from New Jersey. The remaining votes were spread among ten other candidates, including John Jay, John Hancock, Robert Harrison, John Rutledge, and George Clinton.

Although the new government was supposed to open its doors on March 4, 1789, not enough members of Congress had arrived in New York City by that date to achieve a quorum. When the Senate finally convened on April 6 and counted the electoral votes, a messenger was dispatched on horseback to deliver the news to President-elect Washington at his home in Mount Vernon, Virginia. He received the news on April 14.

Washington then set out for New York where he was sworn in on April 30.

Before the end of Washington's first term as president, political divisions developed that would lead to a party system. James Madison emerged as the de facto opposition leader in Congress. Seventeen members of the House of Representatives regularly sided with Madison, and a bloc of fifteen supported the administration. The other dozen or so members of the House switched back and forth between the administration's and Madison's faction.[4]

The election of 1789 demonstrated the potential for partisanship and intrigue in presidential contests. It also revealed the weaknesses of the existing election calendar (which had made it difficult for New York to participate in the election) and reminded participants of the danger of the constitutional "defect" in the selection process that made it possible for the person intended to be vice president to become president.

WASHINGTON'S REELECTION: 1792

George Washington remained first in the hearts of his countrymen when his first term as president drew to a close in 1792. But the facade of national unity was showing signs of crumbling as bitter oppositional factions began to develop. From this arose a system of electoral competition.

Washington won a second unanimous term as president in 1792, but the election did produce competition for vice president. An overtly partisan contest broke out when the Democratic-Republicans, as one faction was now known, decided to challenge the Federalist John Adams. Some of Adams's approving statements about the British angered populists, who campaigned behind the scenes against him. Adams managed to win, but not before bitter partisan identities had developed in response to the nation's only unanimous administration.

The election was different from the 1789 one in another way as well. The election calendar was changed and made more flexible by an act of Congress that allowed states to choose electors within a thirty-four-day span before the first Wednesday in December when the electors met to vote. The new law remained in effect until 1845.

Thomas Jefferson, the leader of the Democratic-Republicans, chose not to run for vice president in 1792, in part because he came from the same state as President Washington. Because electors could vote for only one candidate from their own state, Jefferson was tacitly precluded from receiving the large electoral vote of Virginia. Besides, a "balanced ticket" required regional diversity. Instead, Democratic-Republican leaders from New York, Pennsylvania, Virginia, and South Carolina chose New York governor George Clinton as their candidate at a meeting in Philadelphia in October 1792. The endorsement of Clinton was a milestone in the evolution of the presidential nominating process and a step away from the Framers' original understanding of the selection process.

Both Washington and Adams were reelected, but Clinton scored well in the electoral college. Adams received 77 electoral votes to Clinton's 50 (with four votes going to Jefferson and one to Sen. Aaron Burr of New York), and Washington was reelected president by a unanimous electoral vote of 132.

The political tensions brought out by the Adams-Clinton contest became even tauter as policy controversies arose. Thomas Jefferson resigned as secretary of state in 1793 in protest over Secretary of the Treasury Alexander Hamilton's growing influence in foreign affairs. Jefferson complained: "In place of that noble love of liberty and Republican government which carried us triumphantly through the war, an Anglican, Monarchical, and Aristocratical party has sprung up, whose avowed subject is to draw over us the substance as they have already done the forms of the British government." Even Washington was subject to attacks. A Pennsylvania politician wondered aloud if Washington had not "become the tyrant instead of the saviour of his country."[5]

News of the French Revolution's period of terror divided the nation's political leaders. Federalists recoiled in horror with the news of a democratic revolution gone awry, while democrats such as Thomas Jefferson expressed sympathy for France's struggle. The U.S. government's use of troops to suppress the Whiskey Rebellion of 1794, approval of the Jay Treaty of 1794, and maneuvering between the warring French and British also polarized the young nation into factions. State-level Democratic-Republican societies formed during this period in opposition to the Federalists.

THE FIRST SUCCESSION: 1796

George Washington decided not to run for president again in 1796, even though the Constitution did not bar a third term and public sentiment supported it. With Washington out of the race, the United States witnessed its first partisan contest for president. Washington's Farewell Address, published in the summer of 1796, was "a signal, like dropping a hat, for the party racers to start."[6]

On the Democratic-Republican side, Thomas Jefferson faced no opposition as the presidential candidate; a consensus of party leaders selected him to run in 1796. But a caucus of Democratic-Republican senators was unable to agree on a running mate, producing a tie vote for Sen. Aaron Burr of New York and Sen. Pierce Butler of South Carolina that ended with a walkout by Butler's supporters. As a result, there was no formal Democratic-Republican candidate to run with Jefferson.

The Federalists, by contrast, held what historian Roy F. Nichols has described as a "quasi caucus" of the party's members of Congress in Philadelphia in May 1796.[7] The gathering chose Vice President Adams and Minister to Great Britain Thomas Pinckney of South Carolina as the Federalist presidential and vice-presidential candidates. The choice of Adams was not surprising because he was Washington's vice president. Nevertheless, Adams was unpopular in the South, and he continued to be disliked by Hamilton. As a result, Hamilton tried to use the "defect" in the Constitution to make Pinckney president instead of Adams. He urged northern electors to give equal support to Adams and Pinckney in the hopes that the South would not vote for Adams and that Pinckney would therefore win the most votes.

Had the northern electors followed Hamilton's advice, Pinckney might have won the presidency. Instead, eighteen votes were thrown to other Federalists (thereby preventing a

Thomas Pinckney, the Federalist choice for vice president, was not elected in 1796, although Federalist presidential candidate John Adams won the election. Democratic-Republican Thomas Jefferson won the vice presidency. The Twelfth Amendment (1804) precluded future split-ticket administrations.

Pinckney claim to the presidency), giving Adams the presidency with seventy-one electoral votes. Pinckney—with fifty-nine votes—was not even able to win the vice presidency. Jefferson—the candidate of the opposing Democratic-Republican ticket—came in second with sixty-eight votes and became Adams's vice president. Although the results again played up the defects in the constitutional procedure for electing presidents, Federalists and Democratic-Republicans did not seem unduly concerned that the president and vice president were of opposing parties. Both sides felt that they had prevented the opposition from gaining total victory.

For the first and last time, a foreign figure played an active and public role in the election. French Ambassador Pierre Adet promoted Jefferson's campaign in appearances and in written statements. Whether the Adet effort helped or hurt Jefferson is uncertain. The effort aroused supporters of France but angered others who favored Great Britain or resented outside interference.

JEFFERSON'S REVENGE: 1800

The election of 1800 was the first in which both parties used congressional caucuses to nominate candidates for their tickets. Such caucuses were an important innovation in the presidential selection process because they formalized partisan alignments in Congress and demonstrated the emergence of organized political parties.

President Adams was hated bitterly by farmers, populists, and states' rights advocates. In one of the nation's first professionally run smear campaigns, Adams was denounced as a "hideous hermaphroditical character which has neither the force and firmness of a man, nor the gentleness and sensibility of a woman."[8]

Federalist members of Congress met in the Senate chamber in Philadelphia on May 3, 1800, to choose their candidates. As in previous presidential election years, Federalists were divided in their support of Adams, yet they felt they had to nominate him because he was the incumbent president. Their ambivalence toward Adams was revealed, however, when they nominated both Adams and Maj. Gen. Charles Cotesworth Pinckney of South Carolina without giving preference to one or the other for president. Pinckney was the elder brother of the Federalist vice-presidential candidate in 1796.

The choice of Pinckney was made at Hamilton's insistence. Once again Hamilton was plotting to use the constitutional defect against Adams. In 1796 South Carolina had voted for an all-southern ticket—Jefferson and Thomas Pinckney—even though the two were of opposing parties. Hamilton hoped that South Carolina would vote the same way in 1800, and that all other Federalist electors could be persuaded to vote for Adams and Charles Pinckney. That would give Pinckney more votes than Adams, thus making him president.

Although the deliberations of the Federalist caucus were secret, the existence of the meeting was not. It was described by the local Democratic-Republican paper, the Philadelphia *Aurora,* as a "Jacobinical conclave." Further denunciations by the paper's editor, Benjamin F. Bache, earned him a personal rebuke from the U.S. Senate.

The Democratic-Republicans once again chose Jefferson as the presidential candidate by consensus. On May 11 a caucus of Democratic-Republican members of Congress met at Marache's boarding house in Philadelphia to choose a running mate. Their unanimous choice was Aaron Burr.

Although there was no such thing as a formal party platform in 1800, Jefferson wrote fairly detailed statements of principle in letters to various correspondents. Among other things, the Democratic-Republicans believed in states' rights, a small national government, and a relatively weak executive. They opposed standing armies in peacetime, a large naval force, and alliances with other countries. And they denounced the Alien and Sedition Acts, which had been passed by the Federalists in 1798, ostensibly to protect the nation from subversives given the threat of war with France.

The election in 1800 witnessed other signs of formal public campaigning. Tickets listing the names of Democratic-Republican electors were printed and distributed in a number of states, including New York, Massachusetts, Pennsylvania, and Delaware. Speeches in behalf of the candidates increased markedly. Partisan newspapers also helped to spread the party positions—the number of newspapers in the United States had grown dramatically in the last decade of the century, from 91 to 234.[9] Despite attempts by the Federalist Party to muzzle the opposition press with the passage of the Sedition Act of 1798, partisan newspapers on both sides actively defamed the opposition. Ultimately, the Sedition Act worked against the Federalists by turning the Democratic-Republicans into public champions of a free press.

Increased partisan activity spurred voter participation. Because electors still were chosen indirectly in twelve of the sixteen states, voters often expressed themselves through state legislative elections as a means of influencing future presidential elections.[10] The seeds were being sown for a new phase in the development of the presidential election process.

A harbinger of Democratic-Republican success came in May when the New York state party won state legislative elections. Burr managed the campaign in the state, building a machine with ward and precinct organizations. Burr's efforts showed the importance of large-scale mobilization—a lesson that would not be lost on the party in future years.

When the electors voted in December, the constitutional defect did not work as Hamilton had hoped. Instead of resulting in a Pinckney victory, the defect produced an unexpected tie vote between the two Democratic-Republican candidates, Jefferson and Burr—each of whom had seventy-three electoral votes. Adams came in third with sixty-five, and Pinckney followed with sixty-four. In accord with the Constitution, the election was thrown into the Federalist-controlled House of Representatives.

Some Federalists felt that Burr was the lesser of the two evils and plotted to elect him president instead of Jefferson, even though Jefferson was clearly the presidential candidate. Hamilton helped to squelch the idea. After thirty-six ballots, Jefferson carried a majority in the House of Representatives. The crisis—which could have fatally wounded the nation by calling into question the legitimacy of the new president—was over. Jefferson was elected president and Burr vice president.

The near disaster brought about by the constitutional defect led to the passage of the Twelfth Amendment to the Constitution in September 1804. It called for electors to vote for president and vice president on separate ballots, thereby clarifying who was the presidential candidate and eliminating the possibility of a tie between the principal candidate and the running mate.

JEFFERSON'S REELECTION: 1804

By the 1804 election, President Thomas Jefferson had grudgingly accepted the emergence of a party system. Indeed, the president wrote that year: "The party division in this country is certainly not among its pleasant features. To a certain degree it will always exist."[11]

Jefferson's record—lower taxes, a reduced national debt, repeal of the Alien and Sedition Acts, and purchase of the Louisiana Territory from France—assured him of a second term. Particularly important was Jefferson's willingness to expand the nation's reach and power with the Louisiana Purchase, which compromised his philosophical preference for a small republic. The opposition's case against Jefferson was personal. But

LOOK ON THIS PICTURE,   AND ON THIS.

This 1807 anti-Jefferson cartoon compares Washington and Jefferson in contrasting images of good and evil.

the voters were not convinced of the need to make a change.

The 1804 election was the first one held after the Twelfth Amendment went into effect, requiring electors to cast separate votes for president and vice president. Therefore as of that election parties always specifically designated their presidential and vice-presidential candidates.

The Democratic-Republicans retained the caucus system of nomination in 1804, as they did for the next two decades, and for the first time they publicly reported their deliberations. When the party caucus met on February 25, 1804, it attracted 108 of the party's senators and representatives.

President Jefferson was renominated by acclamation, but Vice President Burr, who had fallen out with his party, was not considered for a second term. On the first nominating roll call publicly reported in U.S. political history, New York governor George Clinton was chosen by the caucus to run for vice president. He received sixty-seven votes and easily defeated Sen. John Breckinridge of Kentucky, who collected twenty votes. To "avoid unpleasant discussions" no names were placed in nomination and the vote was conducted by secret ballot.

Before adjourning, the caucus appointed a thirteen-member committee to conduct the campaign and promote the success of Democratic-Republican candidates. A forerunner of party national committees, the new campaign group included members of both the House and Senate, but with no two persons from the same state. Because the Twelfth Amendment had not yet been passed when the caucus met, the committee was designed to "manage" the vote of Democratic-Republican electors to make

sure that the events of 1800 were not repeated. In fact, that precaution was not necessary because the Twelfth Amendment was ratified in September—well before the electors voted.

By 1804 the Federalist Party had deteriorated badly. The new era of dominance by the Virginia-led Democratic-Republicans had begun. The Federalists did not even hold a congressional caucus to elect their nominees. Instead, Federalist leaders informally chose Charles Cotesworth Pinckney for president and Rufus King of New York for vice president. How the Federalists formulated this ticket is not clear. There is no record in 1804 of any formal meeting to nominate Federalist candidates.

The Federalists then mounted a disorganized and dispirited national campaign. Despite concerted efforts to win at least the votes of New England, the Federalists failed miserably. Pinckney received only 14 electoral votes—those of Connecticut and Delaware, plus 2 from Maryland. Jefferson, the Democratic-Republican candidate, was the overwhelming victor with 162 electoral votes.

MADISON'S 1808 VICTORY

Following George Washington's precedent, Thomas Jefferson refused to seek a third term of office. The nation was bitterly divided over Jefferson's policy toward France and Britain. In an attempt to stay out of their war, Jefferson had supported a trade embargo so that neither country would seize American ships. But the embargo only undermined American business interests. Under attack, Jefferson decided to return to his beloved home of Monticello near Charlottesville, Virginia.

Despite the unpopularity of the administration's European policy, Jefferson's secretary of state and chosen successor, James Madison, won the presidency in 1808. Jefferson's retirement provided a serious test to the authority of the Democratic-Republican congressional caucus to select presidential candidates. The caucus met on January 23, 1808, after, for the first time, a formal call was issued. Sen. Stephen R. Bradley of Vermont, chairman of the 1804 caucus, issued the call to all 146 Democratic-Republicans in Congress and several Federalists sympathetic to the Democratic-Republican cause. A few party leaders questioned Bradley's authority to call the caucus, but various reports indicate that between eighty-nine and ninety-four members of Congress attended.

As in 1804, the balloting took place without names being formally placed in nomination. Madison easily won the presidential nomination with eighty-three votes. Despite earlier support for future Secretary of State James Monroe among Democratic-Republicans in Virginia, and Vice President Clinton's desire to be president, each won only three votes at the caucus. But the caucus overwhelmingly renominated Clinton as vice president, giving him seventy-nine votes; runner-up John Langdon of New Hampshire collected five votes.

The Democratic-Republican caucus also repeated its practice of appointing a committee to conduct the campaign. Membership was expanded from thirteen to fifteen House and Senate members, and it was formally called the "committee of correspondence and arrangement." The committee was authorized to fill vacancies on the national ticket, should any occur. Before the caucus adjourned, it passed a resolution defending the caucus system as "the most practicable mode of consulting and respecting the interest and wishes of all." Later caucuses adopted similar resolutions throughout the history of the system.

Still, the Democratic-Republicans suffered divisions. Forty percent of the Democratic-Republican members of Congress had refused to attend the nominating caucus. Monroe refused to withdraw from the presidential race even after his defeat in the caucus. And Clinton, although he was nominated for vice president, was angry at not being nominated for president—so much so that he publicly denounced the caucus, as did Monroe's supporters. Pro-Clinton newspapers in New York launched harsh attacks on Madison and even suggested a Clinton-Monroe ticket. Some Clinton supporters went so far as to hope that Federalists would nominate Clinton for president later in the year. But such a thought was unpalatable to the Federalists, who ultimately nominated Charles Cotesworth Pinckney.

The Federalists chose their ticket at a secret meeting of party leaders in New York City in August 1808. Initially, the meeting was called by the Federalist members of the Massachusetts legislature. Twenty-five to thirty party leaders from seven states, all north of the Potomac River except South Carolina, attended the national meeting. Despite the suggestion from Massachusetts representatives that Clinton be nominated, the gathering decided to run the same ticket they had chosen in 1804: Pinckney and King.

The Federalists did not actively publicize their ticket. The party itself was divided and devoid of leadership. Indeed, many Virginia Federalists formally endorsed Monroe, even though he was a Democratic-Republican. Others preferred to align themselves with Clinton.

In the end, Madison achieved a wide margin of victory with 122 electoral votes; Pinckney came in second with 47 votes. Monroe received no electoral votes. For the sake of future party unity, Democratic-Republicans had retained Clinton as their vice-presidential nominee even though he had tried to subvert Madison's candidacy. Clinton won, receiving 113 electoral votes for vice president. He even received 6 electoral votes from New York for president.

MADISON'S REELECTION: 1812

The winds of war were sweeping through presidential politics when James Madison sought a second term in 1812. In response to constant agitation by "war hawks," the president asked Congress on June 1 for a declaration of war against Great Britain. Madison, benefiting from the public's willingness to rally in times of national emergency, swept to a second term. The Federalists did not field a candidate but supported a dissident from Madison's party.

The possibility of war had long hung over the United States. Great Britain had taken American ships captive for years—boarding the vessels, taking cargo, and intimidating seamen. Anti-British political forces also charged that the British had encouraged American Indians in their attacks against settlers in the North and West.

The Democratic-Republican Party held its quadrennial nominating caucus on May 18, 1812. Only eighty-three of the 178 Democratic-Republicans in Congress participated. The New England and New York delegations in particular were poorly represented. Many of the New Yorkers supported the candidacy of their state's lieutenant governor, DeWitt Clinton (George Clinton's nephew), who also was maneuvering for the Federalist nomination. New England was noticeably upset with Madison's foreign policy, which was leading to war with England. Others did not attend the caucus because they opposed the system in principle.

Madison won a near-unanimous renomination in the caucus, receiving eighty-two votes. John Langdon of New Hampshire got the vice-presidential nomination by a wide margin, collecting sixty-four votes to sixteen for Gov. Elbridge Gerry of Massachusetts. But Langdon declined the nomination, citing his age (seventy) as the reason. The Democratic-Republicans held a second caucus on June 8 to select another vice-presidential candidate. Gerry was the clear winner with seventy-four votes, and he responded with a formal letter of acceptance. Ten members of Congress who had not been present at the first caucus also took the opportunity to endorse Madison's presidential candidacy.

Democratic-Republicans from New York were unwilling to accept the choice of Madison. They held their own caucus, composed of nearly all party members from the New York state legislature, where they unanimously nominated Clinton, who responded with a written "Address" that was a precursor to party platforms. Clinton won the endorsement of the Federalists as well.

As they had four years earlier, the Federalists convened a three-day secret meeting in New York City. The September meeting was more than twice the size of the 1808 gathering, with seventy representatives from eleven states attending. Delegates were sent to the conference by Federalist general committees, with all but nine of the delegates coming from the New England and Middle Atlantic states.

Debate centered on whether to run a separate Federalist ticket or to endorse Clinton. After much debate, they decided to endorse Clinton, and they nominated Jared Ingersoll of Pennsylvania for vice president. Originally, the caucus's decision was meant to be kept a secret, but leaks eventually were reported by Democratic-Republican newspapers.

The presidential election of 1812 was the first wartime contest for power in the United States. The Federalists, calling Madison a dupe of French emperor Napoleon Bonaparte, aligned themselves with the cause of peace and unimpeded commerce. In some northern states the Federalists even adopted the Peace Party label.

Despite all the opposition to President Madison, he beat Clinton by an electoral vote count of 128–89. The vote reflected the growing split between southern agricultural states, which supported Madison, and northern commercial states, which supported Clinton. Indeed, the common bond that held the Clinton coalition together was a hatred of Virginia—the kingmaker of the Democratic-Republican Party.

The 1812 race was the last real campaign by the Federalists. Disgraced by their obstructionist tactics during the war, isolated by their talk of succession from the Union, and unable to coordinate a national campaign, the Federalists faded from a system increasingly marked by permanent party competition.

MONROE'S 1816 VICTORY

James Monroe, President Madison's old foe who had left the Democratic-Republican Party in 1808, seemed like an unlikely presidential candidate for the party in 1816. But not only did James Monroe return to the Democratic-Republican fold, he also won the White House without any opposition.

The inconclusive War of 1812 colored American politics for years. The United States and Great Britain fought to a stalemate, and then both sides offered conditions for ending the war that the other would not accept. The British, for example, demanded control over the Great Lakes and Mississippi River for commerce, as well as the creation of an Indian state in the Northwest. In the end, both parties simply accepted the end of hostilities. An American representative said the treaty was "a truce rather than a peace."[12] Inconclusive or not, the war sparked a generation of nationalism. Rufus King revived the Federalist Party in 1816 with his race for the governorship of New York. But he lost the race and afterward found the job of maintaining the party a "fruitless struggle." Efforts were made to convene another secret meeting in Philadelphia to nominate candidates for president and vice president, yet the party held no such meeting. With the Federalists not running candidates, nomination by the Democratic-Republican caucus was tantamount to election.

Despite his opposition to Madison in 1808, Monroe had been accepted back into the Democratic-Republican fold in the years that followed. In 1811 Madison had named him secretary of state; by 1816 he was Madison's heir apparent. But many states were increasingly jealous of the Virginia dynasty that had held a grip on the presidency since 1804. Democratic-Republicans in such states opposed Monroe (himself a Virginian) and favored Secretary of War William H. Crawford of Georgia.

A Democratic-Republican caucus met in the House chamber on March 12, 1816, but only fifty-eight members of Congress—mostly Crawford supporters—attended. With the expectation of better attendance, a second caucus was held on March 16. It drew 119 of the 141 Democratic-Republicans in Congress. There, Monroe narrowly defeated Crawford by a vote of 65–54. Forty of Crawford's votes came from five states: Georgia, Kentucky, New Jersey, New York, and North Carolina. The vice-presidential nomination went to New York governor Daniel D. Tompkins, who easily outdistanced Pennsylvania governor Simon Snyder, 85–30.

The nominations of Monroe and Tompkins revived a Virginia-New York alliance that extended back to the late eighteenth century. With the lone exception of 1812, every Democratic-Republican ticket from 1800 to 1820 was composed of a presidential candidate from Virginia and a vice-presidential candidate from New York.

With the Federalist Party still in disarray, the Democratic-Republican ticket won easily. Monroe received 183 electoral votes. The three states—Connecticut, Delaware, and Massachusetts—that had chosen Federalist electors cast their 34 electoral votes for Rufus King.

Although the collapse of the Federalists ensured Democratic-Republican rule, it also increased intraparty friction and spurred further attacks on the caucus system. Twenty-two Democratic-Republican members of Congress had not attended the second party caucus, and at least fifteen were known to be opposed to the system. Mass meetings around the country protested the caucus system.[13] Opponents asserted that the writers of the Constitution did not envision the caucus, that presidential nominating should not be a function of Congress, and that the caucus system encouraged candidates to curry the favor of Congress.

MONROE'S 1820 REELECTION

The 1820 election took place during the "Era of Good Feeling," a phrase coined by a Boston publication, the *Columbian Centinel*, to describe a brief period of virtual one-party rule in the United States. But that phrase glosses over serious sectional divisions that were growing during Monroe's presidency. The divisions, however, did not prevent Monroe from winning another term.

Sectional strife was on the brink of eruption during Monroe's first term over the admission of Missouri as a new state. Tensions between northern and southern states had simmered for years. The emotional core of the struggle was slavery. Therefore whichever region controlled Congress might decide whether slavery was extended into new territories—and the shape of the nation's economy and culture—for years to come.

In the Senate, there was a tenuous balance between the two regions—eleven free states and eleven slave states—but the admission of Missouri threatened that balance. The two sides finally agreed to a compromise in which both Missouri and Maine would apply for statehood at the same time, Maine as a free state and Missouri as a slave state. Monroe remained neutral in the debate leading up to the compromise. Despite a financial panic in 1819, he retained overwhelming popular support, bolstered by peace and a wave of nationalistic feeling that overshadowed any partisan divisions.

While the United States struggled over the slavery issue, President Monroe embarked on a bold new foreign policy. Still smarting over the British presence in North America that had resulted in the War of 1812, the president declared that the United States would view any European attempts to colonize the Western Hemisphere as acts of hostility. The Monroe Doctrine claimed the hemisphere as the preserve of the United States. It was the boldest venture yet of the nation into foreign policy and permanently defined America's role in world affairs.

Although several rival Democratic-Republican candidates aspired to win the presidency when Monroe retired in 1824, none wanted to challenge his reelection in 1820. A nominating caucus was called for early March, but fewer than fifty of the Democratic-Republican Party's 191 members of Congress showed up. The caucus voted unanimously to make no nominations and passed a resolution explaining that it was inexpedient to do so because so few of the party's members were in attendance. Although Monroe and Tompkins were not formally renominated, electoral slates were filed in their behalf.

Because the Federalist Party was finally dead, Monroe ran virtually unopposed. Even John Adams, the last Federalist president, voted for Monroe as an elector from Massachusetts. Only one elector, a Democratic-Republican from New Hampshire, cast a vote against Monroe, supporting instead John Quincy Adams, son of the former president.

LAST OF THE OLD ORDER: 1824

The 1824 election, in an odd way, represented everything that the Framers of the Constitution had hoped to see. Without a permanent party system, a number of candidates vied for the presidency. Unable to win an electoral majority, the top three finishers saw their names submitted to the House of Representatives for a final decision. The candidate representative of elite interests and sensibilities and who had House ties won.

But if the 1824 election of John Quincy Adams represented something old, it also represented something new. The popular winner and House loser, Andrew Jackson, protested loudly that the election had been stolen from the people. In fact, soon he would mobilize the Democratic Party around a populist rallying cry. American politics would never be the same.

In 1824, as in 1820, only one working party existed in the United States: the Democratic-Republican. But that party had an abundance of candidates competing for the presidency: Secretary of State John Quincy Adams of Massachusetts, Sen. Andrew Jackson of Tennessee, Secretary of War John C. Calhoun of South Carolina, House Speaker Henry Clay of Kentucky, and

Secretary of the Treasury William H. Crawford. The number of candidates, coupled with the growing democratization of the U.S. political system, led to the demise of King Caucus in 1824.

Early on, Crawford was the leading candidate. He had strong southern support and appeared likely to win the support of New York's Democratic-Republicans. Because it was assumed that he would win a caucus if one were held, Crawford's opponents joined the growing list of caucus opponents. But Crawford's apparent invincibility suddenly ended in September 1823 when he suffered a paralytic stroke. Nearly blind and unable even to sign his name, he was incapacitated and stayed in seclusion for months.

In early February 1824, eleven Democratic-Republican members of Congress issued a call for a caucus to be held in the middle of the month. Their call was countered by twenty-four other members of Congress from fifteen states who deemed it "inexpedient under existing circumstances" to hold a caucus. They claimed that 181 members of Congress were resolved not to attend if a caucus were held.

The caucus convened in mid-February, but only sixty-six members of Congress showed up. Three-quarters of those attending came from just four states—Georgia, New York, North Carolina, and Virginia. Despite his illness, Crawford won the caucus nomination with sixty-four votes. Albert Gallatin of Pennsylvania was selected for vice president with fifty-seven votes. The caucus adopted a resolution defending its actions as "the best means of collecting and concentrating the feelings and wishes of the people of the Union upon this important subject." The caucus also appointed a committee to write an address to the people. As written, the text of the address viewed with alarm the "dismemberment" of the Democratic-Republican Party.

In fact, the action of the caucus just aggravated splits in the party. Because so few members of Congress attended the caucus—almost all of them Crawford supporters—opponents could argue that the choice was not even representative of the Democratic-Republicans serving in Congress. Crawford was roundly criticized as being an illegitimate candidate. His opponents derided King Caucus, and his physical condition made it even easier for them to reject his nomination. As it stood, other candidates simply refused to follow the caucus's decision. Never again were candidates chosen by the caucus system.

With the caucus devoid of power and the party lacking unity or leadership, there was no chance of rallying behind a single ticket. In addition, many political issues proved to be divisive. Western expansion and protective tariffs, for example, benefited some parts of the country but hurt others. Thus the various candidates came to represent sectional interests.

The candidates themselves recognized that such a crowded field was dangerous. The election would be thrown into the House of Representatives if no candidate received a majority. The candidates therefore made efforts to join forces. Adams tried to lure Jackson as his running mate. Adams was a short, stocky, aloof, well-educated New Englander who came from a family of Federalists, while Jackson was a tall, thin, hot-tempered war hero with little formal education who came to epitomize a new brand of populist democracy. In trying to recruit

This 1836 cartoon depicts Jackson attacking the Bank of the United States with his veto stick. Vice President Van Buren, center, helps to kill the monster, whose heads represent Nicholas Biddle, president of the bank, and directors of the state branches.

Jackson onto their team, Adams supporters envisaged a ticket of "the writer and the fighter." Jackson would have nothing of it.

In the meantime, Crawford dropped Gallatin as his vice-presidential running mate. His supporters then tried to persuade Clay to drop his quest for the presidency and join the Crawford team. They hinted that Crawford's physical condition was such that he would probably not finish out a term of office if elected (in fact, he lived ten more years). But Clay was not swayed. Calhoun then dropped his race for the presidency and joined efforts with Jackson.

Four candidates remained in the field and each collected electoral votes. None, however, received a majority. Jackson received the most with ninety-nine, followed by Adams with eighty-four, Crawford with forty-one, and Clay with thirty-seven. Therefore the election was thrown into the House of Representatives.

In accordance with the Twelfth Amendment, the names of the top three candidates—Jackson, Adams, and Crawford—were placed before the House. Clay, who had come in fourth and was Speaker of the House, would play a major role in tipping the balance in favor of one of the candidates.

In contrast to Jackson, Adams actively lobbied for support, and Washington rocked with rumors of corruption. Clay informed Adams in January that he would support Adams in the House election—a major blow to Jackson. Shortly thereafter, a letter in a Philadelphia newspaper alleged that Adams had offered Clay the post of secretary of state in return for his support. Adams went on to win the House election narrowly by carrying thirteen out of twenty-four state delegations. Jackson came in second with seven, and Crawford third with the remaining four.

Consequently, the candidate who won the most electoral votes and the most popular votes did not win the presidency.

Jackson was furious at what he considered to be unfair bargaining between Adams and Clay. He felt that the will of the people had been thwarted, and he seethed when President Adams proceeded to name Clay secretary of state as rumor had indicated he would. In this way, the events of 1824 kindled the flame of popular democracy. The stage was set for a rematch between Adams and Jackson in 1828.

The Age of Jackson

Andrew Jackson was in many ways the perfect man to usher in an age of popular politics, although his rhetoric was more populist than his style of governing. The textbook version of U.S. history depicts Jackson as a coarse man of the frontier, a war hero, a battler of banks and moneyed interests, and a leader of the unschooled and exploited men who built a mass party on patronage and charismatic leadership. Jackson was the first politician to break the Virginia dynasty that had governed the country since the Revolution. After his bitter defeat in the 1824 election, Jackson fought back and grabbed the reins of government in the turbulent election of 1828. These two elections signaled the passing of elite politics and the rise of popular politics. In 1828 Jackson roused the people to turn Adams and his aristocratic clique out of office.

But the Jacksonian folklore has serious flaws. Jackson traveled in elite business circles, for example, and one of his greatest contributions as president was the creation of a more rationally organized bureaucracy.[14] Still, the textbook depiction of Jackson suffices to show some trends in U.S. politics, including the development of a stable mass party system, sectionalism, urbanization, and shifts in the debate about U.S. expansionism.

While President Adams was struggling with warring factions in Washington, an opposition force was gathering strength, and, in fact, was able to deal the president a number of humiliating defeats. Adams's desire for a national program of roads and canals, education, and research in the arts and sciences antagonized even the most nationalistic groups in the country. U.S. participation in a conference of countries from the Western Hemisphere and the imposition of a tariff (a tax on imported goods designed either to raise revenues or to protect domestic industries from foreign competition) also were divisive issues. But even though Adams was under constant personal attack, the opposition was divided on the same issues. The opposition was united, however, behind "Old Hickory."[15]

Jackson, hero of the Battle of New Orleans in the War of 1812, had a strong appeal to the common man even though he traveled in the circles of southern gentlemen. People who met with Jackson talked of his unerring "intuition" about people and politics. Jackson's decision to push for reforms of the punishment of debtors was an important gesture to small businessmen and workers who were held to a kind of indentured servitude to their creditors. Sen. Martin Van Buren of New York, Jackson's strongest supporter in the Northeast, said the people "were his blood relations—the only blood relations he had."[16]

THE 1828 ELECTION

Jackson and his running mate, John C. Calhoun, easily beat Adams in their 1828 rematch; Jackson won 178 electoral votes, and Adams won 83. (Calhoun also had been vice president under John Quincy Adams.) Of the popular vote, Jackson received 643,000 votes (56.0 percent) to Adams's 501,000 (43.6 percent). Sectional splits showed in the vote distribution. Adams held all but 1 of New England's electoral votes, all of Delaware's and New Jersey's, 16 of New York's 36 votes, and 6 of Maryland's 11 votes. Jackson took all the rest—the South and the West. The election, then, was decided by the newly enfranchised voters in the burgeoning regions of the country. The U.S. electorate, however, was expanding not only in the West but also in the original states. Between 1824 and 1856 voter participation grew from 3.8 percent to 16.7 percent of the total population.[17]

Jackson had only begun to exert electoral influence with his revenge victory over Adams. The expanded pool of politically involved citizens that had brought Jackson victory also brought him demands for patronage jobs with the federal government. Van Buren, a master machine politician from New York State, tutored the beleaguered new president in dealing with the office seekers. Jackson replaced fewer than one-fifth of the government's employees, which he defended as a perfectly reasonable "rotation in office" that would keep the ranks of the bureaucracy fresh. But the effect of his system was greater. Appointees of previous administrations were able to retain their jobs only when they expressed loyalty to Jackson and his party. Far more important than any government turnover, Jackson's spoils system inaugurated an age in which mass party loyalty was a paramount concern in politics.

The increased importance of loyalty, to the president and to the party, became clear with Jackson's dispute with Vice President Calhoun and the subsequent purging of the cabinet. A growing feud between Jackson and Calhoun came to a head when a personal letter in which Calhoun criticized Jackson's conduct of the Seminole Indian campaign and the 1818 invasion of Florida became public. In a letter to Calhoun during the cabinet crisis, Jackson wrote: "Et tu, Brute." A purge of Calhoun men in the cabinet followed the incident. Secretary of State Van Buren enabled the president to make the purge when he and Secretary of War John Eaton, both Jackson allies, resigned their posts; the president then called on the whole cabinet to quit.

The central element of the Jacksonian program was expansion. Much like twentieth-century politicians who would talk about economic growth as the key to opportunity, Jackson maintained that movement West "enlarg[ed] the area of freedom."[18] The administration fought to decentralize the management of expansion. Jackson railed against the "corrupt bargain" between the government and banks, joint-stock companies, and monopolies, which, he said, were squeezing out the average person seeking opportunity.

Indeed, Jackson opposed the Bank of the United States and promoted state banks because of his desire to free finance capital from central control. In his first term, the president carried on a long-running battle with Nicholas Biddle, the head of the Bank of the United States, and with Congress over the status of the bank. Alexander Hamilton had created the bank to manage the nation's monetary policy and investment, but Jackson opposed it as a tool of the eastern financial establishment. Jackson may have failed to close the bank, but he did manage to strip it of much of its basic authority and functions by placing its deposits in a number of regional institutions.

Jackson's presidency was activist from the beginning. His administration negotiated treaties with France, the Ottoman Empire, Russia, and Mexico. Jackson himself established a distinctive interpretation of federalism when he vetoed a number of public improvements bills as unconstitutional infringements of local affairs. He also called for a tariff that would yield revenues for dispersal to the states for their own public projects—an early form of "revenue sharing." And Jackson signed the Indian Removal Act of 1830, which provided for settlement of the territory west of the Mississippi River. Late in his first term, Jackson's strong stand defeated the South Carolina legislature's claim that it could "nullify," or declare "null and void," federal tariff legislation that the state disliked.

JACKSON'S 1832 REELECTION

There was never any doubt that Jackson would be renominated in 1832; in fact, several state legislatures endorsed him before the convention. Jackson's political strength was further underscored with the introduction of a quintessentially party-oriented institution: the national party convention. Jacksonians from New Hampshire proposed the Democratic convention of

1832, and the president and his advisers jumped at the opportunity. The only previous national convention had been held by the Anti-Masonic Party in 1831. Conventions had been the principal means of selecting candidates for local offices since the early part of the century. Especially when compared with the caucus system that preceded it, the convention system was a democratic leap forward.

The convention system enabled the parties to gather partisans from all geographic areas, and it welded them together as a cohesive unit that ultimately was accountable to the electorate, if only in a plebiscitary way. Voters had the opportunity to give approval or disapproval to a party program with one vote. Historian Eugene H. Roseboom has written: "It was representative in character; it divorced nominations from congressional control and added to the independence of the executive; it permitted an authoritative formulation of a party program; and it concentrated the party's strength behind a single ticket, the product of compromise of personal rivalries and group or sectional interests."[19]

Given Jackson's popularity in 1832, the purpose of the convention was to rally behind the president and select a new vice-presidential candidate. Van Buren got the nomination, despite lingering resistance from Calhoun supporters and various "favorite sons" (prominent state and local leaders of state party organizations).

As in 1828, Jackson's political opposition was fragmented. The Whigs—the opposition party that had developed from grassroots protests in the North and West against Jackson's tariff and development policies—held their national convention in Baltimore in December 1831 and unanimously nominated Henry Clay of Kentucky for president. Eighteen states used a variety of selection procedures to determine who would be their convention delegates. The party's platform sharply criticized the Jackson administration's patronage practices, relations with Great Britain, and ill-tempered congressional relations, as well as Supreme Court decisions.

In the election, the incumbent easily dispatched the opposition. "The news from the voting states blows over us like a great cold storm," wrote Rufus Choate, a prominent lawyer, to a friend.[20] Despite last-minute maneuvering to unite the opposition to Jackson and a well-financed campaign by the Bank of the United States, the president won 219 electoral votes to Clay's 49, Independent John Floyd's 11, and Anti-Mason William Wirt's 7. Jackson won all but seven states. Clay won Kentucky, Massachusetts, Rhode Island, Connecticut, and Delaware, plus five electors from Maryland. Jackson won 702,000 popular votes to Clay's 484,000 and Wirt's 101,000.[21]

Jackson, who finally left the political stage in 1837, changed the face of U.S. politics. Even if his pretensions to being an everyman were overstated, he did open up the system to mass participation, and he forced politicians to listen to popular demands. He developed the notion of a strong party organization. He fought, and eventually defeated, the national bank by withdrawing its funds and placing them in state banks. He strongly opposed two forces that could have torn the nation apart—the

nullification principle of state sovereignty and the Supreme Court's bid for broader discretion over political issues (that is, to review legislation and state actions)—by simply proclaiming the law to be "unauthorized by the Constitution" and "therefore null and void."

VAN BUREN'S 1836 WIN

Many historians consider the election of 1836 to be the most important event in the development of the party system. Van Buren, a Democratic follower of Jackson and a theorist on the role of political parties in a democratic system, easily won the election against an uncoordinated Whig Party. The defeat eventually persuaded Whig leaders of the need for a permanent organization for political competition. The emergence of two permanent parties extinguished the American suspicion of the morality of a party system based on unabashed competition for the levers of power.

Van Buren, who had allied with Jackson during the cabinet controversies and promoted his philosophy of parties and patronage, received the Democratic nomination in 1836 at a convention packed with Jackson administration appointees. The vice-presidential nomination of Richard M. Johnson of Kentucky, whose earlier relationship with a mulatto woman caused controversy, damaged the ticket in the South, but the Democrats won anyway.

The Whigs' campaign strategy was to run several favorite sons to prevent any candidate from getting a majority of the electoral votes, thereby throwing the election into the House of Representatives. As one Whig put it: "The disease [Democratic rule] is to be treated as a local disorder—apply local remedies."[22] The Whig expectation was that one of two favorite sons—Gen. William Henry Harrison of Ohio or Hugh Lawson White of Tennessee—would be selected by the House after the electoral college vote proved inconclusive.

Van Buren, however, had Jackson's machine and his personal backing and was able to overcome the Whigs' local strategy. Thus in this race, the last for the White House before presidential elections became dominated by two national parties, Van Buren took 170 electoral votes—22 more than he needed for election. Of the Whig candidates, Harrison received 73 electoral votes; White, 26; and Daniel Webster of Massachusetts, 14. Willie Mangum, an Independent Democrat from North Carolina, received 11 electoral votes from the South Carolina legislature, which was hostile to White because of his role in nullification politics. Van Buren won 764,000 popular votes (50.8 percent); Harrison, 551,000 (36.6 percent); White, 146,000 (9.7 percent); and Webster, 41,000 (2.7 percent). For the only time in history, the Senate selected the vice president, Richard Johnson, who had fallen one vote shy of election by the electoral college. In the Senate, Johnson defeated Francis Granger by a 33–16 vote.

Van Buren was besieged with problems practically from the minute he took the oath of office in March 1837. About midway through his term, the economy crashed after years of feverish business growth, overspeculation in land and business, huge private debt accumulation, and unregulated financial and trade practices. Van Buren's approach to the economic crisis alternated between stubborn refusal to fix a mess that he had not created and action that was guaranteed to antagonize key interest groups.

When Van Buren moved to create an independent treasury to insulate the federal government from state financial institutions, he was opposed by conservative Democrats who were supporters of the state financial institutions that Jackson had promoted in his legendary national bank battles. When Van Buren was not hit from the right, he was hit from the left. The nascent labor movement called for protection of jobs and wages and made protests against monopoly and privilege.

The Idea of a Party System

Whatever problems Van Buren had in governing, he should receive credit at least for helping to establish the principle of party government in the United States. That principle, much derided in the early days of the nation's history, now enjoys widespread allegiance.

Van Buren's arguments for a party system—contained in his book, *An Inquiry into the Origin and Course of Political Parties in the United States*—were similar to the economic principle of Adam Smith, which had held that the pursuit of selfish ends redounded to the good of the entire community. American leaders from George Washington through John Quincy Adams had believed that self-interested factions endangered the functioning and virtue of the Republic. These leaders also had warned against the dangers of democracy, which they often called "mob rule." In the worst possible scenario, permanent parties with strong ideological stances appealed to the mass public for support, undermining the ability of national leaders to guide public virtue.[23]

The basic tension that Van Buren had to resolve was the system's need for stability and responsible leadership and the parties' imperative to gain office. How could a party's selfish desire to run the government and award patronage and contracts to political allies benefit the whole system?

Van Buren argued that the absence of parties—that is, collections of people from disparate backgrounds—resulted in a system of personal politics that fueled demagogy, perpetual campaigns, and a lack of accountability. Personal presidential politics was more polarizing than the politics of consensus or of coalition building. Presidents should be able to do their job without constant carping from outsiders who fancied themselves prospective presidents. Mass parties with certain partisan principles would enable presidents to get the backing they needed to do their work.

Moreover, the existence of two parties would enable the nation to move beyond its many cleavages—that is, toward the general interest and away from simple clashes of particular interests. Competition among parties, like competition among economic enterprises, would bring about a situation in which disparate demands would be promoted by a party. The key was to achieve a balance of competing forces. Summarizing Van Buren, political scientist James W. Ceaser has written:

Established parties . . . may stand 'over' the raw electoral cleavages, possessing some leeway or discretion about which potential issues and electoral divisions will be emphasized and which will be suppressed or kept at the fringes. This discretion is exercised according to the interests of the organizations and the judgement of their leaders. But it is important to keep in mind that the degree of this discretion is limited. . . . Their discretion is always threatened or held in check by the possibility that they might be displaced by a new party having as its goal the advancement of a certain policy. . . . When a sufficiently powerful and enduring issue exists, an impartial reading of American party history suggests that the party system in the end will have to respond to it, regardless of how the established parties initially react.[24]

The Age of Jackson brought a fundamental shift from republican to democratic values as the nation's territory and activities expanded. Republicanism was the product of a variety of strains of thought—from the Romans Cicero and Tacitus and the Greek Polybius to the Frenchman Charles Montesquieu—that stressed the need for a balancing of interests to produce public virtue. Republicans worried about excess in any single form of governance, particularly "mob rule." For them, *democracy* was a term of derision. That is why the Constitution contained many buffers against this and other forms of excess.

Republicanism declined in many stages. A greater stress on the individual's role in society, embodied in the work of Adam Smith and David Hume, restricted the kinds of issues open to public deliberation. At the same time, the pace of economic change undermined established patterns. As the nation demanded large-scale projects (such as canals and railways), and as rival factions looked to the mobilization of larger and larger parts of the electorate to augment their strength, democratic rhetoric gained respectability. Mass party participation became a vehicle for pursuing civic virtue and balance, and the notion of a constant opposition party gained strength. If the democratic process had enough constitutional "checks," political thinkers now reasoned, the harmful "mob" aspects of democracy could be tempered. The development of the Jacksonian party as a way of arbitrating interests was the final stage in republican decline and democratic ascendance.

Political scientist Russell Hanson has noted that the new democratic ethos sprang from one of the same goals as the old republican ethos: development of a public spirit by rising above particular restraints. "Support for popular sovereignty became the lowest common denominator for a Democratic Party composed of interests seeking liberation from a variety of sectionally specific restraints on the 'will of the people.'"[25]

A two-party system persisted as the nation drifted toward civil war, but it was not a simple two-party system. The Democrats and Whigs competed for the presidency and other political offices until 1856, when the Republican Party fielded its first national ticket and made the Whigs obsolete. But the parties were so unstable that their many elements were constantly forming and breaking up coalitions—and threatening to bolt from the system itself. Moreover, a series of third parties entered the national electoral arena for short periods, applying or relieving pressures on the two major parties.[26]

Only by examining the parties and their various factions and struggles can one understand the presidential contests in the two decades before the Civil War, and the way that the Civil War revealed the basic fault lines of U.S. politics.

THE WHIGS' 1840 VICTORY

The Whigs developed to fill the role of their British name-sake, which had been to mount a republican opposition to the royal ruling power. When the rise of Andrew Jackson and his supposedly imperial presidency threatened the "balance" of the United States, the Whigs rose to restore that balance. The Whigs saw Jackson's Democrats as a faction of the most dangerous variety—a majority faction that had the ability to trample liberties in its mad scramble for spoils.

The key to Whiggery was the notion of balanced development. The Whigs opposed the war with Mexico and other expansionist programs because they feared the perils of overextending the nation's abilities and getting entangled with foreign powers. They favored internal improvements, but only as a way of maintaining balance and staving off the corruption of the Jackson era. The protective tariff was central to the Whigs' program of internal development and protection from outsiders. According to Hanson,

even in America, which was uniquely blessed by an abundance of natural resources and a citizenry of hardy stock, there was need for informed guidance and direction of progress. For the Whigs, government was the primary agent of this progress. Government represented a strong and positive force to be used in calling forth a richer society from the unsettled possibilities of America. In the economic realm this meant that government was responsible for providing the essential conditions for a sound economy, namely, a reliable currency, ample credit, and the impetus for internal improvements. And in the social realm, the government was responsible for promoting virtue in its citizenry through education and exhortation.[27]

The Whigs' desire for balance and compromise was intended to give the party a national rather than a sectional identity. Moreover, their tendency to nominate widely popular military heroes helped to create at least the illusion of a party of national dimensions. A series of Senate battles with President Jackson, especially the tariff battles of 1833, which resulted in an unsatisfying compromise, gave impetus to grassroots organizations in the North and West and to southern Democratic opponents. In fact, the Whigs developed first in the South where voters were dissatisfied with Jackson's selection of Van Buren as his running mate. There, loose coalitions elected candidates in the 1834 and 1835 state and congressional elections. Westerners also organized to oppose the Democratic Party, which was headed by a New Yorker.

The first serious Whig presidential contest was a loss, but an encouraging one. In 1836 the Whig tickets headed by Harrison and others had shown surprising appeal in the loss to the Democrat Van Buren. The Whigs had won Jackson's home state of Tennessee and neighboring Georgia, as well as three border slave states, and were strong competitors elsewhere. Harrison had carried the old Northwest (now the Midwest) and had come close in northern states such as Pennsylvania.

Because of the rise of the antislavery "conscience Whigs," the Whigs eventually moved to a completely different base of support—the North rather than the South and West—but their early organizing at least broke the Democratic stranglehold on the latter two regions. The Whigs nominated Harrison in 1840 after a nomination struggle with Henry Clay. A Clay supporter,

John Tyler of Virginia, was the vice-presidential nominee. This time, the popular if politically inexperienced hero of the War of 1812 won his ticket to the White House. Harrison defeated the incumbent Van Buren in an electoral vote landslide, receiving 234 of the 294 electoral votes—all the states except Alabama, Arkansas, Illinois, Missouri, New Hampshire, South Carolina, and Virginia. For the popular vote, Harrison won 1.3 million (52.9 percent) to Van Buren's 1.1 million (46.8 percent).

According to political scientist Richard P. McCormick,

The campaign of 1840 brought the American party system at last to fruition. In every region of the country, and indeed in every state, politics was conducted within the framework of a two-party system, and in all but a handful of states the parties were so closely balanced as to be competitive. In broad terms, it was the contest for the presidency that shaped this party system and defined its essential purpose.[28]

Harrison's campaign was as vague as his government experience was unimpressive. The image of Harrison as a sort of frontier everyman—which received its popular expression when a Baltimore newspaper mocked him as a sedentary man who would sit in a log cabin and drink cider rather than perform great deeds of leadership—was the theme of numerous parades and mass meetings. On issues from banking and currency to slavery, Harrison spoke in generalities. Harrison's strategist acknowledged that he advised the candidate to "say not a single word about his principles or creed. Let him say nothing—promise nothing."[29]

As it happened, Harrison did not have an opportunity to do much as president besides discipline the aggressive Clay. Clay had assumed that he and the rest of the congressional leadership would play the leading role in the government, but Harrison quickly dispelled that notion in a note rebuking him. But one month after his inauguration, the sixty-eight-year-old Harrison developed pneumonia and died. On April 6, 1841, the burdens of the presidency fell on Vice President John Tyler.

The rift between the White House and Congress widened under Tyler. Clay acted as if he were prime minister during a special session of Congress, pushing through a legislative program that included a recharter of the long-controversial Bank of the United States, higher import taxes, and distribution of proceeds from land sales to the states. Tyler, a lifetime states' rights advocate, vetoed two bills for a national bank, and the Whigs in Congress and his cabinet began a bitter feud with the president. In 1842 Clay left the Senate to promote his presidential aspirations, and everyone in the cabinet except Secretary of State Daniel Webster quit. Tyler was all alone, but he did manage to defeat the Whig program in his four years as president.

POLK'S DARK-HORSE VICTORY IN 1844

The Democrats were transformed into a well-organized party by Andrew Jackson and Martin Van Buren between 1828 and 1836. But, like the Whigs, the Democratic Party became vulnerable because of the irreconcilable differences among many of its parts.

From the beginning, the Democratic Party had contained contradictory elements. According to political scientist James L.

Sundquist: "The party had been formed originally as an alliance between Southern planters and New Yorkers and had always spanned both regions. Northern men of abolitionist sympathies were accustomed to sitting with slaveholders in presidential cabinets and collaborating with them in the halls of Congress."[30] But northern Democrats went so far as to organize antiabolitionist rallies in their cities and towns, and newspapers and churches also defended slavery.

The deepest Democratic divisions—which eventually would lead to the failure not only of the party but also of the nation—were the regional differences based on slavery. But other, more complex divisions also affected the operation of the Democratic Party. When the party was able to reconcile or even delay action on the divisive issues, it won. When the divisions burst into the open, the party was in trouble.

James K. Polk of Tennessee, the first "dark-horse" candidate in history, defeated the Whig Henry Clay in 1844 by supporting an expansionist program and winning the support of the solid South. One of the key issues in the campaign was whether Texas should be admitted to the Union and, if so, whether it should be slave or free. President Van Buren in 1840 had opposed annexation—opposition that may have cost him the presidency—and the Democrats and Whigs hedged on the issue for the next eight years. In 1844 Polk endorsed the annexation of Texas as a slave state; that was enough for him to lock up the South.

During the 1844 nominating convention, the Democrats finessed the sectional dangers of the Texas issue by combining it with a call for occupying Oregon and eventually bringing that state into the Union. The Democrats also appealed to Pennsylvania and the rest of the Northeast by supporting a high tariff. Both parties spoke out against the growing foreign elements in the cities, but the Whigs were more effective because of the Democrats' swelling immigrant ranks.

In the election, the Democrat Polk defeated the Whig Clay, winning 1.34 million votes (49.5 percent) to Clay's 1.30 million (48.1 percent) and 170 electoral votes to Clay's 105. Clay received his strongest support from five northeastern states and five border slave states. Of the expansionist Northwest, only Ohio fell in the Clay column.

The Liberty Party—an abolitionist party formed out of more than two hundred antislavery societies in time for the 1840 election—may have been the deciding factor in the 1844 race. Although the party received only 2.3 percent of the popular vote and no electoral votes, it was strong enough in New York to prevent the Whigs from winning that state's crucial thirty-six electoral votes. Those votes went to the Democrat Polk rather than to the Whig Clay.

The depth of the Democrats' divisions were agonizingly evident even when the party won elections and started to pass out spoils and make policy. Like Harrison, the Whig who had won the presidency four years before, President Polk faced the antagonisms of party factions when he began making appointments after his 1844 win. Westerners were angry when they were shut out of the cabinet and Polk vetoed a rivers and harbors bill. Supporters of both Van Buren and John Calhoun were angry that their faction did not win more prominent positions. Northeast-

erners were upset at tariff cuts. The New York split between the reformist "Barnburners" and the party-regular "Hunkers"—who disagreed on every issue, including banks, currency, internal improvements, and political reforms—also disrupted the administration.

Creating still more dissension was the war with Mexico (1846–1848), fought because of the dispute over the Texas border and the possible annexation of California. Northerners resented the country's fighting Mexico over a slave state.

WHIG SUCCESS UNDER TAYLOR IN 1848

In 1848 the Whigs recaptured the White House behind another military hero, Gen. Zachary Taylor, who was vague on most political issues. Hailing from Louisiana, where he was a slave owner, Taylor defeated the irrepressible Clay and Gen. Winfield Scott for the nomination on the fourth convention ballot. His running mate was New Yorker Millard Fillmore. Clay mounted an impressive public campaign that drew large crowds, but the Whigs had lost too many times with Clay.

The Whigs were so determined to avoid sectional and other splits that they not only nominated the popular Taylor but also eschewed writing a platform. Despite such extreme measures to maintain unity, the convention was disturbed by squabbles between pro- and antislavery forces on the question of the Wilmot Proviso, which would ban slavery in any territory the United States obtained from Mexico.

At the Democratic national convention, Sen. Lewis Cass of Michigan defeated Sen. James Buchanan of Pennsylvania and Supreme Court Justice Levi Woodbury for the presidential nomination, and Gen. William Butler was picked as his running mate. (The Democratic incumbent Polk had declared upon entering office that he would not seek a second term.) But the convention experienced splits between two New York factions: the Barnburners, who were part of the antislavery movement, and the more conservative Hunkers, who had ties to southerners. The Barnburners finally defected from the party to become part of the Free Soil Party.

The Democrats behind Cass praised the administration of the beleaguered Polk, defended the war with Mexico, congratulated the French Republic that emerged from the wave of revolution in Europe, and did everything it could to avoid the nasty slavery issue. The nomination of Cass—a "doughface," or northerner with southern principles—was expected to appeal to both sides of the simmering issue.

But Taylor defeated Cass, winning 1.4 million popular votes (47.3 percent) to Cass's 1.2 million (42.5 percent). New York Democrat Martin Van Buren, the former president, running on the Free Soil ticket, won 291,500 votes (10 percent) but no electoral votes. Taylor received 163 electoral votes to Cass's 127, with a strong showing in the North. Taylor won Connecticut, Massachusetts, New Jersey, New York, Pennsylvania, Rhode Island, and Vermont in the North; Delaware, Kentucky, Maryland, North Carolina, and Tennessee in the border states; and Florida, Georgia, and Louisiana in the Deep South. This combination was enough to beat Cass's coalition of seven slave states, six northwestern states, and two New England states.

On July 10, 1850, Fillmore succeeded to the presidency when Taylor died suddenly. After consuming too many refreshments at a Fourth of July celebration, Taylor had developed cramps and then a fatal illness, probably typhoid fever.

Despite this turn of events, Fillmore was unable to secure the party nomination two years later, in 1852, although he had an early lead in convention polling. Gen. Winfield Scott won the nomination, and the Whigs entered into permanent decline.

Slavery Divides the Nation

Try as they might by selecting military heroes as candidates and taking vague stances on issues, the Whigs could not delay facing the nation's disagreements forever. When divisive issues erupted, the party suffered.

The tariff issue and their mildly probusiness stance gave the Whigs strength in the North. But, like the Democrats, they also needed to attract support in the South—a goal they sought by trying to keep the slavery question out of their rhetoric. The Whigs could count on being competitive in the border slave states but not in the rest of Dixie. In 1844 Clay had won only the northern rim of slave states (Delaware, Kentucky, Maryland, North Carolina, and Tennessee).

The abolitionist movement, which may be dated to the founding of William Lloyd Garrison's newspaper, the *Liberator,* in 1831, posed problems for the Whigs that eventually proved fatal. The antislavery belt developed in the Whigs' strongest territory—New England—and westward into the modern-day Midwest. Abolitionism was largely an upper- or middle-class and religious cause. But it also became a partisan issue: the Whigs, the party out of power for years, needed an issue with which to confront the Democrats, and slavery was a useful one, even if the Whigs' antislavery stance in the North contradicted their accommodating stance in the South.

As Sundquist has noted, both the Whig and Democratic Parties in the pre–Civil War era attempted to ignore the slavery issue, but the Whigs had less room to maneuver. The Democrats' agrarian and populist position gave them the solid South as a foundation, and they could make a variety of antiabolitionist appeals to the rest of the electorate. Democrats could argue that their support for slavery in the South was compatible with their many "moderate" positions. The appeal of Senators Stephen A. Douglas of Illinois and Buchanan rested on such a coalition-building strategy. The Whigs, however, included vociferous opponents of slavery who could not be reconciled easily with "moderate" positions. Abolitionism had upper-class and religious roots that were difficult to use as a foundation. The support the Whigs were able to retain in the South was based on their positions on local issues. In sum, the Whigs did not have the same potential to build a national party organization as the Democrats.

Because both parties contained slavery sympathizers and opponents, neither was willing to take a principled stand against the institution, particularly where it already existed. This was not the case, however, for issues such as westward expansion, banking questions, public improvements, the tariff, and foreign relations, where their differences were more evident. But third parties such as the Liberty and Free Soil Parties had no such hesitations about pressing the slavery issue. In fact, sectional cleavages were so strong that in 1836 Congress passed a "gag rule" that forbade the reading of antislavery statements in Congress. Such attempts to silence abolitionist fervor were in vain, however, because politics was entering an age of mass communication and organization. The slavery issue would become irrepressible.

The slavery issue split the Whigs badly with the controversy over the admission of Texas to the Union in 1845. A splinter group of young party members calling themselves the "Conscience Whigs" argued for a straightforward statement of principle against slavery. An opposition group, "Cotton Whigs," wanted to defuse the slavery issue by ignoring moral arguments and simply calling for a halt to annexation. The party split became complete with Clay's Compromise of 1850, which admitted California as a free state, ended slave trade in the District of Columbia, and admitted Texas but reduced its size by splitting off the New Mexico territory. After agitation from Conscience Whigs and General Scott's nomination in 1852, the party was irreparably rent by the slavery issue.

The 1852 Whig convention platform contained several statements supporting states' rights and the principles behind Clay's compromise[31]—concessions made by northern Whigs to win southern support for their presidential favorite, General Scott. But when no Whigs voted for the Kansas-Nebraska Act in 1854, which permitted new states to determine individually the slavery question, the Whigs' remaining ties to Dixie were severed.

The Whigs' strength in the Northwest was almost nonexistent. Only Ohio, in 1844, went for the Whigs even once over the course of the 1844, 1848, and 1852 presidential elections. Previously strong ties between the "lake region" and the South deteriorated as immigrants and others moved from the Northeast to the Northwest and, after the completion of railroad links, the two regions developed strong economic ties.

The Whigs' last gasp came in 1852, when Scott was demolished by Democrat Franklin Pierce, who won all thirty-one states except two in New England (Massachusetts and Vermont) and two border states (Kentucky and Tennessee). In 1856 the Whigs split their votes among Democrat Buchanan, former Whig Millard Fillmore, and Republican John C. Fremont. At that time, not all Whigs were ready yet to join the nascent Republican Party because of the extremism of some of the party's abolitionists. But the majority of Whigs folded into the Republicans in 1860 when Republican presidential candidate Abraham Lincoln avoided a white "backlash" by insisting that he supported slavery where it existed and opposed its spread only because of how it would affect the economic fortunes of poor northern whites.

The Democrats suffered a North-South cleavage that Abraham Lincoln exploited in the 1860 election against Stephen Douglas. Southern Democrats were intent on protecting slavery, and control of Congress was necessary to their strategy. They believed that extension of slavery to the new states joining the Union was needed to maintain their congressional strength. In short, the extension of slavery was the issue that most divided the Democratic Party.

Northern Democrats were willing to allow Dixie to maintain its peculiar institution but were scared about their electoral prospects if slavery should expand. At first they rallied to Douglas's doctrine of "popular sovereignty" (under which the people of new states could decide whether to adopt slavery), but they became nervous when Lincoln hammered away at his argument that any unchecked slavery threatened the freedom of whites as well as blacks. Lincoln argued that Democrats such as Douglas wanted to make slavery a national, rather than an individual state, institution.

Lincoln planted seeds of doubt about partial solutions to the slavery extension question by asserting that slavery could extend to whites if it were nationalized: "If free negroes should be made *things,* how long, think you, before they will begin to make *things* out of poor white men?"[32] Lincoln also maintained that the extension of slavery into new territories would close off those areas for whites seeking upward mobility: "The whole nation is interested that the best use be made of these Territories. We want them for homes of free white people. This they cannot be, to any considerable extent, if slavery shall be planted within them."[33]

Following Lincoln's lead, the growing movement against the extension of slavery was based on a concern for the upward mobility of labor. Rather than stressing the common interests of blacks and poor, northern, white laborers, the antiextension movement played up the competition between the two groups. Horace Greeley's vision of the frontier as "the great regulator of the relations of Labor and Capital, the safety valve of our industrial and social engine" left little room for the extension of slavery into the new territories.[34]

DEMOCRAT PIERCE'S VICTORY: 1852

Clay's congressional compromise on slavery in the territories, known as the Compromise of 1850, turned out to be the major reason for the Democrats' 1852 victory. The compromise addressed the slavery question in all of the new U.S. territories by making concessions to both sides of the struggle. For the North, California would be admitted as a free state, and the slave trade (but not slavery itself) would be abolished in the District of Columbia. For the South, fugitive slave laws would be strengthened, and the New Mexico territory would be divided into two states where the voters, exercising popular sovereignty, would decide the slave issue.

The compromise was designed to settle the issue of slavery in new territories once and for all. But the slavery issue could not be contained by region; it had an increasingly important "spillover" effect. Because of concerns about the congressional balance of power and the difficulties of enforcing slavery provisions such as the fugitive slave law in states that opposed slavery, it was impossible to isolate the slavery question into particular regions as Clay intended.

President Taylor had stalled action on the compromise for months and even suggested that California and New Mexico might become independent nations. But his successor, Millard Fillmore, had thrown his support behind the compromise. The Whigs were divided on the proposal.

General Scott won the Whig nomination in 1852 after platform concessions to the party's southern delegation. Scott's appeal was always limited to the North, while Fillmore appealed to the South and Daniel Webster appealed to New England. Scott won on the fifty-third ballot.

Gov. Franklin Pierce of New Hampshire, a dark horse candidate who gained fame with his Mexican War record, won the Democratic nomination in 1852. His vice-presidential running mate was Sen. William Rufus de Vane King of Alabama. The party held together a coalition of groups with contradictory positions on the slavery issue and regional affairs. The convention, meeting in Baltimore, pledged to "abide by, and adhere to" Clay's compromise and to do what it could to smother the slavery issue.

Attempts to inject issues of economics and foreign affairs into the election failed, and the campaign degenerated into squabbles over personalities. Pierce easily won with 1.6 million popular votes (50.8 percent) to Scott's 1.4 million (43.9 percent). Pierce carried twenty-seven states and 254 electoral votes to Scott's four states and 42 electoral votes.

THE DEMOCRATS' BRUISING 1856 VICTORY

By 1856 the North-South split had eliminated the Whigs as a national party and fatally damaged the Democrats' chances for winning national elections in the decades ahead.

Congress opened the slavery issue by passing the Kansas-Nebraska Act of 1854. The act declared "null and void" the Missouri Compromise of 1820, which had prohibited slavery in new territories north of the 36"30' parallel except in Missouri. The 1854 legislation created two territories (Kansas and Nebraska) from the original Nebraska territory and left the slavery issue to be determined by popular sovereignty there and in the Utah and New Mexico territories.

The Kansas-Nebraska Act was a vehicle to spur the development of the West. Such development was part of a long-standing American approach to creating opportunity and freedom via growth. Sen. Stephen Douglas of Illinois—the promoter of the law and the main advocate of popular sovereignty—held that the law was necessary if the country was to be bound together by rail and telegraph lines and was to drive Great Britain from the continent. The latter goal was based on the widely held suspicion that Britain was exploiting the slavery issue to distract American politics and stunt American growth.

Whatever the economic motives for unification, the Kansas-Nebraska Act was bitterly divisive. Northern state legislatures passed resolutions denouncing the law. The development of sectional parties continued.

A flood of new settlers into Kansas, and the violence that accompanied balloting over whether Kansas was to be a free or a slave state, further inflamed passions. Neighboring Missourians took part in the controversy, arguing that their status as slave owners would be undermined if Kansas voted to be free. Especially in view of the Supreme Court's infamous 1857 *Dred Scott* decision, which denied Congress the power to ban slavery in the territories and barred blacks from citizenship, and the Lincoln-

Douglas debates in Illinois in 1858, the slavery question was becoming decisive in American politics.

The Democrats won the White House in 1856 when the party endorsed the Kansas-Nebraska Act and nominated the pro-South James Buchanan as its presidential candidate. John Breckinridge of Kentucky, who later served as a Confederate general, was Buchanan's running mate. The Democrats, who were becoming mainly a southern party, benefited from close wins in Buchanan's home state of Pennsylvania and in New Jersey, and in western states such as Illinois, Indiana, and California. But the only strong region for the Democrats was the South. Buchanan won all the slave states except Maryland. Overall, Buchanan won 1.8 million popular votes (45.3 percent) to Fremont's 1.3 million (33.1 percent). The electoral college gave Buchanan a 174–114 victory.

The nativist American Party—or the "Know-Nothings," as they were called—nominated former Whig president Millard Fillmore, but the party was never able to move beyond an urban strength based on parochial resistance to immigration and Catholicism. Fillmore won only the state of Maryland; overall, he got 873,000 popular votes (21.5 percent) and 8 electoral votes.

Col. John Charles Fremont was named the Republicans' first presidential candidate. Former Whig senator William Dayton of New Jersey received the vice-presidential nomination. After an 1854 meeting in Ripon, Wisconsin, where a new national party was first proposed, the Republican Party developed quickly. The Republicans had developed a strong grassroots organization in the Northwest after the Kansas-Nebraska Act passed in 1854 and attracted disgruntled abolitionists, Whigs, Know-Nothings, Northern Democrats, and members of the Liberty and Free Soil Parties who were troubled by the possible extension of slavery. Uncertainty about how the extension of slavery would affect laborers who sought opportunity in the territories also helped to unite the new coalition.

The first Republican nominating convention met in Philadelphia in 1856 with delegates from all of the free states, four border states, three territories, and the District of Columbia. The party's opposition to slavery was far from unanimous, but its willingness to address rather than suppress the issue enabled it to redefine the political dialogue. Besides strong antislavery statements, the party platform contained proposals for several internal improvements advantageous to the North. The party did not offer anything to the solidly Democratic South. To win a national election, it would have to sweep the North.

THE FATEFUL ELECTION OF 1860

In 1860 the Democratic split was complete when the party's southern elements supported Vice President Breckinridge and northerners backed Stephen Douglas. The Buchanan administration earlier had waged war on Douglas by ousting his allies from the federal bureaucracy for opposing the administration's prosouthern stance on the Kansas issue.

When the time came for the 1860 presidential campaign, the Democrats were hopelessly split over slavery. The biggest sticking point was the *Dred Scott* decision, which, by decreeing that Congress had no power to prohibit slavery in a territory, was just what southerners favoring popular sovereignty wanted. Yet it also created uncertainty about any legislature's authority over slavery. If Congress could not regulate slavery, could state legislatures? The Republicans were able to use the decision as a rallying point for popular control of government; the Democrats were in the uncustomary position of defending the Supreme Court, which since Thomas Jefferson they had pictured as elitist. Douglas, the eventual Democratic nominee and architect of the platform, insisted on state resolution of the slavery issue. Jefferson Davis of Mississippi, who later became president of the Confederate States of America, fought in Congress for the right of Congress to promote and protect slavery in new territories.

Eventually, the Davis Democrats held their own convention and nominated Vice President Breckinridge for the presidency. Although the Davis Democrats insisted that they were the backbone of the party and had been strong enough to elect Buchanan four years before, the party divided would not be able to win a national election.

And that was the outcome; Democratic Party splits enabled Lincoln to win the 1860 election, resulting in the secession of seven Southern states from the Union even before his inauguration. (The remaining four states forming the Confederacy seceded after the fall of Fort Sumter, on April 13, 1861.)

Because the regional splits that had been tearing the nation apart for decades reached their peak in 1860, none of the four major candidates who were seeking the presidency could compete seriously throughout the nation. The winner was likely to be a candidate from the North, the region with the most electoral votes—that is, either former U.S. representative Abraham Lincoln of Illinois, a Republican, or Stephen Douglas, a Democrat, who defeated Lincoln for the Illinois Senate seat in 1858. Moderate Constitutional Union nominee John Bell of Tennessee and Democrat John Breckinridge of Kentucky were the candidates competing in the South.

The Republicans succeeded in 1860 because they were able to pull together a variety of potentially warring factions. But above all else the Republicans stood against the extension of slavery into new territories. By accepting slavery where it already existed but warning against the spread of the system, the Republicans divided the Democrats and picked up support from a diverse array of otherwise contentious factions—abolitionists, moderate abolitionists, and whites who feared for their position in the economy. Moreover, the *Dred Scott* decision enabled the Republicans to rail publicly against the high court in the tradition of Jefferson and Jackson. While opposing the Democratic doctrine of popular sovereignty, the Republicans picked up some states' rights sympathizers by having a middle-ground slavery stance.

At a frenzied Republican convention in Chicago, which blocked several radical candidates, Lincoln emerged as the consensus compromise choice. The fact that Lincoln was known widely throughout Illinois had improved his chances at the Chicago convention.

Douglas, Lincoln's principal rival, managed several moderate platform victories at the Democratic convention in Charleston, South Carolina, defeating resolutions that called for acceptance

Stephen Douglas, at five feet and four inches, was the 1860 Democratic candidate for president.

of the *Dred Scott* decision and protection of slavery in the territories. But Douglas's success prompted delegates from ten southern states to bolt the convention. After disputes over quorum rules and fifty-seven ballots, the Democrats were unable to muster the necessary two-thirds majority for Douglas. The convention therefore adjourned, reassembled in Baltimore, and faced disputes about the seating of delegates that caused further defections from the South. With southern radicals effectively eliminated from the convention, Douglas swept to a unanimous nomination victory.

The Democratic defectors named Vice President Breckinridge to run for president in the South. The Constitutional Union Party, which developed as a futile attempt to repair the nation's geographic divisions, nominated Bell to oppose Breckinridge. These two candidates were doomed from the start, however, because the South's electoral vote total was significantly below that of the North.

Thanks to the wide-ranging Republican coalition—one that eluded the Whigs in their last years of existence—Lincoln was able to count on strength in the areas that Fremont had won in 1856: New England and the upper Northwest, as well as New York and Ohio. Lincoln's political ties to Illinois, where he practiced law and began his public career, would help in Illinois and Indiana, and his background as a former Whig was a plus in the Ohio valley. The coal and iron regions of Pennsylvania and Ohio were attracted to the party's high-tariff policy. Urban immigrants, particularly Germans, were attracted by the Republican support of homestead (frontier settlement) legislation and the Lincoln campaign's "Vote Yourself a Farm" appeal.[35] The vice-presidential selection of Hannibal Hamlin of Maine, a former Democrat, broadened the coalition beyond partisan lines. Lincoln's oft-stated desire not to challenge slavery where it then existed was an appeal to border states.

Lincoln won easily with a total of 180 electoral votes to Breckinridge's 72, Bell's 39, and Douglas's 12. Lincoln's closest competitor in the popular vote was Douglas. Lincoln had 1.9 million northern popular votes (40.0 percent); Douglas had 1.4 million (29.5 percent) spread out geographically. The two other principal candidates received much less support, which was concentrated in the South: Breckinridge won 848,000 popular votes (18.1 percent); Bell, 591,000 (12.6 percent).

Because some southerners had vowed to secede from the Union if Lincoln won the election, in the period before Lincoln's inauguration congressional committees sought to put together a compromise that would save the nation from civil war. They failed, however, because of Lincoln's refusal to abandon his policy of containing slavery. He rejected proposals for popular sovereignty or a slave-free geographic division of western states, and he would not comment on proposals for constitutional amendments or popular referenda on the issue.

After Lincoln was elected, South Carolina, Louisiana, Mississippi, Alabama, Georgia, Texas, and Florida seceded from the Union and on February 7, 1861, adopted a constitution forming the Confederate States of America. After a protracted standoff between Union soldiers who held Fort Sumter and the Confederate soldiers who controlled South Carolina, the Confederates fired on the fort. Virginia, Arkansas, North Carolina, and Tennessee then joined the Confederacy, and the Civil War was under way.

THE CIVIL WAR ELECTION: 1864

The Union's military difficulties in 1861 and 1862 created resentment against and impatience with President Lincoln. The splits that developed in the Republican Party seemed to imperil his chances for renomination and reelection.

From the very beginning of his administration, Lincoln suffered because of the difficulty he had finding a general who could successfully prosecute the war. Repeated military setbacks and stalemates—such as the Battles of Fredericksburg and Chancellorsville, Confederate general Robert E. Lee's escape after the battle of Antietam (Sharpsburg), and heavy casualties in the drive to Richmond—hurt the Republicans. Publicized conflicts with Union generals such as George McClellan caused further damage. In addition to the military problems, the president's announcement in September 1862 of the emancipation of slaves in rebellious states (the Emancipation Proclamation) created legal and political controversy.

In the 1862 midterm elections, the Republicans experienced widespread losses in congressional and state elections. Among the more bitter defeats for Lincoln was Democrat John Stuart's victory in the president's old congressional district in Illinois. By the time of the presidential election, Stuart, a former law partner of the president, was an ardent political foe.

The military frustrations gave rise to deep divisions within Lincoln's own cabinet. Treasury Secretary Salmon P. Chase was a constant critic of Lincoln's capacity to serve as commander in chief, and the Philadelphia banker Jay Gould briefly led a movement for Chase's nomination for president in 1864. Chase withdrew only after the Lincoln forces dealt him a severe blow at the party caucus in his home state of Ohio. Other radicals met in Cleveland in May 1864 and named John Fremont to run against Lincoln in the fall. Fremont withdrew only after a series of Union military victories strengthened Lincoln's political standing.

The president manipulated the Republican convention in Baltimore brilliantly, ensuring not only his renomination but also the selection of pro-Union governor Andrew Johnson of Union-occupied Tennessee—a lifelong Democrat—as the vice-presidential candidate. Lincoln professed indifference about a possible running mate. "Wish not to interfere about V.P. Cannot interfere about platform," he said in a letter. "Convention must judge for itself."[36] Nevertheless, he maneuvered to build support for Johnson. Johnson's selection was in accord with the desire of the party, which also called itself the Union Party as a way to attract Democrats and to develop nationwide unity. Yet Lincoln's reelection drive was so uncertain that he obliged his cabinet in August 1864 to sign a statement pledging an orderly transition of power if he lost. The statement read: "This morning, as for some days past, it seems exceedingly probable that this Administration will not be reelected. Then it will be my duty to so cooperate with the President-elect, as to save the Union between the election and the inauguration; as he will have secured his elec-

Republican presidential candidate Abraham Lincoln stood tall at six feet and four inches.

President of the Confederacy

Jefferson Davis

In 1861, two weeks before Abraham Lincoln was inaugurated in Washington, D.C., as the sixteenth president of the United States, another president was inaugurated in Montgomery, Alabama. On February 18, 1861, Jefferson Davis became the first and only president of the Confederate States of America.

Davis was born in Christian (now Todd) County, Kentucky, on June 3, 1808. He was the youngest of the ten children of Samuel and Jane Davis, who moved their family to a small Mississippi plantation when Jefferson was a boy. He attended private schools and Transylvania University in Lexington, Kentucky, before his oldest brother, Joseph, secured his appointment to West Point in 1824.

After graduating from the academy, Davis was stationed in Wisconsin under Col. Zachary Taylor. There he saw action in the Black Hawk War during the early 1830s and fell in love with Taylor's daughter, Sarah Knox. In 1835 he left the army, married Sarah, and settled on a one-thousand-acre plantation in Mississippi, which was given to him by his brother Joseph. Tragically, Sarah died from malaria three months after the wedding, and for several years Davis devoted himself to developing his land and wealth.

In 1845 Davis married Varina Howell, a member of the Mississippi aristocracy, and was elected to the U.S. House of Representatives. He served in Washington less than a year before the Mexican War began, and he gave up his seat to accept a commission as a colonel. He became a national hero when his company made a stand at the Battle of Buena Vista that was said to have saved Gen. Zachary Taylor's army from defeat.

In 1847 he left the army and was elected to the Senate. He served there until 1851, when he ran unsuccessfully for governor of Mississippi. He returned to Washington in 1853 after being appointed secretary of war by President Franklin Pierce. Davis was credited with strengthening the armed forces during his time in office. He also was influential in bringing about the Gadsden Purchase from Mexico in 1853, which added southern areas of present-day Arizona and New Mexico to the United States.

In 1857 Davis was reelected to the Senate. Although he became a leading spokesperson for the South, he did not advocate secession until 1860 when it had become inevitable. Davis hoped to be appointed commanding general of the South's army, but instead he was chosen as president by a convention of the seceding states.

Davis believed his first priority as president was to preserve Southern independence. He tried to secure French and British assistance for the Confederacy, but he was largely unsuccessful. Like Lincoln he helped develop military strategy and on occasion interfered with the plans of his generals. In managing the war effort, Davis was hampered by his paradoxical position. The South could fight most effectively as a unified nation run by the central government in Richmond, but the Southern states had succeeded in part to preserve their rights as independent states. Davis took actions, including the suspension of *habeas corpus* and the establishment of conscription, that were regarded as despotic by many Southerners.

When the Union's victory appeared imminent in early 1865, Davis fled south from Richmond and was captured by federal troops. He was indicted for treason and imprisoned for two years, but he never stood trial. He lived in Canada and Europe for several years before retiring to Mississippi. There he wrote his *Rise and Fall of the Confederate Government*, which was published in 1881. He died in New Orleans on December 6, 1889.

tion on such ground that he cannot possibly save it afterwards."[37]

The man for whom Lincoln anticipated arranging a wartime transition was Democratic nominee George McClellan, whom Lincoln had fired as general in January 1863. McClellan had won the Democratic nomination with the strong backing of "peace Democrats" such as Clement L. Vallandigham of Ohio, who was arrested by Union general Ambrose E. Burnside after making a series of antiwar speeches. (Vallandigham later took up exile in Canada.) McClellan's running mate was Rep. George Pendleton of Ohio, who after the war would sponsor landmark civil service reform legislation.

Although popular with his soldiers, General McClellan had not won a single major battle of the war despite many infusions of extra troops. Yet he blamed Lincoln for the losses. Indeed, he was a vocal critic of the administration. McClellan's presidential campaign was built around a call for a cease-fire and a convention to restore the Union. He and his fellow peace Democrats also criticized the administration's violation of civil liberties and other unconstitutional actions.

Lincoln's fortunes improved in the two months before the election. When Gen. William Tecumseh Sherman took Atlanta after a scorched-earth march through the South, the Confederacy was left badly divided geographically. The military victory cut off the Gulf states from the Confederate capital of Richmond. Gen. Philip Sheridan had had important successes in the Shenandoah Valley, and Gen. Ulysses S. Grant had fared well in Virginia.

Not only did the Democrats face a Republican Party reconstituted for the war election as the Union Party and united by recent military victories, but McClellan also had a difficult time developing consistent campaign themes. He was at various times conciliatory toward the Confederacy and solicitous of the soldiers who fought for the Union. The balancing problem was underscored by the inclusion of both war and peace songs in the *McClellan Campaign Songster*, a piece of campaign literature.[38] McClellan also had a difficult time selling his message to Northern industrialists who were profiting from munitions procurement.

Not until the arrival of election results from three state elections on October 11 were Lincoln and the Unionists confident that they would win the national election in November. Republican victories in Indiana, Ohio, and Pennsylvania were the first concrete indications that Lincoln's fortunes had turned around.

Lincoln overwhelmed McClellan by winning all of the loyal states except Delaware, Kentucky, and New Jersey for a 212–21 electoral vote victory. Lincoln garnered 2.2 million popular votes (55.0 percent) to McClellan's 1.8 million (45.0 percent). The electoral votes of Louisiana and Tennessee, the first Confederate states to return to the Union, were not accepted by Congress.

Postwar Radicalism

The end of the Civil War left the nation almost as divided as it had been in the antebellum years. Concerns about punishment of the rebel states, the status of the freedmen, and economic development replaced slavery as the principal sources of disagreement.

The nation undoubtedly would have experienced bitter splits no matter who had served as chief executive, but the assassination of President Lincoln on April 14, 1865, shortly after the Confederate surrender, created a crisis of leadership. Lincoln's vice president, Andrew Johnson, ascended to the presidency and quickly came into conflict with the radical Northern Republicans who controlled Congress. Johnson, a Democrat from Tennessee, was stubborn, which only aggravated the troubles that were inevitable anyway because of his party and regional background.

Johnson intended to continue Lincoln's plans for the reconstruction of the North and South "with malice toward none"; he chafed at the notion of the South as a conquered territory. A states' rights politician, Johnson attempted to put together a coalition of moderates from all parts of the country that would bring about a quick reconciliation between his administration and Congress.

But Congress was intent on establishing political institutions that would respect the rights of former slaves and promote economic growth and vowed to use military occupation to destroy the South's old political elite.[39] Thus Johnson and Congress fought over bills that would extend the life of the Freedmen's Bureau (an agency established to help blacks make the transition from slavery to citizenship) and guarantee the franchise and equal protection to blacks, with the result that Johnson ve-

The 1872 Republican campaign called voters' attention to the humble backgrounds of presidential candidate Ulysses S. Grant and his running mate, Henry Wilson.

toed both bills. Johnson also opposed the Fourteenth Amendment, which guaranteed equal protection, as well as the stipulation that Confederate states approve the amendment as a condition of their readmission to the Union.

When the Radical Republicans took over Congress in the 1866 midterm elections, the war with Johnson began in earnest. In March 1867 Congress established limited military rule in recalcitrant Southern states and in May passed the Tenure of Office Act limiting the president's right to dismiss his appointees. Johnson contemptuously disregarded the tenure act and fired Edwin Stanton, his secretary of war. For this action Johnson was impeached by the House and tried by the Senate. When the Senate voted in May 1868, he avoided the two-thirds total needed for conviction by a single vote (35–19).

THE GRANT VICTORIES: 1868 AND 1872

Ulysses S. Grant was more than a concerned citizen during the dispute between Johnson and Congress. Despite its portrayal in many history books as a clear instance of congressional abuse of power, the affair was more complicated. All of the players in the drama negotiated their way with care, and almost none of them escaped without major scars. Grant was a central figure, and his style of maneuvering was dictated by his ambition to succeed Johnson as president.

Radical Republicans in Congress achieved a lasting victory when they secured passage of the Civil Rights Act of 1866 over President Johnson's veto, but they were increasingly disturbed by reports that the statute was not being enforced. A congressional investigation of violence against blacks in Memphis concluded that the Freedmen's Bureau could not enforce civil rights without help. Radicals began to look to Secretary of War Stanton to enforce the law that the president clearly disliked and repeatedly subverted. When Stanton indicated that he would carry out the law in the Confederacy as Congress intended, Johnson began to think about replacing him. At this point Congress passed the Tenure of Office Act over Johnson's veto in May 1867, reasoning that its constitutional "advise and consent" powers over appointments could be extended to removal as well. Johnson, however, decided to test the law's constitutionality.

In replacing Stanton, Johnson's concern—and indeed the concern of all involved—was who could assume the secretary of war post with minimal threat to Johnson's own position. Johnson first considered General Sherman but decided to appoint Grant on a temporary basis. Originally a Democrat and supporter of moderate policies toward the South, Grant worried about appearing too close to the unpopular president. As a result, after vaguely assuring Johnson that he would accept a temporary appointment, Grant hedged. He increasingly expressed support for the notion that appointees should interpret and obey laws according to congressional intent. Eventually Grant told the president in a letter that he could not accept the appointment.

After the drama of Johnson's impeachment in 1868, Grant was in a good position to seek the White House. He had avoided allying himself with controversy during both Johnson's search for a replacement for Stanton and the ensuing impeachment battle. In fact, he and Chief Justice Salmon Chase were the only ones not tainted by the affair. Grant even managed to maintain his public posture of disinterested duty. Thus during one of the nation's ugliest political episodes, Grant looked clean. He was ready for a presidential campaign.

As Johnson endured his Senate impeachment trial in March, Grant won his first electoral victory. A New Hampshire congressional campaign, which normally would favor the Democrat, became an early Grant referendum when Republican candidate Donald Sickles told voters that a vote for a Republican was a vote for Grant; Sickles won. Just before the Republican convention in May, a Soldiers and Sailors Convention "nominated" Grant. Yet he avoided an excessively military image when he vowed to reduce the size of the standing army. Grant was on his way.

Grant won the presidential nomination without opposition. The real battle at the 1868 Republican convention was for the vice-presidential nomination. Schuyler Colfax of Indiana, the Speaker of the House, won on the sixth ballot; eleven candidates received votes on the initial roll call.

The Democrats had a difficult time finding a nominee. Johnson sought the Democratic nomination, but his appeal was to the South. (Because many Southern states were still outside the Union, Northern politicians were selecting the nominee.) Chief Justice Chase, highly regarded for his fairness during Johnson's Senate trial, was a possibility, but his strong stand for black suffrage was a barrier. Sen. Thomas A. Hendricks of Indiana was strong in the East, and George Pendleton of Ohio, the party's vice-presidential candidate four years earlier, was strong in the West. Gen. Winfield Scott Hancock of Pennsylvania presented the opportunity of running one military hero against another.

After twenty-three bitter ballots in a sweltering New York City, Horatio Seymour, the national party chair and popular war governor of New York, accepted the Democratic nomination against his will. Gen. Francis P. Blair Jr. of Missouri was the vice-presidential nominee. The party platform called for the rapid reentry of Confederate states to the Union, state authority over suffrage questions, and the "Ohio Idea," which promised an inflationary money supply that would help the indebted South.

Both sides were well financed in the election, but the Republicans had the edge. The Republican Party's probusiness positions on the tariff, railroad grants, and the currency attracted millions of dollars. Newspapers and magazines tended to be pro-Republican because of their urban business orientations.

Grant, who ran his campaign from his home in Galena, Illinois, was vague about issues ranging from the currency to voting rights. Appearances in Colorado with fellow generals Sherman and Sheridan were taken to be endorsements. Everything seemed to go Grant's way. Even the traditional campaign gossip about the sexual activities of candidates did not hurt him. Charges that Grant was excessively problack—"I am Captain Grant of the Black Marines, the stupidest man that was ever seen" were the lyrics of one ditty[40]—helped him with the recently enfranchised citizens. Without the black vote, Grant probably would have lost the popular vote and perhaps the electoral vote. Results from October state elections that favored the Republicans created a brief movement for Seymour and Blair to quit the contest so that the Democrats could name a new ticket. Instead Seymour took the October results as an incentive to get to the campaign stump. Seymour was a good speaker, but nothing he could do could help the Democrats.

Grant defeated Seymour by 3.0 million (52.7 percent) to 2.7 million votes (47.3 percent). The electoral vote tally was 214 for Grant and 80 for Seymour. Finally, Grant won all but eight of the thirty-four states taking part in the election. He benefited from Radical Republican reconstructionist sentiment in the North and newly enfranchised blacks in the South.

With Grant's ascension to the presidency in 1869, the Republican Party entered a new era—what the German sociologist Max Weber would have called a shift from "charismatic" to "rational" institutional authority. In other words, the party shifted its devotion from a great moral cause to its own survival as an organization. It had begun as a coalition of activists fervently opposed to the expansion of slavery (many opposed slavery itself) and to the rebellion of Southern states from the Union.

The Republicans' 1868 victory under Grant was the first not dominated wholly by crisis conditions.

The Republicans had a strong base of support: eastern bankers, manufacturers, railroads, and land speculators. With the old Confederacy under the control of military governments and with blacks given the franchise, the Republicans had strength in the South. The West was restive, however, because of depressed farm prices, high taxes, and debt. The industrial-agrarian split between North and South before the Civil War would be resumed as an East-West split in the years after the war.

The Republican leadership itself was changing. Age was claiming a number of the early Republican leaders, such as Thaddeus Stevens, William Seward, Benjamin Wade, Charles Sumner, James Grimes, Edwin Stanton, and Salmon Chase. New party leaders included Senators Roscoe Conkling of New York, Oliver Morton of Indiana, Simon Cameron of Pennsylvania, and Zachariah Chandler of Michigan, and Representatives Benjamin Butler of Massachusetts, John Logan of Illinois, James Garfield of Ohio, and James G. Blaine of Maine.

As for the new Grant administration, it was undistinguished. The new president's inaugural address—spoken without the traditional company of the outgoing president because Grant had neglected to respond to Johnson's polite letters—was decent but uninspiring. Grant vowed that "all laws will be faithfully executed, whether they meet my approval or not," that debtors would not be tolerated, and that blacks should get the vote throughout the country and Indians should be offered "civilization and ultimate citizenship."[41] With a few important exceptions, cabinet positions went to old Grant cronies.

In 1869 the nation experienced a financial panic when financiers Jay Gould and Jim Fisk attempted to corner the world's gold market. Their scheme led to "Black Friday," September 24, 1869. Gould and Fisk had met with President Grant and had urged him not to sell government gold, therefore keeping the price of gold high. At the last minute, however, Grant decided to reject their advice and dumped $4 million worth of gold on the market. That dumping caused a severe drop in gold prices, breaking up the Gould-Fisk conspiracy but also causing tremendous losses for thousands of speculators. It was the worst disaster on Wall Street up to that time. Although it did not cause a depression, the South and West were hard hit by the financial retrenchment program that followed. Tariff rates remained high on most manufactured goods, despite tentative efforts to reform the system.

The spoils system was in full swing during the Grant years. Grant himself was not involved in the scramble for booty, but his family and aides were often shameless in their greed. When Grant learned that liberal Republicans were planning an independent presidential campaign against him in 1872, he took the edge off the spoils issue by creating the Civil Service Reform Commission, but his neglect of the commission made it ineffective.

Before the 1872 election, the *New York Sun* exposed the Crédit Mobilier scandal. The newspaper reported that the firm's board of directors had many of the same members as the Union Pacific Railroad Company, which hired it to build a transcontinental route, and that Crédit Mobilier had paid its board exorbitant profits. To avoid a public investigation, Crédit Mobilier offered stock to Vice President Colfax and Representative (later president) James Garfield. Colfax lost his place on the Republican ticket for his role in the scandal; Sen. Henry Wilson of New Hampshire took his position as the vice-presidential candidate in 1872.

Liberal Republicans, unhappy with protective tariffs, spoils, and the uneven administration of the Southern states, bolted the party in 1872. The group was interested in policies such as civil service and free trade that would promote individual virtue in a laissez-faire economic system. The reformers thought they had a chance to win. The German-born senator Carl Schurz of Missouri wrote to a friend that "the administration with its train of offices and officemongers [is] the great incubus pressing upon the party. . . . The superstition that Grant is the necessary man is rapidly giving way. The spell is broken, and we have only to push through the breach."[42]

Candidates for the nomination from this group of Republicans included former ambassador to Great Britain Charles Francis Adams, son of President John Quincy Adams and grandson of President John Adams; Supreme Court Justice David Davis; Chief Justice Salmon Chase; Sen. Lyman Trumbull of Illinois; and Horace Greeley, editor of the *New York Tribune*. Greeley won the nomination on the sixth ballot and ran as a Democrat and Liberal Republican. The Democrats were so weak that they did not field a candidate of their own. They endorsed the Greeley ticket. (Charles O'Conor of New York was nominated by a group of "Noncoalition Democrats" for president. He did not accept the nomination.)

Since his early days as a newspaper reporter, when he described President Van Buren as an effeminate failure, Greeley had won fame as a pungent social critic. He was a crusading, abolitionist editor and a dedicated reformer, but his rumpled appearance and unpolished speaking style made him appear "unpresidential." Greeley was unable to parlay an amalgam of promises to various interest groups—blacks, soldiers, immigrants, and laborers—into a victory over Grant. Groups that Greeley actively courted found him wanting for a variety of reasons, and even though Greeley advocated the tariff favored by the North, he could not cut into Grant's northeastern strength. One Republican cartoon that revealed Greeley's difficult task showed a fence on which sat a laborer, skeptical because of Greeley's stand against strikes, and a black, concerned because of Greeley's advocacy of amnesty for Confederates. Sitting on the sidelines was a German, upset with Greeley's prohibitionist stance: "Oh! Yaw! You would take my Lager away, den you must get widout me along!"[43]

Even though he went on the stump and delivered a series of impressive speeches, Greeley never had a chance. Republican gubernatorial victories in North Carolina in August and in Pennsylvania, Ohio, and Indiana in October were clear harbingers that the Republican Party would do well in November. Grant took the entire North and the newly admitted South with 3.6 million popular votes (55.6 percent). Greeley won three border states, as well as Tennessee, Texas, and Georgia, with 2.8 million popular votes (43.9 percent). Less than a month after the election, Greeley died. Of the electoral votes, which were cast after Greeley's death, Grant received 286; the Democrats' 63 electoral votes were scattered among various candidates, and 17 Democratic electoral votes were not cast.

THE COMPROMISE OF 1876

The pattern of Republican, northern, and business domination of presidential politics was institutionalized in the 1876 election. Republican Rutherford B. Hayes, the three-time governor of Ohio, lost the popular vote and had a questionable hold on the electoral college vote, but he managed to beat Democrat Samuel J. Tilden for the presidency when the election was settled by a special commission created by Congress. (Hayes won 4.0 million votes to Tilden's 4.3 million—48.0 and 51.0 percent of the popular vote, respectively.) Perhaps the most controversial election outcome in history, some feared it would set off a second civil war.

The problem arose when the vote tallies in Florida, South Carolina, and Louisiana were called into question. Violence had accompanied the voting in all three states, but President Grant had not sent in federal troops to ensure fair balloting. On those states hung the electoral outcome. There was good reason to be suspicious of any vote count in those and other southern states. While the Republicans had controlled the balloting places and mounted vigorous drives to get blacks to the polls, the Democrats had used physical intimidation and bribery to keep blacks away. The bitterness between northern interests and southern whites was apparent in the violence that often took place at polls.

When state election board recounts and investigations did not settle the question of the vote tallies, Congress took up the matter. An electoral commission made up of five senators (three majority-party Republicans, two minority Democrats), five representatives (three majority-party Democrats, two minority Republicans), and five Supreme Court justices (two from each party, one independent) assembled to hear complaints about the disputed states. At the last minute the independent justice disqualified himself, and his place was taken by a Republican who was accepted by Democrats because they considered him to be the most independent of the Republican justices. Weeks of bargaining followed, during which the Republican vote totals of the disputed states were confirmed and the southern Democrats extracted promises of financial aid and political independence from the federal government.

When the validity of the Florida vote count for Hayes was challenged, the commission responded that it did not have the capacity to judge the actual conduct of the balloting, only the validity of the certificates presented to Congress. That decision gave the state to Hayes. Challenges to the vote counts of Louisiana, South Carolina, and Oregon were dismissed in a similar way, so Hayes was awarded the presidency by a single electoral vote, 185 to 184.

The compromise not only settled the partisan dispute between Hayes and Tilden, but also established a rigid alignment of political interests that would dominate U.S. politics for the next half-century. Although Democrats won occasional victories, the Republican, eastern, conservative, business-oriented establishment held sway over the system until Franklin Roosevelt's election in 1932.

The institutional form of the regional splits created by the compromise remained much longer. Historian C. Vann Woodward has argued that secret wheeling and dealing among congressional and party leaders institutionally divided the political system by party, region, economic interest, and governmental branches. Northern Republican industrial interests were given control of the presidential election process, and southern Democratic agricultural interests were given autonomy over their regional politics, which led to domination of Congress.[44] This alignment was not completely dislodged until the passage of important civil rights legislation in the 1960s.

To reward southern Democrats for throwing the 1876 election to the Republican Hayes, northern politicians agreed to pull federal troops out of the South and to allow southern whites to take over the system. Within months southern states were erecting a powerful edifice of racial discrimination that would last until the 1960s. Former South Carolina governor Daniel H. Chamberlain, a Republican, later summed up the deal:

What is the president's Southern policy? [I]t consists in the abandonment of Southern Republicans and especially the colored race, to the control and rule not only of the Democratic Party, but of that class of the South which regarded slavery as a Divine Institution, which waged four years of destructive war for its perpetuation, which steadily opposed citizenship and suffrage for the negro—in a word, a class whose traditions, principles, and history are opposed to every step and feature of what Republicans call our national progress since 1860.[45]

The Age of Republicanism

From 1860 to 1908, the Republicans won eleven elections; the Democrats won only two. Only Grover Cleveland could put together a Democratic win, and he was as conservative on most issues as the Republicans of the period. Presidential election winners after the Great Compromise were Hayes (1876), James Garfield (1880), Cleveland (1884), Benjamin Harrison (1888), Cleveland (1892), William McKinley (1896 and 1900), Theodore Roosevelt (1904), and William Howard Taft (1908).

The political aspirants of the day were required to adhere to the creed of high tariffs, laissez-faire economics, and tight money. Tight money policies—the restricted issuance of currency, which favored bankers and other established interests but hurt debtors and those seeking more rapid expansion of some kinds of investment and spending—provided rare openings for effective Democratic resistance to Republican hegemony. Resistance did develop, however, when the scramble for tariff protections created obvious inequities among businesses and hardships for the consumer. Yet populist uprisings, such as Democrat William Jennings Bryan's 1896 campaign, faltered because of strong mobilization by the Republicans and divisions within the Democratic ranks. Bryan failed to bring a likely Democratic con-

The fiery oratory of 1884 Republican candidate James G. Blaine captured the imagination of the political establishment, but it was not enough to win him the election over Democrat Grover Cleveland.

stituency—the worker—into the fold. Eastern business owners were able to portray their interest in industrial growth as a common concern with labor and Bryan's western agrarian alliance as a danger to that growth.

Although the Republican Party dominated presidential politics, the parties were well balanced in Congress and in state governments until the class and sectional cleavages of the 1890s. The Senate was split evenly in 1881, 37–37, and two years later the Republicans had a 38–36 edge. The Democrats had made gains in northern congressional races, and Republicans were making smaller gains in the South. The House tended to provide a majority for whichever party held the White House.

GARFIELD CARRIES THE REPUBLICAN BANNER: 1880

Hayes honored his pledge to serve only one term, setting off a scramble for both parties' nominations in 1880. When the early momentum for a third term for Grant faltered, the Republican contest became a battle between Grant, Sen. James G. Blaine of Maine, and Treasury Secretary John Sherman of Ohio. Grant was able to muster a first-ballot plurality but could not attract new supporters as the balloting proceeded. A stalemate between Blaine and Sherman ensued.

Rep. James Garfield of Ohio, a former preacher who was impressive in his oratory and organization for Sherman, was the compromise choice for the nomination. He selected as his running mate Chester A. Arthur, the collector of the Port of New York, an important patronage job.

The Democrats named Gen. Winfield Hancock of Pennsylvania and former Indiana representative William English to head their ticket. The Democratic platform advocated the gold standard, a low tariff designed to raise revenue, civil service reform, restrictions on Chinese immigration, and a belated criticism of the 1876 deal that gave the presidency to Hayes. Except for the tariff and 1876 questions, the Democrats' platform was close to the Republicans' statement of principles.

The regional breakdown of support, with most of the North and West falling in Garfield's camp and the South lining up behind Hancock, gave the presidency to Garfield. The popular vote was close—4.45 million (48.27 percent) to 4.44 million (48.25 percent)—but Garfield won a 214–155 electoral vote victory.

The festering issue of patronage and civil service came to a head shortly after Garfield's inauguration. On July 2, 1881, Charles Guiteau, a man later described as a "disappointed office-seeker," shot Garfield while he was en route to Williams College to deliver a commencement address. Garfield died in September, and Arthur became president.

The outstanding feature of Arthur's presidency was the easy passage of the Pendleton Act—legislation that set up a commission to regulate the provision of federal jobs and the behavior of civil servants. The number of federal workers removed from the patronage system was at first small, but successive presidents widened the coverage of nonpartisan workers so that today less than 1 percent of all federal workers are appointed by the president.[46]

The tariff question also emerged as crucial during the Arthur presidency. The Tariff Act of 1883 "gave little or no relief to the consumer and took care of every important industrial interest."[47] The Democrats opposed the bill and later worked for the gradual lowering of rates, but they failed. The tariff would be a major issue in later elections.

DEMOCRAT CLEVELAND WINS: 1884

Arthur wanted the Republican nomination in 1884, and his record as stand-in for the assassinated Garfield arguably should have earned him the nod—even though no successor president during the nineteenth century had been nominated by his party.

Not only was he an important player in civil service reform and the tariff issue, but he initiated modernization of the navy and vetoed the Chinese Exclusion Act of 1882, which prohibited Chinese laborers from entering the United States for ten years. His veto of the $19 million rivers and harbors bill was a model of fiscal probity.

James Blaine of Maine—secretary of state in Arthur's own administration—stood in Arthur's way. After months of public appeals by old-line Republicans interested in stronger leadership and more generous patronage from their party, Blaine quit his administration position and opposed Arthur for the nomination.

Blaine was the most charismatic figure of the period. A former teacher, editor, state legislator, and member of Congress, Blaine's fiery oratory captured the imagination of the political establishment. He had made a national name for himself when he opposed an 1876 congressional resolution expressing forgiveness to Civil War rebels including the Confederate president, Jefferson Davis. Col. Robert G. Ingersoll, a rising political figure in the Republican Party, said of Blaine: "Like an armed warrior, like a plumed knight, James G. Blaine marched down the halls of the American Congress and threw his shining lance full and fair against the brazen forehead of every traitor to his country."[48] The sobriquet "Plumed Knight" caught on.

The Republican convention in Chicago praised Arthur's administration and fudged the tariff issue. The tariff that passed in 1883 was the product of the efforts of swarms of lobbyists for private interests. The Republican platform promised better protection for raw wool interests, angered by their treatment in 1883, and a generally protective stance for domestic industry. The platform also called for an international currency conference, railway regulation, a national agency for labor affairs, and further improvements in the navy.

At a frenzied convention, Blaine took the lead over Arthur on the first ballot. Old-line party leaders quickly united behind Blaine, while Arthur was unable to consolidate the support of reform Republicans still skeptical of his leadership abilities from his days as a patronage politician and collector of the Port of New York. Blaine won the nomination on the fourth ballot. Gen. John Logan of Illinois received the vice-presidential nomination.

The Democrats nominated Grover Cleveland after skirmishes with Sen. Thomas F. Bayard Jr. of Delaware and Sen. Thomas A. Hendricks of Indiana. Hendricks, whose liberal expansionist currency stance would balance the more conservative stance of Cleveland, was named the vice-presidential candidate. The Democratic platform vaguely promised reform of the tariff laws to make them fairer and, even more vaguely, promised a more honest and efficient administration.

Cleveland was a former teacher, lawyer, assistant district attorney, and reform mayor of Buffalo who had won the governorship of New York only two years before. Members of both parties consistently underestimated Cleveland's intellect and resolve. As governor, he had made enemies through his vetoes of low public transit fares and aid to sectarian schools. He also had defied Tammany Hall, the Democratic Party organization that dominated New York politics, especially in New York City.

Cleveland's nomination signaled a triumph for the "educational politics" characteristic of urban progressivism. (Progressives took a patriarchal view of politics in which elites assumed an obligation to better their social underlings through education and various social services.) In a move away from the highly partisan and vitriolic campaigns of the post–Civil War era, Cleveland and other disciples of former New York governor Samuel Tilden promoted their program through a "literary bureau" that distributed pamphlets describing the party's policy positions. Campaign themes were developed at the national level and disseminated via the mails and meetings with the many professional and community organizations. The educational style was adopted by Republican candidate Benjamin Harrison in 1888.[49]

In contrast, Blaine's campaign was one of the dirtiest in U.S. history. He first attempted to spark sectional antagonisms with his "bloody shirt" warnings that the South was trying to reassert its rebel ways through Cleveland. Blaine also tried to rouse the fears of business with claims that Cleveland would institute free trade policies damaging to domestic industries. But that appeal failed because the Democratic platform's plank on the tariff laws specifically supported protection of those interests. Finally, Blaine tried to make a scandal of Cleveland's admission that he had fathered a child out of wedlock years before. Cleveland was charged, among other things, of kidnapping and immuring both the mother and child to cover up the story.

The campaign eventually turned on Cleveland's victory in New York, which resulted from a number of blunders by Blaine. One blunder had occurred years before, when Blaine mocked New York party boss Roscoe Conkling: "The contempt of that large-minded gentleman is so wilted, his haughty disdain, his grandiloquent swell, his majestic, supereminent, overpowering, turkey-gobbler strut, has been so crushing to myself that I know it was an act of the greatest temerity to venture upon a controversy with him."[50] Conkling was so peeved by the turkey image that he spent his whole career battling Blaine, including the presidential campaign of 1884. Blaine's own running mate, Logan, sympathized with Conkling in the dispute.

The other Blaine faux pas occurred a week before the election when a Protestant minister praised Blaine and proclaimed, "We are Republicans, and do not propose to leave our party and identify ourselves with the party whose antecedents have been rum, Romanism, and rebellion." Blaine did not divorce himself from the remark, which angered New York Democrats—and ethnic voters everywhere—and cost him many votes. Later the same day Blaine attended a formal dinner with a number of wealthy persons that became known as "the millionaires dinner." That event belied Blaine's claim to speak for ordinary people.

Of Irish background, Blaine appealed to Irish immigrants in New York for their votes. But Cleveland countered Blaine's Irish tactic by obtaining the last-minute endorsement of the powerful Tammany leader Edward Kelly. On the Saturday before the election, he attended a parade in New York City that attracted forty thousand people chanting: "Blaine, Blaine, James G. Blaine, the Monumental Liar from the State of Maine!" With the help of an economic downturn and the "Mugwumps"—independents and liberal Republicans offended by Blaine—Cleveland won the presidency.

The race, however, was close. Cleveland received 4.9 million votes (48.5 percent) to Blaine's 4.8 million (48.3 percent). He won the solid South, Indiana, Connecticut, New Jersey, and, most important, New York (although by only 1,047 out of 1.13 million votes cast). Still, the election controversy did not end with the balloting. The *New York Tribune* reported that Blaine had won the race, fueling fears about an election deadlock similar to the Hayes-Tilden contest of 1876. But Cleveland received 219 electoral votes to Blaine's 182, making the Democrat the clear winner.

Cleveland's first two years in the White House were productive. His inaugural address and cabinet selections elicited wide praise. And his style of leadership—examined closely in the newspapers—appeared refreshingly unassuming. The Cleveland agenda included issues such as tariff reform (cutting rates on the "necessaries of life"), modernization of the navy, civil service, expansion, and land law reform. The president oversaw passage of the Presidential Succession Act and the Electoral Count Act, changes in currency policy, and labor controversies.

Just as he had done during his terms as mayor of Buffalo and governor of New York, Cleveland icily refused to compromise his values. This steadfastness proved to be a problem, however, for *President* Cleveland. Thousands of Democratic Party workers went to Washington seeking jobs in the new administration only to be disappointed. "Ah, I suppose you mean that I should appoint two horse thieves a day instead of one," Cleveland said in response to one party leader.[51] In vetoing pension bills, Cleveland called their sponsors "blood-suckers," "coffee-boilers," "pension leeches," and "bums."[52] The president appeared just as aloof to labor when a record number of strikes and disturbances swept the nation in 1886; the federal troops that Cleveland sent to the Haymarket riot in Chicago killed thirty people.

When Cleveland did bend to political realities, his timing was off. After standing firm against patronage when party enthusiasm for reform was at its height, Cleveland disappointed reformers when he allowed lieutenants such as First Assistant Postmaster Adlai E. Stevenson to distribute favors.

The biggest controversy of the Cleveland administration involved tariffs. Concerned about federal budget surpluses that threatened to stall economic activity, Cleveland prodded the House of Representatives to pass tariff reductions. The Senate responded with a protective (high) tariff measure.

THE 1888 REPUBLICAN RECOVERY

The tariff issue propelled the two parties into the 1888 election. At their national convention the Democrats nominated Cleveland by acclamation and chose seventy-five-year-old judge Allen G. Thurman of Ohio for the vice presidency. The Democrats tried to soften their low-tariff image by promising that open trade would open world markets to domestic industries. Lower tariffs were said to be necessary for avoiding disastrous federal budget surpluses, preventing the development of monopolies, and ensuring consumers reasonable prices for basic goods.

Captioned "Another Voice for Cleveland," this 1884 cartoon played on Cleveland's admission that he had fathered an illegitimate son.

As for the Republicans, a politics-weary James Blaine sent word from Florence and Paris that he would not be a candidate in 1888, leaving the race open to some lesser political lights, including Sen. John Sherman of Ohio, Gov. Russell Alger of Michigan, Sen. William Allison of Iowa, and Sen. Benjamin Harrison of Indiana. At the Republican national convention Sherman led the early balloting but quickly lost ground to Alger and Harrison. After extensive backroom maneuvering, including a last-minute plea by party members to Blaine to accept the nomination, Harrison, who had the backing of state party bosses, won on the ninth ballot. Levi Morton, a banker, got the vice-presidential nomination.

Harrison, a senator from Indiana, was a former Civil War brigadier and the grandson of President William Henry Harrison. Characterized by a scandal-free if colorless demeanor, Harrison was a good speaker, but he often appeared aloof. One historian wrote: "Those who talked with him were met with a frigid look from two expressionless steel grey eyes; and their remarks were sometimes answered in a few chill monosyllables devoid of the slightest note of interest."[53] Harrison pledged a modernized navy, civil service reforms, and the traditional Republican policies to protect trusts and restrict U.S. markets.

The election turned, as in 1884, on New York and Indiana—both states with extensive evidence of voter intimidation and manipulation of vote counts. Harrison won the two states narrowly—New York by only 14,373 votes out of the 1.3 million cast—and captured the White House. Except for Connecticut and New Jersey, Harrison swept the North and West. Cleveland won the South. Overall, Harrison won 5.4 million popular votes (47.8 percent) and 233 electoral votes; Cleveland won 5.5 million popular votes (48.6 percent) and 168 electoral votes.

Cleveland left the White House with an unusual amount of good will among the public because of his honest tariff campaign. His popularity increased during the next four years as the economy hit slumps and as the former president, while practicing law, delivered speeches calling for a more egalitarian brand of politics. Cleveland would be back in 1892 for vindication.

With a majority in Congress and a president in the White House—the first time the party had accomplished such a feat in a dozen years—the Republicans went about their business briskly after the election. Postmaster General John Wanamaker dispensed patronage with zeal. President Harrison signed into law the McKinley Tariff Act and the Sherman Silver Purchase Act. The former raised duties on manufactured goods to their highest level ever but also included provisions for negotiating with other countries to bring the rates down. The silver act loosened the money supply, which stimulated economic activity but angered creditors and bankers (money, when it is more readily available, is worth less).

CLEVELAND'S COMEBACK: 1892

The 1890 midterm elections brought huge Democratic gains. Voters all over the country—but especially in the depressed farm belt—rebelled against the inflation that high tariffs brought. The Republicans held on to the Senate, but the new House of Representatives had 235 Democrats, 88 Republicans, and 9 Farmers' Alliance members. The brief experiment with party government ended with two years of stalemate.

President Harrison evoked widespread discontent in 1892 for both his demeanor and his policies, but no Republican could mount an effective challenge. Through their strong party government, Republicans had cast their lot with Harrison and had few places to turn for an alternative. Political wizard Mark Hanna, a wealthy coal magnate who had become a powerful behind-the-scenes Republican strategist, promoted Ohio governor William McKinley, and Secretary of State James Blaine became an alternative when he abruptly quit the administration just before the Republican convention. But Harrison received a first-ballot nomination. Former minister to France Whitelaw Reid of New York got the vice-presidential nomination.

In the battle for the Democratic nomination, Cleveland enjoyed widespread backing among rank-and-file voters, but party leaders were suspicious. New York governor David B. Hill got a head start when he called a "snap" state convention and won the delegation. An "anti-snapper" convention from New York sent a rival delegation to the national party convention. Democrats across the country rebelled at Hall's move and rapidly switched their support to Cleveland.

Another problem for Cleveland was the rising sentiment in agrarian states for free and unlimited coinage of silver—a way of boosting sagging farm prices by inducing inflation in the overall economy. Cleveland always had opposed this solution. The former president's consistent, principled stance on the issue not only added to his reputation for integrity but also kept business- and finance-dominated northeastern states in the Democratic camp. Cleveland defeated Hall for the nomination on the

Grover Cleveland is welcomed back on board the "Ship of State" in this 1893 cartoon. Having served as president from 1885 to 1889, he lost the 1888 election but regained the White House in the 1892 contest. Cleveland remains the only president to serve two nonconsecutive terms.

first ballot and selected his former first assistant postmaster Adlai Stevenson of Illinois as his running mate.

The fall campaign was uneventful. Historian Eugene Roseboom wrote: "Honest bearded Benjamin Harrison confronting honest mustached Grover Cleveland in a tariff debate was a repeat performance that did not inspire parades with torches or the chanting of campaign ditties. . . . Democrats, out of power, could assail Republican tariff policy without clarifying their own position."[54]

Cleveland won easily. He received 5.6 million popular votes (46.1 percent) to Harrison's 5.2 million (43.0 percent) and 277 electoral votes to Harrison's 145. Populist general James B. Weaver, advocating expansion of currency and limits on interest rates, won 1.0 million popular votes (8.5 percent) and 22 electoral votes.

The Age of Reform

Throughout the period dominated by Republican conservatism—from Grant's election in 1868 to William McKinley's 1896 win—movements for the reform of political and economic institutions gathered strength at all levels of the American political system. The so-called populists and progressives did not overturn the system, as their rhetoric sometimes suggested, but over time they made major changes in the operation and discourse of U.S. politics.

Depending on the time and place, people who called themselves "populists" and "progressives" promoted such contradictory notions as strict morals and free spirits, tight money and loose money, redistribution to the masses and control of the economy by elites, federal intervention and local control of politics, the opening and closing of electoral participation, technological progress and a return to a long-gone pastoral ideal, individualism and community action, ethnic celebration and immigration barriers, scientific investigation and religion, and internationalism and isolationism.

Reformism was the response to the pressures of national expansion, urban development, and growth. Both major parties had adopted probusiness, laissez-faire policies in the latter part of the nineteenth century; indeed, the parties seemed to exist mainly to ensure the terrain was suitable for economic expansion. But the lack of any program to deal with the undesired consequences of explosive growth led to an accumulation of problems that demanded attention. The most obvious problems evolved on the opposite ends of the rural-urban continuum: on the farms and in the cities.

The farm problem developed as the United States became a major economic power in the world. Agriculture expanded on a vast scale to feed the booming cities and, with international trade, to bring foreign capital to the United States. By 1880, the value of U.S. wheat and flour exports nearly equaled that of cotton exports.[55] As agriculture became part of the international market, farmers became dependent not only on the vagaries of the weather but also on the fluctuations of currency in the larger economy.

In the thirty years after the Civil War, prices for farm staples fell steadily. A debt that could have been paid by producing one thousand bushels of grain immediately after the war required three thousand bushels in 1895. The more farmers produced to meet their obligations, the more prices fell to exacerbate their problems. A solution to the problem required confronting a wide array of issues, including tight money, bankers who charged 20 percent interest for loans, monopolies among farm equipment producers, high tariffs, railroad price gouging, shipping inflation, warehouse monopolies, and land speculation. Throughout the farm belt, particularly in the West, tens of thousands of farmers developed an "intense class consciousness."[56]

All these issues received attention from a variety of third parties and independent organizations, but the two major parties usually were inattentive. The Granger Movement of the 1870s, for example, took hold in several farm states and elected new legislatures and high state officials. The Greenback Party attempted to merge a labor-farmer alliance with a doctrine of silver use for public debts. Later, the Farmers' Alliance politicized the same issues. In 1892 the Populist Party had won 8.5 percent of the vote on a platform calling for free coinage of silver.

Another site of growing reformist strength was the city. The dominance of machines of both parties in the cities established an electoral system based on patronage but stubbornly opposed to any coherent program for addressing urban ills such as poverty, poor housing, unsanitary conditions, transportation, education, and unfair workplace practices. Electoral fraud spurred mostly middle-class reformers to devise new electoral and city government machinery, while social problems incited some insurgent class politics.[57] The labor movement developed strength during this period.[58]

Other parts of the progressive agenda developed with a greater understanding of the nationalization of the economic and political systems. The wider sphere of economic activities created calls for regulation of corporations, railroads, and banks, as well as attention to health and environmental concerns and product safety.

Until the ascendance of William Jennings Bryan, the Democratic presidential nominee in 1896, 1900, and 1908, the reformers had been unable to capture a major party. Partly because political activism was based at the state and local level, neither national party had adopted the reformers' widely variegated program as its own. But the depression of 1888 caused the populist forces to pull together more than they had during previous economic downturns, probably because of the accumulated effects of inaction. The earlier panic of 1873 had created a sectional rather than a party split, with the Democrats eventually adopting a more conservative stance on the debate over whether the currency should be expanded to spur economic activity and redistribute social burdens.[59]

The Republican presidential candidates in the post–Civil War years steadfastly opposed the class-oriented proposals of the progressive movement, especially the loose-money demands. The only Democrat to win the presidency since the Civil War was Cleveland, a stubborn advocate of hard money and other conservative economic policies, in 1884 and 1892. President Cleveland vetoed dozens of private pension bills, only grudgingly accepted railroad regulation, and did not address domestic problems in any comprehensive way. Cleveland's public statements on the currency question were especially strong. He called the use of silver "a dangerous and reckless experiment" that was "unpatriotic."[60] On the question of labor, Cleveland was just as conservative: he called out federal troops to put down the Pullman strike of 1894 and regularly preached about the evils of disorder that the labor movement seemed to foster.

Despite the complexity of the agriculture issue, the most concerted populist action concentrated on the currency question. The drive to overturn the prevailing conventional economic thought by moving from a gold (tight) to a gold and silver (loose) money standard captured the imagination of the entire farm belt stretching from the Southeast to the prairie and silver-producing states of the West. The silver standard was a very simple answer to the problem of farm prices: "If money was scarce, the farmer reasoned, then the logical thing was to increase the money supply."[61]

REPUBLICANS AND MCKINLEY TRIUMPH: 1896 AND 1900

Gold runs on banks, manipulation of the gold crisis by J. P. Morgan and other leading financiers, procorporation Supreme Court decisions, and antilabor actions all stirred up resentment in the South and West. The silver sentiment escalated. The Democratic convention in 1896 called for the issuance of silver and rejected a resolution praising President Cleveland.[62] The movement for a silver currency found an eloquent advocate in Bryan, a member of the House of Representatives from Nebraska, who defeated Richard P. Bland of Missouri for the 1896 Democratic presidential nomination on the strength of his fiery "Cross of Gold" speech.

The speech was one of the most emotional and successful in U.S. history. Bryan attacked eastern financiers and businessmen who exploited farmers. Using a theme to which his fall campaign would return, Bryan sought to expand the traditional Democratic conception of the independent working man to include farmers and factory workers.[63] In his speech's fortissimo, Bryan declared: "You shall not press down upon the brow of labor this crown of thorns, you shall not crucify mankind upon a cross of gold."[64]

In 1896 the Republicans nominated Ohio governor William McKinley after brilliant maneuvering by his manager, Mark Hanna. Hanna's chief strengths were fund raising and his mastery over state party organizations.

McKinley had little difficulty defeating Bryan. McKinley outspent the prairie populist by as much as ten-to-one, and he attracted the disaffected progold wing of the Democratic Party.[65] The Grand Old Party (or GOP as it was by then called) platform called for retention of the gold standard unless international negotiations could produce a bimetallic (silver and gold) currency system. The platform also called for restored tariff protections and an aggressive foreign policy in the Western Hemisphere.

Bryan's campaign was a political hurricane. He spent just $650,000, most of it donated by silver interests, compared with the millions McKinley spent. But Bryan traveled eighteen thousand miles and gave some six hundred speeches, and his campaign staffers put out an impressive quantity of literature. Several million copies of *Coin's Financial School,* a prosilver pamphlet, were distributed during the fall of 1896. Other silverites also maintained busy speaking schedules in the fall.

Bryan's appeal to industrial workers to join his coalition of independent businessmen failed, largely because they depended for their livelihoods on the very eastern interests that Bryan attacked. McKinley won not only the East but also the small cities and towns in Bryan's southern and western belt of support. Bryan was unable to win rural areas in the East. McKinley won the popular vote 7.1 million (51.0 percent) to 6.5 million (46.7 percent) and the electoral vote 271–176.

The effect of the 1896 presidential election was lasting. James Sundquist wrote: "For 20 years the two-party system had been based on dead issues of the past. It had offered the voters no means of expressing a choice on the crucial issues of domestic policy around which the country had been polarizing. . . . Then suddenly, with the nomination of Bryan in 1896, the party system took on meaning once again."[66]

The new Republican coalition included residents of cities, where capital and labor were both reasonably content with the economic growth that the GOP tariff policy promoted; farmers in the East and Midwest, who had strong ties to the "party of Lincoln" and who had come to favor high tariffs; Catholic, German Lutheran, and other liturgical Christian denominations; and some border states. Sundquist noted: "It was the persistence of the Civil War attachments that made the realignment of the North so largely a one-way movement—pro-Republican."[67]

After 1896, the competitive party balance that had prevailed for years gave way to lopsided party strength according to region—Democrats in the South, Republicans in the North. Strong opposition parties disappeared in all regions of the country, vesting political power in the hands of those already part of the system.

As political scientist E. E. Schattschneider has observed:

The 1896 party cleavage resulted from the tremendous reaction of conservatives in both major parties to the Populist movement. . . . [S]outhern conservatives reacted so strongly that they were willing to revive the tensions and animosities of the Civil War and the Reconstruction in order to set up a one-party sectional southern political monopoly in which nearly all Negroes and many poor whites were disenfranchised. One of the most important consequences of the creation of the Solid South was that it severed permanently the connection between the western and the southern wings of the Populist movement.[68]

Conservative Republicans won the White House in all but two (1912 and 1916) of the nine elections from 1896 to 1928. During this period the country experienced economic prosperity that blunted the possible activism of workers and the previous activism of farmers. With good harvests and rising commodity prices, the agrarian revolt fizzled. The development of new ore extraction methods and discovery of new gold deposits made calls for silver to expand the currency supply superfluous. The Spanish-American War in 1898, which McKinley reluctantly entered and the burgeoning mass media publicized, created a patriotic fervor.

McKinley's reelection in 1900 was even stronger than his 1896 election. He won 7.2 million popular votes (51.7 percent) to Bryan's 6.4 million (45.5 percent), and 292 electoral votes to Bryan's 155. McKinley swept to victory with all states except the South and the silver states of the West (Colorado, Montana, Idaho, and Nevada).

THE RISE OF THEODORE ROOSEVELT: 1904

Because Vice President Garret A. Hobart died in office in 1899, the Republicans selected New York's progressive governor, Theodore Roosevelt, to share the ticket with McKinley in the 1900 election. Roosevelt, an independent-minded environmentalist and trust-buster, was promoted for vice president by New York GOP boss Thomas Platt, who wanted to rid the state of him and his progressive politics. Roosevelt was reluctant to take the job: "I am a comparatively young man yet and I like to work. . . . It would not entertain me to preside in the Senate."[69] He accepted, however, when a convention movement and McKinley prevailed on him.

When McKinley was assassinated in 1901 and Roosevelt became president, presidential politics came under the influence of a variant of the progressive movement. As Gabriel Kolko and other historians have demonstrated, Roosevelt's administration

The Democrats selected sober-visaged judge Alton B. Parker to run against the outgoing Theodore Roosevelt in the 1904 election. Roosevelt won by a wide margin.

was friendly to many of the GOP's traditional conservative allies. But Roosevelt's rhetoric and his legacy of regulation and conservation had strong progressive or reformist elements.[70]

Roosevelt's leadership of the progressives was an example of generational politics. (As each generation assumes control over political and social structures, it stamps those institutions with its distinctive style and ethos.) The new president grew up in an era in which economic expansion was straining the nation's fabric, causing political figures to seek idealistic but pragmatic solutions to a wide variety of problems. The previous generation had grown up in a simpler age when "politics were devoid of substance, built around appeals to tradition and old loyalties and aimed at patronage."[71]

Roosevelt steered his party toward conservation of natural resources, enforcement of antitrust laws, promotion of the concerns of labor, and railroad regulation. The government's suit to dissolve the Northern Securities Company under the Sherman Anti-Trust Act and Roosevelt's intervention in the anthracite coal miners' strike, both in 1902, established the tenor for an activist presidency. T R (the first president identified by his initials) also used his office as a "bully pulpit" to promote his progressive ideology.

Roosevelt had no trouble winning the nomination for election as president in his own right in 1904. The Republican convention, arranged in advance at the White House, unanimously voted for Roosevelt and his platform of trust-busting, tariffs, labor relations, and activist foreign policy. Sen. Charles W. Fairbanks of Indiana was the GOP vice-presidential nominee.

To oppose the rambunctious Roosevelt, the Democrats selected a sober-visaged judge. Alton Parker, the chief justice of the New York State Court of Appeals, received the backing of the Democratic Party's conservative establishment when former president Cleveland turned down entreaties to make a fourth presidential run. Parker was opposed by William Randolph Hearst, a member of Congress and newspaper magnate. Bryan forced the party to adopt a liberal platform, as a balance to the conservative judge.

The Roosevelt victory was a landslide. He won 7.6 million votes (56.4 percent) to Parker's 5.1 million (37.6 percent) and carried all but the southern states. Roosevelt won 336 electoral votes to Parker's 140. Both houses of Congress were overwhelmingly Republican. President Roosevelt pledged not to seek a second term of his own because he had served most of McKinley's second term. He occupied himself with his progressive agenda and groomed his secretary of war, William Howard Taft, as his successor.

ROOSEVELT PICKS TAFT: 1908

Roosevelt appeared to be genuinely dismayed by talk in 1907 of a possible third term, so he made public shows of his support for Taft. Because he also was able to line up state delegations for Taft, the nomination was never in doubt. Taft, through Roosevelt, was particularly strong among Republicans in the South. Attempts to restrict southern representation and pass a more liberal party platform were defeated.

Taft had impressive governmental experience. Before joining Roosevelt's cabinet, he had been a Cincinnati judge, U.S. solicitor general, federal circuit judge, head of the U.S. Commission on the Philippines, and the first civil governor of the Philippines.

Roosevelt's only problem in pushing Taft at the convention was avoiding a stampede in his own favor. Despite a highly disciplined convention, the galleries demonstrated wildly for Roosevelt. But Taft—a newcomer to electoral politics—easily won the nomination on the first ballot. He had 702 votes to the runner-up Philander C. Knox's 68. Rep. James S. Sherman of New York was selected as his running mate.

The Democrats nominated William Jennings Bryan for the third time. The electoral disaster that befell Judge Parker in 1904 was said to be evidence that the party needed an aggressive challenger to the Republicans rather than another conservative candidate. The Democrats were bereft of new talent, especially in competitive states in the East and Midwest, and turned to Bryan despite his disastrous campaign record and the warnings of former president Cleveland.

Taft campaigned on the Roosevelt record. Bryan called for government ownership of railroads and other liberal measures—such as a lower tariff, campaign finance reform, a graduated income tax, labor reforms, and greater enforcement of antitrust and other business regulations.

With Roosevelt and Taft promoting much of the progressive agenda, Bryan's message was no longer distinctive, and Taft won easily. He gathered 7.7 million popular votes (51.6 percent) to Bryan's 6.4 million (43.1 percent), and 321 electoral votes to Bryan's 162. The North, most of the West, and the border states went into the Republican column.

WILSON AND THE DIVIDED REPUBLICANS: 1912 AND 1916

Taft was not, by temperament, an ideal executive. His lifelong ambition had been to serve on the Supreme Court, and his disciplined legal mind and collegial nature eventually would enable him to become one of the high court's most able chief justices. (He was appointed to the Court by President Warren G. Harding in 1921.) But Taft foundered in the presidency. He carried out Roosevelt's program of business regulation and conservation, yet Roosevelt responded not with gratitude but with a series of nasty statements and plans for a campaign against Taft.

The tariff issue proved to be Taft's early trouble spot. Taft was committed to reducing tariffs, but he was less cautious than Roosevelt, who had fudged the divisive issue. As a result, Taft quickly became embroiled in a fight with Congress, which wanted to raise tariffs. The Senate remolded House legislation to push up various duties, and Taft publicly promoted the legislation after he managed to secure new corporate taxes and tariff reductions for raw materials. Overall, then, Taft proved ineffective and indecisive on the tariff issue and, as a consequence, began losing his party.

The Glavis-Ballinger affair further muddied the image of the administration. The scandal broke when the chief forester of the Interior Department, Gifford Pinchot, charged that Secretary Richard A. Ballinger had betrayed the cause of conservation and had even engaged in corrupt practices regarding minerals and water power. Pinchot also charged that Ballinger had wrongly fired another Interior official, Louis Glavis, for trying to expose the scandal. Pinchot took his complaints directly to Taft, but Taft sided with Ballinger and urged Pinchot to drop the matter. After an indignant Pinchot went public with the issue, Taft fired him, fueling suspicion of a cover-up at Interior. The incident was a major embarrassment to Taft because of the priority that conservation had received under Roosevelt and because of the inevitable complaints that Taft was betraying his mentor on the issue.[72]

Divisions within the Republican Party eventually created rival Taft and Roosevelt factions. Tariffs, Arizona's new state constitution (which included a provision for recall of the governor which Taft opposed), treaties, and antitrust issues split the former president and the sitting president. In many ways, the dispute was over personalities. Taft carried out Roosevelt's program but lacked his fervor and decisiveness. In a still conserva-

tive age, progressives felt they needed more aggressive leadership than the judicially tempered Taft would ever give them.

Roosevelt spent more than a year of Taft's term hunting in Africa, but he was an active speaker and campaigner when he returned to the United States. He gave a detailed accounting of his philosophy of government in a 1912 speech in Columbus, Ohio, calling for binding votes on public issues, recall of elected officials, and curbs on judicial power. When a dump-Taft movement decided in 1911 that Wisconsin senator Robert La Follette had no chance to defeat the president for the GOP nomination, party discontents turned to the energetic and still young (fifty-two years) Roosevelt.

Roosevelt made an all-out effort for the Republican nomination, entering twelve primaries and winning all but three. More specifically, Roosevelt won 278 delegates in states with primaries to Taft's 48 and La Follette's 36. In today's system, Roosevelt probably would have marched to a first-ballot nomination. (Today, more delegates are allocated by popular votes than by the party organizations, which then dominated the process.) Three crucial Republican states—Pennsylvania, Illinois, and Ohio—went for Roosevelt. He clearly, then, had great popular appeal and vote-getting ability—perhaps more than ever.

But Taft won the nomination. The president controlled the party machinery, and most of the convention's delegates were sent by the state machines. Roosevelt challenged the credentials of Taft delegates at the Chicago convention, and the nomination's outcome turned on battles over almost one-fourth of the delegates. The fight went to the floor of the convention, but Taft's smooth operation defeated Roosevelt. Roosevelt appeared at the convention to buoy his forces and cry foul.

After the defeat, Roosevelt urged his supporters to continue their fight, which motivated some bolting progressive delegates to organize a convention in August to mount a third-party effort. The bolters formed the Progressive Party. When Roosevelt remarked to a reporter during the GOP convention, "I'm feeling like a bull moose," his vigorous campaign had a symbol.

With the Republicans divided, the Democrats saw their first opportunity to win the presidency since Cleveland in 1892. As the 1912 Democratic convention in Baltimore neared, several national candidates and favorite sons were vying for the nomination. The front-runner was House Speaker James Beauchamp "Champ" Clark of Missouri, a party regular who had party organization support and years of experience to recommend him.

Gov. Woodrow Wilson of New Jersey—who held a doctorate in political science and who had moved into politics after a distinguished career as professor and president at Princeton University—was another strong candidate. Wilson's virtues were the opposite of Clark's. He did not have an extensive political record for opponents to attack, and he was supported enthusiastically because of his dynamic presence and reformist rhetoric. Although the New Jersey machine had brought Wilson into politics, he quickly asserted his independence and became something of a crusader.

As a newcomer to national politics, Wilson both refreshed and alienated Democratic crowds in speeches before the convention. He came out strongly for the "radical" platform of referendum, initiative, and recall, prompting a newspaper to report: "The boldness, the directness, the incisiveness, the fearlessness, and the force of the `Virginian-Jerseyan's' words crashed at times through the throng like a series of thunderbolt jolts."[73] But Wilson's embrace of the progressive agenda and attacks on business alienated many southerners; even the delegates from Wilson's home state of Virginia opposed him at the convention.

Other Democratic candidates were the conservative representative Oscar Underwood of Alabama, author of a historic tariff act; another conservative, Gov. Judson Harmon of Ohio; and four favorite-son governors. Clark appeared to have won the nomination when a Tammany bloc of delegates moved to support him after he won a tenth-ballot majority. The requirement for a two-thirds majority, however, gave other candidates time to maneuver. Wilson almost dropped out of the race, but Bryan's late transfer of his support from Clark to Wilson created a bandwagon effect for Wilson. On the forty-sixth ballot, Wilson accumulated the necessary two-thirds of delegates for the nomination. Gov. Thomas Marshall of Indiana, one of the favorite-son candidates, was picked to be the vice-presidential nominee because Underwood, Wilson's choice, would not accept it.

The Democratic platform was progressive. It called for tariff reduction, utility regulation, banking reforms, legislation to curb monopolies, a national income tax, direct election of senators, campaign finance reforms, and a national presidential primary. Theodore Roosevelt actually praised Wilson as "an able man" in the early fall and said he might not have started a third-party effort if he had known Wilson would be the Democrats' candidate. But Wilson and Roosevelt eventually criticized each other's approach to government, especially after Wilson expressed reservations about government activism.[74]

Wilson easily won the election, receiving 435 electoral votes to Roosevelt's 88 and Taft's 8. The Republican split obviously helped Wilson; if Roosevelt and Taft had combined their totals of 4.1 million votes (27.4 percent) and 3.5 million votes (23.2 percent), they would have topped Wilson's 6.3 million (41.8 percent). Yet even though Wilson was a minority president, there was a clear Democratic trend since the Democrats had taken over the House and replaced several Republican governors in the 1910 midterm elections. It was the worst showing ever for an incumbent president—third place with only two states.

Whatever the strength of Wilson's "mandate," he acted as though he had won by a landslide. His first term was one of the most productive in U.S. history. With the Democrats in control of Congress, and with a shrewd political adviser in Col. Edward M. House, Wilson adopted a reform agenda that had been percolating at various levels of government for years. He broke precedent by delivering his first State of the Union message to Congress in person. At the center of the message was a call for reductions in tariff rates. After a bitter fight that raged for a month, Wilson went public with a demand that members of Congress reveal their property holdings. The revelations, in response to public pressure, showed close links between their holdings and the kinds of tariff protections on the books. Congress soon was shamed into passing tariff cuts of 15 percent. Some one hundred items were placed on a free-trade list for the first time.

Woodrow Wilson traveled widely in the 1912 election campaign. His dynamic presence and reformist rhetoric appealed to the crowds who came to hear.

Wilson also addressed other areas successfully: taxes (institution of a graduated income tax in 1913, which replaced reliance on tariffs and various excise and user taxes); banking regulation (the Glass-Owen Act of 1913, which created the Federal Reserve system); antitrust legislation (the Clayton Anti-Trust Act of 1914, creation of the Federal Trade Commission in 1914); labor relations (Section 6 of the Sherman Anti-Trust Act, which exempted unions from antitrust strictures); agriculture (the Smith-Lever Act of 1914, the Federal Farm Loan Act of 1916); conservation (creation of the National Park Service in 1916); and the judiciary (the appointment of Louis Brandeis to the Supreme Court).

Despite his strong leadership—highlighted by his stirring oratory—Wilson still faced the prospect in 1916 of a tough reelection. He had won the presidency in 1912 with only 41.8 percent of the popular vote, and the escalating war in Europe was beginning to disturb the American process of steady economic growth.

Public opinion on the Great War was volatile, largely because more than a third of the U.S. population was either foreign born or the offspring of foreign-born parents. Some eleven million Americans surveyed in the 1910 census were of direct German or Austrian descent, and another five million were from Ireland. Many other immigrants were Russian, Italian, Hungarian, British, and French. Wilson sought to diffuse feelings for the immigrants' native lands when he denounced "hyphenism"—the tendency of many citizens to identify themselves with appellations that linked their ethnic origins and American status—but politicians at lower levels tailored their campaigns to specific nationality voting blocs.[75]

Wilson and Vice President Marshall won renomination without any opposition. The most significant event of the Democratic convention was the passage of the platform, which indicated the party's main campaign theme. By calling for national universal suffrage, Wilson helped himself in the eleven western states where women already had won the vote. The platform praised "the splendid diplomatic victories of our great president, who has preserved the vital interests of our government and its citizens, and kept us out of war." The latter phrase would be repeated endlessly during the fall.[76]

The Republicans gave the presidential nomination to Supreme Court Justice Charles Evans Hughes. Hughes was silent in the months before the convention, but a number of party leaders lined up enough delegates for him to win a third-ballot nomination. Other potential candidates in 1916 included former president Roosevelt, former senator Elihu Root of New York, former vice president Fairbanks, and Senators John Weeks, Albert Cummins, and Lawrence Sherman. Fairbanks won the vice-presidential nomination.

Prosperity and reformism limited the campaign themes available to the Republicans. The GOP railed against Wilson's foreign policy as "shifty expedients" and "phrasemaking" that put the United States in danger of entering the war. Hughes turned out to be a bad campaigner, but he bridged the gap between conservative and progressive Republicans that had cost the party the 1912 election. Wilson was occupied with Congress throughout the summer of 1916, but he emerged to give a series of speeches in the fall. Democratic strategists, meanwhile, conceived and executed a masterful strategy to return Wilson to the White House. The Democrats concentrated all their resources on "swing states" and ignored states they thought Wilson was sure to lose. Illinois, for example, was ignored since it was a certain Republican state. Bryan, Wilson's secretary of state, toured the West.

Wilson won one of the closest elections in history. California, an uncertain state, ensured Wilson's victory when, because of the urban vote, it went the president's way late in the campaign. The margin of victory was 3,420 votes in that state. The president defeated Hughes by a margin of 9.1 million (49.2 percent) to 8.5 million popular votes (46.1 percent). The electoral college gave Wilson 277 votes and Hughes 254.

Even though Wilson's campaign in 1916 was based on his determination to stay out of the Great War, the United States was in the war by 1917. Wilson's conduct of the war won him the status of war hero, but his diplomatic efforts after the war failed. Wilson was the architect of the Treaty of Versailles, which created a League of Nations to prevent future wars. But Wilson was unable to induce the Senate to approve the treaty, and he left office in 1921 a broken and dispirited man.

The "Return to Normalcy" and the Roaring Twenties

After the tumult of Woodrow Wilson's domestic reforms, the First World War, and the divisive battle over the Versailles treaty, the time was ripe for a period of conservatism and Republican government. Deep resentment had developed toward Wilson and the Democratic Party, and the Democrats themselves were divided over many issues, including economic regulation, Prohibition, and race relations.

Blessed with good luck, substantial financial backing, and a strong trend toward split-ticket voting, beginning in the 1920s the Republicans were able to resume their dominance over national politics with three successful presidential campaigns: Warren G. Harding in 1920, Calvin Coolidge in 1924, and Herbert C. Hoover in 1928.

The 1920s are usually pictured as a time of steady, unexciting politics. The conservatives dominated the federal government, and occupying the White House were men who spoke of "normalcy" and a noninterventionist brand of politics in both domestic and foreign affairs. One of the symbols of the age was President Coolidge's program of tax cuts, which reduced the rates on the wealthy. The wartime Revenue Act of 1918 had driven tax rates to the highest point in U.S. history—77 percent in the highest brackets. In 1921, 1923, and 1926, Secretary of the Treasury Andrew Mellon presented to Congress proposals to cut taxes, the most controversial being the reduction in the maximum surtax from 77 to 25 percent. Congress eventually cut the surtax to 40 percent in 1924 and 20 percent in 1926.[77]

But the sober men who filled the presidency in the twenties met challenges from progressives of both parties in Congress and in the state governments. On a wide range of issues—including relief of the poor, subsidies for the depressed farm sector, regulation of utilities, immigration, race relations, states' rights, tax cuts, and Prohibition—the conservative presidents encountered strong challenges. They frequently responded by vetoing legislation, but such an expedient would not prevent the pressures for a more activist government from developing.

HARDING AND "NORMALCY": 1920

Sen. Warren Harding, a product of the GOP machine of Ohio, emerged from a crowded and largely unknown pack to win the Republican nomination in 1920 at a convention dominated by economic interests such as oil, railroads, and steel. The early candidates were Gen. Leonard Wood, an old Roosevelt ally; Gov. Frank Lowden of Illinois, who married into the Pullman family and therefore had ample financing for a campaign; and Sen. Hiram Johnson of California, whose progressive and isolationist stances put him in good stead with voters in many states. A dozen favorite sons hoped that a deadlocked convention might bring the nomination their way. All of the candidates were on hand in Chicago to maneuver for the nomination.

While Wood, Johnson, and Lowden performed reasonably well in the primaries, Harding won only his home state of Ohio and did not arouse much popular enthusiasm. But under the direction of a shrewd campaign manager, Harry Daugherty, Hard-

Democratic presidential candidate James M. Cox of Ohio, left, and vice-presidential candidate Franklin D. Roosevelt (one year before he was stricken with polio), campaign in the 1920 election. They lost to Republican presidential candidate Warren G. Harding and his running mate, Gov. Calvin Coolidge of Massachusetts.

ing gained the support of the party's bosses and won the nomination on the tenth ballot after a brief interview with them in the "smoke-filled room" that was synonymous with boss control. Gov. Calvin Coolidge of Massachusetts, a favorite-son contender for president, became Harding's vice-presidential candidate.

The Democrats selected Gov. James Cox, also from Ohio, after lengthy platform battles and balloting for the nomination. Early ballots put former Treasury secretary William G. McAdoo and Attorney General Mitchell Palmer in the lead, but Cox gained steadily and had the nomination by the forty-fourth roll call. Franklin D. Roosevelt of New York, the assistant secretary of the navy, was rapidly selected to be Cox's running mate.

The image of Woodrow Wilson hung over the convention and would hang over the fall campaign. The Democratic platform praised Wilson's conduct of the war and his domestic reform program. But the results in the November election indicated deep unease over the Democratic administration.

Harding amassed 16.1 million popular votes (60.3 percent) to Cox's 9.1 million (34.2 percent), and 404 electoral votes to Cox's 127. Harding carried the North and West including Oklahoma and all of the southern and border states except Tennessee and Kentucky.

Harding's landslide victory was termed "election by disgust" by political analysts. The wartime sacrifices demanded under Wilson were widely perceived as the cause of Harding's victory rather than a desire for the ideology or policy proposals that Harding was offering. The *New York Post* editorialized: "We are in the backwash from the mighty spiritual and physical effort to which America girded herself when she won the war for the Al-

lies. . . . The war has not been repudiated, though the administration that fought it has been overwhelmed. We are now in the chill that comes with the doctor's bills."[78]

The electorate's ability to shift allegiances from the Republicans to the Democrats and back again—from one period to the next, and from one level of government to the next—suggested a dissolution of partisan alignments. The addition of women to the electorate after passage of the Nineteenth Amendment in 1920 and the increasing independence among all voters induced uncertainty. National exhaustion from the war and the lack of sharp ideological differences between the candidates produced apathy. The electorate's instability was suggested by the divisions within both parties on high-profile issues such as Prohibition, the League of Nations, agricultural policies, and other social and economic matters—among them, technical assistance and trust busting. The appearance of numerous "blocs" in both parties represented "little if anything more than a transitory alignment upon a particular vote or issue."[79]

The shifts in control of congressional and state offices also indicated electoral instability. The Democrats had had comfortable control of Congress under Wilson, but in 1920 the Republicans gained a majority of 301 to 131 in the House and 59 to 37 in the Senate. Impressive liberal gains in congressional and state elections in the midterm election of 1922 appeared to be a slap at the Harding administration. The high turnover of votes also indicated unstable party affiliations: the 14.2 percentage point increase in the Republican vote between the 1916 and 1920 presidential elections was the largest since the Civil War, another time of turmoil.[80]

President Harding died on August 2, 1923, of a heart attack, just as revelations of kickbacks and favoritism in the administration began to surface and several members of the administration quit and two committed suicide. The investigation into the so-called Teapot Dome scandal—so named after the site of naval oil reserves that were transferred to private hands in exchange for bribes—would last five years. The Democrats hoped to make the scandal a major issue in the 1924 election, but Democratic complicity in the wrongdoing and the personal integrity of Harding's successor, Calvin Coolidge, defused the issue.

COOLIDGE CLEANS UP: 1924

President Coolidge fired Attorney General Harry M. Daugherty and other members of Harding's clique and projected an image of puritan cleanliness. Coolidge—a taciturn man who had slowly climbed the political ladder in Massachusetts from city council member to city solicitor, mayor, state legislator, lieutenant governor, and governor before he became vice president—expounded a deeply individualistic Yankee philosophy that helped to separate him from the corrupt men in the Harding White House.

Except for appointing as attorney general Harlan Fiske Stone, former dean of the Columbia University School of Law, Coolidge allowed others to finish cleaning up the mess left behind by Harding. The new president was concerned about unnecessarily alienating himself from party leaders.

By the time Coolidge sought the presidency in his own right in 1924, the economy had rebounded. One of the most conservative presidents ever, Coolidge's platform called for additional tax cuts but said nothing substantive about increasingly salient agriculture and labor issues. Coolidge also pushed an isolationist foreign policy plank. He won the nomination on the first ballot.

While the Republicans were able to "Keep Cool with Coolidge," the Democrats spent sixteen days in a seemingly endless attempt to pick a nominee in New York's sweltering Madison Square Garden. A fight developed because the party was badly split between its northeastern urban bloc and its more conservative southern and western rural bloc. New York governor Alfred E. Smith and former Treasury secretary William McAdoo of California were the key combatants at the convention until the delegates were freed from the instructions of party bosses on the one-hundredth ballot.

Suspicions between the two regional blocs were intense. A platform plank denouncing the Ku Klux Klan created the most controversy. Northerners wanted an explicit repudiation of the society that preached hatred of blacks, Catholics, and Jews; in the end, southerners would settle only for a vaguely worded rebuke. (The Klan had infiltrated the party in many rural areas.) Another divisive issue was Prohibition, with northerners attacking the initiative and southerners supporting it. These sectional splits would cripple the Democrats in the 1924 and 1928 elections.

After the delegates were freed from instructions, a stampede developed for John W. Davis of West Virginia, a lawyer with Wall Street connections. The ticket was balanced with the vice-

"Keep Cool with Coolidge" was the Republican incumbent's 1924 campaign slogan, used on posters, banners, buttons, and decorative stamps such as this one from Wisconsin.

presidential selection of Charles W. Bryan of Nebraska, the younger brother of three-time presidential candidate William Jennings Bryan.

The Progressive candidacy of Robert La Follette complicated the calculations of voters, particularly those on the liberal end of the political spectrum. Because the Democrats had a nearly impenetrable hold on the South, La Follette was not given a reasonable chance of winning. But the conservatism of both Coolidge and Davis meant that La Follette was the only liberal in the race. Still, many liberals voted for Davis or even Coolidge because of the fear of an inconclusive election that would have to be resolved in the House of Representatives.

Coolidge won the election easily, with the Democrats polling their smallest percentage ever. Coolidge won 54.1 percent of the vote, Davis won 28.8 percent, and La Follette won 16.6 percent. Coolidge attracted 15.7 million popular votes and 382 electoral votes; Davis 8.4 million and 136; and La Follette 4.8 million and 13.

On August 2, 1927, when Coolidge announced his decision not to seek reelection by passing out a brief note to reporters and then refusing further comment, the Republicans began jockeying for the nomination for the 1928 election.

THE HOOVER SUCCESSION: 1928

Secretary of Commerce Herbert Hoover was the obvious choice to replace Coolidge at the head of the GOP ticket. A native of Iowa who learned mining engineering at Stanford University, Hoover was immensely popular with most of the party. Hoover's administration of Belgian relief and food distribution programs during World War I had earned him the status of statesman and humanitarian.

Hoover began working for the nomination soon after Coolidge dropped out, spending $400,000 in the nominating phase of the election. He won the nomination on the first ballot over Governors Frank Lowden of Illinois and Charles Curtis of Kansas. Curtis was named Hoover's running mate.

Hoover was religious in his zeal for what he called "the American system" of free enterprise and individualism. He did not see any inconsistency in having the government vigorously support businesses with tax breaks, tariffs, public provision of infrastructures, and police protection, while at the same time denying relief to people in need. Hoover appeared to be less rigid than Coolidge, however. He proposed creation of a special farm board and said he would consider legislation to protect labor unions from abuses in the use of court injunctions.

Al Smith, the Tammany-schooled governor of New York, was the Democratic nominee. Smith had the support of all the party's northern states, and he won a first-ballot nomination. Sen. Joseph T. Robinson of Arkansas was the vice-presidential candidate.

Smith's candidacy polarized the electorate, particularly the South. He was the first Catholic to be nominated for president by a major party, and he endured religious slurs throughout the fall. Moreover, he favored repeal of Prohibition, still a divisive issue, and he was an urbanite, a problem for a nation that had nurtured a rural ideal since Thomas Jefferson. Because he also was a machine politician, he presented a problem for anyone outside (and many people inside) the nation's great cities. He also was a strong opponent of the Klan, which put him in trouble in the South. Finally, he was an unabashed liberal who proposed public works, farm relief programs, stronger protection of workers, and regulation of banking and industry.

During the fall campaign, Hoover acted like the incumbent and Smith barnstormed the country, trying in vain to pick up support in the South and West. The 1928 campaign was the first with extensive radio coverage, and Hoover generally fared better than Smith on the airwaves. Hoover, the small-town boy who made good, represented fulfillment of the American Dream; Smith, the inner-city boy who made good, also embodied that ideal, but he had too many ethnic traits for much of the nation to realize it.

The November election produced another Republican landslide. Hoover carried forty states with 21.4 million popular votes (58.2 percent) and 444 electoral votes, while Smith carried only eight states with 15.0 million popular votes (40.8 percent) and 87 electoral votes. As disastrous as the election appeared to be for the Democrats, it put them in position to build a wide-ranging coalition in future years.

Smith carried only six southern states, but the defection of the others was temporary. More important to the Democrats' long-range fortunes was the movement of cities into the Democratic column, probably for the rest of the century. Immigrants in cities were expanding their vision from local politics to the national stage for the first time. In all, Smith diverted 122 northern counties from the GOP to the Democratic Party. Catholics, whose turnout previously had been low, turned out in record numbers. Smith also seemed to pick up some of the Progressive farm vote that La Follette had tapped before; in Wisconsin, for example, the Democratic vote jumped from 68,000 to 450,000 from 1924 to 1928. Finally, Smith's candidacy put the Democrats solidly in the "wet" column, just as the national temper began to resent Prohibition.

President Hoover impressed political observers with his managerial skills and "coordinating mind." With passage of the Agricultural Marketing Act in June 1929, the administration appeared to address the most pressing economic problem for the business-minded president. He met some legislative setbacks, but, overall, the Great Engineer appeared to be in good political condition as the nation looked back over his record when Congress began its recess in the summer of 1929.

The national economic and social fiesta that had begun at the close of World War I came to an abrupt end on October 29, 1929. After climbing to dizzying new heights for months, the stock market crashed. First described by economists and politicians as a temporary interruption of the good times, the crash quickly led to a wave of business and bank failures, mortgage foreclosures, wage cuts, layoffs, and a crisis of political leadership. By the end of Hoover's term in 1933, more than twelve million workers had lost their jobs; the unemployment rate was approximately 25 percent. An October 1931 advertisement for 6,000 jobs in the Soviet Union brought 100,000 American applications.[81]

President Hoover, who had celebrated his inauguration with a prediction that poverty and hunger were near an end, did not know how to cope with the crisis. In a special session that Hoover called, Congress created the Federal Farm Board to coordinate marketing of agricultural products, but Hoover steadfastly opposed further moves, especially subsidies. In 1930 Hoover signed the Smoot-Hawley Tariff Act to protect manufacturers, but, true to the predictions of economists and bankers, the tariff only aggravated economic conditions by hurting foreign trade.

Hoover later approved agricultural relief and public works programs and established the Reconstruction Finance Corporation. The president refused to approve direct relief to the unemployed and businesses, but he did approve some loans and aid to specific sectors of the economy.

Despite his earnest and tireless efforts, Hoover became a figure of widespread enmity. The low point of his distinguished career came when World War I veterans petitioned for early receipt of their service bonuses, which, by contract, were not to be paid until 1945. They set up camp in Washington, singing old war songs and carrying placards that bore their pleas. The "Bonus Army" numbered twenty thousand at its height. When Hoover feared a protracted protest, he ordered federal troops to take over buildings where some veterans were camping. In two skirmishes, two veterans were killed. The president then sent in Gen. Douglas MacArthur with tanks, infantry, and cavalry soldiers. (MacArthur's junior officers included Dwight D. Eisenhower and George Patton.) After successfully removing the veterans, the military forces overran nearby veterans' camps in a rain of fire and tear gas. Thousands of veterans and their families fled the burning district.

The administration's tough stance against a defeated, ragtag band of former war heroes shocked and embittered the nation. The barricaded White House and administration statements about "insurrectionists" symbolized a dangerous gulf between the government and the people.

Partly because of the economic crisis he did not create, but also because of his dour and unimaginative demeanor, Hoover probably never had a chance to win reelection. The 1930

Gen. Douglas MacArthur, standing against a bridge with a cup of coffee, rests with federal troops during a break in their drive to evacuate World War I veterans camped out in Washington, D.C., in 1932. The veterans, seeking early receipt of their service bonuses, had staged a protest by setting up camps near the Capitol, and President Herbert C. Hoover had ordered troops, headed by MacArthur, to disperse them with tear gas.

midterm elections indicated a loss of confidence in the administration. The House went Democratic, 219 to 214, and the Senate came within a seat of going Democratic as well.

Those election results did not convey the bitterness and despair that the depression would aggravate before the next presidential campaign. Hoover was mercilessly ridiculed in newspapers and in Democratic speeches. The Democratic Party coordinated a comprehensive anti-Hoover campaign that made the president politically impotent.

THE ELECTION OF 1932

Franklin D. Roosevelt, fifth cousin to Theodore Roosevelt, was the perfect candidate to oppose Hoover. The New York governor had been an activist in state politics, first opposing the state's Tammany machine and then pioneering many relief and reconstruction programs that Hoover refused to expand to the national scale. Roosevelt had been the party's vice-presidential candidate twelve years earlier, and he had served in the federal government as assistant secretary of the navy.

Perhaps more important than any of his political accomplishments were FDR's image of strength and optimism and his deft handling of hot issues and disparate members of the potential Democratic coalition. Although he was a polio victim, Roosevelt often smiled—a devastating contrast to Hoover. (Gutzon Borglum, the sculptor, wrote: "If you put a rose in Hoover's hand, it would wilt."[82]) Roosevelt was able to campaign for the presidency without putting forth a comprehensive program: the simple promise of a change in leadership was enough.

Some observers found the man from Hyde Park wanting. Journalist Walter Lippmann, for example, complained that Roosevelt was "a pleasant man who, without any important qualifications for the office, would like very much to be president."[83] But those detractors and a large field of Democratic candidates were not able to keep Roosevelt from his "rendezvous with destiny."[84]

The Democratic field included the 1928 Democratic standard-bearer, Al Smith; John Nance Garner, the Speaker of the House; Gov. Albert Ritchie of Maryland; Gov. George White of Ohio; Gov. Harry Byrd of Virginia; and former Sen. James Reed of Missouri. Most considered Smith more of a "stalking horse" for the anti-FDR forces than a serious candidate in his own right. Garner had impressive backing from the newspaper magnate William Randolph Hearst and former Democratic candidate William McAdoo.

The many favorite sons in the race threatened to deadlock the convention and deny the nomination to the front-runner, as they had done so often in the past. Roosevelt had difficulty with his own region of the country because of his opposition to the Tammany machine in New York. Acquiring the required two-thirds vote of delegates for the nomination was difficult for Roosevelt or any other candidate, but FDR eventually won on the fourth ballot when he promised the vice-presidential slot to Garner.

In U.S. political history, Franklin Roosevelt was the first candidate to appear before the convention that nominated him. In an acceptance speech to the conventioneers who had staged wild rallies in his support, Roosevelt made passing reference to the "new deal" that his administration would offer Americans. That phrase, picked up in a newspaper cartoon the next day, came to symbolize the renewal for which Americans yearned as riots and radicalism seemed to threaten the nation's spirit and the legitimacy of its institutions.

Roosevelt conducted an active fall campaign, traveling twenty-three thousand miles in forty-one states to quell suspicions that his physical handicaps would deter him from performing his job. Besides barnstorming the nation, Roosevelt took to the radio airwaves—he was the first sophisticated electronic media candidate—where he conveyed a sense of warmth and confidence. He also showed an intellectual bent and an open mind when he called on academics and professionals—the famed "brain trust"—for their expert advice on the issues.

Franklin D. Roosevelt campaigns by car in West Virginia, October 19, 1932.

Roosevelt won 22.8 million votes (57.4 percent) to Hoover's 15.8 million (39.6 percent). Forty-two of the forty-eight states and 472 of the 531 electoral votes went for Roosevelt. The election was a landslide and a realignment of the major forces in U.S. politics.

The New Deal Coalition

The profound effect of Roosevelt's victory on U.S. politics can hardly be overstated. The New Deal coalition that Roosevelt assembled shaped the political discourse and electoral competition of the United States until the late 1960s. In many respects, that coalition is a central element of politics today.

The new Democratic coalition brought together a disparate group of interests: southerners, African Americans, immigrants, farmers, capital-intensive producers, international businessmen, financiers, urbanites, trade unions, intellectuals, Catholics, and Jews. Rexford Tugwell called it "the most miscellaneous coalition in history."[85] These blocs were not always in perfect harmony—for example, the Democrats juggled the demands of blacks and white southerners with great difficulty—but they were solid building blocks for national political dominance.

The dominance was impressive. Between 1932 and 1964, the Democrats won seven of nine presidential elections. The only successful Republican, Dwight Eisenhower, could just as easily have run as a Democrat. Party leaders in fact asked him to run as a Democrat in 1948 and 1952, and his name was entered in some Democratic primaries in 1952.

The strength of Roosevelt's rule was attributable partly to the president's personality. He could be soothing. When he gave his first "fireside chat" about the banking crisis, the nation respond-ed with cooperation; the raids and violence at banks ended in a matter of weeks. More important than his soothing nature was his ability to experiment and shift gears. Professor James David Barber described Roosevelt's many public postures:

Founder of the New Deal, modern American democracy's closest approximation to a common political philosophy, Roosevelt came on the scene as the least philosophical of men—"a chameleon in plaid," Hoover called him. Firm fighter of yet another Great War, Roosevelt appeared to H. L. Mencken in 1932 as "far too feeble and wishy-washy a fellow to make a really effective fight." Architect of world organization, he introduced himself as totally concerned with America's domestic drama. His name is inseparable from his generation's great social revolution; in 1932, nearly all the heavy thinkers scoffed at him as just another placebo politician—a "pill to cure an earthquake," said Professor [Harold] Laski.[86]

More important than personality was what Roosevelt had to offer the many groups in his coalition. As historian Richard Hofstadter has noted, the New Deal was "a series of improvisations, many adopted very suddenly, many contradictory."[87] The Roosevelt credo was: "Save the people and the nation, and if we have to change our minds twice a day to accomplish that end, we should do it."[88]

Until the vast expenditures of World War II, there was not enough pump-priming to end the Depression, but Roosevelt's initiatives touched almost everyone affected by the slump.[89] For the jobless, there were unemployment insurance and public works programs such as the Works Progress Administration and the Civilian Conservation Corps. For the poor, there were categorical aid programs. For westerners, there were conservation measures. For the banks, there was the famous holiday that stopped runs on holdings, and there were currency and securities reforms. For farmers, there were incentives and price supports and cooperatives. For the aged, there was Social Security. For southeasterners, there was the Tennessee Valley Authority. For southern whites, there was a hands-off policy on race matters. For blacks, there were sympathy and jobs programs. For those living in rural areas, there was electrification. For families, there were home loans. For the weary worker eager for a few rounds at the local tavern, there was the repeal of Prohibition. For laborers, there was acknowledgment of the right to negotiate for their share of the national wealth. For business, there were the Federal Emergency Relief Act and the National Industrial Recovery Act, as well as diplomatic negotiation to reduce trade barriers.

The remarkably divergent interests in the coalition were underscored by the politics of race. Blacks moved en masse to the Democratic Party from their traditional position in the "Party of Lincoln," partly because of Hoover's failure but also because of the inclusive rhetoric of the New Deal. Yet Roosevelt was too concerned about his bloc of southern support to accept even antilynching legislation.

Scholars have argued that the New Deal coalition did not indicate a wholesale shift in existing political loyalties, but rather that new groups such as urbanites and blacks had joined an already stable alliance to tip the competitive balance of U.S. parties. The political discourse in the United States changed not because all or even most groups changed their behavior but because new groups and issues became involved.[90]

The core of Roosevelt's winning coalition was easy to describe: "Southern white Protestants, Catholics, and non-Southern white Protestants of the lowest socioeconomic stratum together accounted for roughly three-fourths of all Americans of voting age in 1940 who thought of themselves as Democrats. By way of contrast, these three groups provided only about 40 percent of the smaller cadre of Republican identifiers."[91] Within the Democratic coalition, there were both new and old elements.

Although the Democratic Party encompassed new constituencies and addressed new issues, it retained many of its traditional supporters. The segregated "Jim Crow" South had consistently been in the Democratic column; in 1896, for example, the South's percentage support for Democrat William Jennings Bryan exceeded that of the rest of the nation by 15.3 points. Even in 1928, when Al Smith's Catholicism reduced support for the Democrats to under 50 percent for the first time, the Deep South supported the Democrats more than the border South did.[92] To the South, the Democrats were reliably the party of white supremacy and agricultural interests, while Republicans favored the industrial interests of the North.

Outside the South, the Democratic Party was the party of immigrants and Catholics. Since Andrew Jackson's day, the overwhelmingly Democratic voting patterns of Catholics had contrasted with the split vote of Protestants in the United States. The Catholic-Protestant divisions represented "not so much religious as more general ethnocultural traditions."[93] The Democratic hold on the Catholic vote was reinforced by the heavy immigration into northern cities in the last half of the nineteenth century. While the anti-Catholic Ku Klux Klan received Demo-

cratic backing in the South, it received Republican backing in the North, pushing northern Catholics decisively into the Democratic Party.

A steady base in the Democratic Party consisted of laborers and the poor. From the first party machines in the early nineteenth century to William Jennings Bryan's campaign on behalf of the depressed farm belt in 1896 to Woodrow Wilson's acceptance of labor bargaining in 1914, the Democrats had shown sympathy for the less-privileged classes. Such sympathies often were constricted by prejudice or conservatism, but the Democrats offered more hope of representation than the business-oriented Republicans. Roosevelt solidified the support of the poor and laboring classes.[94] Sundquist has written: "The party system undoubtedly reflected some degree of class before the realignment, but there can be little doubt that it was accentuated by the event. It was in the New Deal era that tight bonds were formed between organized labor and the Democratic Party, that ties equally close if less formal and overt were formed between business and the GOP, and that politics for the first time since 1896 sharply accented class issues."[95] Roosevelt consistently received the support of more than two-thirds of the voters of low socioeconomic status.[96]

New converts to the Democratic Party included blacks and Jews. The inclusion of blacks into the New Deal coalition underscored a "multiplier effect" at work within thriving interest group politics. The Republicans received the black vote in the seventeen elections from Reconstruction to 1932. That year, Roosevelt received 35 percent of the black vote, but his black support was as low as 23 percent in Chicago and 29 percent in Cincinnati.[97] Even though Roosevelt did little to promote black interests in the South, where most blacks lived but could not vote, the black vote for him increased to 70 percent in 1936 and 1940. Migration of blacks to the North and the spillover effects of Roosevelt's many domestic programs brought blacks to the Democratic Party.

Jews, who had voted Republican since their numbers swelled during immigration around the turn of the century, turned to the Democrats as they became the more liberal party. Roosevelt got 85 percent of the Jewish vote in 1936 and 84 percent in 1940. New Deal assistance programs and Roosevelt's efforts to fight Nazism appealed to Jews, but perhaps more important was "the historic pattern of discrimination which forced or disposed Jews to oppose conservative parties."[98] The class division that split other social groups was absent in the Jewish population.

In many ways, the whole of the New Deal was greater than the sum of its parts. Political scientist Samuel Beer has argued that two long-competing visions of U.S. politics—the national idea and the democratic idea—at last came together during Roosevelt's administration. With the New Deal, the Democratic Party was able to combine its traditional concern for local, individualistic interests with a national vision. By bringing "locked-out" groups into the system, the Democrats enhanced both nation building and individual freedoms. The parts, put together, created a stronger whole. Beer quotes the French sociologist Emile Durkheim: "The image of the one who completes us becomes inseparable from ours. . . . It thus becomes an integral and permanent part of our conscience. . . ."[99]

The political genius of "interest-group liberalism"[100] was not just that it offered something to everyone, but that it created a new age of consumerism in which everyone's interest was in economic growth rather than structural change. The general good was defined as growth. The potentially divisive competition over restricted and unequally distributed resources was avoided with a general acceptance of growth as the common goal. When there was growth, everyone could get a little more. That public philosophy became a permanent part of American political discourse.

ROOSEVELT'S FIRST REELECTION: 1936

Roosevelt's coalition and leadership were so strong that he became the only president to win more than two elections. He won four elections and served a little more than twelve years in the White House before dying in office.

Roosevelt's four electoral triumphs caused Republicans to fume about his "imperial" presidency; all they could do in response to FDR was to promote a constitutional amendment to limit presidents to two terms. But more important than this perception was the way Roosevelt shaped the American political agenda. For many people of the time, it was difficult to imagine the United States under any other leader.

It is possible that Roosevelt could have forged an even stronger liberal coalition than he did. But Roosevelt was a pragmatist above all else and alternately angered and wooed such groups as business, labor, farmers, and the military. For example, Roosevelt kept his distance from Upton Sinclair's populist campaign for governor of California in 1934. Because he threatened business interests, Sinclair was the target of a sustained personal attack by business and other conservative forces in the state in what one authority has called the first media campaign in American history. Sinclair's losing effort, the historian Greg Mitchell argued, undermined the power of reformers nationally.[101]

Roosevelt's three successful reelection drives evoked a changing response from Republicans. Roosevelt's first reelection opponent, in 1936, was Gov. Alfred M. Landon of Kansas, who strongly criticized every aspect of the New Deal. After 1936, Republican candidates did not criticize federal intervention in economic and social affairs but rather the speed and the skill of Democratic intervention. In the third election the Republicans argued that Roosevelt was a "warmonger" because he tilted toward Great Britain in World War II. The GOP argued in the third and fourth elections that Roosevelt threatened to become a "dictator" by exceeding the traditional two-term limit.

Landon was the early favorite for the Republican nomination in 1936. Sen. Charles McNary of Oregon, Sen. Arthur Vandenberg of Michigan, and *Chicago Daily News* publisher Frank Knox provided weak opposition. A Republican bolter for Theodore Roosevelt's "Bull Moose" candidacy in 1912, Landon was consistently to the left of the GOP. Historian James MacGregor Burns observed: "Landon had just the qualities of common sense, homely competence, cautious liberalism and rock-like 'soundness' that the Republicans hoped would appeal to a people tiring, it was hoped, of the antics and heroics in the White House."[102]

In 1936 the Republicans could not have stated their opposition to the popular New Deal in any stronger terms. The platform read: "America is in peril. The welfare of American men and women and the future of our youth are at stake. We dedicate ourselves to the preservation of their political liberty, their individual opportunity, and their character as free citizens, which today for the first time are threatened by government itself."[103]

The Republicans called for ending a wide range of government regulations, returning relief to state and local governments, replacing Social Security, balancing the budget, and changing tariff and currency policies. Landon's only innovation was to call for a constitutional amendment allowing the states to regulate the labor of women and children; the Supreme Court had struck down a New York minimum wage law in 1935. After Landon won the nomination on the first ballot, he selected Knox as his running mate.

The only time the two presidential candidates met was at a meeting Roosevelt called with state governors in Des Moines to discuss farm relief and a recent drought. FDR hoped to put Landon on the spot about farm relief. But Landon turned out to be the aggressor, demanding that FDR say what to tell 100,000 starving farmers in Oklahoma. FDR responded that he had some federal agencies working on programs "just as fast as the Lord will let them." When Landon said that such an answer was small consolation, Roosevelt retorted: "What more can you say to the hungry farmer, governor? The machinery will be put in gear just as fast as the Lord will let *you*?"[104]

Landon's campaign possessed a lavish war chest of $9 million, benefited from the defections of Democratic stalwarts such as John Davis and Al Smith (the party's presidential nominees in 1924 and 1928) and well-coordinated campaign work by business lobbies, and engaged in smear campaigns that portrayed Social Security as a simple "pay reduction" measure and Roosevelt as physically and mentally ill. Landon also argued that New Deal spending was just another form of spoils politics, a charge Roosevelt addressed by folding postmasters into the civil service system.

The only important innovation at the Democratic convention was the repeal of the party's requirement that a candidate receive two-thirds of the delegates to win the nomination. After some arm twisting, southern delegates backed the change, but the governor of Texas wondered aloud if the change was designed for a third Roosevelt run in 1940. Roosevelt was renominated without opposition. He asked Garner to run with him a second time.

In response to Landon's GOP nomination and agitation by leaders of the left and right—including Huey Long of Louisiana, Father Charles E. Coughlin of Detroit, Dr. Francis Townsend of California (who espoused a federal pension plan for senior citizens), and the Socialist Norman Thomas of New York—President Roosevelt in his acceptance speech launched a rhetorical war against "economic royalists" who opposed his programs. He dropped the idea of a "unity" campaign in favor of a partisan ideological attack intended to gain a mandate for a variety of stalled programs rather than a personal vote of confidence.[105]

President Franklin D. Roosevelt's Republican opponents during his three successful reelection campaigns were, from left: Gov. Alfred M. Landon of Kansas in 1936; former Democrat and business executive Wendell L. Willkie in 1940; and Gov. Thomas E. Dewey of New York in 1944. Dewey ran again and lost against President Truman in 1948.

At first, Roosevelt had planned a low-key campaign of "conciliation," but when Landon got the GOP nomination he decided to wage the more aggressive campaign. After all, Landon had run an impressive nominating campaign and was thought to appeal to American pinings for governmental stability. In the early stages of the fall campaign, Roosevelt pretended not to be a partisan politician. He crisscrossed the country making "official" inspections of drought states and public works programs and delivering speeches on electrical power, conservation, and social welfare programs, among other topics. Roosevelt assigned Postmaster General James Farley the task of addressing party rifts and Republican charges of spoils.

At the end of September, Roosevelt assumed the role of partisan leader. The president answered Republican charges point by point, then lashed out at the Republicans in biting, sarcastic terms. As the campaign progressed and Roosevelt sensed a strong response from the large crowds to his attacks, the attacks became stronger. At the close of the campaign, he said:

We have not come this far without a struggle and I assure you that we cannot go further without a struggle. For twelve years, our nation was afflicted with a hear-nothing, see-nothing, do-nothing government. The nation looked to the government but the government looked away. Nine mocking years with the golden calf and three long years of the scourge! Nine crazy years at the ticker and three long years at the breadlines! Nine mad years of mirage and three long years of despair! And, my friends, powerful influences strive today to restore that kind of government with its doctrine that that government is best which is most indifferent to mankind. . . . Never before in all of our history have these forces been so united against one candidate as they stand today. They are unanimous in their hate for me—and I welcome their hatred.[106]

Especially to sophisticated campaign technicians of the modern age, a poll that predicted a big Landon victory provides some amusement. The *Literary Digest,* which had predicted past elections with accuracy, conducted a postcard poll of its readers

that pointed toward a Landon landslide. But the heavy middle- and upper-class bias of the magazine's readership meant that the views of the voters on the lower rungs of the economic ladder were left out of the sample. To this day, the poll is cited as the prime example of bad survey group selection.

The failure of the *Literary Digest*'s survey pointed to the most salient aspect of the election results: the heavy class divisions among the voters. Polls showed that class divisions widened starting around the midpoint of Roosevelt's first term. The broad support Roosevelt had enjoyed because of a common economic disaster had hardened along class lines by the time of the 1936 election.

In the 1936 election, Roosevelt won 27.7 million popular votes (60.8 percent) to Landon's 16.7 million (36.5 percent). Roosevelt carried all but two of the forty-eight states, and he took 523 of the 531 electoral votes. In addition, the Senate's Democratic majority increased to 75 of 96 seats, and the House majority increased to 333 of 435 seats. Roosevelt even ran ahead of candidates—such as gubernatorial candidate Herbert Lehman of New York—who had been recruited to boost his vote totals in various states. In fact, the Democratic victory was almost too overwhelming, Roosevelt suggested, because it would encourage Democrats to fight among themselves rather than with Republicans.

ROOSEVELT'S THIRD TERM: 1940

Soon after his 1936 landslide, Roosevelt tempted fate with a proposal that would have increased the size of the Supreme Court from nine to fifteen members in order to "pack" the Court with justices closer to the president's political philosophy. In 1935 and 1936, the high court had struck down important New Deal initiatives such as the Agriculture Adjustment Act, the National Recovery Administration, and the tax on food processing.

Roosevelt shrouded his proposal in statements of concern about the capacities of some of the Court's older justices. In a fireside speech, Roosevelt said the Court's failure to keep pace with the other "horses" in the "three-horse team" of the federal government constituted a "quiet crisis."[107] The elderly chief justice, Charles Evans Hughes, belied that charge with the energy he brought to the tribunal. But Roosevelt refused to compromise on the bill, and it became an executive-legislative dispute. The proposal was widely seen as a brazen power play, and Congress defeated it by the summer of 1937.

Nevertheless, President Roosevelt eventually got the judicial approval he wanted for his initiatives—what wags called "the switch in time that saved nine." The Court appeared to shift its philosophy during the court-packing affair, and, before long, enough justices had retired so that Roosevelt could put his own stamp on the Court.

Other problems awaited Roosevelt in the second term. Splits in the labor movement gave rise to violence during organizing drives, and the president responded haltingly. After his rift with business over the full range of New Deal policies, Roosevelt appeared to be drifting. Conservatives in Congress were more assertive than ever in opposing the "socialist" measures of the Roosevelt years. The only major New Deal legislation in the second term was the Fair Labor Standards Act of 1938, which abolished child labor and set a minimum wage and an official rate of time-and-a-half for overtime.

As Roosevelt looked toward a third term in 1940, the widening war in Europe posed a difficult problem. Nazi Germany had invaded the Rhineland, Poland, France, Norway, Denmark, Holland, Belgium, and Luxembourg and had made alliances with Italy and the Soviet Union. Japan had invaded China. Adolf Hitler launched the Battle of Britain in the summer of 1940; allnight air raids of London came soon afterward.

British prime minister Winston Churchill desperately petitioned President Roosevelt to provide fifty naval destroyers. Britain's need for the destroyers was so great that Roosevelt balked at asking Congress for help. He reasoned that congressional action probably would take three months, and isolationists might even block action, dealing a crippling blow to Britain. After lengthy debate within the administration, Roosevelt agreed to send Churchill the destroyers as part of a "lend-lease" agreement. The United States would receive British bases in the Caribbean as part of the deal.

A favorite parlor game as the 1940 election approached was guessing whom Roosevelt might tap as his successor. Roosevelt publicly maintained that he did not want another term, but he refused to issue a definitive statement begging off the race. Despite the historic precedent against third terms, Roosevelt wanted to remain president. And to avoid the appearance of overzealousness, Roosevelt wanted the Democrats to draft him in 1940.

While the nation waited for Roosevelt to act, Vice President Garner announced his candidacy. Postmaster General Farley and Secretary of State Cordell Hull also wanted to be president, and Roosevelt gave both vague assurances of support. Roosevelt, whose relations with Garner had been soured since the court-packing episode (which Garner opposed), simply watched the vice president struggle to gain a respectable public profile. The Farley and Hull prospects withered without the help of the old master.

From a distance, Roosevelt watched state Democratic delegations declare their support. Polls showed Roosevelt's fortunes rising with the deepening European crisis. Just before the GOP convention, Roosevelt appointed Republicans Henry Stimson and Frank Knox to his cabinet. But Roosevelt did not reveal his plans for 1940, even to his closest aides. The president did not forbid aides such as Harry Hopkins to work on a draft, but he did not get involved because he wanted the Democrats to call on him and not the other way around.

At the Chicago convention, Sen. Alben Barkley told the delegates: "The president has never had, and has not today, any desire or purpose to continue in the office of president. . . . He wishes in all earnestness and sincerity to make it clear that all the delegates of this convention are free to vote for any candidate."[108] The statement was followed by an hour-long demonstration and Roosevelt's first-ballot nomination.

The convention mood turned sour, however, when Roosevelt announced that he wanted the liberal secretary of agriculture, Henry Wallace, as his running mate. The announcement disgruntled delegates who already had lined up behind other candidates. But Wallace eventually beat Alabama representative William Bankhead, his strongest opponent for the nomination.

The Republicans mounted their strongest challenge to Roosevelt in 1940, largely based on the charge that Roosevelt was moving the United States toward involvement in the world war. Several moves toward military preparedness had failed at the hands of isolationists in Congress. When Roosevelt asked for increases in defense spending after Gen. Francisco Franco's victory in Spain and Hitler's invasion of Austria in 1938, critics asserted that the president was attempting to cover up domestic failures with foreign adventures. Roosevelt pressed on, however, and Congress passed the Selective Service Act and increases in military spending in 1940.

The Republican field in 1940 included several fresh faces: Sen. Robert A. Taft of Ohio, son of the former president; District Attorney Thomas E. Dewey of New York City; and Sen. Charles L. McNary of Oregon and Sen. Arthur H. Vandenberg of Michigan who had been considered long shots for the Republican nomination in 1936. The freshest face of all was Wendell L. Willkie, a utility executive who had never run for political office. A large, affable man, former Democrat Willkie had barnstormed the country for seven years speaking in opposition to the New Deal.[109] Hundreds of "Willkie clubs" sprang up in the summer of 1940, and a number of publications, including Henry Luce's *Time* magazine, chronicled Willkie's career and encouraged the Willkie groundswell. Despite concern about Willkie's lack of political experience, which led to a "stop Willkie" movement, the Indianan won a sixth-ballot nomination by acclamation. Senator McNary, the Republicans' Senate floor leader, reluctantly accepted the vice-presidential nomination.

Traveling thirty thousand miles in thirty-four states, Willkie gave some 540 speeches. By the time his campaign ended, his already husky voice had turned hoarse. The Republicans spent lavishly and organized grassroots clubs for Willkie across the country. Charges against Roosevelt of managerial incompetence, "warmongering," and imperial ambitions punctuated the Willkie effort. A dramatic moment came when labor leader John L. Lewis called on workers to back Willkie.

After a period of strictly "presidential" behavior, Roosevelt took to the campaign trail with partisan vigor. He answered Willkie's warmongering charges with a promise never to involve the United States in "foreign wars" (which left Roosevelt free to respond to a direct attack).

The alienation of some Democratic and independent voters was symbolized by Vice President Garner, who did not even vote. Roosevelt won, but by the slimmest popular vote margin of any race since 1912. He received 27.3 million popular votes (54.7 percent) to Willkie's 22.3 million (44.8 percent). The electoral vote tally was 449–82.

THE WAR AND ITS LEGACY: 1944

Roosevelt's third term and fourth election were dominated by World War II. Japan attacked U.S. bases at Pearl Harbor, Hawaii, on December 7, 1941. The president, speaking before Congress, declared the date of the surprise attack "a day that will live in infamy." Congress shook off its isolationist inclinations and declared war. A few days after Pearl Harbor, Germany and Italy declared war on the United States, confronting the nation with a two-front war.

The war did for the economy what the New Deal, by itself, could not: it brought economic prosperity. The number of unemployed workers fell from eight million to one million between 1940 and 1944. The boom brought seven million more people, half of them women, into the job market. Inflation, worker shortages, and occasional shortages in raw materials posed problems for wartime agencies. The number of U.S. families paying taxes quadrupled, and by 1945 tax revenues were twenty times their 1940 level. Budget deficits reached new heights.[110]

The fighting in Europe and Asia was grim for the first two years of the president's new term. Isolationist sentiment again built up in Congress, with the Midwest proving the region most resistant to Roosevelt's foreign policy. Criticism of how the Roosevelt administration was managing U.S. participation in the wars on both fronts was rampant. The administration won key congressional votes on the war but faced stubborn resistance on domestic measures. In the 1942 midterm elections, the Republicans gained ten seats in the Senate and forty-seven seats in the House—a major repudiation of Roosevelt.

After several setbacks, the Allied forces won impressive victories. Roosevelt and Churchill worked together closely. Allied forces, led by Gen. Dwight Eisenhower, routed the Axis powers in North Africa in 1942. The Soviet Union beat back a Nazi assault on Stalingrad in the winter of 1942–1943. The Allies took over Italy in 1943 and struggled with the Nazis in France in 1944. In September 1944, British and American troops entered Germany. In the Pacific war, American offensives protected Australia in 1942 and secured the Philippines in 1944.

Despite the bitter opposition that prevailed through much of his third term, Roosevelt had no trouble winning a fourth term in 1944. The Allies found greater success on the battlefield and

on the sea, and the nation did not appear willing to risk untested leadership to prosecute the war. The Republicans turned to the governor of New York, Thomas Dewey. Willkie wanted another shot at the White House, and his best-selling book *One World* put him in the public eye, but old-line conservatives blamed him for the 1940 election defeat. Governors John Bricker of Ohio and Harold Stassen of Minnesota and Gen. Douglas MacArthur were the other hopefuls.

Dewey's primary victories over Willkie in the Wisconsin, Nebraska, and Oregon primaries ended Willkie's public career. Dewey was too far in front to stop. At the convention he won a nearly unanimous first-ballot nomination after Bricker and Stassen dropped out. After Gov. Earl Warren of California refused the vice-presidential nomination, Bricker accepted it.

The party platform extolled the virtues of free enterprise but did not criticize the concept of the New Deal and even made bids for the votes of blacks and women. In his acceptance speech Dewey criticized "stubborn men grown old and tired and quarrelsome in office."[111]

The 1944 election marked the early resistance of the South to the modern Democratic Party. Roosevelt was a shoo-in for the nomination, but southerners wanted a replacement for Wallace as vice president, restoration of the two-thirds nominating rule, and a platform declaration of white supremacy. Dissatisfied southerners threatened to bolt the party in November, but when the party adopted only a vague civil rights plank in its platform, southern discontent dissipated. The rest of the platform called for an internationalist thrust in foreign policy and further New Deal-style reforms domestically.

Roosevelt expressed support for Wallace but said he would allow the convention to pick his running mate. Wallace gave a stirring convention speech but disturbed conservatives with his stand against the poll tax and for equal opportunity for all "regardless of race or sex." Sen. Harry S. Truman of Missouri, who had won fame as a critic of defense spending, beat Wallace for the vice-presidential nomination on the second ballot.

The Democratic campaign was dominated by references to the need for wartime unity and reminders of the Republican rule under Hoover. One leaflet bore the words "Lest We Forget" and a photograph of an unemployed man selling apples in front of a "Hoover Club"; an inset photograph showed Dewey conferring with former president Hoover. The Republicans spent nearly as much money in 1944 as they had in the record-setting 1936 election.

Roosevelt won with 25.6 million popular votes (53.4 percent) to Dewey's 22.0 million (45.9 percent). The electoral vote was 432 to 99. But President Roosevelt, who reshaped U.S. politics at all levels, did not have the opportunity to see the end of the war or to participate in the making of the postwar world. On April 12, 1945, less than three months after his fourth inauguration, he collapsed while sitting for a portrait in Warm Springs, Georgia, and died a few hours later.

THE TRUMAN PRESIDENCY: 1948

The shock of President Roosevelt's death was perhaps greatest for the former haberdasher and machine politician who succeeded him. Truman had been a last-minute choice as FDR's running mate the previous year, and he never became a part of Roosevelt's inner circle. Truman did not know about the most important military program of the age—the Manhattan Project, which, in a race with the Nazis, was developing a nuclear bomb in the secrecy of the brand-new town of Oak Ridge, Tennessee.

Truman also faced a problem of stature. Roosevelt had done nothing less than redefine the presidency in his twelve years in office. He not only effected a partisan realignment in U.S. politics, but he changed the very scope of government activity. As would become clear during the Eisenhower presidency, even Republicans had come to accept, grudgingly, the notion that the government ought to play an active role in stimulating the economy and addressing the needs of specific constituency groups.

Another problem facing Truman: many people could not fathom a presidency without Roosevelt. One member of the White House staff said later: "It was all so sudden, I had completely forgotten about Mr. Truman. Stunned, I realized that I simply couldn't comprehend the presidency as something separate from Roosevelt. The presidency, the White House, the war, our lives—they were all Roosevelt."[112] Other aides could not bring themselves to call Truman "Mr. President," as if so doing would dishonor the late president.

Truman's personality could not have presented a greater contrast to that of Roosevelt. Plain-speaking, blunt, middle-class, midwestern, high school educated, wheeling-and-dealing, and surrounded by old pals from the Pendergast machine of Missouri (the Democratic organization that dominated politics in the state), Truman offended people who had been accustomed to the charisma of Roosevelt. Truman's wife, Bess, also paled in comparison to the dynamic, more public Eleanor Roosevelt as first lady. Nevertheless, Truman showed absolute loyalty to the New Deal, but that would never be enough for many old Roosevelt hands and a nation entering a difficult period of postwar readjustment.

By the time the 1948 election neared, Truman was in grave political shape. He brought former president Hoover back from exile for special projects—one of the many ways he rankled the sensibilities of former Roosevelt aides and Mrs. Roosevelt. Truman also professed a desire to "keep my feet on the ground" and avoid the "crackpots and lunatic fringe" that had surrounded FDR.[113] Toward that end he got rid of Commerce Secretary Henry Wallace and others. The independent journalist I. F. Stone wrote of Truman's personnel moves: "The little nameplates outside the little doors . . . began to change. In Justice, Treasury, Commerce and elsewhere, the New Dealers began to be replaced by the kind of men one was accustomed to meeting in county court-houses."[114]

The politics of postwar adjustment was difficult. The Republican 80th Congress, elected in 1946, sought to dismantle many New Deal programs, and it frustrated anti-inflation efforts. Truman, then, had to duel with Congress, vetoing 250 bills (eleven vetoes were overridden). Tentative civil rights initiatives disgruntled the South. Labor unrest was on the rise. Truman's efforts to "contain" Soviet geopolitical ambitions not only created splits among Democrats but also brought attacks from Republican isolationists. And to make matters worse, Truman was said to have performed inadequately at Potsdam, the conference of World War II victors held in the summer of 1945 that established many geographic borders in Europe.

The situation was so bad that Roosevelt's own son promoted General Eisenhower and Supreme Court Justice William O. Douglas for a 1948 run for the Democratic nomination against Truman. Truman, in other words, was doing a good job antagonizing both the left and the right. In August 1948 the Democratic convention appeared to reflect a dangerously polarized nation. The convention began with a feeling of desperation when Eisenhower and Douglas refused to run. Then a "states' rights" plank offered by southern delegates was defeated, and, after strong speeches by Minneapolis mayor Hubert H. Humphrey and others, a strong northern civil rights plank passed. The party's New Deal and northern machine elements decided that southern defection would be less damaging than northern defection.

Defect is just what some southerners did. The "Dixiecrats," under the leadership of South Carolina's governor J. Strom Thurmond, left the convention to conduct their own fall campaign. Thurmond's candidacy ran under the Democratic Party label in four states (Alabama, Louisiana, Mississippi, and South Carolina) and under the States' Rights Democratic Party elsewhere in the South. Meanwhile, the party's left wing, behind Henry Wallace, protested Truman's Marshall Plan (a multimillion-dollar program to rebuild the economies of western Europe), military buildup, and confrontational stance toward the Soviet Union. It, too, ran its own fall campaign under the banner of the Progressive Citizens of America (the Progressive Party).

The seeds of Dixie defection were planted long before the convention. In 1947 the President's Committee on Civil Rights issued a report calling for the protection of the rights of all minorities. It was just the kind of spark southern segregationists needed to begin a dump-Truman drive and to organize their own campaign in 1948. The Southern Governors Conference in March 1948 recommended that southern states send delegates to the Democratic convention and electors to the electoral college who would refuse to back a pro–civil rights candidate.

As political scientist V. O. Key Jr. has shown, the degree of resistance to civil rights in southern states depended on two basic factors: the proportion of blacks in the population and the strength of the two-party system. Key argued that the existence of a large black population led to stronger Democratic measures against black enfranchisement and led whites to support the Democratic Party in greater numbers. "To them [the whites in such districts], a single Negro vote threatened the whole caste system."[115] Alabama, Louisiana, Mississippi, and South Carolina ended up voting for the Thurmond ticket. Other southern states found broader economic and political issues more compelling than race and voted for Truman.[116]

Many of FDR's old political allies eventually got behind the new man, but Truman's election prospects looked bleak. Some support was grudging—Mrs. Roosevelt offered a straightforward endorsement only to rebut newspaper reports that she fa-

In 1948 pollsters and the media fed Republican candidate Thomas E. Dewey's overconfidence in his campaign to unseat President Harry S. Truman. Truman had the last laugh on the press and his opponent.

vored the Republicans. While the Democratic Party was badly fractured, the Republican Party united behind Dewey.

Dewey, who had been the 1944 GOP candidate, survived a large field in 1948 to become the nominee once again. Senator Taft of Ohio was the main threat, but his isolationism and dull public demeanor were liabilities. The most spirited opposition came from Governor Stassen of Minnesota, who appealed to the more liberal and internationalist wing of the party. An anathema to party bosses, Stassen proved his strength in a series of primary victories. Other candidates or potential convention contenders included Generals Eisenhower and MacArthur, Governor Warren, and Senator Vandenberg. Polls showed all of the Republicans but Taft beating Truman.[117]

Dewey gained the preconvention momentum he needed with an impressive primary victory over Stassen in Oregon. He spent three weeks in the state, while Stassen frittered away his time and resources with a hopeless challenge to Taft in the Ohio primary. Dewey was especially tough in a primary debate with Stassen about communism. With these successes, as well as his impressive organizational strength and mastery over convention mechanics, Dewey won the presidential nomination on the third ballot. Warren was selected as the vice-presidential nominee.

Dewey was part of a new breed of Republican leaders—pragmatic and accepting of the New Deal and the international role that the United States would play in the postwar era. He expressed support for the basic tenets of postwar liberalism, including Social Security, civil rights, and the United Nations. In the 1948 campaign, Dewey planned to put himself above the slashing attack style of President Truman. His constant calls for national unity—spoken in a baritone voice and perfect English—expressed broad public acceptance of the vast changes in U.S. politics over the previous twenty years.

From the beginning of the campaign, the media and professional politicians gave Truman little chance of retaining the White House. Early polls showed Dewey with such a strong lead that pollsters simply stopped surveying voters. But the polls failed because of a bias in the way the questions were asked and a presumption that the large undecided vote would cast their ballots in the same way as the rest of the population, when it in fact heavily favored Truman.[118]

Dewey was so certain of victory that he ran as if he were the incumbent. He made a series of bland, almost diplomatic statements rather than energetic campaign speeches. Dewey appeared confident that his advice to one audience—"Vote your own interests"—would attract an amalgam of disaffected groups. Never even mentioning the president's name, Dewey calmly canvassed the country and just smiled when people called him "President Dewey." Dewey was careful to avoid the overaggressive posture that he thought had ruined his 1944 campaign against Roosevelt. He even made some initial cabinet and policy decisions.

Truman's strategy from the beginning was simply to mobilize the New Deal coalition. The biggest danger was apathy, he and campaign aide Clark Clifford reasoned, so the best strategy was to give the voters a reason to go to the polling booths. Because the Democrats were the majority party, they had to concentrate mainly on getting their longtime supporters to the polls.

Truman ran a scrappy and blunt underdog campaign that could have been mistaken for an outsider's effort. Truman was the president, but he ran against the Washington establishment.

Crisscrossing the nation on a whistle-stop train tour, Truman traveled some 31,000 miles and spoke before six million people. He turned his record of vetoes into an asset, claiming that the "do-nothing" Republican Eightieth Congress made him do it. He assailed the conservative Republican record on inflation, housing, labor, farm issues, and foreign affairs. The president drew large crowds—sometimes many times the size of Dewey's crowds—but he was virtually the only political professional who thought he would win.

Truman himself predicted in October that he had 229 solid electoral votes to Dewey's 109 and Thurmond's 9; 189 votes, he said, could go either way. The best anyone would say about the Truman campaign was that its fighting spirit improved the Democrats' chances to win the Senate. Truman answered the Republicans' claims of liberalism and reformism by criticizing the GOP for obstructing his policies. Truman's outsider taunt was constant: "that no-account, do-nothing, Republican 80th Congress!"[119]

Despite the *Chicago Tribune*'s now-famous headline—"Dewey Defeats Truman"—President Truman prevailed. Early returns put Truman in front, but it was expected that the later-reporting western states would give Dewey the win. When California and Ohio went into the Truman column mid-morning on Wednesday, Dewey conceded defeat.

Considering the Democratic defections, Truman's appeal was widespread. He won twenty-eight states with 24.11 million votes (49.51 percent) and might have won more in the South and North with a united party—as it was, Thurmond won 22 percent of the vote in the South. Dewey won 21.97 million votes (45.12 percent), and Thurmond polled 1.17 million votes (2.40 percent). Henry Wallace won some 1.16 million votes (2.38 percent) but no electoral votes. Wallace's candidacy may have cost Truman New York, Michigan, and Maryland. Yet Wallace may have done Truman a favor by freeing him from the taint of being the most liberal candidate in a time when the electorate was weary of liberalism. Particularly because the Republicans did not have a midwesterner on their ticket and talked about cutting back agricultural subsidies, farmers felt safer with Truman. In all, Truman won 303 electoral votes, Dewey 189, and Thurmond 39.

The Democratic defections may have helped Truman by making him the candidate of the center. The Wallace campaign freed the president from suspicions on the right, and the Thurmond defection strengthened Truman's more liberal northern constituency. In addition, the defections may have inspired Democratic voters to turn out in larger numbers than they would have had victory seemed certain.

In the end the election mostly confirmed long-held partisan allegiances. In the words of political scientist Angus Campbell and his colleagues, it was a "maintaining" election: "The electorate responded to current elements in politics very much in terms of its existing partisan loyalties. Apparently very little of the political landscape attracted strong feeling in that year. But what feeling there was seemed to be governed largely by antecedent attachments to one of the two major parties."[120]

"I LIKE IKE": 1952

Truman's political fortunes worsened during his second term to the extent that he decided belatedly against making a bid for the Democratic nomination. In 1952, for the first time in twenty-four years, neither party had an incumbent president as its nominee.

The Democrats suffered from a weariness that is bound to affect any party that has been in power for twenty years. Problems and opponents' frustrated ambitions were piling up, and in Dwight Eisenhower the Republicans were able to recruit a candidate with universal appeal who was coveted by both parties. The national mood in the years before the 1952 election was sour. The nation was tiring of price controls, recurring scandals among members of the White House staff, and the Korean War, which the Truman administration had begun in 1950 but did not appear interested in either winning or pulling out U.S. troops. The Republicans asked for a chance to "clean up the mess" in Washington and punctuated their appeals with the question: "Had enough?"

The Truman administration had met with repeated frustration in dealing with Congress. On civil rights, tariffs, taxes, labor reform, and the sensationalized question of communist sympathizers in the government, Truman had had to cope with a stubborn Democratic Congress, which, in turn, became more stubborn after Republican gains in the 1950 midterm elections. When Truman seized control of the steel mills because he said the steelworkers' strike threatened the nation's security, he was rebuffed by the Supreme Court.[121]

Truman's biggest problems, however, had concerned cronyism and war. Republicans in congressional investigations and on the stump had hammered away at conflict-of-interest scandals in Truman's administration, creating nationwide sentiment to "clean up" Washington with a new administration. Meanwhile, the United States was mired in a stalemate in Korea—a distant war that was being fought inconclusively under the aegis of the United Nations, with uncertain goals (was it to protect South Korea or to defeat North Korea as well?) and uncertain enemies (was the People's Republic of China an opponent as well as North Korea?). Truman evoked ire with his firing of General MacArthur, who wanted to take the war into China, and with the slow movement toward a settlement. Just as the nation had tired of sacrifices in World War I under Woodrow Wilson, it had tired of sacrifices under Truman.

General Eisenhower—who had just left the presidency of Columbia University to take charge of the forces of the North Atlantic Treaty Organization (NATO)—was recruited by Republicans to run when it appeared that other GOP candidates lacked the national appeal to win the White House. Senator Taft was running again, but his isolationism was considered a liability in the postwar age of internationalism. Stassen, MacArthur, and Warren were other likely Republican candidates.

Eisenhower's popular appeal was revealed when he attracted 50.4 percent of the vote in the New Hampshire primary to Taft's 38.7 percent and Stassen's 7.1 percent. Eisenhower performed well in the northeast area primaries, and Taft generally performed well in the Midwest. A write-in campaign for Eisenhower almost upset Stassen in his home state of Minnesota.

When the GOP convention finally met in Chicago, Taft had the lead in convention delegates. In crucial delegate-seating contests, many of them played out on national television, Eisenhower defeated Taft and won the right to seat pro-Eisenhower insurgents from the South. Taft had relied on the old strategy of mobilizing state machines, but such tactics looked unsavory on television. Eisenhower had undisputed popular appeal, and he won on the first ballot after his early lead turned into a stampede.

Eisenhower selected Sen. Richard Nixon of California as his running mate. The thirty-nine-year-old conservative had won national recognition with his activities on the controversial House Committee on Un-American Activities, which investigated the alleged Soviet ties of Alger Hiss, a former State Department official. Hiss served time for a perjury conviction.

The Democrats moved haltingly toward putting together a ticket. Truman did not announce his decision to stay out of the race until April, after two primary losses. Sen. Estes Kefauver of Tennessee, who had gained fame with his televised hearings on organized crime, ran an aggressive primary campaign and entered the convention with the lead in delegates. Other candidates included Gov. Averell Harriman of New York, Vice President Alben Barkley, Sen. Robert Kerr of Oklahoma, and Sen. Richard Russell of Georgia.

The eventual nominee was Gov. Adlai Stevenson of Illinois, grandson of Grover Cleveland's second vice president. Stevenson had had experience in the navy and State departments before running for governor. President Truman had privately recruited Stevenson for the race—at first unsuccessfully. Then Truman and Illinois backers set up a draft movement for Stevenson, which the governor disavowed until the last minute. Kefauver was the early leader in convention balloting, but Stevenson, always close, pulled into the lead on the third ballot.

Stevenson's campaign was an eloquent call to arms for liberals and reformers. Years later Democrats would recall that the campaign had inspired the generation that would take the reins of power under John F. Kennedy in 1960. Democratic politics at all levels in the 1950s and 1960s would revolve around battles between party regulars and reformers.

Stevenson did not have a chance, however, against the popular Eisenhower. Some southern states bolted the Democratic Party, and the Republicans hammered away at the misdeeds of the Democratic administration under Truman. Such issues as the 1949 communist revolution in China ("Who lost China?"), the protracted Korean War, administration corruption, and the alleged communist infiltration of the government captured the nation's attention more than Stevenson's oratory.

More than anything, however, the desire for party change rather than policy change determined the election. The Republican evocation of the theme of "Corruption, Korea, and Communism" did not challenge the policies that the Democrats offered the nation as much as the way they executed those policies. Eisenhower was a proven administrator and was free of the taint of everyday U.S. politics. Stevenson was a reformer him-self, but his campaign had the conspicuous backing of President Truman. Stevenson's divorce and his public support of Hiss were constant if only vaguely stated issues.

The campaign's biggest controversy developed when newspaper reports alleged that Nixon had used a "secret fund" provided by California millionaires to pay for travel and other expenses. To a Democratic Party weary of charges of impropriety, the revelation offered an opportunity to accuse Nixon of being beholden to special interests. Nixon admitted the existence of the fund but maintained that he used the money solely for travel and that his family did not accept personal gifts.

Nixon originally reacted to the story by asserting that it was a communist smear. When Eisenhower would not publicly back his running mate, speculation developed that Ike would ask Nixon to leave the ticket—and the Republican *New York Herald Tribune* openly called for him to drop out. When Nixon decided to confront his accusers with a television speech, campaign aides told him he would be dropped if the public reaction was not favorable.

Nixon's speech was remarkable. He denied any impropriety and stated that the Stevenson campaign was hypocritical in its criticisms because it had similar funds. More specifically, Nixon denied that he had accepted such gifts as a mink coat for his wife, Pat; he said that his wife wore a "Republican cloth coat." He acknowledged, however, receiving a pet dog named Checkers from a Texas admirer: "And you know, the kids love that dog, and I just want to say this right now, that regardless of what they say about it, we're going to keep it."[122] His folksy message and appeal for telegrams created a wave of sympathy, which Eisenhower rewarded with a pledge of support. The crisis was over.

In a personal victory—surveys showed that the nation still favored the programs of the New Deal but simply wanted to put the cronyism, sacrifices, and Korean War behind it—Eisenhower swept to the White House. Ike won the entire North and West, parts of the South, and some border states—a total of thirty-nine states to Stevenson's nine. His 442 electoral votes and 33.9 million popular votes (55.1 percent) overwhelmed Stevenson's 89 electoral votes and 27.3 million popular votes (44.4 percent). The election of 1956 would bring more of the same.

EISENHOWER'S REELECTION: 1956

Despite his age (sixty-six) and having had a heart attack in 1955, Eisenhower was the strong favorite to be the GOP nominee for another term. Close cooperation with the Democratic congressional leadership and a "hidden-hand" leadership style seemed to comport with the electorate's wishes for normalcy.[123] The White House staff was ably run by the chief of staff, Sherman Adams, and foreign policy was supervised by Secretary of State John Foster Dulles. The genius of Eisenhower's management style was his use of aides as "lightning rods" for unpopular policies.

Even without lightning rods, Eisenhower probably would have fared well. The economy was booming, and Eisenhower had quickly brought the Korean War to a close. His nuclear policy gave the nation a "bigger bang for the buck" in defense spending and kept the troop requirements low. Federal housing and highway programs gave impetus to suburbanization, now considered part of the middle-class American Dream. Issues that would in the future become divisive, such as civil rights, were muffled.

The only unsettled Republican issue was whether Nixon would again be the vice-presidential candidate. Eisenhower offered him a cabinet post, and Stassen mounted a campaign to replace Nixon with Massachusetts governor Christian Herter. After some hesitation, however, Eisenhower stood by his controversial running mate.

In the Democratic camp, Kefauver challenged Stevenson for the right to face Eisenhower in the fall. After impressive primary victories in New Hampshire and Minnesota for Kefauver, the Stevenson campaign fought back with a string of primary wins in states as varied as California, Florida, and Oregon.

Former president Truman endorsed New York governor Harriman—not Stevenson—at the opening of the Democratic convention. A variety of other favorite sons entered the race. But with the help of Eleanor Roosevelt, Stevenson was able to win the nomination for a second time. Stevenson won on the first ballot.

Stevenson left the vice-presidential slot open to the convention delegates. Kefauver, after battling Senators John Kennedy, Albert A. Gore of Tennessee, and Hubert Humphrey and New York mayor Robert Wagner, eventually won. The open contest highlighted the future national political potential of Kennedy, who, according to later accounts, mainly intended not to win the second spot on the ticket but to gain visibility for a 1960 presidential run.

The campaign was bereft of real issues. Eisenhower's campaigning was a tempered appeal to American values and bipartisan consensus. Nixon was left the job of hacking away at the opposition; he called Stevenson "Adlai the Appeaser" and a "Ph.D. graduate of Dean Acheson's cowardly College of Communist Containment."[124] Overall, however, the campaign was an example of what James David Barber has called "the politics of conciliation," with little conflict or desire for change.

Whether or not the electorate was "asleep," as frustrated critics charged, Eisenhower nailed down another strong victory. He won forty-two states, 457 electoral votes, and 35.6 million popular votes (57.4 percent), compared with Stevenson's six states, 73 electoral votes, and 26.0 million popular votes (42.0 percent). In an unprecedented development, however, both houses of Congress went to the opposition.

KENNEDY AND THE POLITICS OF CHANGE: 1960

The periodic national desire for change came at the expense of the Republicans in 1960, when Sen. John F. Kennedy of Massachusetts became the youngest person ever elected president by defeating Vice President Richard Nixon.

The presidential election was foreshadowed by the 1958 midterm election, when the Democrats made impressive gains in Congress. An economic recession and generational politics created the first major shift toward liberalism since the administration of Franklin Roosevelt. The "Class of '58" decisively changed the discourse of U.S. politics. After the election the Democrats held 64 of 98 Senate seats and 283 of 436 House seats, and thirty-five states had Democratic governors. The time appeared ripe for reopening issues that had long been stifled such as civil rights, urban problems, and education.[125]

The 1960 Democratic field was dominated by senators—Kennedy, Lyndon B. Johnson of Texas, Hubert Humphrey of Minnesota, and Stuart Symington of Missouri. Each had important advantages and disadvantages. Kennedy was from a wealthy and politically minded family, but his Catholicism and undistinguished Senate record were liabilities. Johnson was a masterful majority leader, but no southerner had won the White House since James K. Polk in 1844. Humphrey was popular in the Midwest, but he lacked financial backing and was considered too loquacious and liberal. Symington had a strong Senate record and Harry Truman's backing, but he was considered colorless, and Truman's backing carried liabilities.

Former Illinois governor Adlai Stevenson, the party's nominee in 1952 and 1956, stood on the sidelines, hoping that a convention deadlock or draft movement would finally bring him a ticket to the White House. Early speculation was that the convention would be deadlocked and a compromise candidate would have to emerge. It appeared likely that the nomination would go to Symington, Johnson, Humphrey, or to one of the two senior candidates, Stevenson and Kefauver; the other candidates were good bets for the vice-presidential slot.

Kennedy presented the most intriguing candidacy. He was the son of Joseph P. Kennedy, the millionaire who had been Franklin Roosevelt's ambassador to Britain before their bitter break over U.S. involvement in World War II. John Kennedy also was an Ivy League graduate (of Harvard University), a war hero (described in the book *P.T. 109*), and a Pulitzer Prize winner (for *Profiles in Courage*). With an experienced campaign staff, he had won an overwhelming reelection to the Senate in 1958. Moreover, he had been planning a run for the White House for years.

There were Kennedy skeptics, however. No Catholic except Alfred Smith had been a major-party nominee, and Smith's bitter loss and the anti-Catholic sentiments he aroused in 1928 made political professionals wary of naming another Catholic. Some considered Kennedy, at age forty-three, to be too young. Others focused on the influence of Joseph Kennedy, who had bankrolled his son's political career.[126] Truman's comment captured the crux of Kennedy's liabilities: "It's not the Pope I'm afraid of, it's the Pop."[127]

To address the doubts, Kennedy entered political primaries that would enable him to demonstrate vote-getting ability and to confront the religion problem. The two key primaries were Wisconsin and West Virginia. In Wisconsin, Kennedy would answer the charge that he was too conservative. But the Kennedy strategists were divided about whether he should oppose Senator Humphrey of neighboring Minnesota. Wisconsin's growing independence in party politics eventually convinced them, however, that it would present a low risk in return for the possibility of beating Humphrey in his native region. In West Virginia, Kennedy would attempt to blunt the religion issue by attracting the votes of an overwhelmingly Protestant electorate.

In the 1960 presidential campaign John F. Kennedy worked hard to win the West Virginia primary. His victory in this overwhelmingly Protestant state blunted the issue of his Catholicism and set him on the way to a first-ballot nomination.

In the end, Kennedy defeated Humphrey in Wisconsin. Kennedy's impressive campaign treasury enabled him to staff offices in eight of the ten congressional districts in the state; Humphrey had only two offices. Humphrey maintained that the defeat stemmed from crossover Republican Catholic votes and was therefore illegitimate. (Most of the state's Catholics, who made up 31 percent of the population, belonged to the GOP.) But to Kennedy and many political observers, it was still an important victory.

Humphrey wanted to even the score in West Virginia. If Humphrey had quit the campaign and left Kennedy with no opponents, as many advised him to do, a Kennedy victory would have attracted little attention.[128] But Kennedy was able to use the Appalachian state as a way to deflect the religion issue as well as the "can't win" problem. Kennedy had a thorough organization in West Virginia, and he worked hard. He had commissioned polls in the state as far back as 1958 in anticipation of the presidential race.

Kennedy's handling of the religion question in the primaries was shrewd and would be repeated in the fall campaign. He framed the question as one of tolerance—which put Humphrey on the defensive because he had never tried to exploit the religion issue. Kennedy had his campaign workers plant questions about how his religious beliefs would affect his loyalty to the nation, to which the candidate replied with a stock answer: "When any man stands on the steps of the Capitol and takes the oath of office as president, he is swearing to uphold the separation of church and state; he puts one hand on the Bible and raises the other hand to God as he takes the oath. And if he breaks the oath, he is not only committing a crime against the Constitution, for which the Congress can impeach him—but he is committing a sin against God."[129]

Kennedy's direct confrontation of the religion issue worked to his benefit. Kennedy had the money to get his message across: his television expenditures alone in the state totaled $34,000, while Humphrey had only $25,000 for the whole primary campaign in West Virginia.[130] Early polls gave Humphrey wide leads, and interviews elicited strong reservations about Kennedy's Catholicism. As the commercials aired and the primary neared, the lead became smaller, and voters privately said they would vote for Kennedy.

JFK, as he asked headline writers to call him instead of the youthful-sounding "Jack," easily won the primary, taking 61 percent of the vote to Humphrey's 39 percent. He was on his way to a first-ballot nomination.

The Kennedy campaign staffers managed the Democratic convention with consummate skill. Had they failed to gain a majority on the first ballot, pressure might have developed for another candidate. But the Kennedy team efficiently lobbied delegations to augment support; the vice-presidential slot was vaguely offered to several politicians. In the end, Lyndon Johnson was the surprise choice for running mate. Even Kennedy supporters had doubts about Johnson, but the selection of the southerner was a classic ticket-balancing move.[131]

Central to Kennedy's winning campaign was his younger brother Robert F. Kennedy. A former counsel to Republican senator Joseph McCarthy, Robert developed into the consummate political operative. He was JFK's confidant, chief strategist, delegate counter, fund-raiser, taskmaster, and persuader. Biographer Arthur M. Schlesinger Jr. wrote that Robert Kennedy's strength "lay in his capacity to address a specific situation, to assemble an able staff, to inspire and flog them into exceptional deeds, and to prevail through sheer force of momentum."[132]

Vice President Richard Nixon was the overwhelming choice for the Republican nomination. Nelson A. Rockefeller, elected governor of New York in 1958, was a liberal alternative, but he announced in 1959 that he would not run. There was a brief surge for Rockefeller when he criticized the party and its "leading candidate," but meetings with Nixon settled the differences. Some conservatives were disgruntled with Nixon, but their efforts for Sen. Barry Goldwater of Arizona would have to wait until 1964.

Nixon selected United Nations Ambassador Henry Cabot Lodge as his running mate, and the party platform and rhetoric stressed the need for experience in a dangerous world. Nixon promised to continue President Dwight Eisenhower's policies. He attempted to portray Kennedy as an inexperienced upstart, even though he was Kennedy's senior by only four years and the two had entered Congress the same year. Nixon led in the polls at the traditional Labor Day start of the fall campaign.

Kennedy's campaign was based on a promise to "get the nation moving again" after eight years of calm Republican rule. Specifically, he assured voters that he would lead the nation out of a recession. The gross national product increased at a rate of only 2.25 percent annually between 1955 and 1959. Economists puzzled over the simultaneously high unemployment and high inflation rates.[133] Kennedy repeatedly called for two related changes in national policy: pump up the economy and increase defense spending dramatically.

The Democrat faced up to the religion issue again with an eloquent speech before the Greater Houston Ministerial Association, and he attracted attention from civil rights leaders when he offered moral and legal support to the Reverend Martin Luther King Jr. after King was arrested for taking part in a sit-in at an Atlanta restaurant. While Kennedy appealed to the party's more liberal and moderate wing, Johnson toured the South to appeal to regional pride and to assuage fears about an activist government.

The high point of the campaign came on September 26, 1960, when the candidates debated on national television before seventy million viewers. Kennedy was well rested and tanned; he had spent the week before the debate with friends and associates. Nixon was tired from two solid weeks of campaigning; he had spent the preparation period by himself. Their appearances alone greatly influenced the outcome of the debates.

Kennedy's main objective had been simply to look relaxed and "up to" the presidency. He had little to lose. Nixon was always confident of his debating skills, and he performed well in the give-and-take of the debate. But the rules of debating—the way "points" are allocated—are not the same for formal debating and televised encounters. Kennedy's managers prepared their candidate better for the staging of the debate. Nixon's five-o'clock shadow reinforced the cartoon image of him as darkly sinister. As a result of all these factors, polls of radio listeners found that Nixon had "won" the debate, but polls of the more numerous television viewers found that Kennedy had "won." Historian Theodore H. White wrote: "It was the picture image that had done it—and in 1960 it was television that had won the nation away from sound to images, and that was that."[134]

While Kennedy called for a more activist and imaginative approach to world problems, Nixon stressed the candidates' similarities so much that their differences paled into insignificance. Kennedy called for a crusade to eliminate want and to confront tyranny. Nixon responded: "I can subscribe completely to the spirit that Sen. Kennedy has expressed tonight."[135] With ideology an unimportant part of the debate, the images of personal character the candidates were able to project gained in importance.

The candidates held three more debates, addressing issues such as Fidel Castro's Cuba, whether the United States should defend the Chinese offshore islands of Quemoy and Matsu in the event of a military strike by China, and relations with Nikita Khrushchev's Soviet Union. None of the debates had the effect of the first, which neutralized Nixon's quasi-incumbency advantage. Nor was Nixon greatly helped by President Eisenhower, who did not campaign for his protégé until late in the campaign.

The election results were so close that Nixon did not concede his defeat until the afternoon of the day after the election. After a vacation in Florida and Nassau, Nixon returned to Washington on November 19 to consider a series of charges that voter fraud had cost him the election. A shift of between eleven thousand and thirteen thousand votes in a total of five or six states could have given Nixon the electoral vote triumph. Nixon said he decided against demanding a recount because it would take "at least a year and a half" and would throw the federal government into turmoil.[136] Other commentators have pointed out that had Nixon, for instance, challenged voting irregularities in Illinois in Democratic precincts in Chicago, irregularities in Republican rural areas of the state could have been challenged by Kennedy.

When the electoral college voted, Kennedy won 303 electoral votes to Nixon's 219. Democratic senator Harry F. Byrd of Virginia attracted 15 electoral votes. Kennedy won twenty-three states to Nixon's twenty-six. (Six Alabama electors and all eight Mississippi electors, elected as "unpledged Democrats," as well as one Republican elector from Oklahoma, cast their votes for Byrd.) The overall popular vote went 34.2 million for Kennedy and 34.1 million for Nixon. The margin was about two-tenths of 1 percent, or 118,574 votes. Moreover, the margins in many states were very close. Kennedy won Illinois by 8,858 votes and Texas by 46,242 votes. Despite statements that the religion question would hurt Kennedy, it probably helped him by mobilizing Catholics on his behalf. Gallup polls showed that 78 percent of Catholics voted for JFK. Although Catholics were a traditional Democratic constituent group—supporting the party by margins of three or four to one—they had shown support for Republicans Eisenhower and Sen. Joseph McCarthy.[137] In addition, Kennedy put together a predictable coalition: he won the support of voters in the Northeast, in most of the South, and in cities, plus blacks and union workers. Upper New England, the Midwest, and the West went primarily to Nixon.

After the election, Kennedy and Goldwater discussed, in an informal way, how they would conduct their campaigns for the presidency in 1964. The two expected to win their parties' nominations easily, and they talked about crisscrossing the nation in head-to-head debates, which would set a new standard for national campaigns.[138]

The Kennedy-Goldwater campaign never came to be, however. On November 22, 1963, while riding in a motorcade in Dallas, Texas, President Kennedy was assassinated by a gunman named Lee Harvey Oswald.[139] Vice President Johnson assumed the presidency.[140]

In his brief administration, Kennedy had compiled a record disappointing even to many of his supporters. The Bay of Pigs fiasco in which a Central Intelligence Agency plan to overthrow the Cuban government failed miserably, the inability to obtain passage of landmark civil rights legislation, budget deficits and a drain of gold supplies from the United States, confrontations with the Soviet Union in Cuba, Hungary, and Berlin, and the nascent U.S. involvement in the Vietnam War created doubts about the young president's control of the government.

Kennedy had, however, made a start on many important issues. Arms control initiatives such as the test ban treaty, economic growth through tax cuts, modernization of the military, the successful management of the Cuban Missile Crisis, civil rights and other domestic initiatives, the Peace Corps and Alliance for Progress, and growing world stature all offered hope for the second term. It would fall to Johnson, the legendary former Senate majority leader, to bring the Kennedy plans to fruition. First acting as the loyal servant of the slain president, then as his own man, Johnson was able to bring to legislative enactment many of the initiatives long-cherished by liberals—most notably the Civil Rights Act of 1964, which was considerably stronger than the Kennedy bill that had stalled in Congress.

"ALL THE WAY WITH LBJ": 1964

From the time of his sad but graceful ascension to the White House, Johnson was never in doubt as the Democrats' 1964 nominee. He was expected to select an eastern or midwestern liberal as his running mate, and he did so when he tapped Senator Humphrey of Minnesota at the convention, which his campaign organization stage-managed down to the last detail. The only dissent from Democratic unity was provided by Gov.

George C. Wallace of Alabama, whose segregationist campaign took advantage of a backlash against the civil rights movement. Wallace entered three primaries against Johnson-allied favorite sons, and he polled 43 percent of the vote in Maryland. Wallace talked about mounting a third-party bid in the fall, but he backed off.

The Republicans were divided into two bitter camps led by Senator Goldwater of Arizona, the eventual nominee, and by Governor Rockefeller of New York. The nomination contest was a struggle for the soul of the party. Other active and inactive candidates included Ambassador to Vietnam Henry Cabot Lodge, former vice president Nixon, and Gov. William Scranton of Pennsylvania. After a New Hampshire primary victory by Lodge, achieved through a well-organized write-in drive while he was still ambassador to Vietnam, Goldwater and Rockefeller scrapped through a series of primaries. The moderate Lodge later helped Scranton in a late effort to recruit uncommitted delegates to stop Goldwater, but by then it was too late. Goldwater lined up strong delegate support to get the nomination before the primary season even began, but he needed to use the primaries to show that he had vote-getting ability. And the state organizations that backed him needed evidence that his conservative message would find popular acceptance.

In the "mixed" nominating system then in place, candidates were able to pick and choose the primaries that best suited their strategies. Front-runners avoided risks, and long shots entered high-visibility and often risky contests as a way to attract the attention of party professionals. As expected, Goldwater won widespread support in the southern state conventions and had strong primary showings in Illinois and Indiana. Rockefeller beat Lodge in Oregon, but the decisive test came when Goldwater narrowly upset Rockefeller in California.

More important than the confusing preconvention contests was the rhetoric. Both the conservative Goldwater and the liberal Rockefeller vowed to save the party from the other's ideology. Goldwater, who rode the bestseller success of his *Conscience of a Conservative* to hero worship among conservatives, made a vigorous case against New Deal politics and for American sway in world politics: "I don't give a tinker's damn what the rest of the world thinks about the United States, as long as we keep strong militarily."[141] Rockefeller implied that Goldwater would risk nuclear war and would recklessly dismantle basic social programs.

The nominating contest was a regional as well as an ideological struggle. The westerner Goldwater—backed by labor-intensive manufacturers, small business and agricultural enterprises, and domestic oil producers—opposed internationalist banking and commercial interests.[142] Goldwater made eastern media the objects of scorn. Rockefeller and his family, of course, represented the apex of the eastern establishment. Because of his strategy, Goldwater isolated his campaign from the manufacturing and financial interests that were at the center of American economic growth for a generation.

Bitter battles over the party platform and unseemly heckling of Rockefeller displayed the party's divisions at the convention. When the conservatives won the nomination and the platform, there was no reconciliation. Goldwater selected Rep. William

Miller of New York, another conservative, as his running mate and vowed to purge the party of liberal and moderate elements.

In a defiant acceptance speech, Goldwater painted a picture of the United States as inept in international affairs and morally corrupt in domestic pursuits, and he vowed an all-out crusade to change the situation: "Tonight there is violence in our streets, corruption in our highest offices, aimlessness among our youth, anxiety among our elderly, and there's a virtual despair among the many who look beyond the material successes toward the inner meaning of their lives. . . . Extremism in defense of liberty is no vice; moderation in pursuit of justice is no virtue." [143]

To a nation experiencing prosperity and unaware of the true proportions of its involvement in Vietnam, the "choice, not an echo" that Goldwater offered was a moral crusade. But the American consensus was built on material, consumer foundations, and an "outsider" appeal would have to wait until the system's foundations became unstable.

The divided GOP made for easy pickings for Johnson. The fall campaign was dominated by Goldwater's gaffes, which started long before the campaign began. He said, for example, that troops committed to the North Atlantic Treaty Organization (NATO) in Europe probably could be cut by at least one-third if NATO "commanders" had the authority to use tactical nuclear weapons in an emergency.[144] Goldwater also proposed a number of changes in the Social Security system, called for selling off the Tennessee Valley Authority, criticized the civil rights movement, and denounced the Supreme Court, the National Labor Relations Board, and the federal bureaucracy. Except for the use of nuclear weapons and changes in Social Security, most of Goldwater's proposals when taken alone were not shocking. But the sum of his proposals—and his sometimes halting explanations—scared many voters.

President Johnson campaigned very actively to win a mandate for an activist new term. He traveled throughout the country making speeches to build a consensus for his domestic programs as well as his reelection. Johnson resisted Goldwater's frequent calls for televised debates. The nation's prosperity was probably enough to keep the president in the White House.[145]

Johnson desperately wanted a personal mandate to pursue a variety of domestic programs that fell under the rubric of the "Great Society"—a term that Johnson used in a 1964 commencement address (borrowed from a book of the same title by British socialist Graham Wallas). The desired landslide—underscored by his campaign slogan, "All the Way with LBJ"—was essential to initiatives in civil rights, health care, community action, education, welfare, housing, and jobs creation. Central to the landslide was not only economic prosperity but also peace in the world's trouble spots. Johnson therefore ran as a "peace" candidate.

But while he was trying to build a coalition that would sustain his domestic initiatives, Johnson faced an increasingly difficult dilemma about the U.S. role in Vietnam. The United States had been involved in opposing Ho Chi Minh's revolution against French colonial rule in the 1940s and 1950s, and under Presidents Eisenhower and Kennedy the United States had made a commitment to the leaders of South Vietnam (created after

In accepting the 1964 Republican nomination, Sen. Barry Goldwater called for a moral crusade, declaring, "Extremism in defense of liberty is no vice; moderation in pursuit of justice is no virtue."

the failure of the 1954 Geneva accord) as a bastion against communist expansion in Asia. But talk of war would likely imperil the domestic initiatives of the Great Society.

So while Johnson was campaigning as the peace candidate in 1964, he also was preparing for a major increase in U.S. involvement in Vietnam. As early as February 1964, the administration began elaborate covert operations in Southeast Asia and prepared a resolution to give the president a "blank check" in Vietnam.[146] By June, the resolution was ready, and the Pentagon had chosen ninety-four bombing targets in North Vietnam and made provisions for bombing support systems on the ground. But on June 15, Johnson decided to delay major offensives until after the election.[147] In August Johnson sent to Congress what would be known as the Tonkin Gulf resolution, which granted the president broad authority to wage war in Vietnam. The resolution passed quickly and nearly unanimously—after all, the president had instructed congressional leaders to get an overwhelming majority so his policy would be bipartisan.

Johnson also seized on Rockefeller's use of the peace issue during the Republican primaries against Goldwater. He alluded to some of Goldwater's scarier statements about war, and he pledged that "we are not about to send American boys nine or ten thousand miles away from home to do what Asian boys ought to be doing for themselves."[148] A week before the election Johnson said: "The only real issue in this campaign, the only one you ought to get concerned about, is who can best keep the peace."[149]

Johnson's popular vote landslide was the largest in U.S. history. He won 61 percent of the popular vote to Goldwater's

38 percent (or 43.1 million to 27.2 million votes). In the electoral college Johnson received 486 votes to Goldwater's 52, and he carried forty-four states—all but Goldwater's home state of Arizona and five deep South states. In addition, the Democratic Party amassed huge majorities in both the Senate (67–33) and the House of Representatives (295–140).

On election day, Johnson created a working group to study "immediately and intensively" the U.S. options in Southeast Asia.[150] The war was increasing far beyond what most supporters of the Tonkin Gulf resolution or "peace" supporters of the president imagined. In 1965 alone the number of U.S. troops in Vietnam increased from 15,000 to nearly 200,000.[151]

The Breakup of Consensus

A long period of uncertainty in American politics began sometime after Johnson's landslide victory over Goldwater in 1964.

By 1968, some thirty thousand Americans had been killed in action in Vietnam, and television was bringing the war into the living rooms of American families. Despite repeated assertions that the United States was defeating the North Vietnamese enemy, U.S. bombing efforts and ground troops did not break the resolve of the communists in the North or their sympathizers who had infiltrated the South. The corrupt South Vietnamese government and army appeared to lack the will to fight the war on their own.

In the United States, the opposition to the war developed as the casualties mounted, and the administration experienced a "credibility gap" because of its statements about the war. Before the United States left Vietnam in 1975, fifty-five thousand Americans had died in combat. Perhaps more important than the number of casualties—about the same as in the Korean War—was the long-term commitment that the United States appeared to have made with little evidence of progress. The "quagmire," as *New York Times* reporter David Halberstam called the war, was perhaps typified by the program of intense U.S. bombing raids that were judged by many experts to be ineffectual against the North's guerrilla warfare strategy.[152]

As opposition to the war grew among an increasingly vocal and well-organized minority, strains developed in Johnson's economic and domestic programs. Starting with the riots in the Watts section of Los Angeles in 1965, urban areas sizzled with resentment of the mainstream liberal establishment. Detroit, Newark, and many major U.S. cities erupted in other riots that burned miles of city streets and caused millions of dollars in damage. The assassination of civil rights leader Martin Luther King Jr. in Memphis in April 1968, led to riots throughout the nation. Even before the riots, however, a conservative reaction against the Great Society had developed.

The activities of the Great Society were many and varied: the Civil Rights Act of 1964, the Voting Rights Act of 1965, Head Start, Model Cities, mass transit legislation, food stamps, Medicaid, the Elementary and Secondary Education Act, college loans, and housing programs that included subsidies for poor, to name just the most prominent programs.

The conservative backlash was apparent before many programs had time to do their work. Efforts such as the Model Cities program and the Community Action Program, which mandated that poverty programs promote "maximum feasible participation" by the poor themselves, often were badly organized. They also created new struggles over jurisdiction in cities that already were notorious for divisive politics. Liberal efforts that predated the Great Society, such as school desegregation, only added to the tensions in cities.

One of the greatest sources of backlash in the late 1960s was an alarming increase in street crime. Even though blacks and the poor were the chief victims of the increase, the issue was most salient for conservative whites. Many tied the breakdown in order to the growth of the welfare state caused by the Great Society. The crime rate seemed to many to be nothing less than ingratitude on the part of the poor. James Sundquist wrote: "While increasing millions were supported by welfare, rising state and local taxes made the citizen more and more aware of who paid the bill. And while he armed himself for protection against thieves or militants, the liberals were trying to pass legislation to take away his guns."[153]

The crime problem was an important element in both national and metropolitan politics. Polls taken in the late 1960s showed that half the women and a fifth of the men in the country were afraid to walk alone in their own neighborhoods at night.[154] In Alabama, Gov. George Wallace was whipping up his supporters in a frenzy of prejudice and resentment. The fear of crime also would be an important element in Richard Nixon's 1968 campaign.

"NIXON NOW": 1968

With the nation divided over the war and domestic policy, the Democrats entered the 1968 campaign in an increasingly perilous state. In December 1967 Sen. Eugene McCarthy of Minnesota challenged President Johnson for the Democratic nomination, a move based almost entirely on McCarthy's antiwar stance. McCarthy did unexpectedly well against Johnson's write-in candidacy in the New Hampshire primary on March 12, 1968, drawing 42.4 percent of the vote to Johnson's 49.5 percent. Anticipating a devastating defeat in the Wisconsin primary on April 2, Johnson dramatically announced his withdrawal from the campaign in a televised address March 31.

After the New Hampshire primary, New York senator Robert F. Kennedy declared his antiwar candidacy, which put in place all the elements for a Democratic fight of historic proportions. Vice President Humphrey took Johnson's place as the administration's candidate.

McCarthy and Kennedy fought each other in the primaries, and Kennedy appeared to have the upper hand when he closed the primary season with a victory in California on June 5. But after making his acceptance speech, he was assassinated, and the party was in greater turmoil than ever.

At the party convention in Chicago, a site Johnson had chosen for what he thought would be his renomination, Humphrey became the Democratic Party's candidate. He had eschewed the primaries; he won the nomination on the strength of endorsements from state party organizations. The vice president took the nomination on the first ballot after Mayor Richard Daley of Chicago committed the Illinois delegation to his effort. Humphrey won with support from the traditional elements of the Democratic coalition—labor, African Americans, urban voters—plus the backers of President Johnson. Humphrey appealed to many of the party's "moderates" on the issue of the Vietnam War.

Preliminary battles over rules and delegate seating, the representativeness of the party, and the Vietnam War caused ugly skirmishes on the convention floor. The party's platform eventually endorsed the administration's war policy, including bombing, but strong opposition to this plank left the Democrats divided.[155]

Outside the convention halls, demonstrations for civil rights and an end to the war met brutal rejection from the police. After three days of sometimes harsh verbal and physical battles with antiwar demonstrators in city parks, the police charged a group of protesters who planned a march on the convention. Theodore H. White described the scene that played on national television:

Like a fist jolting, like a piston exploding from its chamber, comes a hurtling column of police from off Balbo into the intersection, and all things happen too fast: first the charge as the police wedge cleaves through the mob; then screams, whistles, confusion, people running off into Grant Park, across bridges, into hotel lobbies. And as the scene clears, there are little knots in the open clearing—police clubbing youngsters, police dragging youngsters, police rushing them by their elbows, their heels dragging, to patrol wagons, prodding recalcitrants who refuse to enter quietly.[156]

Humphrey and his running mate, Sen. Edmund S. Muskie of Maine, faced an uphill fight.

The Republicans united behind Richard Nixon, the 1960 nominee whose political career had seemed at an end after he lost in the 1962 California gubernatorial election. The GOP did not have to deal with any of the divisiveness of the 1964 Goldwater-Rockefeller battle.

Nixon outspent Humphrey two-to-one. He also followed a carefully devised script that avoided the exhausting schedule of his 1960 campaign and capitalized on the national discontent created by the Vietnam War, urban riots, political assassinations, and general concern about the speed of change wrought by the Great Society. Nixon traveled the high road in his own campaign by calling for the nation to unite and heal its wounds. Promising an "open administration," Nixon's main offer was change. "I must say the man who helped us get into trouble is not the man to get us out."[157] To avoid scrutiny by the national media, Nixon gave few major addresses, preferring instead a series of interviews with local newspapers and broadcasters.

As President Johnson resisted calls for a halt in the bombing of North Vietnam, Nixon said he had a "secret plan" to end the war. He appealed to weary Democrats with his pledge of an activist administration and alternative approaches to dealing with some of the problems the Great Society addressed. Nixon promised to give blacks, in his words, "a piece of the action with a program to encourage entrepreneurial activity in cities." The

Former vice president Richard Nixon tapped into widespread discontent over the Vietnam War and domestic turmoil to win the 1968 presidential election, one of the closest in U.S. history.

"new Nixon" appeared willing to deal with the Soviet Union, which he had scorned earlier in his career. Meanwhile, his vice-presidential nominee, Gov. Spiro T. Agnew of Maryland, offered a slashing critique of the Democrats to middle-class and blue-collar Americans who resented the civil rights laws, government bureaucracy, Vietnam War protesters, and the young protest generation.

Gov. Wallace of Alabama, heading up one of the strongest third party campaigns in U.S. history, ran as an antiestablishment conservative, railing away at desegregation, crime, taxes, opponents of the war in Vietnam, social programs, and "pointyhead" bureaucrats and "intellectual morons." His American Independent Party was the strongest effort since Robert La Follette's Progressive run in 1924. Like the earlier third-party campaigns, the Wallace run caused concern about the soundness of the electoral college system. Because the race was so close, it was conceivable that no candidate would win an electoral college victory. In that event, Wallace could have held the balance of power.[158]

Despite his early disadvantage, Humphrey made steady inroads into Nixon's support by disassociating himself from Johnson's Vietnam policies. When Johnson on November 1 ordered a halt to all bombing of North Vietnam, Humphrey appeared to be free at last from the stigma of the administration. But this change in policy was not enough to win the election for Humphrey.

The 1968 election was one of the closest in U.S. history. Nixon's victory was not confirmed until the day after the election when California, Ohio, and Illinois—each with very close counts—finally went into the Nixon column. Nixon attracted 31.8 million votes (43.4 percent of all votes cast); Humphrey, 31.3 million votes (42.7 percent); and Wallace, 9.9 million votes (13.5 percent). Nixon won thirty-two states and 301 electoral votes, compared with Humphrey's thirteen states and 191 electoral votes. Nixon won six southern states (Wallace won five others), all of the West except Texas, Washington, and Hawaii, and all the midwestern states except Michigan and Minnesota. Humphrey won all of the East except New Hampshire, Vermont, New Jersey, and Delaware, plus West Virginia, Maryland, and the District of Columbia.

One long-lasting effect of 1968 was a transformation of the nominating process. In response to the bitter complaints about their 1968 convention, the Democratic Party adopted rules that would make the primaries the center of the nominating process. The Chicago convention, dominated by party professionals at the expense of many important constituencies—African Americans, women, youth—had nominated a candidate who did not compete in any primaries. The key reform was a limit on the number of delegates that state committees could choose—after 1968, no more than 10 percent of the delegation.

NIXON'S REELECTION: 1972

Sen. George S. McGovern of South Dakota was the miracle candidate of 1972, but his miracle did not last long enough. Edmund Muskie, a veteran of the U.S. Senate and the vice-presidential nominee in 1968, was the early favorite to win the Democratic nomination. But because of party reforms enacted in response to the disastrous 1968 convention, the nominating process was bound to create surprises and confusion.

No fewer than fifteen contenders announced their candidacy, twelve with serious hopes of winning or influencing the final selection. Some twenty-two primaries to choose 60 percent of the party's delegates—a third more than in 1968—were to take place over four months. The marathon would be decided by accidents, media strategy, and a confusing array of voter choices that changed with each new development.

Muskie was badly damaged before the New Hampshire primary when he appeared to cry while lashing back at the *Manchester Union Leader*'s vicious and unrelenting attacks on his campaign and on his outspoken wife, Jane. The *Union Leader* had printed a series of attacks on Jane and then falsely reported that Muskie had laughed at a derogatory joke about French Canadians. Muskie later said of the incident: "It changed people's minds about me, of what kind of a guy I was. They were looking for a strong, steady man, and here I was weak."[159]

Muskie won the first-in-the-nation New Hampshire primary, but his 46.4 percent of the vote was considered a "disappointing" showing. Senator McGovern, the antiwar candidate who won 37.1 percent of the vote, was pronounced the real winner by media and pundits. He had attracted a corps of youthful volunteers and his strong showing—engineered by imaginative young political operatives led by Gary Hart—was a surprise.

After New Hampshire, the Democrats battled through the summer. Wallace parlayed his antibusing rhetoric into an impressive victory in the Florida primary (41.6 percent). Better organized than the others, McGovern won the Wisconsin delegation by winning 29.6 percent of the state vote. McGovern then won an easy Massachusetts victory with 52.7 percent of the vote to Muskie's 21.3 percent. Humphrey edged McGovern in Ohio by 41.2 to 39.6 percent, but McGovern claimed a moral victory.

In the popular primary vote before the late summer California primary, McGovern actually stood in third place behind Wallace and Humphrey. But the delegate allocation rules gave the edge to the candidate who could squeeze out narrow victories in congressional districts, and that was McGovern. McGovern had 560 delegates to Humphrey's 311. Wallace had 324 delegates, but he was paralyzed after being shot in a Maryland shopping center on May 15, 1972, and therefore no longer appeared to have a chance at the nomination.

The big McGovern-Humphrey showdown was California, which offered 271 delegates to the winner. It was a spirited campaign that included a head-to-head debate and strong Humphrey assaults on McGovern's positions on welfare and defense spending. McGovern went on to beat Humphrey by five percentage points in the winner-take-all primary. McGovern also won a majority of the delegates in New Jersey, South Dakota, and New Mexico on the last day of the primary season.[160]

After platform battles over welfare, busing, and the Vietnam War, McGovern won the nomination handily. He then selected Sen. Thomas Eagleton of Missouri as his running mate after several others declined. McGovern did not get to deliver his acceptance speech—perhaps the best speech of his career—until almost three o'clock in the morning, when most television viewers already were in bed.

President Nixon and Vice President Agnew were renominated with barely a peep out of other Republicans. Rep. Paul N. "Pete" McCloskey Jr. of California opposed Nixon in the primaries but won only one delegate (from New Mexico). Rep. John M. Ashbrook of Ohio also ran in the primaries.

McGovern would have been an underdog in the best of circumstances, but his chances were badly damaged by what came to be known as the "Eagleton affair." As the McGovernites celebrated their hard-won nomination, rumors circulated that Eagleton had been hospitalized for exhaustion in the early 1960s. Eagleton finally told McGovern operatives that he had been hospitalized three times for nervous exhaustion and fatigue, and his treatment included electroshock therapy. Despite McGovern's public statement that he was "1,000 percent for Tom Eagleton, and I have no intention of dropping him," Eagleton left the ticket less than two weeks after his nomination.

McGovern eventually replaced Eagleton with his sixth choice, R. Sargent Shriver, former executive of the Peace Corps and Office of Economic Opportunity. But the aura of confusion that surrounded the Eagleton affair and the search for a new vice-presidential candidate hurt the campaign badly. The columnist Tom Braden likened it to a school teacher who could not control the class: "Nice people, too. One looks back with sympathy and a sense of shame. But at the time—was it that they were too nice?—their classes were a shambles. The erasers flew when they turned their backs."[161]

Nixon was in command of the fall campaign. He paraded a litany of accomplishments—the Paris peace talks over the Vietnam War, the diplomatic opening to China, the arms limitation treaty with the Soviet Union, and a number of domestic initiatives. Most of all, he was a strong figure. And if he still aroused suspicion, he was at least a known commodity.

Nixon won all but Massachusetts and the District of Columbia in the fall election. His popular vote margin was 47.2 million to McGovern's 29.2 million; the electoral college cast 520 votes for Nixon and only 17 for McGovern. Nixon's 60.7 percent share of the popular vote stood second only to Johnson's 61.1 percent in 1964.

On the surface, it appeared in 1972 that American politics was entering an age of calm consensus. At the time of the election, the economy was temporarily strong. Moreover, opposition to the Vietnam War had faded as the two sides negotiated in Paris for an end to the war, and the United States had signed an important nuclear arms treaty with the Soviet Union and had made important diplomatic moves with that country and the People's Republic of China. Nixon's landslide victory appeared to be a mandate and a vote of confidence.

But trouble loomed behind the apparent stability and consensus. The war in Vietnam continued, as did the antiwar protests, and generational cleavages remained. The economy experienced the first of many "shocks" in 1973 when the Organization of Petroleum Exporting Countries agreed to ban oil exports to the United States. The economic turmoil that resulted in the United States was topped off with a wage and price freeze. In addition, a warlike atmosphere between the White House and the media (as well as other perceived enemies of the administration who appeared on Nixon's "enemies list") and the mushrooming Watergate scandal combined to create a dark side to U.S. politics in the 1970s.[162]

The Watergate affair was perhaps the greatest political scandal in U.S. history. For the first time, a president was forced to leave office before his term expired. President Nixon resigned on August 9, 1974, when it became apparent that the House of Representatives would impeach him for "high crimes and misdemeanors" and the Senate would convict him. In addition, a number of Nixon aides, including his first attorney general and campaign manager, John Mitchell, would spend time in jail because of the scandal.

At its simplest, the Watergate affair was "a third-rate burglary," followed by a cover-up by President Nixon and his aides. In the summer of 1972, several employees of the Committee to Re-elect the President (dubbed "CREEP") were arrested after they were discovered breaking into and bugging the Democratic National Committee's offices at the posh Watergate complex in Washington. The break-in was not a major issue in the 1972 election, but the next year a Senate committee began an investigation of the entire affair.

During the investigation, a presidential aide revealed that Nixon had secretly taped Oval Office conversations with aides. When the Watergate special prosecutor, Archibald Cox, ordered Nixon to surrender the tapes in October 1973, Nixon ordered Cox fired. But because Nixon's attorney general, Elliot Richardson, and assistant attorney general, William D. Ruckelshaus, refused to fire Cox, the task was carried out by Solicitor General Robert Bork, igniting a constitutional crisis dubbed the "Saturday night massacre."

Nixon soon handed over the tapes Cox had sought. In the summer of 1974, the Supreme Court ruled that Nixon had to surrender even more tapes, which indicated that he had played an active role in covering up the Watergate scandal. Nixon resigned the presidency when his impeachment and conviction appeared certain. The impeachment articles charged him with obstruction of justice, abuse of presidential powers, and contempt of Congress.

Many students of the Watergate affair maintain that the illegal campaign activities were just part of a tapestry of illegal activities in the Nixon administration—including secretly bombing Cambodia, accepting millions of dollars in illegal campaign contributions, offering government favors in return for contributions, "laundering" money through third parties, wiretapping and burglarizing a wide variety of people thought to be unsupportive of the president, offering executive clemency to convicted campaign workers, engaging in "dirty tricks" to discredit other political figures, compromising criminal investigations by giving information to the people under scrutiny, and using government funds to renovate the president's private residence.[163]

In 1973 Nixon's vice president, Spiro Agnew, resigned after pleading "no contest" to charges of taking bribes while he was governor of Maryland. After Agnew's resignation on October 10, 1973, Nixon named House Minority Leader Gerald Ford, a longtime GOP stalwart, to become vice president under the Twenty-fifth Amendment. Ford, who had never entered a national election, then became president upon Nixon's resignation and quickly attracted the support of the American public with his modest, earnest disposition. He responded to the widespread feeling that Nixon's isolation in the Oval Office had contributed to his downfall by promising to work closely with Congress and to meet with the press regularly.

One month after becoming president, however, Ford ignited a firestorm of criticism with his full pardon of Nixon for all crimes he may have committed while president. Ford testified before Congress that he believed Nixon had suffered enough and that the nation would have been badly torn if a former president were brought to court to face criminal charges. Critics asserted that Ford had made a "deal" in which Nixon resigned the presidency in exchange for the pardon.[164]

Ford selected former New York governor Nelson Rockefeller to be his vice president. Rockefeller received Senate and House confirmation on December 10 and 19, respectively, after long, difficult hearings that centered on his financial dealings.

THE ELECTION OF 1976: JIMMY WHO?

With the benefit of the Watergate scandal and Ford's pardon of Nixon, the Democrats won resounding victories in the 1974 midterm elections. The Democrats' gains of fifty-two House seats and four Senate seats not only created stronger majorities but also reduced the number of members with allegiance to the old system of organizing congressional business.

Virtually unknown to the country at the outset of the campaign, former Georgia governor Jimmy Carter emerged from a field of candidates to win the Democratic nomination and the presidency. His casual and honest approach appealed to many voters.

The moralistic zeal of the "Watergate class" forced major changes on Congress as well as on the presidency and the nation's process of pluralistic political bargaining. The new crop of legislators was so large that it was able to undermine the seniority system that had ordered the way Congress had operated for years. The new system of committee assignments led to a proliferation of subcommittees on which most members had prominent roles. That, in turn, created a fragmented policy-making process—less susceptible to coercion by presidents and party leaders but more susceptible to interest group politics.[165]

The 1976 campaign was the first governed by campaign finance reform legislation enacted in 1971 and 1974. The Federal Election Campaign Act (FECA) of 1971 limited campaign expenditures and required disclosure of campaign receipts and expenditures. The Revenue Act of 1971 created a tax check-off that enabled taxpayers to allocate $1.00 of their taxes for public financing of elections. The FECA amendments of 1974 limited spending and donations for both primary and general election campaigns, established a system of partial public funding of elections, and created the Federal Election Commission to monitor campaign activities.

The Democrats and their eventual nominee, Jimmy Carter, continued to exploit the nation's discontent through the 1976 election. Ronald Reagan, a former movie actor and California governor, added to the Republican Party's vulnerability by waging a stubborn primary campaign against President Ford.

The Democrats appeared headed for a long and bitter nomination struggle for the third time in a row. A few candidates—such as Senators Henry Jackson of Washington and Birch Bayh of Indiana and Governor Wallace of Alabama—had greater stature than others, but their appeal was limited to specific factions of the Democratic coalition. Other candidates included Rep. Morris Udall of Arizona, Sen. Fred Harris of Oklahoma, Sen. Frank Church of Idaho, and Gov. Edmund G. "Jerry" Brown Jr. of California. Church and Brown entered the race late, and Senators Humphrey of Minnesota and Edward M. Kennedy of Massachusetts awaited a draft in the event of a deadlocked convention.

The moderate Carter, whose name recognition in polls stood in single figures when the campaign began, executed a brilliant campaign strategy to win the nomination on the first ballot. Constructing strong organizations for the Iowa caucuses and the New Hampshire primary, Carter won both contests by slim margins. Although liberal candidates Udall and Bayh together polled more votes than Carter, it was Carter who received cover billings on national magazines and live interviews on morning television talk shows.[166] Within a matter of days, Carter went from long shot to front-runner.

Udall performed well in the primaries but never won a single state; he and other liberals were splitting the liberal vote. Udall's chance for a Wisconsin primary win fizzled when Harris refused to back out to create a one-on-one matchup of a liberal with Carter.[167] Carter ran into strong challenges from Church and Brown in later primaries, but he had the delegates and endorsements by the time of the Democratic convention in New York for a first-ballot nomination. The convention itself was a "love fest" with the Democrats united behind Carter and his running mate, Sen. Walter F. Mondale of Minnesota.

The GOP was divided between Ford and Reagan. Ford won the early contests, but Reagan scored big wins in the North Carolina and Texas primaries. Reagan was put on the defensive with his proposals for transferring welfare obligations to the states, but when he focused on foreign policy he had success. For example, he attacked Ford for his policy of détente with the Soviet Union and his negotiation of a treaty that would forfeit U.S. control of the Panama Canal.

In the late summer, with Ford and Reagan locked in a close contest for delegates, Reagan tried to gain the advantage by breaking precedent and naming his vice-presidential candidate before the convention. Reagan's choice—Sen. Richard S. Schweiker of Pennsylvania, a moderate—widened Reagan's ideological appeal but angered many of his conservative supporters. When Reagan tried to force Ford to name a vice-presidential candidate in advance as well, the convention vote on the issue became a crucial test of the candidates' delegate strength. But Ford won that test and the nomination. He selected the acerbic senator Bob Dole of Kansas as his running mate as a consolation prize for disappointed conservatives.

Carter emerged from the Democratic convention with a wide lead over Ford, but the race was too close to call by election day. A number of gaffes—such as Carter's interview with *Playboy* magazine, his ambiguous statements about abortion, and his confused observations on tax reform—hurt the Democratic contender.[168] Ford also gained in the polls when he began to use the patronage powers of the presidency and effectively contrasted his twenty-seven years of Washington experience to Carter's four years as governor of Georgia.

For the first time since 1960, the major candidates took part in televised debates. As the outsider, Carter helped himself by demonstrating a good grasp of national issues and by appealing to Democrats to vote the party line. Ford hurt himself with a claim that Eastern European nations did not consider themselves to be under the control of the Soviet Union.[169] The remark was intended to be testimony to the Europeans' sense of national identity, but it was interpreted as evidence of the president's naiveté.

Carter's main advantage was regional pride. The Democrats had long since lost their hold over the South, but Carter gained widespread support as the first candidate nominated from the region on his own in more than a century. The Democratic Party's many factions—including such big-city mayors as Richard Daley of Chicago and Abraham Beame of New York, civil rights activists, and organized labor—put on a rare display of unity.

Carter defeated Ford by a slim margin, winning 40.8 million votes (50.1 percent) to Ford's 39.1 million (48.0 percent). In the electoral college, 297 votes went to Carter, 240 to Ford. Carter won by pulling together the frazzled New Deal coalition of industrial and urban voters, African Americans, Jews, and southerners. Ford won the West, and Carter won the South, except Virginia. Ford won all the states from the Mississippi River westward except Texas and Hawaii, plus states in his native Midwest like Iowa, Illinois, Michigan, and Indiana. Ford also won Connecticut and the three northernmost New England states—New Hampshire, Vermont, and Maine.

CARTER'S UNCERTAIN LEADERSHIP: 1980

After his election, President Carter's ability to hold the coalition together was limited. The growing influence of the mass media, the fragmenting effects of interest groups, poor relations with Congress, and difficult issues that cut across many different sectors—inflation and unemployment, oil shocks and the more general energy crisis, the Iran hostage crisis, relations with the Soviet Union, and budget austerity moves such as proposed cutbacks in water projects and social welfare—all damaged Carter's governing ability.

As the 1980 election approached, Carter appeared to have lost all but his institutional strength and the reluctance of voters to reject a president for the fourth time in a row. Carter controlled party processes, such as the primary schedule; he had access to key financial support and skilled political operatives; and he shaped much of the political agenda. But Kennedy was hitting him hard from the left, and Reagan and others were hitting him hard from the right. As a result, Carter was unable to forge a lasting consensus on important issues. Kennedy was leading Carter in the polls by a two-to-one margin when he announced

his challenge to the incumbent president in November 1979. But Carter overcame that lead by the start of the nominating season when the seizure of American hostages in Iran rallied the nation around the president and Kennedy made a series of political mistakes. Kennedy was unable to develop campaign themes or answer questions about his personal conduct in the 1969 Chappaquiddick incident in which a woman died after a car he was driving went off a bridge. Other "character" issues, such as Kennedy's alleged "womanizing," and more substantive issues, such as his liberal voting record, also hurt him in a year dominated by conservative themes. Finally, Kennedy's campaign was in financial jeopardy early because of lavish spending on transportation, headquarters, and other expenses.

The campaign of Gov. Jerry Brown of California was unable to find much support for his appeal for recognition of economic and environmental limits. He dropped out of the race in April.

The president was able to manipulate the primary and caucus schedule to bunch together states favorable to him and to match pro-Kennedy states with pro-Carter states. The result was an early, strong Carter lead in delegates. Kennedy came back with some solid primary wins in New York and Pennsylvania, but his campaign by then had been reduced to a vehicle for anti-Carter expressions. Many Kennedy voters hoped for a deadlocked convention at which a third candidate would win the nomination.

Carter won the nomination on the first ballot despite a variety of stop-Carter efforts and Kennedy's attempt to free delegates to vote for any candidate. When Carter won the crucial floor vote on the "open convention" question, Kennedy did not have a chance. The Carter-Mondale ticket entered the fall campaign as a wounded army unable to generate much enthusiasm from the troops.

The Republicans united early behind Reagan. By April 22, 1980, less than two months after the New Hampshire primary, six candidates had dropped out of the race, and George Bush, Reagan's only surviving competitor, was desperately behind in the delegate count. Reagan's campaign experienced an early scare when Bush beat Reagan in the Iowa caucus, but Reagan rebounded, changed campaign managers and tactics, and won a string of primaries and caucuses. By the time of the convention, Reagan was the consensus candidate, and he improved party unity by adding Bush to the fall ticket.

Reagan called on the electorate to replace politics that he said was marked by "pastels," or compromising and uncertain policies, with "bold colors." Reagan's proposed bold strokes included a 30 percent reduction in marginal income tax rates based on a "supply-side" economic theory—which even Bush had said was a dangerous kind of "voodoo economics"—and massive increases in military expenditures. At the same time Reagan criticized Carter's alleged vacillation and his commitment to liberal policies.

President Carter, who was vulnerable as the hostage crisis neared its first anniversary (on November 4, election day) and high inflation and unemployment rates persisted, attempted to portray Reagan as a dangerous, heartless, and inexperienced amateur. Reagan managed to use Carter's attacks to his own advantage by assuming a posture of hurt feelings at the unfair criticism. When in a televised debate Carter attacked Reagan's previous opposition to social welfare programs, Reagan cut him off with a line, "There you go again," that suggested Carter was unfairly and relentlessly distorting Reagan's record.

The greatest controversy of the campaign did not emerge until years later. Books published after the Reagan years charged that the Reagan-Bush campaign negotiated a deal with Iran to delay release of the hostages until after the campaign to embarrass President Carter. Gary Sick, a national security aide for Carter, charged that Reagan campaign officials met with Iranian officials in Europe in the summer of 1980 to arrange weapons sales in exchange for holding the hostages. If true—and many disputed the charges—the deal could have cost Carter the presidency.[170]

Carter strategists also were concerned about the independent candidacy of Rep. John B. Anderson of Illinois, a moderate who dropped out of the Republican race when it became clear that conservatives would dominate that party. After some stronger support in the polls, Anderson stood at about 10 percent for the final two months of the campaign. Carter was concerned that Anderson would take more votes from him than from Reagan, even though analysis of Anderson support suggested otherwise.[171]

Private money almost doubled the amount that Reagan was legally entitled to spend under the federal campaign financing system. Well-organized groups from the "new right," which opposed abortion, gun control, détente, and many social welfare programs, spent lavishly on television commercials and efforts to register like-minded voters. These groups also made a "hit list" of leading liberals in Congress. These candidates were so weakened by the new right's attacks that they put a local and regional drag on an already dragging Democratic ticket.[172]

Polls before election day predicted a close race. Reagan, however, won all but six states and took the White House in an electoral landslide, 489 electoral votes to 49. Reagan won 51 percent of the vote, while Carter managed 41 percent and Anderson 7 percent. Carter ran tight races in ten additional states that could have gone his way with a shift of less than one and a half percentage points. In twenty-one states, Anderson's vote totals made up most or all of the difference between Reagan and Carter. Despite these factors and polls that regularly showed preference for Carter's policy positions, Reagan's victory was impressive. He beat Carter by a better than two-to-one margin in nine states.

Even more surprising than Reagan's electoral landslide was the Republican takeover of the Senate. The new right's targeting of several Senate liberals—such as McGovern, Bayh, Gaylord Nelson of Wisconsin, and John Culver of Iowa—created the biggest Senate turnover since 1958. The Republicans now held the Senate by a 53–46 margin.

President Reagan was able to parlay his claims of an electoral mandate into wide-ranging changes in tax, budget, and military policies. Among other things, he won passage of a three-year, 25 percent cut in tax rates that would reduce federal revenues by $196 billion annually by the time the three-stage program was in place. He also secured omnibus legislation that cut the domestic budget by $140 billion over four years and increased defense spending by $181 billion over the same period. The media hailed Reagan as the most successful handler of Congress since Lyndon Johnson.

The New Conservative Discourse

Reagan's rise ushered in a new age of conservatism in the American political discourse. The vigorous conservative campaigns for the presidency and Congress were accompanied by a host of new "think tanks" and publications with a restyled set of philosophical and policy pronouncements.

The most celebrated event of the conservative revival was the publication in 1980 of George Gilder's *Wealth and Poverty*, a far-reaching attack on welfare state policies that rested on supply-side economic theory. Gilder argued that free markets and low taxes promoted not only economic efficiency and growth but also other benefits such as family strength and artistic creativity. Gilder's book was a central element of Reagan's campaign for major tax cuts.[173] But the supply-side tracts of Gilder and others were only the most visible signs of the conservative movement. Reagan's criticism of the Supreme Court decisions on abortion and school prayer helped to bring evangelical Christians into the political process. Businesses and conservative philanthropists, meanwhile, sponsored an unprecedented level of public policy research that shaped the debate of elections and government policy.[174]

Reagan's political appeal, according to scholar Garry Wills, turned on his ability to blend contradictory elements of American culture such as capitalism, conservatism, and individualism. While Reagan decried the decline of "traditional American values," for example, he extolled the dynamic economic system that demanded constant change. Wills wrote: "There are so many contradictions in this larger construct that one cannot risk entertaining serious challenge to any of its details. In Reagan, luckily, all these clashes are resolved. He is the ideal past, the successful present, the hopeful future all in one."[175]

Using the "bully pulpit" of the presidency, Reagan was able to overwhelm his opponents with his vision. When Democrats criticized specific Reagan policies, Reagan deflated them with expressions of disdain for "little men with loud voices [that] cry doom."[176] Jeane Kirkpatrick's depiction of Democrats as the "blame America first crowd" neatly expressed the way the Reagan rhetoric foreclosed debate on major policy issues such as the budget and trade deficits, military spending, the U.S. role in the third world, and U.S.-Soviet relations.

By the time the 1984 campaign took place, much of the nation had adopted Reagan's terms of debate. Mondale's strongest performance, in fact, was in the first debate when he congratulated Reagan for restoring national pride and suggested not that Reagan should be ousted but rather that he be given a graceful retirement. Mondale's campaign was basically conservative: he did not propose a single new social program and called the federal budget deficit the nation's top problem.

REAGAN'S 1984 LANDSLIDE

Reagan's popularity dipped to 44 percent in 1983—about the average for modern presidents—but it rebounded when the

Democratic presidential candidate Walter F. Mondale and his running mate, Geraldine Ferraro, the first woman to receive a major party nomination for national office, campaign in the 1984 presidential race.

economy later picked up.[177] As the 1984 election approached, Reagan faced no opposition from Republicans, but a large field of Democrats sought the right to oppose him in the fall.

The Democrats' early front-runner was former vice president Mondale, who had accumulated a wide range of endorsements (AFL-CIO, National Education Association, United Mine Workers, and the National Organization for Women) and an impressive campaign treasury. The more conservative senator John Glenn of Ohio, the first American to orbit the earth, was considered a strong challenger. Other candidates included Senators Gary Hart of Colorado, Alan Cranston of California, and Ernest Hollings of South Carolina, civil rights leader Jesse Jackson, former presidential candidate George McGovern, and former governor Reubin Askew of Florida.

The early results eliminated all but Mondale, Hart, and Jackson just sixteen days after the New Hampshire primary. Hart became the serious challenger to Mondale when he finished second in Iowa and first in New Hampshire, creating an explosion of media coverage. After Mondale recovered, the two fought head-to-head until the convention. Jackson, the second African American to run for the presidency, stayed in the race to promote his liberal party agenda.[178]

After interviewing a wide range of candidates, Mondale selected Rep. Geraldine A. Ferraro of New York as his running mate—the first woman ever to receive a major-party nomination for national office. Representative Ferraro's vice-presidential candidacy probably was a drag on the ticket, not so much because she was a woman but because of the controversy created by her husband's finances and her stand on the abortion question. The controversies hindered the Democratic campaign's effort to articulate its own vision for the nation.[179]

Ferraro appeared knowledgeable and strong in her debate with Vice President Bush, and she often drew large and enthusiastic crowds. But she was stuck in controversy when details of her husband's questionable real estate, trusteeship, and tax practices became public. Opponents of abortion held prominent and often loud protests at the sites of her speeches, and she got involved in a lengthy public dispute over abortion with Catholic archbishop John O'Connor. Ferraro also did not help the ticket in regions where the Democrats were weak, such as the South and West.

Mondale ran a generally conservative campaign, concentrating on a proposed tax increase to address the unprecedented budget deficit of more than $200 billion and proposing no new social programs. Mondale criticized Reagan's record on the arms race, but he did not outline basic disagreements on other foreign affairs issues. He charged that Reagan, the oldest president in history, was lazy and out of touch. Only late in the campaign, when his speeches became unabashedly liberal and combative, did Mondale create any excitement.

Just once—in the period after the first presidential debate— did Mondale appear to have a chance to defeat President Reagan. Political pundits had marked Mondale as a poor television performer, but the challenger outfoxed Reagan in the debate and afterward appeared to be gaining ground for a few days. Before the debate, Mondale aides had leaked erroneous information that suggested he would make a slashing attack. But Mondale surprised Reagan by adopting a "gold-watch approach" suitable to a family business retiring an old-timer—"sort of embracing a grandfather, and gently pushing him aside."[180] Mondale gave the president credit for helping to restore national patriotism and beginning a national debate on education reform, but he said it was time for new leadership. Reagan appeared confused and, in the rush to demonstrate statistical knowledge of policies, he failed to outline broad themes.

Although the first debate boosted the Mondale campaign's morale, it never brought Mondale within striking range of Reagan—he never came within ten percentage points of Reagan in the polls. Reagan's campaign was a series of rallies with masses of colorful balloons and confident talk about the United States "standing tall" in domestic and world affairs. Reagan was so sure of victory that he made a last-minute trip to Mondale's home state of Minnesota with the hope of completing a fifty-state sweep of the nation.

As it was, Reagan won forty-nine states, with 2-to-1 margins in eight states. Idaho, Nebraska, and Utah each gave Reagan more than 70 percent of the vote. Mondale won only the District of Columbia and his home state of Minnesota, where he beat Reagan by only two-tenths of a percentage point. As for the popular vote, Reagan won 54.5 million votes (58.8 percent) to Mondale's 37.6 million (40.6 percent). In the electoral college, he received 525 votes to Mondale's 13 votes.

Reagan's two landslides and the conservative discourse of his administration led many experts to wonder if they were witnessing a "realignment"—a major shift in political alliances among a variety of social, economic, and ethnic groups.[181] The trend during the 1970s and 1980s appeared to be one of a Democratic hold on congressional and state elections and Republican dominance of presidential elections. Some experts pointed to the electorate's ticket-splitting tendencies as evidence of "dealignment"—a breakdown of the old system without development of an entirely new system.[182]

Perhaps the most noteworthy development of recent years, which fits the dealignment thesis, has been the convergence of the appeal of the two parties. Michael Barone, in *The Almanac of American Politics,* wrote:

Political preferences in the America of the 1940's correlated to a fair degree with income. Republican strength was greater than average in high income states . . . while Roosevelt and Truman carried virtually every state with incomes below the national average. But today there is virtually no correlation between income level and political preference. Utah, with one of the lowest per capita incomes, was one of the nation's most Republican states in 1980. . . . In the Midwest, high income Illinois is more Democratic than low income Indiana.[183]

BUSH'S ASCENDANCY: 1988

The election of 1988 was the first after 1968 in which an incumbent president did not run. With no major figure and no major issues, the campaign was a tumultuous affair. Fourteen candidates struggled to develop an identity with the voters, and the campaign lurched from one symbolic issue to the next, never developing the overarching themes of previous campaigns.

In the absence of any major new issues, and in a time of general peace and prosperity, Republican vice president George Bush won the presidency. Bush defeated Democratic Massachusetts governor Michael S. Dukakis by a margin of 54 percent to 46 percent—48.9 million votes to 41.8 million votes. Bush's electoral vote margin was more impressive, 426–111. A negative campaign and limited voter registration efforts resulted in the lowest voter turnout rate since the 1920 and 1924 race percentages of 49 percent of all eligible voters. Just a little more than 50 percent of all eligible citizens voted for president in 1988.

Bush, benefiting from the Nixon-Reagan presidential coalition, won all the states of the old Confederacy, the entire West except Oregon and Washington, and several northern industrial states. Dukakis originally had hoped to crack the South by selecting a favorite son, Sen. Lloyd M. Bentsen Jr. of Texas, as his running mate, but that tactic failed. Dukakis lost crucial states that he had fought for to the end, such as California, Pennsylvania, Illinois, Ohio, and Missouri. He won New York, Massachusetts, Wisconsin, Minnesota, Oregon, Washington, West Virginia, Iowa, Rhode Island, Hawaii, and the District of Columbia.

President Ronald Reagan's retirement after two full terms created a political void. By most accounts, Reagan was the most popular president since Dwight Eisenhower. His dominance of national politics left little room for other figures to establish presidential stature.

Reagan's fiscal and social policies reduced the possibility for candidates to offer ambitious new programs. The national government's huge budget deficits—which exceeded $200 billion, compared with about $73 billion in the last year of the Carter administration—checked any grandiose new spending plans. The Reagan debt had exceeded the debt of the previous thirty-eight presidents.

President Reagan also had reshaped the dialogue on foreign affairs. He maintained strong opposition to the Soviet Union and other "Marxist" nations with his policies in Nicaragua, Afghanistan, and Angola. He also had projected an image of strength with military action in Libya and Grenada. At the same time, however, he had co-opted his critics by meeting with Soviet leader Mikhail Gorbachev several times and signing a nuclear arms control agreement. Reagan even asserted that the Gorbachev regime was fundamentally different from previous Soviet regimes, which he had called the "evil empire."

The early Republican front-runners were Bush and Sen. Bob Dole of Kansas; former senator Gary Hart of Colorado was considered the early Democratic leader. The campaign got scrambled before it began, however. Hart left the race in 1987 when the Miami *Herald* augmented rumors of Hart's infidelity with a report that he had spent the night with a young model. The newspaper had staked out Hart's Washington townhouse with two reporters, two editors, and a photographer. The investigators sat in a rental car, loitered nearby, and jogged down the street. Hart, considered by many to be the brightest and most issue-oriented candidate, had long faced criticism about his "character."

The Hart story dominated the political news in 1987. Network news programs devoted 132 minutes to Hart, mostly in the first half of the year and, on the GOP side, 32 minutes to the long-shot television evangelist Marion G. "Pat" Robertson. The two front-runners and eventual nominees, Bush and Dukakis, got 28 and 20 minutes, respectively.[184]

Sen. Joseph R. Biden Jr. of Delaware was the next casualty of the media's 1987 concern with character issues.[185] Media reports that he had committed plagiarism on a law school paper and in campaign speeches led to Biden's early exit from the campaign. Biden had been considered a leading candidate because of his experience and strong speaking style.

With Hart and Biden out of the race, the Democrats were in disarray. Dubbed "dwarfs," the remaining candidates—Rev. Jesse Jackson of Illinois, Gov. Dukakis, Rep. Richard A.

After two popular terms as president, Ronald Reagan and wife Nancy pass leadership of the "Reagan Revolution" to newly inaugurated President George Bush and wife Barbara in 1989.

Gephardt of Missouri, Sen. Albert A. Gore Jr. of Tennessee, Sen. Paul M. Simon of Illinois, and former Arizona governor Bruce Babbitt—lacked the combination of extensive government experience and strong national bases many observers thought necessary to win the presidency.

The Republicans had problems of their own. Vice President Bush was the early favorite, and he benefited from his association with President Reagan. But Bush's public fealty to Reagan also created a problem: he was considered a "wimp," unable to stand on his own. Almost every major position Bush had held in his political career was the result of an appointment: ambassador to the United Nations, chair of the Republican National Committee, envoy to China, director of the Central Intelligence Agency, and vice president. Bush had represented Texas for two terms in the House of Representatives and lost two Senate races.

At the outset of the race, Dole was considered a strong contender. As Republican leader in the Senate, he had a high profile in national politics and proven fund-raising abilities. His wife, Elizabeth, was prominent as secretary of transportation. Dole also had a biting wit, which gave spark to his campaigning style but irritated some voters. Other GOP candidates were Rep. Jack Kemp of New York, former secretary of state Alexander M. Haig Jr. of Pennsylvania, former Delaware governor Pierre S. "Pete" du Pont IV, and television evangelist Pat Robertson of Virginia.

The marathon campaign for the nomination began with the Iowa caucuses, a significant event only because of intense media attention. Gephardt barely edged Simon in the Democratic contests, and Dole won the Republican race. The big story was how badly Bush performed: he finished third behind Dole and Robertson.

The Iowa loss caused Bush to emerge from his isolation and confront his rivals for the nomination. (Bush had been the most restrained and cautious candidate as he tried to benefit from the prestige of the White House.) Bush also became more animated

on the campaign trail. As a result of these changes—and a series of television advertisements charging that Dole would raise taxes—Bush beat Dole in the New Hampshire primary. Dole had failed to respond quickly to the Bush offensive, and when he snapped on national television about Bush's "lying about my record," he reinforced his image as a mean-spirited candidate.

Among the Democrats, Governor Dukakis easily won the New Hampshire primary, capitalizing on his regional popularity. Most of the Democratic fire in that race took place between the two runners-up, Gephardt and Simon. Dukakis escaped without any major criticism, and his already strong fund-raising machine went into high gear.

The decisive stage of the GOP campaign was Super Tuesday—March 8—when twenty-two states held presidential primaries or caucuses. Benefiting from a well-organized campaign and his new aggressiveness on the campaign trail, Bush won seventeen of the eighteen GOP contests. Dole staked his campaign on the ensuing Illinois primary, but he lost badly, and Bush was virtually ensured the Republican nomination.

The one issue that threatened Bush throughout 1988 was the Iran-contra scandal. Revelations that the Reagan administration had traded arms to Iran in exchange for the release of hostages held in Lebanon, then used the proceeds illegally to fund the war in Nicaragua, raised questions about Bush's role in the matter. Administration officials admitted lying to Congress, destroying evidence, and operating outside normal government channels; one top official even attempted suicide. The question of Bush's involvement in the affair, however, fizzled after months of inconclusive questioning.

On Super Tuesday, Democratic front-runner Dukakis won Texas and Florida and five northern states, thereby confirming his shaky front-runner status. Civil rights leader Jesse Jackson was the big surprise, however, winning five southern states. Gore won seven states. Even though it was designed to help conservative candidates, Super Tuesday fit Jackson's strengths. Six of the nine states in which Jackson had scored best in 1984 held their contests on Super Tuesday in 1988. Super Tuesday also was supposed to put the South in the national spotlight, but the region received only a few more candidate visits in 1988 (149) than it had in 1976 (145).[186]

The Democratic marathon continued into Illinois, Michigan, and New York. Dukakis took and maintained the lead in delegates with steady wins over Jackson and Gore. Gore finally dropped out after finishing third in a divisive New York primary, and the rest of the campaign was a one-on-one race between Dukakis and Jackson. Only once—after his victory over Dukakis in the Michigan caucuses—did Jackson appear to have a chance to win the Democratic nomination. But in their next encounter, the Wisconsin primary, Dukakis defeated Jackson.

Jackson was a mixed blessing for the party. An energetic campaigner, he attracted support from blacks and from farmers and blue-collar workers who were disgruntled by the uneven rewards of economic growth. But Jackson was considerably to the left of the rest of the party and never had held any government office. Race also was a factor: no political professional believed that a liberal black could be elected president.

Dukakis practically clinched the nomination with his victory over Jackson in the New York primary. The issue of race was at the center of the campaign. New York City mayor Edward I. Koch, a Gore supporter, called Jackson a "radical" and said Jews would be "crazy" to vote for him. Such remarks aggravated tensions between blacks and Jews that had festered since the 1960s. Dukakis avoided the race issue and won the primary.

As the summer conventions approached, Bush and Dukakis each had the full support of his party. The parties' internal divisions were on display as the prospective nominees considered possible vice-presidential candidates. Blacks lobbied for Jackson's selection by Dukakis, while "new right" GOP leaders lobbied against a "moderate" running mate for Bush.

Dukakis selected conservative senator Lloyd Bentsen of Texas as his running mate before the Atlanta Democratic convention. Jackson complained publicly and privately about the decision, but he eventually embraced Bentsen for the sake of party unity. Dukakis hoped Bentsen would be able to help carry Texas: no Democrat had won the presidency without winning Texas since the state became part of the nation in 1845.

The July convention was a success for the Democrats. After a week of Bush-bashing and Democratic conciliation, Dukakis gave an effective acceptance speech peppered with statements in Spanish and Greek. Dukakis left the convention with a double-digit lead over Bush in the polls.

The Republican convention in August did not start out as well. Bush announced his vice-presidential selection, Sen. James Danforth "Dan" Quayle of Indiana, when he arrived in New Orleans. After revelations that Quayle had avoided military service in the Vietnam War by enlisting in the Indiana National Guard, many Republicans criticized Bush's choice. Some even said that Quayle might have to be dropped from the ticket.[187] By the end of the convention, however, the Republicans had weathered the

storm. Bush delivered a crisp address, which provided the appealing self-portrait the vice president needed, and moved into the fall campaign for a close battle with Dukakis.

Bush took the offensive immediately after the August GOP convention and hit Dukakis as a "liberal" out of touch with American "values." More specifically, Bush attacked Dukakis for his membership in the American Civil Liberties Union, his veto of a bill requiring Massachusetts teachers to lead children in the Pledge of Allegiance, and a Massachusetts program allowing prisoners time off for weekends. The Bush campaign's "Willie Horton" commercial—which told of a black prisoner raping a woman while out on a weekend release program—was particularly controversial. As Bush pounded away at these symbolic issues (effectively drowning out other major issues such as the national debt, trade deficit, housing, education, U.S.-Soviet relations, the environment, and ethics in government), Dukakis's "negative" ratings with voters soared. Roger Ailes, Bush's media adviser, admitted that the Bush camp knew it would have to define Dukakis. The media themselves had no interest in substance, Ailes pointed out, leaving candidates "three ways to get on the air: pictures, attacks, and mistakes." Thus the Bush campaign spent its time "avoiding mistakes, staying on the attack, and giving them pictures."[188]

Not believing the attacks would affect his standing with undecided voters—and believing they might even hurt Bush—Dukakis did not respond forcefully to the frontal assault until October. By then, however, Bush had effectively defined Dukakis as a newcomer to national politics. Dukakis's counteroffensive in the last two weeks of the campaign came too late.

As Dukakis fell behind Bush, his campaign pinned its hopes on two nationally televised debates. Dukakis performed well in the first debate, but Bush appeared to "win" the second debate. Dukakis failed to gain on Bush.

The only major problem for Bush was Quayle. Most political professionals considered Quayle a "lightweight." The forty-one-year-old Quayle had been a poor student and was a marginal member of Congress.[189] Dukakis said Bush's selection of Quayle amounted to failure in his "first presidential decision." Dukakis compared Quayle to the more experienced Bentsen, who performed much better in a vice-presidential debate. Indeed, in that debate Bentsen gave the campaign perhaps its most memorable moment. Responding to Quayle's assertion that he had as much congressional experience as Jack Kennedy had when he sought the presidency, Bentsen said, "Senator, I served with Jack Kennedy. I knew Jack Kennedy. Jack Kennedy was a friend of mine. Senator, you're no Jack Kennedy."[190]

Public polls revealed that most voters thought that Quayle was a bad choice. The Bush campaign tried to minimize the damage by limiting Quayle's public exposure and carefully scripting his statements. Quayle rarely spoke in major media markets; many of his campaign stops were accessible only by bus. While Bush delivered speeches in several states each day, Quayle often made just one speech before schoolchildren or partisan audiences.

After months of inconsistent and confusing strategy, Dukakis finally developed a strong appeal in the last two weeks of the campaign. He told voters he was on their side and portrayed Bush as a toady to the wealthy. Dukakis said the middle class had been "squeezed" by the policies of the Reagan administration and that the Democrats would provide good jobs, affordable housing and health care, and tough enforcement of environmental protection laws.

But it was not enough. Bush, who had made a fortune in the oil business before entering politics and was the son of a former U.S. senator, persuaded more voters that his experience and values were what they wanted in the very personal choice of a president.

Democrats Regain the White House

In March 1991, in the aftermath of the U.S.-led victory over Iraq in the Persian Gulf War, President George Bush received the highest approval ratings since opinion polling began: around 90 percent of respondents said they approved of his performance as president. But just a year later, Bush was struggling to keep his job—and he failed.

Bill Clinton's victory over Bush in 1992 could have been viewed, on the one hand, as a dramatic shift in American politics. Touting his campaign slogan of "change," the forty-six-year-old Arkansas governor repeatedly blasted the Republican White House for its inattention to domestic problems such as the budget deficit, health care, welfare, civil rights, crime, trade, and economic investment. President Bush, Clinton said, was too obsessed with foreign policy and unconcerned with domestic affairs.

On the other hand, Clinton's election could have been viewed as an aberration. Only the second Democrat elected president since 1968, Clinton got only 43 percent of the vote in a three-candidate race. Voters said they voted against Bush, not for Clinton. The independent candidacy of Texas billionaire H. Ross Perot may have cost Bush the election, as much by tarnishing his reputation as by taking away the votes of the angry middle class. Even people who supported Clinton expressed reservations about his character. Voters reacted warily to reports of Clinton's avoidance of military service in Vietnam, marital infidelity, and conflicts of interest while governor, and to his evasiveness about smoking marijuana as a student. On policy questions, Clinton was well informed, but sometimes he appeared insincere. A label pinned on Clinton in Arkansas—"Slick Willie"—stuck.

THE BUSH STRATEGY

President Bush began the election cycle looking unbeatable. Coasting on the apparent success of his leadership during the Gulf War, Bush appeared to have the strength to lead the United States into what he called the "new world order." In 1989 the countries of the so-called Soviet bloc—East Germany, Poland, Czechoslovakia, Romania, Hungary—had broken from communist rule in a series of nonviolent revolutions. In August 1991 an attempted coup against Mikhail Gorbachev's "perestroika" government in the Soviet Union had failed. Afterward, the Soviet regime—Communist Party and all—had collapsed. The Bush

presidency had overseen the most remarkable realignment of world politics since World War II.

Indeed, Bush took credit for presiding over the dramatic changes, but those American "victories" also undermined his position. The Republican Party had dominated recent presidential politics at least partly because of its hawkish policies during the cold war. With the end of the Soviet threat, the GOP no longer had a "gut" issue to use against the Democrats. According to journalist Sidney Blumenthal, "The Cold War's end was not a photo opportunity, a sound bite, a revelation of 'character,' a political consultant's tactic, or even a theme. It was a global sea change as profound as the Cold War's beginning."[191] Bush had a hard time adjusting.

For a while, President Bush looked so strong that many Democrats were reluctant to take him on. The party's leading figures—Gov. Mario Cuomo of New York; Senators Bill Bradley of New Jersey, Al Gore of Tennessee, and Jay Rockefeller of West Virginia; and Rep. Richard Gephardt of Missouri—announced they would not run. Only former senator Paul E. Tsongas of Massachusetts, recently recovered from a bout with cancer, announced his candidacy in spring 1991.

Despite high polling numbers, President Bush might have been doomed from the start. Despite three decades in public life, Bush had never conveyed a coherent identity or campaign theme. His advisers planned to "narrowcast" messages to selected groups until the summer, when Bush would deliver his big "what-I-stand-for" speech. But by that time, Bush's opponent had defined him as weak and unprincipled. His attempt to divert attention to Clinton's foibles only intensified Bush's image as uncertain of his own values and goals.[192]

By the spring of 1992 Bush's base had crumbled. The president had decided to "sit" on his high popularity ratings and win reelection by avoiding mistakes. Bush's chief of staff, John Sununu, summed up the strategy: "There's not another single piece of legislation that needs to be passed in the next two years for this president. In fact, if Congress wants to come together, adjourn, and leave, it's all right with us."[193] The results of this strategy were devastating. In May 1992 a poll found that 76 percent of the public disapproved of the way Bush was handling the economy.[194] His overall approval rating dropped an unprecedented 57 percentage points from the end of the Gulf War to the beginning of the 1992 GOP convention.

A bitter anti-incumbent mood dominated the new campaign year. Nationwide, reformers promoted the idea of term limits for elected officials as a way to sweep out career politicians.[195] Perot, who had parlayed his wealth into a number of headline-grabbing exploits over the years, became a viable independent candidate.[196] His pithy statements about how to "fix" government captured the imagination of the public.

Pennsylvania voters sent a warning shot to the White House when they rejected the 1991 Senate candidacy of Bush's friend and first attorney general, Richard Thornburgh. Democrat Harris Wofford, appointed to the seat that had opened with the death of Sen. John Heinz in April 1991, won on a platform of national health care and a return to domestic priorities—themes that Bill Clinton reprised in 1992. Wofford, a former college president and Kennedy administration official, came from 30 points behind in the polls to win with 55 percent of the vote. It was the highest percentage that any Democrat had received in Pennsylvania senatorial elections. Wofford's campaign was run by a young operative named James Carville.

Bush's major domestic initiative—the budget law passed in October 1990—angered the Republican Party's right wing. Conservatives had long distrusted Bush because of his past moderate positions on taxes, abortion, civil rights, and social programs. The budget act, which increased taxes by $150 billion, broke the pledge of "no new taxes" that Bush had taken in the 1988 presidential campaign.

As the recession and other domestic crises deepened, the president seemed increasingly out of touch. Bush's reported confusion over the use of bar codes at a grocery store symbolized his elite background and isolation. After race riots in Los Angeles drew the nation's attention to the severity of poverty, Bush was photographed teaching baffled-looking urban youths how to use a fishing pole. In a political environment couched in symbolism, these images were ruinous.

Bush had begun his term with less party support than any president in history—the Democrats controlled the Senate by ten seats and the House by eighty-five seats. As a result, Bush's legislative initiatives were routinely labeled "dead on arrival." In 1989, for the first time, the Senate rejected an incoming president's cabinet nominee when it voted down former senator John G. Tower's bid to be secretary of defense. In his dealings with Capitol Hill, Bush had vacillated between confrontation and compromise. In fact, Bush regularly tussled with Congress, vetoing forty-four bills between 1989 and 1992.

THE 1992 PRIMARY SEASON

The Democratic field grew slowly. Besides Clinton and Tsongas, the field included former governor Jerry Brown of California, Senators Thomas Harkin of Iowa and Robert Kerrey of Nebraska, and Gov. L. Douglas Wilder of Virginia. Wilder dropped out, however, before the first contest.

Clinton won the "invisible primaries" before the formal balloting began; he attracted $3.3 million in contributions by the end of 1991. Harkin was second best with a little more than $2 million.[197] The Clinton campaign then organized supporters in most states holding early contests.

By calling himself a "new Democrat," Clinton hoped to separate himself from some of the rejected Democratic candidates of the past: Jimmy Carter, Walter Mondale, and Michael Dukakis. In keeping with this strategy, Clinton promised to move beyond liberal orthodoxy and "reinvent government."[198] His record in Arkansas suggested a willingness to oppose liberal nostrums on issues such as the death penalty, economic growth, and public education.

The centerpiece of Clinton's strategy was to appeal to the "forgotten middle class." Suburbanites, the working class, and southerners and westerners had abandoned the Democratic Party since the late 1960s. Unfortunately for the Democrats, these groups composed a growing part of the electorate. In fact, many pundits argued that these groups gave the Republicans a

"lock" on the presidency.[199] Clinton's goal, then, was to forge a new ideological center and "pick" the lock.

As expected, "favorite-son" Harkin won the Iowa caucuses, winning 76.4 percent of the delegates selected on February 10. Early on, Clinton had led the polling in New Hampshire, but he ran into trouble when the media questioned his character. A woman claimed that she and Clinton had had an affair and that Clinton had helped her to get a state job. Meanwhile, Clinton was reported to have misled an Army Reserves recruiter as part of a scheme to avoid service in Vietnam. And, to make matters worse, at one point Clinton's campaign was almost broke.

But Clinton hit back. Appearing on the television news magazine "60 Minutes" after the January 1992 Super Bowl game, Clinton admitted he had "caused pain" in his marriage but said he and his wife had solved their problems. Hillary Clinton's appearance with her husband seemed to close the matter. Skeptics should vote against Clinton, she said, but they also should drop the character charges.

Tsongas won the New Hampshire primary on February 18 with 33.2 percent of the vote to Clinton's 24.7 percent. Tsongas offered the policy equivalent of castor oil. He said the nation needed to make difficult economic choices such as higher taxes and program cutbacks. He called Clinton, who spoke in favor of a tax cut and the costly Connecticut-built Polaris Navy submarine, a "pander bear."

Clinton, who fell some 20 points in the polls in a month, exuberantly called his second-place finish a victory by noting Tsongas's regional ties and declaring himself the "Comeback Kid." His campaign, however, was out of money and had to be rescued by a $3.5 million line of credit from an Arkansas bank.

Tsongas and Brown won the occasional contest after New Hampshire, but Clinton rolled to the nomination starting with his March 3 victory in the Georgia primary. Kerrey and Harkin dropped out in early March. Clinton's sweep of southern states on "Super Tuesday," March 10, and his decisive wins in Michigan and Illinois on March 17 practically clinched the nomination. But he had a scare when Brown beat him in Connecticut on March 24. He then beat Brown decisively in New York on April 7. Tsongas, by that time an inactive candidate, finished ahead of Brown in New York.

Clinton won thirty-one state primaries with 51.8 percent of the vote; Tsongas, four states with 18.1 percent; and Brown, two states with 20.1 percent.[200] Even as Clinton won state after state and Bush plummeted in the polls, Democratic leaders searched for an alternative; they had grown nervous about Clinton's ability to confront the character issue. In March almost half the Democratic voters in Connecticut's primary said Clinton lacked the "honesty or integrity" to be president.[201] Former governor Brown fed the uncertainty with his relentless attacks on Clinton's ties to special interests. Talk of drafting another candidate continued, but party professionals became resigned to Clinton's nomination.

President Bush faced an unusually pointed challenge from conservative columnist and former White House aide Patrick J. Buchanan, who charged that Bush had betrayed the conservative faith. His main point of attack was the 1990 tax increase. But he also criticized Bush's activism in world affairs, federal support of arts projects that he called "blasphemous," and the nationwide recession.

Buchanan's campaign in New Hampshire, run by his sister, was simple. He wrote his own speeches, showed roughly designed television ads in which people mimicked Bush's "no new taxes" pledge, and mocked Bush's superior campaign organization and resources. According to Buchanan, the "Buchanan brigades" would defeat "King George and his armies." Bush, however, ignored Buchanan's campaign. He sent his wife and other administration representatives to campaign in New Hampshire.

Although in the end Bush won New Hampshire, the media focused on the 37 percent of the vote that the underdog Buchanan received. Buchanan then made a vigorous effort to win some of the southern contests in early March, but he never matched his New Hampshire numbers. Buchanan continued his campaign until June, assured of media attention by virtue of his quixotic quest and uncompromising rhetoric. In the final analysis, however, he did not win any states with his 22 percent of the total primary vote.[202]

Ironically, in taking his hard hits at Bush, Buchanan may have helped to neutralize another protest candidate, former Ku Klux Klan leader David Duke, who had finished second in the Louisiana gubernatorial contest in 1991. Republican leaders were embarrassed by Duke's GOP membership, but he disappeared after a poor showing in New Hampshire.

Perot's on-and-off campaign unsettled Republicans' plans to build on their base in the South and West. Perot's folksy antigovernment rhetoric appealed to voters in the suburbs and high-growth areas of the 1980s—the heart of the GOP base since Richard Nixon's 1968 campaign.

Perot's campaign began where much of the 1992 campaign was waged: on the television talk-show circuit. On the cable TV show "Larry King Live," Perot said in February that he would run for president if volunteers put him on the ballot in all fifty states. He also said he would spend up to $100 million of his own money to fund a "world-class campaign." At one point, Perot appeared to have a chance to win the presidency. Polls in May showed him in second place nationally behind President Bush and winning some southern and western states outright.

As Perot's unofficial campaign progressed, the media raised doubts about his background and grasp of government. For example, Perot had made his fortune by gaining rights to a computer accounting system for government health programs, and it was only his behind-the-scenes lobbying that prompted the Nixon administration to halt a government battle for control of the computer system. On a more personal level, Perot's conspiracy theories about issues such as prisoners of war in Vietnam and political opponents led to speculation about possible paranoia. When asked about the details for his plans to address the budget deficit, improve government efficiency, improve U.S. trade, and address foreign affairs, Perot appeared ill-informed and irritable. Thus by summer more people viewed Perot unfavorably than favorably.

Perot dropped out of the campaign before he had a chance to announce his entry formally. He pointed out that Clinton's se-

Independent H. Ross Perot mounted his 1992 campaign for the presidency by relying on his own money and appearing on the television talk shows, such as here with Larry King.

lection of Sen. Al Gore of Tennessee as his running mate indicated that the Democrats were "getting their act together." He also recognized that his campaign might split the vote badly and send the election into the House of Representatives.

Perot resumed his campaign in the fall, blaming his temporary exit on a Republican "dirty tricks" effort to smear his family. By then the critical reporting had faded. But it was too late for Perot because his erratic behavior had driven away supporters and curious voters alike. Perot also had difficulty finding a credible running mate. His selection of retired admiral James Stockdale became the subject of parody when Stockdale appeared confused and poorly informed during the debate of the vice-presidential candidates.

Even though Perot had no real chance to win, his campaign was significant. He spent $60 million of his own money, mostly to purchase half-hour television advertisements. Some of the ads, dubbed "infomercials," won critical acclaim for their plain talk about the dangers of the federal budget deficit. Perot's bluntness lent credibility to his relentless attacks on Bush.

THE 1992 ELECTION

The communications revolution changed the way the candidates reached voters. For example, candidates appeared in settings once considered undignified for potential presidents. Television talk shows such as "Larry King Live" and "The Arsenio Hall Show," as well as radio programs such as "Imus in the Morning," provided a way for candidates to bypass the establishment media. The blurred lines between news and entertainment were perhaps most evident on cable television in the rock music MTV channel's ongoing coverage of the presidential campaign. New outlets were especially important for candidates facing credibility problems in mainstream media (Clinton) and for the insurgents (Perot and Brown).

Bush's campaign was on the defensive early for using "dirty" campaign tactics. Democrats cited Bush's 1988 "Willie Horton" commercials as evidence of a Republican willingness to appeal to racism and fear. Newspaper citations of the Horton campaign were greater in 1992 than 1988, suggesting that the Democrats eventually got more from the ad's backlash than Republicans got from the original campaign.

Clinton parroted Perot's rhetoric about the evils of special-interest influence in Washington and promised reforms of the campaign finance system. But he also raised money aggressively. The Democrats raised $71 million in 1992, $9 million more than the Republicans.[203] Clinton's selection of moderate senator Gore of Tennessee as a running mate was central to his fall strategy. Gore's service in Vietnam and military expertise countered Clinton's suspect status in foreign policy. Moreover, Gore's Washington experience going back to 1976 helped Clinton to compensate for his own lack of experience. Finally, Gore's reputation as an intellectual—he wrote an acclaimed book about the environment in 1992[204]—contrasted with Vice President Quayle's lightweight reputation.

In his campaign, Clinton benefited from the "year of the woman." Women had supported Democratic candidates in greater numbers than men since the Republican Party dropped its support for the Equal Rights Amendment and abortion rights in 1980. But the Democrats were not able to exploit the "gender gap" until 1992. The galvanizing issue was the allegation that Clarence Thomas, a Bush appointee to the Supreme Court, had sexually harassed a former colleague named Anita Hill. Women were outraged with the Senate Judiciary Committee's handling of the matter, and feminist groups mobilized to increase female representation in politics. The issue put President Bush on the defensive, while Clinton rallied liberals and libertarians alike with his calls for equal opportunity and abortion rights.

The Republican convention in Houston was a turning point in the campaign. Strategists decided to shore up Bush's right-wing support and raise doubts about Clinton's character. The party's platform committee was dominated by the right-wing Christian Coalition. Speeches by Patrick Buchanan, Pat Robertson, and Marilyn Quayle, questioning the Democrats' patriotism and arguing for a rollback of civil liberties, played badly. Bush's lost convention opportunity was apparent in the meager 3 percentage point "bounce" in poll support, compared with Clinton's 17 to 20 percent increase after the Democratic convention.[205]

Clinton ran a sophisticated general election campaign, coordinated from the "war room" in Little Rock by strategists, led by James Carville, who choreographed every aspect of the campaign, from television commercials to talk-show appearances to speechwriting to the bus tours of small towns. The campaign professionals were especially adept at answering charges from the opposition. When Bush attacked, Clintonites issued instant, detailed responses. The quick response prevented Bush's charges from dominating the news cycle.

The Bush-Quayle fall campaign was erratic. Early on, it focused on "family values," critiquing the Democrats as elitists out of touch with ordinary people. Then Bush used the powers of incumbency by announcing billions of dollars in grants to different states. All along, Bush criticized Clinton's character and experience. But the personal attacks often appeared shrill; at one point, he called Clinton and Gore "bozos" and said "my dog Millie" would be better at foreign policy than they. Bush criticized Clinton's visit to the Soviet Union as a student and suggested that he wanted to import British-style socialism to the United States.

Bush's credibility came under fire in the campaign's final days when a special prosecutor indicted former defense secretary Caspar Weinberger and released a memorandum that indicated Bush had participated in the Iran-contra scandal much more actively than he had acknowledged.

The Clinton-Gore ticket gave the Democrats a solid base in the border states to build on. With Arkansas and Tennessee in the Democratic camp, the Democrats could build outward into the old Confederacy (Georgia, Louisiana, Kentucky), north into the industrial states (Illinois, Michigan, Ohio) and west and north into the farm states (Iowa, Minnesota, Wisconsin). The Democrats had consistently lost those states in presidential elections in the past generation, despite strong support in congressional and statewide races.

The Democrats also built on their core of support in the Northeast (winning all the states from Maine to West Virginia) and capitalized on disgruntlement with Bush in the West (California, Colorado, Hawaii, Montana, Nevada, New Mexico, Oregon, and Washington went for Clinton). That was enough to "pick" the Republican "lock" on the electoral college.

Clinton took only 43 percent of the popular vote but garnered 370 electoral votes. This compared with Bush's 38 percent of the popular vote and 168 electoral votes. Perot's 19 percent share of the vote did not win any states.

The hard anti-incumbent mood of the electorate, stoked by Perot, helped to produce the highest voter turnout rate since 1960. Some 55 percent of eligible voters participated in the election. That participation rate was far below rates of other countries and earlier periods in U.S. history. But it seemed to stem, momentarily, the apathy and resignation of American politics.

SETTING THE STAGE FOR 1996

In 1994 many voters sent a strong message of disapproval with President Clinton's record by electing a Republican Congress. That dramatic event led many political analysts to conclude that Clinton would be a one-term president. But what many had not anticipated was that the new GOP Congress, led prominently by controversial House Speaker Newt Gingrich (Georgia), would incorrectly interpret the 1994 elections results as a mandate for their conservative ideological agenda and then push for substantial—and unpopular—policy reform. This miscalculation provided President Clinton with a new opportunity to redefine himself and to rehabilitate his political future.

While the Republicans strove hard for conservative policy change, Clinton adopted more moderate positions and portrayed himself as a check against the "extremism" of the GOP agenda. That tack proved successful by the end of 1995. With the president and Republican legislators feuding over spending priorities, Congress failed to pass a budget in time to avoid two temporary government shutdowns. As the impasse persisted, the Republican Congress began to appear unreason-

Democratic presidential candidate Bill Clinton talks with young people on a program hosted by the MTV cable channel. The 1992 campaign was revolutionary in the way candidates used nontraditional media to reach voters.

able in the public's eye, and the president benefited from the comparison. This budgetary standoff against Congress was perhaps the single most important event to Clinton's political rehabilitation.

The president entered the 1996 election season with renewed political strength and high approval ratings. In addition to the political miscalculations of the majority in Congress, Clinton benefited from a strengthening economy. A third factor also began to weigh in the president's favor: he lacked an intraparty challenge for renomination, while the GOP nomination contest was an expensive, highly negative, and divisive process.

From the beginning Senate Majority Leader Bob Dole (Kansas) was the clear front-runner for the Republican Party's nomination. He had the broadest party support of any announced candidate, the most prominent endorsements, and the best grassroots campaign organization. Although there never was any serious doubt that he would be the Republican nominee, for several months Dole had to fight off a large group of presidential aspirants including television commentator Pat Buchanan, former Department of Education secretary Lamar Alexander, Texas senator Phil Gramm, Indiana senator Richard Lugar, California representative Robert Dornan, and multimillionaire publisher Malcolm S. "Steve" Forbes Jr.

Of these candidates, initially Gramm appeared to be the most formidable because of his status in the Senate and ability to raise huge sums of money for a campaign. Yet Gramm lacked grassroots support and his campaign faded quickly. Colleague Lugar was highly regarded by party moderates and many opinion leaders, but he ran a bland campaign that dwelt on foreign policy issues that were not driving the Republican electorate. Buchanan had support among many of the dedicated antiabortion conservatives in the party, and he fared surprisingly well in some of the early caucuses and primaries, but most in the GOP considered him too extreme and his campaign too faltered.

The most important opponent to Dole ultimately was the publishing tycoon Forbes, who spent an extraordinary sum of his personal fortune to challenge the front-runner with extensive negative television ads. Although Forbes's campaign failed to dislodge Dole from the front of the pack, it succeeded at raising serious doubts about the senator's ability to beat Clinton. The negative ads also hurt Dole's standing with the wider public and forced him to spend his campaign resources on the nomination battle as Clinton amassed campaign funds for the general election.

Dole's eventual nomination—even after losing the traditionally crucial battleground primary in New Hampshire to Buchanan—did not ensure a united Republican Party to challenge the president. Although Dole had long supported the antiabortion stance of many in his party, social conservatives who made up a crucial bloc of the Republican vote were not convinced of his commitment to their cause. Many considered him too moderate in temperament and too willing to compromise principles. Party moderates worried that Dole would allow the Christian right to force his campaign to adopt positions that would enable the Democrats to once again capitalize on the "extremism" charge.[206]

Even after his nomination was ensured, Dole's campaign failed for weeks to capture the public's attention. In part he appeared too much a part of the GOP agenda in Congress that Democrats had successfully defined as harshly conservative. As senate majority leader Dole had found himself in the difficult position of having to manage his official duties while campaigning for president. This involved promoting the GOP agenda in Congress while at the same time trying to distance himself from its less popular elements. Dole made a bold strategic gamble when he decided to resign from the Senate altogether to campaign full time for the presidency. His emotional departure from the Senate on June 11 temporarily energized his campaign.

At his nominating convention in San Diego, Dole performed a tough balancing act in keeping warring moderates and social conservatives from dividing the party. Dole especially sought to avoid the kind of negative publicity that had surrounded "family values night" at the 1992 GOP convention in Houston.[207] The Republicans struck an awkward compromise: although the party platform was very conservative and kept the antiabortion plank, the convention that the country saw on television was moderate in tone and did not feature prime-time addresses by controversial figures such as Buchanan and television evangelist Pat Robertson.

Dole surprised many with two bold campaign moves. First, he selected as his running mate former New York representative and secretary of Housing and Urban Development Jack Kemp, who earlier had endorsed Forbes. Second, Dole proposed an across-the-board 15 percent income tax cut. This proposal was especially surprising because Dole had cultivated a well-deserved reputation as a "deficit hawk" who opposed supply-side economic theory. Yet to energize his lagging campaign, Dole abandoned his lifelong approach to economic policy. Although Dole succeeded in attracting attention with this move, not all of it was positive as many political analysts focused on the contradictions between his tax cut proposal and earlier statements.

CLINTON'S REELECTION

Although polls throughout 1996 showed Clinton with a commanding lead against Dole, those same polls pointed to voter uneasiness with the president's character. Because of continued negative media coverage resulting from Whitewater-related charges, the badly handled White House firing of its travel office staff, and a sexual harassment lawsuit against Clinton, most of the public believed that their president was an individual of unsatisfactory personal character. Yet the polls also indicated that Americans would reelect a flawed president because of their uneasiness with the Republican nominee, their low opinion of the Republican majority in Congress, and their general satisfaction with the state of the economy.

Throughout the campaign season, Clinton often seemed to be running against the unpopular Gingrich and the Republican Congress more than he was taking on Dole. What made Clinton's campaign so strong, in part, was his governing strategy of what one key aide called "triangulation": that is, separating himself from the unpopular elements of both political parties and establishing a less partisan identity at the center of the political spectrum. To achieve that end, Clinton adopted a number of policy initiatives that were conservative, but also largely popular. He signed a welfare reform bill that liberals in his party detested, pushed for imposition of a V-chip in televisions to allow parents to screen program content for children and for a television program rating system, advocated curfews for teenagers and school uniforms as well as mandatory drug tests for sixteen-year-olds applying for driving licenses, proposed a balanced budget by the year 2002, and extolled his record in reducing the federal budget deficit. Clinton also stayed true to his Democratic roots by opposing congressional efforts to reduce Medicare spending and weaken environmental regulation and

by proposing new government programs to make college education more affordable.

Clinton's strategy was brilliant. He effectively took away from Dole's campaign a number of issues that usually help Republican presidential candidates, such as welfare reform, deficit reduction, and family values. He kept his Democratic base by positioning himself as the only viable check against the "extremism" of the Republican Congress.

From a stylistic standpoint, the Clinton and Dole campaigns could not have been more different. Admirers and critics alike agree that Clinton was an effective campaigner and a strong communicator. By contrast, despite protestations by those who know him to be a warm and humorous person, Dole projected the image of a threatening and humorless politician. Despite a vigorous campaign, Dole never overcame the uneasiness that most voters felt about him personally. In past campaigns he had acquired the negative persona of a political "hatchet man" and that image stuck with him throughout the 1996 race. Indeed, Dole tried so hard to change that image that he spent months refusing to attack Clinton's most serious political weakness: his character. When implored by partisan Republicans to attack the president, Dole would reply that he considered Clinton "my opponent, not my enemy." In his two debates with Clinton, Dole did little to improve his public image, as his presentational style was stiff and somewhat harsh—in large contrast to Clinton who projected a much more assuring image.

In the last weeks of the campaign, when it was clear that Dole had no realistic chance of winning, the Republican candidate made a final gamble: he decided finally to attack the president's character and to make it an overriding theme of the campaign. Dole's attacks on the president made a difference in the campaign polls when the news media began to report on questionable fund-raising practices by the Democratic National Committee (DNC) and meetings between foreign lobbyists and Clinton. Stories of unethical and possibly illegal Democratic campaign contributions dovetailed with the Dole message that Clinton lacked good character—and that such a fault was unsuitable for the person serving as president.

Clinton perhaps further hurt himself when he avoided directly confronting the negative stories about the fund-raising practices of his party. Instead, he protested that candidates had no choice but to raise funds and campaign under a flawed system and that, if reelected, he would propose fundamental campaign finance reform. Although this negative publicity and the Dole charges were not enough to deny Clinton's victory, just days before the election one major poll by the Zogby Group for Reuters News Agency placed Clinton's lead at only 7 percent, significantly below the double-digit margins he had maintained throughout the race.[208]

The Reform Party candidate, billionaire Perot, also benefited somewhat from the negative Clinton press. Although he had never been a serious factor in 1996 as he had been as an independent candidate in 1992—and as a result was excluded from the presidential debates—Perot's support increased by several percentage points in the late polls. But in the end, Perot had little impact on the elections. Because of a perceived strong econo-

President Bill Clinton and Vice President Al Gore accept their renomination at the Democratic National Convention in August 1996. In the general election Clinton became the first Democratic president reelected to a second term since Franklin Roosevelt in 1936.

my and a substantial reduction in the federal debt, the public frustration with the two major parties that had given growth to Perot's candidacy in 1992 simply did not exist in 1996.

As the Dole campaign emphasized the character issue, his senior staff were aware that the *Washington Post* was investigating a story about a past marital indiscretion by their candidate. In a controversial decision, the *Post* decided not to publish the information it had gathered about an extramarital affair Dole had in 1969. The newspaper's decision to not publish even after confirming beyond any doubt all the facts angered Clinton partisans who felt that the *Post* had displayed a double standard. Clinton, of course, had been subjected to unrelenting coverage of allegations of extramarital affairs, and these stories had always played a key role in the president's reputation for poor character. Had the newspaper published the story late in the campaign there is little doubt that it would have had an adverse impact on Dole's late surge in the polls that had largely been driven by the character issue. The *Post*'s editor concluded that the story had no relevance to the issue of Dole's qualification to be president—a decision that most journalists thought should have been left to an informed electorate.[209]

Clinton easily won reelection with 49.2 percent of the popular vote and 379 electoral votes to Dole's 40.7 percent and 159 electoral votes. Reform Party candidate Perot polled 8.4 percent of the vote, less than half of his 1992 total, and received no electoral votes.[210] Clinton's victory made him the first Democrat to win reelection since Franklin Roosevelt won his second term in 1936. He became the first Democrat to be elected to the presidency along with a Republican-controlled Congress. Clinton won every state he had captured in 1992, except for Georgia, Montana, and Colorado. However, he picked up Florida and Arizona—becoming the first Democratic presidential candidate to win Florida since 1976 and first to win Arizona since 1948. The so-called gender gap was key to Clinton's victory: while the male vote was evenly split between the two candidates, Clinton won

the female vote by 16 percent, the largest margin ever. Clinton also beat Dole among every age group and was the clear choice of minorities: he received 80 percent of the black vote and 70 percent of the Hispanic vote.[211]

Yet three facts remained discouraging for Clinton. First, for the second straight election he had failed to win a majority of the popular vote. Second, voter turnout was less than 50 percent, the lowest since 1924. Third, Democrats failed to regain control of the Congress, despite the unpopularity of Gingrich and many of his Republican colleagues. Given this scenario, it was difficult for the president to credibly claim that he had achieved any kind of mandate from the American people.

Exit polling data suggested that the incumbent Clinton indeed benefited from positive public feelings about the economy. In one voter poll conducted by numerous news organizations about 60 percent of the respondents said that the economy was doing well. Those respondents heavily favored Clinton. In 1992 the exit polls found that less than 20 percent said the economy was doing well, a situation that had benefited the challenger Clinton.[212]

Perhaps what was most remarkable about the 1996 national elections was just how little had actually changed, despite the two major parties having spent about $500 million on campaign activities. Political analysts have aptly referred to the 1996 elections as reaffirming the status quo, a dramatic difference from both the 1992 and 1994 elections in which voters expressed frustration with the existing political arrangement and sought substantial changes in their government.

2000 Cliffhanger: GOP Retakes the Presidency

The last presidential election of the twentieth century, the closest in forty years, brought the nation to the brink of a constitutional crisis that was narrowly averted only after an unprecedented thirty-six days of rancorous arguing and litigation over who won, Democrat Al Gore or Republican George W. Bush. The eventual outcome, with Texas governor Bush the official winner, did little to unite the electorate, which had split a hundred million votes almost evenly between the two major party candidates. The lingering bitterness put a damper on the January 20, 2001, inauguration of Bush as the forty-third U.S. president.

Although Gore, the departing vice president, clearly won the national popular vote in the 2000 race by more than a half-million votes, Bush claimed the 25 electoral votes of Florida, where the election had been extremely close. Ultimately the state's Republican administration, headed by Gov. Jeb Bush, certified his brother as the popular vote winner in Florida, raising the GOP candidate's nationwide electoral vote total to 271—one more than he needed to win. Gore unsuccessfully contested the election on grounds that the state had stopped the recounts prematurely, leaving thousands of machine-processed ballots not subjected to the scrutiny of human eyes in a hand recount.

In the end, a sharply divided U.S. Supreme Court halted the Florida count, effectively deciding the election in Bush's favor. It was the first time the Court had taken up a disputed presidential election, let alone the first time it had gone against its traditional states' rights principles to overturn a state judiciary in such a matter. And in a historic election studded with anomalies, "firsts," and ironies, the Court for the first time immediately released audio tapes of its hearings on the suit, *Bush v. Gore.*

The tumult focused new attention on proposals to abolish or reform the electoral college system. It also brought to light the need to modernize the problem-prone voting systems still in use in many states besides Florida. And it exposed serious flaws in the technology that broadcast media rely on to project election results minutes after the polls have closed. Repercussions of the event would be felt for many years to come. *(See box, In Wake of 2000 Election "News Disaster," p. 10.)*

During the weeks of contentious legal maneuvering over the Florida vote, partisan tempers flared throughout the United States. Large groups of demonstrators in Florida and Washington, D.C., shouted at the television cameras and waved signs supporting Bush and his vice-presidential choice, Richard B. Cheney, or Gore and his running mate, Joseph I. Lieberman. In a play on the Gore-Lieberman campaign signs, Bush supporters held up "Sore-Loserman" placards. Gore stalwarts retaliated with "Count the Vote" chants and signs.

In the midst of the uproar, Cheney experienced his fourth (an apparently mild) heart attack. Doctors at George Washington University Hospital in Washington used angioplasty to install a stent, an expandable metal tube, in Cheney's heart to open a blocked artery. Within a few days Cheney was back on the job as head of Bush's transition team.

Bush's victory marked the fourth time in U.S. history that the popular vote loser gained the presidency. The first such election, in 1824, was won by John Quincy Adams, who, like Bush (son of former president George Bush), was the son of a president, John Adams. Although Andrew Jackson won the 1824 popular vote, none of the four candidates received the required electoral vote majority and the House of Representatives decided the election in Adams's favor. All four candidates represented factions of the Democratic-Republican Party. In an 1828 rematch with Adams, Jackson won the presidency and changed his party's name to Democratic.

The second contested presidential election, in 1876, was more analogous to the Bush-Gore dispute in that it too involved charges of irregularities in the election process. New York Democrat Samuel J. Tilden won the national vote against Ohio Republican Rutherford B. Hayes, but controversies over the popular votes in three southern states, including Florida, led to rival sets of electoral vote results being sent to Congress from the three states. Lacking a procedure for resolving the dispute, Congress formed a bipartisan special commission, including Supreme Court justices, that gave the votes to Hayes in return for concessions to the South. Hayes thereby won the presidency by a single electoral vote, a margin only one vote lower than Bush's.

In 1887 Congress enacted the Electoral Vote Count Act, specifying procedures for settling electoral vote disputes. One year later Republican Benjamin Harrison won the 1888 presidential election even though Democrat Grover Cleveland received more popular votes. The 1887 act did not come into play, however, because Harrison decisively won the electoral college vote, 233 to 168. *(See "Last of the Old Order: 1824," p. 24; "The Compromise of 1876," p. 40; "The 1888 Republican Recovery," p. 43; and Chapter 5, The Electoral College.)*

Had the Supreme Court not intervened in 2000, it was conceivable that Florida might have sent competing sets of electors' votes to Congress. Although that did not happen, the rules of the 1887 act thwarted efforts by some House members to challenge Florida's electoral votes. In one of the ironies of the election, it fell to Gore as Senate president to reject his supporters' objections.

It was the first time in U.S. history that the outcome of a presidential election had been contested in the courts. And it was the first time that the U.S. Supreme Court had taken up a lawsuit, brought by Bush, related to a presidential election. The Court traditionally had left such matters to Congress or to the states.

THE PRELIMINARIES

The prolonged dispute over Florida's crucial vote overshadowed all other aspects of the 2000 presidential election, including a rather lackluster primary season dominated throughout by Gore on the Democratic side and Bush on the GOP's. Both locked up their nominations early, despite some strong opposition, primarily from Arizona senator John McCain against Bush and former New Jersey senator Bill Bradley against Gore.

Bush entered the race in early 1999 and quickly established himself as the favorite of the Republican establishment and its campaign donors. Without a sitting Democratic president to compete against, the contest attracted a dozen hopefuls for the GOP nomination. But even before the kickoff Iowa caucuses in January 2000 half of the field dropped out, including former vice president Dan Quayle, former Tennessee governor Lamar Alexander, and Elizabeth Dole, head of the Red Cross and wife of 1996 nominee Bob Dole, who said she was unable to compete with Bush's fund-raising prowess. Conservative commentator Pat Buchanan, a past contender, decided instead to seek the Reform Party nomination.

By early February, Bush and McCain remained the only serious contenders. McCain upset Bush in the New Hampshire and Michigan primaries, but Bush went on to win a cluster of March 7 primaries and enough convention delegates to clinch the nomination. Publisher Malcolm S. "Steve" Forbes Jr., who finished third in New Hampshire, ended his campaign after a less impressive showing in Delaware.

McCain, a former Vietnam prisoner of war and cosponsor with Sen. Russell Feingold of Wisconsin of the bipartisan campaign finance reform legislation, was perceived as a moderate despite his solid conservative voting record in the Senate. This, and his penchant for bluntness, appealed to many non-Republicans, who could vote in the growing number of open or semiopen GOP primaries. In all, McCain defeated Bush in seven of the eighteen primaries he entered. But McCain eventually endorsed Bush and was the only member of Congress accorded a

George W. Bush and Al Gore compete for moderator Jim Lehrer's attention during the final presidential debate held October 17 in St. Louis. Although Gore was given a slight edge in most disinterested postdebate analyses of who won or lost, Bush did better than expected, and, presenting a more likable persona, improved his standing with voters over the course of the three debates.

prime-time speaker's slot at the party's nominating convention in Philadelphia.

For Gore, the nomination challenge from Bradley was short and sweet. Bradley failed to win a single primary and dropped out of the race in early March. In a speech to the Democratic convention at Los Angeles, Bradley expressed his support for Gore.

After the conventions Gore, more so than Bush, faced a vote-siphoning threat from the Green Party candidate, consumer advocate Ralph Nader, who received almost 1 percent of the presidential vote in 1996 and was aiming for 5 percent in 2000—a level that would ensure federal campaign funding for the Greens in the 2004 election. Although Republican swing voters were unlikely to switch to corporation-basher Nader, disaffected liberals who supported Bradley found Nader an attractive alternative.

With polls continuing to show the electorate almost evenly divided, the major party race settled down to basically a personality contest between two Ivy Leaguers—Gore (Harvard) and Bush (Yale). The public perceived Bush as personable but perhaps not so intelligent as Gore, despite Bush's master's degree from Harvard's business school. Although known privately as humorous, Gore was seen publicly as somewhat wooden. In the first of their three debates, Gore came off as smart-alecky against Bush, the self-styled "compassionate conservative." In their subsequent debates, Gore toned down his grimacing and head-shaking at Bush's remarks.

Gore's greatest asset was his experience, sixteen years in Congress and eight years in the vice presidency, against Bush's six years as Texas governor. But being vice president was no guarantee of success. Only four sitting vice presidents, including Bush's father in 1988, had been elected president. And the vice presidency was not a compelling qualification for promotion. As political scientist George O. Jones observed, "Most of them couldn't win the nomination on their own without being the vice president."[213]

Both candidates took a lot of negative press and ribbing from late-night comedians about their speaking habits—Bush for malapropisms and Gore for exaggerations. Bush, for example, in one off-hand statement derided people who regard Social Security as "some kind of federal program," which of course it was. Among Bush's other bloopers, as quoted by *Washington Post* columnist Michael Kelly:

On education: "My education program will resignate among all parents." On foreign policy: "A key to foreign policy is to rely on reliance." On whether Social Security recipients will receive the same benefits under his plan as under the current system: "Maybe, maybe not." On his budget proposal: "It's clearly a budget. It's got a lot of numbers in it."[214]

Gore's most ridiculed statement was about his purported claim of "inventing" the Internet. What he actually said on a CNN program, however, was: "During my service in Congress I took the initiative in creating the Internet"—referring to his sponsorship of legislation that funded the early development of the technology. Despite the alleged "liberal bias" of the news media, a preconvention study by the Pew Research Center and the Project for Excellence in Journalism found that most news coverage portrayed Gore as an exaggerator or as scandal tainted (for his role in the Democrats' 1996 fund-raising practices), while Bush was usually referred to more positively as "a different kind of Republican."[215]

The election had been expected to be close. Bush and Gore ran neck-and-neck in public opinion polls, right up to election day. Conditions were also ripe for a tight race. "Not since 1960 has there been a similar convergence of voting trends," political analyst Rhodes Cook wrote two months before the election. He noted that John F. Kennedy won the 1960 popular vote against Richard Nixon by two-tenths of a percentage point (even closer than Gore's five-tenths of a percentage point), although Kennedy had a comfortable lead in electoral votes. "This time the roles of the two parties are reversed," Cook wrote, "as it is the Republicans who are trying to regain the White House after an eight-year absence. And they begin with a larger cache of electoral votes than the Democrats."[216]

From the outset, the election was Gore's to lose. It is almost axiomatic that the party in power retains the White House in times of peace and prosperity. With President Clinton ineligible to succeed himself, Gore stood to inherit the advantage of running on Clinton's successes, especially an economy that had gone from record federal deficits to record surpluses, which opened the prospect of retiring the $3.7 trillion national debt while safeguarding Social Security, Medicare, and other popular but expensive social programs. Clinton could also claim legislative successes in welfare reform and the North American Free Trade Act as well as foreign policy efforts in Bosnia, Kosovo, Northern Ireland, and the Middle East. On the other hand, Republicans controlled Congress for six of Clinton's eight years in office.

Despite his high job approval ratings, Clinton himself was perhaps Gore's biggest handicap. Bush and other Republican candidates tried to saddle Gore with the sins of the Clinton administration, particularly Clinton's December 1998 impeachment for lying under oath about his affair with Monica Lewinsky

Countdown in Florida

The following is a day-by-day chronology of the events surrounding the disputed presidential election results from Florida in the 2000 race between Republican candidate George W. Bush and Democrat Al Gore.

November 7, 2000. Election in Florida too close to call, with Bush holding narrow lead. TV networks retract premature reports declaring Gore winner of state's twenty-five electoral votes.

November 8–10. Gore calls Bush to concede early November 8, then calls back to withdraw concession. Gore seeks hand recounts in four largely Democratic counties. Bush has unofficial 1,784-vote lead November 9. After all but one of Florida's sixty-seven counties complete machine recount required by state law, Bush lead falls to 327 votes.

November 11–14. Broward, Miami-Dade, Palm Beach, and Volusia Counties undertake manual recounts requested by Gore; federal court on November 13 rejects Bush bid to block hand counts; Volusia finishes recount November 14.

November 13. Florida secretary of state Katherine Harris says she will enforce state law deadline of November 14 for counties to submit returns and will not include manual recounts; election boards in Volusia and Palm Beach Counties ask state court judge to overturn deadline.

November 14–16. Leon County Circuit Judge Terry P. Lewis says Harris must justify her position on deadline; Harris reaffirms

decision November 15; Lewis hears new round of arguments November 16.

November 17. Lewis upholds Harris's decision to disregard manual recounts, but Florida supreme court bars certification of state results pending oral arguments on November 20; federal appeals court rejects Bush suit over manual recounts.

November 18. Bush lead grows to 930 votes with absentee ballots; Bush campaign criticizes Democrats for challenging absentee votes from military.

November 21. Florida supreme court rules manual recounts must be included in presidential race if submitted to Harris by 5:00 p.m. Sunday, November 26.

November 22–24. Bush running mate Richard Cheney has heart attack, leaves Washington hospital two days later after surgery to insert stent in artery. Shouting, fist-waving crowd, including Republican congressional aides, tries to enter private room where recounts resume in Miami-Dade. County stops recount, pleading too little time and denying intimidation by the demonstrators. State supreme court on November 23 rejects Gore suit to force Miami-Dade to resume counting. U.S. Supreme Court agrees to hear Bush appeal of Florida supreme court action allowing extended deadline for certifying presidential race.

November 25–26. Manual recounts: Broward finishes November 25; Palm Beach falls just short of completion November

---

when she was a White House intern. The Republicans' strategy was to run against "Clinton-Gore" rather than against Gore alone—even though Gore's marital fidelity was not at issue.

Conservative congressional Republicans were still angry at Clinton for escaping removal from office through the impeachment process. In November 1998, with impeachment looming, Clinton became the first president since Franklin D. Roosevelt in 1934 to gain House seats at a midterm election. He made a net gain of five seats and got rid of his nemesis, Speaker Newt Gingrich, who resigned from Congress in reaction to the GOP setback. The Speaker-designate, Robert L. Livingston of Louisiana, also resigned after admitting an extra-marital affair. Then, in a political twist of the knife, Clinton handily won acquittal from the Senate in his impeachment trial.

In the 2000 campaign, however, neither the Republicans nor the Democrats openly raised the "character issue." (The *Washington Post* called impeachment "2000's Stealth Issue.").[217] But Gore's need to distance himself from Clinton's indiscretions was implicit in his choice of Lieberman as his running mate. An Orthodox Jew, the first of his faith to run on a major party ticket, Lieberman was known for speaking out on moral issues and family values. Although he voted in the Senate to ac-

quit Clinton, Lieberman had publicly taken the president to task for his dalliance with Lewinsky. On the Republican side, Bush's frequent pledges to "restore the honor and dignity" of the presidency also were a thinly veiled reference to impeachment.

Some Gore supporters felt that he perhaps distanced himself from Clinton too much, thereby sacrificing the opportunity to take his share of the credit for the booming economy and other positive aspects of the Clinton legacy. Clinton himself was said to feel "underused" by the Gore campaign. By the final weeks of the campaign Gore became less reluctant to run on Clinton's record, but it was too late to make much of an impression on undecided voters.

With the cold war over and most people better off than they were eight years earlier, traditionally Democratic pocketbook and social issues dominated the campaign—Social Security, education, health care, abortion rights, and gun control. The huge federal surpluses fueled the money issues, with Bush pushing for tax cuts and heavier outlays for antimissile research and development. Gore pledged a "lockbox" for Social Security and criticized Bush's concept of allowing workers to divert part of their trust fund contributions to private investment accounts.

26. Harris announces November 26 that state elections canvassing board certifies Bush as winner by 537-vote margin; Bush claims victory, says he and Cheney are "honored and humbled" to have won Florida's electoral votes.

November 27–29. Gore formally contests the Florida election on November 27. He sues in Leon County Circuit Court, in Tallahassee, claiming the number of legal votes "improperly rejected" and illegal votes counted in Nassau, Palm Beach, and Miami-Dade Counties is enough to change outcome. Judge N. Sanders Sauls orders ballots brought to Tallahassee for possible counting. More than one million ballots are trucked with police escort to the state capital.

December 1. U.S. Supreme Court hears Bush appeal of deadline extension. Florida justices refuse to order revote requested in Palm Beach County because of controversial "butterfly ballot" used there.

December 2–3. Judge Sauls hears testimony on whether 13,000 ballots from Miami-Dade and Palm Beach Counties should be manually counted. Both sides call witnesses on reliability of punch-card voting systems.

December 4. Sauls rejects Gore's request for manual recount and refuses to decertify Bush as winner. U.S. Supreme Court asks state high court to explain its November 21 action allowing manual recounting and extending deadlines.

December 8–9. Florida justices order hand count of ballots on which machines found no vote for president. U.S. Supreme Court unexpectedly halts the hand counts the next day.

December 10–11. U.S. Supreme Court receives briefs and hears arguments in *Bush v. Gore.*

December 12. U.S. Supreme Court splits 5–4 in ruling for Bush against further hand counts. Florida legislature convenes special session to meet the federal deadline for designating presidential electors. Twenty states miss the deadline by a few days.

December 13. Gore concedes election, congratulates Bush and jokingly adds "and I promised him that this time I wouldn't call him back."

December 18. Presidential electors meet in state capitals to cast votes.

January 6, 2001. Congress meets in joint session to count electoral votes. As Senate president, Vice President Gore presides over his own defeat. Twenty Gore supporters, mostly Congressional Black Caucus members, try to block Florida's votes but Gore rejects each representative's objection because none has also been signed by a senator as the 1887 Electoral Vote Count Act requires. One District of Columbia elector, Barbara Lett-Simmons, withholds her vote from Gore in protest of the District's lack of representation in Congress. Final electoral vote tally is 271 for Bush, 266 for Gore with one abstention.

January 20. Inauguration of Bush as president and Cheney as vice president. Protests, largely nonviolent, mar—but do not disrupt—the inaugural parade.

Bush's conservative stance on gun control brought him $1.7 million in support from the National Rifle Association (more than the NRA's independent expenditures for all candidates in 1996). In all, the Bush campaign raised almost $100 million, mostly from individuals, allowing it to decline federal grants and the spending limits that go with them. The Gore campaign accepted federal funding.

THE LONG ELECTION NIGHT

Problems with the crucial Florida vote erupted almost immediately on election day November 7, 2000. Voters in Palm Beach County reported difficulties with an unusual "butterfly" punch-card ballot. Some Democratic voters there thought that they had inadvertently voted for Reform Party nominee Pat Buchanan instead of for Gore. In some of the other twenty-four counties using outmoded punch-card systems, but with regular ballot forms, voters said they were unable to punch out the hole for the candidate of their choice.

Within hours, as news of the problems spread, people around the world became familiar with the obscure noun *chad,* singular or plural, meaning the tiny piece of paper that is pushed out in a punch-card system. If the chad is only dented (dimpled) or partially dislodged, the voting machine may not register the punch as a vote. Therein lay the basis for much of the contention in the days and weeks that were to follow.

Another serious problem emerged shortly after the polls closed, this one having to do with the system—based on exit polling—devised by the news media to project election winners before the votes are counted. The system is uncannily accurate, but its worst and most embarrassing mistake happened at 7:47 p.m. EST when the broadcast networks, using Voter News Service (VNS) data, projected Gore as the winner in Florida. People were still voting in Florida's western panhandle, in the central time zone, when the election was called for Gore. A short time later, the networks retracted and said Florida was too close to call. (*See box, "Countdown in Florida," p. 90.*)

In the early hours of November 8 the news reports put Bush ahead. Gore called Bush from Nashville and told him he was prepared to concede. Later, after being advised that there might be a recount in Florida, Gore called again to Bush in Austin. "You mean you're retracting your concession?" a surprised Bush reportedly asked. "You don't have to get snippy about it," Gore is said to have replied.

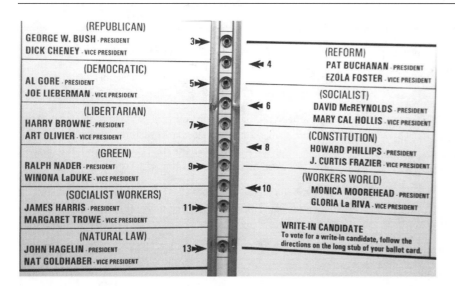

The "butterfly" ballot used in Palm Beach, Florida, confused some voters who, intent on voting for Al Gore, punched out the second hole from the top, recording a vote instead for Reform Party candidate Patrick J. Buchanan (listed on the right side). The confusion probably cost Gore enough votes to swing the state, and thus the electoral college majority to Bush.

Weary television journalists apologized repeatedly for confusing their viewers during the long election night, which finally extended into weeks. "We don't just have egg on our face," said NBC's Tom Brokaw, "we have an omelet." CBS's Dan Rather said, "If you're disgusted with us, frankly I don't blame you."

Besides leading nationwide in the popular vote, Gore outside of Florida led in the electoral college vote, 267 to 246 (after the counting of the absentee vote in Oregon and New Mexico concluded several days later). The entire 2000 presidential election therefore hung on the final results of the popular vote in Florida, which would determine the winner of the state's twenty-five electoral votes.

The close election triggered an automatic machine recount, showing Bush ahead by about 300 votes in Florida. But the Gore camp focused on the thousands of votes that the machines rejected as undervoted, showing no vote for president, or overvoted, showing more than one vote for presidential candidates. Only a manual count of those ballots could discern votes that the machines could not detect, Gore lawyers argued. The Democrats' war cry became, "Every vote counts; count every vote."

In what may have been a tactical mistake, Gore did not request an immediate statewide revote or recount. Instead his lawyers fought to keep hand counts going where Gore was picking up votes, in mostly Democratic counties such as Broward, Miami-Dade, and Volusia, and in Palm Beach County where the butterfly-ballot had recorded an unlikely 3,407 votes for Pat Buchanan, three times more than he received elsewhere in the state. Buchanan himself said it appeared he received votes meant for Gore. Just as fiercely, the Bush forces fought to stop the hand counts. They argued that the votes had been legally counted and recounted, including military and other absentee ballots that favored Bush, and that the canvassers had no uniform standards for gauging the difference between a vote and a nonvote on a punch-card ballot. Allowing more time for recounts, they said, would be changing the rules after the game started.

Both sides assembled high-powered legal teams, each headed by a former secretary of state, James A. Baker III for Bush and Warren N. Christopher for Gore. Both served as above-the-fray spokespeople while the trench warfare fell chiefly to lawyers Barry Richard for Bush and David Boies for Gore. U.S. Supreme Court arguments for Bush were presented by Ted Olson and for Gore initially by Laurence Tribe of Harvard Law School and later by Boies.

But it was a race against the calendar and Katherine Harris was the timekeeper. Harris, Florida's secretary of state and former cochair of Bush's campaign in the state, announced November 13 that counties had until the following day, the date set in state law, to submit their returns, without any manual recount figures. Lawsuits stayed Harris's hand, however, and the manual counts proceeded by fits and starts until Sunday, November 26, under an extension granted by the seven-member Florida supreme court, made up mostly of Democratic appointees. That evening Harris ceremoniously "certified" Bush as the Florida winner by 537 votes out of six million cast.

The battle was by no means over, however. Gore formally contested the election and Bush meanwhile had protested the deadline extension to the U.S. Supreme Court, which heard the arguments December 1. In Tallahassee, after hearing two days of televised testimony, Leon County Circuit Judge N. Sanders Sauls ruled that Gore failed to prove the need for manual recounts. Gore's witnesses had testified that "chad buildup" and poorly maintained equipment could prevent voters from cleanly punching out a machine-read ballot. Gore received another setback the same day, December 4, when the U.S. Supreme Court returned the deadline-extension case to the Florida high court for clarification.

Gore scored a short-lived victory December 8 when the Florida court by a 4–3 vote ordered a resumption of the hand counts, only to have the U.S. Supreme Court quickly halt them the following day, pending its decision in *Bush v. Gore*. In its 5–4 decision, handed down December 12, the Court majority ruled for Bush that the lack of uniform standards for manual recounts denied "equal protection of the laws" to Florida voters. The Court split along ideological lines in the unsigned decision. In the majority were conservatives William Rehnquist, Antonin Scalia, Clarence Thomas, Anthony Kennedy, and Sandra Day O'Connor. Dissenting were liberals or moderates

Stephen Breyer, Ruth Bader Ginsburg, David Souter, and John Paul Stevens.

The Court action left 42,000 Florida undervotes unexamined, including 35,000 from the punch-card counties, but it effectively resolved the 2000 presidential race and possibly averted a constitutional crisis that might have arisen had the dispute resulted in Florida's sending two sets of electoral votes to Congress. The state legislature had already designated a slate of electors committed to Bush. Faced with a hopeless situation, Gore folded his campaign and conceded December 13.

When the presidential electors met in their states December 18 to cast their ballots, one District of Columbia elector, Barbara Lett-Simmons, withheld her vote from Gore in protest of the District's lack of representation in Congress. This reduced Gore's electoral vote total to 266 against 271 for Bush. Gore received 51.0 million votes (48.4 percent) to 50.5 million (47.9 percent) for Bush. Gore's lead in the popular vote was 539,947. Nader"s 2.8 million votes amounted to 2.7 percent of the total. Buchanan received less than 1 percent with 447,798 votes.

An embarrassing loss to Gore was his home state of Tennessee and its eleven electoral votes. Had he won there he would have had an electoral vote majority and the Florida vote would have been irrelevant. Likewise, had Gore received a fraction of the Nader vote in several close states, including Florida, he would have been over the top in electoral votes. Rhodes Cook, however, pointed out while Nader may have siphoned off Gore voters in Florida and elsewhere, Reform Party candidate Pat Buchanan, whose supporters traditionally lean Republican, may have prevented Bush from winning a few states that went closely for Gore. "[T]here were 30 additional electoral votes that Bush may have won if Buchanan had not been in the race, compared to 29 more electoral votes that may have gone to Gore if Nader had not run. In short, the effect of the two third-party candidates on the electoral vote was essentially a wash."[218]

Nationwide, African Americans voted 9 to 1 for Gore. On January 6, 2001, twenty House members, mostly members of the Congressional Black Caucus, tried to disqualify Florida's electoral votes as Congress met in joint session to count the electoral votes. As Senate president by virtue of his being U.S. vice president, Gore one by one ruled the objections out of order because they had not been signed by a senator as required by law. None of the 100 members of the new Senate, evenly divided between Republicans and Democrats, including presidential spouse Hillary Rodham Clinton of New York, had signed a challenge to the Florida votes. Gore in his concession had asked his supporters to accept the Court verdict and the "finality of the outcome."

AFTERMATH

Protests marred President Bush's inauguration on a cold, rainy Saturday January 20, 2001. Thousands of protesters, under tight security, lined the Pennsylvania Avenue parade route to the White House. They were noisy and visible, but there were relatively few arrests and clashes with the police.

Long and bitter as it was, the thirty-six-day 2000 election "night" was shorter and perhaps less vitriolic than its 1876 counterpart, which extended from November 7 to two days before inauguration, then in March. Because March 4, 1877, fell on a Sunday, President Hayes was sworn in privately at the White House and the public ceremonies took place quietly on Monday.

Similarly, the nation witnessed another peaceful transfer of power with the Bush-Cheney inauguration. As historian David McCullough phrased it, the peacefulness was typical of past inaugurations but perhaps for a different reason. "As close as it was, this election was not about visceral issues like slavery or war—things people are really passionate about," McCullough said. "The nation is closely divided, certainly, but we seem to be divided over which party controls the middle of the political spectrum. I'm not sure it's happened quite like that before."[219]

NOTES

1. A. James Reichley, *The Life of the Parties: A History of American Political Parties* (New York: Free Press, 1992), 17.

2. Richard P. McCormick, *The Presidential Game: The Origins of American Presidential Politics* (New York: Oxford University Press, 1982), chap. 1.

3. Ibid., 33–34.

4. Reichley, *Life of the Parties*, 42.

5. Ibid., 49.

6. Robert J. Dinkin, *Campaigning in America: A History of Election Practices* (New York: Greenwood Press, 1989), 18.

7. Roy F. Nichols, *The Invention of the American Political Parties* (New York: Macmillan, 1967), 192.

8. Bruce L. Felkner, *Political Mischief: Smear, Sabotage, and Reform in U.S. Elections* (New York: Praeger, 1992), 31.

9. Dinkin, *Campaigning in America*, 15, 18.

10. Edward Stanwood, *A History of the Presidency* (Boston: Houghton Mifflin, 1898), 63.

11. John F. Hoadley, *Origins of American Party Politics, 1789–1803* (Lexington: University Press of Kentucky, 1986), 191.

12. T. Harry Williams, *The History of American Wars: From Colonial Times to World War I* (New York: Knopf, 1981), 134.

13. Stanwood, *History of the Presidency*, 110.

14. Matthew A. Crenson, *The Federal Machine* (Baltimore: Johns Hopkins University Press, 1971), 11–30.

15. Jackson biographer Robert V. Remini explains the nickname "Old Hickory." In an arduous five-hundred-mile march, Jackson gave his three horses to wounded soldiers and marched on foot with his troops to give them moral support. The soldiers serving under him agreed that their general was as tough as hickory. "Not much later," Remini writes, "they started calling him 'Hickory' as a sign of their respect and regard; then the affectionate 'Old' was added to give Jackson a nickname . . . that admirably served him thereafter throughout his military and political wars" (Robert V. Remini, *Andrew Jackson* [New York: Harper and Row, 1969], 54).

16. Arthur M. Schlesinger Jr., *The Age of Jackson* (New York: New American Library, 1945), 34.

17. *Guide to Congress*, 2nd ed. (Washington, D.C.: Congressional Quarterly, 1982), 613.

18. Russell L. Hanson, *The Democratic Imagination in America: Conversations with Our Past* (Princeton, N.J.: Princeton University Press, 1985), 125.

19. Eugene H. Roseboom, *A History of Presidential Elections* (New York: Macmillan, 1970), 106.

20. Schlesinger, *Age of Jackson*, 55.

21. Estimates of vote totals vary, especially in the years before standardized methods of balloting. Discrepancies developed because of disputes about stuffing ballot boxes, the eligibility of some voters, absentee ballots, and simple counting and reporting difficulties in the premedia age.

22. Roseboom, *History of Presidential Elections*, 112.

23. Hanson, *Democratic Imagination*, 54–120.

24. Ibid., 140–141.

25. Ibid., 130.

26. See Albert O. Hirschman, *Exit, Voice, and Loyalty* (Cambridge, Mass.: Harvard University Press, 1970).

27. Hanson, *Democratic Imagination*, 138.

28. Richard P. McCormick, "Political Development and the Second Party System," in *The American Party Systems: Stages of Development,* ed. William Nisbet Chambers and Walter Dean Burnham (New York: Oxford University Press, 1967), 102.

29. Paul Taylor, *See How They Run: Electing a President in the Age of Mediaocracy* (New York: Knopf, 1991), 4.

30. James L. Sundquist, *Dynamics of the Party System,* rev. ed. (Washington, D.C.: Brookings, 1983), 51.

31. Roseboom, *Presidential Elections,* 143.

32. Richard Hofstadter, *The American Political Tradition* (New York: Vintage, 1948), 113.

33. Ibid.

34. Hanson, *Democratic Imagination*, 176.

35. Roseboom, *History of Presidential Elections,* 177–181.

36. Paul N. Angle, ed., *The Lincoln Reader* (New York: Pocket Books, 1954), 523.

37. Ibid., 531.

38. Roseboom, *History of Presidential Elections,* 201.

39. Eric Foner, *Reconstruction: America's Unfinished Revolution, 1863–1877* (New York: Harper and Row, 1988).

40. William S. McFeely, *Grant* (New York: Norton, 1981), 283.

41. Ibid., 288–289.

42. Ibid., 381.

43. Bernhard Bailyn et al., *The Great Republic: A History of the American People* (Boston: Little, Brown, 1977), 802.

44. C. Vann Woodward, *Reunion and Reaction* (New York: Doubleday Anchor Books, 1951).

45. Kenneth M. Stampp, *The Era of Reconstruction, 1865–1877* (New York: Vintage, 1965), 210–211.

46. Michael Nelson, "A Short, Ironic History of American National Bureaucracy," *Journal of Politics* 44 (winter 1982): 747–777.

47. Roseboom, *History of Presidential Elections,* 264.

48. Harry Thurston Peck, *Twenty Years of the Republic, 1885–1905* (New York: Dodd, Mead, 1906), 20.

49. Michael E. McGerr, *The Decline of Popular Politics: The American North, 1865–1928* (New York: Oxford University Press), 82–106.

50. Peck, *Twenty Years of the Republic,* 41.

51. Ibid., 78.

52. Ibid., 144.

53. Ibid., 169.

54. Roseboom, *History of Presidential Elections,* 290.

55. Bailyn et al., *Great Republic,* 786.

56. Sundquist, *Dynamics of the Party System,* 107.

57. For a concise account of the machine reform struggle, see Dennis R. Judd, *The Politics of American Cities* (Boston: Little, Brown, 1984), 50–110.

58. See David Montgomery, *The Fall of the House of Labor* (New York: Cambridge University Press, 1987).

59. Sundquist, *Dynamics of the Party System,* 116–118.

60. Ibid., 143, 152.

61. Hofstadter, *American Political Tradition,* 187.

62. Sundquist, *Dynamics of the Party System,* 149–152.

63. Hofstadter, *American Political Tradition,* 192–193.

64. See "William Jennings Bryan, Cross of Gold Speech," in *Great Issues in American History: From Reconstruction to the Present Day, 1864–1969,* ed. Richard Hofstadter (New York: Vintage, 1969), 166–173.

65. Jasper B. Shannon, *Money and Politics* (New York: Random House, 1959), 30–32.

66. Sundquist, *Dynamics of the Party System,* 158.

67. Ibid., 169; for a general discussion of the 1896 election's resulting realignment, see pages 160–169.

68. E. E. Schattschneider, *The Semisovereign People* (Hinsdale, Ill.: Dryden Press, 1975), 76–77.

69. Edmund Morris, *The Rise of Theodore Roosevelt* (New York: Ballantine, 1979), 718.

70. See Gabriel Kolko, *The Triumph of Conservatism* (New York: Free Press, 1963).

71. Sundquist, *Dynamics of the Party System,* 176.

72. See Alpheus I. Mason, *Bureaucracy Convicts Itself* (New York: Viking Press, 1941); and James Penick Jr., *Progressive Politics and Conservation* (Chicago: University of Chicago Press, 1968).

73. August Hecksher, *Woodrow Wilson* (New York: Scribner's, 1991), 231–232.

74. Ibid., 259.

75. J. Leonard Bates, *The United States, 1898–1928* (New York: McGraw-Hill, 1976), 187.

76. Roseboom, *History of Presidential Elections,* 384.

77. John L. Shover, ed., *Politics of the Nineteen Twenties* (Waltham, Mass.: Ginn-Blaisdell, 1970), 148.

78. Ibid., 4.

79. Ibid., 12.

80. Ibid., 10.

81. James David Barber, *The Pulse of Politics: Electing Presidents in the Media Age* (New York: Norton, 1980), 239.

82. William E. Leuchtenberg, *Franklin D. Roosevelt and the New Deal* (New York: Harper and Row, 1963), 13.

83. Frank Friedel, *Franklin D. Roosevelt: The Triumph* (Boston: Little, Brown, 1956), 248–249.

84. Barber, *Pulse of Politics,* 243.

85. Ibid., 244.

86. Ibid., 238.

87. Hofstadter, *American Political Tradition,* 332.

88. Barber, *Pulse of Politics,* 244.

89. See Robert Lekachman, *The Age of Keynes* (New York: Random House, 1966).

90. Schattschneider argues in *The Semisovereign People* that the key element of any conflict is the extent to which the protagonists are able to control how many people get involved. Every "scope of conflict" has a bias. The size of the group involved in the conflict is almost always open to change. Schattschneider writes: "A look at political literature shows that there has indeed been a long-standing struggle between the conflicting tendencies toward the privatization and socialization of conflict" (p. 7). The New Deal was a stage of socialization of conflict.

91. Everett Carll Ladd Jr. and Charles D. Hadley, *Transformations of the American Party System* (New York: Norton, 1978), 86.

92. Ibid., 43.

93. Ibid., 46.

94. Ibid., 64–74, 112; Sundquist, *Dynamics of the Party System,* 214–224.

95. Sundquist, *Dynamics of the Party System,* 217.

96. Ladd and Hadley, *Transformations,* 82.

97. Ibid., 58–59.

98. Ibid., 63.

99. Samuel H. Beer, "Liberalism and the National Interest," *Public Interest,* no. 1 (fall 1966): 81.

100. Theodore J. Lowi, *The End of Liberalism* (New York: Norton, 1969). See also Hanson, *Democratic Imagination*, 257–292.

101. Greg Mitchell, *The Campaign of the Century: Upton Sinclair's Race for Governor of California and the Birth of Modern Media Politics* (New York: Random House, 1992).

102. James MacGregor Burns, *Roosevelt: The Lion and the Fox* (New York: Harcourt Brace and World, 1956), 282–283.

103. Roseboom, *History of Presidential Elections,* 447.

104. Burns, *Roosevelt,* 277–278.

105. Ibid., 269–271.

106. Ibid., 282–283.

107. Ibid., 300.

108. Ibid., 427.

109. Barber, *Pulse of Politics.* This book tells the story behind the Willkie movement and the role played by Henry R. Luce, the founder of Time Inc.

110. See Lekachman, *Age of Keynes,* esp. chaps. 5 and 6.

111. Roseboom, *History of Presidential Elections,* 483.

112. William E. Leuchtenberg, *In the Shadow of F.D.R.: From Harry Truman to Ronald Reagan* (Ithaca, N.Y.: Cornell University Press, 1983), 1–2.

113. Ibid., 15.

114. Ibid., 21.

115. V. O. Key Jr., *Southern Politics in State and Nation* (Knoxville: University of Tennessee Press, 1984), 649.

116. Ibid., 330–344.

117. Barber, *Pulse of Politics,* 50.

118. Nelson W. Polsby and Aaron Wildavsky, *Presidential Elections* (New York: Scribner's, 1984), 205–206.

119. Barber, *Pulse of Politics,* 61.

120. Angus Campbell, Philip E. Convers, Warren E. Miller, and Donald E. Stokes, *The American Voter* (New York: Wiley, 1960), 532.

121. Richard Neustadt, *Presidential Power* (New York: Wiley, 1980), 10, 12–14, 16, 18, 19, 22–25, 43, 67–68, 178.

122. Garry Wills, *Nixon Agonistes* (New York: New American Library, 1969), 91.

123. Fred Greenstein, *The Hidden-Hand Presidency* (New York: Basic Books, 1982).

124. Barber, *Pulse of Politics,* 269.

125. Eric F. Goldman quipped, "The returns, as the gangsters said, made even Alf Landon look good," in *The Crucial Decade* (New York: Vintage, 1960), 326.

126. The elder Kennedy always had planned for his sons to enter national politics. He originally pushed his eldest son, Joseph Jr., but the son died in combat in World War II. John was next; he ran for Congress in 1946. Robert, the third Kennedy son, served as an aide to Sen. Joseph McCarthy before managing John's 1960 presidential campaign and serving as his attorney general. Edward, the youngest, worked on the 1960 campaign and won a Senate seat in 1962.

127. Merle Miller, *Plain Speaking* (New York: Berkeley, 1974), 199.

128. Theodore H. White, *The Making of the President 1960* (New York: Atheneum, 1961), 114–116.

129. Ibid., 128.

130. Ibid., 130.

131. Ibid., 198–204.

132. Arthur M. Schlesinger Jr., *Robert F. Kennedy and His Times* (Boston: Houghton Mifflin, 1978), 193.

133. Henry Fairlie, *The Kennedy Promise* (New York: Dell, 1972), 30–31.

134. White, *Making of the President 1960,* 329.

135. Ibid., 327.

136. Richard M. Nixon, *Six Crises* (Garden City, N.Y.: Doubleday, 1962), 412.

137. White, *Making of the President 1960,* 397–401.

138. Sen. Barry Goldwater, letter to the author, January 25, 1988.

139. The Warren Commission, appointed by Johnson, concluded that Oswald acted alone, but Oswald himself was killed before he had a chance to give full testimony. Many experts dispute the Warren Commission conclusion.

140. The Kennedy assassination fomented passage of the Twenty-fifth Amendment, which provides for a more orderly system of replacement. Previously, when a vice president ascended to the White House after the death or removal of a president, the vice presidency was left vacant. The amendment provides for presidential appointment of a vice president to fill the vacant spot. It also provides for at least temporary replacement of the president in the case of disability. The latter provision developed out of a concern that the country could have become leaderless had Kennedy been physically or mentally impaired but not killed.

141. Barber, *Pulse of Politics,* 167.

142. Thomas Ferguson and Joel Rogers, *Right Turn: The Decline of the Democrats and the Future of American Politics* (New York: Hill and Wang, 1986), 53.

143. Theodore H. White, *The Making of the President 1964* (New York: New American Library, 1965), 261.

144. Ibid., 353.

145. The central importance of economic conditions to electoral politics is widely documented. See, for example, Stanley Kelley Jr., *Interpreting Elections* (Princeton, N.J.: Princeton University Press, 1983); Edward R. Tufte, *Political Control of the Economy* (Princeton, N.J.: Princeton University Press, 1978); and Campbell, et al., *The American Voter.* On the link between economic conditions and the 1964 election, see Kelley, *Interpreting Elections,* 194.

146. Stanley Karnow, *Vietnam: A History* (New York: Viking, 1983), 358.

147. Ibid., 362.

148. Ibid., 395.

149. James David Barber, *The Presidential Character* (Englewood Cliffs, N.J.: Prentice-Hall, 1972), 34.

150. Karnow, *Vietnam,* 403.

151. Ibid., 479.

152. David Halberstam, *The Best and the Brightest* (New York: Random House, 1969).

153. Sundquist, *Dynamics of the Party System,* 384.

154. Ibid., 383.

155. The administration plank supported a bombing halt only when it "would not endanger the lives of our troops in the field," did not call for a reduction in search-and-destroy missions or a withdrawal of troops until the end of the war, and advocated a new government in Saigon only after the war had ended. The minority plank, drafted by McCarthy and McGovern, called for an immediate halt to the bombing, reduction of offensive operations in the South Vietnamese countryside, a negotiated troop withdrawal, and encouragement of the South Vietnamese government to negotiate with communist insurgents. After nearly three hours of debate, the minority plank was defeated, 1,567¾ to 1,041¼.

156. Theodore H. White, *The Making of the President 1968* (New York, Atheneum, 1969), 371.

157. Roseboom, *History of Presidential Elections,* 603.

158. See Russell Baker, *The Next President* (New York: Dell, 1968).

159. David Broder, "The Story That Still Nags at Me," *Washington Monthly,* February 1987, 29–32 .See also Theodore H. White, *Making of the President 1972* (New York: New American Library, 1973), 82.

160. White, *Making of the President 1972,* 129.

161. Ibid., 207.

162. On the politics of the period, see Sundquist, *Dynamics of the Party System,* 393–411; and Theodore H. White, *America in Search of Itself* (New York: Harper and Row, 1981). Good accounts of the Watergate scandal include those by Theodore H. White, *Breach of Faith* (New York: Atheneum, 1975); Jonathan Schell, *The Time of Illusion* (New York: Knopf, 1976); and Lewis Chester et al., *Watergate* (New York: Ballantine, 1973).

163. See Bruce Odes, ed., *From the President: Richard Nixon's Secret Files* (New York: Harper and Row, 1989).

164. Seymour Hersch, "The Pardon," *Atlantic,* August 1983, 55–78.

165. David J. Vogler, *The Politics of Congress* (Boston: Allyn and Bacon, 1977), 15–20, 25–26, 34, 147–155, 243–245.

166. For a good account of Jimmy Carter's 1976 Iowa victory, see Hugh Winebrenner, *The Iowa Precinct Caucuses* (Ames: University of Iowa Press, 1987), 67–93.

167. Jules Witcover, *Marathon* (New York: Viking, 1977), 274–288.

168. Ibid., 545–560.

169. Responding to a question during a debate, Ford said: "There is no Soviet domination of Eastern Europe, and there never will be under a Ford administration. . . . I don't believe . . . that the Yugoslavians consider themselves dominated by the Soviet Union. I don't believe that the Romanians consider themselves dominated by the Soviet Union. I don't believe that the Poles consider themselves dominated by the Soviet Union" (ibid., 597, 598).

170. See Gary Sick, *October Surprise: America's Hostages in Iran and the Election of Ronald Reagan* (New York: Times Books, 1992).

171. Richard Harwood, ed., *The Pursuit of the Presidency 1980* (New York: Berkeley, 1980), 305–307.

172. Thomas Byrne Edsall, *The New Politics of Inequality* (New York: Norton, 1984), 77–78.

173. George Gilder, *Wealth and Poverty* (New York: Basic Books, 1980). Another prominent supply-side tract is that by Jude Wanniski, *The Way the World Works* (New York: Basic Books, 1978). A sympathetic summary of the whole movement can be found in Robert Craig Paul, *The Supply-Side Revolution* (Cambridge, Mass.: Harvard University Press, 1984).

174. Ferguson and Rogers, *Right Turn*, 86–88, n. 245.

175. Garry Wills, *Reagan's America: Innocents at Home* (Garden City, N.Y.: Doubleday, 1987), 387.

176. Ibid., 385.

177. Ferguson and Rogers, *Right Turn*.

178. Rep. Shirley Chisholm of Brooklyn, New York, was the first African American to seek a major-party nomination. Her participation in the 1972 Democratic primaries won 151 delegates.

179. Geraldine Ferraro, with Linda Bird Francke, *Ferraro: My Story* (New York: Bantam, 1985), 164.

180. Paul R. Abramson, John H. Aldrich, and David W. Rohde, *Change and Continuity in the 1984 Elections,* rev. ed. (Washington, D.C.: CQ Press, 1986), 58.

181. V. O. Key Jr., "A Theory of Critical Elections," *Journal of Politics* 17 (February 1955): 3–18.

182. Abramson et al., *Change and Continuity*, 286–287.

183. Michael Barone and Grant Ujifusa, *The Almanac of American Politics: 1984* (Washington, D.C.: National Journal, 1983), xiv. See also Ladd and Hadley, *American Party System*, 237–249.

184. Taylor, *See How They Run*, 76.

185. Also that year, two Supreme Court nominees, Robert H. Bork and Douglas H. Ginsburg, failed to win Senate confirmation. Bork lost because of his views on a wide variety of social issues, but many criticisms focused on his personality. Ginsburg withdrew from consideration after revelations that he had smoked marijuana as a student and law school professor.

186. Barbara Norrander, *Super Tuesday: Regional Politics and Presidential Primaries* (Lexington: University Press of Kentucky, 1992), 101.

187. In the twelve days after Bush picked Quayle, ABC, CBS, and NBC aired ninety-three stories about him—more than Michael Dukakis received during the whole primary season. Two-thirds of the stories were negative. See Taylor, *See How They Run*, 162.

188. Nelson W. Polsby and Aaron Wildavsky, *Presidential Elections: Contemporary Strategies of American Electoral Politics,* 8th ed. (New York: Basic Books, 1991), 248.

189. Quayle did not meet the requirements set for political science majors and failed the first general examination at DePauw University in Indiana. He also failed to gain admission to law school under the usual application procedure. A study of Quayle's congressional career concludes that Quayle had no policy achievements in the House of Representatives but mastered some policy issues in the Senate. See Anthony Lewis, "The Intimidated Press," *New York Times,* January 19, 1989, 27; and Richard F. Fenno Jr., *The Making of a Senator: Dan Quayle* (Washington, D.C.: CQ Press, 1988).

190. *The Presidency A to Z* (Washington, D.C.: Congressional Quarterly, 1992), 29.

191. Sidney Blumenthal, *Pledging Allegiance: The Last Campaign of the Cold War* (New York: HarperCollins, 1990), 317.

192. Michael Duffy and Dan Goodgame, *Marching in Place: The Status Quo Presidency of George Bush* (New York: Simon and Schuster, 1992), 267–268.

193. Quoted in Michael Nelson, "The Presidency: Clinton and the Cycle of Politics and Policy," in *The Elections of 1992*, ed. Michael Nelson (Washington, D.C.: CQ Press, 1993), 144.

194. Paul J. Quirk and Jon K. Dalager, "The Election: A 'New Democrat' and a New Kind of Presidential Campaign," in Nelson, *Elections of 1992*, 61.

195. The unofficial manifesto of this movement is that by George F. Will, *Restoration: Congress, Term Limits, and the Recovery of Deliberative Democracy* (New York: Free Press, 1993).

196. Perot's rescue of his employees from Tehran during the 1979 Iranian revolution, for example, resulted in a best-selling book—Ken Follett's *On Wings of Eagles* (New York: Morrow, 1983)—and a made-for-TV movie. Earlier, he had founded a national organization to support President Nixon's Vietnam policy. Later, his company's merger with General Motors provoked a public dispute that cast him as the problem solver and GM officials as entrenched bureaucrats.

197. Ryan J. Barilleaux and Randall E. Adkins, "The Nominations: Process and Patterns," in Nelson, *Elections of 1992,* 38–39.

198. See David Osborne and Ted Gaebler, *Reinventing Government: How the Entrepreneurial Spirit Is Transforming the Public Sector* (Reading, Mass.: Addison-Wesley, 1992), for a manifesto of Clinton's approach to government reform.

199. For an excellent treatment of the importance of the middle class and suburbanism on modern American politics, see Thomas Byrne Edsall and Mary D. Edsall, *Chain Reaction: The Impact of Race, Rights, and Taxes on American Politics* (New York: Norton, 1991).

200. Barilleaux and Adkins, "The Nominations," 48–49.

201. Duffy and Goodgame, *Marching in Place*.

202. *Congressional Quarterly Weekly Report,* supplements, July 4, 1992, 71, and August 8, 1992, 67.

203. Daniel Hellinger and Dennis R. Judd, *The Democratic Facade* (Belmont, Calif.: Wadsworth, 1994), 180.

204. Al Gore, *Earth in the Balance: Ecology and the Human Spirit* (Boston: Houghton Mifflin, 1992).

205. Ross K. Barker, "Sorting Out and Suiting Up: The Presidential Nominations," in *The Election of 1992*, ed. Gerald M. Pomper (Chatham, N.J.: Chatham House, 1993), 67.

206. See Mark J. Rozell and Clyde Wilcox, "It Isn't the Old Christian Right Anymore," *Los Angeles Times,* April 29, 1996, B5.

207. See Clyde Wilcox and Mark J. Rozell, "Dole's Delicate Balancing Act," *Christian Science Monitor,* June 4, 1996, 20.

208 ."Polls and the Election," *The Public Perspective,* December 1996/January 1997, 58.

209. Howard Kurtz, "A Big Story: But Only Behind the Scenes; Media Fretted Over Reporting Dole Affair," *Washington Post,* November 13, 1996, D1.

210. Green Party candidate Ralph Nader polled 0.7 percent and Libertarian Harry Browne polled 0.5 percent. Rhodes Cook, "Even with Higher Vote, Clinton Remains Minority President," *Congressional Quarterly Weekly Report,* January 18, 1997, 185–188.

211. Howard Fineman, "Clinton's Big Win," *Newsweek,* November 18, 1996, 8–13; Rhodes Cook, "Clinton's Easy Second-Term Win Riddles GOP Electoral Map," *Congressional Quarterly Weekly Report,* November 9, 1996, 3189–3194.

212. See Richard L. Berke, "Clinton Wins Second Term by Solid Margin," *New York Times,* November 6, 1996.

213. See Gregory L. Giroux, "In His Own Right," *Congressional Quarterly Democratic Convention Guide,* August 12, 2000, 9.

214. Michael Kelly, "The Democrats' Delusion," *Washington Post,* November 1, 2000, A33.

215. Jane Hall, "Gore Media Coverage: Playing Hardball," *Columbia Journalism Review,* September/October 2000, 30.

216. Rhodes Cook, "A Reprise of '60?" *The Rhodes Cook Letter,* September 2000, 4.

217. Matthew Vita, "2000's Stealth Issue: Impeachment's Effects Are Playing Out in Races from National to District Level," *Washington Post,* November 1, 2000, A1.

218. Rhodes Cook, "The Nader Factor: Overrated?" *The Rhodes Cook Letter,* January 2001, 7.

219. See Ken Ringle, "For Jan. 20, a Peaceful Precedent," *Washington Post,* January 10, 2001, C9.

3

Presidential Primaries

THE QUADRENNIAL PROCESS of electing a president has two distinct parts—the nominating process and the general election. Yet while the latter has been generally static in form—a one-day nationwide vote on the first Tuesday after the first Monday in November—the former is constantly evolving.

The changes in the nominating process over the course of the nation's history have been dramatic—from congressional caucuses in the early nineteenth century, through the heyday of the national conventions over the next century and a half, to the present nominating system, where conventions merely ratify the choices made months earlier in the election year by Democratic and Republican primary voters.

Nominations are now decided in the presidential primaries. And they have been since the Democrats' tumultuous convention in Chicago in 1968 encouraged both parties, but the Democrats in particular, to look for ways to open the nominating process to greater grass-roots participation.

The principal way to more voter involvement has been through the proliferation of presidential primaries. While a product of the Progressive Era in the early twentieth century, primaries were few and far between until the late 1960s. But after that, they quickly mushroomed in number—from fifteen in 1968, to thirty-six in 1980, to more than forty in 1996.

As the number of primaries grew, power in the nominating process quickly shifted from party kingmakers at the national conventions to voters in the primary states. Gone were the days when candidates could win their party's nomination without entering the primaries. No nominee of either major party has done so since Democrat Hubert H. Humphrey in 1968. Gone too were the days when candidates could win their party's nomination without first proving broad-based popularity among millions of voters. Since Democrat George McGovern in 1972, every major-party nominee has first been their party's highest vote-getter in the primaries. In the process, the once climactic conventions have become little more than giant pep rallies, ratifying the choices of Democratic and Republican primary voters.

"Front-Loaded" Process

As the number of primaries has grown, nominations have been settled earlier and earlier as more and more states have moved their primaries forward to dates near the beginning of the election year in a bid to heighten their influence (a process that has become known as "front-loading.")

In 1968 only one presidential primary (New Hampshire's) was held before the end of March. In 1980 ten states held primaries so early. By 1988 the number surpassed twenty, and in 2000, more than half the country held primary elections before the end of March.

The result has been an increasingly truncated nominating process that has followed a clear pattern. Early votes in Iowa and New Hampshire have winnowed the field to a handful of candidates. Then, after a short period of unpredictability, one candidate has scored a knockout in the glut of March primaries, with their victory ratified by a string of essentially meaningless primary votes over the spring months.

That is what happened in the campaign for the Republican nomination in 2000. Sen. John McCain of Arizona routed the GOP front-runner, Gov. George W. Bush of Texas, in New Hampshire, and battled him ballot for ballot in the array of Republican primaries scattered across the rest of February. But once the calendar flipped to March, Bush's superior organization and resources kicked in. On March 7 alone, eleven primaries were held from Maine to California. Bush triumphed convincingly in most of them—including the featured events in California, New York, and Ohio—driving McCain from the race and essentially wrapping up the nomination.

The Democratic presidential contest ended at the same time, as Vice President Al Gore defeated former Sen. Bill Bradley of New Jersey in all eleven of the day's Democratic primaries. Roughly five months remained before both parties' national conventions, but the nominations for both parties were settled.

Cut out of any meaningful role in the year's nominating process were Florida, Illinois, New Jersey, North Carolina, Pennsylvania, Wisconsin, and more than a dozen other states, which held their primaries after the competitive stage of the primary season had ended.

The last time that either the Democratic or Republican party had an elongated tug-of-war for its presidential nomination was 1984, when former vice president Walter F. Mondale and Sen. Gary Hart of Colorado battled into the final week of Democratic primaries before Mondale won the final delegates needed to nail down his nomination. Neither party has had a nominating contest that was even vaguely competitive at the time of its national convention since the 1976 Republican race between President Gerald R. Ford and actor and former Gov. Ronald Reagan of California.

REVERSAL OF FORTUNE

When they were regularly winning the White House in the 1970s and 1980s, Republicans showed little interest in tinkering with the nominating process; they were happy to leave that as a concern of the Democrats. But once the GOP began to lose

Types of Primaries and Procedures

In many respects, the presidential nominating process is like a modern-day Alice in Wonderland. Its basic dynamics do not always appear very logical. Primaries and caucuses are strewn across the calendar from January to June, culminating with party conventions in the summer. A nomination is won by a candidate attaining a majority of delegates, an honor that is formally bestowed at the conventions but for years has informally occurred much earlier during the primary season.

Size is less important in determining a state's importance in the nominating process than its tradition and place on the calendar (early is best). Hence, the quadrennial starring role for Iowa and New Hampshire, and the bit parts frequently assigned California and New York.

States have different ground rules in the nominating process. Some have caucuses, many more have primaries. Most primaries allocate a state's delegates, but some are nonbinding "beauty contests," with the delegates elected independently of the preference vote for presidential candidates.

Rules on voter participation vary from state to state. Some states hold "closed" contests, which are open only to a party's registered voters. Some hold "semi-open" events, which allow independent voters to participate along with registered members of the party. About half the states have "open" primaries or caucuses, in which any registered voter can participate. (The bulk of these states do not have party registration to begin with.)

The parties themselves also have different playing fields. Since 1980, Democrats have not allowed any states except Iowa, New Hampshire, and sometimes Maine, to hold a primary or caucus before early March. Republicans have had no such restriction, and in some years a state or two on the GOP side has voted in advance of Iowa and New Hampshire.

Since 1984, Democrats have reserved between 10 and 20 percent of their delegate seats for high-level party and elected officials (such as Democratic governors, members of Congress, and members of the party's national committee). Often called "superdelegates," these automatic delegates do not have to declare a presidential preference. (Republicans did not have "superdelegates" until the 2000 GOP convention approved automatic delegate seats for RNC members in 2004.) Since 1992, Democrats have required states to distribute delegates among their candidates in

proportion to their vote, statewide and in congressional districts, with 15 percent required to win a share.

Republicans, in contrast, allow a variety of delegate allocation methods, including proportional representation, statewide winner-take-all (in which the candidate winning the most votes statewide wins all the delegates), congressional district, and statewide winner-take-all (in which the high vote-getter in a district wins that district's delegates and the high vote-getter statewide wins all the at-large delegates), or some combination of the three.

Still another method is the selection of individual delegates in a "loophole," or direct election, primary. And in Republican caucus states, delegates often run as individuals and frequently are not officially allocated to any candidate.

How delegates are actually elected can vary from state to state. Most primary states hold presidential preference votes, in which voters choose among the candidates who have qualified for the ballot in their states. Although preference votes may be binding or nonbinding, in most states the vote is binding on the delegates, who are elected in the primary itself or chosen outside of it by a caucus process, by a state committee or by the candidates who have qualified to win delegates.

For those primaries in which the preference vote is binding upon delegates, state laws may vary as to the number of ballots through which delegates at the convention must remain committed. Delegates may be bound for as short as one ballot or as long as a candidate remains in the race. National Democratic rules were changed in 1980 to bind delegates for one ballot unless released by the candidate they were elected to support. The rule, though, became a flash point of controversy between the front-runner, President Jimmy Carter, and his major challenger, Sen. Edward M. Kennedy of Massachusetts. The Carter forces prevailed in having the rule sustained at the 1980 convention, but it was subsequently dropped during the quadrennial review of party rules after the election.

Until 1980 the Republicans had a rule requiring delegates bound to a specific candidate by state law in primary states to vote for that candidate at the convention regardless of their personal presidential preferences. That rule was repealed at the party's July 1980 convention.

presidential elections in the 1990s, many Republicans began to decry the "front-loaded" primary calendar that produced nominees within a few weeks of voting.

At their convention in San Diego in 1996, Republicans approved a rules change designed to help spread out the calendar. States were offered bonus delegates the later they held their primary or caucus. It did not get many takers, though, in 2000.

But in the wake of that year's Bush-McCain contest, a party commission headed by former Tennessee senator and national GOP chairman Bill Brock recommended that the presidential primary calendar be dramatically overhauled, so that small

states would vote first in 2004 and large states would vote last.

States were to be grouped into four "pods" of roughly equal number, with each pod voting over the course of a month. The initial calendar called for voting from March to June, but in the course of discussion the calendar was moved up a month to start in February and end in May. Still, the fourth pod was to be comprised of the largest states, holding roughly half the delegates. The idea was to slow the rush to judgment evident in the "front-loaded" primary system by making it mathematically impossible for a candidate to amass a majority of delegates before most, if not all, of the states had voted.

Table 3-1
Votes Cast and Delegates Selected in Presidential Primaries, 1912–2000

| Year | Democratic Party | | | Republican Party | | | Total | |
	Number of primaries	Votes cast	Delegates selected through primaries (%)	Number of primaries	Votes cast	Delegates selected through primaries (%)	Votes cast	Delegates selected through primaries (%)
1912	12	974,775	32.9	13	2,261,240	41.7	3,236,015	37.3
1916	20	1,187,691	53.5	20	1,923,374	58.9	3,111,065	56.2
1920	16	571,671	44.6	20	3,186,248	57.8	3,757,919	51.2
1924	14	763,858	35.5	17	3,525,185	45.3	4,289,043	40.4
1928	16	1,264,220	42.2	15	4,110,288	44.9	5,374,508	43.5
1932	16	2,952,933	40.0	14	2,346,996	37.7	5,299,929	38.8
1936	14	5,181,808	36.5	12	3,319,810	37.5	8,501,618	37.0
1940	13	4,468,631	35.8	13	3,227,875	38.8	7,696,506	37.3
1944	14	1,867,609	36.7	13	2,271,605	38.7	4,139,214	37.7
1948	14	2,151,865	36.3	12	2,653,255	36.0	4,805,120	36.1
1952	16	4,928,006	38.7	13	7,801,413	39.0	12,729,419	38.8
1956	19	5,832,592	42.7	19	5,828,272	44.8	11,660,864	43.7
1960	16	5,687,742	38.3	15	5,537,967	38.6	11,224,631	38.5
1964	16	6,247,435	45.7	16	5,935,339	45.6	12,182,774	45.6
1968	15	7,535,069	40.2	15	4,473,551	38.1	12,008,620	39.1
1972	21	15,993,965	65.3	20	6,188,281	56.8	22,182,246	61.0
1976	27	16,052,652	76.0	26	10,374,125	71.0	26,426,777	73.5
1980	34	18,747,825	71.8	34	12,690,451	76.0	31,438,276	73.7
1984	29	18,009,217	52.4	25	6,575,651	71.0	24,584,868	59.6
1988	36	22,961,936	66.6	36	12,165,115	76.9	35,127,051	70.2
1992	39	20,239,385	66.9	38	12,696,547	83.9	32,935,932	72.7
1996	35	10,996,395	65.3	42	14,233,939	84.6	25,230,334	69.2
2000	40	14,045,745	64.6	43	17,156,117	83.8	31,201,862	70.8

Source: Percentages of delegates selected are from Congressional Quarterly.

The idea, dubbed the "Delaware Plan" because of its state of origin, was controversial, particularly among the larger states, who feared a loss of influence if they were required to vote en masse at the end of the primary season. The "Delaware Plan," though, did win the approval of the rules committee of the Republican National Committee (RNC) in May 2000 and the full RNC itself on the eve of the party's convention that summer.

But the plan was defeated in the convention rules committee July 28, after the Bush campaign shifted from a position of neutrality to opposition. Several reasons were cited for the eleventh hour change of heart, including complaints from the big states over their potential loss of influence, the lack of an agreement with the Democrats over a common course of action, and a loss of control by the states over their primary or caucus dates if the "Delaware Plan" were imposed. But it was also obvious that the Bush campaign wanted an harmonious convention without any contested issues on the floor.

CHANGE CERTAIN IN FUTURE

Even if the "Delaware Plan" had been approved by the Republican convention, it still would have faced an uncertain future. Earlier in 2000, the rules committee of the Democratic Party had expressed support for the status quo and urged Republicans to embrace the Democratic primary calendar, which allowed Iowa and New Hampshire to vote first but prohibited other states from voting before the first Tuesday in March. Meanwhile, the nation's secretaries of state recommended a different solution, a system of regional primaries, whose order would be rotated every four years. Yet with neither of the major parties rallying behind it, the secretaries' plan had little chance of being embraced.

Still, even without the Democrats or Republicans opting for bold changes, the nominating process is by nature evolutionary. Every four years at least a few states move their primary or caucus date, creating a new calendar. And nearly every four years, at least one of the parties makes a change in their rules that proves significant. In 2000 Republicans added four delegates to each state's total in 2004 and created automatic delegate seats for the members of the RNC.

An Evolutionary Process

During the early years of the nation, presidential nominations were decided by party caucuses in Congress (derided by their critics as "King Caucus"). At the dawn of the Jacksonian era in the 1830s, though, the nominating role shifted to national conventions, a broader-based venue where party leaders from around the country held sway.

In the early twentieth century, presidential primaries appeared on the scene, adding a new element of grass-roots democracy and voter input. But for the next half century, the primaries were relatively few in number and played a limited advisory role. Nominations continued to be settled in the party conventions.

After World War II American society became more mobile and media-oriented, and once-powerful party organizations began to lose their clout. An increasing number of presidential as-

Democrat Hubert H. Humphrey in 1968 was the last candidate to win a major party's presidential nomination without entering the primaries.

pirants saw the primaries as a way to generate popular support that might overcome the resistance of party leaders. Both Republican Dwight D. Eisenhower in 1952 and Democrat John F. Kennedy in 1960 scored a string of primary victories that demonstrated their vote-getting appeal and made their nominations possible.

Yet the conventions continued to reign supreme through the 1960s, although 1968 proved to be a watershed year in the evolution of the nominating process. Sens. Eugene McCarthy of Minnesota and Robert F. Kennedy of New York used the handful of Democratic primaries that spring to protest the war in Vietnam, together taking more than two-thirds of the party's primary vote and driving President Lyndon B. Johnson from the race.

History might have been different if Kennedy had not been assassinated after his victory in the California primary that June. But without Kennedy on the scene, the party's embattled leadership was able to maintain a tenuous control of the convention that August in Chicago, nominating Vice President Humphrey, who had not competed in a single primary state.

But Humphrey's nomination came at a price. For the first time in several generations, the legitimacy of the convention itself was thrown into question. And as an outgrowth, a series of Democratic rules review commissions began to overhaul the presidential nominating process to encourage much greater grass-roots participation.

CHANGE COMES QUICKLY

The immediate result was a dramatic increase in presidential primaries that enhanced the chances of long-shot outsiders, such as George McGovern and Jimmy Carter, who captured the Democratic nomination in 1972 and 1976, respectively.

In the 1970s, the primary calendar started slowly, giving little-known candidates the time to raise money and momentum after doing well in the early rounds. Most of the primaries then were held in May and June.

But the layout of the nominating process has been less favorable to dark horses since then. In the 1980s Democrats reinserted party and elected officials into the process, creating a new category of automatic delegate seats for them that have come to be known as "superdelegates." And states began to move forward on the calendar in a bid to increase their influence, heightening the need for candidates to be well organized and well funded at the beginning of the primary season.

Democrats sought to put a brake on the calendar sprawl toward the beginning of the election year by instituting the "window," which prohibited any of the party's primaries or caucuses from being held before early March, with the exception of Iowa, New Hampshire, and for a while, Maine.

With the creation of that early March firewall, many states parked their primary in March—gradually at first, but then in tidal wave proportions in 1988, with the creation of a full-scale primary vote across the South on the second Tuesday in March that came to be known as "Super Tuesday."

The event did not have the effect that its Democratic sponsors had hoped for, in terms of steering the nomination toward a centrist son of the South, such as Sen. Al Gore of Tennessee. In the early 1990s, the early March southern primary lost some of its members.

But the concept of early regional primaries took hold elsewhere. In 1996 all of New England except New Hampshire voted on the first Tuesday in March. Six southern states, led by Texas and Florida, voted on the second Tuesday. Four states in the industrial Midwest—Illinois, Michigan, Ohio, and Wisconsin—voted on the third Tuesday in March. And California anchored a three-state western primary on the fourth Tuesday.

In 2000 the bulk of the New England states continued to vote on the first Tuesday in March, and much of the South on the second Tuesday. But the big story was the dramatic movement toward a broad-based, coast-to-coast vote on the first Tuesday in March. The day's primaries and caucuses involved states with nearly 40 percent of the nation's population, including three of the seven most populous states—California, New York, and Ohio.

Current Arrangement

Even though much of the primary calendar has changed dramatically over the last few decades, the accepted starting points have remained Iowa and New Hampshire (even though other states have occasionally voted before them).

Both states have made their early events into cottage industries, but the candidates and the media have helped make them so. More than ever, Iowa and New Hampshire are about the only places left where candidates have some control over their destinies. They can woo voters one-on-one, whether in bowling alleys, coffee shops, or the frequent gatherings in neighborhood living rooms.

For if there is one thing that has become certain in recent years, once the New Hampshire primary is over and candidates must compete in several states simultaneously, there is a frenetic burst of tarmac-to-tarmac campaigning heavily dependent on media advertising.

With one exception, every presidential nominee since 1976 has won either Iowa or New Hampshire, and finished no lower than third in the other. The exception was Bill Clinton in 1992, who did not seriously contest Iowa in deference to the home-state appeal of Sen. Tom Harkin and finished second in New Hampshire behind former Sen. Paul E. Tsongas of Massachusetts.

Iowa and New Hampshire illustrate the two different types of delegate-selection processes that states have to choose from. Iowa is a caucus; New Hampshire is a primary. Primaries require voters only to cast a ballot, an exercise that usually takes just a few minutes. The deliberative nature of a neighborhood caucus, though, often requires the commitment of an afternoon or evening.

A SMALL SLICE OF THE ELECTORATE

Voter turnout is usually much higher in a primary than a caucus, but even in primaries the turnout is much lower than a general election. In New Hampshire, for instance, where interest in the presidential primary is probably greater than any other state, nearly 400,000 voters turned out in February 2000 for the presidential primary.

The disparity is much greater in many other states. Roughly 35 million votes were cast in all the presidential primaries in 2000. Meanwhile, turnout in the handful of states that held caucuses was no more than several hundred thousand more voters. By comparison, 96 million voters turned out for the 1996 general election.

Rules governing voter participation play a role in the comparatively low turnouts for the nominating process. Every primary is not as open as a general election, where any registered voter can participate. A number of states limit participation to registered Democratic and Republican voters. Some others allow independents to participate, but list them on the voting rolls afterward as members of the party in which they cast their primary ballot.

Still, the vast majority of registered voters across the country can participate in a presidential primary or caucus if they want. The fact that more do not has generated the conventional wisdom that the nominating process is dominated by ideological activists—liberals on the Democratic side, conservatives on the Republican.

That is debatable in the primaries, where the winners in recent years have been from the mainstreams of both parties. An ideological bent is usually more evident in the low-turnout world of the caucuses, where a small cadre of dedicated voters can significantly affect the outcome.

When religious broadcaster Pat Robertson tried for the Republican presidential nomination in 1988, for instance, he won first-round caucus voting in three states and finished second in three others, including Iowa. But Robertson did not come close that year to winning a presidential primary.

CLUES TO THE FALL

It has been a matter of debate within the political community whether the current primary-dominated nominating process is better than the old system, in which party leaders controlled the selection process.

But it is a fact that the increased number of primaries helps provide valuable clues about the vote-getting potential of candidates in the general election. Nominees that have exhibited broad-based appeal among the diverse array of primary voters in the winter and spring have gone on to be quite competitive in the fall, while those nominees who have struggled through the primaries showing limited appeal among one or two of their party's major constituency groups have usually been buried under landslides in November.

A less reliable indicator of what will happen in the fall is the number of votes cast in each party's primaries. In every year from 1956 through 1992, more ballots were cast in Democratic than Republican primaries. In part, it was due to the simple fact that through much of this period, Democrats outnumbered Republicans.

But it also reflected the fact that the Democratic primaries drew more voter interest because they often exhibited more conflict between competing constituencies within the party. That kind of political drama and angst was good for primary turnout, but not for the party's chances in the fall elections, as Republicans won most of the presidential contests in this period.

Legacy of the Progressive Era

Yet, entrenched as they now are in the electoral process, primaries are still relatively recent replacements for the old smoke-filled rooms where party bosses once dictated the choice of presidential nominees.

Presidential primaries originated as an outgrowth of the Progressive movement in the early twentieth century. Progressives, populists, and reformers in general were fighting state and municipal corruption. They objected to the links between political bosses and big business and advocated returning the government to the people.

Part of this "return to the people" was a turn away from what were looked upon as boss-dominated conventions. It was only a matter of time before the primary idea spread from state and local elections to presidential contests. Because there was no provision for a nationwide primary, state primaries were initiated to choose delegates to the national party conventions (delegate-selection primaries) and to register voters' preferences on their parties' eventual presidential nominees (preference primaries).

Florida enacted the first presidential primary law in 1901. The law gave party officials an option of holding a party primary to choose any party candidate for public office, as well as del-

Selection by Caucus Method

In the current primary-dominated era of presidential politics, which began two decades ago, caucuses have survived in the quiet backwater of the nominating process.

The impact of caucuses decreased in the 1970s as the number of primaries grew dramatically. Previously, a candidate sought to run well in primary states mainly to have a bargaining chip with which to deal with powerful leaders in the caucus states. Republicans Barry Goldwater in 1964 and Richard Nixon in 1968 and Democrat Hubert H. Humphrey in 1968 all built up solid majorities among caucus state delegates that carried them to their parties' nominations. Humphrey did not compete in a single primary state in 1968.

After 1968, candidates placed their principal emphasis on primaries. First George McGovern in 1972—and then incumbent Republican President Gerald R. Ford and Democratic challenger Jimmy Carter in 1976—won nomination by securing large majorities of the primary state delegates. Neither McGovern nor Ford won a majority of the caucus state delegates. Carter was able to win a majority only after his opponents' campaigns collapsed.

Complex Method

Compared with a primary, the caucus system is complicated. Instead of focusing on a single primary election ballot, the caucus presents a multitiered system that involves meetings scheduled over several weeks, sometimes even months. There is mass participation at the first level only, with meetings often lasting several hours and attracting only the most enthusiastic and dedicated party members.

The operation of the caucus varies from state to state, and each party has its own set of rules. Most begin with precinct caucuses or some other type of local mass meeting open to all party voters.

Participants, often publicly declaring their votes, elect delegates to the next stage in the process.

In smaller states such as Delaware and Hawaii, delegates are elected directly to a state convention, where the national convention delegates are chosen. In larger states such as Iowa, there is at least one, sometimes two, more steps. Delegates in Iowa are elected at the precinct caucuses to county conventions, which are followed by congressional district conventions and the state convention, the two levels where the national convention delegates are chosen.

Participation, even at the first level of the caucus process, is much lower than in primaries. Caucus participants usually are local party leaders and activists. Many rank-and-file voters find a caucus complex, confusing, or intimidating.

As a result, caucuses are usually considered tailor-made for candidates with a cadre of passionately dedicated supporters. That was evident as long ago as 1972, when a surprisingly strong showing in the Iowa precinct caucuses helped to propel Sen. George McGovern of South Dakota, an ardent foe of the Vietnam War, toward the Democratic nomination.

In a caucus state the focus is on one-on-one campaigning. Time, not money, is usually the most valuable resource. Because organization and personal campaigning are so important, an early start is far more crucial in a caucus state than in a primary. And because only a small segment of the electorate is targeted in most caucus states, candidates usually use media advertising sparingly.

The lone exception is Iowa. As the kick-off point for the quadrennial nominating process, Iowa has recently become a more expensive stop for ambitious presidential candidates, as they must shell out money for everything from straw votes to radio and TV advertising. But the accent in Iowa, as in other caucus states, is

egates to the national conventions. However, there was no provision for placing names of presidential candidates on the ballot—either in the form of a preference vote or with information indicating the preference of the candidates for convention delegates.

Wisconsin's progressive Republican politician, Gov. Robert M. La Follette, gave a major boost to the presidential primary following the 1904 Republican National Convention. It was at that convention that the credentials of La Follette's progressive delegation were rejected and a regular Republican delegation from Wisconsin was seated. Angered by what he considered his unfair treatment, La Follette returned to his home state and began pushing for a presidential primary law. The result was the Wisconsin law of 1905 mandating the direct election of national convention delegates. The law, however, did not include a provision for indicating the delegates' presidential preference.

Pennsylvania followed Wisconsin in 1906 with a statute providing that each candidate for delegate to a national convention

could have printed beside his name on the official primary ballot the name of the presidential candidate he would support at the convention. However, no member of either party exercised this option in the 1908 primary.

La Follette's sponsorship of the delegate-selection primary helped make the concept a part of the progressive political program. The growth of the Progressive movement rapidly resulted in the enactment of presidential primary laws in other states.

The next step in presidential primaries—the preferential vote for president—took place in Oregon. There, in 1910, Sen. Jonathan Bourne, a progressive Republican colleague of La Follette (then a senator), sponsored a referendum to establish a presidential preference primary, with delegates legally bound to support the primary winner. By 1912, with Oregon in the lead, fully a dozen states had enacted presidential primary laws that provided for either direct election of delegates, a preferential vote, or both. The number had expanded to twenty-six states by 1916.

still on grass-roots organization. That was underscored in 1996, when the late-starting campaign of wealthy publisher Steve Forbes spent lavishly on an Iowa media blitz that netted only 10 percent of the Republican caucus vote.

Although the basic steps in the caucus process are the same for both parties, the rules that govern them are vastly different. Democratic rules have been revamped substantially since 1968, establishing national standards for grass-roots participation. Republican rules have remained largely unchanged, with the states given wide latitude in drawing up their delegate-selection plans.

Caucuses

For both the Republican and Democratic parties, the percentage of delegates elected from caucus states was on a sharp decline throughout the 1970s. But the Democrats broke the downward trend and elected more delegates by the caucus process in 1980 than in 1976.

Between 1980 and 1984 six states switched from a primary to a caucus system; none the other way. Since 1984 the trend has turned back toward primaries. In 1996 primaries were held in forty-one states, the District of Columbia, and Puerto Rico. The Democrats elected 65.3 percent of their national convention delegates in primaries, against only 16.8 percent in caucuses. (The remaining 17.9 percent were "superdelegate" party and elected officials.) The Republicans in 1992 chose 84.6 percent of delegates in primaries and the rest by caucus or state committee, with no superdelegates. And the proportions have stayed roughly the same since then.

A strong showing in the caucuses by Walter F. Mondale in 1984 led many Democrats—and not only supporters of his rivals—to conclude that caucuses are inherently unfair. The mainstream Democratic coalition of party activists, labor union members, and teachers dominated the caucuses in Mondale's behalf.

The caucus also came in for criticism in 1988. The Iowa Democratic caucuses were seen as an unrepresentative test dominated by liberal interest groups. And the credibility of the caucuses was shaken by the withdrawal from the race of the two winners—Democrat Richard A. Gephardt and Republican Robert Dole—within a month after the caucuses were held. Furthermore, several other state caucuses featured vicious infighting between supporters of various candidates.

In 1992 the presence of a favorite son, Sen. Tom Harkin, among the leading Democratic candidates for president, further diminished the Iowa caucus' significance as a rival to the New Hampshire primary as an early indicator of the candidate to beat for the nomination. Harkin easily won his state's party caucus, but he soon dropped out after fading in the primaries elsewhere.

Yet in 1996 and again in 2000, Iowa was back enjoying center stage. And in both years, the campaigns of the Republican nominee—Dole and Gov. George W. Bush of Texas, respectively—were successfully launched in Iowa, as was the campaign of Vice President Al Gore in 2000 on the Democratic side.

The major complaint about the caucus process is that it does not involve enough voters, and that the low turnouts are not so representative of voter sentiment as a higher-turnout primary. The combined turnout for both parties for the Iowa caucuses in 2000, for example, was roughly 150,000, less than half the number that turned out for the New Hampshire primary a week later.

Staunch defenders, however, believe a caucus has party-building attributes a primary cannot match. They note that several hours at a caucus can involve voters in a way that quickly casting a primary ballot does not. Following caucus meetings, the state party comes away with lists of thousands of voters who can be tapped to volunteer time or money, or even to run for local office. And, while the multitiered caucus process is often a chore for the state party to organize, a primary is substantially more expensive.

PRIMARIES AND CONVENTIONS

The first major test of the impact of presidential primary laws—in 1912—demonstrated that victories in the primaries did not ensure a candidate's nomination. Former President Theodore Roosevelt, campaigning in twelve Republican primaries, won nine of them, including Ohio, the home state of incumbent Republican president William Howard Taft. Roosevelt lost to Taft by a narrow margin in Massachusetts and to La Follette in North Dakota and Wisconsin.

Despite this impressive string of primary victories, the convention rejected Roosevelt in favor of Taft. Taft supporters dominated the Republican National Committee, which ran the convention, and the convention's credentials committee, which ruled on contested delegates. Moreover, Taft was backed by many state organizations, especially in the South, where most delegates were chosen by caucuses or conventions dominated by party leaders.

On the Democratic side, the convention more closely reflected the primary results. Gov. Woodrow Wilson of New Jersey and Speaker of the House Champ Clark of Missouri were closely matched in total primary votes, with Wilson only 29,632 votes ahead of Clark. Wilson emerged with the nomination after a long convention struggle with Clark.

Likewise, in 1916, Democratic primary results foreshadowed the winner of the nomination, although Wilson, who was then the incumbent, had no major opposition for renomination. But once again, Republican presidential primaries had little impact upon the nominating process at the convention. The eventual nominee, Supreme Court Justice Charles Evans Hughes, had won only two primaries.

In 1920 presidential primaries did not play a major role in determining the winner of either party's nomination. James M. Cox, the eventual Democratic nominee, ran in only one primary, his home state of Ohio. Most of the Democratic primaries featured favorite-son candidates, unpledged delegate slates, or write-in votes. And at the convention Democrats took forty-four ballots to settle on Cox.

Choosing a Running Mate: The Balancing Act

In modern times, with presidential candidates wrapping up their party's nominations early in the primary season, the greatest suspense before a national convention has centered on the selection of a running mate. But this closely watched selection process is a recent development.

During the country's first years, the runner-up for the presidency automatically took the second slot, although that system did not last long. In 1800 Thomas Jefferson and Aaron Burr found themselves in a tie for electoral votes. Neither man's supporters were willing to settle for the lesser office. The deadlock went to the House of Representatives, where Jefferson needed thirty-six ballots to clinch the presidency. It also led to the Twelfth Amendment to the U.S. Constitution, ratified in 1804, providing for separate Electoral College balloting for president and vice president. With the emergence of political parties after 1800, candidates ran as teams. Once party conventions began in 1831, delegates, with the guidance of party bosses, began to do the choosing.

In fact, it was only in 1940 that presidential nominees began regularly hand-picking their running mates. That year, after failing to persuade Secretary of State Cordell Hull to accept the vice presidency, Franklin D. Roosevelt forced Henry A. Wallace on a reluctant Democratic convention by threatening to not run a third time if Wallace was rejected. The only exception to the practice Roosevelt established came in 1956, when Democrat Adlai E. Stevenson left the choice up to the convention.

If the selection of a running mate often seemed like something of an afterthought, it could be because the position itself was not especially coveted. John Adams, the first to hold the job, once complained, "My country has in its wisdom contrived for me the most insignificant office that ever the intention of man contrived or his imagination conceived." More than a century later Thomas R. Marshall, Woodrow Wilson's vice president, expressed a similarly dismal view: "Once there were two brothers. One ran away to sea; the other was elected Vice President. And nothing was ever heard of either of them again."

Writing in *Atlantic* in 1974, historian Arthur Schlesinger Jr. suggested the office be done away with. "It is a doomed office," he commented. "The Vice President has only one serious thing to do: that is, to wait around for the President to die." But there is a reasonable chance that whoever fills the position will get a chance to move up, either by succession or election. As of 2000, fourteen presidents had held the second-ranking post, seven in the twentieth century.

Also, since the 1970s the vice presidency has evolved from the somnolent office it once was; during this period four vice presidents enjoyed responsibility their predecessors did not. Nelson A. Rockefeller, who served under Gerald R. Ford, was given considerable authority in domestic policy coordination. Walter F. Mondale and George Bush helped to set policy for their respective presidents. And Bill Clinton placed Al Gore in charge of a "reinventing government" task force as well as environmental and high-tech initiatives. Many aspiring politicians now see the office as the premier base from which to campaign for the presidency.

Yet whoever is selected is often scrutinized for how well the choice balances (or unbalances) the ticket. One important factor is geography, which Clinton of Arkansas used unconventionally in choosing Sen. Gore of Tennessee to form the first successful all-southern ticket in 164 years. Other traditional factors weighed by nominees are religion and ethnicity. In modern national politics, however, those considerations seemed to be losing their place to race, gender, and age. In 1984, for example, the Democrats chose Rep. Geraldine A. Ferraro of New York to be their vice-presidential candidate, the first woman to receive a major party nomination.

Although no African American has so far been selected by either party, many Democrats thought that Jesse Jackson deserved second place on the ticket in 1988. Jackson had received 29 percent of the primary vote to 43 percent for Michael Dukakis. Instead, the fifty-four-year-old Dukakis chose Sen. Lloyd Bentsen of Texas, then sixty-seven, balancing the Democratic ticket by age as well as geographically and philosophically.

In 1988 George Bush surprised many by selecting Sen. Dan Quayle of Indiana. Quayle was forty-one years old and had a relatively brief career in politics—two terms in the House of Representatives before his election to the Senate in 1980. Because of Quayle's youth and good looks, it was even suggested by some critics that Bush had selected him to appeal to young voters and women. Some disturbing revelations about Quayle's education and National Guard service along with his tendency to misspeak fostered doubts that he was qualified to serve a "heartbeat" away from the presidency. But Bush vigorously defended his choice, and the two won in 1988, before losing their bid for reelection in 1992.

For his running mate, the forty-six-year-old Clinton, in another unbalancing act, selected someone in his own age group (Gore, forty-four) rather than an elder statesman like Bentsen (who served as Clinton's first secretary of the Treasury). But what the Clinton-Gore ticket lacked in the traditional sense, it made up with a balance of the candidate's other attributes. As governor of Arkansas, Clinton lacked foreign policy experience and had a mixed environmental record. Gore had a strong foreign policy and environmental record in Congress.

In 2000 Vice President Gore ran for the White House against Bush's son, Texas governor George W. Bush, who went a different direction from his father in choosing a running mate. The younger Bush chose an experienced Washington hand, Richard B. Cheney, who was a former Wyoming representative and defense secretary in the elder Bush's administration.

As for Gore, he too broke new ground. Rather than pick a southern baby-boomer as Clinton had, he chose Connecticut Senator Joseph I. Lieberman, the fifty-eight-year-old chair of the centrist Democratic Leadership Council and the first member of the Jewish faith to win a place on the national ticket of either major party.

Similarly, the main entrants in the Republican presidential primaries that year failed to capture their party's nomination. Sen. Warren G. Harding of Ohio, the compromise choice, won the primary in his home state but lost badly in Indiana and garnered only a handful of votes elsewhere. The three primary leaders—Sen. Hiram Johnson of California, Gen. Leonard Wood of New Hampshire, and Gov. Frank O. Lowden of Illinois—lost out in the end.

After the first wave of enthusiasm for presidential primaries, interest in them waned. By 1935, eight states had repealed their presidential primary laws. The diminution of reform zeal during the 1920s, the preoccupation of the country with the Great Depression in the 1930s, and war in the 1940s appeared to have been leading factors in this decline. Also, party leaders were not enthusiastic about primaries; the cost of conducting them was relatively high, both for the candidates and the states. Many presidential candidates ignored the primaries, and voter participation often was low.

But after World War II, interest picked up again. Some politicians with presidential ambitions, knowing the party leadership was not enthusiastic about their candidacies, entered the primaries to try to generate a bandwagon effect. In 1948 Harold Stassen, Republican governor of Minnesota from 1939 to 1943, entered presidential primaries in opposition to the Republican organization and made some headway before losing in Oregon to Gov. Thomas E. Dewey of New York. And in 1952, Sen. Estes Kefauver, D-Tenn., riding a wave of public recognition as head of the Senate Organized Crime Investigating Committee, challenged Democratic Party leaders by winning several primaries, including an upset of President Harry S. Truman in New Hampshire. The Eisenhower-Taft struggle for the Republican Party nomination that year also stimulated interest in the primaries.

In 1960 Sen. John F. Kennedy of Massachusetts challenged Sen. Hubert Humphrey of Minnesota in two primaries: Wisconsin, which bordered on Humphrey's home state, and West Virginia, a labor state with few Catholic voters. (Kennedy was Roman Catholic, and some questioned whether voters would elect a Catholic president.) After Kennedy won both primaries, Humphrey withdrew from the race. The efforts of party leaders to draft an alternative to Kennedy came to be viewed as undemocratic by rank-and-file voters. The primary now significantly challenged approval by party leaders as the preferred route to the nomination.

Similarly, Sen. Barry M. Goldwater, R-Ariz., in 1964, former vice president Richard Nixon in 1968, and Sen. George S. McGovern, D-S.D., in 1972, were able to use the primaries to show their vote-getting and organizational abilities on the way to becoming their party's presidential nominees.

THE DEMOCRATS BEGIN TO TINKER

Despite the growing importance of primaries, party leaders until 1968 maintained some control of the nominating process. With only a handful of the fifteen to twenty primaries regularly contested, candidates could count on a short primary season. They began in New Hampshire in March, then tested their appeal during the spring in Wisconsin, Nebraska, Oregon, and

---

Presidents' Reelection Chances

The record of twentieth-century U.S. presidential elections indicates that a smooth path to renomination is essential for incumbents seeking reelection. Every president who actively sought renomination this century was successful. And those who were virtually unopposed within their own party won another term. But all the presidents who faced significant opposition for renomination ended up losing in the general election.

The following chart shows the presidents who sought reelection to a second term since 1900, whether they had "clear sailing" or "tough sledding" for renomination and their fate in the general election.

A president with an asterisk (*) next to his name was, like Ronald Reagan in 1984, completing his first full four-year term when he sought reelection. A dash (—) indicates there were no presidential preference primaries. The primary vote for President Lyndon B. Johnson in 1964 included the vote cast for favorite sons and uncommitted delegate slates; Johnson was subsequently nominated by acclamation at the Democratic convention. George Bush in 1992 had to fight off a significant challenge by Patrick J. Buchanan in the Republican primaries before he went on to win 95 percent of the convention delegates.

	Incumbent's Percentage of:		
	Primary vote	Convention delegates	General election result
'Clear Sailing'			
William McKinley (1900) *	—	100%	Won
Theodore Roosevelt (1904)	—	100	Won
Woodrow Wilson (1916) *	99%	99	Won
Calvin Coolidge (1924)	68	96	Won
Franklin D. Roosevelt (1936) *	93	100	Won
Franklin D. Roosevelt (1940)	72	86	Won
Franklin D. Roosevelt (1944)	71	92	Won
Harry S. Truman (1948)	64	75	Won
Dwight D. Eisenhower (1956) *	86	100	Won
Lyndon B. Johnson (1964)	88	100	Won
Richard Nixon (1972) *	87	99	Won
Ronald Reagan (1984) *	99	100	Won
Bill Clinton (1996) *	88	100	Won
'Tough Sledding'			
William H. Taft (1912) *	34%	52%	Lost
Herbert Hoover (1932) *	33	98	Lost
Gerald R. Ford (1976)	53	53	Lost
Jimmy Carter (1980) *	51	64	Lost
George Bush (1992) *	72	95	Lost

California before resuming their courtship of party leaders. In 1968—admittedly an unusual year, with incumbent Democratic president Lyndon B. Johnson suddenly withdrawing from his race for reelection, and the leading Democratic candidate (Sen. Robert F. Kennedy of New York) assassinated a few weeks before the convention—Vice President Humphrey was able to gain the party's nomination without entering a single primary.

But after 1968, the Democrats began tinkering with the nominating rules, in an effort to reduce the alienation of liberals and minorities from the political system and to allow the people to

VPs Who Have Become President

Fourteen men who served as vice president have become president: John Adams, Thomas Jefferson, Martin Van Buren, John Tyler, Millard Fillmore, Andrew Johnson, Chester A. Arthur, Theodore Roosevelt, Calvin Coolidge, Harry S. Truman, Richard M. Nixon, Lyndon B. Johnson, Gerald R. Ford, and George Bush.

Of those, all but Adams, Jefferson, Van Buren, Nixon, and Bush first became president on the death or resignation of their predecessor. Nine vice presidents since 1900 have run unsuccessfully for president:

• Thomas R. Marshall, Democratic vice president under Woodrow Wilson from 1913 to 1921, failed to win the nomination in 1920.

• Charles G. Dawes, Republican vice president under Coolidge from 1925 to 1929, unsuccessfully sought the nomination in 1928 and 1932.

• John Nance Garner, Democratic vice president under Franklin D. Roosevelt from 1933 to 1941, ran unsuccessfully for the nomination in 1940.

• Henry A. Wallace, Democratic vice president under Roosevelt from 1941 to 1945, was Progressive Party nominee in 1948.

• Alben W. Barkley, Democratic vice president under Truman from 1949 to 1953, failed to win the 1952 nomination.

• Nixon, Republican vice president under Dwight D. Eisenhower from 1953 to 1961, was the GOP nominee in 1960. (He won in 1968 and 1972.)

• Hubert H. Humphrey, Democratic vice president under Lyndon Johnson from 1965 to 1969, was the Democratic nominee in 1968.

• Walter F. Mondale, Democratic vice president under Jimmy Carter from 1977 to 1981, was the Democratic nominee in 1984.

• Al Gore, Democratic vice president under Bill Clinton from 1993 to 2001, was the Democratic nominee in 2000.

Sen. Edward M. Kennedy of Massachusetts. With no opposition in the late primary contests, Reagan emerged as a more one-sided choice of GOP primary voters. He finished nearly 4.8 million votes ahead of his closest competitor, George Bush.

Disheartened by Carter's massive defeat in 1980, the Democrats revised their nominating rules for the 1984 election. The party created a new bloc of so-called "superdelegates"—that is, delegate seats were reserved for party leaders who were not formally committed to any presidential candidate. This reform had two main goals. First, Democratic leaders wanted to ensure that the party's elected officials would participate at the convention. Second, they wanted to ensure that these uncommitted party leaders could play a major role in selecting the presidential nominee if no candidate was a clear front-runner.

While the reforms of the 1970s were designed to give more influence to grass-roots activists and less to party regulars, this revision was intended to bring about a deliberative process in which experienced party leaders could help select a consensus Democratic nominee with a strong chance to win the presidency.

The Democrats' new rules had some expected, as well as unexpected, results. For the first time since 1968, the number of primaries declined and the number of caucuses increased. The Democrats held only thirty primaries in 1984 (including the District of Columbia and Puerto Rico). Yet, like McGovern in 1972 and Carter in 1976, Colorado Sen. Gary Hart used the primaries to pull ahead (temporarily) of former vice president Walter F. Mondale, an early front-runner whose strongest ties were to the party leadership and its traditional core elements. In 1984 the presence of superdelegates was important because about four out of five backed Mondale. (But Mondale did wind up with more primary votes than Hart.)

A few critics regarded the seating of superdelegates as undemocratic, and there were calls for reducing their numbers. Yet to those of most influence within the party, the superdelegates had served their purpose. The Democratic National Committee (DNC) set aside additional seats for party leaders, increasing the number of superdelegates from 14 percent of the delegates in 1984 to 18 percent in 1996. All members of the DNC were guaranteed convention seats, as were all Democratic governors and members of Congress.

The Republican Party did not guarantee delegate seats to its leaders until the 2000 convention voted to make members of the RNC automatic "superdelegates" at the party's convention in 2004. Republicans had not acted before that, in part because their rules permit less rigid pledging of delegates, which generally has led to substantial participation by Republican leaders, despite the absence of such guarantees.

Regional Primaries and Super Tuesday

In addition to the Democrats' internal party concerns with the nominating process, other critics often cited the length of the primary season (nearly twice as long as the general election campaign), the expense, the physical strain on the candidates and the variations and complexities of state laws as problems of presidential primaries.

choose their own leaders. Victors in 1968, and four of the five presidential elections that followed, the Republicans were slow to make any changes in their rules. This era of grass-roots control produced for the Democrats presidential candidates such as McGovern, a liberal from South Dakota who lost in a landslide to Nixon in 1972, and Jimmy Carter, a former governor of Georgia, who beat incumbent President Gerald R. Ford in 1976 but lost to Ronald Reagan in 1980.

With a then-record high of thirty-seven primaries held in 1980 (including the District of Columbia and Puerto Rico), the opportunity for mass participation in the nominating process was greater than ever before. President Carter and Republican nominee Reagan were the clear winners of the long 1980 primary season. Although Carter received a bare majority of the cumulative Democratic primary vote, he amassed a plurality of more than two and one-half million votes over his major rival,

Republican presidential candidates face off in debate before the 1996 primaries. Left to right: Alan Keyes, Morry Taylor, Steve Forbes, Robert Dornan, Bob Dole, Richard Lugar, Lamar Alexander, and Pat Buchanan.

To deal with these problems, several states in 1974 and 1975 discussed the feasibility of creating regional primaries, in which individual states within a geographical region would hold their primaries on the same day. Supporters of the concept believed it would reduce candidate expenses and strain and would permit concentration on regional issues.

The idea achieved some limited success in 1976 when three western states (Idaho, Nevada, and Oregon) and three southern states (Arkansas, Kentucky, and Tennessee)—decided to organize regional primaries in each of their areas. However, the two groups chose May 25 to hold their primaries, thus defeating one of the main purposes of the plan by forcing candidates to shuttle across the country to cover both areas.

Attempts also were made in New England to construct a regional primary. But New Hampshire would not participate because its law required the state to hold its primary at least one week before any other state. Hesitancy by the other New England state legislatures defeated the idea. Only Vermont joined Massachusetts, on March 2, in holding a simultaneous presidential primary, although New Hampshire voted only one week earlier.

In 1980 and 1984, limited regional primaries were held again in several areas of the country. Probably the most noteworthy was the trio of southern states (Alabama, Florida, and Georgia) that voted on the second Tuesday in March—first, in 1980; then again in 1984. It became the basis for "Super Tuesday," which became a full-blown southern-oriented regional primary in 1988.

But the biggest change was that more and more states, hoping to increase their impact on the presidential campaign, decided to hold their primaries early. When South Dakota announced that it would hold its presidential primary in 1988 on Feb. 23, New Hampshire moved its date to Feb. 16.

Sixteen states—a dozen from the South—held primaries on Super Tuesday, March 8, 1988. The long-held goal of many southern political leaders to hold an early regional primary was finally realized. Most of the GOP primaries were winner-take-all, and when Vice President George Bush swept every Republican primary on Super Tuesday, he effectively locked up the GOP nomination. His major opponent, Sen. Robert Dole of Kansas, withdrew by the end of the month. For the Democrats, Massachusetts Gov. Michael S. Dukakis also fared well on Super Tuesday. But the Rev. Jesse Jackson—the first serious black candidate for a major-party presidential nomination—kept the contest going into June.

'MARCH MADNESS'

In 1992 Super Tuesday had become part of a general rush among states to hold their primaries as early as possible. Dubbed "March Madness," the early clustering of primaries—seventeen states held primaries in February or March—was viewed with dismay by some political analysts. They said it could lead to nominees being locked in before most voters knew what was happening, resulting in less informed and deliberative voting in the general election.

As winner in the eight Super Tuesday primaries (six of which were again in the South) on March 10, 1992, President Bush was well on his way to renomination on the GOP side. Although he lost the two New England primaries (Massachusetts and Rhode Island) that day, Bill Clinton by winning all six southern primaries (Florida, Louisiana, Mississippi, Oklahoma, Tennessee, and Texas) established himself as the Democratic front-runner. Most of his competitors had dropped out of the race by the end of the following week. Former Gov. Jerry Brown of California held out until the Democratic convention, but Brown was never able to establish any sort of momentum to overtake Clinton.

In 1996 the process was even more heavily weighted in favor of early primaries, as more than two-thirds of them were held before the end of March. The idea of regional primaries also came the closest to fruition in 1996. "Junior Tuesday Week"

Growth of Presidential Primaries: More and More, Earlier and Earlier

Over the years, there have been more and more states holding primaries earlier and earlier in the presidential election year. The result is that a nominating system that once featured primaries sprinkled across the spring is now front-loaded with the bulk of the primaries held during the winter months of February and March.

Following is a list of primaries held in each month of every nominating season from 1968 through 2000. Primaries included are those in the fifty states and the District of Columbia in which at least one of the parties permitted a direct vote for presidential candidates, or there was an aggregated statewide vote for delegates.

	1968	1972	1976	1980	1984	1988	1992	1996	2000
February	0	0	1	1	1	2	2	5	7
March	1	3	5	9	8	20	15	24	20
April	3	3	2	4	3	3	5	1	2
May	7	11	13	13	11	7	10	8	9
June	4	4	6	9	7	5	7	4	5
Total	15	21	27	36	30	37	39	42	43

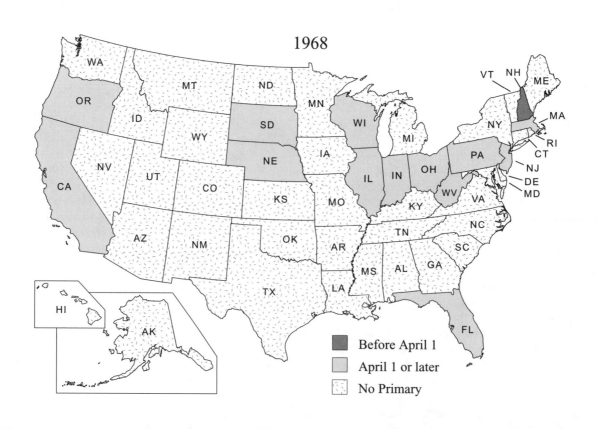

1968

Before April 1
April 1 or later
No Primary

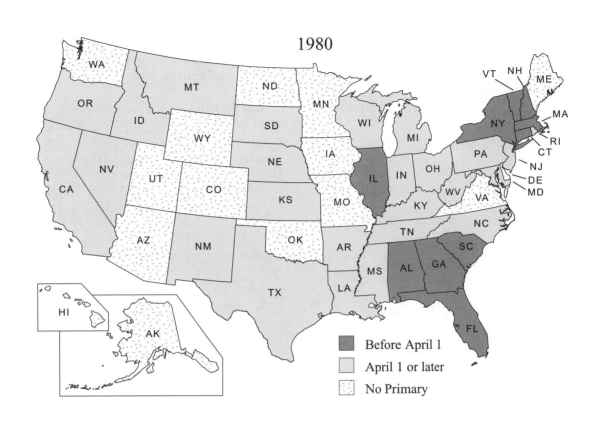

1980

Before April 1

April 1 or later

No Primary

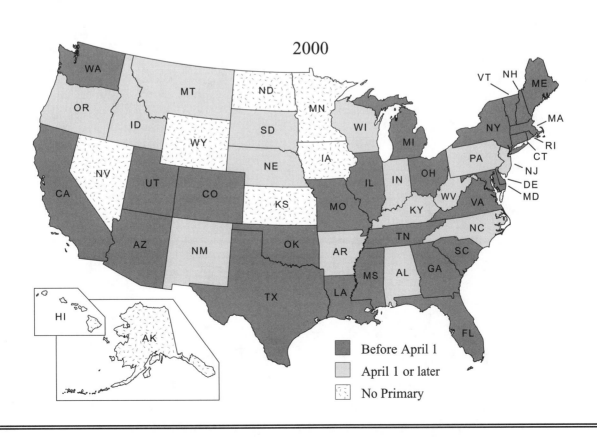

2000

Before April 1

April 1 or later

No Primary

(March 2–7) featured primary voting in ten states (five of which were in New England); Super Tuesday (March 12) had seven primaries (six of which were in the South); and "Big Ten" Tuesday (March 19) had four primaries in important midwestern states. By the time California (which had moved it primary forward in the hope of increasing its sway on the nominating process) had its primary on March 26 (along with two other western states—Nevada and Washington), Dole had all but clinched the Republican nomination.

2000 OUTCOME

In 2000 there were not only a glut of early primaries, but a large concentration on a single day, the first Tuesday in March (March 7). The clustering on this date was not coincidental. It was the earliest date allowed by Democratic rules for states other than Iowa and New Hampshire to hold their primary or caucus. Eleven states scheduled primaries on March 7, 2000, creating a de facto national primary that became variously known as "Titanic Tuesday" or the new "Super Tuesday," although the large southern-oriented vote of the same name remained on the second Tuesday in March.

Political analysts predicted the huge volume of early primaries would result in both parties' nominations being decided by the ides of March. And they were right. George W. Bush and John McCain battled almost evenly through the seven states that held Republican primaries in February—Bush winning four, McCain, three. But once the calendar turned to March, Bush's superior organization and financial resources proved decisive as he dominated the vote March 7 and drove McCain from the race.

With Democratic rules preventing a wholesale movement of states into February, the early Democratic calendar was quite different from the Republican one. The Democratic campaign essentially went "dark" from the early February voting in New Hampshire until the huge array of primaries March 7.

But the result was the same on the Democratic side as it was on the Republican, an early knockout by the front-runner. Vice President Al Gore was closely contested by his major challenger, former Sen. Bill Bradley of New Jersey, in raising funds and drawing media attention during the long stretch before the primaries. But once the balloting began, Bradley proved no match for Gore. The vice president won the late January caucuses in Iowa decisively, the New Hampshire primary narrowly, and swept all the Democratic primaries and caucuses March 7, driving Bradley to the sidelines. Only half the states had voted by then, but the Democratic and Republican races were over.

4

Popular Vote Returns for President

POPULAR VOTE RETURNS for all presidential elections from 1824 to 2000 are presented in this section (pages 644–700). The presidential returns, except where indicated by a footnote, were obtained from three sources. The returns for 1824 to 1916 are from Inter-University Consortium for Political and Social Research (ICPSR) at the University of Michigan. The returns from 1920 to 1992 are from Richard M. Scammon and Alice V. McGillivray, *America at the Polls* (Washington, D.C.: Congressional Quarterly, 1994). The returns for 1996 and 2000 are from the *America Votes* series, compiled biennially by Rhodes Cook for Congressional Quarterly in Washington, D.C. For this edition, elections historian Michael J. Dubin supplemented this source material with new elections data research. CQ editors felt the new data was of scholarly merit and worthy of inclusion—much of it filling the gaps or correcting errors in previous editions of *Guide to U.S. Elections*. Dubin's original sources are also listed in the footnotes.

The 1824 starting date for the ICPSR collection was based on factors such as the pronounced trend by 1824 for the election of presidential electors by popular vote, as well as the availability, accessibility, and quality of the returns. The bulk of the ICPSR election data collection consists of returns at the county level in computer-readable form.

TABLE ORGANIZATION

For each presidential election from 1824 to 2000, the following information is provided in the tables for the popular returns:

- Names and party affiliations of major candidates.
- Total state-by-state popular vote for president.
- State-by-state breakdown of the popular vote and the percentage of the vote received by each candidate.
- The aggregate vote and percentage of the total vote received in each state by minor party candidates, minor parties running unpledged electors, or unidentified votes. These figures appear in the column designated "Other."
- The plurality received by the candidate who carried each state, along with the candidate's party designation.
- The total national popular vote for president, the total national popular vote and percentage of the vote received by each candidate, and the nationwide plurality of the candidate who received the greatest number of votes.

The omission of popular vote returns for a state *after 1824* indicates an absence of popular voting for that election. The South Carolina legislature, for example, chose the state's presidential electors until 1860, and the state did not participate in the 1864 presidential election because of the Civil War. Thus, the first popular vote returns shown for South Carolina are for the 1868 election.

PARTY DESIGNATION

In many cases presidential candidates appeared on state ballots under different, even *multiple* party designations. Thus, in the returns for 1968, George C. Wallace ran for president under a variety of party designations in different states: Democratic, American, American Independent, Independent, George Wallace Party, Conservative, American Party of Missouri, Independent American, Courage, and George Wallace and Independent.

To provide one party designation for presidential candidates for the elections 1824 through 1916, Congressional Quarterly has aggregated under a single party designation the votes of candidates who are listed in the ICPSR data as receiving votes under more than one party designation. The source used for assigning party designation for these years is Svend Petersen, *A Statistical History of the American Presidential Elections* (Westport, Conn.: Greenwood Press, 1981). For the 1920 to 1992 elections, the source for party designation is Scammon and McGillivray, *America at the Polls*. For 1968 Scammon lists Wallace as an American Independent, and Congressional Quarterly follows this usage. For the 1996 and 2000 elections, the source for party designation is Cook, the *America Votes* series.

VOTE TOTALS AND PERCENTAGES

The total popular vote for each candidate in a given election was determined by adding the votes received by that candidate in each state (including write-in votes where available), even though the vote totals for some states may have come from sources other than ICPSR, Scammon, or Cook.

The percentages of the vote received in each state and nationally by any candidate or party has been calculated to two decimal places and rounded to one place; thus, 0.05 percent is listed as 0.1 percent. Due to rounding, state and national percentages do not always equal 100 percent.

PLURALITIES

The plurality column represents the differences between the vote received by the first- and second-place finishers in each state and in the nation. In most cases, most notably in 1912 and 1924, a losing major party candidate finished in third place in a state. In those few cases where votes from the "Other" column were needed to calculate the plurality, a footnote provides an explanation.

1824 Presidential Election

STATE	TOTAL VOTE	JOHN Q. ADAMS (Democratic-Republican)		ANDREW JACKSON (Democratic-Republican)		HENRY CLAY (Democratic-Republican)		WILLIAM H. CRAWFORD (Democratic-Republican)		OTHER		PLURALITY[1]	
		Votes	%	Votes	%	Votes	%	Votes	%	Votes	%		
Alabama	13,603	2,422	17.8	9,429	69.3	96	0.7	1,656	12.2	—	0.0	7,007	AJ
Connecticut	10,647	7,494	70.4	—	0.0	—	0.0	1,965	18.5	1,188	11.2	5,529	JQA
Illinois	4,671	1,516	32.5	1,272	27.2	1,036	22.2	847	18.1	—	0.0	244	JQA
Indiana	15,838	3,071	19.4	7,444	47.0	5,316	33.6	—	0.0	7	0.0	2,128	AJ
Kentucky	23,338	—	0.0	6,356	27.2	16,982	72.8	—	0.0	—	0.0	10,626	HC
Maine[2]	12,625	10,289	81.5	—	0.0	—	0.0	2,336	18.5	—	0.0	7,953	JQA
Maryland[2]	33,214	14,632	44.1	14,523	43.7	695	2.1	3,364	10.1	—	0.0	109	JQA
Massachusetts	42,056	30,687	73.0	—	0.0	—	0.0	—	0.0	11,369	27.0	24,071	JQA[3]
Mississippi	4,894	1,654	33.8	3,121	63.8	—	0.0	119	2.4	—	0.0	1,467	AJ
Missouri	3,432	159	4.6	1,166	34.0	2,042	59.5	32	0.9	33	1.0	876	HC
New Hampshire[2]	10,032	9,389	93.6	—	0.0	—	0.0	643	6.4	—	0.0	8,746	JQA
New Jersey	19,837	8,309	41.9	10,332	52.1	—	0.0	1,196	6.0	—	0.0	2,023	AJ
North Carolina	36,109	—	0.0	20,231	56.0	—	0.0	15,622	43.3	256	0.7	4,609	AJ
Ohio[2]	50,024	12,280	24.5	18,489	37.0	19,255	38.5	—	0.0	—	0.0	766	HC
Pennsylvania	47,073	5,441	11.6	35,736	75.9	1,690	3.6	4,206	8.9	—	0.0	30,295	AJ
Rhode Island	2,344	2,144	91.5	—	0.0	—	0.0	—	0.0	200	8.5	1,944	JQA
Tennessee[2]	20,725	216	1.0	20,197	97.5	—	0.0	312	1.5	—	0.0	19,885	AJ
Virginia	15,371	3,419	22.2	2,975	19.4	419	2.7	8,558	55.7	—	0.0	5,139	WHC
Totals	**365,833**	**113,122**	**30.9**	**151,271**	**41.3**	**47,531**	**13.0**	**40,856**	**11.2**	**13,053**	**3.6**	**38,149**	**AJ**

1. For the 1824 plurality winner the designations are JQA (John Quincy Adams), AJ (Andrew Jackson), WHC (William H. Crawford), and HC (Henry Clay). Adams was elected president by the House of Representatives.

2. Figures from Svend Petersen, *A Statistical History of the American Presidential Elections* (Westport, Conn.: Greenwood Press, 1981), 18.

3. Plurality of 24,071 votes is calculated on the basis of 6,616 for unpledged electors.

1828 Presidential Election

STATE	TOTAL VOTE	ANDREW JACKSON (Democratic-Republican)		JOHN Q. ADAMS (National Republican)		OTHER		PLURALITY	
		Votes	%	Votes	%	Votes	%		
Alabama	18,618	16,736	89.9	1,878	10.1	4	0.0	14,858	DR
Connecticut	19,378	4,448	23.0	13,829	71.4	1,101	5.7	9,381	NR
Georgia[1]	20,004	19,362	96.8	642	3.2	—	0.0	18,720	DR
Illinois	14,222	9,560	67.2	4,662	32.8	—	0.0	4,898	DR
Indiana	39,210	22,201	56.6	17,009	43.4	—	0.0	5,192	DR
Kentucky	70,776	39,308	55.5	31,468	44.5	—	0.0	7,840	DR
Louisiana	8,687	4,605	53.0	4,082	47.0	—	0.0	523	DR
Maine	34,789	13,927	40.0	20,773	59.7	89	0.3	6,846	NR
Maryland	45,796	22,782	49.7	23,014	50.3	—	0.0	232	NR
Massachusetts	39,074	6,012	15.4	29,836	76.4	3,226	8.3	23,824	NR
Mississippi	8,344	6,763	81.1	1,581	18.9	—	0.0	5,182	DR
Missouri	11,654	8,232	70.6	3,422	29.4	—	0.0	4,810	DR
New Hampshire	44,035	20,212	45.9	23,823	54.1	—	0.0	3,611	NR
New Jersey	45,570	21,809	47.9	23,753	52.1	8	0.0	1,944	NR
New York	270,975	139,412	51.4	131,563	48.6	—	0.0	7,849	DR
North Carolina	51,747	37,814	73.1	13,918	26.9	15	0.0	23,896	DR
Ohio	131,049	67,596	51.6	63,453	48.4	—	0.0	4,143	DR
Pennsylvania	152,220	101,457	66.7	50,763	33.3	—	0.0	50,694	DR
Rhode Island	3,580	820	22.9	2,755	77.0	5	0.1	1,935	NR
Tennessee[1]	46,533	44,293	95.2	2,240	4.8	—	0.0	42,053	DR
Vermont	32,833	8,350	25.4	24,363	74.2	120	0.4	16,013	NR
Virginia	38,924	26,854	69.0	12,070	31.0	—	0.0	14,784	DR
Totals	**1,148,018**	**642,553**	*56.0*	**500,897**	*43.6*	**4,568**	*0.4*	**141,656**	**DR**

1. Figures from Svend Petersen, *A Statistical History of the American Presidential Elections* (Westport, Conn.: Greenwood Press, 1981), 20.

1832 Presidential Election

STATE	TOTAL VOTE	ANDREW JACKSON (Democrat)		HENRY CLAY (National Republican)		WILLIAM WIRT (Anti-Mason)		OTHER		PLURALITY	
		Votes	%	Votes	%	Votes	%	Votes	%		
Alabama	14,291	14,286	100.0	5	0.0	—	0.0	—	0.0	14,281	D
Connecticut	32,833	11,269	34.3	18,155	55.3	3,409	10.4	—	0.0	6,886	NR
Delaware	8,386	4,110	49.0	4,276	51.0	—	0.0	—	0.0	166	NR
Georgia[1]	20,750	20,750	100.0	—	0.0	—	0.0	—	0.0	20,750	D
Illinois	21,481	14,609	68.0	6,745	31.4	97	0.5	30	0.1	7,864	D
Indiana	57,152	31,652	55.4	25,473	44.6	27	0.0	—	0.0	6,179	D
Kentucky	79,741	36,292	45.5	43,449	54.5	—	0.0	—	0.0	7,157	NR
Louisiana	6,337	3,908	61.7	2,429	38.3	—	0.0	—	0.0	1,479	D
Maine	62,153	33,978	54.7	27,331	44.0	844	1.4	—	0.0	6,647	D
Maryland	38,316	19,156	50.0	19,160	50.0	—	0.0	—	0.0	4	NR
Massachusetts	67,619	13,933	20.6	31,963	47.3	14,692	21.7	7,031	10.4	17,271	NR
Mississippi	5,750	5,750	100.0	—	0.0	—	0.0	—	0.0	5,750	D
Missouri[1]	5,192	5,192	100.0	—	0.0	—	0.0	—	0.0	5,192	D
New Hampshire	43,793	24,855	56.8	18,938	43.2	—	0.0	—	0.0	5,917	D
New Jersey	47,760	23,826	49.9	23,466	49.1	468	1.0	—	0.0	360	D
New York	323,393	168,497	52.1	154,896	47.9	—	0.0	—	0.0	13,601	D
North Carolina	29,799	25,261	84.8	4,538	15.2	—	0.0	—	0.0	20,723	D
Ohio	158,350	81,246	51.3	76,566	48.4	538	0.3	—	0.0	4,680	D
Pennsylvania	157,679	90,973	57.7	—	0.0	66,706	42.3	—	0.0	24,267	D
Rhode Island	5,747	2,051	35.7	2,871	50.0	819	14.3	6	0.1	820	NR
Tennessee	29,425	28,078	95.4	1,347	4.6	—	0.0	—	0.0	26,731	D
Vermont	32,344	7,865	24.3	11,161	34.5	13,112	40.5	206	0.6	1,951	AM
Virginia	45,682	34,243	75.0	11,436	25.0	3	0.0	—	0.0	22,807	D
Totals	**1,293,973**	**701,780**	*54.2*	**484,205**	*37.4*	**100,715**	*7.8*	**7,273**	*0.6*	**217,575**	**D**

1. Figures from Svend Petersen, *A Statistical History of the American Presidential Elections* (Westport, Conn.: Greenwood Press, 1981), 21.

1836 Presidential Election

STATE	TOTAL VOTE	MARTIN VAN BUREN (Democrat)		WILLIAM H. HARRISON (Whig)		HUGH L. WHITE (Whig)		DANIEL WEBSTER (Whig)		OTHER		PLURALITY[1]	
		Votes	%	Votes	%	Votes	%	Votes	%	Votes	%		
Alabama	37,296	20,638	55.3	—	0.0	16,658	44.7	—	0.0	—	0.0	3,980	MBV
Arkansas	3,714	2,380	64.1	—	0.0	1,334	35.9	—	0.0	—	0.0	1,046	MBV
Connecticut	38,093	19,294	50.6	18,799	49.4	—	0.0	—	0.0	—	0.0	495	MBV
Delaware	8,895	4,154	46.7	4,736	53.2	—	0.0	—	0.0	5	0.1	582	WHH
Georgia	47,259	22,778	48.2	—	0.0	24,481	51.8	—	0.0	—	0.0	1,703	HLW
Illinois	33,589	18,369	54.7	15,220	45.3	—	0.0	—	0.0	—	0.0	3,149	MBV
Indiana	74,423	33,084	44.5	41,339	55.5	—	0.0	—	0.0	—	0.0	8,255	WHH
Kentucky	70,090	33,229	47.4	36,861	52.6	—	0.0	—	0.0	—	0.0	3,632	WHH
Louisiana	7,425	3,842	51.7	—	0.0	3,583	48.3	—	0.0	—	0.0	259	MBV
Maine	38,740	22,825	58.9	14,803	38.2	—	0.0	—	0.0	1,112	2.9	8,022	MBV
Maryland	48,119	22,267	46.3	25,852	53.7	—	0.0	—	0.0	—	0.0	3,585	WHH
Massachusetts	74,732	33,486	44.8	—	0.0	—	0.0	41,201	55.1	45	0.1	33,486	DW
Michigan	12,052	6,507	54.0	5,545	46.0	—	0.0	—	0.0	—	0.0	962	MBV
Mississippi	20,079	10,297	51.3	—	0.0	9,782	48.7	—	0.0	—	0.0	515	MBV
Missouri[2]	18,332	10,995	60.0	—	0.0	7,337	40.0	—	0.0	—	0.0	3,658	MBV
New Hampshire	24,925	18,697	75.0	6,228	25.0	—	0.0	—	0.0	—	0.0	12,469	MBV
New Jersey	51,729	25,592	49.5	26,137	50.5	—	0.0	—	0.0	—	0.0	545	WHH
New York	305,343	166,795	54.6	138,548	45.4	—	0.0	—	0.0	—	0.0	28,247	MBV
North Carolina	50,153	26,631	53.1	—	0.0	23,521	46.9	—	0.0	1	0.0	3,110	MBV
Ohio	202,931	97,122	47.9	105,809	52.1	—	0.0	—	0.0	—	0.0	8,687	WHH
Pennsylvania	178,701	91,466	51.2	87,235	48.8	—	0.0	—	0.0	—	0.0	4,231	MBV
Rhode Island	5,673	2,962	52.2	2,710	47.8	—	0.0	—	0.0	1	0.0	252	MBV
Tennessee	62,197	26,170	42.1	—	0.0	36,027	57.9	—	0.0	—	0.0	9,857	HLW
Vermont	35,099	14,040	40.0	20,994	59.8	—	0.0	—	0.0	65	0.2	6,954	WHH
Virginia	53,945	30,556	56.6	—	0.0	23,384	43.3	—	0.0	5	0.0	7,172	MBV
Totals	1,503,534	764,176	50.8	550,816	36.6	146,107	9.7	41,201	2.7	1,234	0.1	213,360	MBV

1. For the 1836 plurality winner, the designations are MVB (Martin Van Buren), WHH (William Henry Harrison), HLW (Hugh L. White), and DW (Daniel Webster).
2. Figures from Svend Petersen, *A Statistical History of the American Presidential Elections* (Westport, Conn.: Greenwood Press, 1981), 22.

1840 Presidential Election

STATE	TOTAL VOTE	WILLIAM H. HARRISON (Whig)		MARTIN VAN BUREN (Democrat)		JAMES G. BIRNEY (Liberty)		OTHER		PLURALITY	
		Votes	%	Votes	%	Votes	%	Votes	%		
Alabama	62,511	28,515	45.6	33,996	54.4	—	0.0	—	0.0	5,481	D
Arkansas	11,839	5,160	43.6	6,679	56.4	—	0.0	—	0.0	1,519	D
Connecticut	56,879	31,598	55.6	25,281	44.4	—	0.0	—	0.0	6,317	W
Delaware	10,852	5,967	55.0	4,872	44.9	—	0.0	13	0.1	1,095	W
Georgia	72,322	40,339	55.8	31,983	44.2	—	0.0	—	0.0	8,356	W
Illinois	93,175	45,574	48.9	47,441	50.9	160	0.2	—	0.0	1,867	D
Indiana	117,605	65,280	55.5	51,696	44.0	30	0.0	599	0.5	13,584	W
Kentucky	91,104	58,488	64.2	32,616	35.8	—	0.0	—	0.0	25,872	W
Louisiana	18,912	11,296	59.7	7,616	40.3	—	0.0	—	0.0	3,680	W
Maine	92,802	46,612	50.2	46,190	49.8	—	0.0	—	0.0	422	W
Maryland	62,280	33,528	53.8	28,752	46.2	—	0.0	—	0.0	4,776	W
Massachusetts	126,825	72,852	57.4	52,355	41.3	1,618	1.3	—	0.0	20,497	W
Michigan	44,029	22,933	52.1	21,096	47.9	—	0.0	—	0.0	1,837	W
Mississippi	36,525	19,515	53.4	17,010	46.6	—	0.0	—	0.0	2,505	W
Missouri	52,923	22,954	43.4	29,969	56.6	—	0.0	—	0.0	7,015	D
New Hampshire	59,956	26,310	43.9	32,774	54.7	872	1.5	—	0.0	6,464	D
New Jersey	64,454	33,351	51.7	31,034	48.1	69	0.1	—	0.0	2,317	W
New York	441,543	226,001	51.2	212,733	48.2	2,809	0.6	—	0.0	13,268	W
North Carolina	80,735	46,567	57.7	34,168	42.3	—	0.0	—	0.0	12,399	W
Ohio	272,890	148,043	54.3	123,944	45.4	903	0.3	—	0.0	24,099	W
Pennsylvania	287,695	144,023	50.1	143,672	49.9	—	0.0	—	0.0	351	W
Rhode Island	8,631	5,213	60.4	3,263	37.8	19	0.2	136	1.6	1,950	W
Tennessee	108,145	60,194	55.7	47,951	44.3	—	0.0	—	0.0	12,243	W
Vermont	50,782	32,440	63.9	18,006	35.5	317	0.6	19	0.0	14,434	W
Virginia	86,394	42,637	49.4	43,757	50.6	—	0.0	—	0.0	1,120	D
Totals	2,411,808	1,275,390	52.9	1,128,854	46.8	6,797	0.3	767	0.0	146,536	W

1844 Presidential Election

STATE	TOTAL VOTE	JAMES K. POLK (Democrat)		HENRY CLAY (Whig)		JAMES G. BIRNEY (Liberty)		OTHER		PLURALITY	
		Votes	%	Votes	%	Votes	%	Votes	%		
Alabama	63,403	37,401	59.0	26,002	41.0	—	0.0	—	0.0	11,399	D
Arkansas	15,150	9,546	63.0	5,604	37.0	—	0.0	—	0.0	3,942	D
Connecticut	64,616	29,841	46.2	32,832	50.8	1,943	3.0	—	0.0	2,991	W
Delaware	12,247	5,970	48.7	6,271	51.2	—	0.0	6	0.0	301	W
Georgia	86,247	44,147	51.2	42,100	48.8	—	0.0	—	0.0	2,047	D
Illinois	109,057	58,795	53.9	45,854	42.0	3,469	3.2	939	0.9	12,941	D
Indiana	140,157	70,183	50.1	67,866	48.4	2,108	1.5	—	0.0	2,317	D
Kentucky	113,237	51,988	45.9	61,249	54.1	—	0.0	—	0.0	9,261	W
Louisiana	26,865	13,782	51.3	13,083	48.7	—	0.0	—	0.0	699	D
Maine	84,933	45,719	53.8	34,378	40.5	4,836	5.7	—	0.0	11,341	D
Maryland	68,690	32,706	47.6	35,984	52.4	—	0.0	—	0.0	3,278	W
Massachusetts	132,037	53,039	40.2	67,062	50.8	10,830	8.2	1,106	0.8	14,023	W
Michigan	55,560	27,737	49.9	24,185	43.5	3,638	6.5	—	0.0	3,552	D
Mississippi	45,004	25,846	57.4	19,158	42.6	—	0.0	—	0.0	6,688	D
Missouri	72,522	41,322	57.0	31,200	43.0	—	0.0	—	0.0	10,122	D
New Hampshire	49,187	27,160	55.2	17,866	36.3	4,161	8.5	—	0.0	9,294	D
New Jersey	75,944	37,495	49.4	38,318	50.5	131	0.2	—	0.0	823	W
New York	485,882	237,588	48.9	232,482	47.8	15,812	3.3	—	0.0	5,106	D
North Carolina	82,521	39,287	47.6	43,232	52.4	—	0.0	2	0.0	3,945	W
Ohio	312,300	149,127	47.8	155,091	49.7	8,082	2.6	—	0.0	5,964	W
Pennsylvania	331,645	167,311	50.4	161,195	48.6	3,139	0.9	—	0.0	6,116	D
Rhode Island	12,194	4,867	39.9	7,322	60.0	—	0.0	5	0.0	2,455	W
Tennessee	119,957	59,917	49.9	60,040	50.1	—	0.0	—	0.0	123	W
Vermont	48,765	18,041	37.0	26,770	54.9	3,954	8.1	—	0.0	8,729	W
Virginia	95,539	50,679	53.0	44,860	47.0	—	0.0	—	0.0	5,819	D
Totals	2,703,659	1,339,494	49.5	1,300,004	48.1	62,103	2.3	2,058	0.1	39,490	D

1848 Presidential Election

STATE	TOTAL VOTE	ZACHARY TAYLOR (Whig)		LEWIS CASS (Democrat)		MARTIN VAN BUREN (Free Soil)		OTHER		PLURALITY	
		Votes	%	Votes	%	Votes	%	Votes	%		
Alabama	61,659	30,482	49.4	31,173	50.6	—	0.0	4	0.0	691	D
Arkansas	16,888	7,587	44.9	9,301	55.1	—	0.0	—	0.0	1,714	D
Connecticut	62,398	30,318	48.6	27,051	43.4	5,005	8.0	24	0.0	3,267	W
Delaware	12,432	6,440	51.8	5,910	47.5	82	0.7	—	0.0	530	W
Florida	7,203	4,120	57.2	3,083	42.8	—	0.0	—	0.0	1,037	W
Georgia	92,317	47,532	51.5	44,785	48.5	—	0.0	—	0.0	2,747	W
Illinois	124,596	52,853	42.4	55,952	44.9	15,702	12.6	89	0.1	3,099	D
Indiana	152,394	69,668	45.7	74,695	49.0	8,031	5.3	—	0.0	5,027	D
Iowa	22,271	9,930	44.6	11,238	50.5	1,103	5.0	—	0.0	1,308	D
Kentucky	116,865	67,145	57.5	49,720	42.5	—	0.0	—	0.0	17,425	W
Louisiana	33,866	18,487	54.6	15,379	45.4	—	0.0	—	0.0	3,108	W
Maine	87,625	35,273	40.3	40,195	45.9	12,157	13.9	—	0.0	4,922	D
Maryland	72,359	37,702	52.1	34,528	47.7	129	0.2	—	0.0	3,174	W
Massachusetts	134,748	61,072	45.3	35,281	26.2	38,333	28.4	62	0.0	22,739	W
Michigan	65,082	23,947	36.8	30,742	47.2	10,393	16.0	—	0.0	6,795	D
Mississippi	52,456	25,911	49.4	26,545	50.6	—	0.0	—	0.0	634	D
Missouri	72,748	32,671	44.9	40,077	55.1	—	0.0	—	0.0	7,406	D
New Hampshire	50,104	14,781	29.5	27,763	55.4	7,560	15.1	—	0.0	12,982	D
New Jersey	77,745	40,015	51.5	36,901	47.5	829	1.1	—	0.0	3,114	W
New York	455,944	218,583	47.9	114,319	25.1	120,497	26.4	2,545	0.6	98,086	W
North Carolina	79,826	44,054	55.2	35,772	44.8	—	0.0	—	0.0	8,282	W
Ohio	328,987	138,656	42.1	154,782	47.0	35,523	10.8	26	0.0	16,126	D
Pennsylvania	369,092	185,730	50.3	172,186	46.7	11,176	3.0	—	0.0	13,544	W
Rhode Island	11,049	6,705	60.7	3,613	32.7	726	6.6	5	0.0	3,092	W
Tennessee	122,463	64,321	52.5	58,142	47.5	—	0.0	—	0.0	6,179	W
Texas	17,000	5,281	31.1	11,644	68.5	—	0.0	75	0.4	6,363	D
Vermont	47,897	23,117	48.3	10,943	22.8	13,837	28.9	—	0.0	9,280	W
Virginia	92,004	45,265	49.2	46,739	50.8	—	0.0	—	0.0	1,474	D
Wisconsin	39,166	13,747	35.1	15,001	38.3	10,418	26.6	—	0.0	1,254	D
Totals	2,879,184	1,361,393	47.3	1,223,460	42.5	291,501	10.1	2,830	0.1	137,933	W

1852 Presidential Election

STATE	TOTAL VOTE	FRANKLIN PIERCE (Democrat)		WINFIELD SCOTT (Whig)		JOHN P. HALE (Free Soil)		OTHER		PLURALITY	
		Votes	%	Votes	%	Votes	%	Votes	%		
Alabama	44,147	26,881	60.9	15,061	34.1	—	0.0	2,205	5.0	11,820	D
Arkansas	19,577	12,173	62.2	7,404	37.8	—	0.0	—	0.0	4,769	D
California	76,810	40,721	53.0	35,972	46.8	61	0.1	56	0.1	4,749	D
Connecticut	66,781	33,249	49.8	30,359	45.5	3,161	4.7	12	0.0	2,890	D
Delaware	12,673	6,318	49.9	6,293	49.7	62	0.5	—	0.0	25	D
Florida	7,193	4,318	60.0	2,875	40.0	—	0.0	—	0.0	1,443	D
Georgia[1]	62,626	40,516	64.7	16,660	26.6	—	0.0	5,450	8.7	23,856	D
Illinois	154,974	80,378	51.9	64,733	41.8	9,863	6.4	—	0.0	15,645	D
Indiana	183,176	95,340	52.0	80,907	44.2	6,929	3.8	—	0.0	14,433	D
Iowa	35,364	17,763	50.2	15,856	44.8	1,606	4.5	139	0.4	1,907	D
Kentucky	111,643	53,949	48.3	57,428	51.4	266	0.2	—	0.0	3,479	W
Louisiana	35,902	18,647	51.9	17,255	48.1	—	0.0	—	0.0	1,392	D
Maine	82,182	41,609	50.6	32,543	39.6	8,030	9.8	—	0.0	9,066	D
Maryland	75,120	40,022	53.3	35,077	46.7	21	0.0	—	0.0	4,945	D
Massachusetts	127,103	44,569	35.1	52,683	41.4	28,023	22.0	1,828	1.4	8,114	W
Michigan	82,939	41,842	50.4	33,860	40.8	7,237	8.7	—	0.0	7,982	D
Mississippi	44,454	26,896	60.5	17,558	39.5	—	0.0	—	0.0	9,338	D
Missouri	68,801	38,817	56.4	29,984	43.6	—	0.0	—	0.0	8,833	D
New Hampshire	50,535	28,503	56.4	15,486	30.6	6,546	13.0	—	0.0	13,017	D
New Jersey	83,926	44,301	52.8	38,551	45.9	336	0.4	738	0.9	5,750	D
New York	522,294	262,083	50.2	234,882	45.0	25,329	4.8	—	0.0	27,201	D
North Carolina	78,891	39,788	50.4	39,043	49.5	—	0.0	60	0.1	745	D
Ohio	352,903	169,193	47.9	152,577	43.2	31,133	8.8	—	0.0	16,616	D
Pennsylvania	387,920	198,568	51.2	179,182	46.2	8,500	2.2	1,670	0.4	19,386	D
Rhode Island	17,005	8,735	51.4	7,626	44.8	644	3.8	—	0.0	1,109	D
Tennessee	115,486	56,900	49.3	58,586	50.7	—	0.0	—	0.0	1,686	W
Texas	20,223	14,857	73.5	5,356	26.5	—	0.0	10	0.0	9,501	D
Vermont	43,838	13,044	29.8	22,173	50.6	8,621	19.7	—	0.0	9,129	W
Virginia	132,604	73,872	55.7	58,732	44.3	—	0.0	—	0.0	15,140	D
Wisconsin	64,740	33,658	52.0	22,240	34.4	8,842	13.7	—	0.0	11,418	D
Totals	3,161,830	1,607,510	50.8	1,386,942	43.9	155,210	4.9	12,168	0.4	220,568	D

1. Figures from Svend Petersen, *A Statistical History of the American Presidential Elections* (Westport, Conn.: Greenwood Press, 1981), 31.

1856 Presidential Election

STATE	TOTAL VOTE	JAMES BUCHANAN (Democrat)		JOHN C. FREMONT (Republican)		MILLARD FILLMORE (Whig-American)		OTHER		PLURALITY	
		Votes	%	Votes	%	Votes	%	Votes	%		
Alabama	75,291	46,739	62.1	—	0.0	28,552	37.9	—	0.0	18,187	D
Arkansas	32,642	21,910	67.1	—	0.0	10,732	32.9	—	0.0	11,178	D
California	110,255	53,342	48.4	20,704	18.8	36,195	32.8	14	0.0	17,147	D
Connecticut	80,360	35,028	43.6	42,717	53.2	2,615	3.3	—	0.0	7,689	R
Delaware	14,598	8,004	54.8	310	2.1	6,275	43.0	9	0.1	1,729	D
Florida	11,191	6,358	56.8	—	0.0	4,833	43.2	—	0.0	1,525	D
Georgia	99,020	56,581	57.1	—	0.0	42,439	42.9	—	0.0	14,142	D
Illinois	239,334	105,528	44.1	96,275	40.2	37,531	15.7	—	0.0	9,253	D
Indiana	235,401	118,670	50.4	94,375	40.1	22,356	9.5	—	0.0	24,295	D
Iowa	92,310	37,568	40.7	45,073	48.8	9,669	10.5	—	0.0	7,505	R
Kentucky	142,058	74,642	52.5	—	0.0	67,416	47.5	—	0.0	7,226	D
Louisiana	42,873	22,164	51.7	—	0.0	20,709	48.3	—	0.0	1,455	D
Maine	109,689	39,140	35.7	67,279	61.3	3,270	3.0	—	0.0	28,139	R
Maryland	86,860	39,123	45.0	285	0.3	47,452	54.6	—	0.0	8,329	WA
Massachusetts	170,048	39,244	23.1	108,172	63.6	19,626	11.5	3,006	1.8	68,928	R
Michigan	125,558	52,136	41.5	71,762	57.2	1,660	1.3	—	0.0	19,626	R
Mississippi	59,647	35,456	59.4	—	0.0	24,191	40.6	—	0.0	11,265	D
Missouri	106,486	57,964	54.4	—	0.0	48,522	45.6	—	0.0	9,442	D
New Hampshire	69,774	31,891	45.7	37,473	53.7	410	0.6	—	0.0	5,582	R
New Jersey	99,396	46,943	47.2	28,338	28.5	24,115	24.3	—	0.0	18,605	D
New York	596,486	195,878	32.8	276,004	46.3	124,604	20.9	—	0.0	80,126	R
North Carolina	84,963	48,243	56.8	—	0.0	36,720	43.2	—	0.0	11,523	D
Ohio	386,640	170,874	44.2	187,497	48.5	28,121	7.3	148	0.0	16,623	R
Pennsylvania	460,937	230,772	50.1	147,963	32.1	82,202	17.8	—	0.0	82,809	D
Rhode Island	19,822	6,680	33.7	11,467	57.8	1,675	8.5	—	0.0	4,787	R
Tennessee	133,582	69,704	52.2	—	0.0	63,878	47.8	—	0.0	5,826	D
Texas	48,005	31,995	66.6	—	0.0	16,010	33.4	—	0.0	15,985	D
Vermont	50,675	10,569	20.9	39,561	78.1	545	1.1	—	0.0	28,992	R
Virginia	150,233	90,083	60.0	—	0.0	60,150	40.0	—	0.0	29,933	D
Wisconsin	120,513	52,843	43.8	67,090	55.7	580	0.5	—	0.0	14,247	R
Totals	4,054,647	1,836,072	45.3	1,342,345	33.1	873,053	21.5	3,177	0.1	493,727	D

1860 Presidential Election

STATE	TOTAL VOTE	ABRAHAM LINCOLN (Republican)		STEPHEN A. DOUGLAS (Democrat)		JOHN C. BRECKINRIDGE (Southern Democrat)		JOHN BELL (Constitutional (Union)		OTHER		PLURALITY	
		Votes	%	Votes	%	Votes	%	Votes	%	Votes	%		
Alabama	90,122	—	0.0	13,618	15.1	48,669	54.0	27,835	30.9	—	0.0	20,834	SD
Arkansas	54,152	—	0.0	5,357	9.9	28,732	53.1	20,063	37.0	—	0.0	8,669	SD
California	119,827	38,733	32.3	37,999	31.7	33,969	28.3	9,111	7.6	15	0.0	734	R
Connecticut	74,819	43,488	58.1	15,431	20.6	14,372	19.2	1,528	2.0	—	0.0	28,057	R
Delaware	16,115	3,822	23.7	1,066	6.6	7,339	45.5	3,888	24.1	—	0.0	3,451	SD
Florida	13,301	—	0.0	223	1.7	8,277	62.2	4,801	36.1	—	0.0	3,476	SD
Georgia	106,717	—	0.0	11,581	10.9	52,176	48.9	42,960	40.3	—	0.0	9,216	SD
Illinois	339,666	172,171	50.7	160,215	47.2	2,331	0.7	4,914	1.4	35	0.0	11,956	R
Indiana	272,143	139,033	51.1	115,509	42.4	12,295	4.5	5,306	1.9	—	0.0	23,524	R
Iowa	128,739	70,302	54.6	55,639	43.2	1,035	0.8	1,763	1.4	—	0.0	14,663	R
Kentucky[1]	146,216	1,364	0.9	25,651	17.5	53,143	36.3	66,058	45.2	—	0.0	12,915	CU
Louisiana	50,510	—	0.0	7,625	15.1	22,681	44.9	20,204	40.0	—	0.0	2,477	SD
Maine	100,918	62,811	62.2	29,693	29.4	6,368	6.3	2,046	2.0	—	0.0	33,118	R
Maryland	92,502	2,294	2.5	5,966	6.4	42,482	45.9	41,760	45.1	—	0.0	722	SD
Massachusetts	169,876	106,684	62.8	34,370	20.2	6,163	3.6	22,331	13.1	328	0.2	72,314	R
Michigan	154,758	88,481	57.2	65,057	42.0	805	0.5	415	0.3	—	0.0	23,424	R
Minnesota	34,804	22,069	63.4	11,920	34.2	748	2.1	50	0.1	17	0.0	10,149	R
Mississippi	69,095	—	0.0	3,282	4.7	40,768	59.0	25,045	36.2	—	0.0	15,723	SD
Missouri	165,563	17,028	10.3	58,801	35.5	31,362	18.9	58,372	35.3	—	0.0	429	D
New Hampshire	65,943	37,519	56.9	25,887	39.3	2,125	3.2	412	0.6	—	0.0	11,632	R
New Jersey[1]	121,215	58,346	48.1	62,869	51.9	—	0.0	—	0.0	—	0.0	4,523	D
New York	675,156	362,646	53.7	312,510	46.3	—	0.0	—	0.0	—	0.0	50,136	R
North Carolina	96,712	—	0.0	2,737	2.8	48,846	50.5	45,129	46.7	—	0.0	3,717	SD
Ohio	442,866	231,709	52.3	187,421	42.3	11,406	2.6	12,194	2.8	136	0.0	44,288	R
Oregon	14,758	5,329	36.1	4,136	28.0	5,075	34.4	218	1.5	—	0.0	254	R
Pennsylvania	476,442	268,030	56.3	16,765	3.5	178,871	37.5	12,776	2.7	—	0.0	89,159	R
Rhode Island	19,951	12,244	61.4	7,707	38.6	—	0.0	—	0.0	—	0.0	4,537	R
Tennessee	146,106	—	0.0	11,281	7.7	65,097	44.6	69,728	47.7	—	0.0	4,631	CU
Texas	62,855	—	0.0	18	0.0	47,454	75.5	15,383	24.5	—	0.0	32,071	SD
Vermont	44,644	33,808	75.7	8,649	19.4	218	0.5	1,969	4.4	—	0.0	25,159	R
Virginia	166,891	1,887	1.1	16,198	9.7	74,325	44.5	74,481	44.6	—	0.0	156	CU
Wisconsin	152,179	86,110	56.6	65,021	42.7	887	0.6	161	0.1	—	0.0	21,089	R
Totals	4,685,561	1,865,908	39.9	1,380,202	29.5	848,019	18.1	590,901	12.6	531	0.0	485,706	R

1. Figures from Svend Petersen, *A Statistical History of the American Presidential Elections* (Westport, Conn.: Greenwood Press, 1981), 37.

1864 Presidential Election

STATE[1]	TOTAL VOTE	ABRAHAM LINCOLN (Republican)		GEORGE B. McCLELLAN (Democrat)		OTHER		PLURALITY	
		Votes	%	Votes	%	Votes	%		
California	105,890	62,053	58.6	43,837	41.4	—	0.0	18,216	R
Connecticut	86,958	44,673	51.4	42,285	48.6	—	0.0	2,388	R
Delaware	16,922	8,155	48.2	8,767	51.8	—	0.0	612	D
Illinois	348,236	189,512	54.4	158,724	45.6	—	0.0	30,788	R
Indiana	280,117	149,887	53.5	130,230	46.5	—	0.0	19,657	R
Iowa[2]	138,025	88,500	64.1	49,525	35.9	—	0.0	38,975	R
Kansas	21,580	17,089	79.2	3,836	17.8	655	3.0	13,253	R
Kentucky	92,088	27,787	30.2	64,301	69.8	—	0.0	36,514	D
Maine[3]	115,099	68,104	59.2	46,995	40.8	—	0.0	21,109	R
Maryland	72,892	40,153	55.1	32,739	44.9	—	0.0	7,414	R
Massachusetts	175,493	126,742	72.2	48,745	27.8	6	0.0	77,997	R
Michigan[4]	160,023	88,551	55.3	71,472	44.7	—	0.0	17,079	R
Minnesota	42,433	25,031	59.0	17,376	40.9	26	0.1	7,655	R
Missouri	104,346	72,750	69.7	31,596	30.3	—	0.0	41,154	R
Nevada	16,420	9,826	59.8	6,594	40.2	—	0.0	3,232	R
New Hampshire	69,630	36,596	52.6	33,034	47.4	—	0.0	3,562	R
New Jersey	128,744	60,724	47.2	68,020	52.8	—	0.0	7,296	D
New York	730,721	368,735	50.5	361,986	49.5	—	0.0	6,749	R
Ohio	471,283	265,674	56.4	205,609	43.6	—	0.0	60,065	R
Oregon	18,350	9,888	53.9	8,457	46.1	5	0.0	1,431	R
Pennsylvania[5]	572,707	296,391	51.7	276,316	48.3	—	0.0	20,075	R
Rhode Island	23,067	14,349	62.2	8,718	37.8	—	0.0	5,631	R
Vermont	55,740	42,419	76.1	13,321	23.9	—	0.0	29,098	R
West Virginia	34,877	23,799	68.2	11,078	31.8	—	0.0	12,721	R
Wisconsin	149,342	83,458	55.9	65,884	44.1	—	0.0	17,574	R
Totals	4,030,291	2,220,846	55.1	1,809,445	44.9	692	0.0	411,401	R

1. Eleven Confederate states did not participate in the election because of the Civil War.
2. Figures from *Iowa Official Register, 1913–1914.*
3. Figures from Maine's Executive Council minutes.
4. Figures from *Michigan Manual 1913,* p. 689.
5. Figures from Pennsylvania's *Manual,* 1865.

1868 Presidential Election

STATE[1]	TOTAL VOTE	ULYSSES S. GRANT (Republican)		HORATIO SEYMOUR (Democrat)		OTHER		PLURALITY	
		Votes	%	Votes	%	Votes	%		
Alabama	149,594	76,667	51.3	72,921	48.7	6	0.0	3,746	R
Arkansas	41,190	22,112	53.7	19,078	46.3	—	0.0	3,034	R
California	108,656	54,588	50.2	54,068	49.8	—	0.0	520	R
Connecticut	98,570	50,789	51.5	47,781	48.5	—	0.0	3,008	R
Delaware	18,571	7,614	41.0	10,957	59.0	—	0.0	3,343	D
Georgia	159,816	57,109	35.7	102,707	64.3	—	0.0	45,598	D
Illinois	449,420	250,304	55.7	199,116	44.3	—	0.0	51,188	R
Indiana	343,528	176,548	51.4	166,980	48.6	—	0.0	9,568	R
Iowa	194,439	120,399	61.9	74,040	38.1	—	0.0	46,359	R
Kansas	43,630	30,027	68.8	13,600	31.2	3	0.0	16,427	R
Kentucky	155,455	39,566	25.5	115,889	74.5	—	0.0	76,323	D
Louisiana	113,488	33,263	29.3	80,225	70.7	—	0.0	46,962	D
Maine	112,962	70,502	62.4	42,460	37.6	—	0.0	28,042	R
Maryland	92,795	30,438	32.8	62,357	67.2	—	0.0	31,919	D
Massachusetts	195,508	136,379	69.8	59,103	30.2	26	0.0	77,276	R
Michigan	225,632	128,563	57.0	97,069	43.0	—	0.0	31,494	R
Minnesota	71,620	43,545	60.8	28,075	39.2	—	0.0	15,470	R
Missouri	152,488	86,860	57.0	65,628	43.0	—	0.0	21,232	R
Nebraska	15,291	9,772	63.9	5,519	36.1	—	0.0	4,253	R
Nevada	11,689	6,474	55.4	5,215	44.6	—	0.0	1,259	R
New Hampshire	68,304	37,718	55.2	30,575	44.8	11	0.0	7,143	R
New Jersey	163,133	80,132	49.1	83,001	50.9	—	0.0	2,869	D
New York	849,771	419,888	49.4	429,883	50.6	—	0.0	9,995	D
North Carolina	181,498	96,939	53.4	84,559	46.6	—	0.0	12,380	R
Ohio	518,665	280,159	54.0	238,506	46.0	—	0.0	41,653	R
Oregon	22,086	10,961	49.6	11,125	50.4	—	0.0	164	D
Pennsylvania	655,662	342,280	52.2	313,382	47.8	—	0.0	28,898	R
Rhode Island	19,511	13,017	66.7	6,494	33.3	—	0.0	6,523	R
South Carolina	107,538	62,301	57.9	45,237	42.1	—	0.0	17,064	R
Tennessee	82,757	56,628	68.4	26,129	31.6	—	0.0	30,499	R
Vermont	56,224	44,173	78.6	12,051	21.4	—	0.0	32,122	R
West Virginia	49,321	29,015	58.8	20,306	41.2	—	0.0	8,709	R
Wisconsin	193,628	108,920	56.3	84,708	43.7	—	0.0	24,212	R
Totals	5,722,440	3,013,650	52.7	2,708,744	47.3	46		304,906	R

1. Mississippi, Texas, and Virginia did not participate in the election due to Reconstruction. In Florida the state legislature cast the electoral vote.

1872 Presidential Election

STATE	TOTAL VOTE	ULYSSES S. GRANT (Republican)		HORACE GREELEY (Democrat, Liberal Republican)		CHARLES O'CONOR (Straight Out Democrat)		OTHER		PLURALITY	
		Votes	%	Votes	%	Votes	%	Votes	%		
Alabama	169,716	90,272	53.2	79,444	46.8	—	0.0	—	0.0	10,828	R
Arkansas	79,300	41,373	52.2	37,927	47.8	—	0.0	—	0.0	3,446	R
California	95,785	54,007	56.4	40,717	42.5	1,061	1.1	—	0.0	13,290	R
Connecticut	95,992	50,307	52.4	45,685	47.6	—	0.0	—	0.0	4,622	R
Delaware	21,822	11,129	51.0	10,205	46.8	488	2.2	—	0.0	924	R
Florida	33,190	17,763	53.5	15,427	46.5	—	0.0	—	0.0	2,336	R
Georgia	138,906	62,550	45.0	76,356	55.0	—	0.0	—	0.0	13,806	D
Illinois	429,971	241,936	56.3	184,884	43.0	3,151	0.7	—	0.0	57,052	R
Indiana	349,779	186,147	53.2	163,632	46.8	—	0.0	—	0.0	22,515	R
Iowa	216,365	131,566	60.8	71,189	32.9	2,221	1.0	11,389	5.3	60,377	R
Kansas	100,512	66,805	66.5	32,970	32.8	156	0.2	581	0.6	33,835	R
Kentucky	191,552	88,970	45.5	100,208	54.5	2,374	1.2	—	0.0	11,238	D
Louisiana	128,692	71,663	55.7	57,029	44.3	—	0.0	—	0.0	14,634	R
Maine	90,523	61,426	67.9	29,097	32.1	—	0.0	—	0.0	32,329	R
Maryland	134,447	66,760	49.7	67,687	50.3	—	0.0	—	0.0	927	D
Massachusetts	192,650	133,455	69.3	59,195	30.7	—	0.0	—	0.0	74,260	R
Michigan	221,569	138,768	62.6	78,651	35.5	2,879	1.3	1,271	0.6	60,117	R
Minnesota	91,339	56,040	61.4	35,131	38.5	—	0.0	168	0.2	20,909	R
Mississippi	129,457	82,175	63.5	47,282	36.5	—	0.0	—	0.0	34,893	R
Missouri	273,059	119,196	43.7	151,434	55.5	2,429	0.9	—	0.0	32,238	D
Nebraska	25,932	18,329	70.7	7,603	29.3	—	0.0	—	0.0	10,726	R
Nevada	14,649	8,413	57.4	6,236	42.6	—	0.0	—	0.0	2,177	R
New Hampshire	68,906	37,168	53.9	31,425	45.6	—	0.0	313	0.5	5,743	R
New Jersey[1]	168,467	91,666	54.5	76,801	45.5	—	0.0	—	0.0	14,865	R
New York	829,692	440,758	53.1	387,279	46.7	1,454	0.2	201	0.0	53,479	R
North Carolina	165,163	94,772	57.4	70,130	42.5	261	0.2	—	0.0	24,642	R
Ohio	529,435	281,852	53.2	244,320	46.1	1,163	0.2	2,100	0.4	37,532	R
Oregon	20,107	11,818	58.8	7,742	38.5	547	2.7	—	0.0	4,076	R
Pennsylvania	561,629	349,589	62.2	212,040	37.8	—	0.0	—	0.0	137,549	R
Rhode Island	18,994	13,665	71.9	5,329	28.1	—	0.0	—	0.0	8,336	R
South Carolina	95,452	72,290	75.7	22,699	23.8	204	0.2	259	0.3	49,591	R
Tennessee	179,046	85,655	47.8	93,391	52.2	—	0.0	—	0.0	7,736	D
Texas	115,700	47,910	41.4	67,675	58.5	115	0.1	—	0.0	19,765	D
Vermont	52,961	41,480	78.3	10,926	20.6	553	1.0	—	0.0	30,554	R
Virginia	185,195	93,463	50.5	91,647	49.5	85	0.0	—	0.0	1,816	R
West Virginia	62,467	32,320	51.7	29,532	47.3	615	1.0	—	0.0	2,788	R
Wisconsin	192,255	105,012	54.6	86,390	44.9	853	0.4	—	0.0	18,622	R
Totals	6,470,674	3,598,468	55.6	2,835,315	43.8	20,609	0.3	16,282	0.3	763,153	R

1. Figures from New Jersey's *Manual, 1873*.

1876 Presidential Election

STATE	TOTAL VOTE	RUTHERFORD B. HAYES [1] (Republican) Votes	%	SAMUEL J. TILDEN [1] (Democrat) Votes	%	PETER COOPER (Greenback) Votes	%	OTHER Votes	%	PLURALITY	
Alabama	171,699	68,708	40.0	102,989	60.0	—	0.0	2	0.0	34,281	D
Arkansas	96,946	38,649	39.9	58,086	59.9	211	0.2	—	0.0	19,437	D
California	155,784	79,258	50.9	76,460	49.1	47	0.0	19	0.0	2,798	R
Connecticut	122,134	59,033	48.3	61,927	50.7	774	0.6	400	0.3	2,894	D
Delaware	24,133	10,752	44.6	13,381	55.4	—	0.0	—	0.0	2,629	D
Florida	46,776	23,849	51.0	22,927	49.0	—	0.0	—	0.0	922	R
Georgia	180,690	50,533	28.0	130,157	72.0	—	0.0	—	0.0	79,624	D
Illinois	554,368	278,232	50.2	258,611	46.6	17,207	3.1	318	0.1	19,621	R
Indiana	430,020	206,971	48.1	213,516	49.7	9,533	2.2	—	0.0	6,545	D
Iowa	293,398	171,326	58.4	112,121	38.2	9,431	3.2	520	0.2	59,205	R
Kansas	124,134	78,324	63.1	37,902	30.5	7,770	6.3	138	0.1	40,422	R
Kentucky	259,614	97,156	37.4	159,696	61.5	1,944	0.7	818	0.3	62,540	D
Louisiana	145,823	75,315	51.6	70,508	48.4	—	0.0	—	0.0	4,807	R
Maine[2]	117,045	66,300	56.6	49,917	42.6	662	0.6	166	0.1	16,383	R
Maryland	163,759	71,980	44.0	91,779	56.0	—	0.0	—	0.0	19,799	D
Massachusetts	259,619	150,063	57.8	108,777	41.9	—	0.0	779	0.3	41,286	R
Michigan	318,426	166,901	52.4	141,665	44.5	9,023	2.8	837	0.3	25,236	R
Minnesota[3]	124,119	72,982	58.8	48,816	39.3	2,321	1.9	—	0.0	24,166	R
Mississippi	164,776	52,603	31.9	112,173	68.1	—	0.0	—	0.0	59,570	D
Missouri	350,610	145,027	41.4	202,086	57.6	3,497	1.0	—	0.0	57,059	D
Nebraska	49,258	31,915	64.8	17,343	35.2	—	0.0	—	0.0	14,572	R
Nevada	19,691	10,383	52.7	9,308	47.3	—	0.0	—	0.0	1,075	R
New Hampshire	80,143	41,540	51.8	38,510	48.1	—	0.0	93	0.1	3,030	R
New Jersey	220,193	103,517	47.0	115,962	52.7	714	0.3	—	0.0	12,445	D
New York	1,015,503	489,207	48.2	521,949	51.4	1,978	0.2	2,369	0.2	32,742	D
North Carolina	233,911	108,484	46.4	125,427	53.6	—	0.0	—	0.0	16,943	D
Ohio	658,650	330,698	50.2	323,182	49.1	3,058	0.5	1,712	0.3	7,516	R
Oregon	29,873	15,207	50.9	14,157	47.4	509	1.7	—	0.0	1,050	R
Pennsylvania	758,973	384,157	50.6	366,204	48.2	7,209	0.9	1,403	0.2	17,953	R
Rhode Island	26,499	15,787	59.6	10,712	40.4	—	0.0	—	0.0	5,075	R
South Carolina	182,683	91,786	50.2	90,897	49.8	—	0.0	—	0.0	889	R
Tennessee	222,743	89,566	40.2	133,177	59.8	—	0.0	—	0.0	43,611	D
Texas	151,431	45,013	29.7	106,372	70.2	—	0.0	46	0.0	61,359	D
Vermont	64,460	44,092	68.4	20,254	31.4	—	0.0	114	0.2	23,838	R
Virginia	236,288	95,518	40.4	140,770	59.6	—	0.0	—	0.0	45,252	D
West Virginia	99,647	41,997	42.1	56,546	56.7	1,104	1.1	—	0.0	14,549	D
Wisconsin[4]	257,799	130,668	50.7	123,927	48.1	1,509	0.6	1,695	0.7	6,741	R
Totals	8,411,618	4,033,497	48.0	4,288,191	51.0	78,501	0.9	11,429	0.1	254,694	D

1. Hayes won the election. For resolution of disputed 1876 election, see p. 166.
2. Figures from *Maine Register, 1945.*
3. Figures from *Minnesota Votes.*
4. Figures from *Wisconsin Blue Book 1997,* p. 677.

1880 Presidential Election

STATE	TOTAL VOTE	JAMES A. GARFIELD (Republican) Votes	%	WINFIELD S. HANCOCK (Democrat) Votes	%	JAMES B. WEAVER (Greenback) Votes	%	OTHER Votes	%	PLURALITY	
Alabama	151,902	56,350	37.1	91,130	60.0	4,422	2.9	—	0.0	34,780	D
Arkansas[1]	108,870	42,436	39.0	60,775	55.9	4,116	3.8	1,543	1.4	18,339	D
California	164,218	80,282	48.9	80,426	49.0	3,381	2.1	129	0.1	144	D
Colorado	53,546	27,450	51.3	24,647	46.0	1,435	2.7	14	0.0	2,803	R
Connecticut	132,798	67,071	50.5	64,411	48.5	868	0.7	448	0.3	2,660	R
Delaware	29,458	14,148	48.0	15,181	51.5	129	0.4	—	0.0	1,033	D
Florida	51,618	23,654	45.8	27,964	54.2	—	0.0	—	0.0	4,310	D
Georgia	157,451	54,470	34.6	102,981	65.4	—	0.0	—	0.0	48,511	D
Illinois	622,305	318,036	51.1	277,321	44.6	26,358	4.2	590	0.1	40,715	R
Indiana	470,758	232,169	49.3	225,523	47.9	13,066	2.8	—	0.0	6,646	R
Iowa	323,140	183,904	56.9	105,845	32.8	32,327	10.0	1,064	0.3	78,059	R
Kansas	201,054	121,520	60.4	59,789	29.7	19,710	9.8	35	0.0	61,731	R
Kentucky	266,884	106,059	39.7	149,068	55.9	11,499	4.3	258	0.1	43,009	D
Louisiana	104,462	38,978	37.3	65,047	62.3	437	0.4	—	0.0	26,069	D
Maine	143,903	74,052	51.5	65,211	45.3	4,409	3.1	231	0.2	8,841	R
Maryland	173,049	78,515	45.4	93,706	54.1	828	0.5	—	0.0	15,191	D
Massachusetts	282,505	165,198	58.5	111,960	39.6	4,548	1.6	799	0.3	53,238	R
Michigan	353,076	185,335	52.5	131,596	37.3	34,895	9.9	1,250	0.4	53,739	R
Minnesota	150,806	93,939	62.3	53,314	35.4	3,267	2.2	286	0.2	40,625	R
Mississippi	117,068	34,844	29.8	75,750	64.7	5,797	5.0	677	0.6	40,906	D
Missouri	397,289	153,647	38.7	208,600	52.5	35,042	8.8	—	0.0	54,953	D
Nebraska	87,355	54,979	62.9	28,523	32.7	3,853	4.4	—	0.0	26,456	R
Nevada	18,343	8,732	47.6	9,611	52.4	—	0.0	—	0.0	879	D
New Hampshire	86,361	44,856	51.9	40,797	47.2	528	0.6	180	0.2	4,059	R
New Jersey	245,928	120,555	49.0	122,565	49.8	2,617	1.1	191	0.1	2,010	D
New York	1,103,945	555,544	50.3	534,511	48.4	12,373	1.1	1,517	0.1	21,033	R
North Carolina	240,946	115,616	48.0	124,204	51.5	1,126	0.5	—	0.0	8,588	D
Ohio	724,984	375,048	51.7	340,867	47.0	6,456	0.9	2,613	0.4	34,181	R
Oregon	40,841	20,619	50.5	19,955	48.9	267	0.7	—	0.0	664	R
Pennsylvania	874,783	444,704	50.8	407,428	46.6	20,667	2.4	1,984	0.2	37,276	R
Rhode Island	29,235	18,195	62.2	10,779	36.9	236	0.8	25	0.1	7,416	R
South Carolina	169,793	57,954	34.1	111,236	65.5	567	0.3	36	0.0	53,282	D
Tennessee	243,263	107,677	44.3	129,569	53.3	6,017	2.5	—	0.0	21,892	D
Texas[1]	240,659	57,225	23.8	155,963	64.8	27,471	11.4	—	0.0	98,738	D
Vermont	65,098	45,567	70.0	18,316	28.1	1,215	1.9	—	0.0	27,251	R
Virginia[1]	212,660	83,634	39.3	128,647[2]	60.5	—	0.0	379	0.2	45,013	D
West Virginia	112,641	46,243	41.1	57,390	50.9	9,008	8.0	—	0.0	11,147	D
Wisconsin	267,202	144,406	54.0	114,650	42.9	7,986	3.0	160	0.1	29,756	R
Totals	9,220,197	4,453,611	48.3	4,445,256	48.2	306,921	3.3	14,409	0.2	8,355	R

1. Figures from W. Dean Burnham, *Presidential Ballots 1836–1892* (New York: Arno Press, 1976).
2. According to Burnham there were two Democratic slates—regular with 96,594 votes and Readjuster Democrats with 32,053 votes—and he does not combine the two. They are combined here. It is not entirely clear if they ran the same set of electors.

1884 Presidential Election

STATE	TOTAL VOTE	GROVER CLEVELAND (Democrat)		JAMES G. BLAINE (Republican)		BENJAMIN F. BUTLER (Greenback)		JOHN P. ST. JOHN (Prohibition)		OTHER		PLURALITY	
		Votes	%	Votes	%	Votes	%	Votes	%	Votes	%		
Alabama	153,624	92,736	60.4	59,444	38.7	762	0.5	610	0.4	72	0.0	33,292	D
Arkansas	125,779	72,734	57.8	51,198	40.7	1,847	1.5	—	0.0	—	0.0	21,536	D
California	196,988	89,288	45.3	102,369	52.0	2,037	1.0	2,965	1.5	329	0.2	13,081	R
Colorado	66,519	27,723	41.7	36,084	54.2	1,956	2.9	756	1.1	—	0.0	8,361	R
Connecticut	137,221	67,167	48.9	65,879	48.0	1,682	1.2	2,493	1.8	—	0.0	1,288	D
Delaware	29,984	16,957	56.6	12,953	43.2	10	0.0	64	0.2	—	0.0	4,004	D
Florida	59,990	31,769	53.0	28,031	46.7	—	0.0	72	0.1	118	0.2	3,738	D
Georgia	143,610	94,667	65.9	48,603	33.8	145	0.1	195	0.1	—	0.0	46,064	D
Illinois	672,670	312,351	46.4	337,469	50.2	10,776	1.6	12,074	1.8	—	0.0	25,118	R
Indiana[1]	495,423	245,041	49.5	238,511	48.1	8,820	1.8	3,051	0.6	—	0.0	6,530	D
Iowa	393,542	177,316	45.1	197,089	50.1	16,341	4.2	1,499	0.4	1,297	0.3	19,773	R
Kansas	250,991	90,111	35.9	154,410	61.5	1,691	0.7	4,311	1.7	468	0.2	64,299	R
Kentucky	276,503	152,894	55.3	118,822	43.0	1,690	0.6	3,097	1.1	—	0.0	34,072	D
Louisiana	109,399	62,594	57.2	46,347	42.4	120	0.1	338	0.3	—	0.0	16,247	D
Maine[2]	130,489	52,153	40.0	72,217	55.3	3,953	3.0	2,160	1.7	6	0.0	20,064	R
Maryland	185,838	96,941	52.2	85,748	46.1	347	0.2	2,802	1.5	—	0.0	11,193	D
Massachusetts[3]	303,383	122,352	40.3	146,724	48.4	24,382	8.0	9,923	3.3	2	0.0	24,372	R
Michigan[4]	401,186	189,361	47.2	192,669	48.0	753	0.2	18,403	4.6	—	0.0	3,308	R
Minnesota[5]	190,236	70,135	36.7	111,819	58.8	3,583	1.9	4,696	2.5	—	0.0	41,684	R
Mississippi	120,688	77,653	64.3	43,035	35.7	—	0.0	—	0.0	—	0.0	34,618	D
Missouri	441,268	236,023	53.5	203,081	46.0	—	0.0	2,164	0.5	—	0.0	32,942	D
Nebraska	134,202	54,391	40.5	76,912	57.3	—	0.0	2,899	2.2	—	0.0	22,521	R
Nevada	12,779	5,577	43.6	7,176	56.2	26	0.2	—	0.0	—	0.0	1,599	R
New Hampshire	84,586	39,198	46.3	43,254	51.1	554	0.7	1,580	1.9	—	0.0	4,056	R
New Jersey	260,853	127,747	49.0	123,436	47.3	3,486	1.3	6,156	2.4	28	0.0	4,311	D
New York	1,167,003	563,048	48.2	562,001	48.2	16,955	1.5	24,999	2.1	—	0.0	1,047	D
North Carolina	268,356	142,905	53.3	125,021	46.6	—	0.0	430	0.2	—	0.0	17,884	D
Ohio	784,620	368,280	46.9	400,092	51.0	5,179	0.7	11,069	1.4	—	0.0	31,812	R
Oregon	52,683	24,598	46.7	26,845	51.0	726	1.4	479	0.9	35	0.1	2,247	R
Pennsylvania[6]	899,563	392,915	43.7	474,350	52.7	16,992	1.9	15,306	1.7	—	0.0	81,435	R
Rhode Island	32,771	12,391	37.8	19,030	58.1	422	1.3	928	2.8	—	0.0	6,639	R
South Carolina	92,812	69,845	75.3	21,730	23.4	—	0.0	—	0.0	1,237	1.3	48,115	D
Tennessee	259,978	133,770	51.5	124,101	47.7	957	0.4	1,150	0.4	—	0.0	9,669	D
Texas[1]	326,458	226,375	69.3	93,345	28.6	3,221	1.0	3,517	1.1	—	0.0	133,030	D
Vermont	59,409	17,331	29.2	39,514	66.5	785	1.3	1,752	2.9	27	0.0	22,183	R
Virginia	284,977	145,491	51.1	139,356	48.9	—	0.0	130	0.0	—	0.0	6,135	D
West Virginia	132,145	67,311	50.9	63,096	47.7	799	0.6	939	0.7	—	0.0	4,215	D
Wisconsin	319,847	146,447	45.8	161,155	50.4	4,594	1.4	7,651	2.4	—	0.0	14,708	R
Totals	10,058,373	4,915,586	48.9	4,852,916	48.2	135,594	1.3	150,658	1.5	3,619	0.0	62,670	D

1. Figures from W. Dean Burnham, *Presidential Ballots 1836–1892* (New York: Arno Press, 1976).
2. Figures from Svend Petersen, *A Statistical History of the American Presidential Elections* (Westport, Conn.: Greenwood Press, 1981); *Maine Register, 1945.*
3. Figures from *Manual, 1885.*
4. Figures from *Michigan Manual, 1913,* p. 689. For Michigan's Democratic total, twelve out of thirteen electors ran on both the Democratic and Greenback ticket (a Fusion slate); the Fusion electors vote is used here. The vote listed under Greenback was solely for the "straight" Greenback slate.
5. Figures from *Minnesota Votes.*
6. Figures from Pennsylvania's *Manual, 1885.*

1888 Presidential Election

STATE	TOTAL VOTE	BENJAMIN HARRISON[1] (Republican) Votes	%	GROVER CLEVELAND[1] (Democrat) Votes	%	CLINTON B. FISK (Prohibition) Votes	%	ALSON J. STREETER (Union Labor) Votes	%	OTHER Votes	%	PLURALITY	
Alabama	175,085	57,177	32.7	117,314	67.0	594	0.3	—	0.0	—	0.0	60,137	D
Arkansas	157,058	59,752	38.0	86,062	54.8	614	0.4	10,630	6.8	—	0.0	26,310	D
California	251,339	124,816	49.7	117,729	46.8	5,761	2.3	—	0.0	3,033	1.2	7,087	R
Colorado	91,946	50,772	55.2	37,549	40.8	2,182	2.4	1,266	1.4	177	0.2	13,223	R
Connecticut	153,978	74,584	48.4	74,920	48.7	4,234	2.7	240	0.2	—	0.0	336	D
Delaware	29,764	12,950	43.5	16,414	55.1	399	1.3	—	0.0	1	0.0	3,464	D
Florida	66,500	26,529	39.9	39,557	59.5	414	0.6	—	0.0	—	0.0	13,028	D
Georgia	142,936	40,499	28.3	100,493	70.3	1,808	1.3	136	0.1	—	0.0	59,994	D
Illinois	747,813	370,475	49.5	348,351	46.6	21,703	2.9	7,134	1.0	150	0.0	22,124	R
Indiana	536,988	263,366	49.0	260,990	48.6	9,939	1.9	2,693	0.5	—	0.0	2,376	R
Iowa	404,694	211,607	52.3	179,876	44.4	3,550	0.9	9,105	2.2	556	0.1	31,731	R
Kansas	331,133	182,845	55.2	102,739	31.0	6,774	2.0	37,838	11.4	937	0.3	80,106	R
Kentucky	344,868	155,138	45.0	183,830	53.3	5,223	1.5	677	0.2	—	0.0	28,692	D
Louisiana	115,891	30,660	26.5	85,032	73.4	160	0.1	39	0.0	—	0.0	54,372	D
Maine	128,253	73,730	57.5	50,472	39.4	2,691	2.1	1,344	1.0	16	0.0	23,258	R
Maryland	210,941	99,986	47.4	106,188	50.3	4,767	2.3	—	0.0	—	0.0	6,202	D
Massachusetts	344,243	183,892	53.4	151,590	44.0	8,701	2.5	—	0.0	60	0.0	32,302	R
Michigan	475,356	236,387	49.7	213,469	44.9	20,945	4.4	4,555	1.0	—	0.0	22,918	R
Minnesota	263,162	142,492	54.1	104,372	39.7	15,201	5.8	1,097	0.4	—	0.0	38,120	R
Mississippi	115,786	30,095	26.0	85,451	73.8	240	0.2	—	0.0	—	0.0	55,356	D
Missouri	521,359	236,252	45.3	261,943	50.2	4,539	0.9	18,625	3.6	—	0.0	25,691	D
Nebraska	202,630	108,417	53.5	80,552	39.8	9,435	4.7	4,226	2.1	—	0.0	27,865	R
Nevada	12,573	7,229	57.5	5,303	42.2	41	0.3	—	0.0	—	0.0	1,926	R
New Hampshire	90,770	45,734	50.4	43,382	47.8	1,596	1.8	—	0.0	58	0.1	2,352	R
New Jersey[2]	303,801	144,360	47.5	151,508	49.9	7,933	2.6	—	0.0	—	0.0	7,148	D
New York[3]	1,321,270	650,338	49.2	635,965	48.1	30,231	2.3	627	0.0	4,736	0.4	14,373	R
North Carolina[4]	285,946	134,784	47.1	148,336	51.9	2,789	1.0	—	0.0	37	0.0	13,552	D
Ohio	839,357	416,054	49.6	395,456	47.1	24,356	2.9	3,491	0.4	—	0.0	20,598	R
Oregon	61,889	33,291	53.8	26,518	42.8	1,676	2.7	—	0.0	404	0.7	6,773	R
Pennsylvania	997,568	526,091	52.7	446,633	44.8	20,947	2.1	3,873	0.4	24	0.0	79,458	R
Rhode Island	40,775	21,969	53.9	17,530	43.0	1,251	3.1	18	0.0	7	0.0	4,439	R
South Carolina	79,997	13,736	17.2	65,824	82.3	—	0.0	—	0.0	437	0.5	52,088	D
Tennessee[4]	304,313	139,511	45.8	158,779	52.2	5,975	2.0	48	0.0	—	0.0	19,268	D
Texas[5]	363,484	93,991	25.9	236,290	65.0	4,739	1.3	28,459	7.8	—	0.0	142,299	D
Vermont	63,476	45,193	71.2	16,788	26.4	1,460	2.3	—	0.0	35	0.1	28,405	R
Virginia	304,087	150,399	49.5	152,004	50.0	1,684	0.6	—	0.0	—	0.0	1,605	D
West Virginia	159,440	78,171	49.0	78,677	49.3	1,084	0.7	1,508	0.9	—	0.0	506	D
Wisconsin	354,614	176,553	49.8	155,232	43.8	14,277	4.0	8,552	2.4	—	0.0	21,321	R
Totals	11,395,705	5,449,825	47.8	5,539,118	48.6	249,492	2.2	146,602	1.3	10,668	0.1	89,293	D

1. Harrison won the election. See p. 198.
2. Figures from *Manual, 1889.*
3. Figures from *New York Legislative Manual, 1889.*
4. Figures from Svend Petersen, *A Statistical History of the American Presidential Elections* (Westport, Conn.: Greenwood Press, 1981).
5. Figures from W. Dean Burnham, *Presidential Ballots 1836–1892* (New York: Arno Press, 1976).

1892 Presidential Election

STATE	TOTAL VOTE	GROVER CLEVELAND (Democrat) Votes	%	BENJAMIN HARRISON (Republican) Votes	%	JAMES B. WEAVER (Populist) Votes	%	JOHN BIDWELL (Prohibition) Votes	%	OTHER Votes	%	PLURALITY	
Alabama	232,543	138,135	59.4	9,184	3.9	84,984	36.5	240	0.1	—	0.0	53,151	D
Arkansas	148,117	87,834	59.3	47,072	31.8	11,831	8.0	113	0.1	1,267	0.9	40,762	D
California	269,585	118,151	43.8	118,027	43.8	25,311	9.4	8,096	3.0	—	0.0	124	D
Colorado	93,881	—	0.0	38,620	41.1	53,584	57.1	1,677	1.8	—	0.0	14,964	POP
Connecticut	164,593	82,395	50.1	77,030	46.8	809	0.5	4,026	2.4	333	0.2	5,365	D
Delaware	37,235	18,581	49.9	18,077	48.5	—	0.0	564	1.5	13	0.0	504	D
Florida[1]	35,567	30,154	84.8	—	0.0	4,843	13.6	570	1.6	—	0.0	25,311	D
Georgia[1]	223,961	129,386	57.8	48,305	21.6	42,937	19.2	988	0.4	2,345	1.0	81,081	D
Idaho	19,407	—	0.0	8,599	44.3	10,520	54.2	288	1.5	—	0.0	1,921	POP
Illinois	873,667	426,281	48.8	399,308	45.7	22,207	2.5	25,871	3.0	—	0.0	26,973	D
Indiana	553,613	262,740	47.5	255,615	46.2	22,208	4.0	13,050	2.4	—	0.0	7,125	D
Iowa	443,159	196,367	44.3	219,795	49.6	20,595	4.6	6,402	1.4	—	0.0	23,428	R
Kansas	323,591	—	0.0	156,134	48.3	162,888	50.3	4,569	1.4	—	0.0	6,754	POP
Kentucky	340,864	175,461	51.5	135,462	39.7	23,500	6.9	6,441	1.9	—	0.0	39,999	D
Louisiana[1]	118,287	87,922	74.3	27,903	23.6	2,462	2.1	—	0.0	—	0.0	60,023	D
Maine[2]	116,013	48,024	41.4	62,878	54.2	2,045	1.8	3,062	2.6	4	0.0	14,854	R
Maryland	213,275	113,866	53.4	92,736	43.5	796	0.4	5,877	2.8	—	0.0	21,130	D
Massachusetts	391,028	176,813	45.2	202,814	51.9	3,210	0.8	7,539	1.9	652	0.2	26,001	R
Michigan	466,917	202,396	43.3	222,708	47.7	20,031	4.3	20,857	4.5	925	0.2	20,312	R
Minnesota[3]	267,461	101,055	37.8	122,836	45.9	29,336	11.0	14,234	5.3	—	0.0	21,781	R
Mississippi	52,519	40,030	76.2	1,398	2.7	10,118	19.3	973	1.9	—	0.0	29,912	D
Missouri	541,583	268,400	49.6	227,646	42.0	41,204	7.6	4,333	0.8	—	0.0	40,754	D
Montana	44,461	17,690	39.8	18,871	42.4	7,338	16.5	562	1.3	—	0.0	1,181	R
Nebraska	200,205	24,956	12.5	87,213	43.6	83,134	41.5	4,902	2.4	—	0.0	4,079	R
Nevada	10,826	703	6.5	2,811	26.0	7,226	66.7	86	0.8	—	0.0	4,415	POP
New Hampshire	89,328	42,081	47.1	45,658	51.1	292	0.3	1,297	1.5	—	0.0	3,577	R
New Jersey	337,485	170,987	50.7	156,059	46.2	969	0.3	8,133	2.4	1,337	0.4	14,928	D
New York	1,336,793	654,868	49.0	609,350	45.6	16,429	1.2	38,190	2.9	17,956	1.3	45,518	D
North Carolina	280,270	132,951	47.4	100,346	35.8	44,336	15.8	2,637	0.9	—	0.0	32,605	D
North Dakota[1]	36,118	—	0.0	17,519	48.5	17,700	49.0	899	2.5	—	0.0	181	POP
Ohio	850,164	404,115	47.5	405,187	47.7	14,850	1.7	26,012	3.1	—	0.0	1,072	R
Oregon	78,378	14,243	18.2	35,002	44.7	26,875	34.3	2,258	2.9	—	0.0	8,127	R
Pennsylvania	1,003,000	452,264	45.1	516,011	51.4	8,714	0.9	25,123	2.5	888	0.1	63,747	R
Rhode Island	53,196	24,336	45.7	26,975	50.7	228	0.4	1,654	3.1	3	0.0	2,639	R
South Carolina	70,504	54,680	77.6	13,345	18.9	2,407	3.4	—	0.0	72	0.1	41,335	D
South Dakota	70,513	9,081	12.9	34,888	49.5	26,544	37.6	—	0.0	—	0.0	8,344	R
Tennessee	265,732	136,468	51.4	100,537	37.8	23,918	9.0	4,809	1.8	—	0.0	35,931	D
Texas[4]	422,447	239,148	56.6	77,478	18.3	99,688	23.6	2,165	0.5	3,968	1.0	161,670	D
Vermont	55,793	16,325	29.3	37,992	68.1	42	0.1	1,424	2.6	10	0.0	21,667	R
Virginia	292,238	164,136	56.2	113,098	38.7	12,275	4.2	2,729	0.9	—	0.0	51,038	D
Washington	87,968	29,802	33.9	36,459	41.4	19,165	21.8	2,542	2.9	—	0.0	6,657	R
West Virginia	171,079	84,467	49.4	80,292	46.9	4,167	2.4	2,153	1.3	—	0.0	4,175	D
Wisconsin	371,481	177,325	47.7	171,101	46.1	9,919	2.7	13,136	3.5	—	0.0	6,224	D
Wyoming	16,703	—	0.0	8,454	50.6	7,722	46.2	498	3.0	29	0.2	732	R
Totals	12,071,548	5,554,617	46.0	5,186,793	43.0	1,024,280	8.5	270,979	2.2	29,802	0.2	367,824	D

1. Figures from Svend Petersen, *A Statistical History of the American Presidential Elections* (Westport, Conn.: Greenwood Press, 1981), p. 60.
2. Figures from *Maine Register, 1945.*
3. Figures from *Minnesota Votes.*
4. Figures from *The Texas Almanac's Political History of Texas.*

1896 Presidential Election

STATE	TOTAL VOTE	WILLIAM McKINLEY (Republican)		WILLIAM J. BRYAN (Democrat, Populist)[1]		JOHN M. PALMER (National Democrat)		JOSHUA LEVERING (Prohibition)		OTHER		PLURALITY	
		Votes	%	Votes	%	Votes	%	Votes	%	Votes	%		
Alabama	194,580	55,673	28.6	130,298	67.0	6,375	3.3	2,234	1.1	—	0.0	74,625	D
Arkansas	149,396	37,512	25.1	110,103	73.7	—	0.0	889	0.6	892	0.6	72,591	D
California[2]	299,374	146,688	49.1	123,143	41.2	2,006	0.7	2,573	0.9	24,285	8.2	23,545	R
Colorado	189,539	26,271	13.9	161,005	84.9	1	0.0	1,717	0.9	545	0.3	134,734	D
Connecticut	174,394	110,285	63.2	56,740	32.5	4,336	2.5	1,806	1.0	1,227	0.7	53,545	R
Delaware[3]	31,538	16,883	53.5	13,425	42.6	877	2.8	355	1.1	—	0.0	3,458	R
Florida[2]	46,468	11,298	24.3	30,683	66.0	1,778	3.8	656	1.4	2,053	4.4	19,385	D
Georgia[4]	163,309	60,107	36.8	94,733	58.0	2,809	1.7	5,613	3.4	47	0.0	34,626	D
Idaho	29,631	6,324	21.3	23,135	78.1	—	0.0	172	0.6	—	0.0	16,811	D
Illinois	1,090,766	607,130	55.7	465,593	42.7	6,307	0.6	9,796	0.9	1,940	0.2	141,537	R
Indiana	637,089	323,754	50.8	305,538	48.0	2,145	0.3	3,061	0.5	2,591	0.4	18,216	R
Iowa	521,550	289,293	55.5	223,744	42.9	4,516	0.9	3,192	0.6	805	0.2	65,549	R
Kansas	336,085	159,484	47.5	173,049	51.5	1,209	0.4	1,723	0.5	620	0.2	13,565	D
Kentucky	445,928	218,171	48.9	217,894	48.9	5,084	1.1	4,779	1.1	—	0.0	277	R
Louisiana	101,046	22,037	21.8	77,175	76.4	1,834	1.8	—	0.0	—	0.0	55,138	D
Maine	118,419	80,403	67.9	34,587	29.2	1,867	1.6	1,562	1.3	—	0.0	45,816	R
Maryland	250,249	136,959	54.7	104,150	41.6	2,499	1.0	5,918	2.4	723	0.3	32,809	R
Massachusetts	401,269	278,976	69.5	105,414	26.3	11,749	2.9	2,998	0.7	2,132	0.5	173,562	R
Michigan	545,583	293,336	53.8	237,164	43.5	6,923	1.3	4,978	0.9	3,182	0.6	56,172	R
Minnesota	341,762	193,503	56.6	139,735	40.9	3,222	0.9	4,348	1.3	954	0.3	53,768	R
Mississippi	69,591	4,819	6.9	63,355	91.0	1,021	1.5	396	0.6	—	0.0	58,536	D
Missouri	674,032	304,940	45.2	363,667	54.0	2,365	0.4	2,169	0.3	891	0.1	58,727	D
Montana	53,330	10,509	19.7	42,628	79.9	—	0.0	193	0.4	—	0.0	32,119	D
Nebraska	223,181	103,064	46.2	115,007	51.5	2,885	1.3	1,242	0.6	983	0.4	11,943	D
Nevada[5]	10,314	1,938	18.8	7,802	75.6	—	0.0	—	0.0	574	5.6	5,864	D
New Hampshire[2]	83,670	57,444	68.7	21,271	25.4	3,520	4.2	779	0.9	656	0.8	36,173	R
New Jersey	371,014	221,367	59.7	133,675	36.0	6,373	1.7	—	0.0	9,599	2.6	87,692	R
New York	1,423,876	819,838	57.6	551,369	38.7	18,950	1.3	16,052	1.1	17,667	1.2	268,469	R
North Carolina	331,337	155,122	46.8	174,408	52.6	578	0.2	635	0.2	594	0.2	19,286	D
North Dakota	47,391	26,335	55.6	20,686	43.6	—	0.0	358	0.8	12	0.0	5,649	R
Ohio[2]	1,014,295	525,991	51.9	474,882	46.8	1,858	0.2	5,068	0.5	6,496	0.6	51,109	R
Oregon	97,335	48,700	50.0	46,739	48.0	977	1.0	919	0.9	—	0.0	1,961	R
Pennsylvania[6]	1,194,355	728,300	61.0	427,125	35.8	11,000	0.9	19,274	1.6	8,656	0.7	301,175	R
Rhode Island	54,785	37,437	68.3	14,459	26.4	1,166	2.1	1,160	2.1	563	1.0	22,978	R
South Carolina	68,938	9,313	13.5	58,801	85.3	824	1.2	—	0.0	—	0.0	49,488	D
South Dakota	82,937	41,040	49.5	41,225	49.7	—	0.0	672	0.8	—	0.0	185	D
Tennessee	320,903	148,683	46.3	167,168	52.1	1,953	0.6	3,099	1.0	—	0.0	18,485	D
Texas[7]	515,987	163,413	31.7	267,803	51.9	4,989	1.0	1,797	0.3	77,985	15.1	104,390	D
Utah	78,098	13,491	17.3	64,607	82.7	—	0.0	—	0.0	—	0.0	51,116	D
Vermont[8]	63831	51,127	80.1	10,179	15.9	1,331	2.1	733	1.1	461	0.7	40,948	R
Virginia	294,674	135,379	45.9	154,708	52.5	2,129	0.7	2,350	0.8	108	0.0	19,329	D
Washington[2]	93,583	39,153	41.8	51,646	55.2	—	0.0	968	1.0	1,668	1.8	12,493	D
West Virginia	201,757	105,379	52.2	94,480	46.8	678	0.3	1,220	0.6	—	0.0	10,899	R
Wisconsin	447,409	268,135	59.9	165,523	37.0	4,584	1.0	7,507	1.7	1,660	0.4	102,612	R
Wyoming[2]	21,093	10,072	47.8	10,376	49.3	—	0.0	159	0.8	486	2.3	304	D
Totals	13,905,691	7,105,144	51.1	6,370,897	45.8	132,718	1.0	125,118	0.9	171,814	1.2	734,247	R

1. Bryan was nominated by both the Democrats and the Populists but with different running mates. In several states different slates of electors were entered by each party. It is legally incorrect to combine the vote. The separate vote for Bryan usually under the Populist ticket is listed under "Other." In other states it appears that the two slates of electors were the same and it is correct to combine the vote.
2. Figures from Edgar E. Robinson, *The Presidential Vote 1896–1932* (Stanford, Calif.: Stanford University Press, 1934).
3. The vote of Kent County was excluded from the official tally because two sets of returns were sent to the state. The vote of the county as reported would have made the vote: McKinley, 20,685; Bryan, 16,708; Palmer, 968; and Levering, 469.
4. Figures from Svend Petersen, *A Statistical History of the American Presidential Elections* (Westport, Conn.: Greenwood Press, 1981).
5. Figures from *Political History of Nevada* (Secretary of State).
6. Figures from *Manual, 1897.*
7. There were two separate Bryan slates in Texas with various sources offering widely different totals. Figures here are from Robinson, *The Presidential Vote,* supplemented with manuscript returns supplied by the Texas secretary of state.
8. Figures from *Vermont Legislative Directory.*

1900 Presidential Election

STATE	TOTAL VOTE	WILLIAM McKINLEY (Republican) Votes	%	WILLIAM J. BRYAN (Democrat) Votes	%	JOHN G. WOOLEY (Prohibition) Votes	%	EUGENE V. DEBS (Socialist) Votes	%	OTHER Votes	%	PLURALITY	
Alabama[1]	160,477	55,634	34.7	96,368	60.1	3,796	2.4	928	0.6	3,751	2.3	40,734	D
Arkansas	127,966	44,800	35.0	81,242	63.5	584	0.5	—	0.0	1,340	1.0	36,442	D
California[2]	302,399	164,755	54.5	124,985	41.3	5,087	1.7	7,572	2.50	—	0.0	39,770	R
Colorado	220,895	92,701	42.0	122,705	55.5	3,790	1.7	686	0.3	1,013	0.5	30,004	D
Connecticut	180,195	102,572	56.9	74,014	41.1	1,617	0.9	1,029	0.6	963	0.5	28,558	R
Delaware	41,989	22,535	53.7	18,852	44.9	546	1.3	56	0.1	—	0.0	3,683	R
Florida[1]	39,777	7,463	18.8	28,273	71.1	2,244	5.7	654	1.6	1,143	2.9	20,810	D
Georgia	121,410	34,260	28.2	81,180	66.9	1,402	1.2	—	0.0	4,568	3.8	46,920	D
Idaho[1]	56,760	27,198	47.9	28,260	49.8	857	1.5	—	0.0	445	0.8	1,062	D
Illinois	1,131,898	597,985	52.8	503,061	44.4	17,626	1.6	9,687	0.9	3,539	0.3	94,924	R
Indiana	664,094	336,063	50.6	309,584	46.6	13,718	2.1	2,374	0.4	2,355	0.4	26,479	R
Iowa	530,345	307,799	58.0	209,261	39.5	9,502	1.8	2,743	0.5	1,040	0.2	98,538	R
Kansas[3]	353,766	185,955	52.6	162,601	46.0	3,605	1.0	1,605	0.5	—	0.0	23,354	R
Kentucky[4]	467,580	226,801	48.5	234,889	50.2	2,814	0.6	—	0.0	3,076	0.7	8,008	D
Louisiana	67,906	14,234	21.0	53,668	79.0	—	0.0	—	0.0	4	0.0	39,434	D
Maine[5]	107,698	66,413	61.7	37,822	35.1	2,585	2.4	878	0.8	—	0.0	28,591	R
Maryland	264,386	136,151	51.5	122,237	46.2	4,574	1.7	900	0.3	524	0.2	13,914	R
Massachusetts	414,804	238,866	57.6	156,997	37.8	6,202	1.5	9,607	2.3	3,132	0.8	81,869	R
Michigan	543,789	316,014	58.1	211,432	38.9	11,804	2.2	2,820	0.5	1,719	0.3	104,582	R
Minnesota	316,311	190,461	60.2	112,901	35.7	8,555	2.7	3,065	1.0	1,329	0.4	77,560	R
Mississippi	59,055	5,707	9.7	51,706	87.6	—	0.0	—	0.0	1,642	2.8	45,999	D
Missouri	683,658	314,092	45.9	351,922	51.5	5,965	0.9	6,139	0.9	5,540	0.8	37,830	D
Montana	63,856	25,409	39.8	37,311	58.4	306	0.5	711	1.1	119	0.2	11,902	D
Nebraska	241,430	121,835	50.5	114,013	47.2	3,655	1.5	823	0.3	1,104	0.5	7,822	R
Nevada	10,196	3,849	37.8	6,347	62.2	—	0.0	—	0.0	—	0.0	2,498	D
New Hampshire	92,364	54,799	59.3	35,489	38.4	1,270	1.4	790	0.9	16	0.0	19,310	R
New Jersey	401,050	221,707	55.3	164,808	41.1	7,183	1.8	4,609	1.1	2,743	0.7	56,899	R
New York	1,548,043	822,013	53.1	678,462	43.8	22,077	1.4	12,869	0.8	12,622	0.8	143,551	R
North Carolina	292,518	132,997	45.5	157,733	53.9	990	0.3	—	0.0	798	0.3	24,736	D
North Dakota	57,783	35,898	62.1	20,524	35.5	735	1.3	517	0.9	109	0.2	15,374	R
Ohio	1,040,073	543,918	52.3	474,882	45.7	10,203	1.0	4,847	0.5	6,223	0.6	69,036	R
Oregon[6]	84,216	46,526	55.2	33,385	39.6	2,536	3.1	1,494	1.8	275	0.3	13,141	R
Pennsylvania	1,173,210	712,665	60.7	424,232	36.2	27,908	2.4	4,831	0.4	3,574	0.3	288,433	R
Rhode Island	56,548	33,784	59.7	19,812	35.0	1,529	2.7	—	0.0	1,423	2.5	13,972	R
South Carolina	50,698	3,525	7.0	47,173	93.0	—	0.0	—	0.0	—	0.0	43,648	D
South Dakota	96,169	54,574	56.7	39,538	41.1	1,541	1.6	176	0.2	340	0.4	15,036	R
Tennessee	273,860	123,108	45.0	145,240	53.0	3,844	1.4	346	0.1	1,322	0.5	22,132	D
Texas	424,334	131,174	30.9	267,945	63.1	2,642	0.6	1,846	0.4	20,727	4.9	136,771	D
Utah	93,071	47,089	50.6	44,949	48.3	205	0.2	717	0.8	111	0.1	2,140	R
Vermont	56,212	42,569	75.7	12,849	22.9	383	0.7	39	0.1	372	0.7	29,720	R
Virginia	264,208	115,769	43.8	146,079	55.3	2,130	0.8	—	0.0	230	0.1	30,310	D
Washington	107,523	57,455	53.4	44,833	41.7	2,363	2.2	2,006	1.9	866	0.8	12,622	R
West Virginia	220,796	119,829	54.3	98,807	44.8	1,628	0.7	286	0.1	246	0.1	21,022	R
Wisconsin	442,501	265,760	60.1	159,163	36.0	10,027	2.3	7,048	1.6	503	0.1	106,597	R
Wyoming	24,708	14,482	58.6	10,164	41.1	—	0.0	21	0.1	41	0.2	4,318	R
Totals	13,972,525	7,219,193	51.7	6,357,698	45.5	210,028	1.5	94,719	0.7	90,887	0.7	861,495	R

1. Figures from Edgar E. Robinson, *The Presidential Vote 1896–1932* (Stanford, Calif.: Stanford University Press, 1934).
2. Figures from Svend Petersen, *A Statistical History of the American Presidential Elections* (Westport, Conn.: Greenwood Press, 1981); *Blue Book, 1908*, p. 700.
3. Figures from Petersen, *A Statistical History*, p. 67.
4. Figures from *Official Manual, 1904*, pp. 118–121.
5. Figures from *Maine Register*, 1945.
6. Figures from Petersen, *A Statistical History*; Robinson, *The Presidential Vote*.

1904 Presidential Election

STATE	TOTAL VOTE	THEODORE ROOSEVELT (Republican)		ALTON B. PARKER (Democrat)		EUGENE V. DEBS (Socialist)		SILAS C. SWALLOW (Prohibition)		OTHER		PLURALITY	
		Votes	%	Votes	%	Votes	%	Votes	%	Votes	%		
Alabama	108,785	22,472	20.7	79,797	73.4	853	0.8	612	0.6	5,051	4.6	57,325	D
Arkansas	116,328	46,760	40.2	64,434	55.4	1,816	1.6	992	0.9	2,326	2.0	17,674	D
California	331,768	205,226	61.9	89,294	26.9	29,535	8.9	7,380	2.2	333	0.1	115,932	R
Colorado	243,667	134,661	55.3	100,105	41.1	4,304	1.8	3,438	1.4	1,159	0.5	34,556	R
Connecticut	191,136	111,089	58.1	72,909	38.1	Z8	2.4	1,506	0.8	1,089	0.6	38,180	R
Delaware	43,856	23,705	54.1	19,347	44.1	146	0.3	607	1.4	51	0.1	4,358	R
Florida[1]	39,302	8,314	21.2	27,046	68.8	2,337	6.0	—	0.0	1,605	4.1	18,732	D
Georgia	130,986	24,004	18.3	83,466	63.7	196	0.1	685	0.5	22,635	17.3	59,462	D
Idaho	72,577	47,783	65.8	18,480	25.5	4,949	6.8	1,013	1.4	352	0.5	29,303	R
Illinois	1,076,495	632,645	58.8	327,606	30.4	69,225	6.4	34,770	3.2	12,249	1.1	305,039	R
Indiana	682,206	368,289	54.0	274,356	40.2	12,023	1.8	23,496	3.4	4,042	0.6	93,933	R
Iowa	485,703	307,907	63.4	149,141	30.7	14,847	3.1	11,601	2.4	2,207	0.5	158,766	R
Kansas	329,047	213,455	64.9	86,164	26.2	15,869	4.8	7,306	2.2	6,253	1.9	127,291	R
Kentucky	435,946	205,457	47.1	217,170	49.8	3,599	0.8	6,603	1.5	3,117	0.7	11,713	D
Louisiana	53,908	5,205	9.7	47,708	88.5	995	1.8	—	0.0	—	0.0	42,503	D
Maine[2]	96,036	64,438	67.1	27,648	28.8	2,103	2.2	1,510	1.6	337	0.3	36,790	R
Maryland	224,229	109,497	48.8	109,446	48.8	2,247	1.0	3,034	1.4	5	0.0	51	R
Massachusetts	445,100	257,813	57.9	165,746	37.2	13,604	3.1	4,279	1.0	3,658	0.8	92,067	R
Michigan	520,443	361,863	69.5	134,163	25.8	8,942	1.7	13,312	2.6	2,163	0.4	227,700	R
Minnesota	292,860	216,651	74.0	55,187	18.8	11,692	4.0	6,253	2.1	3,077	1.1	161,464	R
Mississippi	58,721	3,280	5.6	53,480	91.1	462	0.8	—	0.0	1,499	2.6	50,200	D
Missouri	643,861	321,449	49.9	296,312	46.0	13,009	2.0	7,191	1.1	5,900	0.9	25,137	R
Montana	63,568	33,994	53.5	21,816	34.3	5,675	8.9	339	0.5	1,744	2.7	12,178	R
Nebraska	225,732	138,558	61.4	52,921	23.4	7,412	3.3	6,323	2.8	20,518	9.1	85,637	R
Nevada	12,115	6,864	56.7	3,982	32.9	925	7.6	—	0.0	344	2.8	2,882	R
New Hampshire	90,151	54,157	60.1	34,071	37.8	1,090	1.2	750	0.8	83	0.1	20,086	R
New Jersey[3]	432,547	245,164	56.7	164,566	38.0	9,587	2.2	6,845	1.6	6,385	1.5	80,598	R
New York	1,617,765	859,533	53.1	683,981	42.3	36,883	2.3	20,787	1.3	16,581	1.0	175,552	R
North Carolina	207,818	82,442	39.7	124,091	59.7	124	0.1	342	0.2	819	0.4	41,649	D
North Dakota[2]	70,279	52,595	74.8	14,273	20.3	2,009	2.9	1,137	1.6	165	0.2	38,322	R
Ohio	1,004,395	600,095	59.7	344,674	34.3	36,260	3.6	19,339	1.9	4,027	0.4	255,421	R
Oregon	89,656	60,309	67.3	17,327	19.3	7,479	8.3	3,795	4.2	746	0.8	42,982	R
Pennsylvania	1,236,738	840,949	68.0	337,998	27.3	21,863	1.8	33,717	2.7	2,211	0.2	502,951	R
Rhode Island	68,656	41,605	60.6	24,839	36.2	956	1.4	768	1.1	488	0.7	16,766	R
South Carolina	55,890	2,570	4.6	53,320	95.4	—	0.0	—	0.0	—	0.0	50,750	D
South Dakota	101,395	72,083	71.1	21,969	21.7	3,138	3.1	2,965	2.9	1,240	1.2	50,114	R
Tennessee	242,750	105,363	43.4	131,653	54.2	1,354	0.6	1,889	0.8	2,491	1.0	26,290	D
Texas	233,609	51,307	22.0	167,088	71.5	2,788	1.2	3,933	1.7	8,493	3.6	115,781	D
Utah	101,626	62,446	61.4	33,413	32.9	5,767	5.7	—	0.0	—	0.0	29,033	R
Vermont	51,888	40,459	78.0	9,777	18.8	859	1.7	792	1.5	1	0.0	30,682	R
Virginia	130,410	48,180	36.9	80,649	61.8	202	0.2	1,379	1.1	—	0.0	32,469	D
Washington	145,151	101,540	70.0	28,098	19.4	10,023	6.9	3,229	2.2	2,261	1.6	73,442	R
West Virginia	239,986	132,620	55.3	100,855	42.0	1,573	0.7	4,599	1.9	339	0.1	31,765	R
Wisconsin	443,440	280,314	63.2	124,205	28.0	28,240	6.4	9,872	2.2	809	0.2	156,109	R
Wyoming	30,614	20,489	66.9	8,930	29.2	987	3.2	208	0.7	—	0.0	11,559	R
Totals	13,519,039	7,625,599	56.4	5,083,501	37.6	402,490	3.0	258,596	1.9	148,853	1.1	2,542,098	R

1. Figures from Svend Petersen, *A Statistical History of the American Presidential Elections* (Westport, Conn.: Greenwood Press, 1981).
2. Figures from *Maine Register, 1945.*
3. Figures from *Manual, 1905.*

1908 Presidential Election

STATE	TOTAL VOTE	WILLIAM H. TAFT (Republican)		WILLIAM J. BRYAN (Democrat)		EUGENE V. DEBS (Socialist)		EUGENE W. CHAFIN (Prohibition)		OTHER		PLURALITY	
		Votes	%	Votes	%	Votes	%	Votes	%	Votes	%		
Alabama	105,152	25,561	24.3	74,391	70.7	1,450	1.4	690	0.7	3,060	2.9	48,830	D
Arkansas	151,845	56,684	37.3	87,020	57.3	5,842	3.8	1,026	0.7	1,273	0.8	30,336	D
California	386,625	214,398	55.5	127,492	33.0	28,659	7.4	11,770	3.0	4,306	1.1	86,906	R
Colorado	263,858	123,693	46.9	126,644	48.0	7,960	3.0	5,559	2.1	2	0.0	2,951	D
Connecticut	189,903	112,815	59.4	68,255	35.9	5,113	2.7	2,380	1.3	1,340	0.7	44,560	R
Delaware	48,007	25,014	52.1	22,055	45.9	239	0.5	670	1.4	29	0.1	2,959	R
Florida	49,360	10,654	21.6	31,104	63.0	3,747	7.6	1,356	2.7	2,499	5.1	20,450	D
Georgia[1]	132,794	41,692	31.4	72,413	54.5	584	0.4	1,059	0.8	17,046	12.8	30,721	D
Idaho	97,293	52,621	54.1	36,162	37.2	6,400	6.6	1,986	2.0	124	0.1	16,459	R
Illinois	1,155,254	629,932	54.5	450,810	39.0	34,711	3.0	29,364	2.5	10,437	0.9	179,122	R
Indiana	721,117	348,993	48.4	338,262	46.9	13,476	1.9	18,036	2.5	2,350	0.3	10,731	R
Iowa	494,770	275,210	55.6	200,771	40.6	8,287	1.7	9,837	2.0	665	0.1	74,439	R
Kansas	376,043	197,316	52.5	161,209	42.9	12,420	3.3	5,030	1.3	68	0.0	36,107	R
Kentucky	490,719	235,711	48.0	244,092	49.7	4,093	0.8	5,885	1.2	938	0.2	8,381	D
Louisiana	75,117	8,958	11.9	63,568	84.6	2,514	3.3	—	0.0	77	0.1	54,610	D
Maine	106,335	66,987	63.0	35,403	33.3	1,758	1.7	1,487	1.4	700	0.7	31,584	R
Maryland	238,531	116,513	48.8	115,908	48.6	2,323	1.0	3,302	1.4	485	0.2	605	R
Massachusetts	456,905	265,966	58.2	155,533	34.0	10,778	2.4	4,373	1.0	20,255	4.4	110,433	R
Michigan	538,124	333,313	61.9	174,619	32.4	11,527	2.1	16,785	3.1	1,880	0.3	158,694	R
Minnesota[2]	331,328	195,846	59.1	109,411	33.0	14,528	4.4	11,114	3.4	429	0.1	86,435	R
Mississippi	66,904	4,363	6.5	60,287	90.1	978	1.5	—	0.0	1,276	1.9	55,924	D
Missouri	715,841	347,203	48.5	346,574	48.4	15,431	2.2	4,209	0.6	2,424	0.3	629	R
Montana	69,233	32,471	46.9	29,511	42.6	5,920	8.6	838	1.2	493	0.7	2,960	R
Nebraska	266,799	126,997	47.6	131,099	49.1	3,524	1.3	5,179	1.9	—	0.0	4,102	D
Nevada	24,526	10,775	43.9	11,212	45.7	2,103	8.6	—	0.0	436	1.8	437	D
New Hampshire	89,595	53,144	59.3	33,655	37.6	1,299	1.4	905	1.0	592	0.7	19,489	R
New Jersey	467,111	265,298	56.8	182,522	39.1	10,249	2.2	4,930	1.1	4,112	0.9	82,776	R
New York	1,638,350	870,070	53.1	667,468	40.7	38,451	2.3	22,667	1.4	39,694	2.4	202,602	R
North Carolina	252,554	114,887	45.5	136,928	54.2	372	0.1	354	0.1	13	0.0	22,041	D
North Dakota	94,524	57,680	61.0	32,884	34.8	2,421	2.6	1,496	1.6	43	0.0	24,796	R
Ohio	1,121,552	572,312	51.0	502,721	44.8	33,795	3.0	11,402	1.0	1,322	0.1	69,591	R
Oklahoma	254,260	110,473	43.4	122,362	48.1	21,425	8.4	—	0.0	—	0.0	11,889	D
Oregon	110,539	62,454	56.5	37,792	34.2	7,322	6.6	2,682	2.4	289	0.3	24,662	R
Pennsylvania	1,267,450	745,779	58.8	448,782	35.4	33,914	2.7	36,694	2.9	2,281	0.2	296,997	R
Rhode Island	72,317	43,942	60.8	24,706	34.2	1,365	1.9	1,016	1.4	1,288	1.8	19,236	R
South Carolina	66,379	3,945	5.9	62,288	93.8	100	0.2	—	0.0	46	0.1	58,343	D
South Dakota	114,775	67,536	58.8	40,266	35.1	2,846	2.5	4,039	3.5	88	0.1	27,270	R
Tennessee	257,180	117,977	45.9	135,608	52.7	1,870	0.7	301	0.1	1,424	0.6	17,631	D
Texas	292,913	65,605	22.4	216,662	74.0	7,779	2.7	1,626	0.6	1,241	0.4	151,057	D
Utah	108,757	61,165	56.2	42,610	39.2	4,890	4.5	—	0.0	92	0.1	18,555	R
Vermont	52,680	39,552	75.1	11,496	21.8	—	0.0	799	1.5	833	1.6	28,056	R
Virginia	137,065	52,572	38.4	82,946	60.5	255	0.2	1,111	0.8	181	0.1	30,374	D
Washington	183,570	106,062	57.8	58,383	31.8	14,177	7.7	4,700	2.6	248	0.1	47,679	R
West Virginia	258,098	137,869	53.4	111,410	43.2	3,679	1.4	5,140	2.0	—	0.0	26,459	R
Wisconsin	454,438	247,744	54.5	166,662	36.7	28,147	6.2	11,565	2.5	320	0.1	81,082	R
Wyoming	37,608	20,846	55.4	14,918	39.7	1,715	4.6	66	0.2	63	0.2	5,928	R
Totals	14,884,098	7,676,598	51.6	6,406,874	43.0	420,436	2.8	253,428	1.7	126,762	0.9	1,269,724	R

1. Figures from Svend Petersen, *A Statistical History of the American Presidential Elections* (Westport, Conn.: Greenwood Press, 1981).
2. Figures from *Minnesota Votes*.

1912 Presidential Election

STATE	TOTAL VOTE	WOODROW WILSON (Democrat) Votes	%	THEODORE ROOSEVELT (Progressive) Votes	%	WILLIAM H. TAFT (Republican) Votes	%	EUGENE V. DEBS (Socialist) Votes	%	OTHER Votes	%	PLURALITY	
Alabama	117,959	82,438	69.9	22,680	19.2	9,807	8.3	3,029	2.6	5	0.0	59,758	D
Arizona	23,687	10,324	43.6	6,949	29.3	2,986	12.6	3,163	13.4	265	1.1	3,375	D
Arkansas	125,104	68,814	55.0	21,644	17.3	25,585	20.5	8,153	6.5	908	0.7	43,229	D
California	677,877	283,436	41.8	283,610	41.8	3,847	0.6	79,201	11.7	27,783	4.1	174	PR
Colorado	265,954	113,912	42.8	71,752	27.0	58,386	22.0	16,366	6.2	5,538	2.1	42,160	D
Connecticut	190,404	74,561	39.2	34,129	17.9	68,324	35.9	10,056	5.3	3,334	1.8	6,237	D
Delaware	48,690	22,631	46.5	8,886	18.3	15,997	32.9	556	1.1	620	1.3	6,634	D
Florida[1]	51,911	36,417	70.2	4,555	8.8	4,279	8.2	4,806	9.3	1,854	3.6	31,862	D
Georgia	121,470	93,087	76.6	21,985	18.1	5,191	4.3	1,058	0.9	149	0.1	71,102	D
Idaho	105,754	33,921	32.1	25,527	24.1	32,810	31.0	11,960	11.3	1,536	1.5	1,111	D
Illinois	1,146,173	405,048	35.3	386,478	33.7	253,593	22.1	81,278	7.1	19,776	1.7	18,570	D
Indiana	654,474	281,890	43.1	162,007	24.8	151,267	23.1	36,931	5.6	22,379	3.4	119,883	D
Iowa	492,353	185,322	37.6	161,819	32.9	119,805	24.3	16,967	3.4	8,440	1.7	23,503	D
Kansas	365,560	143,663	39.3	120,210	32.9	74,845	20.5	26,779	7.3	63	0.0	23,453	D
Kentucky[2]	453,707	219,585	48.4	102,766	22.7	115,520	25.5	11,647	2.6	4,189	0.9	104,065	D
Louisiana	79,248	60,871	76.8	9,283	11.7	3,833	4.8	5,261	6.6	—	0.0	51,588	D
Maine	129,641	51,113	39.4	48,495	37.4	26,545	20.5	2,541	2.0	947	0.7	2,618	D
Maryland	231,981	112,674	48.6	57,789	24.9	54,956	23.7	3,996	1.7	2,566	1.1	54,885	D
Massachusetts	488,056	173,408	35.5	142,228	29.1	155,948	32.0	12,616	2.6	3,856	0.8	17,460	D
Michigan	547,971	150,201	27.4	213,243	38.9	151,434	27.6	23,060	4.2	10,033	1.8	61,809	PR
Minnesota	334,219	106,426	31.8	125,856	37.7	64,334	19.2	27,505	8.2	10,098	3.0	19,430	PR
Mississippi	64,483	57,324	88.9	3,549	5.5	1,560	2.4	2,050	3.2	—	0.0	53,775	D
Missouri	698,566	330,746	47.3	124,375	17.8	207,821	29.7	28,466	4.1	7,158	1.0	122,925	D
Montana	80,256	28,129	35.0	22,709	28.3	18,575	23.1	10,811	13.5	32	0.0	5,420	D
Nebraska	249,483	109,008	43.7	72,681	29.1	54,226	21.7	10,185	4.1	3,383	1.4	36,327	D
Nevada	20,115	7,986	39.7	5,620	27.9	3,196	15.9	3,313	16.5	—	0.0	2,366	D
New Hampshire	87,961	34,724	39.5	17,794	20.2	32,927	37.4	1,981	2.3	535	0.6	1,797	D
New Jersey	433,663	178,638	41.2	145,679	33.6	89,066	20.5	15,948	3.7	4,332	1.0	32,959	D
New Mexico	48,807	20,437	41.9	8,347	17.1	17,164	35.2	2,859	5.9	—	0.0	3,273	D
New York	1,588,315	655,573	41.3	390,093	24.6	455,487	28.7	63,434	4.0	23,728	1.5	200,086	D
North Carolina	243,776	144,407	59.2	69,135	28.4	29,129	11.9	987	0.4	118	0.0	75,272	D
North Dakota	86,474	29,549	34.2	25,726	29.7	22,990	26.6	6,966	8.1	1,243	1.4	3,823	D
Ohio	1,037,114	424,834	41.0	229,807	22.2	278,168	26.8	90,164	8.7	14,141	1.4	146,666	D
Oklahoma	253,694	119,143	47.0	—	0.0	90,726	35.8	41,630	16.4	2,195	0.9	28,417	D
Oregon	137,040	47,064	34.3	37,600	27.4	34,673	25.3	13,343	9.7	4,360	3.2	9,464	D
Pennsylvania	1,217,736	395,637	32.5	444,894	36.5	273,360	22.4	83,614	6.9	20,231	1.7	49,257	PR
Rhode Island	77,894	30,412	39.0	16,878	21.7	27,703	35.6	2,049	2.6	852	1.1	2,709	D
South Carolina	50,403	48,355	95.9	1,293	2.6	536	1.1	164	0.3	55	0.1	47,062	D
South Dakota	116,327	48,942	42.1	58,811	50.6	—	0.0	4,664	4.0	3,910	3.4	9,869	PR
Tennessee	251,933	133,021	52.8	54,041	21.5	60,475	24.0	3,564	1.4	832	0.3	72,546	D
Texas	300,961	218,921	72.7	26,715	8.9	28,310	9.4	24,884	8.3	2,131	0.7	190,611	D
Utah	112,272	36,576	32.6	24,174	21.5	42,013	37.4	8,999	8.0	510	0.5	5,437	R
Vermont	62,804	15,350	24.4	22,129	35.2	23,303	37.1	928	1.5	1,094	1.7	1,174	R
Virginia	136,975	90,332	65.9	21,776	15.9	23,288	17.0	820	0.6	759	0.6	67,044	D
Washington	322,799	86,840	26.9	113,698	35.2	70,445	21.8	40,134	12.4	11,682	3.6	26,858	PR
West Virginia	268,728	113,097	42.1	79,112	29.4	56,754	21.1	15,248	5.7	4,517	1.7	33,985	D
Wisconsin	399,975	164,230	41.1	62,448	15.6	130,596	32.7	33,476	8.4	9,225	2.3	33,634	D
Wyoming	42,283	15,310	36.2	9,232	21.8	14,560	34.4	2,760	6.5	421	1.0	750	D
Totals	15,043,029	6,294,326	41.8	4,120,207	27.4	3,486,343	23.2	900,370	6.0	241,783	1.6	2,174,119	D

1. Figures from Svend Petersen, *A Statistical History of the American Presidential Elections* (Westport, Conn.: Greenwood Press, 1981); Edgar E. Robinson, *The Presidential Vote 1896–1932* (Stanford, Calif.: Stanford University Press, 1934).
2. Figures from *Kentucky Directory 1916,* pp. 145–149.

1916 Presidential Election

STATE	TOTAL VOTE	WOODROW WILSON (Democrat) Votes	%	CHARLES E. HUGHES (Republican) Votes	%	ALLAN L. BENSON (Socialist) Votes	%	J. FRANK HANLY (Prohibition) Votes	%	OTHER Votes	%	PLURALITY	
Alabama[1]	131,142	99,409	75.6	28,809	21.9	1,925	1.5	999	0.8	—	0.0	70,600	D
Arizona	58,019	33,170	57.2	20,522	35.4	3,174	5.5	1,153	2.0	—	0.0	12,648	D
Arkansas[2]	168,348	112,186	66.6	47,148	28.0	6,999	4.2	2,015	1.2	—	0.0	65,038	D
California	999,250	465,936	46.6	462,516	46.3	42,898	4.3	27,713	2.8	187	0.0	3,420	D
Colorado[2]	294,375	178,816	60.5	102,308	34.8	10,049	3.4	2,793	0.9	409	0.1	76,508	D
Connecticut	213,874	99,786	46.7	106,514	49.8	5,179	2.4	1,789	0.8	606	0.3	6,728	R
Delaware	51,810	24,753	47.8	26,011	50.2	480	0.9	566	1.1	—	0.0	1,258	R
Florida	80,734	55,984	69.3	14,611	18.1	5,353	6.6	4,786	5.9	—	0.0	41,373	D
Georgia[3]	158,690	125,845	79.3	11,225	7.1	967	0.6	—	0.0	20,653	12.9	105,192	D
Idaho	134,615	70,054	52.0	55,368	41.1	8,066	6.0	1,127	0.8	—	0.0	14,686	D
Illinois	2,192,707	950,229	43.3	1,152,549	52.6	61,394	2.8	26,047	1.2	2,488	0.1	202,320	R
Indiana	718,853	334,063	46.5	341,005	47.4	21,860	3.0	16,368	2.3	5,557	0.8	6,942	R
Iowa	518,738	221,699	42.7	280,439	54.1	10,976	2.1	3,371	0.6	2,253	0.4	58,740	R
Kansas	629,813	314,588	49.9	277,658	44.1	24,685	3.9	12,882	2.0	—	0.0	36,930	D
Kentucky	520,078	269,990	51.9	241,854	46.5	4,734	0.9	3,039	0.6	461	0.1	28,136	D
Louisiana	92,974	79,875	85.9	6,466	7.0	284	0.3	—	0.0	6,349	6.8	73,409	D
Maine	136,314	64,033	47.0	69,508	51.0	2,177	1.6	596	0.4	—	0.0	5,475	R
Maryland	262,039	138,359	52.8	117,347	44.8	2,674	1.0	2,903	1.1	756	0.3	21,012	D
Massachusetts	531,822	247,885	46.6	268,784	50.5	11,058	2.1	2,993	0.6	1,102	0.2	20,899	R
Michigan	646,873	283,993	43.9	337,952	52.2	16,012	2.5	8,085	1.2	831	0.1	53,959	R
Minnesota	387,367	179,155	46.2	179,544	46.3	20,117	5.2	7,793	2.0	758	0.2	389	R
Mississippi	86,679	80,422	92.8	4,253	4.9	1,484	1.7	—	0.0	520	0.6	76,169	D
Missouri	786,773	398,032	50.6	369,339	46.9	14,612	1.9	3,887	0.5	903	0.1	28,693	D
Montana	178,009	101,104	56.8	66,933	37.6	9,634	5.4	—	0.0	338	0.2	34,171	D
Nebraska	287,315	158,827	55.3	117,771	41.0	7,141	2.5	2,952	1.0	624	0.2	41,056	D
Nevada	33,314	17,776	53.4	12,127	36.4	3,065	9.2	346	1.0	—	0.0	5,649	D
New Hampshire	89,127	43,781	49.1	43,725	49.1	1,318	1.5	303	0.3	—	0.0	56	D
New Jersey	494,442	211,018	42.7	268,982	54.4	10,405	2.1	3,182	0.6	855	0.2	57,964	R
New Mexico	66,879	33,693	50.4	31,097	46.5	1,977	3.0	112	0.2	—	0.0	2,596	D
New York	1,706,305	759,426	44.5	879,238	51.5	45,944	2.7	19,031	1.1	2,666	0.2	119,812	R
North Carolina	289,837	168,383	58.1	120,890	41.7	509	0.2	55	0.0	—	0.0	47,493	D
North Dakota	115,390	55,206	47.8	53,471	46.3	5,716	5.0	997	0.9	—	0.0	1,735	D
Ohio	1,165,091	604,161	51.9	514,753	44.2	38,092	3.3	8,085	0.7	—	0.0	89,408	D
Oklahoma	292,327	148,123	50.7	97,233	33.3	45,091	15.4	1,646	0.6	234	0.1	50,890	D
Oregon	261,650	120,087	45.9	126,813	48.5	9,711	3.7	4,729	1.8	310	0.1	6,726	R
Pennsylvania	1,297,189	521,784	40.2	703,823	54.3	42,638	3.3	28,525	2.2	419	0.0	182,039	R
Rhode Island	87,816	40,394	46.0	44,858	51.1	1,914	2.2	470	0.5	180	0.2	4,464	R
South Carolina	63,950	61,845	96.7	1,550	2.4	135	0.2	—	0.0	420	0.7	60,295	D
South Dakota	128,942	59,191	45.9	64,217	49.8	3,760	2.9	1,774	1.4	—	0.0	5,026	R
Tennessee	272,190	153,280	56.3	116,223	42.7	2,542	0.9	145	0.1	—	0.0	37,057	D
Texas[4]	372,467	286,514	76.9	64,999	17.5	18,969	5.1	1,985	0.5	—	0.0	221,515	D
Utah	143,145	84,145	58.8	54,137	37.8	4,460	3.1	149	0.1	254	0.2	30,008	D
Vermont	64,475	22,708	35.2	40,250	62.4	798	1.2	709	1.1	10	0.0	17,542	R
Virginia[1]	153,993	102,825	66.8	49,358	32.1	1,060	0.7	683	0.4	67	0.0	53,467	D
Washington	380,994	183,388	48.1	167,208	43.9	22,800	6.0	6,868	1.8	730	0.2	16,180	D
West Virginia	289,671	140,403	48.5	143,124	49.4	6,144	2.1	—	0.0	—	0.0	2,721	R
Wisconsin	447,134	191,363	42.8	220,822	49.4	27,631	6.2	7,318	1.6	—	0.0	29,459	R
Wyoming	51,906	28,376	54.7	21,698	41.8	1,459	2.8	373	0.7	—	0.0	6,678	D
Totals	18,535,445	9,126,063	49.2	8,547,039	46.1	590,110	3.2	221,293	1.2	50,940	0.3	579,024	D

1. Figures from Svend Petersen, *A Statistical History of the American Presidential Elections* (Westport, Conn.: Greenwood Press, 1981); Edgar E. Robinson, *The Presidential Vote 1896–1932* (Stanford, Calif.: Stanford University Press, 1934).
2. Figures from Petersen, *A Statistical History*.
3. Figures from Petersen, *A Statistical History*. Plurality of 105,192 votes is calculated on the basis of 20,653 votes cast for the Progressive Party.
4. Figures from Petersen, *A Statistical History*; *Texas Almanac*.

1920 Presidential Election

STATE	TOTAL VOTE	WARREN G. HARDING (Republican)		JAMES M. COX (Democrat)		EUGENE V. DEBS (Socialist)		PARLEY P. CHRISTENSEN (Farmer-Labor)		OTHER		PLURALITY	
		Votes	%	Votes	%	Votes	%	Votes	%	Votes	%		
Alabama	233,951	74,719	31.9	156,064	66.7	2,402	1.0	—	0.0	766	0.3	81,345	D
Arizona	66,803	37,016	55.4	29,546	44.2	222	0.3	15	0.0	4	0.0	7,470	R
Arkansas[1]	183,637	71,117	38.7	107,409	58.5	5,111	2.8	—	0.0	—	0.0	36,292	D
California	943,463	624,992	66.2	229,191	24.3	64,076	6.8	—	0.0	25,204	2.7	395,801	R
Colorado	292,053	173,248	59.3	104,936	35.9	8,046	2.8	3,016	1.0	2,807	1.0	68,312	R
Connecticut	365,518	229,238	62.7	120,721	33.0	10,350	2.8	1,947	0.5	3,262	0.9	108,517	R
Delaware	94,875	52,858	55.7	39,911	42.1	988	1.0	93	0.1	1,025	1.1	12,947	R
Florida	145,684	44,853	30.8	90,515	62.1	5,189	3.6	—	0.0	5,127	3.5	45,662	D
Georgia	149,558	42,981	28.7	106,112	71.0	465	0.3	—	0.0	—	0.0	63,131	D
Idaho[2]	138,359	91,351	66.0	46,930	33.9	38	0.3	6	0.0	34	0.2	44,421	R
Illinois	2,094,714	1,420,480	67.8	534,395	25.5	74,747	3.6	49,630	2.4	15,462	0.7	886,085	R
Indiana	1,262,974	696,370	55.1	511,364	40.5	24,713	2.0	16,499	1.3	14,028	1.1	185,006	R
Iowa	894,959	634,674	70.9	227,804	25.5	16,981	1.9	10,321	1.2	5,179	0.6	406,870	R
Kansas	570,243	369,268	64.8	185,464	32.5	15,511	2.7	—	0.0	—	0.0	183,804	R
Kentucky	918,636	452,480	49.3	456,497	49.7	6,409	0.7	—	0.0	3,250	0.4	4,017	D
Louisiana	126,397	38,539	30.5	87,519	69.2	—	0.0	—	0.0	339	0.3	48,980	D
Maine	197,840	136,355	68.9	58,961	29.8	2,214	1.1	—	0.0	310	0.2	77,394	R
Maryland	428,443	236,117	55.1	180,626	42.2	8,876	2.1	1,645	0.4	1,179	0.3	55,491	R
Massachusetts	993,718	681,153	68.5	276,691	27.8	32,267	3.2	—	0.0	3,607	0.4	404,462	R
Michigan	1,048,411	762,865	72.8	233,450	22.3	28,947	2.8	10,480	1.0	12,669	1.2	529,415	R
Minnesota	735,838	519,421	70.6	142,994	19.4	56,106	7.6	—	0.0	17,317	2.4	376,427	R
Mississippi	82,351	11,576	14.1	69,136	84.0	1,639	2.0	—	0.0	—	0.0	57,560	D
Missouri	1,332,140	727,252	54.6	574,699	43.1	20,342	1.5	3,108	0.2	6,739	0.5	152,553	R
Montana	179,006	109,430	61.1	57,372	32.1	—	0.0	12,204	6.8	—	0.0	52,058	R
Nebraska	382,743	247,498	64.7	119,608	31.3	9,600	2.5	—	0.0	6,037	1.6	127,890	R
Nevada	27,194	15,479	56.9	9,851	36.2	1,864	6.9	—	0.0	—	0.0	5,628	R
New Hampshire	159,092	95,196	59.8	62,662	39.4	1,234	0.8	—	0.0	—	0.0	32,534	R
New Jersey	910,251	615,333	67.6	258,761	28.4	27,385	3.0	2,264	0.2	6,508	0.7	356,572	R
New Mexico	105,412	57,634	54.7	46,668	44.3	2	0.0	1,104	1.0	4	0.0	10,966	R
New York	2,898,513	1,871,167	64.6	781,238	27.0	203,201	7.0	18,413	0.6	24,494	0.8	1,089,929	R
North Carolina	538,649	232,819	43.2	305,367	56.7	446	0.1	—	0.0	17	0.0	72,548	D
North Dakota	205,786	160,082	77.8	37,422	18.2	8,282	4.0	—	0.0	—	0.0	122,660	R
Ohio	2,021,653	1,182,022	58.5	780,037	38.6	57,147	2.8	—	0.0	2,447	0.1	401,985	R
Oklahoma	485,678	243,840	50.2	216,122	44.5	25,716	5.3	—	0.0	—	0.0	27,718	R
Oregon	238,522	143,592	60.2	80,019	33.5	9,801	4.1	—	0.0	5,110	2.1	63,573	R
Pennsylvania	1,851,248	1,218,215	65.8	503,202	27.2	70,021	3.8	15,642	0.8	44,168	2.4	715,013	R
Rhode Island	167,981	107,463	64.0	55,062	32.8	4,351	2.6	—	0.0	1,105	0.7	52,401	R
South Carolina[2]	66,808	2,610	3.9	64,170	96.1	28	0.0	—	0.0	—	0.0	61,560	D
South Dakota	182,237	110,692	60.7	35,938	19.7	—	0.0	34,707	19.0	900	0.5	74,754	R
Tennessee	428,036	219,229	51.2	206,558	48.3	2,249	0.5	—	0.0	—	0.0	12,671	R
Texas	486,109	114,658	23.6	287,920	59.2	8,124	1.7	—	0.0	75,407	15.5	173,262	D
Utah	145,828	81,555	55.9	56,639	38.8	3,159	2.2	4,475	3.1	—	0.0	24,916	R
Vermont	89,961	68,212	75.8	20,919	23.3	—	0.0	—	0.0	830	0.9	47,293	R
Virginia	231,000	87,456	37.9	141,670	61.3	808	0.3	240	0.1	826	0.4	54,214	D
Washington	398,715	223,137	56.0	84,298	21.1	8,913	2.2	77,246	19.4	5,121	1.3	138,839	R
West Virginia	509,936	282,007	55.3	220,785	43.3	5,618	1.1	—	0.0	1,526	0.3	61,222	R
Wisconsin	701,281	498,576	71.1	113,422	16.2	80,635	11.5	—	0.0	8,648	1.2	385,154	R
Wyoming	56,253	35,091	62.4	17,429	31.0	1,288	2.3	2,180	3.9	265	0.5	17,662	R
Totals	26,768,457	16,151,916	60.3	9,134,074	34.1	915,511	3.4	265,235	1.0	301,721	1.1	7,017,842	R

1. Figures from Svend Petersen, *A Statistical History of the American Presidential Elections* (Westport, Conn.: Greenwood Press, 1981); *America at the Polls 1920-1956* (Washington, D.C.: Congressional Quarterly, 1994).
2. Two sets of Harding electors are combined here: Republican, 2,244; Insurgent Referendum, 366.

1924 Presidential Election

STATE	TOTAL VOTE	CALVIN COOLIDGE (Republican) Votes	%	JOHN W. DAVIS (Democrat) Votes	%	ROBERT M. LA FOLLETTE (Progressive) Votes	%	HERMAN P. FARIS (Prohibition) Votes	%	OTHER Votes	%	PLURALITY	
Alabama[1]	166,593	45,005	27.0	112,966	67.8	8,084	4.9	538	0.3	—	0.0	67,961	D
Arizona	73,961	30,516	41.3	26,235	35.5	17,210	23.3	—	0.0	—	0.0	4,281	R
Arkansas	138,540	40,583	29.3	84,790	61.2	13,167	9.5	—	0.0	—	0.0	44,207	D
California	1,281,778	733,250	57.2	105,514	8.2	424,649	33.1	18,365	1.4	—	0.0	308,601	R
Colorado[2]	342,261	195,171	57.0	75,238	22.0	69,945	20.4	966	0.3	940	0.3	119,933	R
Connecticut	400,396	246,322	61.5	110,184	27.5	42,416	10.6	—	0.0	1,474	0.4	136,138	R
Delaware	90,885	52,441	57.7	33,445	36.8	4,979	5.5	—	0.0	20	0.0	18,996	R
Florida	109,158	30,633	28.1	62,083	56.9	8,625	7.9	5,498	5.0	2,319	2.1	31,450	D
Georgia	166,635	30,300	18.2	123,262	74.0	12,687	7.6	231	0.1	155	0.1	92,962	D
Idaho	147,690	69,791	47.3	23,951	16.2	53,948	36.5	—	0.0	—	0.0	15,843	R
Illinois	2,470,067	1,453,321	58.8	576,975	23.4	432,027	17.5	2,367	0.1	5,377	0.2	876,346	R
Indiana	1,272,390	703,042	55.3	492,245	38.7	71,700	5.6	4,416	0.3	987	0.1	210,797	R
Iowa	976,770	537,458	55.0	160,382	16.4	274,448	28.1	—	0.0	4,482	0.5	263,010	R
Kansas	662,456	407,671	61.5	156,320	23.6	98,461	14.9	—	0.0	4	0.0	251,351	R
Kentucky[3]	816,070	398,966	48.9	375,593	46.0	38,465	4.7	—	0.0	3,046	0.4	23,373	R
Louisiana	121,951	24,670	20.2	93,218	76.4	—	0.0	—	0.0	4,063	3.3	68,548	D
Maine	192,192	138,440	72.0	41,964	21.8	11,382	5.9	—	0.0	406	0.2	96,476	R
Maryland	358,630	162,414	45.3	148,072	41.3	47,157	13.1	—	0.0	987	0.3	14,342	R
Massachusetts	1,129,837	703,476	62.3	280,831	24.9	141,225	12.5	—	0.0	4,305	0.4	422,645	R
Michigan	1,160,419	874,631	75.4	152,359	13.1	122,014	10.5	6,085	0.5	5,330	0.5	722,272	R
Minnesota	822,146	420,759	51.2	55,913	6.8	339,192	41.3	—	0.0	6,282	0.8	81,567	R
Mississippi	112,442	8,494	7.6	100,474	89.4	3,474	3.1	—	0.0	—	0.0	91,980	D
Missouri[4]	1,310,095	648,488	49.5	574,962	43.9	83,986	6.4	1,418	0.1	1,231	0.1	73,526	R
Montana[5]	174,425	74,138	42.5	33,805	19.4	65,876	37.9	—	0.0	358	0.2	8,014	R
Nebraska	463,559	218,985	47.2	137,299	29.6	105,681	22.8	1,594	0.3	—	0.0	81,686	R
Nevada	26,921	11,243	41.8	5,909	21.9	9,769	36.3	—	0.0	—	0.0	1,474	R
New Hampshire	164,769	98,575	59.8	57,201	34.7	8,993	5.5	—	0.0	—	0.0	41,374	R
New Jersey	1,088,054	676,277	62.2	298,043	27.4	109,028	10.0	1,660	0.2	3,046	0.3	378,234	R
New Mexico	112,830	54,745	48.5	48,542	43.0	9,543	8.5	—	0.0	—	0.0	6,203	R
New York[6]	3,263,939	1,820,058	55.8	950,796	29.1	474,913	14.6	—	0.0	18,172	0.6	869,262	R
North Carolina	481,608	190,754	39.6	284,190	59.0	6,651	1.4	13	0.0	—	0.0	93,436	D
North Dakota	199,081	94,931	47.7	13,858	7.0	89,922	45.2	—	0.0	370	0.2	5,009	R
Ohio	2,016,296	1,176,130	58.3	477,887	23.7	358,008	17.8	—	0.0	4,271	0.2	698,243	R
Oklahoma[7]	527,928	225,755	42.8	255,798	48.4	41,141	7.8	—	0.0	5,234	1.0	30,043	D
Oregon	279,488	142,579	51.0	67,589	24.2	68,403	24.5	—	0.0	917	0.3	74,176	R
Pennsylvania[8]	2,144,850	1,401,481	65.3	409,192	19.1	307,567	14.3	9,779	0.5	16,831	0.8	992,289	R
Rhode Island	210,115	125,286	59.6	76,606	36.5	7,628	3.6	—	0.0	595	0.3	48,680	R
South Carolina	50,755	1,123	2.2	49,008	96.6	623	1.2	—	0.0	1	0.0	47,885	D
South Dakota	203,868	101,299	49.7	27,214	13.3	75,355	37.0	—	0.0	—	0.0	25,944	R
Tennessee	301,030	130,831	43.5	159,339	52.9	10,666	3.5	94	0.0	100	0.0	28,508	D
Texas	657,054	130,794	19.9	483,381	73.6	42,879	6.5	—	0.0	—	0.0	352,587	D
Utah	156,990	77,327	49.3	47,001	29.9	32,662	20.8	—	0.0	—	0.0	30,326	R
Vermont	102,917	80,498	78.2	16,124	15.7	5,964	5.8	326	0.3	5	0.0	64,374	R
Virginia	223,603	73,328	32.8	139,717	62.5	10,369	4.6	—	0.0	189	0.1	66,389	D
Washington	421,549	220,224	52.2	42,842	10.2	150,727	35.8	—	0.0	7,756	1.8	69,497	R
West Virginia[9]	583,662	288,635	49.5	257,232	44.1	36,723	6.3	—	0.0	1,072	0.2	31,403	R
Wisconsin	840,827	311,614	37.1	68,115	8.1	453,678	54.0	2,918	0.3	4,502	0.5	142,064	P
Wyoming	79,900	41,858	52.4	12,868	16.1	25,174	31.5	—	0.0	—	0.0	16,684	R
Totals	29,099,380	15,724,310	54.0	8,386,532	28.8	4,827,184	16.6	56,268	0.2	104,827	0.4	7,337,778	R

1. Figures from Svend Petersen, *A Statistical History of the American Presidential Elections* (Westport, Conn.: Greenwood Press, 1981); Clerk of the House of Representatives, *Statistics of the Congressional and Presidential Election* (Washington, D.C.: U.S. Government Printing Office, 1924).
2. Two sets of La Follette electors are combined here: Colorado Independent Progressive, 57,368; Farmer-Labor, 12,577.
3. Figures from Petersen, *A Statistical History*; Clerk of the House, *Congressional and Presidential Election*; *Kentucky Directory 1925*, p. 142.
4. Two sets of La Follette electors are combined here: Missouri Socialist, 56,723; Liberal, 27,263.
5. Two sets of La Follette electors are combined here: Montana Independent Progressive, 61,105; Farmer-Labor, 4,771.
6. Two sets of La Follette electors are combined here: New York Socialist, 268,518; Progressive, 206,395.
7. There were two separate slates of electors pledged to La Follette in Oklahoma that could not legally be combined. State Election Board *Directory of Oklahoma 1973*, p. 343.
8. Two sets of La Follette electors are combined here: Pennsylvania Socialist, 93,441; Labor, 214,126.
9. Two sets of La Follette electors are combined here: West Virginia Socialist, 14,903; Farmer-Labor, 21,820.

1928 Presidential Election

STATE	TOTAL VOTE	HERBERT C. HOOVER (Republican)		ALFRED E. SMITH (Democrat)		NORMAN M. THOMAS (Socialist)		WILLIAM Z. FOSTER (Communist)		OTHER		PLURALITY	
		Votes	%	Votes	%	Votes	%	Votes	%	Votes	%		
Alabama	248,981	120,725	48.5	127,796	51.3	460	0.2	—	0.0	—	0.0	7,071	D
Arizona	91,254	52,533	57.6	38,537	42.2	—	0.0	184	0.2	—	0.0	13,996	R
Arkansas	197,726	77,784	39.3	119,196	60.3	429	0.2	317	0.2	—	0.0	41,412	D
California	1,796,656	1,162,323	64.7	614,365	34.2	19,595	1.1	—	0.0	373	0.0	547,958	R
Colorado	392,242	253,872	64.7	133,131	33.9	3,472	0.9	675	0.2	1,092	0.3	120,741	R
Connecticut	553,118	296,641	53.6	252,085	45.6	3,029	0.5	738	0.1	625	0.1	44,556	R
Delaware	104,602	68,860	65.8	35,354	33.8	329	0.3	59	0.1	—	0.0	33,506	R
Florida[1]	253,672	144,168	56.8	101,764	40.1	4,036	1.6	3,704	1.5	—	0.0	42,404	R
Georgia[2]	231,592	101,800	44.0	129,604	56.0	124	0.1	64	0.0	—	0.0	27,804	D
Idaho[3]	154,230	99,848	64.7	53,074	34.4	1,308	0.8	—	0.0	—	0.0	46,774	R
Illinois	3,107,489	1,769,141	56.9	1,313,817	42.3	19,138	0.6	3,581	0.1	1,812	0.1	455,324	R
Indiana	1,421,314	848,290	59.7	562,691	39.6	3,871	0.3	321	0.0	6,141	0.4	285,599	R
Iowa	1,009,189	623,570	61.8	379,011	37.6	2,960	0.3	328	0.0	3,320	0.3	244,559	R
Kansas	713,200	513,672	72.0	193,003	27.1	6,205	0.9	320	0.0	—	0.0	320,669	R
Kentucky	940,521	558,064	59.3	381,070	40.5	783	0.1	288	0.0	316	0.0	176,994	R
Louisiana	215,833	51,160	23.7	164,655	76.3	—	0.0	—	0.0	18	0.0	113,495	D
Maine	262,170	179,923	68.6	81,179	31.0	1,068	0.4	—	0.0	—	0.0	98,744	R
Maryland	528,348	301,479	57.1	223,626	42.3	1,701	0.3	636	0.1	906	0.2	77,853	R
Massachusetts	1,577,823	775,566	49.2	792,758	50.2	6,262	0.4	2,461	0.2	776	0.0	17,192	D
Michigan	1,372,082	965,396	70.4	396,762	28.9	3,516	0.3	2,881	0.2	3,527	0.3	568,634	R
Minnesota	970,976	560,977	57.8	396,451	40.8	6,774	0.7	4,853	0.5	1,921	0.2	164,526	R
Mississippi[4]	151,568	27,030	17.8	124,538	82.2	—	0.0	—	0.0	—	0.0	97,508	D
Missouri	1,500,845	834,080	55.6	662,684	44.2	3,739	0.2	—	0.0	342	0.0	171,396	R
Montana	194,108	113,300	58.4	78,578	40.5	1,667	0.9	563	0.3	—	0.0	34,722	R
Nebraska	547,128	345,745	63.2	197,950	36.2	3,433	0.6	—	0.0	—	0.0	147,795	R
Nevada	32,417	18,327	56.5	14,090	43.5	—	0.0	—	0.0	—	0.0	4,237	R
New Hampshire	196,757	115,404	58.7	80,715	41.0	465	0.2	173	0.1	—	0.0	34,689	R
New Jersey	1,549,381	926,050	59.8	616,517	39.8	4,897	0.3	1,257	0.1	660	0.0	309,533	R
New Mexico	118,077	69,708	59.0	48,211	40.8	—	0.0	158	0.1	—	0.0	21,497	R
New York	4,405,626	2,193,344	49.8	2,089,863	47.4	107,332	2.4	10,876	0.2	4,211	0.1	103,481	R
North Carolina	635,150	348,923	54.9	286,227	45.1	—	0.0	—	0.0	—	0.0	62,696	R
North Dakota	239,845	131,419	54.8	106,648	44.5	936	0.4	842	0.4	—	0.0	24,771	R
Ohio	2,508,346	1,627,546	64.9	864,210	34.5	8,683	0.3	2,836	0.1	5,071	0.2	763,336	R
Oklahoma	618,427	394,046	63.7	219,174	35.4	3,924	0.6	—	0.0	1,283	0.2	174,872	R
Oregon	319,942	205,341	64.2	109,223	34.1	2,720	0.9	1,094	0.3	1,564	0.5	96,118	R
Pennsylvania	3,150,612	2,055,382	65.2	1,067,586	33.9	18,647	0.6	4,726	0.2	4,271	0.1	987,796	R
Rhode Island	237,194	117,522	49.5	118,973	50.2	—	0.0	283	0.1	416	0.2	1,451	D
South Carolina[5]	68,605	5,858	8.5	62,700	91.4	47	0.1	—	0.0	—	0.0	56,842	D
South Dakota	261,857	157,603	60.2	102,660	39.2	443	0.2	224	0.1	927	0.4	54,943	R
Tennessee	353,192	195,388	55.3	157,143	44.5	567	0.2	94	0.0	—	0.0	38,245	R
Texas[6]	708,999	367,036	51.8	341,032	48.1	722	0.1	209	0.0	—	0.0	26,004	R
Utah	176,603	94,618	53.6	80,985	45.9	954	0.5	46	0.0	—	0.0	13,633	R
Vermont	135,191	90,404	66.9	44,440	32.9	—	0.0	—	0.0	347	0.3	45,964	R
Virginia	305,364	164,609	53.9	140,146	45.9	249	0.1	179	0.1	181	0.1	24,463	R
Washington	500,840	335,844	67.1	156,772	31.3	2,615	0.5	1,541	0.3	4,068	0.8	179,072	R
West Virginia	642,752	375,551	58.4	263,784	41.0	1,313	0.2	401	0.1	1,703	0.3	111,767	R
Wisconsin	1,016,831	544,205	53.5	450,259	44.3	18,213	1.8	1,528	0.2	2,626	0.3	93,946	R
Wyoming	82,835	52,748	63.7	29,299	35.4	788	1.0	—	0.0	—	0.0	23,449	R
Totals	36,801,510	21,432,823	58.2	15,004,336	40.8	267,414	0.7	48,440	0.1	48,497	0.1	6,428,487	R

1. Figures from Clerk of the House of Representatives, *Statistics of the Congressional and Presidential Election* (Washington, D.C.: U.S. Government Printing Office, 1928).
2. Two sets of Hoover electors are combined here: Republican, 65,423; Anti-Smith, 36,377.
3. Figures from Clerk of the House, *Congressional and Presidential Election*.
4. Three sets of Hoover electors are combined here: Republican, 26,222; Ligon electors, 544; Rogers electors, 264.
5. Two sets of Hoover electors are combined here: Republican, 3,188; Anti-Smith, 2,670.
6. Figures from Svend Petersen, *A Statistical History of the American Presidential Elections* (Westport, Conn.: Greenwood Press, 1981); Clerk of the House, *Congressional and Presidential Election*; *Texas Almanac*.

1932 Presidential Election

STATE	TOTAL VOTE	FRANKLIN D. ROOSEVELT (Democrat) Votes	%	HERBERT C. HOOVER (Republican) Votes	%	NORMAN M. THOMAS (Socialist) Votes	%	WILLIAM Z. FOSTER (Communist) Votes	%	OTHER Votes	%	PLURALITY	
Alabama	245,303	207,910	84.8	34,675	14.1	2,030	0.8	675	0.3	13	0.0	173,235	D
Arizona	118,251	79,264	67.0	36,104	30.5	2,618	2.2	256	0.2	9	0.0	43,160	D
Arkansas	216,569	186,829	86.3	27,465	12.7	1,166	0.5	157	0.1	952	0.4	159,364	D
California	2,266,972	1,324,157	58.4	847,902	37.4	63,299	2.8	1,023	0.0	30,591	1.3	476,255	D
Colorado	457,696	250,877	54.8	189,617	41.4	13,591	3.0	787	0.2	2,824	0.6	61,260	D
Connecticut	594,183	281,632	47.4	288,420	48.5	20,480	3.4	1,364	0.2	2,287	0.4	6,788	R
Delaware	112,901	54,319	48.1	57,073	50.6	1,376	1.2	133	0.1	—	0.0	2,754	R
Florida	276,943	206,307	74.5	69,170	25.0	775	0.3	—	0.0	691	0.2	137,137	D
Georgia	255,590	234,118	91.6	19,863	7.8	461	0.2	23	0.0	1,125	0.4	214,255	D
Idaho	186,520	109,479	58.7	71,312	38.2	526	0.3	491	0.3	4,712	2.5	38,167	D
Illinois	3,407,926	1,882,304	55.2	1,432,756	42.0	67,258	2.0	15,582	0.5	10,026	0.3	449,548	D
Indiana	1,576,927	862,054	54.7	677,184	42.9	21,388	1.4	2,187	0.1	14,114	0.9	184,870	D
Iowa	1,036,687	598,019	57.7	414,433	40.0	20,467	2.0	559	0.1	3,209	0.3	183,586	D
Kansas	791,978	424,204	53.6	349,498	44.1	18,276	2.3	—	0.0	—	0.0	74,706	D
Kentucky	983,059	580,574	59.1	394,716	40.2	3,853	0.4	271	0.0	3,645	0.4	185,858	D
Louisiana	268,804	249,418	92.8	18,853	7.0	—	0.0	—	0.0	533	0.2	230,565	D
Maine	298,444	128,907	43.2	166,631	55.8	2,489	0.8	162	0.1	255	0.1	37,724	R
Maryland	511,054	314,314	61.5	184,184	36.0	10,489	2.1	1,031	0.2	1,036	0.2	130,130	D
Massachusetts	1,580,114	800,148	50.6	736,959	46.6	34,305	2.2	4,821	0.3	3,881	0.2	63,189	D
Michigan	1,664,765	871,700	52.4	739,894	44.4	39,205	2.4	9,318	0.6	4,648	0.3	131,806	D
Minnesota	1,002,843	600,806	59.9	363,959	36.3	25,476	2.5	6,101	0.6	6,501	0.6	236,847	D
Mississippi[1]	146,034	140,168	96.0	5,180	3.5	686	0.5	—	0.0	—	0.0	134,988	D
Missouri	1,609,894	1,025,406	63.7	564,713	35.1	16,374	1.0	568	0.0	2,833	0.2	460,693	D
Montana	216,479	127,286	58.8	78,078	36.1	7,891	3.6	1,775	0.8	1,449	0.7	49,208	D
Nebraska	570,135	359,082	63.0	201,177	35.3	9,876	1.7	—	0.0	—	0.0	157,905	D
Nevada	41,430	28,756	69.4	12,674	30.6	—	0.0	—	0.0	—	0.0	16,082	D
New Hampshire	205,520	100,680	49.0	103,629	50.4	947	0.5	264	0.1	—	0.0	2,949	R
New Jersey	1,630,063	806,630	49.5	775,684	47.6	42,998	2.6	2,915	0.2	1,836	0.1	30,946	D
New Mexico	151,606	95,089	62.7	54,217	35.8	1,776	1.2	135	0.1	389	0.3	40,872	D
New York	4,688,614	2,534,959	54.1	1,937,963	41.3	177,397	3.8	27,956	0.6	10,339	0.2	596,996	D
North Carolina	711,498	497,566	69.9	208,344	29.3	5,588	0.8	—	0.0	—	0.0	289,222	D
North Dakota	256,290	178,350	69.6	71,772	28.0	3,521	1.4	830	0.3	1,817	0.7	106,578	D
Ohio	2,609,728	1,301,695	49.9	1,227,319	47.0	64,094	2.5	7,231	0.3	9,389	0.4	74,376	D
Oklahoma	704,633	516,468	73.3	188,165	26.7	—	0.0	—	0.0	—	0.0	328,303	D
Oregon	368,751	213,871	58.0	136,019	36.9	15,450	4.2	1,681	0.5	1,730	0.5	77,852	D
Pennsylvania	2,859,021	1,295,948	45.3	1,453,540	50.8	91,119	3.2	5,658	0.2	12,756	0.4	157,592	R
Rhode Island	266,170	146,604	55.1	115,266	43.3	3,138	1.2	546	0.2	616	0.2	31,338	D
South Carolina	104,407	102,347	98.0	1,978	1.9	82	0.1	—	0.0	—	0.0	100,369	D
South Dakota	288,438	183,515	63.6	99,212	34.4	1,551	0.5	364	0.1	3,796	1.3	84,303	D
Tennessee	390,273	259,473	66.5	126,752	32.5	1,796	0.5	254	0.1	1,998	0.5	132,721	D
Texas[2]	863,406	760,348	88.1	97,959	11.3	4,450	0.5	207	0.0	442	0.0	662,389	D
Utah	206,578	116,750	56.5	84,795	41.0	4,087	2.0	946	0.5	—	0.0	31,955	D
Vermont	136,980	56,266	41.1	78,984	57.7	1,533	1.1	195	0.1	2	0.0	22,718	R
Virginia	297,942	203,979	68.5	89,637	30.1	2,382	0.8	86	0.0	1,858	0.6	114,342	D
Washington	614,814	353,260	57.5	208,645	33.9	17,080	2.8	2,972	0.5	32,857	5.3	144,615	D
West Virginia	743,774	405,124	54.5	330,731	44.5	5,133	0.7	444	0.1	2,342	0.3	74,393	D
Wisconsin	1,114,814	707,410	63.5	347,741	31.2	53,379	4.8	3,105	0.3	3,179	0.3	359,669	D
Wyoming	96,962	54,370	56.1	39,583	40.8	2,829	2.9	180	0.2	—	0.0	14,787	D
Totals	39,747,783	22,818,740	57.4	15,760,425	39.6	884,685	2.2	103,253	0.3	180,680	0.5	7,058,315	D

1. Two sets of Hoover electors are combined here: Lily White, 3,210; Black and Tan, 1,970.
2. Figures from Svend Petersen, *A Statistical History of the American Presidential Elections* (Westport, Conn.: Greenwood Press, 1981); Clerk of the House of Representatives, *Statistics of the Congressional and Presidential Election* (Washington, D.C.: U.S. Government Printing Office, 1932); *Texas Almanac.*

1936 Presidential Election

STATE	TOTAL VOTE	FRANKLIN D. ROOSEVELT (Democrat)		ALFRED M. LANDON (Republican)		WILLIAM LEMKE (Union)		NORMAN M. THOMAS (Socialist)		OTHER		PLURALITY	
		Votes	%	Votes	%	Votes	%	Votes	%	Votes	%		
Alabama	275,744	238,196	86.4	35,358	12.8	551	0.2	242	0.1	1,397	0.5	202,838	D
Arizona	124,163	86,722	69.8	33,433	26.9	3,307	2.7	317	0.3	384	0.3	53,289	D
Arkansas	179,431	146,765	81.8	32,049	17.9	4	0.0	446	0.2	167	0.1	114,716	D
California	2,638,882	1,766,836	67.0	836,431	31.7	—	0.0	11,331	0.4	24,284	0.9	930,405	D
Colorado	488,685	295,021	60.4	181,267	37.1	9,962	2.0	1,594	0.3	841	0.2	113,754	D
Connecticut	690,723	382,129	55.3	278,685	40.3	21,805	3.2	5,683	0.8	2,421	0.4	103,444	D
Delaware[1]	127,603	69,702	54.6	54,014	42.3	442	0.3	172	0.1	3,273	2.6	15,688	D
Florida	327,436	249,117	76.1	78,248	23.9	—	0.0	—	0.0	71	0.0	170,869	D
Georgia	293,170	255,363	87.1	36,943	12.6	136	0.0	68	0.0	660	0.2	218,420	D
Idaho	199,617	125,683	63.0	66,256	33.2	7,678	3.8	—	0.0	—	0.0	59,427	D
Illinois	3,956,522	2,282,999	57.7	1,570,393	39.7	89,439	2.3	7,530	0.2	6,161	0.2	712,606	D
Indiana	1,650,897	934,974	56.6	691,570	41.9	19,407	1.2	3,856	0.2	1,090	0.1	243,404	D
Iowa	1,142,737	621,756	54.4	487,977	42.7	29,687	2.6	1,373	0.1	1,944	0.2	133,779	D
Kansas	865,507	464,520	53.7	397,727	46.0	494	0.1	2,766	0.3	—	0.0	66,793	D
Kentucky	926,214	541,944	58.5	369,702	39.9	12,501	1.3	627	0.1	1,440	0.2	172,242	D
Louisiana	329,778	292,894	88.8	36,791	11.2	—	0.0	—	0.0	93	0.0	256,103	D
Maine	304,240	126,333	41.5	168,823	55.5	7,581	2.5	783	0.3	720	0.2	42,490	R
Maryland	624,896	389,612	62.3	231,435	37.0	—	0.0	1,629	0.3	2,220	0.4	158,177	D
Massachusetts	1,840,357	942,716	51.2	768,613	41.8	118,639	6.4	5,111	0.3	5,278	0.3	174,103	D
Michigan	1,805,098	1,016,794	56.3	699,733	38.8	75,795	4.2	8,208	0.5	4,568	0.3	317,061	D
Minnesota	1,129,975	698,811	61.8	350,461	31.0	74,296	6.6	2,872	0.3	3,535	0.3	348,350	D
Mississippi	162,142	157,333	97.0	4,467	2.8	—	0.0	342	0.2	—	0.0	152,866	D
Missouri	1,828,635	1,111,043	60.8	697,891	38.2	14,630	0.8	3,454	0.2	1,617	0.1	413,152	D
Montana	230,502	159,690	69.3	63,598	27.6	5,539	2.4	1,066	0.5	609	0.3	96,092	D
Nebraska	608,023	347,445	57.1	247,731	40.7	12,847	2.1	—	0.0	—	0.0	99,714	D
Nevada	43,848	31,925	72.8	11,923	27.2	—	0.0	—	0.0	—	0.0	20,002	D
New Hampshire	218,114	108,460	49.7	104,642	48.0	4,819	2.2	—	0.0	193	0.1	3,818	D
New Jersey	1,820,437	1,083,850	59.5	720,322	39.6	9,407	0.5	3,931	0.2	2,927	0.2	363,528	D
New Mexico	169,135	106,037	62.7	61,727	36.5	924	0.5	343	0.2	104	0.1	44,310	D
New York	5,596,398	3,293,222	58.8	2,180,670	39.0	—	0.0	86,897	1.6	35,609	0.6	1,112,552	D
North Carolina	839,475	616,141	73.4	223,294	26.6	2	0.0	21	0.0	17	0.0	392,847	D
North Dakota	273,716	163,148	59.6	72,751	26.6	36,708	13.4	552	0.2	557	0.2	90,397	D
Ohio	3,012,660	1,747,140	58.0	1,127,855	37.4	132,212	4.4	167	0.0	5,286	0.2	619,285	D
Oklahoma	749,740	501,069	66.8	245,122	32.7	—	0.0	2,221	0.3	1,328	0.2	255,947	D
Oregon	414,021	266,733	64.4	122,706	29.6	21,831	5.3	2,143	0.5	608	0.1	144,027	D
Pennsylvania	4,138,105	2,353,788	56.9	1,690,300	40.8	67,467	1.6	14,375	0.3	12,175	0.3	663,488	D
Rhode Island	310,278	164,338	53.0	125,031	40.3	19,569	6.3	—	0.0	1,340	0.4	39,307	D
South Carolina	115,437	113,791	98.6	1,646	1.4	—	0.0	—	0.0	—	0.0	112,145	D
South Dakota	296,452	160,137	54.0	125,977	42.5	10,338	3.5	—	0.0	—	0.0	34,160	D
Tennessee[2]	475,533	327,083	68.8	146,516	30.8	296	0.1	687	0.1	951	0.2	180,567	D
Texas[3]	843,482	734,485	87.1	103,874	12.3	3,281	0.4	1,075	0.1	767	0.1	630,611	D
Utah	216,679	150,248	69.3	64,555	29.8	1,121	0.5	432	0.2	323	0.1	85,693	D
Vermont	143,689	62,124	43.2	81,023	56.4	—	0.0	—	0.0	542	0.4	18,899	R
Virginia	334,590	234,980	70.2	98,336	29.4	233	0.1	313	0.1	728	0.2	136,644	D
Washington	692,338	459,579	66.4	206,892	29.9	17,463	2.5	3,496	0.5	4,908	0.7	252,687	D
West Virginia	829,945	502,582	60.6	325,358	39.2	—	0.0	832	0.1	1,173	0.1	177,224	D
Wisconsin	1,258,560	802,984	63.8	380,828	30.3	60,297	4.8	10,626	0.8	3,825	0.3	422,156	D
Wyoming	103,382	62,624	60.6	38,739	37.5	1,653	1.6	200	0.2	166	0.2	23,885	D
Totals	45,656,991	27,750,866	60.8	16,679,683	36.5	892,361	2.0	187,781	0.4	136,300	0.3	11,071,183	D

1. Figures from Clerk of the House of Representatives, *Statistics of the Congressional and Presidential Election* (Washington, D.C.: U.S. Government Printing Office, 1936). Two sets of Landon electors—Republican and Independent Republican—are combined here.
2. Figures from Svend Petersen, *A Statistical History of the American Presidential Elections* (Westport, Conn.: Greenwood Press, 1981); Clerk of the House, *Congressional and Presidential Election*.
3. Figures from Petersen, *A Statistical History*; Clerk of the House, *Congressional and Presidential Election*; *Texas Almanac*.

1940 Presidential Election

STATES	TOTAL VOTE	FRANKLIN D. ROOSEVELT (Democrat) Votes	%	WENDELL WILLKIE (Republican) Votes	%	NORMAN M. THOMAS (Socialist) Votes	%	ROGER W. BABSON (Prohibition) Votes	%	OTHER Votes	%	PLURALITY	
Alabama	294,219	250,726	85.2	42,184	14.3	100	0.0	700	0.2	509	0.2	208,542	D
Arizona	150,039	95,267	63.5	54,030	36.0	—	0.0	742	0.5	—	0.0	41,237	D
Arkansas	200,429	157,213	78.4	42,122	21.0	301	0.2	793	0.4	—	0.0	115,091	D
California	3,268,791	1,877,618	57.4	1,351,419	41.3	16,506	0.5	9,400	0.3	13,848	0.4	526,199	D
Colorado	549,004	265,554	48.4	279,576	50.9	1,899	0.3	1,597	0.3	378	0.1	14,022	R
Connecticut	781,502	417,621	53.4	361,819	46.3	—	0.0	—	0.0	2,062	0.3	55,802	D
Delaware	136,374	74,599	54.7	61,440	45.1	115	0.1	220	0.2	—	0.0	13,159	D
Florida	485,640	359,334	74.0	126,158	26.0	—	0.0	—	0.0	148	0.0	233,176	D
Georgia[1]	312,686	265,194	84.8	46,495	14.9	—	0.0	983	0.3	14	0.0	218,699	D
Idaho	235,168	127,842	54.4	106,553	45.3	497	0.2	—	0.0	276	0.1	21,289	D
Illinois	4,217,935	2,149,934	51.0	2,047,240	48.5	10,914	0.3	9,190	0.2	657	0.0	102,694	D
Indiana	1,782,747	874,063	49.0	899,466	50.5	2,075	0.1	6,437	0.4	706	0.0	25,403	R
Iowa	1,215,432	578,802	47.6	632,370	52.0	—	0.0	2,284	0.2	1,976	0.2	53,568	R
Kansas	860,297	364,725	42.4	489,169	56.9	2,347	0.3	4,056	0.5	—	0.0	124,444	R
Kentucky	970,163	557,322	57.4	410,384	42.3	1,014	0.1	1,443	0.1	—	0.0	146,938	D
Louisiana	372,305	319,751	85.9	52,446	14.1	—	0.0	—	0.0	108	0.0	267,305	D
Maine	320,840	156,478	48.8	163,951	51.1	—	0.0	—	0.0	411	0.1	7,473	R
Maryland	660,104	384,546	58.3	269,534	40.8	4,093	0.6	—	0.0	1,931	0.3	115,012	D
Massachusetts	2,026,993	1,076,522	53.1	939,700	46.4	4,091	0.2	1,370	0.1	5,310	0.3	136,822	D
Michigan	2,085,929	1,032,991	49.5	1,039,917	49.9	7,593	0.4	1,795	0.1	3,633	0.2	6,926	R
Minnesota	1,251,188	644,196	51.5	596,274	47.7	5,454	0.4	—	0.0	5,264	0.4	47,922	D
Mississippi	175,824	168,267	95.7	7,364	4.2	193	0.1	—	0.0	—	0.0	160,903	D
Missouri	1,833,729	958,476	52.3	871,009	47.5	2,226	0.1	1,809	0.1	209	0.0	87,467	D
Montana	247,873	145,698	58.8	99,579	40.2	1,443	0.6	664	0.3	489	0.2	46,119	D
Nebraska	615,878	263,677	42.8	352,201	57.2	—	0.0	—	0.0	—	0.0	88,524	R
Nevada	53,174	31,945	60.1	21,229	39.9	—	0.0	—	0.0	—	0.0	10,716	D
New Hampshire	235,419	125,292	53.2	110,127	46.8	—	0.0	—	0.0	—	0.0	15,165	D
New Jersey	1,972,552	1,016,808	51.5	945,475	47.9	2,433	0.1	873	0.0	6,963	0.4	71,333	D
New Mexico	183,258	103,699	56.6	79,315	43.3	144	0.1	100	0.1	—	0.0	24,384	D
New York	6,301,596	3,251,918	51.6	3,027,478	48.0	18,950	0.3	3,250	0.1	—	0.0	224,440	D
North Carolina	822,648	609,015	74.0	213,633	26.0	—	0.0	—	0.0	—	0.0	395,382	D
North Dakota	280,775	124,036	44.2	154,590	55.1	1,279	0.5	325	0.1	545	0.2	30,554	R
Ohio	3,319,912	1,733,139	52.2	1,586,773	47.8	—	0.0	—	0.0	—	0.0	146,366	D
Oklahoma	826,212	474,313	57.4	348,872	42.2	—	0.0	3,027	0.4	—	0.0	125,441	D
Oregon	481,240	258,415	53.7	219,555	45.6	398	0.1	154	0.0	2,718	0.6	38,860	D
Pennsylvania	4,078,714	2,171,035	53.2	1,889,848	46.3	10,967	0.3	—	0.0	6,864	0.2	281,187	D
Rhode Island	321,152	182,181	56.7	138,654	43.2	—	0.0	74	0.0	243	0.1	43,527	D
South Carolina	99,830	95,470	95.6	4,360	4.4	—	0.0	—	0.0	—	0.0	91,110	D
South Dakota	308,427	131,362	42.6	177,065	57.4	—	0.0	—	0.0	—	0.0	45,703	R
Tennessee	522,823	351,601	67.3	169,153	32.4	463	0.1	1,606	0.3	—	0.0	182,448	D
Texas[2]	1,041,168	840,151	80.7	199,152	19.1	728	0.1	925	0.1	212	0.0	640,999	D
Utah	247,819	154,277	62.3	93,151	37.6	200	0.1	—	0.0	191	0.1	61,126	D
Vermont	143,062	64,269	44.9	78,371	54.8	—	0.0	—	0.0	422	0.3	14,102	R
Virginia	346,608	235,961	68.1	109,363	31.6	282	0.1	882	0.3	120	0.0	126,598	D
Washington	793,833	462,145	58.2	322,123	40.6	4,586	0.6	1,686	0.2	3,293	0.4	140,022	D
West Virginia	868,076	495,662	57.1	372,414	42.9	—	0.0	—	0.0	—	0.0	123,248	D
Wisconsin	1,405,522	704,821	50.1	679,206	48.3	15,071	1.1	2,148	0.2	4,276	0.3	25,615	D
Wyoming	112,240	59,287	52.8	52,633	46.9	148	0.1	172	0.2	—	0.0	6,654	D
Totals	49,817,149	27,343,218	54.7	22,334,940	44.8	116,510	0.2	58,705	0.1	63,776	0.1	5,008,278	D

1. Two sets of Willkie electors are combined here: Republican, 23,934; Independent Democrat, 22,561.
2. Figures from Svend Petersen, *A Statistical History of the American Presidential Elections* (Westport, Conn.: Greenwood Press, 1981); Clerk of the House of Representatives, *Statistical of the Congressional and Presidential Election* (Washington, D.C.: U.S. Government Printing Office, 1940); *Texas Almanac.*

1944 Presidential Election

STATE	TOTAL VOTE	FRANKLIN D. ROOSEVELT (Democrat) Votes	%	THOMAS E. DEWEY (Republican) Votes	%	NORMAN THOMAS (Socialist) Votes	%	CLAUDE A. WATSON (Prohibition) Votes	%	OTHER Votes	%	PLURALITY	
Alabama	244,743	198,918	81.3	44,540	18.2	190	0.1	1,095	0.4	—	0.0	154,378	D
Arizona	137,634	80,926	58.8	56,287	40.9	—	0.0	421	0.3	—	0.0	24,639	D
Arkansas	212,954	148,965	70.0	63,551	29.8	438	0.2	—	0.0	—	0.0	85,414	D
California	3,520,875	1,988,564	56.5	1,512,965	43.0	2,515	0.1	14,770	0.4	2,061	0.1	475,599	D
Colorado	505,039	234,331	46.4	268,731	53.2	1,977	0.4	—	0.0	—	0.0	34,400	R
Connecticut	831,990	435,146	52.3	390,527	46.9	5,097	0.6	—	0.0	1,220	0.1	44,619	D
Delaware	125,361	68,166	54.4	56,747	45.3	154	0.1	294	0.2	—	0.0	11,419	D
Florida	482,803	339,377	70.3	143,215	29.7	—	0.0	—	0.0	211	0.0	196,162	D
Georgia[1]	328,129	268,187	81.7	56,506	17.2	6	0.0	36	0.0	3,373	1.0	211,681	D
Idaho	208,321	107,399	51.6	100,137	48.1	282	0.1	503	0.2	—	0.0	7,262	D
Illinois	4,036,061	2,079,479	51.5	1,939,314	48.0	180	0.0	7,411	0.2	9,677	0.2	140,165	D
Indiana	1,672,091	781,403	46.7	875,891	52.4	2,223	0.1	12,574	0.8	—	0.0	94,488	R
Iowa	1,052,599	499,876	47.5	547,267	52.0	1,511	0.1	3,752	0.4	193	0.0	47,391	R
Kansas	733,776	287,458	39.2	442,096	60.2	1,613	0.2	2,609	0.4	—	0.0	154,638	R
Kentucky	867,924	472,589	54.5	392,448	45.2	535	0.1	2,023	0.2	329	0.0	80,141	D
Louisiana	349,383	281,564	80.6	67,750	19.4	—	0.0	—	0.0	69	0.0	213,814	D
Maine	296,400	140,631	47.4	155,434	52.4	—	0.0	—	0.0	335	0.1	14,803	R
Maryland	608,439	315,490	51.9	292,949	48.1	—	0.0	—	0.0	—	0.0	22,541	D
Massachusetts	1,960,665	1,035,296	52.8	921,350	47.0	—	0.0	973	0.0	3,046	0.2	113,946	D
Michigan	2,205,223	1,106,899	50.2	1,084,423	49.2	4,598	0.2	6,503	0.3	2,800	0.1	22,476	D
Minnesota	1,125,504	589,864	52.4	527,416	46.9	5,048	0.4	—	0.0	3,176	0.3	62,448	D
Mississippi	180,234	168,621	93.6	11,613	6.4	—	0.0	—	0.0	—	0.0	157,008	D
Missouri	1,571,697	807,356	51.4	761,175	48.4	1,751	0.1	1,195	0.1	220	0.0	46,181	D
Montana	207,355	112,556	54.3	93,163	44.9	1,296	0.6	340	0.2	—	0.0	19,393	D
Nebraska	563,126	233,246	41.4	329,880	58.6	—	0.0	—	0.0	—	0.0	96,634	R
Nevada	54,234	29,623	54.6	24,611	45.4	—	0.0	—	0.0	—	0.0	5,012	D
New Hampshire	229,625	119,663	52.1	109,916	47.9	46	0.0	—	0.0	—	0.0	9,747	D
New Jersey	1,963,761	987,874	50.3	961,335	49.0	3,358	0.2	4,255	0.2	6,939	0.4	26,539	D
New Mexico	152,225	81,389	53.5	70,688	46.4	—	0.0	148	0.1	—	0.0	10,701	D
New York	6,316,790	3,304,238	52.3	2,987,647	47.3	10,553	0.2	—	0.0	14,352	0.2	316,591	D
North Carolina	790,554	527,399	66.7	263,155	33.3	—	0.0	—	0.0	—	0.0	264,244	D
North Dakota	220,182	100,144	45.5	118,535	53.8	954	0.4	549	0.2	—	0.0	18,391	R
Ohio	3,153,056	1,570,763	49.8	1,582,293	50.2	—	0.0	—	0.0	—	0.0	11,530	R
Oklahoma	722,636	401,549	55.6	319,424	44.2	—	0.0	1,663	0.2	—	0.0	82,125	D
Oregon	480,147	248,635	51.8	225,365	46.9	3,785	0.8	2,362	0.5	—	0.0	23,270	D
Pennsylvania	3,794,793	1,940,479	51.1	1,835,054	48.4	11,721	0.3	5,750	0.2	1,789	0.0	105,425	D
Rhode Island	299,276	175,356	58.6	123,487	41.3	—	0.0	433	0.1	—	0.0	51,869	D
South Carolina[2]	103,382	90,601	87.6	4,554	4.4	—	0.0	365	0.4	7,862	7.6	82,802	D
South Dakota	232,076	96,711	41.7	135,365	58.3	—	0.0	—	0.0	—	0.0	38,654	R
Tennessee	510,692	308,707	60.4	200,311	39.2	792	0.2	882	0.2	—	0.0	108,396	D
Texas	1,150,334	821,605	71.4	191,423	16.6	594	0.1	1,018	0.1	135,694	11.8	630,182	D
Utah	248,319	150,088	60.4	97,891	39.4	340	0.1	—	0.0	—	0.0	52,197	D
Vermont	125,361	53,820	42.9	71,527	57.1	—	0.0	—	0.0	14	0.0	17,707	R
Virginia	388,485	242,276	62.4	145,243	37.4	417	0.1	459	0.1	90	0.0	97,033	D
Washington	856,328	486,774	56.8	361,689	42.2	3,824	0.4	2,396	0.3	1,645	0.2	125,085	D
West Virginia	715,596	392,777	54.9	322,819	45.1	—	0.0	—	0.0	—	0.0	69,958	D
Wisconsin	1,339,152	650,413	48.6	674,532	50.4	13,205	1.0	—	0.0	1,002	0.1	24,119	R
Wyoming	101,340	49,419	48.8	51,921	51.2	—	0.0	—	0.0	—	0.0	2,502	R
Totals	47,976,670	25,612,610	53.4	22,021,053	45.9	79,003	0.2	74,779	0.2	196,097	0.4	3,591,557	D

1. Clerk of the House of Representatives, *Statistics of the Congressional and Presidential Election* (Washington, D.C.: U.S. Government Printing Office, 1944). There were two separate slates of electors pledged to Dewey in Georgia that could not legally be combined: Republican, 56,606; Independent Democrat, 3,373.

2. Clerk of the House, *Congressional and Presidential Election*. There were two separate slates of electors pledged to Dewey in South Carolina that could not legally be combined: Republican, 4,554; Tobert Faction, 63. Plurality of 82,802 votes is calculated on the basis of 7,799 votes cast for the Southern Democrats Party.

1948 Presidential Election

STATE	TOTAL VOTE	HARRY S. TRUMAN (Democrat)		THOMAS E. DEWEY (Republican)		J. STROM THURMOND (States' Rights Democrat)		HENRY A. WALLACE (Progressive)		OTHER		PLURALITY
		Votes	%	Votes	%	Votes	%	Votes	%	Votes	%	
Alabama	214,980	—	0.0	40,930	19.0	171,443	79.7	1,522	0.7	1,085	0.5	130,513 SR
Arizona	177,065	95,251	53.8	77,597	43.8	—	0.0	3,310	1.9	907	0.5	17,654 D
Arkansas	242,475	149,659	61.7	50,959	21.0	40,068	16.5	751	0.3	1,038	0.4	98,700 D
California	4,021,538	1,913,134	47.6	1,895,269	47.1	1,228	0.0	190,381	4.7	21,526	0.5	17,865 D
Colorado	515,237	267,288	51.9	239,714	46.5	—	0.0	6,115	1.2	2,120	0.4	27,574 D
Connecticut	883,518	423,297	47.9	437,754	49.5	—	0.0	13,713	1.6	8,754	1.0	14,457 R
Delaware	139,073	67,813	48.8	69,588	50.0	—	0.0	1,050	0.8	622	0.4	1,775 R
Florida	577,643	281,988	48.8	194,280	33.6	89,755	15.5	11,620	2.0	—	0.0	87,708 D
Georgia	418,844	254,646	60.8	76,691	18.3	85,135	20.3	1,636	0.4	736	0.2	169,511 D
Idaho	214,816	107,370	50.0	101,514	47.3	—	0.0	4,972	2.3	960	0.4	5,856 D
Illinois	3,984,046	1,994,715	50.1	1,961,103	49.2	—	0.0	—	0.0	28,228	0.7	33,612 D
Indiana	1,656,212	807,831	48.8	821,079	49.6	—	0.0	9,649	0.6	17,653	1.1	13,248 R
Iowa	1,038,264	522,380	50.3	494,018	47.6	—	0.0	12,125	1.2	9,741	0.9	28,362 D
Kansas	788,819	351,902	44.6	423,039	53.6	—	0.0	4,603	0.6	9,275	1.2	71,137 R
Kentucky	822,658	466,756	56.7	341,210	41.5	10,411	1.3	1,567	0.2	2,714	0.3	125,546 D
Louisiana	416,336	136,344	32.7	72,657	17.5	204,290	49.1	3,035	0.7	10	0.0	67,946 SR
Maine	264,787	111,916	42.3	150,234	56.7	—	0.0	1,884	0.7	753	0.3	38,318 R
Maryland	596,748	286,521	48.0	294,814	49.4	2,489	0.4	9,983	1.7	2,941	0.5	8,293 R
Massachusetts	2,107,146	1,151,788	54.7	909,370	43.2	—	0.0	38,157	1.8	7,831	0.4	242,418 D
Michigan	2,109,609	1,003,448	47.6	1,038,595	49.2	—	0.0	46,515	2.2	21,051	1.0	35,147 R
Minnesota	1,212,226	692,966	57.2	483,617	39.9	—	0.0	27,866	2.3	7,777	0.6	209,349 D
Mississippi	192,190	19,384	10.1	5,043	2.6	167,538	87.2	225	0.1	—	0.0	148,154 SR
Missouri	1,578,628	917,315	58.1	655,039	41.5	—	0.0	3,998	0.3	2,276	0.1	262,276 D
Montana	224,278	119,071	53.1	96,770	43.1	—	0.0	7,313	3.3	1,124	0.5	22,301 D
Nebraska	488,940	224,165	45.8	264,774	54.2	—	0.0	—	0.0	1	0.0	40,609 R
Nevada	62,117	31,291	50.4	29,357	47.3	—	0.0	1,469	2.4	—	0.0	1,934 D
New Hampshire	231,440	107,995	46.7	121,299	52.4	7	0.0	1,970	0.9	169	0.1	13,304 R
New Jersey	1,949,555	895,455	45.9	981,124	50.3	—	0.0	42,683	2.2	30,293	1.6	85,669 R
New Mexico	187,063	105,464	56.4	80,303	42.9	—	0.0	1,037	0.6	259	0.1	25,161 D
New York	6,177,337	2,780,204	45.0	2,841,163	46.0	—	0.0	509,559	8.2	46,411	0.8	60,959 R
North Carolina	791,209	459,070	58.0	258,572	32.7	69,652	8.8	3,915	0.5	—	0.0	200,498 D
North Dakota	220,716	95,812	43.4	115,139	52.2	374	0.2	8,391	3.8	1,000	0.5	19,327 R
Ohio	2,936,071	1,452,791	49.5	1,445,684	49.2	—	0.0	37,596	1.3	—	0.0	7,107 D
Oklahoma	721,599	452,782	62.7	268,817	37.3	—	0.0	—	0.0	—	0.0	183,965 D
Oregon	524,080	243,147	46.4	260,904	49.8	—	0.0	14,978	2.9	5,051	1.0	17,757 R
Pennsylvania	3,735,348	1,752,426	46.9	1,902,197	50.9	—	0.0	55,161	1.5	25,564	0.7	149,771 R
Rhode Island	327,702	188,736	57.6	135,787	41.4	—	0.0	2,619	0.8	560	0.2	52,949 D
South Carolina	142,571	34,423	24.1	5,386	3.8	102,607	72.0	154	0.1	1	0.0	68,184 SR
South Dakota	250,105	117,653	47.0	129,651	51.8	—	0.0	2,801	1.1	—	0.0	11,998 R
Tennessee	550,283	270,402	49.1	202,914	36.9	73,815	13.4	1,864	0.3	1,288	0.2	67,488 D
Texas[1]	1,147,245	750,700	65.4	282,240	24.6	106,909	9.3	3,764	0.3	3,632	0.3	468,460 D
Utah	276,306	149,151	54.0	124,402	45.0	—	0.0	2,679	1.0	74	0.0	24,749 D
Vermont	123,382	45,557	36.9	75,926	61.5	—	0.0	1,279	1.0	620	0.5	30,369 R
Virginia	419,256	200,786	47.9	172,070	41.0	43,393	10.4	2,047	0.5	960	0.2	28,716 D
Washington	905,058	476,165	52.6	386,314	42.7	—	0.0	31,692	3.5	10,887	1.2	89,851 D
West Virginia	748,750	429,188	57.3	316,251	42.2	—	0.0	3,311	0.4	—	0.0	112,937 D
Wisconsin	1,276,800	647,310	50.7	590,959	46.3	—	0.0	25,282	2.0	13,249	1.0	56,351 D
Wyoming	101,425	52,354	51.6	47,947	47.3	—	0.0	931	0.9	193	0.2	4,407 D
Totals	48,691,494	24,105,810	49.5	21,970,064	45.1	1,169,114	2.4	1,157,172	2.4	289,334	0.6	2,135,746 D

1. Figures from Svend Petersen, *A Statistical History of the American Presidential Elections* (Westport, Conn.: Greenwood Press, 1981); Clerk of the House of Representatives, *Statistics of the Congressional and Presidential Election* (Washington, D.C.: U.S. Government Printing Office, 1948); *Texas Almanac*. Totals do not include the vote in thirty-five counties that were excluded from the official returns. Had these counties been counted, the vote in Texas would have been as follows: Total, 1,249,577; Truman, 824,235; Dewey, 303,467; Thurmond, 113,920; Wallace, 3,918; Other, 4,037; Plurality, 520,768 D. The totals for the nation would have been as follows: Total, 48,793,826; Truman, 24,179,345; Dewey, 21,991,291; Thurmond, 1,176,125; Wallace, 1,157,326; Other, 289,739; Plurality, 2,188,054 D.

1952 Presidential Election

STATE	TOTAL VOTE	DWIGHT D. EISENHOWER (Republican)		ADLAI E. STEVENSON (Democrat)		VINCENT HALLINAN (Progressive)		STUART HAMBLEN (Prohibition)		OTHER		PLURALITY	
		Votes	%	Votes	%	Votes	%	Votes	%	Votes	%		
Alabama	426,120	149,231	35.0	275,075	64.6	—	0.0	1,814	0.4	—	0.0	125,844	D
Arizona	260,570	152,042	58.3	108,528	41.7	—	0.0	—	0.0	—	0.0	43,514	R
Arkansas	404,800	177,155	43.8	226,300	55.9	—	0.0	886	0.2	459	0.1	49,145	D
California	5,141,849	2,897,310	56.3	2,197,548	42.7	24,106	0.5	15,653	0.3	7,232	0.1	699,762	R
Colorado	630,103	379,782	60.3	245,504	39.0	1,919	0.3	—	0.0	2,898	0.5	134,278	R
Connecticut	1,096,911	611,012	55.7	481,649	43.9	1,466	0.1	—	0.0	2,784	0.3	129,363	R
Delaware	174,025	90,059	51.8	83,315	47.9	155	0.1	234	0.1	262	0.2	6,744	R
Florida	989,337	544,036	55.0	444,950	45.0	—	0.0	—	0.0	351	0.0	99,086	R
Georgia	655,785	198,961	30.3	456,823	69.7	—	0.0	—	0.0	1	0.0	257,862	D
Idaho	276,254	180,707	65.4	95,081	34.4	443	0.2	—	0.0	23	0.0	85,626	R
Illinois	4,481,058	2,457,327	54.8	2,013,920	44.9	—	0.0	—	0.0	9,811	0.2	443,407	R
Indiana	1,955,049	1,136,259	58.1	801,530	41.0	1,085	0.1	15,335	0.8	840	0.0	334,729	R
Iowa	1,268,773	808,906	63.8	451,513	35.6	5,085	0.4	2,882	0.2	387	0.0	357,393	R
Kansas	896,166	616,302	68.8	273,296	30.5	—	0.0	6,038	0.7	530	0.1	343,006	R
Kentucky	993,148	495,029	49.8	495,729	49.9	336	0.0	1,161	0.1	893	0.1	700	D
Louisiana	651,952	306,925	47.1	345,027	52.9	—	0.0	—	0.0	—	0.0	38,102	D
Maine	351,786	232,353	66.0	118,806	33.8	332	0.1	—	0.0	295	0.1	113,547	R
Maryland	902,074	499,424	55.4	395,337	43.8	7,313	0.8	—	0.0	—	0.0	104,087	R
Massachusetts	2,383,398	1,292,325	54.2	1,083,525	45.5	4,636	0.2	886	0.0	2,026	0.1	208,800	R
Michigan	2,798,592	1,551,529	55.4	1,230,657	44.0	3,922	0.1	10,331	0.4	2,153	0.1	320,872	R
Minnesota	1,379,483	763,211	55.3	608,458	44.1	2,666	0.2	2,147	0.2	3,001	0.2	154,753	R
Mississippi	285,532	112,966	39.6	172,566	60.4	—	0.0	—	0.0	—	0.0	59,600	D
Missouri	1,892,062	959,429	50.7	929,830	49.1	987	0.1	885	0.0	931	0.0	29,599	R
Montana	265,037	157,394	59.4	106,213	40.1	723	0.3	548	0.2	159	0.1	51,181	R
Nebraska	609,660	421,603	69.2	188,057	30.8	—	0.0	—	0.0	—	0.0	233,546	R
Nevada	82,190	50,502	61.4	31,688	38.6	—	0.0	—	0.0	—	0.0	18,814	R
New Hampshire	272,950	166,287	60.9	106,663	39.1	—	0.0	—	0.0	—	0.0	59,624	R
New Jersey	2,418,554	1,373,613	56.8	1,015,902	42.0	5,589	0.2	989	0.0	22,461	0.9	357,711	R
New Mexico	238,608	132,170	55.4	105,661	44.3	225	0.1	297	0.1	255	0.1	26,509	R
New York	7,128,239	3,952,813	55.5	3,104,601	43.6	64,211	0.9	—	0.0	6,614	0.1	848,212	R
North Carolina	1,210,910	558,107	46.1	652,803	53.9	—	0.0	—	0.0	—	0.0	94,696	D
North Dakota	270,127	191,712	71.0	76,694	28.4	344	0.1	302	0.1	1,075	0.4	115,018	R
Ohio	3,700,758	2,100,391	56.8	1,600,367	43.2	—	0.0	—	0.0	—	0.0	500,024	R
Oklahoma	948,984	518,045	54.6	430,939	45.4	—	0.0	—	0.0	—	0.0	87,106	R
Oregon	695,059	420,815	60.5	270,579	38.9	3,665	0.5	—	0.0	—	0.0	150,236	R
Pennsylvania	4,580,969	2,415,789	52.7	2,146,269	46.9	4,222	0.1	8,951	0.2	5,738	0.1	269,520	R
Rhode Island	414,498	210,935	50.9	203,293	49.0	187	0.0	—	0.0	83	0.0	7,642	R
South Carolina[1]	341,087	9,793	2.9	173,004	50.7	—	0.0	1	0.0	158,289	46.4	4,922	D
South Dakota	294,283	203,857	69.3	90,426	30.7	—	0.0	—	0.0	—	0.0	113,431	R
Tennessee	892,553	446,147	50.0	443,710	49.7	885	0.1	1,432	0.2	379	0.0	2,437	R
Texas	2,075,946	1,102,878	53.1	969,228	46.7	294	0.0	1,983	0.1	1,563	0.1	133,650	R
Utah	329,554	194,190	58.9	135,364	41.1	—	0.0	—	0.0	—	0.0	58,826	R
Vermont	153,557	109,717	71.5	43,355	28.2	282	0.2	—	0.0	203	0.1	66,362	R
Virginia	619,689	349,037	56.3	268,677	43.4	311	0.1	—	0.0	1,664	0.3	80,360	R
Washington	1,102,708	599,107	54.3	492,845	44.7	2,460	0.2	—	0.0	8,296	0.8	106,262	R
West Virginia	873,548	419,970	48.1	453,578	51.9	—	0.0	—	0.0	—	0.0	33,608	D
Wisconsin	1,607,370	979,744	61.0	622,175	38.7	2,174	0.1	—	0.0	3,277	0.2	357,569	R
Wyoming	129,253	81,049	62.7	47,934	37.1	—	0.0	194	0.2	76	0.1	33,115	R
Totals	61,550,918	33,777,945	54.9	27,314,992	44.4	140,023	0.2	72,949	0.1	245,009	0.4	6,462,953	R

1. There were two separate slates of electors pledged to Eisenhower in South Carolina that could not legally be combined: Republican, 9,793; Independent slate, 158,289. Had these two been combined Eisenhower would have totaled 168,082 in the state and 33,936,234 nationally.

1956 Presidential Election

STATE	TOTAL VOTE	DWIGHT D. EISENHOWER (Republican) Votes	%	ADLAI E. STEVENSON (Democrat) Votes	%	T. COLEMAN ANDREWS (Constitution) Votes	%	ERIC HASS (Socialist Labor) Votes	%	OTHER Votes	%	PLURALITY	
Alabama	496,861	195,694	39.4	280,844	56.5	—	0.0	—	0.0	20,323	4.1	885,150	D
Arizona	290,173	176,990	61.0	112,880	38.9	303	0.1	—	0.0	—	0.0	64,110	R
Arkansas	406,572	186,287	45.8	213,277	52.5	7,008	1.7	—	0.0	—	0.0	26,990	D
California	5,466,355	3,027,668	55.4	2,420,135	44.3	6,087	0.1	300	0.0	12,165	0.2	607,533	R
Colorado	657,074	394,479	60.0	257,997	39.3	759	0.1	3,308	0.5	531	0.1	136,482	R
Connecticut	1,117,121	711,837	63.7	405,079	36.3	—	0.0	—	0.0	205	0.0	306,758	R
Delaware	177,988	98,057	55.1	79,421	44.6	—	0.0	110	0.1	400	0.2	18,636	R
Florida	1,125,762	643,849	57.2	480,371	42.7	—	0.0	—	0.0	1,542	0.1	163,478	R
Georgia	669,655	222,778	33.3	444,688	66.4	2,096	0.3	—	0.0	93	0.0	221,910	D
Idaho	272,989	166,979	61.2	105,868	38.8	126	0.0	—	0.0	16	0.0	61,111	R
Illinois	4,407,407	2,623,327	59.5	1,775,682	40.3	—	0.0	8,342	0.2	56	0.0	847,645	R
Indiana	1,974,607	1,182,811	59.9	783,908	39.7	—	0.0	1,334	0.1	6,554	0.3	398,903	R
Iowa	1,234,564	729,187	59.1	501,858	40.7	3,202	0.3	125	0.0	192	0.0	227,329	R
Kansas	866,243	566,878	65.4	296,317	34.2	—	0.0	—	0.0	3,048	0.4	270,561	R
Kentucky	1,053,805	572,192	54.3	476,453	45.2	—	0.0	358	0.0	4,802	0.5	95,739	R
Louisiana	617,544	329,047	53.3	243,977	39.5	—	0.0	—	0.0	44,520	7.2	85,070	R
Maine	351,706	249,238	70.9	102,468	29.1	—	0.0	—	0.0	—	0.0	146,770	R
Maryland	932,827	559,738	60.0	372,613	39.9	—	0.0	—	0.0	476	0.1	187,125	R
Massachusetts	2,348,506	1,393,197	59.3	948,190	40.4	—	0.0	5,573	0.2	1,546	0.1	445,007	R
Michigan	3,080,468	1,713,647	55.6	1,359,898	44.1	—	0.0	—	0.0	6,923	0.2	353,749	R
Minnesota	1,340,005	719,302	53.7	617,525	46.1	—	0.0	2,080	0.2	1,098	0.1	101,777	R
Mississippi	248,104	60,685	24.5	144,453	58.2	—	0.0	—	0.0	42,966	17.3	83,768	D
Missouri	1,832,562	914,289	49.9	918,273	50.1	—	0.0	—	0.0	—	0.0	3,984	D
Montana	271,171	154,933	57.1	116,238	42.9	—	0.0	—	0.0	—	0.0	38,695	R
Nebraska	577,137	378,108	65.5	199,029	34.5	—	0.0	—	0.0	—	0.0	179,079	R
Nevada	96,689	56,049	58.0	40,640	42.0	—	0.0	—	0.0	—	0.0	15,409	R
New Hampshire	266,994	176,519	66.1	90,364	33.8	111	0.0	—	0.0	—	0.0	86,155	R
New Jersey	2,484,312	1,606,942	64.7	850,337	34.2	5,317	0.2	6,736	0.3	14,980	0.6	756,605	R
New Mexico	253,926	146,788	57.8	106,098	41.8	364	0.1	69	0.0	607	0.2	40,690	R
New York	7,095,971	4,345,506	61.2	2,747,944	38.7	1,027	0.0	150	0.0	1,344	0.0	1,597,562	R
North Carolina	1,165,592	575,062	49.3	590,530	50.7	—	0.0	—	0.0	—	0.0	15,468	D
North Dakota	253,991	156,766	61.7	96,742	38.1	483	0.2	—	0.0	—	0.0	60,024	R
Ohio	3,702,265	2,262,610	61.1	1,439,655	38.9	—	0.0	—	0.0	—	0.0	822,955	R
Oklahoma	859,350	473,769	55.1	385,581	44.9	—	0.0	—	0.0	—	0.0	88,188	R
Oregon	736,132	406,393	55.2	329,204	44.7	—	0.0	—	0.0	535	0.1	77,189	R
Pennsylvania	4,576,503	2,585,252	56.5	1,981,769	43.3	—	0.0	7,447	0.2	2,035	0.0	603,483	R
Rhode Island	387,609	225,819	58.3	161,790	41.7	—	0.0	—	0.0	—	0.0	64,029	R
South Carolina[1]	300,583	75,700	25.2	136,372	45.4	2	0.0	—	0.0	88,509	29.4	47,863	D
South Dakota	293,857	171,569	58.4	122,288	41.6	—	0.0	—	0.0	—	0.0	49,281	R
Tennessee	939,404	462,288	49.2	456,507	48.6	19,820	2.1	—	0.0	789	0.1	5,781	R
Texas	1,955,168	1,080,619	55.3	859,958	44.0	14,591	0.7	—	0.0	—	0.0	220,661	R
Utah	333,995	215,631	64.6	118,364	35.4	—	0.0	—	0.0	—	0.0	97,267	R
Vermont	152,978	110,390	72.2	42,549	27.8	—	0.0	—	0.0	39	0.0	67,841	R
Virginia	697,978	386,459	55.4	267,760	38.4	42,964	6.2	351	0.1	444	0.1	118,699	R
Washington	1,150,889	620,430	53.9	523,002	45.4	—	0.0	7,457	0.6	—	0.0	97,428	R
West Virginia	830,831	449,297	54.1	381,534	45.9	—	0.0	—	0.0	—	0.0	67,763	R
Wisconsin	1,550,558	954,844	61.6	586,768	37.8	6,918	0.4	710	0.0	1,318	0.1	368,076	R
Wyoming	124,127	74,573	60.1	49,554	39.9	—	0.0	—	0.0	—	0.0	25,019	R
Totals	62,026,908	35,590,472	57.4	26,022,752	42.0	111,178	0.2	44,450	0.1	258,056	0.4	9,567,720	R

1. Plurality of 47,863 votes is calculated on the basis of Stevenson's vote and the 88,509 votes cast for unpledged electors.

1960 Presidential Election

STATE	TOTAL VOTE	JOHN F. KENNEDY (Democrat)		RICHARD M. NIXON (Republican)		ERIC HASS (Socialist Labor)		(UNPLEDGED)		OTHER		PLURALITY	
		Votes	%	Votes	%	Votes	%	Votes	%	Votes	%		
Alabama	570,225	324,050	56.8	237,981	41.7	—	0.0	—	0.0	8,194	1.4	86,069	D
Alaska	60,762	29,809	49.1	30,953	50.9	—	0.0	—	0.0	—	0.0	1,144	R
Arizona	398,491	176,781	44.4	221,241	55.5	469	0.1	—	0.0	—	0.0	44,460	R
Arkansas	428,509	215,049	50.2	184,508	43.1	—	0.0	—	0.0	28,952	6.8	30,541	D
California	6,506,578	3,224,099	49.6	3,259,722	50.1	1,051	0.0	—	0.0	21,706	0.3	35,623	R
Colorado	736,236	330,629	44.9	402,242	54.6	2,803	0.4	—	0.0	562	0.1	71,613	R
Connecticut	1,222,883	657,055	53.7	565,813	46.3	—	0.0	—	0.0	15	0.0	91,242	D
Delaware	196,683	99,590	50.6	96,373	49.0	82	0.0	—	0.0	638	0.3	3,217	D
Florida	1,544,176	748,700	48.5	795,476	51.5	—	0.0	—	0.0	—	0.0	46,776	R
Georgia	733,349	458,638	62.5	274,472	37.4	—	0.0	—	0.0	239	0.0	184,166	D
Hawaii	184,705	92,410	50.0	92,295	50.0	—	0.0	—	0.0	—	0.0	115	D
Idaho	300,450	138,853	46.2	161,597	53.8	—	0.0	—	0.0	—	0.0	22,744	R
Illinois	4,757,409	2,377,846	50.0	2,368,988	49.8	10,560	0.2	—	0.0	15	0.0	8,858	D
Indiana	2,135,360	952,358	44.6	1,175,120	55.0	1,136	0.1	—	0.0	6,746	0.3	222,762	R
Iowa	1,273,810	550,565	43.2	722,381	56.7	230	0.0	—	0.0	634	0.0	171,816	R
Kansas	928,825	363,213	39.1	561,474	60.4	—	0.0	—	0.0	4,138	0.4	198,261	R
Kentucky	1,124,462	521,855	46.4	602,607	53.6	—	0.0	—	0.0	—	0.0	80,752	R
Louisiana	807,891	407,339	50.4	230,980	28.6	—	0.0	—	0.0	169,572	21.0	176,359	D
Maine	421,767	181,159	43.0	240,608	57.0	—	0.0	—	0.0	—	0.0	59,449	R
Maryland	1,055,349	565,808	53.6	489,538	46.4	—	0.0	—	0.0	3	0.0	76,270	D
Massachusetts	2,469,480	1,487,174	60.2	976,750	39.6	3,892	0.2	—	0.0	1,664	0.1	510,424	D
Michigan	3,318,097	1,687,269	50.9	1,620,428	48.8	1,718	0.1	—	0.0	8,682	0.3	66,841	D
Minnesota	1,541,887	779,933	50.6	757,915	49.2	962	0.1	—	0.0	3,077	0.2	22,018	D
Mississippi[1]	298,171	108,362	36.3	73,561	24.7	—	0.0	116,248	39.0	—	0.0	7,886	U
Missouri	1,934,422	972,201	50.3	962,221	49.7	—	0.0	—	0.0	—	0.0	9,980	D
Montana	277,579	134,891	48.6	141,841	51.1	—	0.0	—	0.0	847	0.3	6,950	R
Nebraska	613,095	232,542	37.9	380,553	62.1	—	0.0	—	0.0	—	0.0	148,011	R
Nevada	107,267	54,880	51.2	52,387	48.8	—	0.0	—	0.0	—	0.0	2,493	D
New Hampshire	295,761	137,772	46.6	157,989	53.4	—	0.0	—	0.0	—	0.0	20,217	R
New Jersey	2,773,111	1,385,415	50.0	1,363,324	49.2	4,262	0.2	—	0.0	20,110	0.7	22,091	D
New Mexico	311,107	156,027	50.2	153,733	49.4	570	0.2	—	0.0	777	0.2	2,294	D
New York	7,291,079	3,830,085	52.5	3,446,419	47.3	—	0.0	—	0.0	14,575	0.2	383,666	D
North Carolina	1,368,556	713,136	52.1	655,420	47.9	—	0.0	—	0.0	—	0.0	57,716	D
North Dakota	278,431	123,963	44.5	154,310	55.4	—	0.0	—	0.0	158	0.1	30,347	R
Ohio	4,161,859	1,944,248	46.7	2,217,611	53.3	—	0.0	—	0.0	—	0.0	273,363	R
Oklahoma	903,150	370,111	41.0	533,039	59.0	—	0.0	—	0.0	—	0.0	162,928	R
Oregon	776,421	367,402	47.3	408,060	52.6	—	0.0	—	0.0	959	0.1	40,658	R
Pennsylvania	5,006,541	2,556,282	51.1	2,439,956	48.7	7,185	0.1	—	0.0	3,118	0.1	116,326	D
Rhode Island	405,535	258,032	63.6	147,502	36.4	—	0.0	—	0.0	1	0.0	110,530	D
South Carolina	386,688	198,129	51.2	188,558	48.8	—	0.0	—	0.0	1	0.0	9,571	D
South Dakota	306,487	128,070	41.8	178,417	58.2	—	0.0	—	0.0	—	0.0	50,347	R
Tennessee	1,051,792	481,453	45.8	556,577	52.9	—	0.0	—	0.0	13,762	1.3	75,124	R
Texas	2,311,084	1,167,567	50.5	1,121,310	48.5	—	0.0	—	0.0	22,207	1.0	46,257	D
Utah	374,709	169,248	45.2	205,361	54.8	—	0.0	—	0.0	100	0.0	36,113	R
Vermont	167,324	69,186	41.3	98,131	58.6	—	0.0	—	0.0	7	0.0	28,945	R
Virginia	771,449	362,327	47.0	404,521	52.4	397	0.1	—	0.0	4,204	0.5	42,194	R
Washington	1,241,572	599,298	48.3	629,273	50.7	10,895	0.9	—	0.0	2,106	0.2	29,975	R
West Virginia	837,781	441,786	52.7	395,995	47.3	—	0.0	—	0.0	—	0.0	45,791	D
Wisconsin	1,729,082	830,805	48.0	895,175	51.8	1,310	0.1	—	0.0	1,792	0.1	64,370	R
Wyoming	140,782	63,331	45.0	77,451	55.0	—	0.0	—	0.0	—	0.0	14,120	R
Totals	68,838,219	34,226,731	49.7	34,108,157	49.5	47,522	0.1	116,248	0.2	339,561	0.5	118,574	D

1. Votes for unpledged electors who carried the state and cast electoral votes for Harry F. Byrd (D Va.).

1964 Presidential Election

STATE	TOTAL VOTE	LYNDON B. JOHNSON (Democrat) Votes	%	BARRY M. GOLDWATER (Republican) Votes	%	ERIC HASS (Socialist Labor) Votes	%	CLIFTON DeBERRY (Socialist Workers) Votes	%	OTHER Votes	%	PLURALITY	
Alabama[1]	689,818	—	0.0	479,085	69.5	—	0.0	—	0.0	210,732	30.5	268,353	R
Alaska	67,259	44,329	65.9	22,930	34.1	—	0.0	—	0.0	—	0.0	21,399	D
Arizona	480,770	237,753	49.5	242,535	50.4	482	0.1	—	0.0	—	0.0	4,782	R
Arkansas	560,426	314,197	56.1	243,264	43.4	—	0.0	—	0.0	2,965	0.5	70,933	D
California	7,057,586	4,171,877	59.1	2,879,108	40.8	489	0.0	378	0.0	5,734	0.1	1,292,769	D
Colorado	776,986	476,024	61.3	296,767	38.2	302	0.0	2,537	0.3	1,356	0.2	179,257	D
Connecticut	1,218,578	826,269	67.8	390,996	32.1	—	0.0	—	0.0	1,313	0.1	435,273	D
Delaware	201,320	122,704	60.9	78,078	38.8	113	0.1	—	0.0	425	0.2	44,626	D
Florida	1,854,481	948,540	51.1	905,941	48.9	—	0.0	—	0.0	—	0.0	42,599	D
Georgia	1,139,335	522,556	45.9	616,584	54.1	—	0.0	—	0.0	195	0.0	94,028	R
Hawaii	207,271	163,249	78.8	44,022	21.2	—	0.0	—	0.0	—	0.0	119,227	D
Idaho	292,477	148,920	50.9	143,557	49.1	—	0.0	—	0.0	—	0.0	5,363	D
Illinois	4,702,841	2,796,833	59.5	1,905,946	40.5	—	0.0	—	0.0	62	0.0	890,887	D
Indiana	2,091,606	1,170,848	56.0	911,118	43.6	1,374	0.1	—	0.0	8,266	0.4	259,730	D
Iowa	1,184,539	733,030	61.9	449,148	37.9	182	0.0	159	0.0	2,020	0.2	283,882	D
Kansas	857,901	464,028	54.1	386,579	45.1	1,901	0.2	—	0.0	5,393	0.6	77,449	D
Kentucky	1,046,105	669,659	64.0	372,977	35.7	—	0.0	—	0.0	3,469	0.3	296,682	D
Louisiana	896,293	387,068	43.2	509,225	56.8	—	0.0	—	0.0	—	0.0	122,157	R
Maine	380,965	262,264	68.8	118,701	31.2	—	0.0	—	0.0	—	0.0	143,563	D
Maryland	1,116,457	730,912	65.5	385,495	34.5	—	0.0	—	0.0	50	0.0	345,417	D
Massachusetts	2,344,798	1,786,422	76.2	549,727	23.4	4,755	0.2	—	0.0	3,894	0.2	1,236,695	D
Michigan	3,203,102	2,136,615	66.7	1,060,152	33.1	1,704	0.1	3,817	0.1	814	0.0	1,076,463	D
Minnesota	1,554,462	991,117	63.8	559,624	36.0	2,544	0.2	1,177	0.1	—	0.0	431,493	D
Mississippi	409,146	52,618	12.9	356,528	87.1	—	0.0	—	0.0	—	0.0	303,910	R
Missouri	1,817,879	1,164,344	64.0	653,535	36.0	—	0.0	—	0.0	—	0.0	510,809	D
Montana	278,628	164,246	58.9	113,032	40.6	—	0.0	332	0.1	1,018	0.4	51,214	D
Nebraska	584,154	307,307	52.6	276,847	47.4	—	0.0	—	0.0	—	0.0	30,460	D
Nevada	135,433	79,339	58.6	56,094	41.4	—	0.0	—	0.0	—	0.0	23,245	D
New Hampshire	288,093	184,064	63.9	104,029	36.1	—	0.0	—	0.0	—	0.0	80,035	D
New Jersey	2,847,663	1,868,231	65.6	964,174	33.9	7,075	0.2	8,183	0.3	—	0.0	904,057	D
New Mexico	328,645	194,015	59.0	132,838	40.4	1,217	0.4	—	0.0	575	0.2	61,177	D
New York	7,166,275	4,913,102	68.6	2,243,559	31.3	6,118	0.1	3,228	0.0	268	0.0	2,669,543	D
North Carolina	1,424,983	800,139	56.2	624,844	43.8	—	0.0	—	0.0	—	0.0	175,295	D
North Dakota	258,389	149,784	58.0	108,207	41.9	—	0.0	224	0.1	174	0.1	41,577	D
Ohio	3,969,196	2,498,331	62.9	1,470,865	37.1	—	0.0	—	0.0	—	0.0	1,027,466	D
Oklahoma	932,499	519,834	55.7	412,665	44.3	—	0.0	—	0.0	—	0.0	107,169	D
Oregon	786,305	501,017	63.7	282,779	36.0	—	0.0	—	0.0	2,509	0.3	218,238	D
Pennsylvania	4,822,690	3,130,954	64.9	1,673,657	34.7	5,092	0.1	10,456	0.2	2,531	0.1	1,457,297	D
Rhode Island	390,091	315,463	80.9	74,615	19.1	—	0.0	—	0.0	13	0.0	240,848	D
South Carolina	524,779	215,723	41.1	309,048	58.9	—	0.0	—	0.0	8	0.0	93,325	R
South Dakota	293,118	163,010	55.6	130,108	44.4	—	0.0	—	0.0	—	0.0	32,902	D
Tennessee	1,143,946	634,947	55.5	508,965	44.5	—	0.0	—	0.0	34	0.0	125,982	D
Texas	2,626,811	1,663,185	63.3	958,566	36.5	—	0.0	—	0.0	5,060	0.2	704,619	D
Utah	401,413	219,628	54.7	181,785	45.3	—	0.0	—	0.0	—	0.0	37,843	D
Vermont	163,089	108,127	66.3	54,942	33.7	—	0.0	—	0.0	20	0.0	53,185	D
Virginia	1,042,267	558,038	53.5	481,334	46.2	2,895	0.3	—	0.0	—	0.0	76,704	D
Washington	1,258,556	779,881	62.0	470,366	37.4	7,772	0.6	537	0.0	—	0.0	309,515	D
West Virginia	792,040	538,087	67.9	253,953	32.1	—	0.0	—	0.0	—	0.0	284,134	D
Wisconsin	1,691,815	1,050,424	62.1	638,495	37.7	1,204	0.1	1,692	0.1	—	0.0	411,929	D
Wyoming	142,716	80,718	56.6	61,998	43.4	—	0.0	—	0.0	—	0.0	18,720	D
Dist. of Col.	198,597	169,796	85.5	28,801	14.5	—	0.0	—	0.0	—	0.0	140,995	D
Totals	70,644,592	43,129,566	61.1	27,178,188	38.5	45,219	0.1	32,720	0.0	258,899	0.4	15,951,378	D

1. Plurality of 268,353 votes is calculated on the basis of Goldwater's vote and the 210,732 votes cast for the unpledged Democratic elector ticket.

1968 Presidential Election

STATE	TOTAL VOTE	RICHARD M. NIXON (Republican) Votes	%	HUBERT H. HUMPHREY (Democrat) Votes	%	GEORGE C. WALLACE (American Independent) Votes	%	HENNING A. BLOMEN (Socialist Labor) Votes	%	OTHER Votes	%	PLURALITY	
Alabama	1,049,922	146,923	14.0	196,579	18.7	691,425	65.9	—	0.0	14,995	1.4	494,846	A
Alaska	83,035	37,600	45.3	35,411	42.6	10,024	12.1	—	0.0	—	0.0	2,189	R
Arizona	486,936	266,721	54.8	170,514	35.0	46,573	9.6	75	0.0	3,053	0.6	96,207	R
Arkansas	619,969	190,759	30.8	188,228	30.4	240,982	38.9	—	0.0	—	0.0	50,223	A
California	7,251,587	3,467,664	47.8	3,244,318	44.7	487,270	6.7	341	0.0	51,994	0.7	223,346	R
Colorado	811,199	409,345	50.5	335,174	41.3	60,813	7.5	3,016	0.4	2,851	0.4	74,171	R
Connecticut	1,256,232	556,721	44.3	621,561	49.5	76,650	6.1	—	0.0	1,300	0.1	64,840	D
Delaware	214,367	96,714	45.1	89,194	41.6	28,459	13.3	—	0.0	—	0.0	7,520	R
Florida	2,187,805	886,804	40.5	676,794	30.9	624,207	28.5	—	0.0	—	0.0	210,010	R
Georgia	1,250,266	380,111	30.4	334,440	26.7	535,550	42.8	—	0.0	165	0.0	155,439	A
Hawaii	236,218	91,425	38.7	141,324	59.8	3,469	1.5	—	0.0	—	0.0	49,899	D
Idaho	291,183	165,369	56.8	89,273	30.7	36,541	12.5	—	0.0	—	0.0	76,096	R
Illinois	4,619,749	2,174,774	47.1	2,039,814	44.2	390,958	8.5	13,878	0.3	325	0.0	134,960	R
Indiana	2,123,597	1,067,885	50.3	806,659	38.0	243,108	11.4	—	0.0	5,945	0.3	261,226	R
Iowa	1,167,931	619,106	53.0	476,699	40.8	66,422	5.7	241	0.0	5,463	0.5	142,407	R
Kansas	872,783	478,674	54.8	302,996	34.7	88,921	10.2	—	0.0	2,192	0.3	175,678	R
Kentucky	1,055,893	462,411	43.8	397,541	37.6	193,098	18.3	—	0.0	2,843	0.3	64,870	R
Louisiana	1,097,450	257,535	23.5	309,615	28.2	530,300	48.3	—	0.0	—	0.0	220,685	A
Maine	392,936	169,254	43.1	217,312	55.3	6,370	1.6	—	0.0	—	0.0	48,058	D
Maryland	1,235,039	517,995	41.9	538,310	43.6	178,734	14.5	—	0.0	—	0.0	20,315	D
Massachusetts	2,331,752	766,844	32.9	1,469,218	63.0	87,088	3.7	6,180	0.3	2,422	0.1	702,374	D
Michigan	3,306,250	1,370,665	41.5	1,593,082	48.2	331,968	10.0	1,762	0.1	8,773	0.3	222,417	D
Minnesota	1,588,506	658,643	41.5	857,738	54.0	68,931	4.3	285	0.0	2,909	0.2	199,095	D
Mississippi	654,509	88,516	13.5	150,644	23.0	415,349	63.5	—	0.0	—	0.0	264,705	A
Missouri	1,809,502	811,932	44.9	791,444	43.7	206,126	11.4	—	0.0	—	0.0	20,488	R
Montana	274,404	138,835	50.6	114,117	41.6	20,015	7.3	—	0.0	1,437	0.5	24,718	R
Nebraska	536,851	321,163	59.8	170,784	31.8	44,904	8.4	—	0.0	—	0.0	150,379	R
Nevada	154,218	73,188	47.5	60,598	39.3	20,432	13.2	—	0.0	—	0.0	12,590	R
New Hampshire	297,298	154,903	52.1	130,589	43.9	11,173	3.8	—	0.0	633	0.2	24,314	R
New Jersey	2,875,395	1,325,467	46.1	1,264,206	44.0	262,187	9.1	6,784	0.2	16,751	0.6	61,261	R
New Mexico	327,350	169,692	51.8	130,081	39.7	25,737	7.9	—	0.0	1,840	0.6	39,611	R
New York	6,791,688	3,007,932	44.3	3,378,470	49.7	358,864	5.3	8,432	0.1	37,990	0.6	370,538	D
North Carolina	1,587,493	627,192	39.5	464,113	29.2	496,188	31.3	—	0.0	—	0.0	131,004	R
North Dakota	247,882	138,669	55.9	94,769	38.2	14,244	5.7	—	0.0	200	0.1	43,900	R
Ohio	3,959,698	1,791,014	45.2	1,700,586	42.9	467,495	11.8	120	0.0	483	0.0	90,428	R
Oklahoma	943,086	449,697	47.7	301,658	32.0	191,731	20.3	—	0.0	—	0.0	148,039	R
Oregon	819,622	408,433	49.8	358,866	43.8	49,683	6.1	—	0.0	2,640	0.3	49,567	R
Pennsylvania	4,747,928	2,090,017	44.0	2,259,405	47.6	378,582	8.0	4,977	0.1	14,947	0.3	169,388	D
Rhode Island	385,000	122,359	31.8	246,518	64.0	15,678	4.1	—	0.0	445	0.1	124,159	D
South Carolina	666,978	254,062	38.1	197,486	29.6	215,430	32.3	—	0.0	—	0.0	38,632	R
South Dakota	281,264	149,841	53.3	118,023	42.0	13,400	4.8	—	0.0	—	0.0	31,818	R
Tennessee	1,248,617	472,592	37.8	351,233	28.1	424,792	34.0	—	0.0	—	0.0	47,800	R
Texas	3,079,216	1,227,844	39.9	1,266,804	41.1	584,269	19.0	—	0.0	299	0.0	38,960	D
Utah	422,568	238,728	56.5	156,665	37.1	26,906	6.4	—	0.0	269	0.1	82,063	R
Vermont	161,404	85,142	52.8	70,255	43.5	5,104	3.2	—	0.0	903	0.6	14,887	R
Virginia	1,361,491	590,319	43.4	442,387	32.5	321,833	23.6	4,671	0.3	2,281	0.2	147,932	R
Washington	1,304,281	588,510	45.1	616,037	47.2	96,990	7.4	488	0.0	2,256	0.2	27,527	D
West Virginia	754,206	307,555	40.8	374,091	49.6	72,560	9.6	—	0.0	—	0.0	66,536	D
Wisconsin	1,691,538	809,997	47.9	748,804	44.3	127,835	7.6	1,338	0.1	3,564	0.2	61,193	R
Wyoming	127,205	70,927	55.8	45,173	35.5	11,105	8.7	—	0.0	—	0.0	25,754	R
Dist. of Col.	170,578	31,012	18.2	139,566	81.8	—	0.0	—	0.0	—	0.0	108,554	D
Totals	73,211,875	31,785,480	43.4	31,275,166	42.7	9,906,473	13.5	52,588	0.1	192,168	0.3	510,314	R

1972 Presidential Election

STATE	TOTAL VOTE	RICHARD M. NIXON (Republican)		GEORGE S. McGOVERN (Democrat)		JOHN G. SCHMITZ (American)		BENJAMIN SPOCK (People's)		OTHER		PLURALITY	
		Votes	%	Votes	%	Votes	%	Votes	%	Votes	%		
Alabama	1,006,111	728,701	72.4	256,923	25.5	11,928	1.2	—	0.0	8,559	0.9	471,778	R
Alaska	95,219	55,349	58.1	32,967	34.6	6,903	7.2	—	0.0	—	0.0	22,382	R
Arizona	622,926	402,812	64.7	198,540	31.9	21,208	3.4	—	0.0	366	0.1	204,272	R
Arkansas	651,320	448,541	68.9	199,892	30.7	2,887	0.4	—	0.0	—	0.0	248,649	R
California	8,367,862	4,602,096	55.0	3,475,847	41.5	232,554	2.8	55,167	0.7	2,198	0.0	1,126,249	R
Colorado	953,884	597,189	62.6	329,980	34.6	17,269	1.8	2,403	0.3	7,043	0.7	267,209	R
Connecticut	1,384,277	810,763	58.6	555,498	40.1	17,239	1.2	—	0.0	777	0.1	255,265	R
Delaware	235,516	140,357	59.6	92,283	39.2	2,638	1.1	—	0.0	238	0.1	48,074	R
Florida	2,583,283	1,857,759	71.9	718,117	27.8	—	0.0	—	0.0	7,407	0.3	1,139,642	R
Georgia	1,174,772	881,496	75.0	289,529	24.6	812	0.1	—	0.0	2,935	0.2	591,967	R
Hawaii	270,274	168,865	62.5	101,409	37.5	—	0.0	—	0.0	—	0.0	67,456	R
Idaho	310,379	199,384	64.2	80,826	26.0	28,869	9.3	903	0.3	397	0.1	118,558	R
Illinois	4,723,236	2,788,179	59.0	1,913,472	40.5	2,471	0.1	—	0.0	19,114	0.4	874,707	R
Indiana	2,125,529	1,405,154	66.1	708,568	33.3	—	0.0	4,544	0.2	7,263	0.3	696,586	R
Iowa	1,225,944	706,207	57.6	496,206	40.5	22,056	1.8	—	0.0	1,475	0.1	210,001	R
Kansas	916,095	619,812	67.7	270,287	29.5	21,808	2.4	—	0.0	4,188	0.5	349,525	R
Kentucky	1,067,499	676,446	63.4	371,159	34.8	17,627	1.7	1,118	0.1	1,149	0.1	305,287	R
Louisiana	1,051,491	686,852	65.3	298,142	28.4	52,099	5.0	—	0.0	14,398	1.4	388,710	R
Maine	417,042	256,458	61.5	160,584	38.5	—	0.0	—	0.0	—	0.0	95,874	R
Maryland	1,353,812	829,305	61.3	505,781	37.4	18,726	1.4	—	0.0	—	0.0	323,524	R
Massachusetts	2,458,756	1,112,078	45.2	1,332,540	54.2	2,877	0.1	101	0.0	11,160	0.5	220,462	D
Michigan	3,489,727	1,961,721	56.2	1,459,435	41.8	63,321	1.8	—	0.0	5,250	0.2	502,286	R
Minnesota	1,741,652	898,269	51.6	802,346	46.1	31,407	1.8	2,805	0.2	6,825	0.4	95,923	R
Mississippi	645,963	505,125	78.2	126,782	19.6	11,598	1.8	—	0.0	2,458	0.4	378,343	R
Missouri	1,855,803	1,153,852	62.2	697,147	37.6	—	0.0	—	0.0	4,804	0.3	456,705	R
Montana	317,603	183,976	57.9	120,197	37.8	13,430	4.2	—	0.0	—	0.0	63,779	R
Nebraska	576,289	406,298	70.5	169,991	29.5	—	0.0	—	0.0	—	0.0	236,307	R
Nevada	181,766	115,750	63.7	66,016	36.3	—	0.0	—	0.0	—	0.0	49,734	R
New Hampshire	334,055	213,724	64.0	116,435	34.9	3,386	1.0	—	0.0	510	0.2	97,289	R
New Jersey	2,997,229	1,845,502	61.6	1,102,211	36.8	34,378	1.1	5,355	0.2	9,783	0.3	743,291	R
New Mexico	386,241	235,606	61.0	141,084	36.5	8,767	2.3	—	0.0	784	0.2	94,522	R
New York	7,165,919	4,192,778	58.5	2,951,084	41.2	—	0.0	—	0.0	22,057	0.3	1,241,694	R
North Carolina	1,518,612	1,054,889	69.5	438,705	28.9	25,018	1.6	—	0.0	—	0.0	616,184	R
North Dakota	280,514	174,109	62.1	100,384	35.8	5,646	2.0	—	0.0	375	0.1	73,725	R
Ohio	4,094,787	2,441,827	59.6	1,558,889	38.1	80,067	2.0	—	0.0	14,004	0.3	882,938	R
Oklahoma	1,029,900	759,025	73.7	247,147	24.0	23,728	2.3	—	0.0	—	0.0	511,878	R
Oregon	927,946	486,686	52.4	392,760	42.3	46,211	5.0	—	0.0	2,289	0.2	93,926	R
Pennsylvania	4,592,106	2,714,521	59.1	1,796,951	39.1	70,593	1.5	—	0.0	10,041	0.2	917,570	R
Rhode Island	415,808	220,383	53.0	194,645	46.8	25	0.0	5	0.0	750	0.2	25,738	R
South Carolina	673,960	477,044	70.8	186,824	27.7	10,075	1.5	—	0.0	17	0.0	290,220	R
South Dakota	307,415	166,476	54.2	139,945	45.5	—	0.0	—	0.0	994	0.3	26,531	R
Tennessee	1,201,182	813,147	67.7	357,293	29.7	30,373	2.5	—	0.0	369	0.0	455,854	R
Texas	3,471,281	2,298,896	66.2	1,154,289	33.3	6,039	0.2	—	0.0	12,057	0.3	1,144,607	R
Utah	478,476	323,643	67.6	126,284	26.4	28,549	6.0	—	0.0	—	0.0	197,359	R
Vermont	186,947	117,149	62.7	68,174	36.5	—	0.0	1,010	0.5	614	0.3	48,975	R
Virginia	1,457,019	988,493	67.8	438,887	30.1	19,721	1.4	—	0.0	9,918	0.7	549,606	R
Washington	1,470,847	837,135	56.9	568,334	38.6	58,906	4.0	2,644	0.2	3,828	0.3	268,801	R
West Virginia	762,399	484,964	63.6	277,435	36.4	—	0.0	—	0.0	—	0.0	207,529	R
Wisconsin	1,852,890	989,430	53.4	810,174	43.7	47,525	2.6	2,701	0.1	3,060	0.2	179,256	R
Wyoming	145,570	100,464	69.0	44,358	30.5	748	0.5	—	0.0	—	0.0	56,106	R
Dist. of Col.	163,421	35,226	21.6	127,627	78.1	—	0.0	—	0.0	568	0.3	92,401	D
Totals	77,718,554	47,169,911	60.7	29,170,383	37.5	1,099,482	1.4	78,756	0.1	200,022	0.3	17,999,528	R

1976 Presidential Election

STATE	TOTAL VOTE	JIMMY CARTER (Democrat)		GERALD R. FORD (Republican)		EUGENE J. McCARTHY (Independent)		ROGER MacBRIDE (Libertarian)		OTHER		PLURALITY	
		Votes	%	Votes	%	Votes	%	Votes	%	Votes	%		
Alabama	1,182,850	659,170	55.7	504,070	42.6	99	0.0	1,481	0.1	18,030	1.5	155,100	D
Alaska	123,574	44,058	35.7	71,555	57.9	—	0.0	6,785	5.5	1,176	1.0	27,497	R
Arizona	742,719	295,602	39.8	418,642	56.4	19,229	2.6	7,647	1.0	1,599	0.2	123,040	R
Arkansas	767,535	498,604	65.0	267,903	34.9	639	0.1	—	0.0	389	0.1	230,701	D
California	7,867,117	3,742,284	47.6	3,882,244	49.3	58,412	0.7	56,388	0.7	127,789	1.6	139,960	R
Colorado	1,081,554	460,353	42.6	584,367	54.0	26,107	2.4	5,330	0.5	5,397	0.5	124,014	R
Connecticut	1,381,526	647,895	46.9	719,261	52.1	3,759	0.3	209	0.0	10,402	0.8	71,366	R
Delaware	235,834	122,596	52.0	109,831	46.6	2,437	1.0	—	0.0	970	0.4	12,765	D
Florida	3,150,631	1,636,000	51.9	1,469,531	46.6	23,643	0.8	103	0.0	21,354	0.7	166,469	D
Georgia	1,467,458	979,409	66.7	483,743	33.0	991	0.1	175	0.0	3,140	0.2	495,666	D
Hawaii	291,301	147,375	50.6	140,003	48.1	—	0.0	3,923	1.3	—	0.0	7,372	D
Idaho	344,071	126,549	36.8	204,151	59.3	1,194	0.3	3,558	1.0	8,619	2.5	77,602	R
Illinois	4,718,914	2,271,295	48.1	2,364,269	50.1	55,939	1.2	8,057	0.2	19,354	0.4	92,974	R
Indiana	2,220,362	1,014,714	45.7	1,183,958	53.3	—	0.0	—	0.0	21,690	1.0	169,244	R
Iowa	1,279,306	619,931	48.5	632,863	49.5	20,051	1.6	1,452	0.1	5,009	0.4	12,932	R
Kansas	957,845	430,421	44.9	502,752	52.5	13,185	1.4	3,242	0.3	8,245	0.9	72,331	R
Kentucky	1,167,142	615,717	52.8	531,852	45.6	6,837	0.6	814	0.1	11,922	1.0	83,865	D
Louisiana	1,278,439	661,365	51.7	587,446	46.0	6,588	0.5	3,325	0.3	19,715	1.5	73,919	D
Maine	483,216	232,279	48.1	236,320	48.9	10,874	2.3	11	0.0	3,732	0.8	4,041	R
Maryland	1,439,897	759,612	52.8	672,661	46.7	4,541	0.3	255	0.0	2,828	0.2	86,951	D
Massachusetts	2,547,558	1,429,475	56.1	1,030,276	40.4	65,637	2.6	135	0.0	22,035	0.9	399,199	D
Michigan	3,653,749	1,696,714	46.4	1,893,742	51.8	47,905	1.3	5,406	0.1	9,982	0.3	197,028	R
Minnesota	1,949,931	1,070,440	54.9	819,395	42.0	35,490	1.8	3,529	0.2	21,077	1.1	251,045	D
Mississippi	769,361	381,309	49.6	366,846	47.7	4,074	0.5	2,788	0.4	14,344	1.9	14,463	D
Missouri	1,953,600	998,387	51.1	927,443	47.5	24,029	1.2	—	0.0	3,741	0.2	70,944	D
Montana	328,734	149,259	45.4	173,703	52.8	—	0.0	—	0.0	5,772	1.8	24,444	R
Nebraska	607,668	233,692	38.5	359,705	59.2	9,409	1.5	1,482	0.2	3,380	0.6	126,013	R
Nevada	201,876	92,479	45.8	101,273	50.2	—	0.0	1,519	0.8	6,605	3.3	8,794	R
New Hampshire	339,618	147,635	43.5	185,935	54.7	4,095	1.2	936	0.3	1,017	0.3	38,300	R
New Jersey	3,014,472	1,444,653	47.9	1,509,688	50.1	32,717	1.1	9,449	0.3	17,965	0.6	65,035	R
New Mexico	418,409	201,148	48.1	211,419	50.5	1,161	0.3	1,110	0.3	3,571	0.9	10,271	R
New York	6,534,170	3,389,558	51.9	3,100,791	47.5	4,303	0.1	12,197	0.2	27,321	0.4	288,767	D
North Carolina	1,678,914	927,365	55.2	741,960	44.2	780	0.0	2,219	0.1	6,590	0.4	185,405	D
North Dakota	297,188	136,078	45.8	153,470	51.6	2,952	1.0	253	0.1	4,435	1.5	17,392	R
Ohio	4,111,873	2,011,621	48.9	2,000,505	48.7	58,258	1.4	8,961	0.2	32,528	0.8	11,116	D
Oklahoma	1,092,251	532,442	48.7	545,708	50.0	14,101	1.3	—	0.0	—	0.0	13,266	R
Oregon	1,029,876	490,407	47.6	492,120	47.8	40,207	3.9	—	0.0	7,142	0.7	1,713	R
Pennsylvania	4,620,787	2,328,677	50.4	2,205,604	47.7	50,584	1.1	—	0.0	35,922	0.8	123,073	D
Rhode Island	411,170	227,636	55.4	181,249	44.1	479	0.1	715	0.2	1,091	0.3	46,387	D
South Carolina	802,583	450,807	56.2	346,149	43.1	289	0.0	53	0.0	5,285	0.7	104,658	D
South Dakota	300,678	147,068	48.9	151,505	50.4	—	0.0	1,619	0.5	486	0.2	4,437	R
Tennessee	1,476,345	825,879	55.9	633,969	42.9	5,004	0.3	1,375	0.1	10,118	0.7	191,910	D
Texas	4,071,884	2,082,319	51.1	1,953,300	48.0	20,118	0.5	189	0.0	15,958	0.4	129,019	D
Utah	541,198	182,110	33.6	337,908	62.4	3,907	0.7	2,438	0.5	14,835	2.7	155,798	R
Vermont	187,765	80,954	43.1	102,085	54.4	4,001	2.1	—	0.0	725	0.4	21,131	R
Virginia	1,697,094	813,896	48.0	836,554	49.3	—	0.0	4,648	0.3	41,996	2.5	22,658	R
Washington	1,555,534	717,323	46.1	777,732	50.0	36,986	2.4	5,042	0.3	18,451	1.2	60,409	R
West Virginia	750,964	435,914	58.0	314,760	41.9	113	0.0	16	0.0	161	0.0	121,154	D
Wisconsin	2,104,175	1,040,232	49.4	1,004,987	47.8	34,943	1.7	3,814	0.2	20,199	1.0	35,245	D
Wyoming	156,343	62,239	39.8	92,717	59.3	624	0.4	89	0.1	674	0.4	30,478	R
Dist. of Col.	168,830	137,818	81.6	27,873	16.5	—	0.0	274	0.2	2,865	1.7	109,945	D
Totals	81,555,889	40,830,763	50.1	39,147,793	48.0	756,691	0.9	173,011	0.2	647,631	0.8	1,682,970	D

1980 Presidential Election

STATE	TOTAL VOTE	RONALD REAGAN (Republican) Votes	%	JIMMY CARTER (Democrat) Votes	%	JOHN B. ANDERSON (Independent) Votes	%	ED CLARK (Libertarian) Votes	%	OTHER Votes	%	PLURALITY	
Alabama	1,341,929	654,192	48.8	636,730	47.4	16,481	1.2	13,318	1.0	21,208	1.6	17,462	R
Alaska	158,445	86,112	54.3	41,842	26.4	11,155	7.0	18,479	11.7	857	0.5	44,270	R
Arizona	873,945	529,688	60.6	246,843	28.2	76,952	8.8	18,784	2.1	1,678	0.2	282,845	R
Arkansas	837,582	403,164	48.1	398,041	47.5	22,468	2.7	8,970	1.1	4,939	0.6	5,123	R
California	8,587,063	4,524,858	52.7	3,083,661	35.9	739,833	8.6	148,434	1.7	90,277	1.1	1,441,197	R
Colorado	1,184,415	652,264	55.1	367,973	31.1	130,633	11.0	25,744	2.2	7,801	0.7	284,291	R
Connecticut	1,406,285	677,210	48.2	541,732	38.5	171,807	12.2	8,570	0.6	6,966	0.5	135,478	R
Delaware	235,900	111,252	47.2	105,754	44.8	16,288	6.9	1,974	0.8	632	0.3	5,498	R
Florida	3,686,930	2,046,951	55.5	1,419,475	38.5	189,692	5.1	30,524	0.8	288	0.0	627,476	R
Georgia	1,596,695	654,168	41.0	890,733	55.8	36,055	2.3	15,627	1.0	112	0.0	236,565	D
Hawaii	303,287	130,112	42.9	135,879	44.8	32,021	10.6	3,269	1.1	2,006	0.7	5,767	D
Idaho	437,431	290,699	66.5	110,192	25.2	27,058	6.2	8,425	1.9	1,057	0.2	180,507	R
Illinois	4,749,721	2,358,049	49.6	1,981,413	41.7	346,754	7.3	38,939	0.8	24,566	0.5	376,636	R
Indiana	2,242,033	1,255,656	56.0	844,197	37.7	111,639	5.0	19,627	0.9	10,914	0.5	411,459	R
Iowa	1,317,661	676,026	51.3	508,672	38.6	115,633	8.8	13,123	1.0	4,207	0.3	167,354	R
Kansas	979,795	566,812	57.9	326,150	33.3	68,231	7.0	14,470	1.5	4,132	0.4	240,662	R
Kentucky	1,294,627	635,274	49.1	616,417	47.6	31,127	2.4	5,531	0.4	6,278	0.5	18,857	R
Louisiana	1,548,591	792,853	51.2	708,453	45.7	26,345	1.7	8,240	0.5	12,700	0.8	84,400	R
Maine	523,011	238,522	45.6	220,974	42.3	53,327	10.2	5,119	1.0	5,069	1.0	17,548	R
Maryland	1,540,496	680,606	44.2	726,161	47.1	119,537	7.8	14,192	0.9	—	0.0	45,555	D
Massachusetts[1]	2,522,890	1,057,631	41.9	1,053,802	41.7	382,539	15.2	22,038	0.9	6,880	0.3	3,829	R
Michigan	3,909,725	1,915,225	49.0	1,661,532	42.5	275,223	7.0	41,597	1.1	16,148	0.4	253,693	R
Minnesota	2,051,980	873,268	42.6	954,174	46.5	174,990	8.5	31,592	1.5	17,956	0.9	80,906	D
Mississippi	892,620	441,089	49.4	429,281	48.1	12,036	1.3	5,465	0.6	4,749	0.5	11,808	R
Missouri	2,099,824	1,074,181	51.2	931,182	44.3	77,920	3.7	14,422	0.7	2,119	0.1	142,999	R
Montana	363,952	206,814	56.8	118,032	32.4	29,281	8.0	9,825	2.7	—	0.0	88,782	R
Nebraska	640,854	419,937	65.5	166,851	26.0	44,993	7.0	9,073	1.4	—	0.0	253,086	R
Nevada	247,885	155,017	62.5	66,666	26.9	17,651	7.1	4,358	1.8	4,193	1.7	88,351	R
New Hampshire	383,990	221,705	57.7	108,864	28.4	49,693	12.9	2,064	0.5	1,664	0.4	112,841	R
New Jersey	2,975,684	1,546,557	52.0	1,147,364	38.6	234,632	7.9	20,652	0.7	26,479	0.9	399,193	R
New Mexico	456,971	250,779	54.9	167,826	36.7	29,459	6.4	4,365	1.0	4,542	1.0	82,953	R
New York	6,201,959	2,893,831	46.7	2,728,372	44.0	467,801	7.5	52,648	0.8	59,307	1.0	165,459	R
North Carolina	1,855,833	915,018	49.3	875,635	47.2	52,800	2.8	9,677	0.5	2,703	0.1	39,383	R
North Dakota	301,545	193,695	64.2	79,189	26.3	23,640	7.8	3,743	1.2	1,278	0.4	114,506	R
Ohio	4,283,603	2,206,545	51.5	1,752,414	40.9	254,472	5.9	49,033	1.1	21,139	0.5	454,131	R
Oklahoma	1,149,708	695,570	60.5	402,026	35.0	38,284	3.3	13,828	1.2	—	0.0	293,544	R
Oregon	1,181,516	571,044	48.3	456,890	38.7	112,389	9.5	25,838	2.2	15,355	1.3	114,154	R
Pennsylvania	4,561,501	2,261,872	49.6	1,937,540	42.5	292,921	6.4	33,263	0.7	35,905	0.8	324,332	R
Rhode Island	416,072	154,793	37.2	198,342	47.7	59,819	14.4	2,458	0.6	660	0.2	43,549	D
South Carolina	894,071	441,841	49.4	430,385	48.1	14,153	1.6	5,139	0.6	2,553	0.3	11,456	R
South Dakota	327,703	198,343	60.5	103,855	31.7	21,431	6.5	3,824	1.2	250	0.1	94,488	R
Tennessee	1,617,616	787,761	48.7	783,051	48.4	35,991	2.2	7,116	0.4	3,697	0.2	4,710	R
Texas	4,541,636	2,510,705	55.3	1,881,147	41.4	111,613	2.5	37,643	0.8	528	0.0	629,558	R
Utah	604,222	439,687	72.8	124,266	20.6	30,284	5.0	7,226	1.2	2,759	0.5	315,421	R
Vermont	213,299	94,628	44.4	81,952	38.4	31,761	14.9	1,900	0.9	3,058	1.4	12,676	R
Virginia	1,866,032	989,609	53.0	752,174	40.3	95,418	5.1	12,821	0.7	16,010	0.9	237,435	R
Washington	1,742,394	865,244	49.7	650,193	37.3	185,073	10.6	29,213	1.7	12,671	0.7	215,051	R
West Virginia	737,715	334,206	45.3	367,462	49.8	31,691	4.3	4,356	0.6	—	0.0	33,256	D
Wisconsin	2,273,221	1,088,845	47.9	981,584	43.2	160,657	7.1	29,135	1.3	13,000	0.6	107,261	R
Wyoming	176,713	110,700	62.6	49,427	28.0	12,072	6.8	4,514	2.6	—	0.0	61,273	R
Dist. of Col.	175,237	23,545	13.4	131,113	74.8	16,337	9.3	1,114	0.6	3,128	1.8	107,568	D
Totals	86,513,813	43,904,153	50.7	35,483,883	41.0	5,720,060	6.6	921,299	1.1	484,418	0.6	8,420,270	R

1. Figures from Clerk of the House of Representatives, *Statistics of the Congressional and Presidential Election* (Washington, D.C.: U.S. Government Printing Office, 1980); *Massachusetts Election Statistics, 1980*.

1984 Presidential Election

STATE	TOTAL VOTE	RONALD REAGAN (Republican) Votes	%	WALTER F. MONDALE (Democrat) Votes	%	DAVID BERGLAND (Libertarian) Votes	%	LYNDON H. LaROUCHE JR. (Independent) Votes	%	OTHER Votes	%	PLURALITY	
Alabama	1,441,713	872,849	60.5	551,899	38.3	9,504	0.7	—	0.0	7,461	0.5	320,950	R
Alaska	207,605	138,377	66.7	62,007	29.9	6,378	3.1	—	0.0	843	0.4	76,370	R
Arizona	1,025,897	681,416	66.4	333,854	32.5	10,585	1.0	—	0.0	42	0.0	347,562	R
Arkansas	884,406	534,774	60.5	338,646	38.3	2,221	0.3	1,890	0.2	6,875	0.8	196,128	R
California	9,505,423	5,467,009	57.5	3,922,519	41.3	49,951	0.5	—	0.0	65,944	0.7	1,544,490	R
Colorado	1,295,380	821,817	63.4	454,975	35.1	11,257	0.9	4,662	0.4	2,669	0.2	366,842	R
Connecticut	1,466,900	890,877	60.7	569,597	38.8	204	0.0	—	0.0	6,222	0.4	321,280	R
Delaware	254,572	152,190	59.8	101,656	39.9	268	0.1	—	0.0	458	0.2	50,534	R
Florida	4,180,051	2,730,350	65.3	1,448,816	34.7	754	0.0	—	0.0	131	0.0	1,281,534	R
Georgia	1,776,120	1,068,722	60.2	706,628	39.8	152	0.0	34	0.0	584	0.0	362,094	R
Hawaii	335,846	185,050	55.1	147,154	43.8	2,167	0.6	654	0.2	821	0.2	37,896	R
Idaho	411,144	297,523	72.4	108,510	26.4	2,823	0.7	—	0.0	2,288	0.6	189,013	R
Illinois	4,819,088	2,707,103	56.2	2,086,499	43.3	10,086	0.2	—	0.0	15,400	0.3	620,604	R
Indiana	2,233,069	1,377,230	61.7	841,481	37.7	6,741	0.3	—	0.0	7,617	0.3	535,749	R
Iowa	1,319,805	703,088	53.3	605,620	45.9	1,844	0.1	6,248	0.5	3,005	0.2	97,468	R
Kansas	1,021,991	677,296	66.3	333,149	32.6	3,329	0.3	—	0.0	8,217	0.8	344,147	R
Kentucky	1,369,345	821,702	60.0	539,539	39.4	—	0.0	1,776	0.1	6,328	0.5	282,163	R
Louisiana	1,706,822	1,037,299	60.8	651,586	38.2	1,876	0.1	3,552	0.2	12,509	0.7	385,713	R
Maine	553,144	336,500	60.8	214,515	38.8	—	0.0	—	0.0	2,129	0.4	121,985	R
Maryland	1,675,873	879,918	52.5	787,935	47.0	5,721	0.3	—	0.0	2,299	0.1	91,983	R
Massachusetts	2,559,453	1,310,936	51.2	1,239,606	48.4	—	0.0	—	0.0	8,911	0.3	71,330	R
Michigan	3,801,658	2,251,571	59.2	1,529,638	40.2	10,055	0.3	3,862	0.1	6,532	0.2	721,933	R
Minnesota	2,084,449	1,032,603	49.5	1,036,364	49.7	2,996	0.1	3,865	0.2	8,621	0.4	3,761	D
Mississippi	941,104	582,377	61.9	352,192	37.4	2,336	0.2	1,001	0.1	3,198	0.3	230,185	R
Missouri	2,122,783	1,274,188	60.0	848,583	40.0	—	0.0	—	0.0	12	0.0	425,605	R
Montana	384,377	232,450	60.5	146,742	38.2	5,185	1.3	—	0.0	—	0.0	85,708	R
Nebraska	652,090	460,054	70.6	187,866	28.8	2,079	0.3	—	0.0	2,091	0.3	272,188	R
Nevada	286,667	188,770	65.8	91,655	32.0	2,292	0.8	—	0.0	3,950	1.4	97,115	R
New Hampshire	389,066	267,051	68.6	120,395	30.9	735	0.2	467	0.1	418	0.1	146,656	R
New Jersey	3,217,862	1,933,630	60.1	1,261,323	39.2	6,416	0.2	—	0.0	16,493	0.5	672,307	R
New Mexico	514,370	307,101	59.7	201,769	39.2	4,459	0.9	—	0.0	1,041	0.2	105,332	R
New York	6,806,810	3,664,763	53.8	3,119,609	45.8	11,949	0.2	—	0.0	10,489	0.2	545,154	R
North Carolina	2,175,361	1,346,481	61.9	824,287	37.9	3,794	0.2	—	0.0	799	0.0	522,194	R
North Dakota	308,971	200,336	64.8	104,429	33.8	703	0.2	1,278	0.4	2,225	0.7	95,907	R
Ohio	4,547,619	2,678,560	58.9	1,825,440	40.1	5,886	0.1	10,693	0.2	27,040	0.6	853,120	R
Oklahoma	1,255,676	861,530	68.6	385,080	30.7	9,066	0.7	—	0.0	—	0.0	476,450	R
Oregon	1,226,527	685,700	55.9	536,479	43.7	—	0.0	—	0.0	4,348	0.4	149,221	R
Pennsylvania	4,844,903	2,584,323	53.3	2,228,131	46.0	6,982	0.1	—	0.0	25,467	0.5	356,192	R
Rhode Island	410,492	212,080	51.7	197,106	48.0	277	0.1	—	0.0	1,029	0.3	14,974	R
South Carolina	968,529	615,539	63.6	344,459	35.6	4,359	0.5	—	0.0	4,172	0.4	271,080	R
South Dakota	317,867	200,267	63.0	116,113	36.5	—	0.0	—	0.0	1,487	0.5	84,154	R
Tennessee	1,711,994	990,212	57.8	711,714	41.6	3,072	0.2	1,852	0.1	5,144	0.3	278,498	R
Texas	5,397,571	3,433,428	63.6	1,949,276	36.1	—	0.0	14,613	0.3	254	0.0	1,484,152	R
Utah	629,656	469,105	74.5	155,369	24.7	2,447	0.4	—	0.0	2,735	0.4	313,736	R
Vermont	234,561	135,865	57.9	95,730	40.8	1,002	0.4	423	0.2	1,541	0.7	40,135	R
Virginia	2,146,635	1,337,078	62.3	796,250	37.1	—	0.0	13,307	0.6	—	0.0	540,828	R
Washington	1,883,910	1,051,670	55.8	807,352	42.9	8,844	0.5	4,712	0.3	11,332	0.6	244,318	R
West Virginia	735,742	405,483	55.1	328,125	44.6	—	0.0	—	0.0	2,134	0.3	77,358	R
Wisconsin	2,211,689	1,198,584	54.2	995,740	45.0	4,883	0.2	3,791	0.2	8,691	0.4	202,844	R
Wyoming	188,968	133,241	70.5	53,370	28.2	2,357	1.2	—	0.0	—	0.0	79,871	R
Dist. of Col.	211,288	29,009	13.7	180,408	85.4	279	0.1	127	0.1	1,465	0.7	151,399	D
Totals	92,652,842	54,455,075	58.8	37,577,185	40.6	228,314	0.2	78,807	0.1	313,461	0.3	16,877,890	R

1988 Presidential Election

STATE	TOTAL VOTE	GEORGE BUSH (Republican) Votes	%	MICHAEL S. DUKAKIS (Democrat) Votes	%	RON PAUL (Libertarian) Votes	%	LENORA B. FULANI (New Alliance) Votes	%	OTHER Votes	%	PLURALITY	
Alabama	1,378,476	815,576	59.2	549,506	39.9	8,460	0.6	3,311	0.2	1,623	0.1	266,070	R
Alaska	200,116	119,251	59.6	72,584	36.3	5,484	2.7	1,024	0.5	1,773	0.9	46,667	R
Arizona	1,171,873	702,541	60.0	454,029	38.7	13,351	1.1	1,662	0.1	290	0.0	248,512	R
Arkansas	827,738	466,578	56.4	349,237	42.2	3,297	0.4	2,161	0.3	6,465	0.8	117,341	R
California	9,887,065	5,054,917	51.1	4,702,233	47.6	70,105	0.7	31,181	0.3	28,629	0.3	352,684	R
Colorado	1,372,394	728,177	53.1	621,453	45.3	15,482	1.1	2,539	0.2	4,743	0.3	106,724	R
Connecticut	1,443,394	750,241	52.0	676,584	46.9	14,071	1.0	2,491	0.2	7	0.0	73,657	R
Delaware	249,891	139,639	55.9	108,647	43.5	1,162	0.5	443	0.2	—	0.0	30,992	R
Florida	4,302,313	2,618,885	60.9	1,656,701	38.5	19,796	0.5	6,655	0.2	276	0.0	962,184	R
Georgia	1,809,672	1,081,331	59.8	714,792	39.5	8,435	0.5	5,099	0.3	15	0.0	366,539	R
Hawaii	354,461	158,625	44.8	192,364	54.3	1,999	0.6	1,003	0.3	470	0.1	33,739	D
Idaho	408,968	253,881	62.1	147,272	36.0	5,313	1.3	2,502	0.6	—	0.0	106,609	R
Illinois	4,559,120	2,310,939	50.7	2,215,940	48.6	14,944	0.3	10,276	0.2	7,021	0.2	94,999	R
Indiana	2,168,621	1,297,763	59.8	860,643	39.7	—	0.0	10,215	0.5	—	0.0	437,120	R
Iowa	1,225,614	545,355	44.5	670,557	54.7	2,494	0.2	540	0.0	6,668	0.5	125,202	D
Kansas	993,044	554,049	55.8	422,636	42.6	12,553	1.3	3,806	0.4	—	0.0	131,413	R
Kentucky	1,322,517	734,281	55.5	580,368	43.9	2,118	0.2	1,256	0.1	4,494	0.3	153,913	R
Louisiana	1,628,202	883,702	54.3	717,460	44.1	4,115	0.3	2,355	0.1	20,570	1.3	166,242	R
Maine	555,035	307,131	55.3	243,569	43.9	2,700	0.5	1,405	0.3	230	0.0	63,562	R
Maryland	1,714,358	876,167	51.1	826,304	48.2	6,748	0.4	5,115	0.3	24	0.0	49,863	R
Massachusetts	2,632,805	1,194,635	45.4	1,401,415	53.2	24,251	0.9	9,561	0.4	2,943	0.1	206,780	D
Michigan	3,669,163	1,965,486	53.6	1,675,783	45.7	18,336	0.5	2,513	0.1	7,045	0.2	289,703	R
Minnesota	2,096,790	962,337	45.9	1,109,471	52.9	5,109	0.2	1,734	0.1	18,139	0.9	147,134	D
Mississippi	931,527	557,890	59.9	363,921	39.1	3,329	0.4	2,155	0.2	4,232	0.5	193,969	R
Missouri	2,093,713	1,084,953	51.8	1,001,619	47.8	434	0.0	6,656	0.3	51	0.0	83,334	R
Montana	365,674	190,412	52.1	168,936	46.2	5,047	1.4	1,279	0.3	—	0.0	21,476	R
Nebraska	661,465	397,956	60.2	259,235	39.2	2,534	0.4	1,740	0.3	—	0.0	138,721	R
Nevada	350,067	206,040	58.9	132,738	37.9	3,520	1.0	835	0.2	6,934	2.0	73,302	R
New Hampshire	451,074	281,537	62.4	163,696	36.3	4,502	1.0	790	0.2	549	0.1	117,841	R
New Jersey	3,099,553	1,743,192	56.2	1,320,352	42.6	8,421	0.3	5,139	0.2	22,449	0.7	422,840	R
New Mexico	521,287	270,341	51.9	244,497	46.9	3,268	0.6	2,237	0.4	944	0.2	25,844	R
New York	6,485,683	3,081,871	47.5	3,347,882	51.6	12,109	0.2	15,845	0.2	27,976	0.4	266,011	D
North Carolina	2,134,370	1,237,258	58.0	890,167	41.7	1,263	0.1	5,682	0.3	—	0.0	347,091	R
North Dakota	297,261	166,559	56.0	127,739	43.0	1,315	0.4	396	0.1	1,252	0.4	38,820	R
Ohio	4,393,699	2,416,549	55.0	1,939,629	44.1	11,989	0.3	12,017	0.3	13,515	0.3	476,920	R
Oklahoma	1,171,036	678,367	57.9	483,423	41.3	6,261	0.5	2,985	0.3	—	0.0	194,944	R
Oregon	1,201,694	560,126	46.6	616,206	51.3	14,811	1.2	6,487	0.5	4,064	0.3	56,080	D
Pennsylvania	4,536,251	2,300,087	50.7	2,194,944	48.4	12,051	0.3	4,379	0.1	24,790	0.5	105,143	R
Rhode Island	404,620	177,761	43.9	225,123	55.6	825	0.2	280	0.1	631	0.2	47,362	D
South Carolina	986,009	606,443	61.5	370,554	37.6	4,935	0.5	4,077	0.4	—	0.0	235,889	R
South Dakota	312,991	165,415	52.8	145,560	46.5	1,060	0.3	730	0.2	226	0.1	19,855	R
Tennessee	1,636,250	947,233	57.9	679,794	41.5	2,041	0.1	1,334	0.1	5,848	0.4	267,439	R
Texas	5,427,410	3,036,829	56.0	2,352,748	43.3	30,355	0.6	7,208	0.1	270	0.0	684,081	R
Utah	647,008	428,442	66.2	207,343	32.0	7,473	1.2	455	0.1	3,295	0.5	221,099	R
Vermont	243,328	124,331	51.1	115,775	47.6	1,000	0.4	205	0.1	2,017	0.8	8,556	R
Virginia	2,191,609	1,309,162	59.7	859,799	39.2	8,336	0.4	14,312	0.7	—	0.0	449,363	R
Washington	1,865,253	903,835	48.5	933,516	50.0	17,240	0.9	3,520	0.2	7,142	0.4	29,681	D
West Virginia	653,311	310,065	47.5	341,016	52.2	—	0.0	2,230	0.3	—	0.0	30,951	D
Wisconsin	2,191,608	1,047,499	47.8	1,126,794	51.4	5,157	0.2	1,953	0.1	10,205	0.5	79,295	D
Wyoming	176,551	106,867	60.5	67,113	38.0	2,026	1.1	545	0.3	—	0.0	39,754	R
Dist. of Col.	192,877	27,590	14.3	159,407	82.6	554	0.3	2,901	1.5	2,425	1.3	131,817	D
Totals	91,594,809	48,886,097	53.4	41,809,074	45.6	432,179	0.5	217,219	0.2	250,240	0.3	7,077,023	R

1992 Presidential Election

STATE	TOTAL VOTE	BILL CLINTON (Democrat) Votes	%	GEORGE BUSH (Republican) Votes	%	ROSS PEROT (Independent) Votes	%	ANDRE V. MARROU (Libertarian) Votes	%	OTHER Votes	%	PLURALITY	
Alabama	1,688,060	690,080	40.9	804,283	47.6	183,109	10.8	5,737	0.3	4,851	0.3	114,203	R
Alaska	258,506	78,294	30.3	102,000	39.5	73,481	28.4	1,378	0.5	3,353	1.3	23,706	R
Arizona	1,486,975	543,050	36.5	572,086	38.5	353,741	23.8	6,759	0.5	11,339	0.8	29,036	R
Arkansas	950,653	505,823	53.2	337,324	35.5	99,132	10.4	1,261	0.1	7,113	0.7	168,499	D
California	11,131,721	5,121,325	46.0	3,630,574	32.6	2,296,006	20.6	48,139	0.4	35,677	0.3	1,490,751	D
Colorado	1,569,180	629,681	40.1	562,850	35.9	366,010	23.3	8,669	0.6	1,970	0.1	66,831	D
Connecticut	1,616,332	682,318	42.2	578,313	35.8	348,771	21.6	5,391	0.3	1,539	0.1	104,005	D
Delaware	289,735	126,054	43.5	102,313	35.3	59,213	20.4	935	0.3	1,220	0.4	23,741	D
Florida	5,314,392	2,072,698	39.0	2,173,310	40.9	1,053,067	19.8	15,079	0.3	238		100,612	R
Georgia	2,321,125	1,008,966	43.5	995,252	42.9	309,657	13.3	7,110	0.3	140		13,714	D
Hawaii	372,842	179,310	48.1	136,822	36.7	53,003	14.2	1,119	0.3	2,588	0.7	42,488	D
Idaho	482,142	137,013	28.4	202,645	42.0	130,395	27.0	1,167	0.2	10,922	2.3	65,632	R
Illinois	5,050,157	2,453,350	48.6	1,734,096	34.3	840,515	16.6	9,218	0.2	12,978	0.3	719,254	D
Indiana	2,305,871	848,420	36.8	989,375	42.9	455,934	19.8	7,936	0.3	4,206	0.2	140,955	R
Iowa	1,354,607	586,353	43.3	504,891	37.3	253,468	18.7	1,076	0.1	8,819	0.7	81,462	D
Kansas	1,157,335	390,434	33.7	449,951	38.9	312,358	27.0	4,314	0.4	278		59,517	R
Kentucky	1,492,900	665,104	44.6	617,178	41.3	203,944	13.7	4,513	0.3	2,161	0.1	47,926	D
Louisiana	1,790,017	815,971	45.6	733,386	41.0	211,478	11.8	3,155	0.2	26,027	1.5	82,585	D
Maine	679,499	263,420	38.8	206,504	30.4	206,820	30.4	1,681	0.2	1,074	0.2	56,600	D
Maryland	1,985,046	988,571	49.8	707,094	35.6	281,414	14.2	4,715	0.2	3,252	0.2	281,477	D
Massachusetts	2,773,700	1,318,662	47.5	805,049	29.0	630,731	22.7	9,024	0.3	10,234	0.4	513,613	D
Michigan	4,274,673	1,871,182	43.8	1,554,940	36.4	824,813	19.3	10,175	0.2	13,563	0.3	316,242	D
Minnesota	2,347,948	1,020,997	43.5	747,841	31.9	562,506	24.0	3,374	0.1	13,230	0.6	273,156	D
Mississippi	981,793	400,258	40.8	487,793	49.7	85,626	8.7	2,154	0.2	5,962	0.6	87,535	R
Missouri	2,391,565	1,053,873	44.1	811,159	33.9	518,741	21.7	7,497	0.3	295		242,714	D
Montana	410,611	154,507	37.6	144,207	35.1	107,225	26.1	986	0.2	3,686	0.9	10,300	D
Nebraska	737,546	216,864	29.4	343,678	46.6	174,104	23.6	1,340	0.2	1,560	0.2	126,814	R
Nevada	506,318	189,148	37.4	175,828	34.7	132,580	26.2	1,835	0.4	6,927	1.4	13,320	D
New Hampshire	537,943	209,040	38.9	202,484	37.6	121,337	22.6	3,548	0.7	1,534	0.3	6,556	D
New Jersey	3,343,594	1,436,206	43.0	1,356,865	40.6	521,829	15.6	6,822	0.2	21,872	0.7	79,341	D
New Mexico	569,986	261,617	45.9	212,824	37.3	91,895	16.1	1,615	0.3	2,035	0.4	48,793	D
New York	6,926,925	3,444,450	49.7	2,346,649	33.9	1,090,721	15.7	13,451	0.2	31,654	0.5	1,097,801	D
North Carolina	2,611,850	1,114,042	42.7	1,134,661	43.4	357,864	13.7	5,171	0.2	112		20,619	R
North Dakota	308,133	99,168	32.2	136,244	44.2	71,084	23.1	416	0.1	1,221	0.4	37,076	R
Ohio	4,939,967	1,984,942	40.2	1,894,310	38.3	1,036,426	21.0	7,252	0.1	17,037	0.3	90,632	D
Oklahoma	1,390,359	473,066	34.0	592,929	42.6	319,878	23.0	4,486	0.3	—		119,863	R
Oregon	1,462,643	621,314	42.5	475,757	32.5	354,091	24.2	4,277	0.3	7,204	0.5	145,557	D
Pennsylvania	4,959,810	2,239,164	45.1	1,791,841	36.1	902,667	18.2	21,477	0.4	4,661	0.1	447,323	D
Rhode Island	453,477	213,299	47.0	131,601	29.0	105,045	23.2	571	0.1	2,961	0.7	81,698	D
South Carolina	1,202,527	479,514	39.9	577,507	48.0	138,872	11.5	2,719	0.2	3,915	0.3	97,993	R
South Dakota	336,254	124,888	37.1	136,718	40.7	73,295	21.8	814	0.2	539	0.2	11,830	R
Tennessee	1,982,638	933,521	47.1	841,300	42.4	199,968	10.1	1,847	0.1	6,002	0.3	92,221	D
Texas	6,154,018	2,281,815	37.1	2,496,071	40.6	1,354,781	22.0	19,699	0.3	1,652		214,256	R
Utah	743,999	183,429	24.7	322,632	43.4	203,400	27.3	1,900	0.3	32,638	4.4	119,232	R
Vermont	289,701	133,592	46.1	88,122	30.4	65,991	22.8	501	0.2	1,495	0.5	45,470	D
Virginia	2,558,665	1,038,650	40.6	1,150,517	45.0	348,639	13.6	5,730	0.2	15,129	0.6	111,867	R
Washington	2,288,230	993,037	43.4	731,234	32.0	541,780	23.7	7,533	0.3	14,646	0.6	261,803	D
West Virginia	683,762	331,001	48.4	241,974	35.4	108,829	15.9	1,873	0.3	85		89,027	D
Wisconsin	2,531,114	1,041,066	41.1	930,855	36.8	544,479	21.5	2,877	0.1	11,837	0.5	110,211	D
Wyoming	200,598	68,160	34.0	79,347	39.6	51,263	25.6	844	0.4	984	0.5	11,187	R
Dist. of Col.	227,572	192,619	84.6	20,698	9.1	9,681	4.3	467	0.2	4,107	1.8	171,921	D
Totals	104,425,014	44,909,326	43.0	39,103,882	37.4	19,741,657	18.9	291,627	0.3	378,522	0.4	5,805,444	D

1996 Presidential Election

STATE	TOTAL VOTE	BILL CLINTON (Democrat)		BOB DOLE (Republican)		ROSS PEROT (Reform)		RALPH NADER (Green)		OTHER		PLURALITY	
		Votes	%	Votes	%	Votes	%	Votes	%	Votes	%		
Alabama	1,534,349	662,165	43.2	769,044	50.1	92,149	6.0	—		10,991	0.7	106,879	R
Alaska	241,620	80,380	33.3	122,746	50.8	26,333	10.9	7,597	3.1	4,564	1.9	42,366	R
Arizona	1,404,405	653,288	46.5	622,073	44.3	112,072	8.0	2,062	0.1	14,910	1.1	31,215	D
Arkansas	884,262	475,171	53.7	325,416	36.8	69,884	7.9	3,649	0.4	10,142	1.1	149,755	D
California	10,019,484	5,119,835	51.1	3,828,380	38.2	697,847	7.0	237,016	2.4	136,406	1.4	1,291,455	D
Colorado	1,510,704	671,152	44.4	691,848	45.8	99,629	6.6	25,070	1.7	23,005	1.5	20,696	R
Connecticut	1,392,614	735,740	52.8	483,109	34.7	139,523	10.0	24,321	1.7	9,921	0.7	252,631	D
Delaware	270,845	140,355	51.8	99,062	36.6	28,719	10.6	18		2,691	1.0	41,293	D
Florida	5,303,794	2,546,870	48.0	2,244,536	42.3	483,870	9.1	4,101	0.1	24,417	0.5	302,334	D
Georgia	2,299,071	1,053,849	45.8	1,080,843	47.0	146,337	6.4	—		18,042	0.8	26,994	R
Hawaii	360,120	205,012	56.9	113,943	31.6	27,358	7.6	10,386	2.9	3,421	0.9	91,069	D
Idaho	491,719	165,443	33.6	256,595	52.2	62,518	12.7	—		7,163	1.5	91,152	R
Illinois	4,311,391	2,341,744	54.3	1,587,021	36.8	346,408	8.0	1,447		34,771	0.8	754,723	D
Indiana	2,135,431	887,424	41.6	1,006,693	47.1	224,299	10.5	895		16,120	0.8	119,269	R
Iowa	1,234,075	620,258	50.3	492,644	39.9	105,159	8.5	6,550	0.5	9,464	0.8	127,614	D
Kansas	1,074,300	387,659	36.1	583,245	54.3	92,639	8.6	914	0.1	9,843	0.9	195,586	R
Kentucky	1,388,708	636,614	45.8	623,283	44.9	120,396	8.7	701	0.1	7,714	0.6	13,331	D
Louisiana	1,783,959	927,837	52.0	712,586	39.9	123,293	6.9	4,719	0.3	15,524	0.9	215,251	D
Maine	605,897	312,788	51.6	186,378	30.8	85,970	14.2	15,279	2.5	5,482	0.9	126,410	D
Maryland	1,780,870	966,207	54.3	681,530	38.3	115,812	6.5	2,606	0.1	14,715	0.8	284,677	D
Massachusetts	2,556,786	1,571,763	61.5	718,107	28.1	227,217	8.9	4,565	0.2	35,134	1.4	853,656	D
Michigan	3,848,844	1,989,653	51.7	1,481,212	38.5	336,670	8.7	2,322	0.1	38,987	1.0	508,441	D
Minnesota	2,192,640	1,120,438	51.1	766,476	35.0	257,704	11.8	24,908	1.1	23,114	1.1	353,962	D
Mississippi	893,857	394,022	44.1	439,838	49.2	52,222	5.8	—		7,775	0.9	45,816	R
Missouri	2,158,065	1,025,935	47.5	890,016	41.2	217,188	10.1	534		24,392	1.1	135,919	D
Montana	407,261	167,922	41.3	179,652	44.1	55,229	13.6	—		4,458	1.1	11,730	R
Nebraska	677,415	236,761	35.0	363,467	53.7	71,278	10.5	—		5,909	0.9	126,706	R
Nevada	464,279	203,974	43.9	199,244	42.9	43,986	9.5	4,730	1.0	12,345	2.7	4,730	D
New Hampshire	499,175	246,214	49.3	196,532	39.4	48,390	9.7	—		8,039	1.6	49,682	D
New Jersey	3,075,807	1,652,329	53.7	1,103,078	35.9	262,134	8.5	32,465	1.1	25,801	0.8	549,251	D
New Mexico	556,074	273,495	49.2	232,751	41.9	32,257	5.8	13,218	2.4	4,353	0.8	40,744	D
New York	6,316,129	3,756,177	59.5	1,933,492	30.6	503,458	8.0	75,956	1.2	47,046	0.7	1,822,685	D
North Carolina	2,515,807	1,107,849	44.0	1,225,938	48.7	168,059	6.7	2,108	0.1	11,853	0.4	118,089	R
North Dakota	266,411	106,905	40.1	125,050	46.9	32,515	12.2	—		1,941	0.7	18,145	R
Ohio	4,534,434	2,148,222	47.4	1,859,883	41.0	483,207	10.7	2,962	0.1	40,160	0.9	288,339	D
Oklahoma	1,206,713	488,105	40.4	582,315	48.3	130,788	10.8	—		5,505	0.5	94,210	R
Oregon	1,377,760	649,641	47.2	538,152	39.1	121,221	8.8	49,415	3.6	19,331	1.4	111,489	D
Pennsylvania	4,506,118	2,215,819	49.2	1,801,169	40.0	430,984	9.6	3,086	0.1	55,060	1.2	414,650	D
Rhode Island	390,284	233,050	59.7	104,683	26.8	43,723	11.2	6,040	1.5	2,788	0.7	128,367	D
South Carolina	1,151,689	506,283	44.0	573,458	49.8	64,386	5.6	—		7,562	0.7	67,175	R
South Dakota	323,826	139,333	43.0	150,543	46.5	31,250	9.7	—		2,700	0.8	11,210	R
Tennessee	1,894,105	909,146	48.0	863,530	45.6	105,918	5.6	6,427	0.3	9,084	0.4	45,616	D
Texas	5,611,644	2,459,683	43.8	2,736,167	48.8	378,537	6.7	4,810	0.1	32,447	0.6	276,484	R
Utah	665,629	221,633	33.3	361,911	54.4	66,461	10.0	4,615	0.7	11,009	1.7	140,278	R
Vermont	258,449	137,894	53.4	80,352	31.1	31,024	12.0	5,585	2.2	3,594	1.4	57,542	D
Virginia	2,416,642	1,091,060	45.1	1,138,350	47.1	159,861	6.6	—		27,371	1.1	47,290	R
Washington	2,253,837	1,123,323	49.8	840,712	37.3	201,003	8.9	60,322	2.7	28,477	1.3	282,611	D
West Virginia	636,459	327,812	51.5	233,946	36.8	71,639	11.3	—		3,062	0.5	93,866	D
Wisconsin	2,196,169	1,071,971	48.8	845,029	38.5	227,339	10.4	28,723	1.3	23,107	1.1	226,942	D
Wyoming	211,571	77,934	36.8	105,388	49.8	25,928	12.3	—		2,321	1.1	27,454	R
Dist. of Col.	185,726	158,220	85.2	17,339	9.3	3,611	1.9	4,780	2.6	1,776	1.0	140,881	D
Totals	96,277,223	47,402,357	49.2	39,198,755	40.7	8,085,402	8.4	684,902	0.7	905,807	0.9	8,203,602	D

2000 Presidential Election

STATE	TOTAL VOTE	GEORGE W. BUSH (Republican)		AL GORE (Democrat)		RALPH NADER (Green)		PATRICK J. BUCHANAN (Reform)		OTHER		PLURALITY	
		Votes	%	Votes	%	Votes	%	Votes	%	Votes	%		
Alabama	1,666,272	941,173	56.5	692,611	41.6	18,323	1.1	6,351	0.4	7,814	0.5	248,562	R
Alaska	285,560	167,398	58.6	79,004	27.7	28,747	10.1	5,192	1.8	5,219	1.8	88,394	R
Arizona	1,532,016	781,652	51.0	685,341	44.7	45,645	3.0	12,373	0.8	7,005	0.5	96,311	R
Arkansas	921,781	472,940	51.3	422,768	45.9	13,421	1.5	7,358	0.8	5,294	0.6	50,172	R
California	10,965,856	4,567,429	41.7	5,861,203	53.4	418,707	3.8	44,987	0.4	75,530	0.7	1,293,774	D
Colorado	1,741,368	883,748	50.8	738,227	42.4	91,434	5.3	10,465	0.6	17,494	1.0	145,521	R
Connecticut	1,459,525	561,094	38.4	816,015	55.9	64,452	4.4	4,731	0.3	13,233	0.9	254,921	D
Delaware	327,622	137,288	41.9	180,068	55.0	8,307	2.5	777	0.2	1,182	0.4	42,780	D
Florida	5,963,110	2,912,790	48.8	2,912,253	48.8	97,488	1.6	17,484	0.3	23,095	0.4	537	R
Georgia	2,596,645	1,419,720	54.7	1,116,230	43.0	13,273	0.5	10,926	0.4	36,496	1.4	303,490	R
Hawaii	367,951	137,845	37.5	205,286	55.8	21,623	5.9	1,071	0.3	2,126	0.6	67,441	D
Idaho	501,621	336,937	67.2	138,637	27.6	12,292	2.5	7,615	1.5	6,140	1.2	198,300	R
Illinois	4,742,123	2,019,421	42.6	2,589,026	54.6	103,759	2.2	16,106	0.3	13,811	0.3	569,605	D
Indiana	2,199,302	1,245,836	56.6	901,980	41.0	18,531	0.8	16,959	0.8	15,996	0.7	343,856	R
Iowa	1,315,563	634,373	48.2	638,517	48.5	29,374	2.2	5,731	0.4	7,568	0.6	4,144	D
Kansas	1,072,218	622,332	58.0	399,276	37.2	36,086	3.4	7,370	0.7	7,154	0.7	223,056	R
Kentucky	1,544,187	872,492	56.5	638,898	41.4	23,192	1.5	4,173	0.3	5,432	0.4	233,594	R
Louisiana	1,765,656	927,871	52.6	792,344	44.9	20,473	1.2	14,356	0.8	10,612	0.6	135,527	R
Maine	651,817	286,616	44.0	319,951	49.1	37,127	5.7	4,443	0.7	3,680	0.6	33,335	D
Maryland	2,020,480	813,797	40.3	1,140,782	56.5	53,768	2.7	4,248	0.2	7,885	0.4	326,985	D
Massachusetts	2,702,984	878,502	32.5	1,616,487	59.8	173,564	6.4	11,149	0.4	23,282	0.9	737,985	D
Michigan	4,232,711	1,953,139	46.1	2,170,418	51.3	84,165	2.0	2,061	0.0	22,928	0.5	217,279	D
Minnesota	2,438,685	1,109,659	45.5	1,168,266	47.9	126,696	5.2	22,166	0.9	11,898	0.5	58,607	D
Mississippi	994,184	572,844	57.6	404,614	40.7	8,122	0.8	2,265	0.2	6,339	0.6	168,230	R
Missouri	2,359,892	1,189,924	50.4	1,111,138	47.1	38,515	1.6	9,818	0.4	10,497	0.4	78,786	R
Montana	410,997	240,178	58.4	137,126	33.4	24,437	5.9	5,697	1.4	3,559	0.9	103,052	R
Nebraska	697,019	433,862	62.2	231,780	33.3	24,540	3.5	3,646	0.5	3,191	0.5	202,082	R
Nevada	608,970	301,575	49.5	279,978	46.0	15,008	2.5	4,747	0.8	7,662	1.3	21,597	R
New Hampshire	569,081	273,559	48.1	266,348	46.8	22,198	3.9	2,615	0.5	4,361	0.8	7,211	R
New Jersey	3,187,226	1,284,173	40.3	1,788,850	56.1	94,554	3.0	6,989	0.2	12,660	0.4	504,677	D
New Mexico	598,605	286,417	47.8	286,783	47.9	21,251	3.6	1,392	0.2	2,762	0.5	366	D
New York	6,821,999	2,403,374	35.2	4,107,697	60.2	244,030	3.6	31,599	0.5	35,299	0.5	1,704,323	D
North Carolina	2,911,262	1,631,163	56.0	1,257,692	43.2	—	0.0	8,874	0.3	13,533	0.5	373,471	R
North Dakota	288,256	174,852	60.7	95,284	33.1	9,486	3.3	7,288	2.5	1,346	0.5	79,568	R
Ohio	4,701,998	2,350,363	50.0	2,183,628	46.4	117,799	2.5	26,721	0.6	23,484	0.5	166,735	R
Oklahoma	1,234,229	744,337	60.3	474,276	38.4	—	0.0	9,014	0.7	6,602	0.5	270,061	R
Oregon	1,533,968	713,577	46.5	720,342	47.0	77,357	5.0	7,063	0.5	15,629	1.0	6,765	D
Pennsylvania	4,913,119	2,281,127	46.4	2,485,967	50.6	103,392	2.1	16,023	0.3	26,610	0.5	204,840	D
Rhode Island	409,047	130,555	31.9	249,508	61.0	25,052	6.1	2,273	0.6	1,659	0.4	118,953	D
South Carolina	1,382,717	785,937	56.8	565,561	40.9	20,200	1.5	3,519	0.3	7,500	0.5	220,376	R
South Dakota	316,269	190,700	60.3	118,804	37.6	—	0.0	3,322	1.1	3,443	1.1	71,896	R
Tennessee	2,076,181	1,061,949	51.1	981,720	47.3	19,781	1.0	4,250	0.2	8,481	0.4	80,229	R
Texas	6,407,637	3,799,639	59.3	2,433,746	38.0	137,994	2.2	12,394	0.2	23,864	0.4	1,365,893	R
Utah	770,754	515,096	66.8	203,053	26.3	35,850	4.7	9,319	1.2	7,436	1.0	312,043	R
Vermont	294,308	119,775	40.7	149,022	50.6	20,374	6.9	2,192	0.7	2,945	1.0	29,247	D
Virginia	2,739,447	1,437,490	52.5	1,217,290	44.4	59,398	2.2	5,455	0.2	19,814	0.7	220,200	R
Washington	2,487,433	1,108,864	44.6	1,247,652	50.2	103,002	4.1	7,171	0.3	20,744	0.8	138,788	D
West Virginia	648,124	336,475	51.9	295,497	45.6	10,680	1.6	3,169	0.5	2,303	0.4	40,978	R
Wisconsin	2,598,607	1,237,279	47.6	1,242,987	47.8	94,070	3.6	11,446	0.4	12,825	0.5	5,708	D
Wyoming	218,351	147,947	67.8	60,481	27.7	4,625	2.1	2,724	1.2	2,574	1.2	87,466	R
Dist. of Col.	201,894	18,073	9.0	171,923	85.2	10,576	5.2	—	0.0	1,322	0.7	153,850	D
Totals	105,396,627	50,455,156	47.9	50,992,335	48.4	2,882,738	2.7	449,077	0.4	617,321	0.6	537,179	D

5

The Electoral College

FOR MORE THAN TWO CENTURIES, Americans have been electing their presidents through the electoral college. Created by the framers of the Constitution as a compromise between selection by Congress and election by direct popular vote, the system has continued to function even though the United States has undergone radical transformation from an agricultural seaboard nation to a world power.

But despite its durability the electoral college is perhaps the least cherished of the United States' venerable political institutions. Thomas Jefferson called it "the most dangerous blot on our Constitution," and people have been calling for its abolition or reform ever since.

Under the electoral college system, each state is entitled to electoral votes equal in number to its congressional delegation—that is, the number of representatives from the state, plus two for the state's two senators. (The District of Columbia has three electoral votes, the number it would have if it were a state, making the total electoral college membership 538.) As it works today, the electoral college is a "winner-take-all" system. The party that receives a plurality of a state's popular vote is virtually assured of receiving all of that state's electoral votes. Exceptions are Maine and Nebraska, where two electoral votes are awarded to the statewide winner and the others are allocated by presidential election districts that match the states' congressional districts (two in Maine and three in Nebraska). In the past there were even more variations of today's procedure, including choosing electors by congressional district, voting statewide for each individual elector, and selection of electors by state legislatures. There also have been several cases of a so-called faithless elector, who cast his or her electoral vote for a candidate other than the one who won the popular vote in the elector's state. (See box, Splitting of States' Electoral Votes, p. 158.)

Critics call the electoral college anachronistic and antidemocratic. Many believe that direct election is fairer and more likely to express the will of the people. Public opinion polls consistently show that most Americans favor switching to direct popular vote. Supporters, however, view the college as a bulwark of federalism and the two-party system. They note that most of the time it works flawlessly. They maintain that the system forces a winning candidate to build a national coalition covering many states, which usually enables the president to govern from a wide base even if the popular vote margin of victory was close. Only in four elections has the popular vote winner not won the presidency.

Constitutional Background

The method of selecting a president was the subject of long debate at the Constitutional Convention of 1787. Several plans were proposed and rejected before a compromise solution, which was modified only slightly in later years, was adopted (Article II, Section I, Clause 2).

Facing the convention when it opened May 25 was the question of whether the chief executive should be chosen by direct popular election, by the Congress, by state legislatures, or by intermediate electors. Direct election was opposed because it was felt generally that the people lacked sufficient knowledge of the character and qualifications of possible candidates to make an intelligent choice. Many delegates also feared that the people of the various states would be unlikely to agree on a single person, usually casting their votes for favorite-son candidates well known to them.

The possibility of giving Congress the power to choose the president also received consideration. This plan was rejected, however, largely because of fear that it would jeopardize the principle of executive independence. Similarly, a plan favored by many delegates, to let state legislatures choose the president, was turned down because the delegates thought the president might feel so indebted to the states as to allow them to encroach on federal authority.

Unable to agree on a plan, the convention August 31 appointed a "Committee of Eleven" to solve the problem. On September 4 it suggested a compromise under which each state would appoint presidential electors equal to the total number of its representatives and senators. The electors, chosen in a manner set forth by each state legislature, would meet in their own states and each cast votes for two persons. The votes would be counted in Congress, with the candidate receiving a majority elected president and the second-highest candidate becoming vice president.

No distinction was made between ballots for president and vice president. Moreover, the development of national political parties and the nomination of tickets for president and vice president created further confusion in the electoral system. All the electors of one party tended to cast ballots for their two party nominees. But with no distinction between the presidential and vice-presidential nominees, the danger arose of a tie vote between the two. That actually happened in 1800, leading to a change in the original electoral system with ratification of the Twelfth Amendment in 1804.

The committee's compromise plan constituted a great concession to the less populous states, because it ensured them a

Splitting of States' Electoral Votes: Factionalism and "Faithless Electors"

Throughout the history of presidential elections, there have been numerous occurrences when the U.S. electoral votes from an individual state have been divided among two or more candidates. These cases of split electoral votes occurred for a variety of reasons.

Electoral Vote Splits, 1789–1836

Splits of a state's electoral votes cast for president before 1836 occurred for these reasons:

• For the first four presidential elections (1789–1800) held under Article II, Section 1 of the Constitution, each elector cast two votes without designating which vote was for president and which for vice president. As a result, electoral votes for each state were often scattered among several candidates. The Twelfth Amendment, ratified in 1804, required electors to vote separately for president and vice president.

• The district system of choosing electors, in which different candidates each could carry several districts. This system is the explanation for the split electoral votes in Maryland in 1804, 1808, 1812, 1824, 1828, and 1832; North Carolina in 1808; Illinois in 1824; Maine in 1828; and New York in 1828.

• The selection of electors by the legislatures of some states. This system sometimes led to party factionalism or political deals that resulted in the choice of electors loyal to more than one presidential candidate. This was the cause for the division of electoral votes in New York in 1808 and 1824, Delaware in 1824, and Louisiana in 1824.

• The vote of an individual elector for someone other than his party's candidate. This happened in New Hampshire in 1820 when one Democratic-Republican elector voted for John Quincy Adams instead of the party nominee, James Monroe, to preserve George Washington's distinction as the only unanimously elected president. Three other electors did not vote in 1820.

Voting for Individual Electors

By 1836 all states except South Carolina, which selected its electors by the state legislature until after the Civil War, had established a system of statewide popular election of electors. The new system limited the frequency of electoral vote splits. Nevertheless, a few states on occasion still divided their electoral votes among different presidential candidates. This occurred because of the practice of listing on the ballot the names of all electors and allowing voters to cross off the names of any particular electors they did not like, or, alternatively, requiring voters to vote for each individual elector. In a close election, electors of different parties sometimes were chosen. An example occurred in California in 1880, when one Democratic elector ran behind the Republican thus:

Winning votes	Party	Losing electors	Party
80,443	Democratic	80,282	Republican
80,426	Democratic	80,252	Republican
80,420	Democratic	80,242	Republican
80,413	Democratic	80,228	Republican
80,348	Republican	79,885	Democratic

• *New Jersey, 1860.* Four Republican and three Douglas Democratic electors won.

• *California, 1892.* Eight Democratic electors and one Republican won.

• *North Dakota, 1892.* Two Fusionists (Democrats and Populists) and one Republican won. One of the Fusion electors voted for Democrat Grover Cleveland, and the other voted for Populist James B. Weaver, while the Republican elector voted for Benjamin Harrison, thus splitting the state's electoral vote three ways.

• *Ohio, 1892.* Twenty-two Republicans and one Democratic elector won.

• *Oregon, 1892.* Three Republicans and one Populist with Democratic support won.

---

minimum of three votes (two for their two senators and at least one for their representative) however small their populations might be. The plan also left important powers with the states by giving complete discretion to state legislatures to determine the method of choosing electors.

The only part of the committee's plan that aroused serious opposition was a provision giving the Senate the right to decide presidential elections in which no candidate received a majority of electoral votes. Some delegates feared that the Senate, which already had been given treaty ratification powers and the responsibility to "advise and consent" on all important executive appointments, might become too powerful. A proposal was made and accepted to let the House of Representatives decide the winner in instances when the electors failed to give a majority of their votes to a single candidate. The interests of the small states were preserved by giving each state's delegation only one vote in the House on roll calls to elect a president.

The system adopted by the Constitutional Convention was a compromise born out of problems involved in diverse state voting requirements, the slavery problem, big-state versus small-state rivalries, and the complexities of the balance of power among different branches of the government. Moreover, it was probably as close to a direct popular election as the men who wrote the Constitution thought possible and appropriate at the time.

The term *electoral college* itself does not appear in the Constitution. It was first used unofficially in the early 1800s and became the official designation for the electoral body in 1845.

THE TWELFTH AMENDMENT

Only once since ratification of the Constitution has an amendment been adopted that substantially altered the method of electing the president. In the 1800 presidential election, the

- *California, 1896.* Eight Republicans and one Democratic elector won
- *Kentucky, 1896.* Twelve Republicans and one Democratic elector won.
- *Maryland, 1904.* Seven Democratic electors and one Republican won.
- *Maryland, 1908.* Six Democratic and two Republican electors won.
- *California, 1912.* Eleven Progressive and two Democratic electors won.
- *West Virginia, 1916.* Seven Republicans and one Democratic elector won.

The increasing use of voting machines and straight-ticket voting—where the pull of a lever or the marking of an "X" results in automatically casting a vote for every elector—led to the decline in split electoral votes.

"Faithless Electors"

Yet another cause for occasional splits in a state's electoral vote is the so-called faithless elector. Legally, electors are not bound to vote for any particular candidate; they may cast their ballots any way they wish. By 2000 twenty-nine states and the District of Columbia had laws requiring electors to vote for the state's popular vote winner. These states were Alabama, Alaska, California, Colorado, Connecticut, Delaware, Florida, Hawaii, Maine, Maryland, Massachusetts, Michigan, Mississippi, Montana, Nebraska, Nevada, New Mexico, North Carolina, Ohio, Oklahoma, Oregon, South Carolina, Tennessee, Utah, Vermont, Virginia, Washington, Wisconsin, and Wyoming.

In Michigan, North Carolina, and Utah a "faithless elector" was not to be counted with the remaining electors filling the vacancy. New Mexico, North Carolina, Oklahoma, South Carolina, and Washington provided criminal penalties or fines for violations. However, no faithless elector has ever been punished and experts doubt that it would be constitutionally possible to do so.

In reality, electors are almost always faithful to the candidate of the party with which they are affiliated, law or no law. But at times in American political history electors have broken ranks to vote for candidates not supported by their parties. In 1796 a Pennsylvania Federalist elector voted for Democratic-Republican Thomas Jefferson instead of Federalist John Adams. And some historians and political scientists claim that three Democratic-Republican electors voted for Adams. However, the fluidity of political party lines at that early date and the well-known personal friendship between Adams and at least one of the electors make the claim of their being faithless electors one of continuing controversy. In 1820 a New Hampshire Democratic-Republican elector voted for John Quincy Adams instead of the party nominee, James Monroe.

There was no further occurrence until 1948, when Preston Parks, a Truman elector in Tennessee, voted for Gov. Strom Thurmond of South Carolina, the States Rights Democratic Party (Dixiecrat) presidential nominee. Since then, there have been the following instances:

- In 1956 W. F. Turner, a Stevenson elector in Alabama, voted for a local judge, Walter B. Jones.
- In 1960 Henry D. Irwin, a Nixon elector in Oklahoma, voted for Sen. Harry F. Byrd, Virginia Democrat.
- In 1968 Dr. Lloyd W. Bailey, a Nixon elector in North Carolina, voted for George C. Wallace, the American Independent Party candidate.
- In 1972 Roger L. MacBride, a Nixon elector in Virginia, voted for John Hospers, the Libertarian Party candidate.
- In 1976 Mike Padden, a Ford elector in the state of Washington, voted for former governor Ronald Reagan of California.
- In 1988 Margaret Leach, a Dukakis elector in West Virginia, voted for Dukakis's running mate, Sen. Lloyd Bentsen of Texas.
- In 2000 Barbara Lett-Simmons, a Gore elector in Washington, D.C., withheld her vote from Gore.

Democratic-Republican electors inadvertently caused a tie in the electoral college by casting equal numbers of votes for Thomas Jefferson, whom they wished to be elected president, and Aaron Burr, whom they wished to elect vice president. The election was thrown into the House, and thirty-six ballots were required before Jefferson was finally elected president. The Twelfth Amendment, ratified in 1804, sought to prevent a recurrence of this incident by providing that the electors should vote separately for president and vice president.

Other changes in the system evolved over the years. The authors of the Constitution, for example, had intended that each state should choose its most distinguished citizens as electors and that they would deliberate and vote as individuals in electing the president. But as strong political parties began to appear, the electors came to be chosen merely as representatives of the parties; independent voting by electors disappeared almost entirely.

Methods of Choosing Electors

In the early years of the Republic, states used a variety of methods to select presidential electors. For the first presidential election, in 1789, four states held direct popular elections to choose their electors: Pennsylvania and Maryland (at large) as well as Virginia and Delaware (by district). In five states—Connecticut, Georgia, New Jersey, New York, and South Carolina—the state legislatures were to make the choice.

New Hampshire and Massachusetts adopted a combination of the legislative and popular methods. New Hampshire held a statewide popular vote for presidential electors with the stipulation that any elector would have to win a majority of the popular vote to be elected; otherwise, the legislature would choose. In Massachusetts the arrangement was for the voters in each congressional district to vote for the two persons they wanted to be presidential electors. From the two individuals in each district receiving the highest number of votes, the legislature, by joint ballot of both houses, was to choose one. In addition, the legislature was to choose two electors at large.

Because of a dispute between the two chambers, the New York legislature failed to choose electors. The state Senate insisted on full equality with the Assembly (lower house); that is, the Senate wanted each house to take a separate ballot and to resolve any differences between them by agreement rather than by having one house impose its will on the other. The Assembly, on the other hand, wanted a joint ballot, on which the lower house's larger numbers would prevail, or it was willing to divide the electors with the Senate. The failure to compromise cost the state its vote in the first presidential election.

The twelfth and thirteenth states—North Carolina and Rhode Island—had not ratified the Constitution by the time the electors were chosen, and so they did not participate.

Generally similar arrangements prevailed for the election of 1792. Massachusetts, while continuing to choose electors by district, changed the system somewhat to provide for automatic election of any candidate for elector who received a majority of the popular vote. New Hampshire continued the system of popular election at large, but substituted a popular runoff election in place of legislative choice, if no candidate received a majority of the popular vote.

Besides Massachusetts and New Hampshire, electors were chosen in 1792 by popular vote in Maryland and Pennsylvania (at large) and Virginia and Kentucky (by district). State legislatures chose electors in Connecticut, Delaware, Georgia, New Jersey, New York, North Carolina, Rhode Island, South Carolina, and Vermont.

By 1796 several changes had occurred. New Hampshire switched back to legislative choice for those electors who failed to receive a majority of the popular vote. Tennessee entered the Union (1796) with a unique system for choosing presidential electors: the state legislature appointed three persons in each county, who in turn chose the presidential electors. Massachusetts retained the system used in 1792. Other states chose their electors as follows: at-large popular vote: Georgia, Pennsylvania; district popular vote: Kentucky, Maryland, North Carolina, Virginia; state legislature: Connecticut, Delaware, New Jersey, New York, Rhode Island, South Carolina, Vermont.

POLITICAL PARTIES AND ELECTORS: 1800

As political parties gained power, manipulation of the system of choosing electors became increasingly widespread. For example, in 1800 Massachusetts switched from popular voting to legislative selection of electors because of recent successes by the Democratic-Republican Party in that state. The Federalists, still in firm control of the legislature, sought to secure the state's entire electoral vote for its presidential candidate, native son John Adams. New Hampshire did likewise.

The rival Democratic-Republicans were not innocent of this kind of political maneuver. In Virginia, where that party was in control, the legislature changed the system for choosing electors from districts to a statewide at-large ballot. That way, the expected statewide Democratic-Republican majority could overcome Federalist control in some districts and garner a unanimous vote for Jefferson, the Democratic-Republican presidential candidate.

In Pennsylvania the two houses of the state legislature could not agree on legislation providing for popular ballots, the system used in the first three elections, so the legislature itself chose the electors, dividing them between the parties.

In other changes in 1800, Rhode Island switched to popular election and Georgia reverted to legislative elections. The sixteen states used the following methods of choosing presidential electors in 1800:

- By popular vote: Kentucky, Maryland, North Carolina (by district); Rhode Island, Virginia (at large).
- By the legislature: Connecticut, Delaware, Georgia, Massachusetts, New Hampshire, New Jersey, New York, Pennsylvania, South Carolina, Tennessee (indirectly, as in 1796), Vermont.

TREND TO WINNER-TAKE-ALL SYSTEM

For the next third of a century, the states moved slowly but inexorably toward a standard system of choosing presidential electors—the statewide, winner-take-all popular ballot. The development of political parties resulted in the adoption of slates of electors pledged to vote for the parties' presidential candidates. Each party organization saw a statewide ballot as being in its best interest, with the hope of sweeping in all its electors and preventing the opposition group from capitalizing on local areas of strength (which could result in winning only part of the electoral vote under the districting system).

From 1804 to 1832 the states used three basic methods of choosing presidential electors—at-large popular vote, district popular vote, and election by the state legislature. The following list shows the changing methods of choosing presidential electors for each state from 1804 to 1832:

1804

Popular vote, at large: New Hampshire, New Jersey, Ohio, Pennsylvania, Rhode Island, Virginia.

Popular vote, by district: Kentucky, Maryland, Massachusetts, North Carolina, Tennessee.

State legislature: Connecticut, Delaware, Georgia, New York, South Carolina, Vermont.

1808

Popular vote, at large: New Hampshire, New Jersey, Ohio, Pennsylvania, Rhode Island, Virginia.

Popular vote, by district: Kentucky, Maryland, North Carolina, Tennessee.

State legislature: Connecticut, Delaware, Georgia, Massachusetts, New York, South Carolina, Vermont.

1812

Popular vote, at large: New Hampshire, Ohio, Pennsylvania, Rhode Island, Virginia.

Popular vote, by district: Kentucky, Maryland, Massachusetts, Tennessee.

State legislature: Connecticut, Delaware, Georgia, Louisiana, New Jersey, New York, North Carolina, South Carolina, Vermont.

1816

Popular vote, at large: New Hampshire, New Jersey, North Carolina, Ohio, Pennsylvania, Rhode Island, Virginia.

Popular vote, by district: Kentucky, Maryland, Tennessee.

State legislature: Connecticut, Delaware, Georgia, Indiana, Louisiana, Massachusetts, New York, South Carolina, Vermont.

1820

Popular vote, at large: Connecticut, Mississippi, New Hampshire, New Jersey, North Carolina, Ohio, Pennsylvania, Rhode Island, Virginia.

Popular vote, by district: Illinois, Kentucky, Maine, Maryland, Massachusetts, Tennessee.

State legislature: Alabama, Delaware, Georgia, Indiana, Louisiana, Missouri, New York, South Carolina, Vermont.

1824

Popular vote, at large: Alabama, Connecticut, Indiana, Massachusetts, Mississippi, New Hampshire, New Jersey, North Carolina, Ohio, Pennsylvania, Rhode Island, Virginia.

Popular vote, by district: Illinois, Kentucky, Maine, Maryland, Missouri, Tennessee.

State legislature: Delaware, Georgia, Louisiana, New York, South Carolina, Vermont.

1828

Popular vote, at large: Alabama, Connecticut, Georgia, Illinois, Indiana, Kentucky, Louisiana, Massachusetts, Mississippi, Missouri, New Hampshire, New Jersey, North Carolina, Ohio, Pennsylvania, Rhode Island, Vermont, Virginia.

Popular vote, by district: Maine, Maryland, New York, Tennessee.

State legislature: Delaware, South Carolina.

1832

Popular vote, at large: All states except Maryland and South Carolina.

Popular vote, by district: Maryland.

State legislature: South Carolina.

By 1836 Maryland switched to the system of choosing its electors by statewide popular vote. This left only South Carolina selecting its electors through the state legislature. The state continued this practice through the election of 1860. Only after the Civil War was popular voting for presidential electors instituted in South Carolina.

Since 1836 the statewide, winner-take-all popular vote for electors has been the almost universal practice. Exceptions include the following:

• *Massachusetts, 1848.* Three slates of electors ran—Whig, Democratic, and Free Soil—none of which received a majority of the popular vote. Under the law then in force, the state legislature was to choose in such a case. It chose the Whig electors.

• *Florida, 1868.* The state legislature chose the electors.

• *Colorado, 1876.* The state legislature chose the electors because the state had just been admitted to the Union, had held state elections in August and did not want to go to the trouble and expense of holding a popular vote for the presidential election so soon thereafter.

• *Michigan, 1892.* Republicans had been predominant in the state since the 1850s. However, in 1890 the Democrats gained control of the legislature and the governorship and enacted a districting system of choosing presidential electors in the expectation that the Democrats could carry some districts and thus some electoral votes in 1892. They were correct; the Republicans won nine and the Democrats five electoral votes that year. But the Republicans soon regained control of the state and reenacted the at-large system for the 1896 election.

• *Maine, 1972.* In 1969 the Maine legislature enacted a district system for choosing presidential electors. Two of the state's four electors were selected on the basis of the statewide vote, and the other two were determined by which party carried each of the state's two congressional districts. The system is still in force. Although the district system allowed splitting electoral votes, from its inception through 2000 the system had not produced a split vote in Maine.

• *Nebraska, 1992.* Nebraska, with five electoral votes, adopted an allocation system similar to Maine's. Like Maine, Nebraska had not split its electoral votes under the new system through the 2000 presidential election..

• *Florida, 2000.* The Republican-controlled legislature met in special session to choose the state's twenty-five electors. The action ensured that Florida's electoral votes would not be disqualified if the winner of the state's popular vote had not been determined by the federal date for counting electoral votes. Florida is one of twenty-nine states that bind electors to the popular vote winner, but the constitutionality of such laws has not been tested.

Historical Anomalies

The complicated and indirect system of electing the president has led to anomalies from time to time. In 1836, for example, the Whigs sought to take advantage of the electoral system by running different presidential candidates in different parts of the country. William Henry Harrison ran in most of New England, the mid-Atlantic states, and the Midwest; Daniel Webster ran in Massachusetts; Hugh White of Tennessee ran in the South.

The theory was that each candidate could capture electoral votes for the Whig Party in the region where he was strongest. Then the Whig electors could combine on one candidate or, alternatively, throw the election into the House, whichever

Electoral College Chronology

Before 1800. U.S. Constitution establishes the electoral college system for electing the president.

1787. Constitution provides for president to be named by state-appointed "electors"; each state free to determine method of choosing electors; plan calls for second-place finisher to become vice president and for House of Representatives to elect president if no candidate has majority.

1800s. Electoral college is tested in three contentious elections but survives with one significant modification effective 1804; states gradually move to winner-take-all system, giving electoral votes to winner of the state's popular vote for president.

1800. Presidential election is thrown into House, which takes thirty-six ballots to pick Thomas Jefferson over Aaron Burr.

1804. The Twelfth Amendment provides for separate election of vice president.

1824–1825. John Quincy Adams trails in popular vote and electoral vote to Andrew Jackson but is elected president after one House ballot.

1830s. Most states adopt popular election of presidential elections; by 1860 only South Carolina lets state legislature choose.

1845. Congress adopts uniform national election day: first Tuesday after first Monday in November in even-numbered years.

1876–1877. Rutherford B. Hayes is elected president with one-vote electoral college majority, 185–184, after a fifteen-member commission splits along party lines in awarding him disputed votes from three southern states.

1887. Electoral Vote Count Act specifies states' authority to determine legality of their choices for electors.

1900s. Proposals to abolish electoral college surface periodically, but no constitutional amendment emerges from Congress.

1950. Senate approves "proportional vote" plan to divide state electors on basis of popular vote; House kills measure.

1960. John F. Kennedy wins electoral college majority over Richard M. Nixon, 303–219; Kennedy's popular vote margin is closest in twentieth century. Fourteen unpledged electors and one "faithless" Republican elector vote for Sen. Harry F. Byrd, Virginia Democrat.

1968. Nixon wins electoral college majority over Democrat Hubert H. Humphrey and third-party candidate George Wallace (301–191–46); both Nixon and Humphrey had vowed not to negotiate with Wallace if election were thrown into House.

1969. House approves constitutional amendment to shift to direct popular election of president; measure dies after Senate filibuster in 1970. Maine, in 1969, replaces winner-take-all with district-by-district system.

1980–1988. Electoral college issue fades as Republican candidates win three successive elections with decisive popular votes and electoral majorities. One Democratic elector in 1988 votes for vice-presidential nominee Lloyd Bentsen to protest system.

1992. Strong third-party bid by H. Ross Perot stirs fears of throwing election to House, but Bill Clinton wins electoral college majority as Perot fails to carry any state. Nebraska adopts district voting for electors.

2000–2001. Democrat Al Gore surpasses Republican George W. Bush in popular vote, but electoral college outcome turns on close count in Florida; Gore and Bush vie in state and federal courts over recount. U.S. Supreme Court halts count, settling election contest in Bush's favor. Final electoral vote tally is Bush 271 (one more than he needed to win) and Gore 266 (one fewer than he was entitled to because a District of Columbia elector withheld her vote to protest the District's lack of congressional representation). When Congress meets to count the electoral votes, several minority and women House members object to Florida's votes. Gore, presiding, rules each objection out of order because it was not also signed by a senator as the 1887 law requires.

seemed to their advantage. However, the scheme did not work because Martin Van Buren, the Democratic nominee, captured a majority of the electoral vote.

Another quirk in the system surfaced in 1872. The Democratic presidential nominee, Horace Greeley, died between the time of the popular vote and the meeting of the presidential electors. The Democratic electors had no party nominee to vote for, and each was left to his own judgment. Forty-two of the sixty-six Democratic electors chose to vote for the Democratic governor-elect of Indiana, Thomas Hendricks. The rest of the electors split their votes among three other politicians: eighteen for B. Gratz Brown of Missouri, the Democratic vice-presidential nominee; two for Charles J. Jenkins of Georgia, and one for David Davis of Illinois. Three Georgia electors insisted on casting their votes for Greeley, but Congress refused to count them. Counting Republican Ulysses S. Grant, who won, five candidates received electoral votes in 1872, tied for the largest number in U.S. history (five candidates also received electoral votes in 1800 and 1836).

In four elections the electoral college has chosen presidents who ran behind their opponents in the popular vote. In two of these instances—Republican Rutherford B. Hayes in 1876 and Republican Benjamin Harrison in 1888—the winning candidate carried a number of key states by close margins, while losing other states by wide margins. In the third instance—Democratic-Republican John Quincy Adams in 1824—the House chose the new president after no candidate had achieved a majority in the electoral college. In the fourth instance, the 2000 election hinged on Florida's twenty-five electoral votes, which went to Republican George W. Bush when the U.S. Supreme Court rejected Democrat Al Gore's contest of the state's vote count. *(See Chapter 2, Chronology of Presidential Elections.)*

Election by Congress

Under the Constitution, Congress has two major responsibilities relating to the election of the president and vice president. First, it is directed to receive and, in joint session, count the electoral votes certified by the states. Second, if no candidate has a majority of the electoral vote, the House of Representatives must elect the president and the Senate the vice president.

Although many of the framers of the Constitution apparently thought that most elections would be decided by Congress, the House actually has chosen a president only twice, in 1801 and 1825. But a number of campaigns have been deliberately designed to throw elections into the House, where each state has one vote and a majority of states is needed to elect.

In modern times the formal counting of electoral votes has been largely a ceremonial function, but the congressional role can be decisive when votes are contested. The preeminent example is the Hayes-Tilden contest of 1876, when congressional decisions on disputed electoral votes from four states gave the election to Republican Hayes despite the fact that Democrat Samuel J. Tilden had a majority of the popular vote. *(See "Hayes-Tilden Contest," p. 166.)*

From the beginning, the constitutional provisions governing the selection of the president have had few defenders, and many efforts at electoral college reform have been undertaken. Although prospects for reform seemed favorable after the close 1968 presidential election, the Ninety-first Congress (1969–1971) did not take final action on a proposed constitutional amendment that would have provided for direct popular election of the president and eliminated the existing provision for contingent election by the House. Reform legislation was reintroduced in the Senate during the Ninety-fourth Congress (1975–1977) and Ninety-fifth Congress (1977–1979). In the 107th Congress (2001–2003) more talk of reforming or replacing the electoral college system followed the fiercely fought 2000 election.

In addition to its role in electing the president, Congress bears responsibility in the related areas of presidential succession and disability. The Twelfth Amendment empowers Congress to decide what to do if the president-elect and the vice president-elect both fail to qualify by the date prescribed for commencement of their terms; it also gives Congress authority to settle problems arising from the death of candidates in cases where the election devolves upon Congress. Under the Twenty-fifth Amendment, Congress has ultimate responsibility for resolving disputes over presidential disability. It also must confirm presidential nominations to fill a vacancy in the vice presidency.

JEFFERSON-BURR DEADLOCK

The election of 1800 was the first in which the Constitution's contingent election procedures were put to the test and the House elected the president. The Federalists, a declining but still potent political force, nominated John Adams for a second term and chose Charles Cotesworth Pinckney as his running mate. A Democratic-Republican congressional caucus chose Vice President Jefferson for president and Burr, who had been instrumental in winning the New York legislature for the Democratic-Republicans earlier in 1800, for vice president.

The electors met in each state on December 4, with the following results: Jefferson and Burr, 73 electoral votes each; Adams, 65; Pinckney, 64; and John Jay, 1. The Federalists had lost, but because the Democratic-Republicans had neglected to withhold one electoral vote from Burr, their presidential and vice-presidential candidates were tied, and the election was thrown into the House.

The lame-duck Congress, with a partisan Federalist majority, was still in office for the electoral count, and the possibilities for intrigue were only too apparent. After toying with and rejecting a proposal to block any election until March 4, when Adams's term expired, the Federalists decided to support Burr and thereby elect a relatively pliant politician over a man they considered a "dangerous radical." Alexander Hamilton opposed this move. "I trust the Federalists will not finally be so mad as to vote for Burr," he wrote. "I speak with intimate and accurate knowledge of his character. His elevation can only promote the purposes of the desperate and the profligate. If there be a man in the world I ought to hate, it is Jefferson. With Burr I have always been personally well. But the public good must be paramount to every private consideration."

On February 11, 1801, Congress met in joint session—with Jefferson, the outgoing vice president, in the chair—to count the electoral vote. This ritual ended, the House retired to its own chamber to elect a president. When the House met, it became apparent that Hamilton's advice had been rejected; a majority of Federalists insisted on backing Burr over Jefferson, the man they despised more. Indeed, if Burr had given clear assurances that he would run the country as a Federalist, he might have been elected. But Burr was unwilling to make those assurances; and, as one chronicler put it, "No one knows whether it was honor or a wretched indecision which gagged Burr's lips."

In all, there were 106 members of the House at the time, 58 Federalists and 48 Democratic-Republicans. If the ballots had been cast per capita Burr would have been elected, but the Constitution provided that each state should cast a single vote and that a majority of states was necessary for election.

On the first ballot Jefferson received the votes of eight states, one short of a majority of the sixteen states then in the Union. Six states backed Burr. The representatives of Vermont and Maryland were equally divided and, therefore, could not cast

Presidential Election by the House

The following rules, reprinted from Hinds' *Precedents of the House of Representatives,* were adopted by the House in 1825 for use in deciding the presidential election of 1824. They would provide a precedent for any future House election of a president, although the House could change them.

1. In the event of its appearing, on opening all the certificates, and counting the votes given by the electors of the several States for President, that no person has a majority of the votes of the whole number of electors appointed, the same shall be entered on the Journals of this House.

2. The roll of the House shall then be called by States; and, on its appearing that a Member or Members from two-thirds of the States are present, the House shall immediately proceed, by ballot, to choose a President from the persons having the highest numbers, not exceeding three, on the list of those voted for as President; and, in case neither of those persons shall receive the votes of a majority of all the states on the first ballot, the House shall continue to ballot for a President, without interruption by other business, until a President be chosen.

3. The doors of the Hall shall be closed during the balloting, except against the Members of the Senate, stenographers, and the officers of the House.

4. From the commencement of the balloting until an election is made no proposition to adjourn shall be received, unless on the motion of one State, seconded by another State, and the question shall be decided by States. The same rule shall be observed in regard to any motion to change the usual hour for the meeting of the House.

5. In balloting the following mode shall be observed, to wit:

The Representatives of each State shall be arranged and seated together, beginning with the seats at the right hand of the Speaker's chair, with the Members from the State of Maine; thence, proceeding with the Members from the States, in the order the States are usually named for receiving petitions[1] around the Hall of the House, until all are seated.

A ballot box shall be provided for each State.

The Representatives of each State shall, in the first instance, ballot among themselves, in order to ascertain the vote of their State; and they may, if necessary, appoint tellers of their ballots.

After the vote of each State is ascertained, duplicates thereof shall be made out; and in case any one of the persons from whom the choice is to be made shall receive a majority of the votes given, on any one balloting by the Representatives of a State, the name of that person shall be written on each of the duplicates; and in case the votes so given shall be divided so that neither of said persons shall have a majority of the whole number of votes given by such State, on any one balloting, then the word "divided" shall be written on each duplicate.

After the delegation from each State shall have ascertained the vote of their State, the Clerk shall name the States in the order they are usually named for receiving petitions; and as the name of each is called the Sergeant-at-Arms shall present to the delegation of each two ballot boxes, in each of which shall be deposited, by some Representative of the State, one of the duplicates made as aforesaid of the vote of said State, in the presence and subject to the examination of all the Members from said State then present; and where there is more than one Representative from a State, the duplicates shall not both be deposited by the same person.

When the votes of the States are thus all taken in, the Sergeant-at-Arms shall carry one of said ballot boxes to one table and the other to a separate and distinct table.

One person from each State represented in the balloting shall be appointed by the Representatives to tell off said ballots; but, in case the Representatives fail to appoint a teller, the Speaker shall appoint.

The said tellers shall divide themselves into two sets, as nearly equal in number as can be, and one of the said sets of tellers shall proceed to count the votes in one of said boxes, and the other set the votes in the other box.

When the votes are counted by the different sets of tellers, the result shall be reported to the House; and if the reports agree, the same shall be accepted as the true votes of the States; but if the reports disagree, the States shall proceed, in the same manner as before, to a new ballot.

6. All questions arising after the balloting commences, requiring the decision of the House, which shall be decided by the House, voting per capita, to be incidental to the power of choosing a President, shall be decided by States without debate; and in case of an equal division of the votes of States, the question shall be lost.

7. When either of the persons from whom the choice is to be made shall have received a majority of all the States, the Speaker shall declare the same, and that that person is elected President of the United States.

8. The result shall be immediately communicated to the Senate by message, and a committee of three persons shall be appointed to inform the President of the United States and the President-elect of said election.

On Feb. 9, 1825, the election of John Quincy Adams took place in accordance with these rules.

1. Petitions are no longer introduced in this way. This old procedure of calling the states beginning with Maine proceeded through the original thirteen states and then through the remaining states in the order of their admission to the Union.

their states' votes. By midnight of the first day of voting, nineteen ballots had been taken, and the deadlock remained.

In all, thirty-six ballots were taken before the House came to a decision on February 17. Predictably, there were men who sought to exploit the situation for personal gain. Jefferson wrote: "Many attempts have been made to obtain terms and promises from me. I have declared to them unequivocally that I would not receive the Government on capitulation; that I would not go in with my hands tied."

The impasse was broken finally when Vermont and Maryland switched to support Jefferson. Delaware and South Carolina also withdrew their support from Burr by casting blank ballots. The final vote: ten states for Jefferson, four (all in New England) for Burr. Jefferson became president, and Burr, under the Constitution as it then stood, automatically became vice president.

Federalist James A. Bayard of Delaware, who had played an important role in breaking the deadlock, wrote to Hamilton: "The means existed of electing Burr, but this required his cooperation. By deceiving one man (a great blockhead) and tempting two (not incorruptible), he might have secured a majority of the states. He will never have another chance of being president of the United States; and the little use he has made of the one which has occurred gives me but an humble opinion of the talents of an unprincipled man."

The Jefferson-Burr contest clearly illustrated the dangers of the double-balloting system established by the original Constitution, and pressure began to build for an amendment requiring separate votes for president and vice president. Congress approved the Twelfth Amendment in December 1803, and the states—acting with unexpected speed—ratified it in time for the 1804 election.

JOHN QUINCY ADAMS ELECTION

The only other time the House of Representatives elected a president was in 1825. There were many contenders in the 1824 election, but four predominated: John Quincy Adams, Henry Clay, William H. Crawford, and Andrew Jackson. Crawford, secretary of the Treasury under President James Monroe, was the early front-runner, but his candidacy faltered after he suffered an incapacitating illness in 1823.

When the electoral votes were counted, Jackson had ninety-nine, Adams eighty-four, Crawford forty-one, and Clay thirty-seven. With eighteen of the twenty-four states choosing their electors by popular vote, Jackson also led in the popular voting, although the significance of the popular vote was open to challenge. Under the Twelfth Amendment, the names of the three top contenders—Jackson, Adams, and the ailing Crawford—were placed before the House. Clay's support was vital to either of the two front-runners.

From the start, Clay apparently intended to support Adams as the lesser of two evils. But before the House voted, a great scandal erupted. A Philadelphia newspaper published an anonymous letter alleging that Clay had agreed to support Adams in return for being made secretary of state. The letter alleged also that Clay would have been willing to make the same deal with Jackson. Clay immediately denied the charge and pronounced the writer of the letter "a base and infamous character, a dastard and a liar."

When the House met to vote, Adams was supported by the six New England states and New York and, in large part through Clay's backing, by Maryland, Ohio, Kentucky, Illinois, Missouri, and Louisiana. A majority of thirteen delegations voted for him—the bare minimum he needed for election, because there were twenty-four states in the Union at the time. The election was accomplished on the first ballot, but Adams took office under a cloud from which his administration never emerged.

Jackson had believed the charges and found his suspicions vindicated when Adams, after the election, did appoint Clay as secretary of state. "Was there ever witnessed such a bare-faced corruption in any country before?" Jackson wrote to a friend. Jackson's successful 1828 campaign made much of his contention that the House of Representatives had thwarted the will of the people by denying him the presidency in 1825, even though he had been the leader in the popular and electoral votes.

OTHER ANOMALIES

The Senate has chosen the vice president only once. That was in 1837, when Van Buren was elected president with 170 of the 294 electoral votes while his vice-presidential running mate, Richard M. Johnson, received only 147 electoral votes—one less than a majority. This discrepancy occurred because Van Buren electors from Virginia boycotted Johnson, reportedly in protest against his social behavior. The Senate elected Johnson, 33–16, over Francis Granger of New York, the runner-up in the electoral vote for vice president.

In 1912 President William Howard Taft's vice president, James S. Sherman, died in October after he and Taft won renomination by the Republican Party. Taft and his substitute running mate, Nicholas Murray Butler, lost the election to Democrats Woodrow Wilson and Thomas R. Marshall. But because it had been too late to change the GOP state ballots, Butler won Sherman's eight electoral votes.

Although only two presidential elections actually have been decided by the House, a number of others—including those of 1836, 1856, 1860, 1892, 1948, 1960, and 1968—could have been thrown into the House by only a small shift in the popular vote.

The threat of House election was most clearly evident in 1968, when Democrat George C. Wallace of Alabama ran as a strong third-party candidate. Wallace frequently asserted that he could win an outright majority in the electoral college by the addition of key Midwestern and Mountain states to his hoped-for base in the South and border states. In reality, the Wallace campaign had a narrower goal: to win the balance of power in electoral college voting, thereby depriving either major party of the clear electoral majority required for election. Wallace made it clear that he then would expect one of the major party candidates to make concessions in return for enough votes from Wallace electors to win the election. Wallace indicated that he expected the election to be settled in the electoral college and not in the House of Representatives. At the end of the campaign it was disclosed that Wallace had obtained written affidavits from all of his electors in which they promised to vote for Wallace "or whomsoever he may direct" in the electoral college.

In response to the Wallace challenge, both major party candidates, Republican Richard Nixon and Democrat Hubert H. Humphrey, maintained that they would refuse to bargain with Wallace for his electoral votes. Nixon asserted that the House, if the decision rested there, should elect the popular-vote winner. Humphrey said the representatives should select "the president they believe would be best for the country." Bipartisan efforts to obtain advance agreements from House candidates to vote for the national popular-vote winner if the election should go to the House ended in failure. Neither Nixon nor Humphrey replied to suggestions that they pledge before the election to swing enough electoral votes to the popular-vote winner to ensure his election without help from Wallace.

In the end Wallace received only 13.5 percent of the popular vote and forty-six electoral votes (including the vote of one Republican defector), all from southern states. He failed to win the balance of power in the electoral college, which he had hoped to use to wring policy concessions from one of the major party candidates. If Wallace had won a few border states, or if a few thousand more Democratic votes had been cast in northern states barely carried by Nixon, reducing Nixon's electoral vote below 270, Wallace would have been in a position to bargain off his electoral votes or to throw the election into the House for final settlement. Wallace later told journalist Neal R. Peirce that he would have tried to instruct his electors to vote for Nixon rather than to have the election go to the House.

Counting the Electoral Vote

Over the years Congress has mandated a variety of dates for the casting of popular votes, the meeting of the electors to cast ballots in the various states, and the official counting of the electoral votes before both houses of Congress.

The Continental Congress made the provisions for the first election. On September 13, 1788, it directed that each state choose its electors on the first Wednesday in January 1789. It further directed these electors to cast their ballots on the first Wednesday in February 1789.

In 1792 the Second Congress passed legislation setting up a permanent calendar for choosing electors. Allowing some flexibility in dates, the law directed that states choose their electors within the thirty-four days preceding the first Wednesday in December of each presidential election year. Then the electors would meet in their various states and cast their ballots on the first Wednesday in December. On the second Wednesday of the following February, the votes were to be opened and counted before a joint session of Congress. Provision also was made for a special presidential election in case of the removal, death, resignation, or disability of both the president and vice president.

Under that system, states chose presidential electors at various times. For instance, in 1840 the popular balloting for electors began in Pennsylvania and Ohio on October 30 and ended in North Carolina on November 12. South Carolina, the only state still choosing presidential electors through its state legislature, appointed its electors on November 26.

Congress modified the system in 1845, providing that each state choose its electors on the same day—the Tuesday next after the first Monday in November—a provision that still remains in force. Otherwise, the days for casting and counting the electoral votes remained the same.

The next change occurred in 1887, when Congress provided that electors were to meet and cast their ballots on the second Monday in January instead of the first Wednesday in December. Congress also dropped the provision for a special presidential election.

In 1934 Congress again revised the law. The new arrangements, still in force, directed the electors to meet on the first Monday after the second Wednesday in December. The ballots are opened and counted before Congress on January 6 (the next day if January 6 falls on a Sunday).

The Constitution states: "The President of the Senate shall, in the presence of the Senate and House of Representatives, open all the certificates, and the votes shall then be counted." It gives no guidance on disputed ballots. Early objections to electoral votes usually arose from disputes about whether a state had fully qualified for statehood. After the Civil War, some southern votes were contested on grounds that the states were still considered in "insurrection" against the United Sates.

Before counting the electoral votes in 1865, Congress adopted the Twenty-second Joint Rule, which provided that no electoral votes objected to in joint session could be counted except by the concurrent votes of both the Senate and House. The rule was pushed by congressional Republicans to ensure rejection of the electoral votes from the newly reconstructed states of Louisiana and Tennessee. Under this rule, Congress in 1873 also threw out the electoral votes of Louisiana and Arkansas and three from Georgia.

The rule lapsed at the beginning of 1876, however, when the Senate refused to readopt it because the House was under Democratic control. As a consequence, Congress had no rules to guide it following the 1876 Hayes-Tilden election, when it became apparent that for the first time the outcome of an election would be determined by decisions on disputed electoral votes.

HAYES-TILDEN CONTEST

The 1876 campaign pitted Republican Hayes against Democrat Tilden. Early returns indicated that Tilden had been elected. He had won the swing states of Indiana, New York, Connecticut, and New Jersey. Those states plus his expected southern support would give Tilden the election. However, by the following morning it became apparent that if the Republicans could hold South Carolina, Florida, and Louisiana, Hayes would be elected with 185 electoral votes to 184 for Tilden. But if a single elector in any of these states voted for Tilden, he would throw the election to the Democrats. Tilden led in the popular-vote count by more than a quarter million votes.

The situation was much the same in each of the three contested states. Historian Eugene H. Roseboom described it as follows:

The Republicans controlled the state governments and the election machinery, had relied upon the Negro masses for votes, and had practiced frauds as in the past. The Democrats used threats, intimidation, and even violence when necessary, to keep Negroes from the polls; and where they were in a position to do so they resorted to fraud also. The firm determination of the whites to overthrow carpetbag rule contributed to make a full and fair vote impossible; carpetbag hold on the state governments made a fair count impossible. Radical reconstruction was reaping its final harvest.

Both parties pursued the votes of the three states with a fine disregard for propriety or legality, and in the end double sets of elector returns were sent to Congress from all three. Oregon also sent two sets of returns. Although Hayes carried that state, the Democratic governor discovered that one of the Hayes electors was a postmaster and therefore ineligible under the Constitution, so he certified the election of the top-polling Democratic elector. However, the Republican electors met, received the resignation of their ineligible colleague, then reappointed him to the vacancy because he had in the meantime resigned his postmastership.

Had the Twenty-second Joint Rule remained in effect, the Democratic House of Representatives could have objected to any of Hayes's disputed votes. But because the rule had lapsed, Congress had to find a new method of resolving electoral disputes. A joint committee was created to work out a plan, and the resulting Electoral Commission Law was approved by large majorities and signed into law January 29, 1877—only days before the date scheduled for counting the electoral votes.

The law, which applied only to the 1876 electoral vote count, established a fifteen-member commission that was to have final authority over disputed electoral votes, unless both houses of Congress agreed to overrule it. The commission was to consist of five senators, five representatives, and five Supreme Court justices. Each chamber was to appoint its own members of the commission, with the understanding that the majority party would have three members and the minority two. Four justices, two from each party, were named in the bill, and these four were to select the fifth. It was expected that they would choose Justice David Davis, who was considered a political independent, but he disqualified himself when the Illinois legislature named him to a seat in the Senate. Justice Joseph P. Bradley, a Republican, then was named to the fifteenth seat. The Democrats supported his selection because they considered him the most independent of the remaining justices, all of whom were Republicans. However, he was to vote with the Republicans on every dispute and thus ensure the victory of Hayes.

The electoral count began in Congress February 1 (moved up from the second Wednesday in February for this one election), and the proceedings continued until March 2. States were called in alphabetical order, and as each disputed state was reached objections were raised to both the Hayes and Tilden electors. The question was then referred to the electoral commission, which in every case voted 8–7 for Hayes. In each case, the Democratic House rejected the commission's decision, but the Republican Senate upheld it, so the decision stood.

As the count went on, Democrats in the House threatened to launch a filibuster to block resumption of joint sessions so that the count could not be completed before Inauguration Day. The threat was never carried out because of an agreement reached between the Hayes forces and southern conservatives. The southerners agreed to let the electoral count continue without obstruction. In return Hayes agreed that, as president, he would withdraw federal troops from the South, end Reconstruction, and make other concessions. The southerners, for their part, pledged to respect Negro rights, a pledge they did not carry out.

Consequently, at 4 a.m. March 2, 1877, the president of the Senate was able to announce that Hayes had been elected president with 185 electoral votes, as against 184 for Tilden. Later that day Hayes arrived in Washington. The next evening he took the oath of office privately at the White House, because March 4 fell on a Sunday. His formal inauguration followed on Monday. The country acquiesced. So ended a crisis that could have resulted in civil war.

Not until 1887 did Congress enact permanent legislation on the handling of disputed electoral votes. The Electoral Count Act of that year gave each state final authority in determining the legality of its choice of electors and required a concurrent majority of both the Senate and House to reject any electoral votes. It also established procedures for counting electoral votes in Congress. (See box, Law for Counting Electoral Votes in Congress, p. 168.)

APPLICATION OF 1887 LAW IN 1969

The procedures relating to disputed electoral votes were used for the first time after the election of 1968. When Congress met in joint session January 6, 1969, to count the electoral votes, Sen. Edmund S. Muskie of Maine and Rep. James G. O'Hara of Michigan, both Democrats, joined by six other senators and thirty-seven other representatives, filed a written objection to the vote cast by a North Carolina elector, Lloyd W. Bailey of Rocky Mount. He had been elected as a Republican but chose to vote for George Wallace and Curtis LeMay, the candidates of the American Independent Party, instead of Republican Nixon and his running mate, Spiro T. Agnew.

Acting under the 1887 law, Muskie and O'Hara objected to Bailey's vote on the grounds that it was "not properly given" because a plurality of the popular votes in North Carolina were cast for Nixon-Agnew and the state's voters had chosen electors to vote for Nixon and Agnew only. Muskie and O'Hara asked that Bailey's vote not be counted at all by Congress.

The 1887 statute stipulated that "no electoral vote or votes from any State which shall have been regularly given by electors whose appointment has been lawfully certified . . . from which but one return has been received shall be rejected, but the two Houses concurrently may reject the vote or votes when they agree that such vote or votes have not been so regularly given by electors whose appointment has been so certified." The statute did not define the term "regularly given," although at the time of its adoption the chief concern centered on problems of dual sets of electoral vote returns from a state, votes cast on an improper day, or votes disputed because of uncertainty about whether a state lawfully was in the Union when the vote was cast.

The 1887 statute provided that if written objection to any state's vote was received from at least one member of both the Senate and House, the two legislative bodies were to retire immediately to separate sessions, debate for two hours with a five-minute limitation on speeches, and each decide the issue by vote

Law for Counting Electoral Votes in Congress

Following is the complete text of Title 3, section 15 of the U.S. Code, enacted originally in 1887, governing the counting of electoral votes in Congress:

Congress shall be in session on the sixth day of January succeeding every meeting of the electors. The Senate and House of Representatives shall meet in the Hall of the House of Representatives at the hour of 1 o'clock in the afternoon on that day, and the President of the Senate shall be their presiding officer. Two tellers shall be previously appointed on the part of the Senate and two on the part of the House of Representatives, to whom shall be handed, as they are opened by the President of the Senate, all the certificates and papers purporting to be certificates of the electoral votes, which certificates and papers shall be opened, presented, and acted upon in the alphabetical order of the States, beginning with the letter A; and said tellers, having then read the same in the presence and hearing of the two Houses, shall make a list of the votes as they shall appear from the said certificates; and the votes having been ascertained and counted according to the rules in this subchapter provided, the result of the same shall be delivered to the President of the Senate, who shall thereupon announce the state of the vote, which announcement shall be deemed a sufficient declaration of the persons, if any, elected President and Vice President of the United States, and, together with a list of votes, be entered on the Journals of the two Houses. Upon such reading of any such certificate or paper, the President of the Senate shall call for objections, if any. Every objection shall be made in writing, and shall state clearly and concisely, and without argument, the ground thereof, and shall be signed by at least one Senator and one Member of the House of Representatives before the same shall be received. When all objections so made to any vote or paper from a State shall have been received and read, the Senate shall thereupon withdraw, and such objections shall be submitted to the Senate for its decision; and the Speaker of the House of Representatives shall, in like manner, submit such objections to the House of Representatives for its decision; and no electoral vote or votes from any State which shall have been regularly given by electors whose appointment has been lawfully certified to according to section 6[1] of this title from which but one return has been received shall be rejected, but the two Houses concurrently may re-

ject the vote or votes when they agree that such vote or votes have not been so regularly given by electors whose appointment has been so certified. If more than one return or paper purporting to be a return from a State shall have been received by the President of the Senate, those votes, and those only, shall be counted which shall have been regularly given by the electors who are shown by the determination mentioned in section 5[2] of this title to have been appointed, if the determination in said section provided for shall have been made, or by such successors or substitutes, in case of a vacancy in the board of electors so ascertained, as have been appointed to fill such vacancy in the mode provided by the laws of the State; but in case there shall arise the question which of two or more of such State authorities determining what electors have been appointed, as mentioned in section 5 of this title, is the lawful tribunal of such State, the votes regularly given of those electors, and those only, of such State shall be counted whose title as electors the two Houses, acting separately, shall concurrently decide is supported by the decision of such State so authorized by its law; and in such case of more than one return or paper purporting to be a return from a State, if there shall have been no such determination of the question in the State aforesaid, then those votes, and those only, shall be counted which the two Houses shall concurrently decide were cast by lawful electors appointed in accordance with the laws of the State, unless the two Houses, acting separately, shall concurrently decide such votes not to be the lawful votes of the legally appointed electors of such State. But if the two Houses shall disagree in respect of the counting of such votes, then, and in that case, the votes of the electors whose appointment shall have been certified by the executive of the State, under the seal thereof, shall be counted. When the two Houses have voted, they shall immediately again meet, and the presiding officer shall then announce the decision of the questions submitted. No votes or papers from any other State shall be acted upon until the objections previously made to the votes or papers from any State shall have been finally disposed of.

1. Section 6 provides for certification of votes by electors by state governors.
2. Section 5 provides that if state law specifies a method for resolving disputes concerning the vote for presidential electors, Congress must respect any determination so made by a state.

before resuming the joint session. The statute made clear that both the Senate and House had to reject a challenged electoral vote (or votes) for such action to prevail.

At the January 6 joint session, with Senate President Pro Tempore Richard B. Russell, Georgia Democrat, presiding, the counting of the electoral vote proceeded smoothly through the alphabetical order of states until the North Carolina result was announced, at which time O'Hara rose to announce filing of the complaint. The two houses then reassembled in joint session at which the results of the separate deliberations were announced

and the count of the electoral vote by state proceeded without event. At the conclusion, Russell announced the vote and declared Nixon and Agnew elected.

APPLICATION OF THE 1887 LAW IN 2001

The U.S. Supreme Court's peremptory 5–4 vote ending the recount of Florida's extremely close presidential vote left many Americans angry and embittered. Vice President Al Gore, the Democratic nominee, had defeated Texas's Republican governor, George W. Bush, by more than a half-million votes in the popular election and also led in the electoral vote, pending determination of the Florida winner. African Americans were particularly dissatisfied with the result. They had overwhelmingly supported Gore nationally, and in Florida their votes made up a disproportionately large share of the ballots not counted because of problems with the obsolete punch-card voting system used in many counties. They and many others felt that the majority had been disfranchised and that Gore might have won had the Court not stopped the recount.

But the ruling in *Bush v. Gore* left no recourse through the judicial system. Only one step remained before the 2000 election was officially closed: the formal counting of the 538 electoral votes by both chambers of Congress. When that day came, on January 5, 2001, twenty House members, mostly members of the Congressional Black Caucus, made a last-ditch effort to deny Florida's twenty-five electoral votes to Bush. With Gore presiding, each one submitted a written objection to the counting of Florida's votes. Gore asked each representative if the objection was also signed by a senator, as the 1887 law required. When each responded no, Gore ruled the objection out of order. At one point he thanked Rep. Jesse L. Jackson Jr., Illinois Democrat, for his remarks and said, "But, hey," and spread his arms in a gesture of futility.

It was the first time since the 1969 faithless elector incident that there had been any objections to the counting of electoral votes. In the 2001 counting there was one abstention, by a District of Columbia elector for Gore, resulting in a total of 537 electoral votes being cast.

Reform Proposals

Since January 6, 1797, when Rep. William L. Smith, a South Carolina Federalist, introduced in Congress the first proposed constitutional amendment for reform of the electoral college system, hardly a session of Congress has passed without the introduction of one or more resolutions of this nature. In all, more than seven hundred such proposals have been submitted. But only one—the Twelfth Amendment, ratified in 1804—ever has been approved.

In recent years, public interest in a change in the electoral college system was spurred by the close 1960, 1968, and 2000 elections, by a series of Supreme Court rulings relating to apportionment and redistricting, and by the introduction of unpledged elector systems in the southern states.

HOUSE APPROVAL OF AMENDMENT

Early in 1969 President Nixon asked Congress to take prompt action on electoral college reform. He said he would support any plan that would eliminate individual electors and distribute among the presidential candidates the electoral vote of every state and the District of Columbia in a manner more closely approximating the popular vote.

Later that year the House approved, 338–70, a resolution proposing a constitutional amendment to eliminate the electoral college and to provide instead for direct popular election of the president and vice president. The measure set a minimum of 40 percent of the popular vote as sufficient for election and provided for a runoff election between the two top candidates for the presidency if no candidate received 40 percent. Under this plan the House of Representatives could no longer be called upon to select a president. The proposed amendment also authorized Congress to provide a method of filling vacancies caused by the death, resignation, or disability of presidential nominees before the election and a method of filling postelection vacancies caused by the death of the president-elect or vice president-elect.

Nixon, who previously had favored a proportional plan of allocating each state's electoral votes, endorsed the House resolution and urged the Senate to adopt it. To become effective, the proposed amendment had to be approved by a two-thirds majority in both the Senate and House and be ratified by the legislatures of three-fourths of the states. When the proposal reached the Senate floor in September 1970, senators from small states and the South succeeded in blocking final action. The resolution was laid aside October 5, after two unsuccessful efforts to cut off debate by invoking cloture.

CARTER ENDORSEMENT OF PLAN

Another major effort to eliminate the electoral college occurred in 1977, when President Jimmy Carter included such a proposal in his election reform package, unveiled March 22. Carter endorsed the amendment approved by the House in 1969 to replace the electoral college with direct popular election of the president and vice president, and provide for a runoff if no candidate received at least 40 percent of the vote. Because the Senate again was seen as the major stumbling block, the House waited to see what the Senate would do before beginning any deliberation of its own.

After several months of deadlock, the Senate Judiciary Committee approved September 15 the direct presidential election plan by a 9–8 vote. But Senate opponents threatened a filibuster, and the Senate leadership decided it could not spare the time or effort to try to break it. The measure was never brought to the floor and died when the Ninety-fifth Congress adjourned in 1978.

On January 15, 1979, the opening day of the Ninety-sixth Congress, Sen. Birch Bayh, Indiana Democrat, began another effort to abolish the electoral college through a constitutional amendment. In putting off action in the previous Congress, Senate leaders had agreed to try for early action in the Ninety-sixth.

A proposed constitutional amendment to abolish the electoral college and elect the president by popular vote did reach the Senate floor in July 1979. The Senate voted in favor of the measure, 51 to 48, fifteen votes short of the required two-thirds majority of those present and voting needed to approve a constitutional amendment.

Supporters of the resolution blamed defections by several northern liberals for the margin of defeat. Major Jewish and black groups extensively lobbied the northern senators, arguing that the voting strength of black and Jewish voters is maximized under the electoral college system because both groups are concentrated in urban areas of the large electoral vote states.

ALTERNATIVE PLANS

Besides direct election of the president and vice president, two other major proposals to replace the electoral college have gained considerable support. One is the district plan, similar to the Maine and Nebraska systems, that would award an electoral vote to the candidate who carried a congressional district and two to the candidate who carried the state as a whole. The other is the proportional plan that would distribute a state's electoral votes on the basis of the proportion of the vote each candidate received.

Had any of the three plans been in effect since 1960, the outcome of several close elections would have been different, according to Stephen J. Wayne, professor of American Government at Georgetown University. In his book *The Road to the White House, 2000*, Wayne calculates that the district plan would have elected Richard Nixon in 1960 over John F. Kennedy, and that in 1976 it would have resulted in an electoral college tie between Gerald R. Ford and Jimmy Carter. The proportional plan would have thrown the 1960, 1968, 1992, and 1996 elections to the House of Representatives, because none of the candidates would have received an electoral vote majority.

Wayne advocated direct election, which he said would requires national systems of voting and tabulating of the results. The United States had neither at the beginning of the twenty-first century. Of the eleven presidential elections since 1960, only the 2000 election would have had a different result under direct election. As the popular vote winner, Gore would have been elected over Bush. Although the 1960 popular vote was even closer, Kennedy won both the popular and electoral college votes.

As in the 1969 plan, most of the direct election proposals call for a minimum plurality, usually 40 percent, with a runoff election to be held if no candidate receives the minimum percentage.

Presidential Disability

A decade of congressional concern over the question of presidential disability was eased in 1967 by ratification of the Twenty-fifth Amendment to the Constitution. The amendment for the first time provided for continuity in carrying out the functions of the presidency in the event of presidential disability and for filling a vacancy in the vice presidency. The amendment was approved by the Senate and House in 1965 and took effect February 10, 1967, after ratification by thirty-eight states. Congressional consideration of the problem of presidential disability had been prompted by President Dwight D. Eisenhower's heart attack in 1955. The ambiguity of the language of the disability clause (Article II, Section 1, Clause 5) of the Constitution had provoked occasional debate ever since the Constitutional Convention of 1787. But it never had been decided how far the term *disability* extended or who would be the judge of it.

Clause 5 provided that Congress should decide who was to succeed to the presidency if both the president and the vice president died, resigned, or became disabled. Congress enacted succession laws three times. By the Act of March 1, 1792, it provided for succession (after the vice president) of the president pro tempore of the Senate, then of the House Speaker; if those offices were vacant, states were to send electors to Washington to choose a new president.

That law stood until passage of the Presidential Succession Act of January 19, 1886, which changed the line of succession to run from the vice president to the secretary of state, secretary of the Treasury, and so on through the cabinet in order of rank. Sixty-one years later the Presidential Succession Act of July 18, 1947, (still in force) placed the Speaker of the House and the president pro tempore of the Senate ahead of cabinet officers in succession after the vice president.

Before ratification of the Twenty-fifth Amendment, no procedures had been laid down to govern situations arising in the event of presidential incapacity or of a vacancy in the office of vice president. Two presidents had had serious disabilities—James A. Garfield, shot in 1881 and confined to his bed until he died two and a half months later, and Woodrow Wilson, who suffered a stroke in 1919. In each case the vice president did not assume any duties of the presidency for fear he would appear to be usurping the powers of that office.

Ratification of the Twenty-fifth Amendment established procedures that clarified these areas of uncertainty in the Constitution. The amendment provided that the vice president should become acting president under either one of two circumstances: (1) if the president informed Congress of inability to perform duties, the vice president would become acting president until the president could resume normal responsibilities; (2) if the vice president and a majority of the cabinet, or another body designated by Congress, found the president to be incapacitated, the vice president would become acting president until the president informed Congress that the disability had ended. Congress was given twenty-one days to resolve any dispute over the president's disability; a two-thirds vote of both chambers was required to overrule the president's declaration of being no longer incapacitated.

VACANCY IN THE VICE PRESIDENCY

The Twenty-fifth Amendment also specified what to do when a vacancy occurred in the office of the vice president, by death, succession to the presidency, or resignation. Through February 2001, the United States has been without a vice president eighteen times for a total of forty years, but since the amendment went into effect such vacancies have been brief. Under the amendment, the president nominates a replacement vice president, with the nomination subject to confirmation by a majority vote of both chambers of Congress. Within only eight years after ratification, two presidents used the power to appoint a new vice president.

In October 1973 when Vice President Agnew resigned, President Nixon nominated Gerald Ford as the new vice president. Ford was confirmed by both houses of Congress and sworn in

Immediately after President Ronald Reagan was shot on March 30, 1981, there was some confusion at the White House over who was in charge while the president was at a Washington, D.C., hospital.

December 6, 1973. On Nixon's resignation August 9, 1974, Ford succeeded to the presidency, becoming the first president in American history who was elected neither to the presidency nor to the vice presidency. President Ford chose as his new vice president Nelson A. Rockefeller, former governor of New York, who was sworn in December 19, 1974.

With both the president and vice president holding office through appointment rather than election, members of Congress and the public expressed concern about the power of a president to appoint, in effect, his own successor. Accordingly, Sen. John O. Pastore, Rhode Island Democrat, introduced a proposed constitutional amendment February 3, 1975, to provide for a special national election for president when more than one year remained in a presidential term. Hearings were held before the Senate Judiciary Subcommittee on Constitutional Amendments, but no action was taken.

CONFUSION AFTER REAGAN SHOOTING

In the aftermath of the attempted assassination of President Ronald Reagan in March 1981, there was no need to invoke the presidential disability provisions of the Twenty-fifth Amendment. However, some of the public statements made by administration officials immediately after the president was shot by John W. Hinckley Jr. reflected continuing confusion over the issue of who is in charge when the president temporarily is unable to function. Soon after news of the shooting became known, the members of the Reagan cabinet gathered in the White House, ready to invoke the amendment's procedures, if necessary. Vice President George Bush was on an Air Force jet returning to Washington from Texas.

At a televised press briefing later that afternoon, Secretary of State Alexander M. Haig Jr. confirmed that Reagan was in surgery and under anesthesia. It was clear that he temporarily was unable to make presidential decisions should the occasion—such as a foreign attack or other national emergency—require them. Attempting to reassure the country, Haig stated that he was in control in the White House pending the return of Vice President Bush, with whom he was in contact.

This assertion was followed by a question from the press about who was making administration decisions. Haig responded, "Constitutionally, gentlemen, you have the president, the vice president, and the secretary of state in that order, and should the president decide he wants to transfer the helm to the vice president, he will do so. He has not done that. As of now, I am in control here, in the White House, pending the return of the vice president and in close touch with him. If something came up, I would check with him, of course." Actually, the Constitution is silent on the order of succession beyond the vice president. Haig was referring to succession under laws superseded by the 1947 act, which specifies that the line of succession is the vice president, the Speaker of the House, the president pro tempore of the Senate, and then the cabinet officials in order of rank.

Criticism of the administration's failure to act after Reagan was shot shaped its response to the second instance of presidential disability, Reagan's cancer surgery on July 13, 1985. This time Reagan did relinquish his powers and duties to Bush before undergoing anesthesia. Curiously, however, he did not explicitly invoke the Twenty-fifth Amendment, saying instead that he was not convinced that the amendment was meant to apply to "such brief and temporary periods of incapacity." Still, a precedent was established that the Twenty-fifth Amendment would work as intended in future administrations. This precedent was followed in May 1991 when President Bush said he would turn power over to Vice President Dan Quayle if his irregular heartbeat required electroshock therapy. It did not.

Electoral Votes for President, 1789–2000

Electoral maps and vote charts for all presidential elections from 1789 to 2000 are presented in this section (pages 173–230). The sources for electoral votes cast for presidential candidates are the *Senate Manual* (Washington, D.C., U.S. Government Printing Office, 1997), and *CQ Weekly Report*.

Article II, Section 1 of the Constitution gives each state a number of electors equal to the number of senators and representatives to which it is entitled. Total electoral votes for each state through the 2000 election were compiled from a chart of each apportionment of the House of Representatives, published in Kenneth C. Martis and Gregory A. Elmes, *The Historical Atlas of State Power in Congress, 1790–1990* (Washington, D.C., Congressional Quarterly, 1993), pp. 6–7.

Under the Constitution (Article II, Section 1) each presidential elector was originally given two votes and was required to cast each vote for a different person. The person receiving the highest number of votes from a majority of electors was elected president; the person receiving the second highest total became vice president. For the first presidential election in 1789, there were 69 electors, and Washington's 69 votes constituted a unanimous election. After ratification of the Twelfth Amendment in 1804, electors were required to designate which of their two votes was for president and which was for vice president. The electoral college charts on pages 174–177 show *all* electoral votes cast in the elections of 1789, 1792, 1796, and 1800; the charts for 1804 and thereafter show electoral votes cast only for president.

For electoral votes cast for vice-presidential candidates, see pages 228–230 at the end of this chapter.

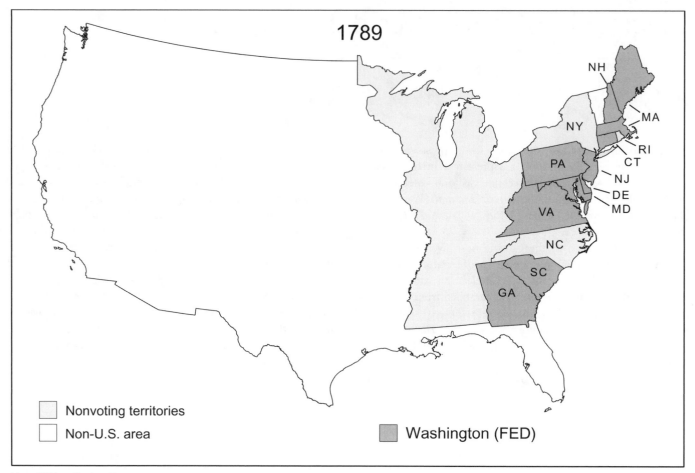

Key: FED—Federalist

States	Electoral votes[1]	Washington	Adams	Jay	Harrison	Rutledge	Hancock	Clinton	Huntington	Milton	Armstrong	Lincoln	Telfair
Connecticut[2]	(14)	7	5	–	–	–	–	–	2	–	–	–	–
Delaware	(6)	3	–	3	–	–	–	–	–	–	–	–	–
Georgia[2]	(10)	5	–	–	–	–	–	–	–	2	1	1	1
Maryland[3]	(16)	6	–	–	6	–	–	–	–	–	–	–	–
Massachusetts	(20)	10	10	–	–	–	–	–	–	–	–	–	–
New Hampshire	(10)	5	5	–	–	–	–	–	–	–	–	–	–
New Jersey[2]	(12)	6	1	5	–	–	–	–	–	–	–	–	–
New York[4]	(16)	–	–	–	–	–	–	–	–	–	–	–	–
North Carolina[5]	(14)	–	–	–	–	–	–	–	–	–	–	–	–
Pennsylvania[2]	(20)	10	8	–	–	–	2	–	–	–	–	–	–
Rhode Island[5]	(6)	–	–	–	–	–	–	–	–	–	–	–	–
South Carolina[2]	(14)	7	–	–	–	6	1	–	–	–	–	–	–
Virginia[6]	(24)	10	5	1	–	–	1	3	–	–	–	–	–
Totals	(182)	69	34	9	6	6	4	3	2	2	1	1	1

1. Two votes for each elector; see explanation, p. 172.
2. For explanation of split electoral votes, see p. 158.
3. Two Maryland electors did not vote.
4. Not voting. Because of a dispute between its two chambers, the New York legislature failed to choose electors.
5. Not voting because had not yet ratified the Constitution.
6. Two Virginia electors did not vote. For explanation of split electoral votes, see p. 158.

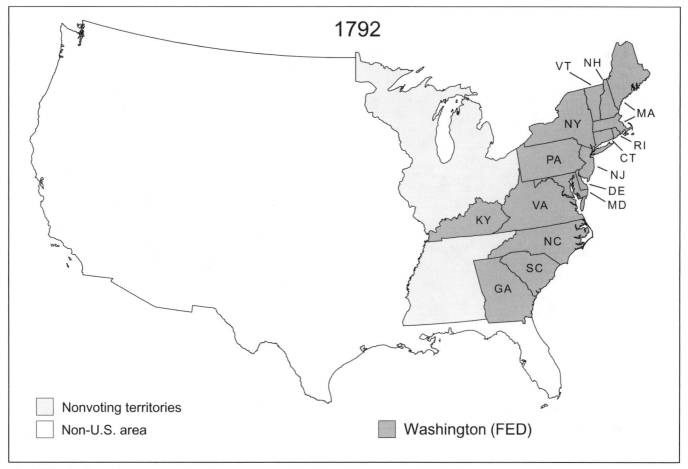

1792

Nonvoting territories
Non-U.S. area

Washington (FED)

Key: FED—Federalist

States	Electoral votes[1]	Washington	Adams	Clinton	Jefferson	Burr
Connecticut	(18)	9	9	–	–	–
Delaware	(6)	3	3	–	–	–
Georgia	(8)	4	–	4	–	–
Kentucky	(8)	4	–	–	4	–
Maryland[2]	(20)	8	8	–	–	–
Massachusetts	(32)	16	16	–	–	–
New Hampshire	(12)	6	6	–	–	–
New Jersey	(14)	7	7	–	–	–
New York	(24)	12	–	12	–	–
North Carolina	(24)	12	–	12	–	–
Pennsylvania3	(30)	15	14	1	–	–
Rhode Island	(8)	4	4	–	–	–
South Carolina3	(16)	8	7	–	–	1
Vermont2	(8)	3	3	–	–	–
Virginia	(42)	21	–	21	–	–
Totals	(270)	132	77	50	4	1

1. Two votes for each elector; see explanation, p. 172.
2. Two Maryland electors and one Vermont elector did not vote.
3. For explanation of split electoral votes, see p. 158.

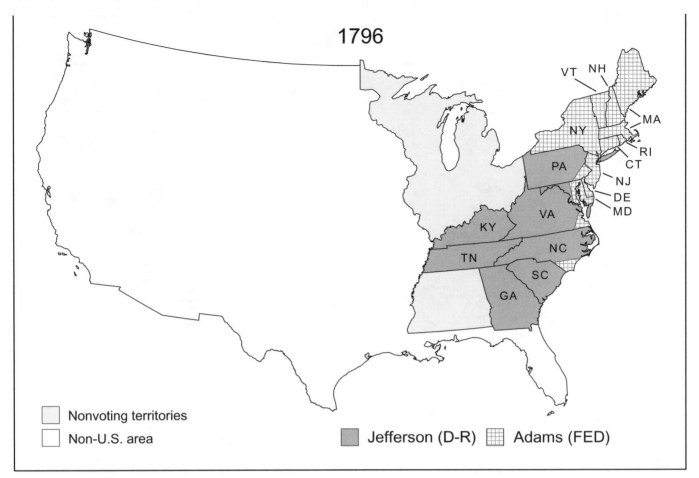

1796

Nonvoting territories

Non-U.S. area

Jefferson (D-R) ⊞ Adams (FED)

Key: D-R—Democratic-Republican; FED—Federalist

States	Electoral votes[1]	J. Adams	Jefferson	T. Pinckney	Burr	S. Adams	Ellsworth	Clinton	Jay	Iredell	Henry	Johnston	Washington	C. Pinckney
Connecticut[2]	(18)	9	–	4	–	–	–	–	5	–	–	–	–	–
Delaware	(6)	3	–	3	–	–	–	–	–	–	–	–	–	–
Georgia	(8)	–	4	–	–	–	–	4	–	–	–	–	–	–
Kentucky	(8)	–	4	–	4	–	–	–	–	–	–	–	–	–
Maryland[2]	(20)	7	4	4	3	–	–	–	–	–	2	–	–	–
Massachusetts[2]	(32)	16	–	13	–	–	1	–	–	–	–	2	–	–
New Hampshire	(12)	6	–	–	–	–	6	–	–	–	–	–	–	–
New Jersey	(14)	7	–	7	–	–	–	–	–	–	–	–	–	–
New York	(24)	12	–	12	–	–	–	–	–	–	–	–	–	–
North Carolina[2]	(24)	1	11	1	6	–	–	–	–	3	–	–	1	1
Pennsylvania[2]	(30)	1	14	2	13	–	–	–	–	–	–	–	–	–
Rhode Island	(8)	4	–	–	–	–	4	–	–	–	–	–	–	–
South Carolina	(16)	–	8	8	–	–	–	–	–	–	–	–	–	–
Tennessee	(6)	–	3	–	3	–	–	–	–	–	–	–	–	–
Vermont	(8)	4	–	4	–	–	–	–	–	–	–	–	–	–
Virginia[2]	(42)	1	20	1	1	15	–	3	–	–	–	–	1	–
Totals	(276)	71	68	59	30	15	11	7	5	3	2	2	2	1

1. Two votes for each elector; see explanation, p. 172.
2. For explanation of split electoral votes, see p. 158.

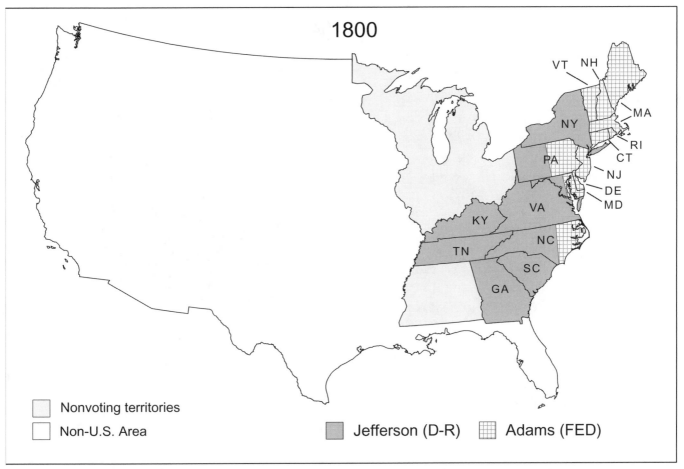

Key: D-R—Democratic-Republican; FED—Federalist

States	Electoral Vote[1]	Jefferson[2]	Burr[2]	Adams	Pinckney	Jay	States	Electoral votes[1]	Jefferson[2]	Burr[2]	Adams	Pinckney	Jay
Connecticut	(18)	–	–	9	9	–	North Carolina[3]	(24)	8	8	4	4	–
Delaware	(6)	–	–	3	3	–	Pennsylvania[3]	(30)	8	8	7	7	–
Georgia	(8)	4	4	–	–	–	Rhode Island[3]	(8)	–	–	4	3	1
Kentucky	(8)	4	4	–	–	–	South Carolina	(16)	8	8	–	–	–
Maryland[3]	(20)	5	5	5	5	–	Tennessee	(6)	3	3	–	–	–
Massachusetts	(32)	–	–	16	16	–	Vermont	(8)	–	–	4	4	–
New Hampshire	(12)	–	–	6	6	–	Virginia	(42)	21	21	–	–	–
New Jersey	(14)	–	–	7	7	–							
New York	(24)	12	12	–	–	–	Totals	(276)	73	73	65	64	1

1. Two votes for each elector; see explanation, p. 172.
2. Since Jefferson and Burr tied in the electoral college, the election was decided (in Jefferson's favor) by the House of Representatives. See "Jefferson's Revenge: 1800," p. 19.
3. For explanation of split electoral votes, see p. 158.

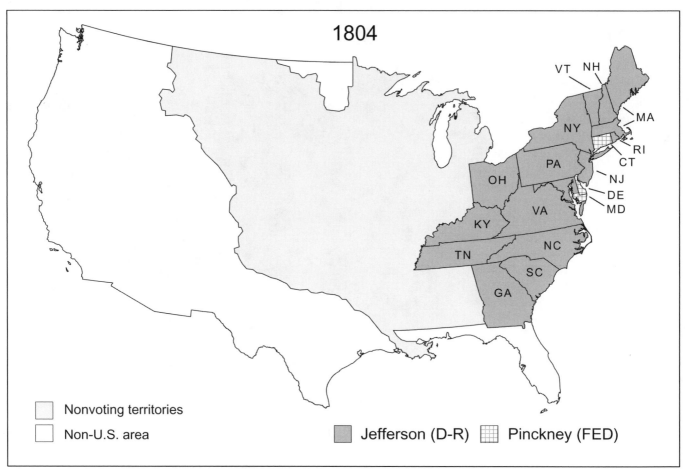

1804

Nonvoting territories

Non-U.S. area

Jefferson (D-R)   Pinckney (FED)

Key: D-R—Democratic-Republican; FED—Federalist

States	Electoral votes	Jefferson	Pinckney	States	Electoral votes	Jefferson	Pinckney
Connecticut	(9)	–	9	Ohio	(3)	3	–
Delaware	(3)	–	3	Pennsylvania	(20)	20	–
Georgia	(6)	6	–	Rhode Island	(4)	4	–
Kentucky	(8)	8	–	South Carolina	(10)	10	–
Maryland[1]	(11)	9	2	Tennessee	(5)	5	–
Massachusetts	(19)	19	–	Vermont	(6)	6	–
New Hampshire	(7)	7	–	Virginia	(24)	24	–
New Jersey	(8)	8	–				
New York	(19)	19	–	Totals	(176)	162	14
North Carolina	(14)	14	–				

1. For explanation of split electoral votes, see p. 158.

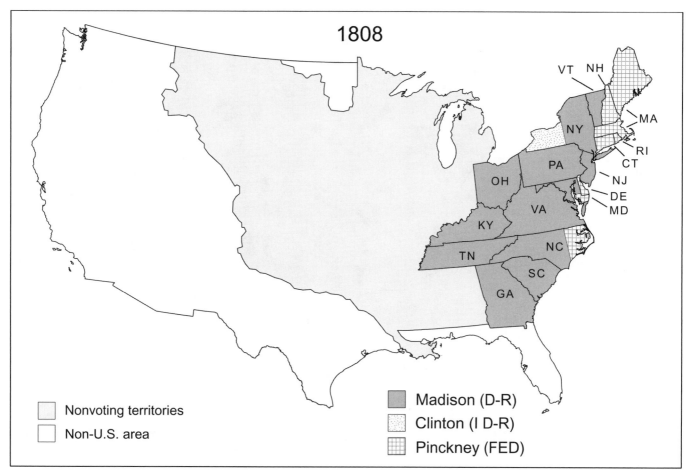

1808

Nonvoting territories

Non-U.S. area

Madison (D-R)

Clinton (I D-R)

Pinckney (FED)

Key: D-R—Democratic-Republican; FED—Federalist; I D-R—Independent Democratic-Republican

States	Electoral votes	Madison	Pinckney	Clinton	States	Electoral votes	Madison	Pinckney	Clinton
Connecticut	(9)	–	9	–	Ohio	(3)	3	–	–
Delaware	(3)	–	3	–	Pennsylvania	(20)	20	–	–
Georgia	(6)	6	–	–	Rhode Island	(4)	–	4	–
Kentucky[1]	(8)	7	–	–	South Carolina	(10)	10	–	–
Maryland[2]	(11)	9	2	–	Tennessee	(5)	5	–	–
Massachusetts	(19)	–	19	–	Vermont	(6)	6	–	–
New Hampshire	(7)	–	7	–	Virginia	(24)	24	–	–
New Jersey	(8)	8	–	–					
New York[2]	(19)	13	–	6	Totals	(176)	122	47	6
North Carolina[2]	(14)	11	3	–					

1. One Kentucky elector did not vote.
2. For explanation of split electoral votes, see p. 158.

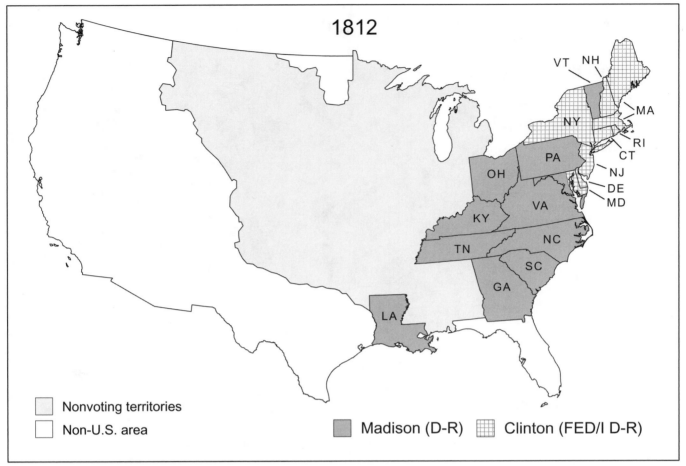

Key: D-R—Democratic-Republican; FED/I D-R—Federalist/Independent Democratic-Republican

States	Electoral votes	Madison	Clinton	States	Electoral votes	Madison	Clinton
Connecticut	(9)	–	9	North Carolina	(15)	15	–
Delaware	(4)	–	4	Ohio[2]	(8)	7	–
Georgia	(8)	8	–	Pennsylvania	(25)	25	–
Kentucky	(12)	12	–	Rhode Island	(4)	–	4
Louisiana	(3)	3	–	South Carolina	(11)	11	–
Maryland[1]	(11)	6	5	Tennessee	(8)	8	–
Massachusetts	(22)	–	22	Vermont	(8)	8	–
New Hampshire	(8)	–	8	Virginia	(25)	25	–
New Jersey	(8)	–	8				
New York	(29)	–	29	Totals	(218)	128	89

1. For explanation of split electoral votes, see p. 158.
2. One Ohio elector did not vote.

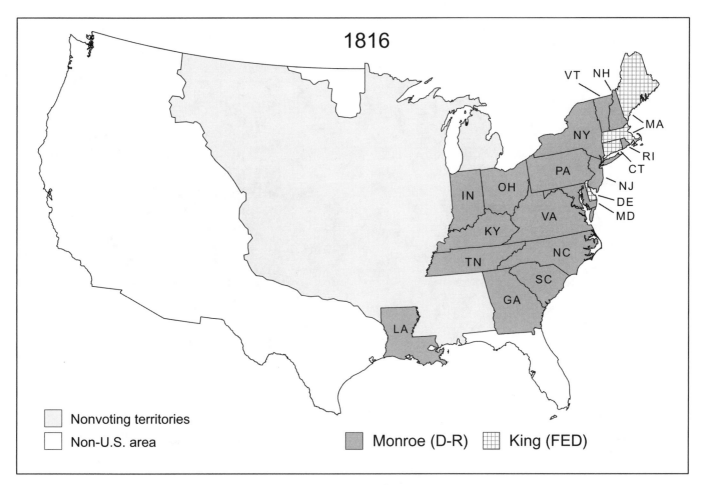

1816

Nonvoting territories

Non-U.S. area

Monroe (D-R)   King (FED)

Key: D-R—Democratic-Republican; FED—Federalist

States	Electoral votes	Monroe	King	States	Electoral votes	Monroe	King
Connecticut	(9)	–	9	North Carolina	(15)	15	–
Delaware[1]	(4)	–	3	Ohio	(8)	8	–
Georgia	(8)	8	–	Pennsylvania	(25)	25	–
Indiana	(3)	3	–	Rhode Island	(4)	4	–
Kentucky	(12)	12	–	South Carolina	(11)	11	–
Louisiana	(3)	3	–	Tennessee	(8)	8	–
Maryland[1]	(11)	8	–	Vermont	(8)	8	–
Massachusetts	(22)	–	22	Virginia	(25)	25	–
New Hampshire	(8)	8	–				
New Jersey	(8)	8	–	Totals	(221)	183	34
New York	(29)	29	–				

1. One Delaware and three Maryland electors did not vote.

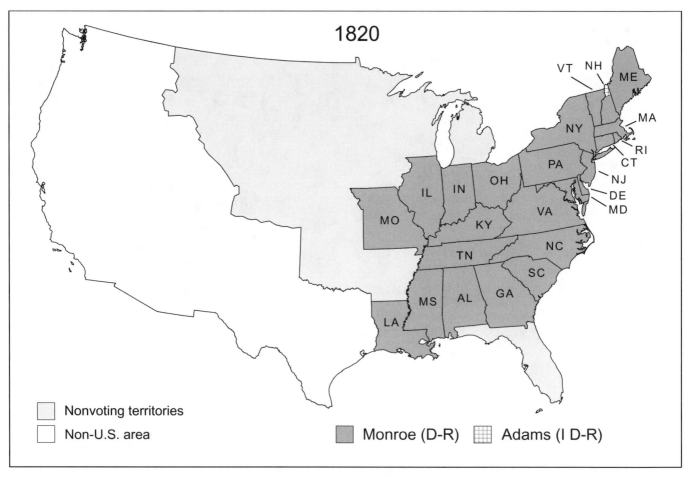

1820

Key: Nonvoting territories
Non-U.S. area
Monroe (D-R) Adams (I D-R)

Key: D-R—Democratic-Republican; I D-R Independent Democratic-Republican

States	Electoral votes	Monroe	Adams	States	Electoral votes	Monroe	Adams
Alabama	(3)	3	–	New Hampshire[2]	(8)	7	1
Connecticut	(9)	9	–	New Jersey	(8)	8	–
Delaware	(4)	4	–	New York	(29)	29	–
Georgia	(8)	8	–	North Carolina	(15)	15	–
Illinois	(3)	3	–	Ohio	(8)	8	–
Indiana	(3)	3	–	Pennsylvania[1]	(25)	24	–
Kentucky	(12)	12	–	Rhode Island	(4)	4	–
Louisiana	(3)	3	–	South Carolina	(11)	11	–
Maine	(9)	9	–	Tennessee[1]	(8)	7	–
Maryland	(11)	11	–	Vermont	(8)	8	–
Massachusetts	(15)	15	–	Virginia	(25)	25	–
Mississippi[1]	(3)	2	–				
Missouri	(3)	3	–	Totals	(235)	231	1

1. One elector each from Mississippi, Pennsylvania, and Tennessee did not vote.
2. For explanation of split electoral votes, see p. 158.

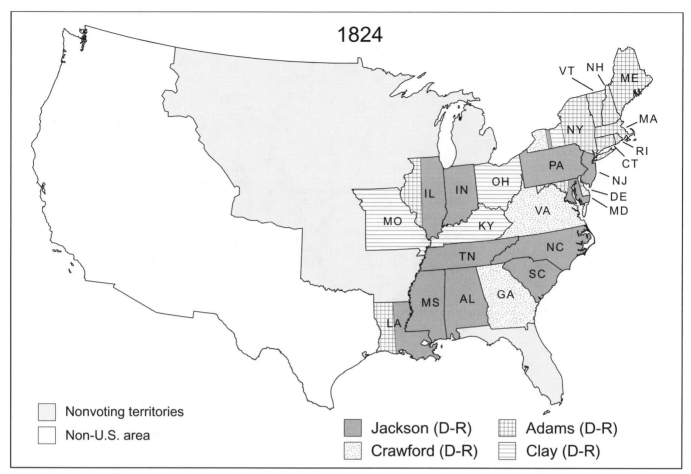

1824

Nonvoting territories

Non-U.S. area

Jackson (D-R)   Adams (D-R)

Crawford (D-R)   Clay (D-R)

Key: D-R—Democratic-Republican

States	Electoral votes	Jackson	Adams	Crawford	Clay	States	Electoral votes	Jackson	Adams	Crawford	Clay
Alabama	(5)	5	–	–	–	New Hampshire	(8)	–	8	–	–
Connecticut	(8)	–	8	–	–	New Jersey	(8)	8	–	–	–
Delaware[1]	(3)	–	1	2	–	New York[1]	(36)	1	26	5	4
Georgia	(9)	–	–	9	–	North Carolina	(15)	15	–	–	–
Illinois[1]	(3)	2	1	–	–	Ohio	(16)	–	–	–	16
Indiana	(5)	5	–	–	–	Pennsylvania	(28)	28	–	–	–
Kentucky	(14)	–	–	–	14	Rhode Island	(4)	–	4	–	–
Louisiana[1]	(5)	3	2	–	–	South Carolina	(11)	11	–	–	–
Maine	(9)	–	9	–	–	Tennessee	(11)	11	–	–	–
Maryland[1]	(11)	7	3	1	–	Vermont	(7)	–	7	–	–
Massachusetts	(15)	–	15	–	–	Virginia	(24)	–	–	24	–
Mississippi	(3)	3	–	–	–						
Missouri	(3)	–	–	–	3	Totals	(261)	99[2]	84	41	37

1.   For explanation of split electoral votes, see p. 158.

2.   As no candidate received a majority of the electoral votes, the election was decided (in Adams's favor) by the House of Representatives.

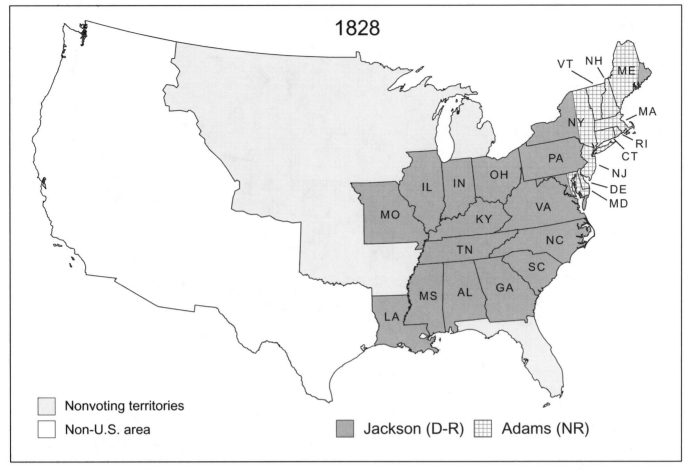

1828

Nonvoting territories

Non-U.S. area

Jackson (D-R)   Adams (NR)

Key: D-R—Democratic-Republican; NR—National Republican

States	Electoral votes	Jackson	Adams	States	Electoral votes	Jackson	Adams
Alabama	(5)	5	–	New Hampshire	(8)	–	8
Connecticut	(8)	–	8	New Jersey	(8)	–	8
Delaware	(3)	–	3	New York[1]	(36)	20	16
Georgia	(9)	9	–	North Carolina	(15)	15	–
Illinois	(3)	3	–	Ohio	(16)	16	–
Indiana	(5)	5	–	Pennsylvania	(28)	28	–
Kentucky	(14)	14	–	Rhode Island	(4)	–	4
Louisiana	(5)	5	–	South Carolina	(11)	11	–
Maine[1]	(9)	1	8	Tennessee	(11)	11	–
Maryland[1]	(11)	5	6	Vermont	(7)	–	7
Massachusetts	(15)	–	15	Virginia	(24)	24	–
Mississippi	(3)	3	–				
Missouri	(3)	3	–	Totals	(261)	178	83

1. For explanation of split electoral votes, see p. 158.

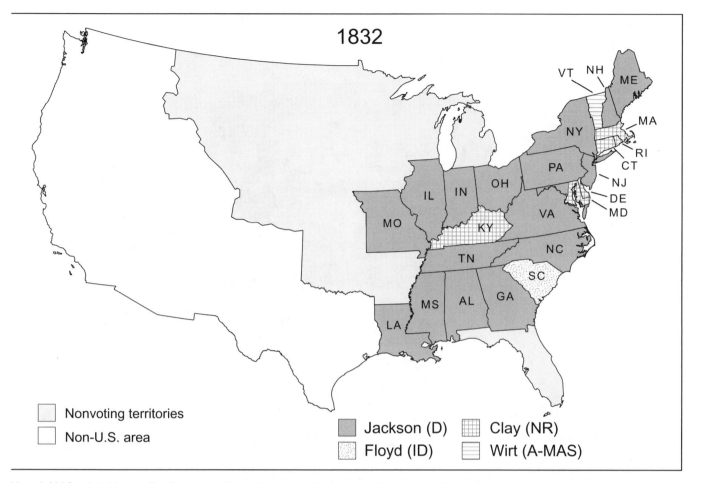

1832

Nonvoting territories
Non-U.S. area

Jackson (D)   Clay (NR)
Floyd (ID)   Wirt (A-MAS)

Key: A-MAS—Anti-Mason; D—Democrat; ID—Independent Democrat; NR—National Republican

States	Electoral votes	Jackson	Clay	Floyd	Wirt	States	Electoral votes	Jackson	Clay	Floyd	Wirt
Alabama	(7)	7	–	–	–	New Hampshire	(7)	7	–	–	–
Connecticut	(8)	–	8	–	–	New Jersey	(8)	8	–	–	–
Delaware	(3)	–	3	–	–	New York	(42)	42	–	–	–
Georgia	(11)	11	–	–	–	North Carolina	(15)	15	–	–	–
Illinois	(5)	5	–	–	–	Ohio	(21)	21	–	–	–
Indiana	(9)	9	–	–	–	Pennsylvania	(30)	30	–	–	–
Kentucky	(15)	–	15	–	–	Rhode Island	(4)	–	4	–	–
Louisiana	(5)	5	–	–	–	South Carolina	(11)	–	–	11	–
Maine	(10)	10	–	–	–	Tennessee	(15)	15	–	–	–
Maryland[1]	(10)	3	5	–	–	Vermont	(7)	–	–	–	7
Massachusetts	(14)	–	14	–	–	Virginia	(23)	23	–	–	–
Mississippi	(4)	4	–	–	–						
Missouri	(4)	4	–	–	–	Totals	(288)	219	49	11	7

1. Two Maryland electors did not vote. For explanation of split electoral votes, see p. 158.

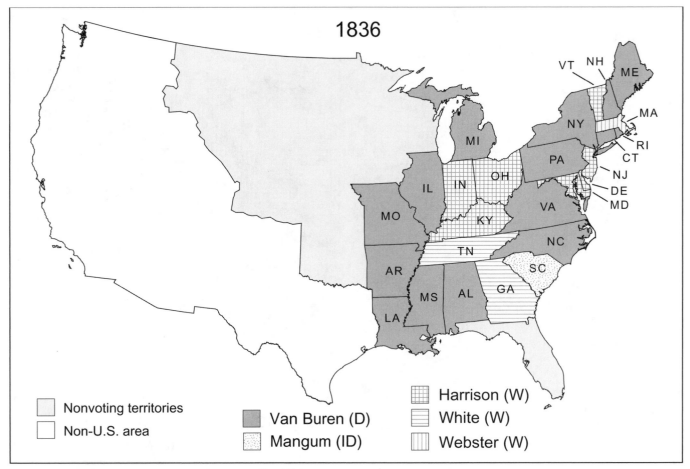

1836

Key: D—Democrat; ID—Independent Democrat; W—Whig

States	Electoral votes	Van Buren	Harrison[1]	White[1]	Webster[1]	Mangum
Alabama	(7)	7	–	–	–	–
Arkansas	(3)	3	–	–	–	–
Connecticut	(8)	8	–	–	–	–
Delaware	(3)	–	3	–	–	–
Georgia	(11)	–	–	11	–	–
Illinois	(5)	5	–	–	–	–
Indiana	(9)	–	9	–	–	–
Kentucky	(15)	–	15	–	–	–
Louisiana	(5)	5	–	–	–	–
Maine	(10)	10	–	–	–	–
Maryland	(10)	–	10	–	–	–
Massachusetts	(14)	–	–	–	14	–
Michigan	(3)	3	–	–	–	–
Mississippi	(4)	4	–	–	–	–
Missouri	(4)	4	–	–	–	–
New Hampshire	(7)	7	–	–	–	–
New Jersey	(8)	–	8	–	–	–
New York	(42)	42	–	–	–	–
North Carolina	(15)	15	–	–	–	–
Ohio	(21)	–	21	–	–	–
Pennsylvania	(30)	30	–	–	–	–
Rhode Island	(4)	4	–	–	–	–
South Carolina	(11)	–	–	–	–	11
Tennessee	(15)	–	–	15	–	–
Vermont	(7)	–	7	–	–	–
Virginia	(23)	23	–	–	–	–
Totals	(294)	170	73	26	14	11

1. For an explanation of the Whigs' strategy in running several candidates, see "Van Buren's 1836 Win," p. 27.

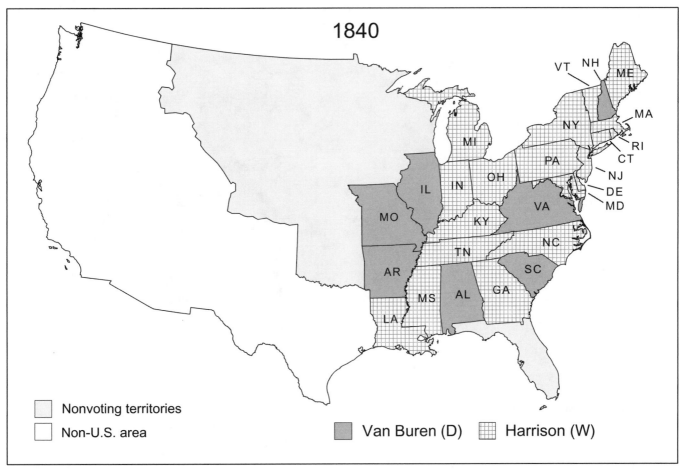

Key: D—Democrat; W—Whig

States	Electoral votes	Harrison	Van Buren	States	Electoral votes	Harrison	Van Buren
Alabama	(7)	–	7	Missouri	(4)	–	4
Arkansas	(3)	–	3	New Hampshire	(7)	–	7
Connecticut	(8)	8	–	New Jersey	(8)	8	–
Delaware	(3)	3	–	New York	(42)	42	–
Georgia	(11)	11	–	North Carolina	(15)	15	–
Illinois	(5)	–	5	Ohio	(21)	21	–
Indiana	(9)	9	–	Pennsylvania	(30)	30	–
Kentucky	(15)	15	–	Rhode Island	(4)	4	–
Louisiana	(5)	5	–	South Carolina	(11)	–	11
Maine	(10)	10	–	Tennessee	(15)	15	–
Maryland	(10)	10	–	Vermont	(7)	7	–
Massachusetts	(14)	14	–	Virginia	(23)	–	23
Michigan	(3)	3	–				
Mississippi	(4)	4	–	Totals	(294)	234	60

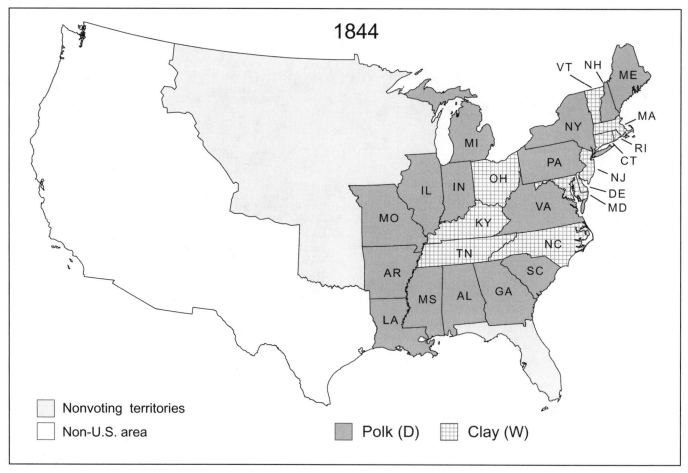

1844

Nonvoting territories

Non-U.S. area

Polk (D)   Clay (W)

Key: D—Democrat; W—Whig

States	Electoral votes	Polk	Clay	States	Electoral votes	Polk	Clay
Alabama	(9)	9	–	Missouri	(7)	7	–
Arkansas	(3)	3	–	New Hampshire	(6)	6	–
Connecticut	(6)	–	6	New Jersey	(7)	–	7
Delaware	(3)	–	3	New York	(36)	36	–
Georgia	(10)	10	–	North Carolina	(11)	–	11
Illinois	(9)	9	–	Ohio	(23)	–	23
Indiana	(12)	12	–	Pennsylvania	(26)	26	–
Kentucky	(12)	–	12	Rhode Island	(4)	–	4
Louisiana	(6)	6	–	South Carolina	(9)	9	–
Maine	(9)	9	–	Tennessee	(13)	–	13
Maryland	(8)	–	8	Vermont	(6)	–	6
Massachusetts	(12)	–	12	Virginia	(17)	17	–
Michigan	(5)	5	–				
Mississippi	(6)	6	–	Totals	(275)	170	105

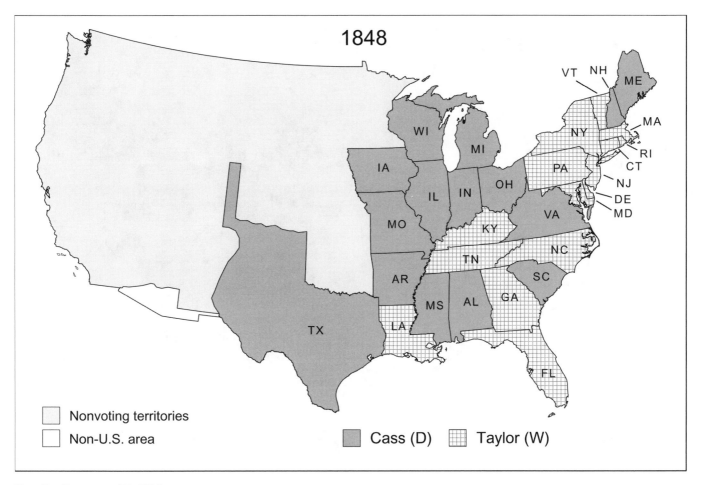

Key: D—Democrat; W—Whig

States	Electoral votes	Taylor	Cass	States	Electoral votes	Taylor	Cass
Alabama	(9)	–	9	Missouri	(7)	–	7
Arkansas	(3)	–	3	New Hampshire	(6)	–	6
Connecticut	(6)	6	–	New Jersey	(7)	7	–
Delaware	(3)	3	–	New York	(36)	36	–
Florida	(3)	3	–	North Carolina	(11)	11	–
Georgia	(10)	10	–	Ohio	(23)	–	23
Illinois	(9)	–	9	Pennsylvania	(26)	26	–
Indiana	(12)	–	12	Rhode Island	(4)	4	–
Iowa	(4)	–	4	South Carolina	(9)	–	9
Kentucky	(12)	12	–	Tennessee	(13)	13	–
Louisiana	(6)	6	–	Texas	(4)	–	4
Maine	(9)	–	9	Vermont	(6)	6	–
Maryland	(8)	8	–	Virginia	(17)	–	17
Massachusetts	(12)	12	–	Wisconsin	(4)	–	4
Michigan	(5)		5				
Mississippi	(6)	–	6	Totals	(290)	163	127

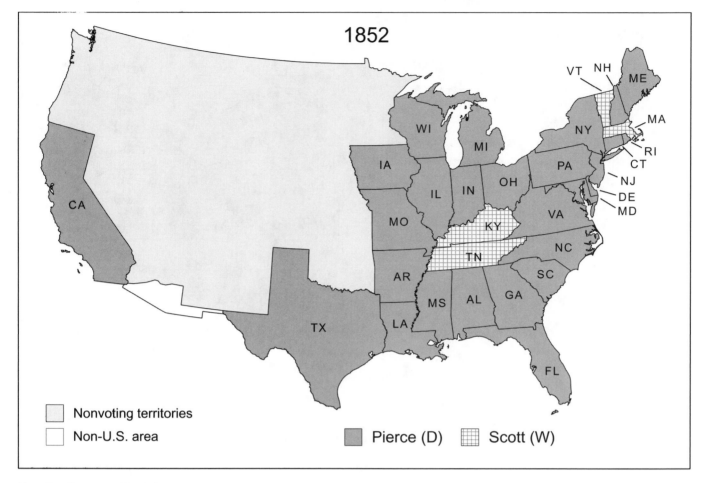

1852

Nonvoting territories

Non-U.S. area

Pierce (D)   Scott (W)

Key: D—Democrat; W—Whig

States	Electoral votes	Pierce	Scott	States	Electoral votes	Pierce	Scott
Alabama	(9)	9	–	Missouri	(9)	9	–
Arkansas	(4)	4	–	New Hampshire	(5)	5	–
California	(4)	4	–	New Jersey	(7)	7	–
Connecticut	(6)	6	–	New York	(35)	35	–
Delaware	(3)	3	–	North Carolina	(10)	10	–
Florida	(3)	3	–	Ohio	(23)	23	–
Georgia	(10)	10	–	Pennsylvania	(27)	27	–
Illinois	(11)	11	–	Rhode Island	(4)	4	–
Indiana	(13)	13	–	South Carolina	(8)	8	–
Iowa	(4)	4	–	Tennessee	(12)	–	12
Kentucky	(12)	–	12	Texas	(4)	4	–
Louisiana	(6)	6	–	Vermont	(5)	–	5
Maine	(8)	8	–	Virginia	(15)	15	–
Maryland	(8)	8	–	Wisconsin	(5)	5	–
Massachusetts	(13)	–	13				
Michigan	(6)	6	–	Totals	(296)	254	42
Mississippi	(7)	7	–				

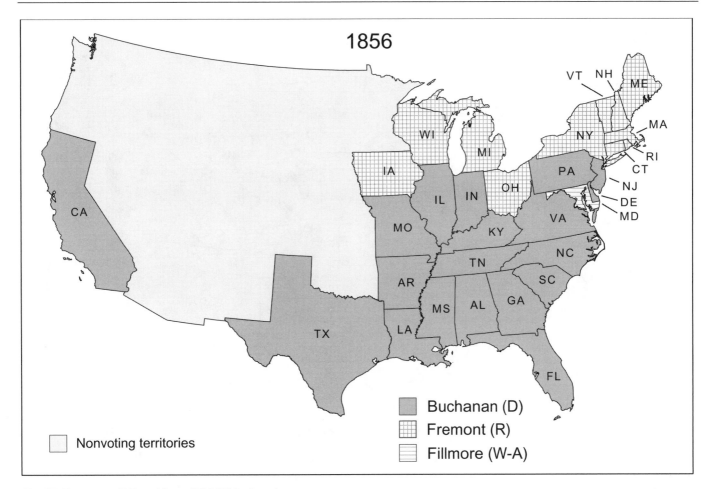

1856

Buchanan (D)
Fremont (R)
Fillmore (W-A)

Nonvoting territories

Key:°D Democrat; R Republican; W-A Whig-American

States	Electoral votes	Buchanan	Fremont	Fillmore	States	Electoral votes	Buchanan	Fremont	Fillmore
Alabama	(9)	9	–	–	Missouri	(9)	9	–	–
Arkansas	(4)	4	–	–	New Hampshire	(5)	–	5	–
California	(4)	4	–	–	New Jersey	(7)	7	–	–
Connecticut	(6)	–	6	–	New York	(35)	–	35	–
Delaware	(3)	3	–	–	North Carolina	(10)	10	–	–
Florida	(3)	3	–	–	Ohio	(23)	–	23	–
Georgia	(10)	10	–	–	Pennsylvania	(27)	27	–	–
Illinois	(11)	11	–	–	Rhode Island	(4)	–	4	–
Indiana	(13)	13	–	–	South Carolina	(8)	8	–	–
Iowa	(4)	–	4	–	Tennessee	(12)	12	–	–
Kentucky	(12)	12	–	–	Texas	(4)	4	–	–
Louisiana	(6)	6	–	–	Vermont	(5)	–	5	–
Maine	(8)	–	8	–	Virginia	(15)	15	–	–
Maryland	(8)	–	–	8	Wisconsin	(5)	–	5	–
Massachusetts	(13)	–	13	–					
Michigan	(6)	–	6	–	Totals	(296)	174	114	8
Mississippi	(7)	7	–	–					

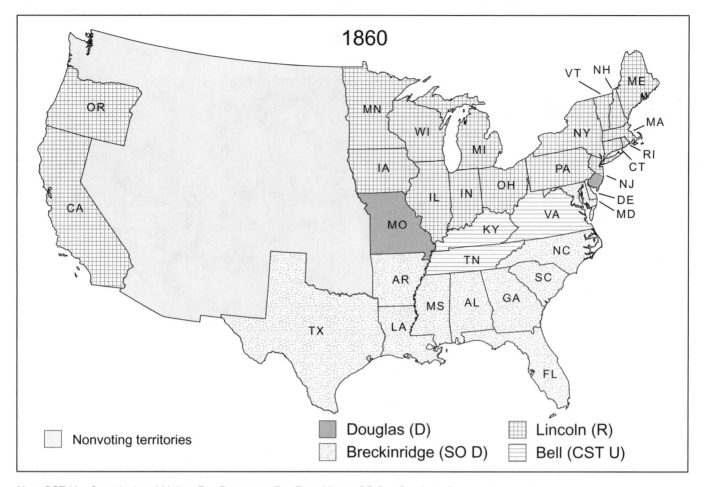

1860

Nonvoting territories

Douglas (D)

Breckinridge (SO D)

Lincoln (R)

Bell (CST U)

Key: CST U—Constitutional Union; D—Democrat; R—Republican; SO D—Southern Democrat

States	Electoral votes	Lincoln	Breckinridge	Bell	Douglas	States	Electoral votes	Lincoln	Breckinridge	Bell	Douglas
Alabama	(9)	–	9	–	–	Missouri	(9)	–	–	–	9
Arkansas	(4)	–	4	–	–	New Hampshire	(5)	5	–	–	–
California	(4)	4	–	–	–	New Jersey[1]	(7)	4	–	–	3
Connecticut	(6)	6	–	–	–	New York	(35)	35	–	–	–
Delaware	(3)	–	3	–	–	North Carolina	(10)	–	10	–	–
Florida	(3)	–	3	–	–	Ohio	(23)	23	–	–	–
Georgia	(10)	–	10	–	–	Oregon	(3)	3	–	–	–
Illinois	(11)	11	–	–	–	Pennsylvania	(27)	27	–	–	–
Indiana	(13)	13	–	–	–	Rhode Island	(4)	4	–	–	–
Iowa	(4)	4	–	–	–	South Carolina	(8)	–	8	–	–
Kentucky	(12)	–	–	12	–	Tennessee	(12)	–	–	12	–
Louisiana	(6)	–	6	–	–	Texas	(4)	–	4	–	–
Maine	(8)	8	–	–	–	Vermont	(5)	5	–	–	–
Maryland	(8)	–	8	–	–	Virginia	(15)	–	–	15	–
Massachusetts	(13)	13	–	–	–	Wisconsin	(5)	5	–	–	–
Michigan	(6)	6	–	–	–						
Minnesota	(4)	4	–	–	–	Totals	(303)	180	72	39	12
Mississippi	(7)	–	7	–	–						

1. For explanation of split electoral votes, see p. 158

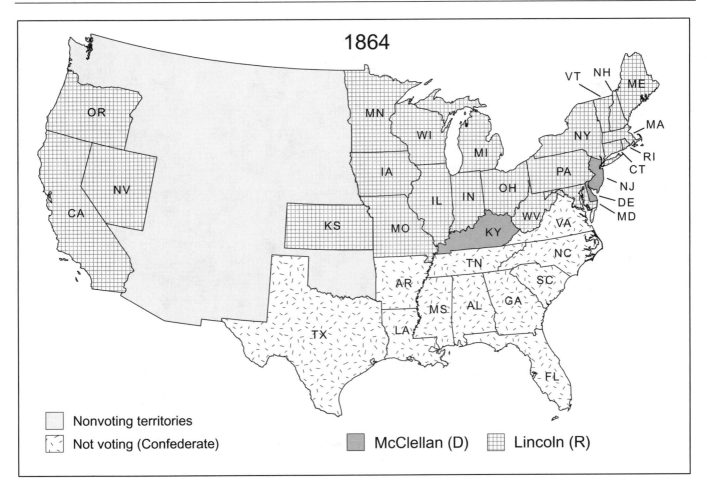

Key: D—Democrat; R—Republican

States[1]	Electoral votes	Lincoln	McClellan	States[1]	Electoral votes	Lincoln	McClellan
California	(5)	5	–	Nevada[2]	(3)	2	–
Connecticut	(6)	6	–	New Hampshire	(5)	5	–
Delaware	(3)	–	3	New Jersey	(7)	–	7
Illinois	(16)	16	–	New York	(33)	33	–
Indiana	(13)	13	–	Ohio	(21)	21	–
Iowa	(8)	8	–	Oregon	(3)	3	–
Kansas	(3)	3	–	Pennsylvania	(26)	26	–
Kentucky	(11)	–	11	Rhode Island	(4)	4	–
Maine	(7)	7	–	Vermont	(5)	5	–
Maryland	(7)	7	–	West Virginia	(5)	5	–
Massachusetts	(12)	12	–	Wisconsin	(8)	8	–
Michigan	(8)	8	–				
Minnesota	(4)	4	–	Totals	(234)	212	21
Missouri	(11)	11	–				

1. Eleven southern states—Alabama, Arkansas, Florida, Georgia, Louisiana, Mississippi, North Carolina, South Carolina, Tennessee, Texas, and Virginia—had seceded from the Union and did not vote.
2. One Nevada elector did not vote.

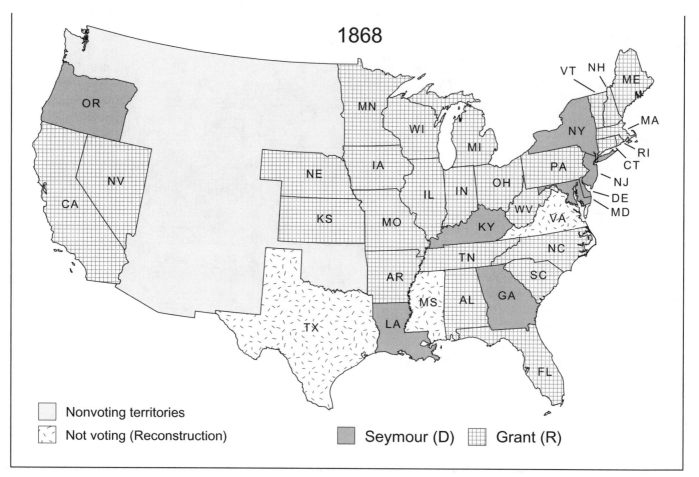

1868

Key: D—Democrat; R—Republican

States[1]	Electoral votes	Grant	Seymour	States[1]	Electoral votes	Grant	Seymour
Alabama	(8)	8	–	Missouri	(11)	11	–
Arkansas	(5)	5	–	Nebraska	(3)	3	–
California	(5)	5	–	Nevada	(3)	3	–
Connecticut	(6)	6	–	New Hampshire	(5)	5	–
Delaware	(3)	–	3	New Jersey	(7)	–	7
Florida	(3)	3	–	New York	(33)	–	33
Georgia	(9)	–	9	North Carolina	(9)	9	–
Illinois	(16)	16	–	Ohio	(21)	21	–
Indiana	(13)	13	–	Oregon	(3)	–	3
Iowa	(8)	8	–	Pennsylvania	(26)	26	–
Kansas	(3)	3	–	Rhode Island	(4)	4	–
Kentucky	(11)	–	11	South Carolina	(6)	6	–
Louisiana	(7)	–	7	Tennessee	(10)	10	–
Maine	(7)	7	–	Vermont	(5)	5	–
Maryland	(7)	–	7	West Virginia	(5)	5	–
Massachusetts	(12)	12	–	Wisconsin	(8)	8	–
Michigan	(8)	8	–				
Minnesota	(4)	4	–	Totals	(294)	214	80

1. Mississippi, Texas, and Virginia were not yet readmitted to the Union and did not participate in the election.

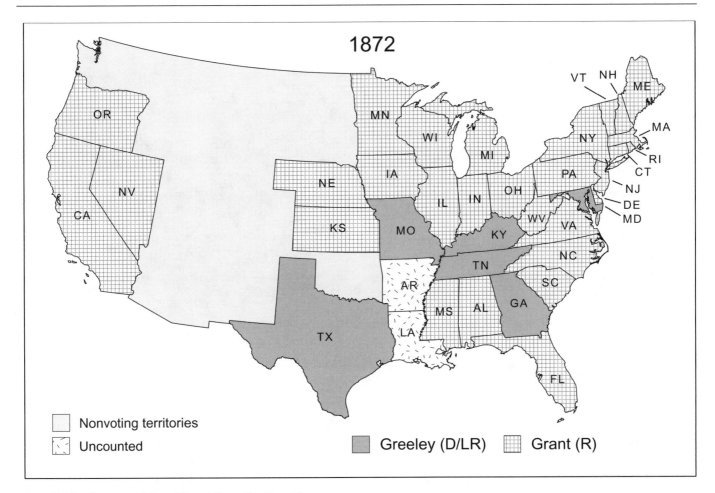

1872

Key: D/LR—Democrat/Liberal Republican; R—Republican

States	Electoral votes	Grant	Hendricks[1]	Brown[1]	Jenkins[1]	Davis[1]	States	Electoral votes	Grant	Hendricks[1]	Brown[1]	Jenkins[1]	Davis[1]
Alabama	(10)	10	–	–	–	–	Nebraska	(3)	3	–	–	–	–
Arkansas[2]	(6)	–	–	–	–	–	Nevada	(3)	3	–	–	–	–
California	(6)	6	–	–	–	–	New Hampshire	(5)	5	–	–	–	–
Connecticut	(6)	6	–	–	–	–	New Jersey	(9)	9	–	–	–	–
Delaware	(3)	3	–	–	–	–	New York	(35)	35	–	–	–	–
Florida	(4)	4	–	–	–	–	North Carolina	(10)	10	–	–	–	–
Georgia[3]	(11)	–	–	6	2	–	Ohio	(22)	22	–	–	–	–
Illinois	(21)	21	–	–	–	–	Oregon	(3)	3	–	–	–	–
Indiana	(15)	15	–	–	–	–	Pennsylvania	(29)	29	–	–	–	–
Iowa	(11)	11	–	–	–	–	Rhode Island	(4)	4	–	–	–	–
Kansas	(5)	5	–	–	–	–	South Carolina	(7)	7	–	–	–	–
Kentucky	(12)	–	8	4	–	–	Tennessee	(12)	–	12	–	–	–
Louisiana[2]	(8)	–	–	–	–	–	Texas	(8)	–	8	–	–	–
Maine	(7)	7	–	–	–	–	Vermont	(5)	5	–	–	–	–
Maryland	(8)	–	8	–	–	–	Virginia	(11)	11	–	–	–	–
Massachusetts	(13)	13	–	–	–	–	West Virginia	(5)	5	–	–	–	–
Michigan	(11)	11	–	–	–	–	Wisconsin	(10)	10	–	–	–	–
Minnesota	(5)	5	–	–	–	–							
Mississippi	(8)	8	–	–	–	–	Totals	(366)	286	42	18	2	1
Missouri	(15)	–	6	8	–	1							

1. Liberal Republican and Democratic presidential candidate Horace Greeley died November 29, 1872. In the electoral college, the electors who had been pledged to Greeley split their presidential electoral votes among four candidates, including 18 for Benjamin Gratz Brown, Greeley's running mate.
2. Congress refused to accept the electoral votes of Arkansas and Louisiana because of disruptive conditions during Reconstruction
3. Three Georgia electoral votes cast for Greeley were not counted.

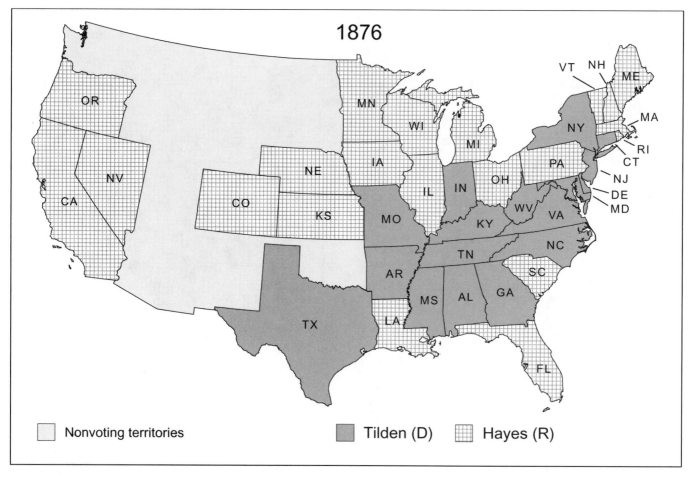

1876

| | Nonvoting territories | | ■ Tilden (D) | ▦ Hayes (R) |

Key: D—Democrat; R—Republican

States	Electoral votes	Hayes	Tilden	States	Electoral votes	Hayes	Tilden
Alabama	(10)	–	10	Missouri	(15)	–	15
Arkansas	(6)	–	6	Nebraska	(3)	3	–
California	(6)	6	–	Nevada	(3)	3	–
Colorado	(3)	3	–	New Hampshire	(5)	5	–
Connecticut	(6)	–	6	New Jersey	(9)	–	9
Delaware	(3)	–	3	New York	(35)	–	35
Florida[1]	(4)	4	–	North Carolina	(10)	–	10
Georgia	(11)	–	11	Ohio	(22)	22	–
Illinois	(21)	21	–	Oregon[1]	(3)	3	–
Indiana	(15)	–	15	Pennsylvania	(29)	29	–
Iowa	(11)	11	–	Rhode Island	(4)	4	–
Kansas	(5)	5	–	South Carolina[1]	(7)	7	–
Kentucky	(12)	–	12	Tennessee	(12)	–	12
Louisiana[1]	(8)	8	–	Texas	(8)	–	8
Maine	(7)	7	–	Vermont	(5)	5	–
Maryland	(8)	–	8	Virginia	(11)	–	11
Massachusetts	(13)	13	–	West Virginia	(5)	–	5
Michigan	(11)	11	–	Wisconsin	(10)	10	–
Minnesota	(5)	5	–				
Mississippi	(8)	–	8	Totals	(369)	185	184

1. The electoral votes of Florida, Louisiana, Oregon, and South Carolina were disputed. See "The Compromise of 1876," p. 40.

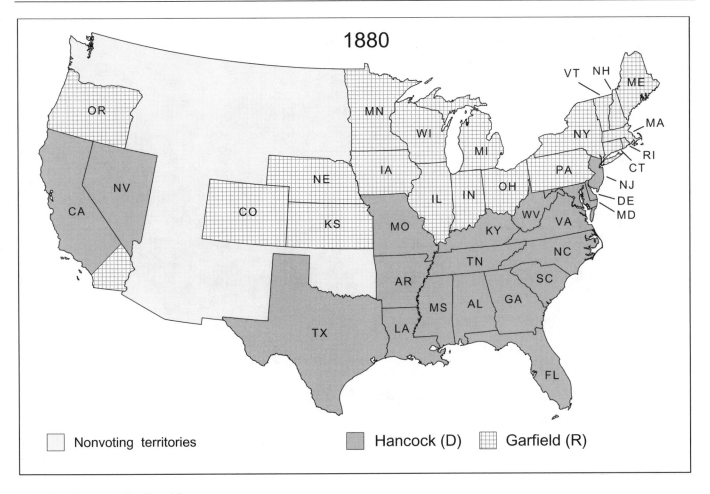

1880

Key: D—Democrat; R—Republican

States	Electoral votes	Garfield	Hancock	States	Electoral votes	Garfield	Hancock
Alabama	(10)	–	10	Missouri	(15)	–	15
Arkansas	(6)	–	6	Nebraska	(3)	3	–
California[1]	(6)	1	5	Nevada	(3)	–	3
Colorado	(3)	3	–	New Hampshire	(5)	5	–
Connecticut	(6)	6	–	New Jersey	(9)	–	9
Delaware	(3)	–	3	New York	(35)	35	–
Florida	(4)	–	4	North Carolina	(10)	–	10
Georgia	(11)	–	11	Ohio	(22)	22	–
Illinois	(21)	21	–	Oregon	(3)	3	–
Indiana	(15)	15	–	Pennsylvania	(29)	29	–
Iowa	(11)	11	–	Rhode Island	(4)	4	–
Kansas	(5)	5	–	South Carolina	(7)	–	7
Kentucky	(12)	–	12	Tennessee	(12)	–	12
Louisiana	(8)	–	8	Texas	(8)	–	8
Maine	(7)	7	–	Vermont	(5)	5	–
Maryland	(8)	–	8	Virginia	(11)	–	11
Massachusetts	(13)	13	–	West Virginia	(5)	–	5
Michigan	(11)	11	–	Wisconsin	(10)	10	–
Minnesota	(5)	5	–				
Mississippi	(8)	–	8	Totals	(369)	214	155

1. For explanation of split electoral votes, see p. 158.

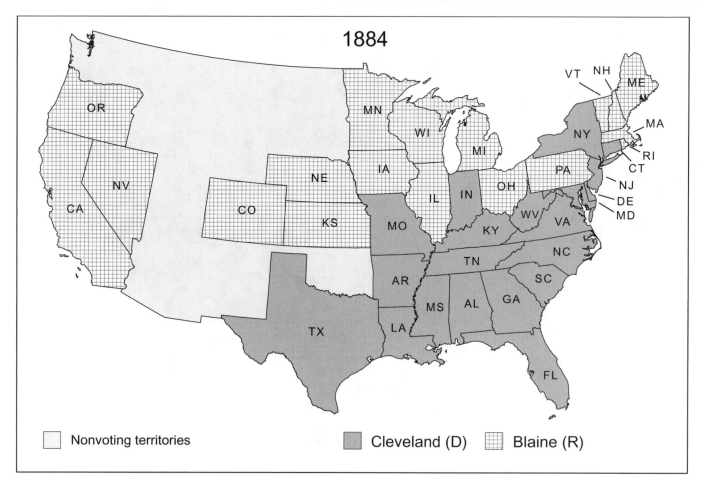

1884

Key: D—Democrat; R—Republican

States	Electoral votes	Cleveland	Blaine	States	Electoral votes	Cleveland	Blaine
Alabama	(10)	10	–	Missouri	(16)	16	–
Arkansas	(7)	7	–	Nebraska	(5)	–	5
California	(8)	–	8	Nevada	(3)	–	3
Colorado	(3)	–	3	New Hampshire	(4)	–	4
Connecticut	(6)	6	–	New Jersey	(9)	9	–
Delaware	(3)	3	–	New York	(36)	36	–
Florida	(4)	4	–	North Carolina	(11)	11	–
Georgia	(12)	12	–	Ohio	(23)	–	23
Illinois	(22)	–	22	Oregon	(3)	–	3
Indiana	(15)	15	–	Pennsylvania	(30)	–	30
Iowa	(13)	–	13	Rhode Island	(4)	–	4
Kansas	(9)	–	9	South Carolina	(9)	9	–
Kentucky	(13)	13	–	Tennessee	(12)	12	–
Louisiana	(8)	8	–	Texas	(13)	13	–
Maine	(6)	–	6	Vermont	(4)	–	4
Maryland	(8)	8	–	Virginia	(12)	12	–
Massachusetts	(14)	–	14	West Virginia	(6)	6	–
Michigan	(13)	–	13	Wisconsin	(11)	–	11
Minnesota	(7)	–	7				
Mississippi	(9)	9	–	Totals	(401)	219	182

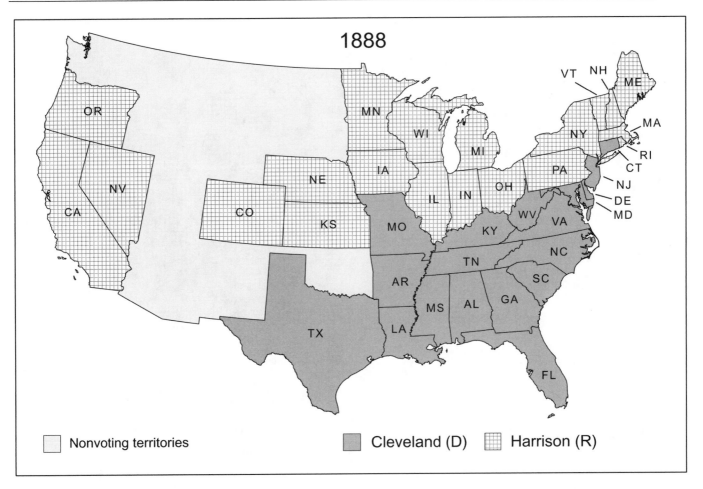

1888

Nonvoting territories   Cleveland (D)   Harrison (R)

Key: D—Democrat; R—Republican

States	Electoral votes	Harrison	Cleveland	States	Electoral votes	Harrison	Cleveland
Alabama	(10)	–	10	Missouri	(16)	–	16
Arkansas	(7)	–	7	Nebraska	(5)	5	–
California	(8)	8	–	Nevada	(3)	3	–
Colorado	(3)	3	–	New Hampshire	(4)	4	–
Connecticut	(6)	–	6	New Jersey	(9)	–	9
Delaware	(3)	–	3	New York	(36)	36	–
Florida	(4)	–	4	North Carolina	(11)	–	11
Georgia	(12)	–	12	Ohio	(23)	23	–
Illinois	(22)	22	–	Oregon	(3)	3	–
Indiana	(15)	15	–	Pennsylvania	(30)	30	–
Iowa	(13)	13	–	Rhode Island	(4)	4	–
Kansas	(9)	9	–	South Carolina	(9)	–	9
Kentucky	(13)	–	13	Tennessee	(12)	–	12
Louisiana	(8)	–	8	Texas	(13)	–	13
Maine	(6)	6	–	Vermont	(4)	4	–
Maryland	(8)	–	8	Virginia	(12)	–	12
Massachusetts	(14)	14	–	West Virginia	(6)	–	6
Michigan	(13)	13	–	Wisconsin	(11)	11	–
Minnesota	(7)	7	–				
Mississippi	(9)	–	9	Totals	(401)	233	168

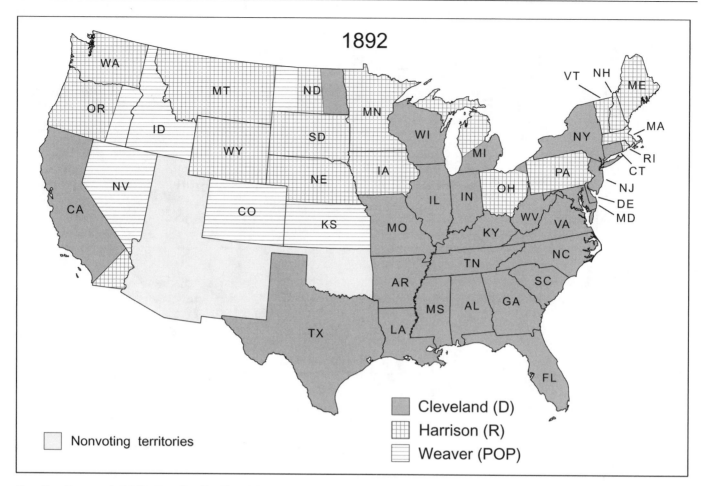

1892

Cleveland (D)

Harrison (R)

Weaver (POP)

Nonvoting territories

Key: D—Democrat; POP—Populist; R—Republican

States	Electoral votes	Cleveland	Harrison	Weaver	States	Electoral votes	Cleveland	Harrison	Weaver
Alabama	(11)	11	–	–	Nebraska	(8)	–	8	–
Arkansas	(8)	8	–	–	Nevada	(3)	–	–	3
California[1]	(9)	8	1	–	New Hampshire	(4)	–	4	–
Colorado	(4)	–	–	4	New Jersey	(10)	10	–	–
Connecticut	(6)	6	–	–	New York	(36)	36	–	–
Delaware	(3)	3	–	–	North Carolina	(11)	11	–	–
Florida	(4)	4	–	–	North Dakota[1]	(3)	1	1	1
Georgia	(13)	13	–	–	Ohio[1]	(23)	1	22	–
Idaho	(3)	–	–	3	Oregon[1]	(4)	–	3	1
Illinois	(24)	24	–	–	Pennsylvania	(32)	–	32	–
Indiana	(15)	15	–	–	Rhode Island	(4)	–	4	–
Iowa	(13)	–	13	–	South Carolina	(9)	9	–	–
Kansas	(10)	–	–	10	South Dakota	(4)	–	4	–
Kentucky	(13)	13	–	–	Tennessee	(12)	12	–	–
Louisiana	(8)	8	–	–	Texas	(15)	15	–	–
Maine	(6)	–	6	–	Vermont	(4)	–	4	–
Maryland	(8)	8	–	–	Virginia	(12)	12	–	–
Massachusetts	(15)	–	15	–	Washington	(4)	–	4	–
Michigan[1]	(14)	5	9	–	West Virginia	(6)	6	–	–
Minnesota	(9)	–	9	–	Wisconsin	(12)	12	–	–
Mississippi	(9)	9	–	–	Wyoming	(3)	–	3	–
Missouri	(17)	17	–	–					
Montana	(3)	–	3	–	Totals	(444)	277	145	22

1. For explanation of split electoral votes, see p. 158.

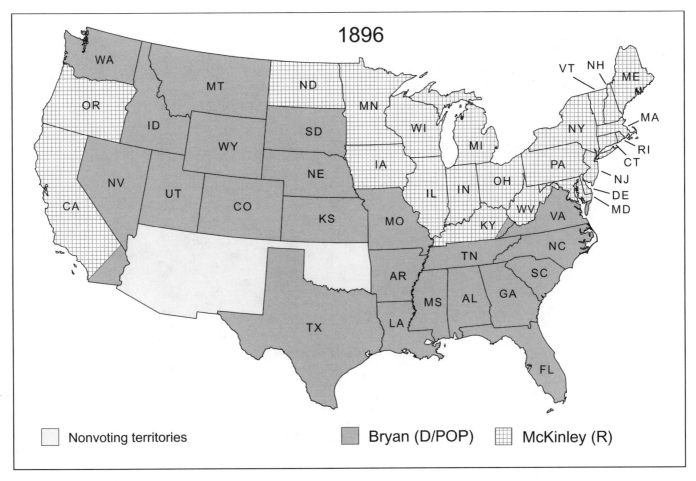

1896

Nonvoting territories   Bryan (D/POP)   McKinley (R)

Key: D/POP—Democrat/Populist; R—Republican

States	Electoral votes	McKinley	Bryan	States	Electoral votes	McKinley	Bryan
Alabama	(11)	–	11	Nevada	(3)	–	3
Arkansas	(8)	–	8	New Hampshire	(4)	4	–
California[1]	(9)	8	1	New Jersey	(10)	10	–
Colorado	(4)	–	4	New York	(36)	36	–
Connecticut	(6)	6	–	North Carolina	(11)	–	11
Delaware	(3)	3	–	North Dakota	(3)	3	–
Florida	(4)	–	4	Ohio	(23)	23	–
Georgia	(13)	–	13	Oregon	(4)	4	–
Idaho	(3)	–	3	Pennsylvania	(32)	32	–
Illinois	(24)	24	–	Rhode Island	(4)	4	–
Indiana	(15)	15	–	South Carolina	(9)	–	9
Iowa	(13)	13	–	South Dakota	(4)	–	4
Kansas	(10)	–	10	Tennessee	(12)	–	12
Kentucky[1]	(13)	12	1	Texas	(15)	–	15
Louisiana	(8)	–	8	Utah	(3)	–	3
Maine	(6)	6	–	Vermont	(4)	4	–
Maryland	(8)	8	–	Virginia	(12)	–	12
Massachusetts	(15)	15	–	Washington	(4)	–	4
Michigan	(14)	14	–	West Virginia	(6)	6	–
Minnesota	(9)	9	–	Wisconsin	(12)	12	–
Mississippi	(9)	–	9	Wyoming	(3)	–	3
Missouri	(17)	–	17				
Montana	(3)	–	3	Totals	(447)	271	176
Nebraska	(8)	–	8				

1. For explanation of split electoral votes, see p. 158.

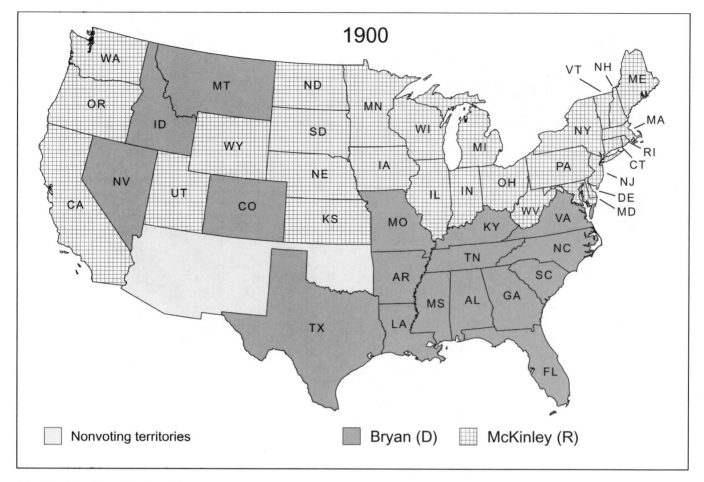

1900

Nonvoting territories   Bryan (D)   McKinley (R)

Key: D—Democrat; R—Republican

States	Electoral votes	McKinley	Bryan	States	Electoral votes	McKinley	Bryan
Alabama	(11)	–	11	Nevada	(3)	–	3
Arkansas	(8)	–	8	New Hampshire	(4)	4	–
California	(9)	9	–	New Jersey	(10)	10	–
Colorado	(4)	–	4	New York	(36)	36	–
Connecticut	(6)	6	–	North Carolina	(11)	–	11
Delaware	(3)	3	–	North Dakota	(3)	3	–
Florida	(4)	–	4	Ohio	(23)	23	–
Georgia	(13)	–	13	Oregon	(4)	4	–
Idaho	(3)	–	3	Pennsylvania	(32)	32	–
Illinois	(24)	24	–	Rhode Island	(4)	4	–
Indiana	(15)	15	–	South Carolina	(9)	–	9
Iowa	(13)	13	–	South Dakota	(4)	4	–
Kansas	(10)	10	–	Tennessee	(12)	–	12
Kentucky	(13)	–	13	Texas	(15)	–	15
Louisiana	(8)	–	8	Utah	(3)	3	–
Maine	(6)	6	–	Vermont	(4)	4	–
Maryland	(8)	8	–	Virginia	(12)	–	12
Massachusetts	(15)	15	–	Washington	(4)	4	–
Michigan	(14)	14	–	West Virginia	(6)	6	–
Minnesota	(9)	9	–	Wisconsin	(12)	12	–
Mississippi	(9)	–	9	Wyoming	(3)	3	–
Missouri	(17)		17				
Montana	(3)	–	3	Totals	(447)	292	155
Nebraska	(8)	8	–				

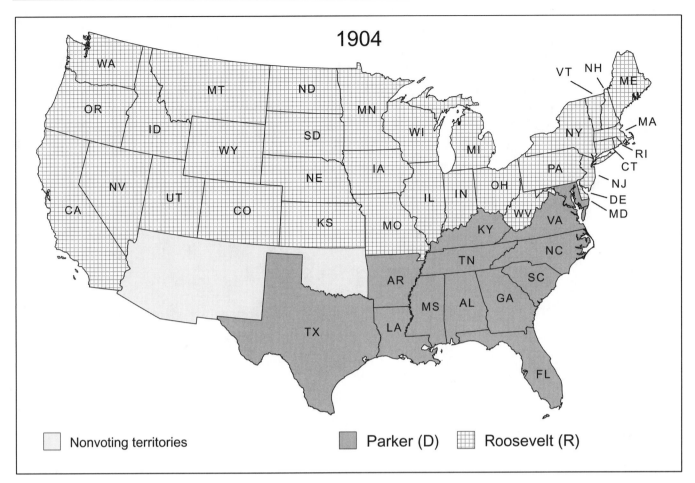

1904

Nonvoting territories   Parker (D)   Roosevelt (R)

Key: D—Democrat; R—Republican

States	Electoral votes	Roosevelt	Parker	States	Electoral votes	Roosevelt	Parker
Alabama	(11)	–	11	Nevada	(3)	3	–
Arkansas	(9)	–	9	New Hampshire	(4)	4	–
California	(10)	10	–	New Jersey	(12)	12	–
Colorado	(5)	5	–	New York	(39)	39	–
Connecticut	(7)	7	–	North Carolina	(12)	–	12
Delaware	(3)	3	–	North Dakota	(4)	4	–
Florida	(5)	–	5	Ohio	(23)	23	–
Georgia	(13)	–	13	Oregon	(4)	4	–
Idaho	(3)	3	–	Pennsylvania	(34)	34	–
Illinois	(27)	27	–	Rhode Island	(4)	4	–
Indiana	(15)	15	–	South Carolina	(9)	–	9
Iowa	(13)	13	–	South Dakota	(4)	4	–
Kansas	(10)	10	–	Tennessee	(12)	–	12
Kentucky	(13)	–	13	Texas	(18)	–	18
Louisiana	(9)	–	9	Utah	(3)	3	–
Maine	(6)	6	–	Vermont	(4)	4	–
Maryland[1]	(8)	1	7	Virginia	(12)	–	12
Massachusetts	(16)	16	–	Washington	(5)	5	–
Michigan	(14)	14	–	West Virginia	(7)	7	–
Minnesota	(11)	11	–	Wisconsin	(13)	13	–
Mississippi	(10)	–	10	Wyoming	(3)	3	–
Missouri	(18)	18	–				
Montana	(3)	3	–	Totals	(476)	336	140
Nebraska	(8)	8	–				

1. For explanation of split electoral votes, see p. 158.

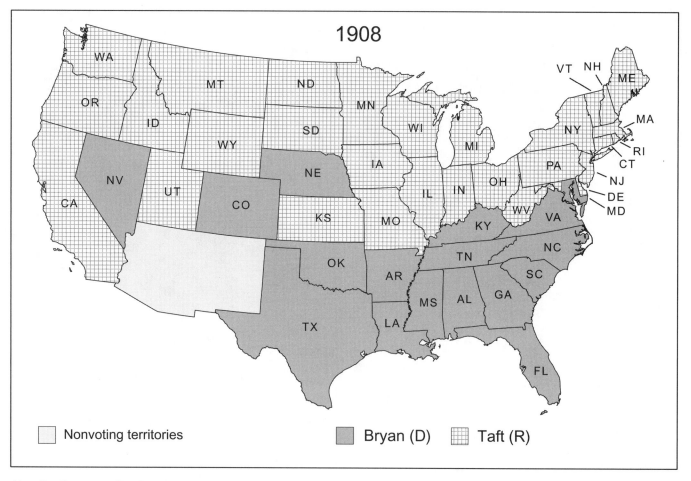

1908

Nonvoting territories   Bryan (D)   Taft (R)

Key: D—Democrat; R—Republican

States	Electoral votes	Taft	Bryan	States	Electoral votes	Taft	Bryan
Alabama	(11)	–	11	Nevada	(3)	–	3
Arkansas	(9)	–	9	New Hampshire	(4)	4	–
California	(10)	10	–	New Jersey	(12)	12	–
Colorado	(5)	–	5	New York	(39)	39	–
Connecticut	(7)	7	–	North Carolina	(12)	–	12
Delaware	(3)	3	–	North Dakota	(4)	4	–
Florida	(5)	–	5	Ohio	(23)	23	–
Georgia	(13)	–	13	Oklahoma	(7)	–	7
Idaho	(3)	3	–	Oregon	(4)	4	–
Illinois	(27)	27	–	Pennsylvania	(34)	34	–
Indiana	(15)	15	–	Rhode Island	(4)	4	–
Iowa	(13)	13	–	South Carolina	(9)	–	9
Kansas	(10)	10	–	South Dakota	(4)	4	–
Kentucky	(13)	–	13	Tennessee	(12)	–	12
Louisiana	(9)	–	9	Texas	(18)	–	18
Maine	(6)	6	–	Utah	(3)	3	–
Maryland[1]	(8)	2	6	Vermont	(4)	4	–
Massachusetts	(16)	16	–	Virginia	(12)	–	12
Michigan	(14)	14	–	Washington	(5)	5	–
Minnesota	(11)	11	–	West Virginia	(7)	7	–
Mississippi	(10)	–	10	Wisconsin	(13)	13	–
Missouri	(18)	18	–	Wyoming	(3)	3	–
Montana	(3)	3	–				
Nebraska	(8)	–	8	Totals	(483)	321	162

1. For explanation of split electoral votes, see p. 158.

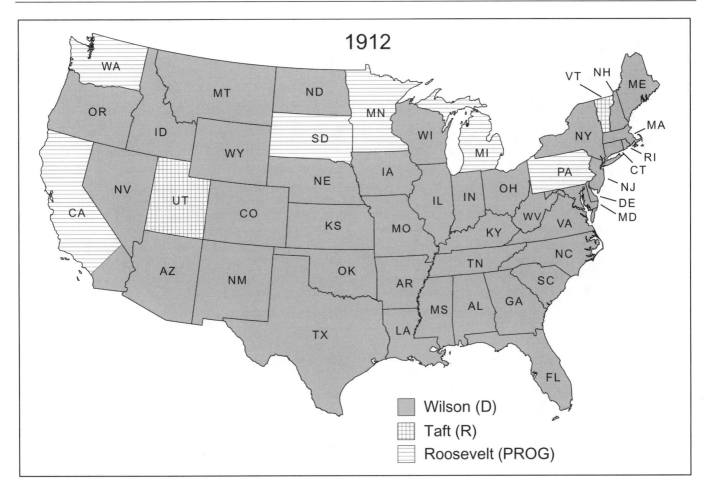

1912

Wilson (D)
Taft (R)
Roosevelt (PROG)

Key: D—Democrat; PROG—Progressive; R—Republican

States	Electoral votes	Wilson	Roosevelt	Taft	States	Electoral votes	Wilson	Roosevelt	Taft
Alabama	(12)	12	–	–	Nevada	(3)	3	–	–
Arizona	(3)	3	–	–	New Hampshire	(4)	4	–	–
Arkansas	(9)	9	–	–	New Jersey	(14)	14	–	–
California[1]	(13)	2	11	–	New Mexico	(3)	3	–	–
Colorado	(6)	6	–	–	New York	(45)	45	–	–
Connecticut	(7)	7	–	–	North Carolina	(12)	12	–	–
Delaware	(3)	3	–	–	North Dakota	(5)	5	–	–
Florida	(6)	6	–	–	Ohio	(24)	24	–	–
Georgia	(14)	14	–	–	Oklahoma	(10)	10	–	–
Idaho	(4)	4	–	–	Oregon	(5)	5	–	–
Illinois	(29)	29	–	–	Pennsylvania	(38)	–	38	–
Indiana	(15)	15	–	–	Rhode Island	(5)	5	–	–
Iowa	(13)	13	–	–	South Carolina	(9)	9	–	–
Kansas	(10)	10	–	–	South Dakota	(5)	–	5	–
Kentucky	(13)	13	–	–	Tennessee	(12)	12	–	–
Louisiana	(10)	10	–	–	Texas	(20)	20	–	–
Maine	(6)	6	–	–	Utah	(4)	–	–	4
Maryland	(8)	8	–	–	Vermont	(4)	–	–	4
Massachusetts	(18)	18	–	–	Virginia	(12)	12	–	–
Michigan	(15)	–	15	–	Washington	(7)	–	7	–
Minnesota	(12)	–	12	–	West Virginia	(8)	8	–	–
Mississippi	(10)	10	–	–	Wisconsin	(13)	13	–	–
Missouri	(18)	18	–	–	Wyoming	(3)	3	–	–
Montana	(4)	4	–	–					
Nebraska	(8)	8	–	–	Totals	(531)	435	88	8

1. For explanation of split electoral votes, see p. 158.

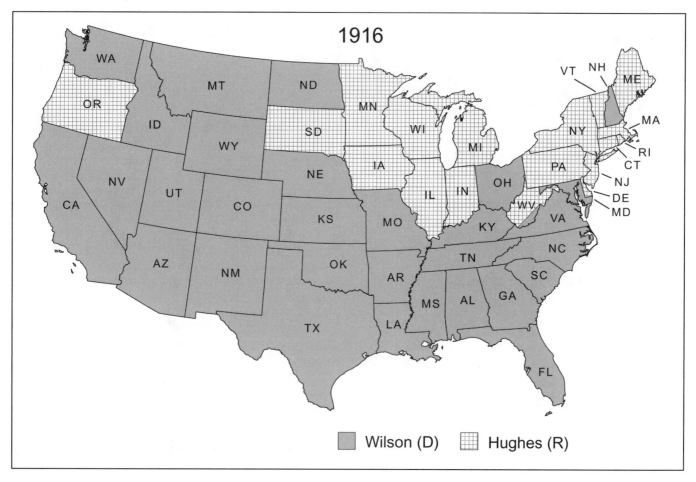

1916

| | Wilson (D) | | Hughes (R) |

Key: D—Democrat; R—Republican

States	Electoral votes	Wilson	Hughes	States	Electoral votes	Wilson	Hughes
Alabama	(12)	12	–	Nevada	(3)	3	–
Arizona	(3)	3	–	New Hampshire	(4)	4	–
Arkansas	(9)	9	–	New Jersey	(14)	–	14
California	(13)	13	–	New Mexico	(3)	3	–
Colorado	(6)	6	–	New York	(45)	–	45
Connecticut	(7)	–	7	North Carolina	(12)	12	–
Delaware	(3)	–	3	North Dakota	(5)	5	–
Florida	(6)	6	–	Ohio	(24)	24	–
Georgia	(14)	14	–	Oklahoma	(10)	10	–
Idaho	(4)	4	–	Oregon	(5)	–	5
Illinois	(29)	–	29	Pennsylvania	(38)	–	38
Indiana	(15)	–	15	Rhode Island	(5)	–	5
Iowa	(13)	–	13	South Carolina	(9)	9	–
Kansas	(10)	10	–	South Dakota	(5)	–	5
Kentucky	(13)	13	–	Tennessee	(12)	12	–
Louisiana	(10)	10	–	Texas	(20)	20	–
Maine	(6)	–	6	Utah	(4)	4	–
Maryland	(8)	8	–	Vermont	(4)	–	4
Massachusetts	(18)	–	18	Virginia	(12)	12	–
Michigan	(15)	–	15	Washington	(7)	7	–
Minnesota	(12)	–	12	West Virginia[1]	(8)	1	7
Mississippi	(10)	10	–	Wisconsin	(13)	–	13
Missouri	(18)	18	–	Wyoming	(3)	3	–
Montana	(4)	4	–				
Nebraska	(8)	8	–	Totals	(531)	277	254

1. For explanation of split electoral votes, see p. 158.

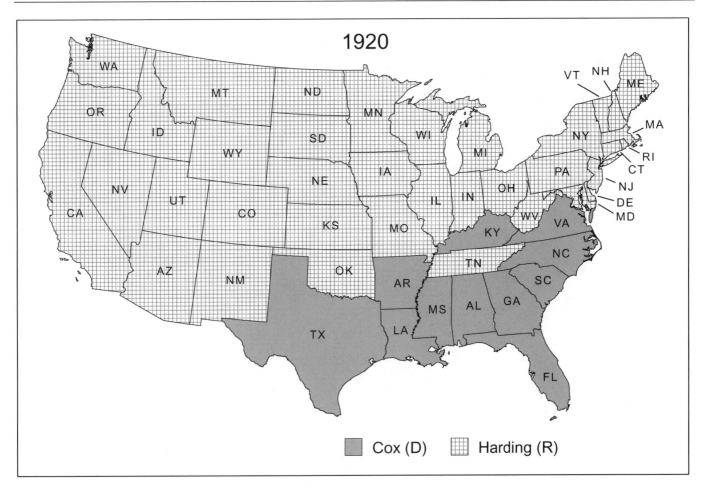

1920

Key: D—Democrat; R—Republican

States	Electoral votes	Harding	Cox	States	Electoral votes	Harding	Cox
Alabama	(12)	–	12	Nevada	(3)	3	–
Arizona	(3)	3	–	New Hampshire	(4)	4	–
Arkansas	(9)	–	9	New Jersey	(14)	14	–
California	(13)	13	–	New Mexico	(3)	3	–
Colorado	(6)	6	–	New York	(45)	45	–
Connecticut	(7)	7	–	North Carolina	(12)	–	12
Delaware	(3)	3	–	North Dakota	(5)	5	–
Florida	(6)	–	6	Ohio	(24)	24	–
Georgia	(14)	–	14	Oklahoma	(10)	10	–
Idaho	(4)	4	–	Oregon	(5)	5	–
Illinois	(29)	29	–	Pennsylvania	(38)	38	–
Indiana	(15)	15	–	Rhode Island	(5)	5	–
Iowa	(13)	13	–	South Carolina	(9)	–	9
Kansas	(10)	10	–	South Dakota	(5)	5	–
Kentucky	(13)	–	13	Tennessee	(12)	12	–
Louisiana	(10)	–	10	Texas	(20)	–	20
Maine	(6)	6	–	Utah	(4)	4	–
Maryland	(8)	8	–	Vermont	(4)	4	–
Massachusetts	(18)	18	–	Virginia	(12)	–	12
Michigan	(15)	15	–	Washington	(7)	7	–
Minnesota	(12)	12	–	West Virginia	(8)	8	–
Mississippi	(10)	–	10	Wisconsin	(13)	13	–
Missouri	(18)	18	–	Wyoming	(3)	3	–
Montana	(4)	4	–				
Nebraska	(8)	8	–	Totals	(531)	404	127

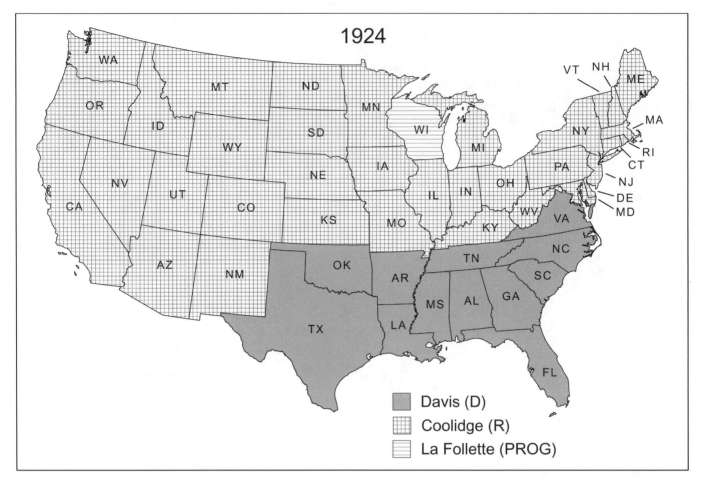

1924

Davis (D)
Coolidge (R)
La Follette (PROG)

Key: D—Democrat; P—Progressive; R—Republican

States	Electoral votes	Coolidge	Davis	La Follette	States	Electoral votes	Coolidge	Davis	La Follette
Alabama	(12)	–	12	–	Nevada	(3)	3	–	–
Arizona	(3)	3	–	–	New Hampshire	(4)	4	–	–
Arkansas	(9)	–	9	–	New Jersey	(14)	14	–	–
California	(13)	13	–	–	New Mexico	(3)	3	–	–
Colorado	(6)	6	–	–	New York	(45)	45	–	–
Connecticut	(7)	7	–	–	North Carolina	(12)	–	12	–
Delaware	(3)	3	–	–	North Dakota	(5)	5	–	–
Florida	(6)	–	6	–	Ohio	(24)	24	–	–
Georgia	(14)	–	14	–	Oklahoma	(10)	–	10	–
Idaho	(4)	4	–	–	Oregon	(5)	5	–	–
Illinois	(29)	29	–	–	Pennsylvania	(38)	38	–	–
Indiana	(15)	15	–	–	Rhode Island	(5)	5	–	–
Iowa	(13)	13	–	–	South Carolina	(9)	–	9	–
Kansas	(10)	10	–	–	South Dakota	(5)	5	–	–
Kentucky	(13)	13	–	–	Tennessee	(12)	–	12	–
Louisiana	(10)	–	10	–	Texas	(20)	–	20	–
Maine	(6)	6	–	–	Utah	(4)	4	–	–
Maryland	(8)	8	–	–	Vermont	(4)	4	–	–
Massachusetts	(18)	18	–	–	Virginia	(12)	–	12	–
Michigan	(15)	15	–	–	Washington	(7)	7	–	–
Minnesota	(12)	12	–	–	West Virginia	(8)	8	–	–
Mississippi	(10)	–	10	–	Wisconsin	(13)	–	–	13
Missouri	(18)	18	–	–	Wyoming	(3)	3	–	–
Montana	(4)	4	–	–					
Nebraska	(8)	8	–	–	Totals	(531)	382	136	13

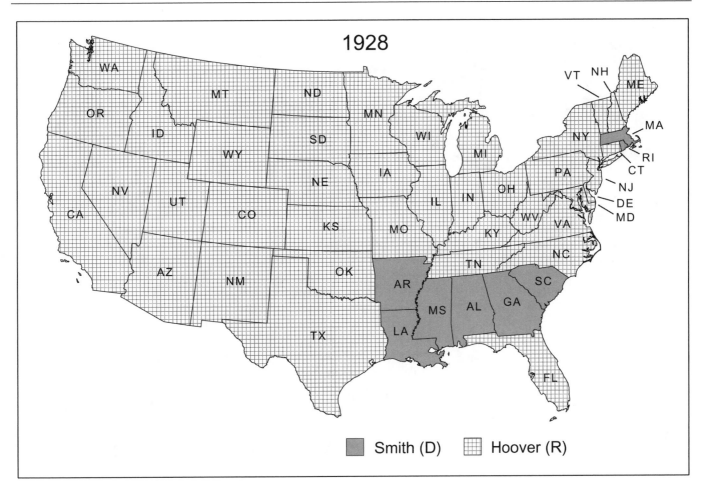

1928

Smith (D)   Hoover (R)

Key: D—Democrat; R—Republican

States	Electoral votes	Hoover	Smith	States	Electoral votes	Hoover	Smith
Alabama	(12)	–	12	Nevada	(3)	3	–
Arizona	(3)	3	–	New Hampshire	(4)	4	–
Arkansas	(9)	–	9	New Jersey	(14)	14	–
California	(13)	13	–	New Mexico	(3)	3	–
Colorado	(6)	6	–	New York	(45)	45	–
Connecticut	(7)	7	–	North Carolina	(12)	12	–
Delaware	(3)	3	–	North Dakota	(5)	5	–
Florida	(6)	6	–	Ohio	(24)	24	–
Georgia	(14)	–	14	Oklahoma	(10)	10	–
Idaho	(4)	4	–	Oregon	(5)	5	–
Illinois	(29)	29	–	Pennsylvania	(38)	38	–
Indiana	(15)	15	–	Rhode Island	(5)	–	5
Iowa	(13)	13	–	South Carolina	(9)	–	9
Kansas	(10)	10	–	South Dakota	(5)	5	–
Kentucky	(13)	13	–	Tennessee	(12)	12	–
Louisiana	(10)	–	10	Texas	(20)	20	–
Maine	(6)	6	–	Utah	(4)	4	–
Maryland	(8)	8	–	Vermont	(4)	4	–
Massachusetts	(18)	–	18	Virginia	(12)	12	–
Michigan	(15)	15	–	Washington	(7)	7	–
Minnesota	(12)	12	–	West Virginia	(8)	8	–
Mississippi	(10)	–	10	Wisconsin	(13)	13	–
Missouri	(18)	18	–	Wyoming	(3)	3	–
Montana	(4)	4	–				
Nebraska	(8)	8	–	Totals	(531)	444	87

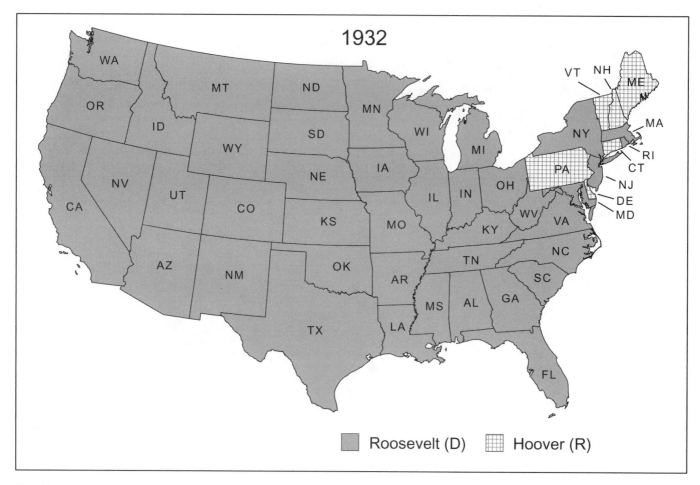

1932

Roosevelt (D)   Hoover (R)

Key: D—Democrat; R—Republican

States	Electoral votes	Roosevelt	Hoover	States	Electoral votes	Roosevelt	Hoover
Alabama	(11)	11	–	Nevada	(3)	3	–
Arizona	(3)	3	–	New Hampshire	(4)	–	4
Arkansas	(9)	9	–	New Jersey	(16)	16	–
California	(22)	22	–	New Mexico	(3)	3	–
Colorado	(6)	6	–	New York	(47)	47	–
Connecticut	(8)	–	8	North Carolina	(13)	13	–
Delaware	(3)	–	3	North Dakota	(4)	4	–
Florida	(7)	7	–	Ohio	(26)	26	–
Georgia	(12)	12	–	Oklahoma	(11)	11	–
Idaho	(4)	4	–	Oregon	(5)	5	–
Illinois	(29)	29	–	Pennsylvania	(36)	–	36
Indiana	(14)	14	–	Rhode Island	(4)	4	–
Iowa	(11)	11	–	South Carolina	(8)	8	–
Kansas	(9)	9	–	South Dakota	(4)	4	–
Kentucky	(11)	11	–	Tennessee	(11)	11	–
Louisiana	(10)	10	–	Texas	(23)	23	–
Maine	(5)	–	5	Utah	(4)	4	–
Maryland	(8)	8	–	Vermont	(3)	–	3
Massachusetts	(17)	17	–	Virginia	(11)	11	–
Michigan	(19)	19	–	Washington	(8)	8	–
Minnesota	(11)	11	–	West Virginia	(8)	8	–
Mississippi	(9)	9	–	Wisconsin	(12)	12	–
Missouri	(15)	15	–	Wyoming	(3)	3	–
Montana	(4)	4	–				
Nebraska	(7)	7	–	Totals	(531)	472	59

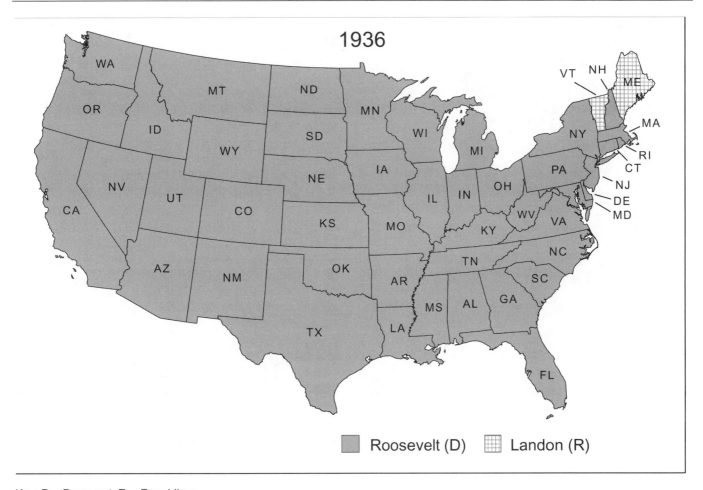

1936

Roosevelt (D)   Landon (R)

Key: D—Democrat; R—Republican

States	Electoral votes	Roosevelt	Landon	States	Electoral votes	Roosevelt	Landon
Alabama	(11)	11	–	Nevada	(3)	3	–
Arizona	(3)	3	–	New Hampshire	(4)	4	–
Arkansas	(9)	9	–	New Jersey	(16)	16	–
California	(22)	22	–	New Mexico	(3)	3	–
Colorado	(6)	6	–	New York	(47)	47	–
Connecticut	(8)	8	–	North Carolina	(13)	13	–
Delaware	(3)	3	–	North Dakota	(4)	4	–
Florida	(7)	7	–	Ohio	(26)	26	–
Georgia	(12)	12	–	Oklahoma	(11)	11	–
Idaho	(4)	4	–	Oregon	(5)	5	–
Illinois	(29)	29	–	Pennsylvania	(36)	36	–
Indiana	(14)	14	–	Rhode Island	(4)	4	–
Iowa	(11)	11	–	South Carolina	(8)	8	–
Kansas	(9)	9	–	South Dakota	(4)	4	–
Kentucky	(11)	11	–	Tennessee	(11)	11	–
Louisiana	(10)	10	–	Texas	(23)	23	–
Maine	(5)	–	5	Utah	(4)	4	–
Maryland	(8)	8	–	Vermont	(3)	–	3
Massachusetts	(17)	17	–	Virginia	(11)	11	–
Michigan	(19)	19	–	Washington	(8)	8	–
Minnesota	(11)	11	–	West Virginia	(8)	8	–
Mississippi	(9)	9	–	Wisconsin	(12)	12	–
Missouri	(15)	15	–	Wyoming	(3)	3	–
Montana	(4)	4	–				
Nebraska	(7)	7	–	Totals	(531)	523	8

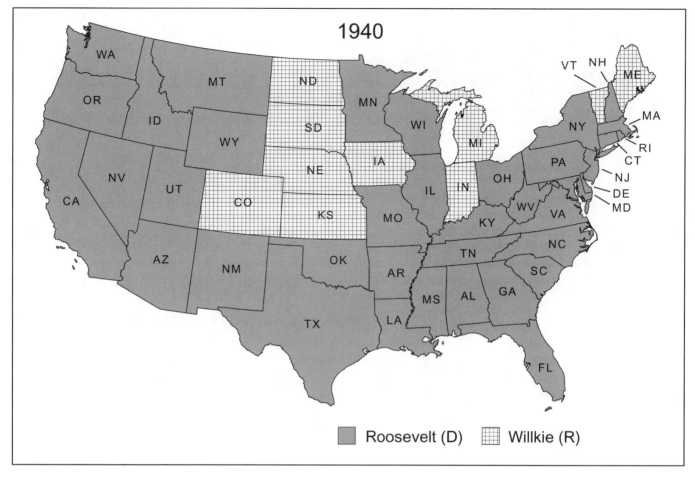

1940

Roosevelt (D)   Willkie (R)

Key: D—Democrat; R—Republican

States	Electoral votes	Roosevelt	Willkie	States	Electoral votes	Roosevelt	Willkie
Alabama	(11)	11	–	Nevada	(3)	3	–
Arizona	(3)	3	–	New Hampshire	(4)	4	–
Arkansas	(9)	9	–	New Jersey	(16)	16	–
California	(22)	22	–	New Mexico	(3)	3	–
Colorado	(6)	–	6	New York	(47)	47	–
Connecticut	(8)	8	–	North Carolina	(13)	13	–
Delaware	(3)	3	–	North Dakota	(4)	–	4
Florida	(7)	7	–	Ohio	(26)	26	–
Georgia	(12)	12	–	Oklahoma	(11)	11	–
Idaho	(4)	4	–	Oregon	(5)	5	–
Illinois	(29)	29	–	Pennsylvania	(36)	36	–
Indiana	(14)	–	14	Rhode Island	(4)	4	–
Iowa	(11)	–	11	South Carolina	(8)	8	–
Kansas	(9)	–	9	South Dakota	(4)	–	4
Kentucky	(11)	11	–	Tennessee	(11)	11	–
Louisiana	(10)	10	–	Texas	(23)	23	–
Maine	(5)	–	5	Utah	(4)	4	–
Maryland	(8)	8	–	Vermont	(3)	–	3
Massachusetts	(17)	17	–	Virginia	(11)	11	–
Michigan	(19)	–	19	Washington	(8)	8	–
Minnesota	(11)	11	–	West Virginia	(8)	8	–
Mississippi	(9)	9	–	Wisconsin	(12)	12	–
Missouri	(15)	15	–	Wyoming	(3)	3	–
Montana	(4)	4	–				
Nebraska	(7)	–	7	Totals	(531)	449	82

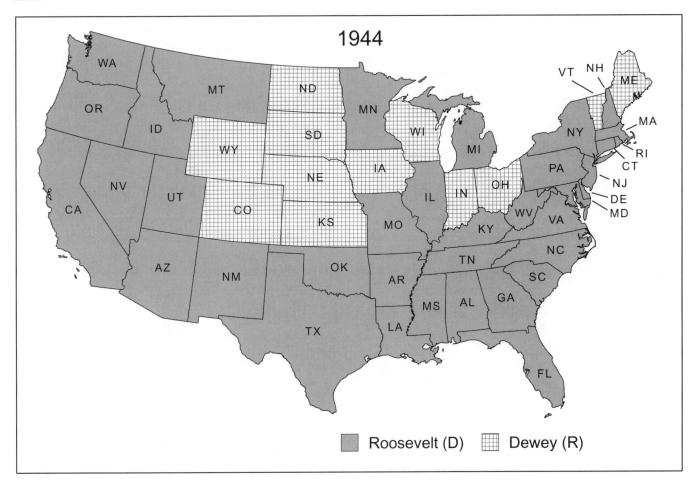

1944

Roosevelt (D)   Dewey (R)

Key: D—Democrat; R—Republican

States	Electoral votes	Roosevelt	Dewey	States	Electoral votes	Roosevelt	Dewey
Alabama	(11)	11	–	Nevada	(3)	3	–
Arizona	(4)	4	–	New Hampshire	(4)	4	–
Arkansas	(9)	9	–	New Jersey	(16)	16	–
California	(25)	25	–	New Mexico	(4)	4	–
Colorado	(6)	–	6	New York	(47)	47	–
Connecticut	(8)	8	–	North Carolina	(14)	14	–
Delaware	(3)	3	–	North Dakota	(4)	–	4
Florida	(8)	8	–	Ohio	(25)	–	25
Georgia	(12)	12	–	Oklahoma	(10)	10	–
Idaho	(4)	4	–	Oregon	(6)	6	–
Illinois	(28)	28	–	Pennsylvania	(35)	35	–
Indiana	(13)	–	13	Rhode Island	(4)	4	–
Iowa	(10)	–	10	South Carolina	(8)	8	–
Kansas	(8)	–	8	South Dakota	(4)	–	4
Kentucky	(11)	11	–	Tennessee	(12)	12	–
Louisiana	(10)	10	–	Texas	(23)	23	–
Maine	(5)	–	5	Utah	(4)	4	–
Maryland	(8)	8	–	Vermont	(3)	–	3
Massachusetts	(16)	16	–	Virginia	(11)	11	–
Michigan	(19)	19	–	Washington	(8)	8	–
Minnesota	(11)	11	–	West Virginia	(8)	8	–
Mississippi	(9)	9	–	Wisconsin	(12)	–	12
Missouri	(15)	15	–	Wyoming	(3)	–	3
Montana	(4)	4	–				
Nebraska	(6)	–	6	Totals	(531)	432	99

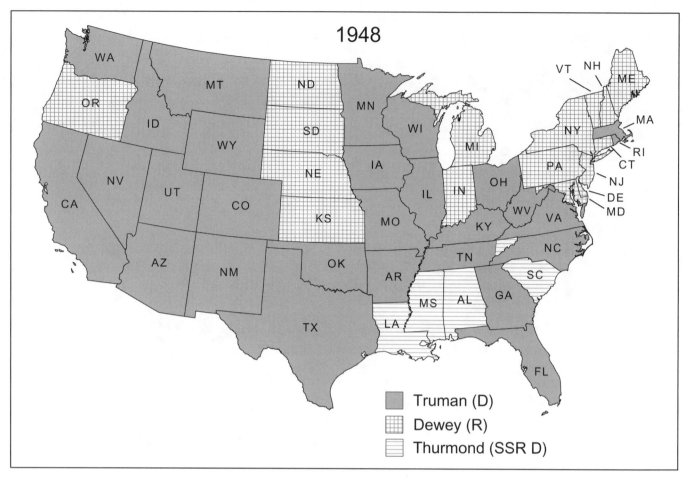

1948

Truman (D)
Dewey (R)
Thurmond (SSR D)

Key: D—Democrat; R—Republican; SSR D—States' Rights Democrat

States	Electoral votes	Truman	Dewey	Thurmond	States	Electoral votes	Truman	Dewey	Thurmond
Alabama	(11)	–	–	11	Nevada	(3)	3	–	–
Arizona	(4)	4	–	–	New Hampshire	(4)	–	4	–
Arkansas	(9)	9	–	–	New Jersey	(16)	–	16	–
California	(25)	25	–	–	New Mexico	(4)	4	–	–
Colorado	(6)	6	–	–	New York	(47)	–	47	–
Connecticut	(8)	–	8	–	North Carolina	(14)	14	–	–
Delaware	(3)	–	3	–	North Dakota	(4)	–	4	–
Florida	(8)	8	–	–	Ohio	(25)	25	–	–
Georgia	(12)	12	–	–	Oklahoma	(10)	10	–	–
Idaho	(4)	4	–	–	Oregon	(6)	–	6	–
Illinois	(28)	28	–	–	Pennsylvania	(35)	–	35	–
Indiana	(13)	–	13	–	Rhode Island	(4)	4	–	–
Iowa	(10)	10	–	–	South Carolina	(8)	–	–	8
Kansas	(8)	–	8	–	South Dakota	(4)	–	4	–
Kentucky	(11)	11	–	–	Tennessee[1]	(12)	11	–	1
Louisiana	(10)	–	–	10	Texas	(23)	23	–	–
Maine	(5)	–	5	–	Utah	(4)	4	–	–
Maryland	(8)	–	8	–	Vermont	(3)	–	3	–
Massachusetts	(16)	16	–	–	Virginia	(11)	11	–	–
Michigan	(19)	–	19	–	Washington	(8)	8	–	–
Minnesota	(11)	11	–	–	West Virginia	(8)	8	–	–
Mississippi	(9)	–	–	9	Wisconsin	(12)	12	–	–
Missouri	(15)	15	–	–	Wyoming	(3)	3	–	–
Montana	(4)	4	–	–					
Nebraska	(6)	–	6	–	Totals	(531)	303	189	39

1. For explanation of split electoral votes, see p. 158.

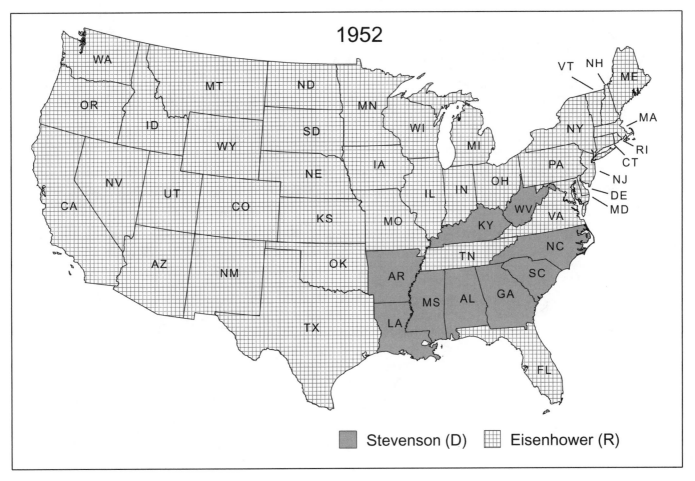

1952

Stevenson (D)   Eisenhower (R)

Key: D—Democrat; R—Republican

States	Electoral votes	Eisenhower	Stevenson	States	Electoral votes	Eisenhower	Stevenson
Alabama	(11)	–	11	Nevada	(3)	3	–
Arizona	(4)	4	–	New Hampshire	(4)	4	–
Arkansas	(8)	–	8	New Jersey	(16)	16	–
California	(32)	32	–	New Mexico	(4)	4	–
Colorado	(6)	6	–	New York	(45)	45	–
Connecticut	(8)	8	–	North Carolina	(14)	–	14
Delaware	(3)	3	–	North Dakota	(4)	4	–
Florida	(10)	10	–	Ohio	(25)	25	–
Georgia	(12)	–	12	Oklahoma	(8)	8	–
Idaho	(4)	4	–	Oregon	(6)	6	–
Illinois	(27)	27	–	Pennsylvania	(32)	32	–
Indiana	(13)	13	–	Rhode Island	(4)	4	–
Iowa	(10)	10	–	South Carolina	(8)	–	8
Kansas	(8)	8	–	South Dakota	(4)	4	–
Kentucky	(10)	–	10	Tennessee	(11)	11	–
Louisiana	(10)	–	10	Texas	(24)	24	–
Maine	(5)	5	–	Utah	(4)	4	–
Maryland	(9)	9	–	Vermont	(3)	3	–
Massachusetts	(16)	16	–	Virginia	(12)	12	–
Michigan	(20)	20	–	Washington	(9)	9	–
Minnesota	(11)	11	–	West Virginia	(8)	–	8
Mississippi	(8)	–	8	Wisconsin	(12)	12	–
Missouri	(13)	13	–	Wyoming	(3)	3	–
Montana	(4)	4	–				
Nebraska	(6)	6	–	Totals	(531)	442	89

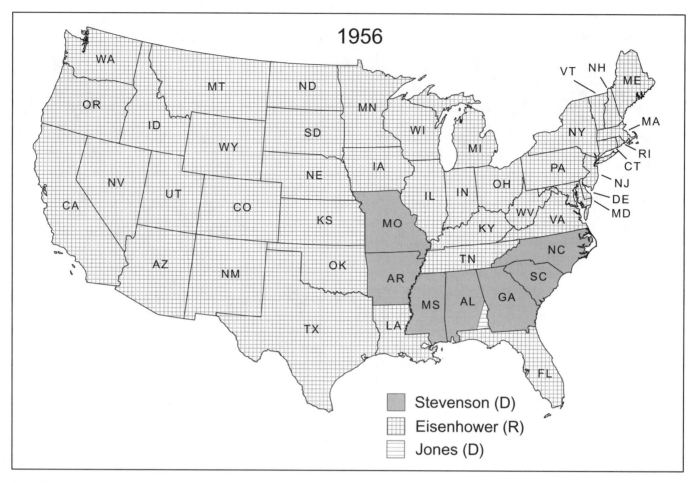

1956

Key: D—Democrat; R—Republican

States	Electoral votes	Eisenhower	Stevenson	Jones	States	Electoral votes	Eisenhower	Stevenson	Jones
Alabama[1]	(11)	–	10	1	Nevada	(3)	3	–	–
Arizona	(4)	4	–	–	New Hampshire	(4)	4	–	–
Arkansas	(8)	–	8	–	New Jersey	(16)	16	–	–
California	(32)	32	–	–	New Mexico	(4)	4	–	–
Colorado	(6)	6	–	–	New York	(45)	45	–	–
Connecticut	(8)	8	–	–	North Carolina	(14)	–	14	–
Delaware	(3)	3	–	–	North Dakota	(4)	4	–	–
Florida	(10)	10	–	–	Ohio	(25)	25	–	–
Georgia	(12)	–	12	–	Oklahoma	(8)	8	–	–
Idaho	(4)	4	–	–	Oregon	(6)	6	–	–
Illinois	(27)	27	–	–	Pennsylvania	(32)	32	–	–
Indiana	(13)	13	–	–	Rhode Island	(4)	4	–	–
Iowa	(10)	10	–	–	South Carolina	(8)	–	8	–
Kansas	(8)	8	–	–	South Dakota	(4)	4	–	–
Kentucky	(10)	10	–	–	Tennessee	(11)	11	–	–
Louisiana	(10)	10	–	–	Texas	(24)	24	–	–
Maine	(5)	5	–	–	Utah	(4)	4	–	–
Maryland	(9)	9	–	–	Vermont	(3)	3	–	–
Massachusetts	(16)	16	–	–	Virginia	(12)	12	–	–
Michigan	(20)	20	–	–	Washington	(9)	9	–	–
Minnesota	(11)	11	–	–	West Virginia	(8)	8	–	–
Mississippi	(8)	–	8	–	Wisconsin	(12)	12	–	–
Missouri	(13)	–	13	–	Wyoming	(3)	3	–	–
Montana	(4)	4	–	–					
Nebraska	(6)	6	–	–	Totals	(531)	457	73	1

1. For explanation of split electoral votes, see p. 158

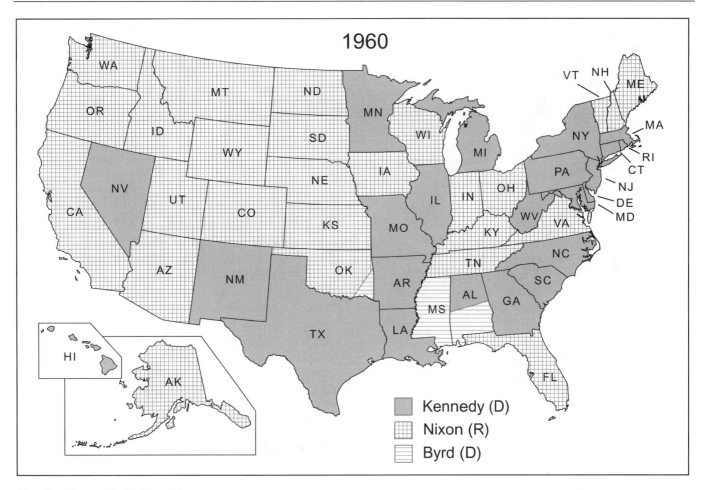

1960

Key: D—Democrat; R—Republican

States	Electoral votes	Kennedy	Nixon	Byrd	States	Electoral votes	Kennedy	Nixon	Byrd
Alabama[1]	(11)	5	–	6	Nebraska	(6)	–	6	–
Alaska	(3)	–	3	–	Nevada	(3)	3	–	–
Arizona	(4)	–	4	–	New Hampshire	(4)	–	4	–
Arkansas	(8)	8	–	–	New Jersey	(16)	16	–	–
California	(32)	–	32	–	New Mexico	(4)	4	–	–
Colorado	(6)	–	6	–	New York	(45)	45	–	–
Connecticut	(8)	8	–	–	North Carolina	(14)	14	–	–
Delaware	(3)	3	–	–	North Dakota	(4)	–	4	–
Florida	(10)	–	10	–	Ohio	(25)	–	25	–
Georgia	(12)	12	–	–	Oklahoma[2]	(8)	–	7	1
Hawaii	(3)	3	–	–	Oregon	(6)	–	6	–
Idaho	(4)	–	4	–	Pennsylvania	(32)	32	–	–
Illinois	(27)	27	–	–	Rhode Island	(4)	4	–	–
Indiana	(13)	–	13	–	South Carolina	(8)	8	–	–
Iowa	(10)	–	10	–	South Dakota	(4)	–	4	–
Kansas	(8)	–	8	–	Tennessee	(11)	–	11	–
Kentucky	(10)	–	10	–	Texas	(24)	24	–	–
Louisiana	(10)	10	–	–	Utah	(4)	–	4	–
Maine	(5)	–	5	–	Vermont	(3)	–	3	–
Maryland	(9)	9	–	–	Virginia	(12)	–	12	–
Massachusetts	(16)	16	–	–	Washington	(9)	–	9	–
Michigan	(20)	20	–	–	West Virginia	(8)	8	–	–
Minnesota	(11)	11	–	–	Wisconsin	(12)	–	12	–
Mississippi[1]	(8)	–	–	8	Wyoming	(3)	–	3	–
Missouri	(13)	13	–	–					
Montana	(4)	–	4	–	Totals	(537)	303	219	15

1. Six Alabama electors and all eight Mississippi electors, elected as "unpledged Democrats," cast their votes for Byrd.
2. For explanation of split electoral votes, see p. 158.

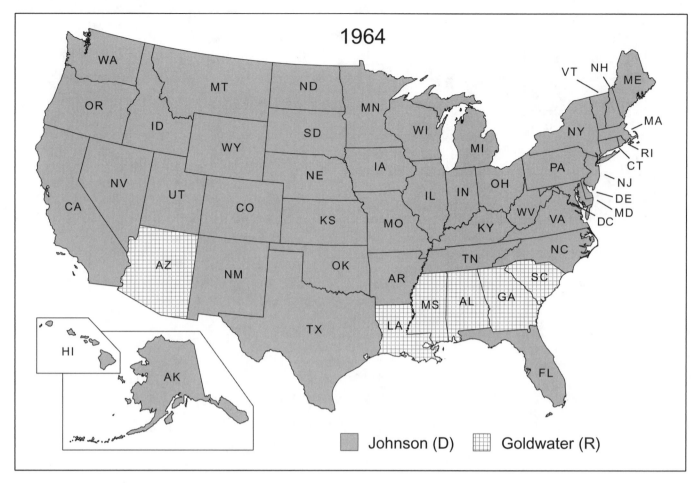

1964

Johnson (D)   Goldwater (R)

Key: D—Democrat; R—Republican

States	Electoral votes	Johnson	Goldwater	States	Electoral votes	Johnson	Goldwater
Alabama	(10)	–	10	Nebraska	(5)	5	–
Alaska	(3)	3	–	Nevada	(3)	3	–
Arizona	(5)	–	5	New Hampshire	(4)	4	–
Arkansas	(6)	6	–	New Jersey	(17)	17	–
California	(40)	40	–	New Mexico	(4)	4	–
Colorado	(6)	6	–	New York	(43)	43	–
Connecticut	(8)	8	–	North Carolina	(13)	13	–
Delaware	(3)	3	–	North Dakota	(4)	4	–
District of Columbia	(3)	3	–	Ohio	(26)	26	–
Florida	(14)	14	–	Oklahoma	(8)	8	–
Georgia	(12)	–	12	Oregon	(6)	6	–
Hawaii	(4)	4	–	Pennsylvania	(29)	29	–
Idaho	(4)	4	–	Rhode Island	(4)	4	–
Illinois	(26)	26	–	South Carolina	(8)	–	8
Indiana	(13)	13	–	South Dakota	(4)	4	–
Iowa	(9)	9	–	Tennessee	(11)	11	–
Kansas	(7)	7	–	Texas	(25)	25	–
Kentucky	(9)	9	–	Utah	(4)	4	–
Louisiana	(10)	–	10	Vermont	(3)	3	–
Maine	(4)	4	–	Virginia	(12)	12	–
Maryland	(10)	10	–	Washington	(9)	9	–
Massachusetts	(14)	14	–	West Virginia	(7)	7	–
Michigan	(21)	21	–	Wisconsin	(12)	12	–
Minnesota	(10)	10	–	Wyoming	(3)	3	–
Mississippi	(7)	–	7				
Missouri	(12)	12	–	Totals	(538)	486	52
Montana	(4)	4	–				

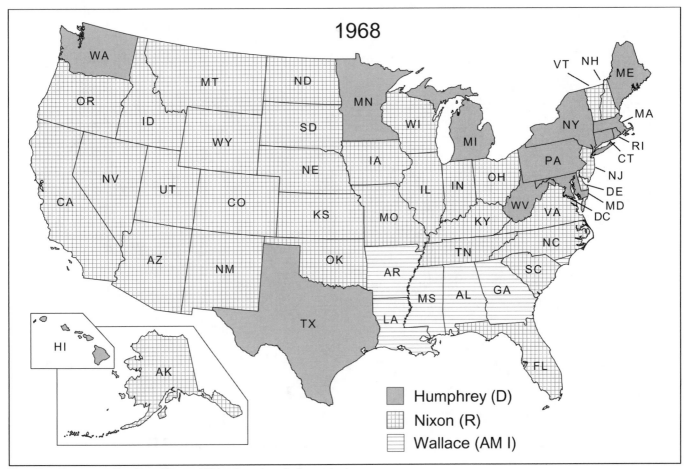

Key: D—Democrat; R—Republican; AM I—American Independent

States	Electoral votes	Nixon	Humphrey	Wallace	States	Electoral votes	Nixon	Humphrey	Wallace
Alabama	(10)	-	-	10	Nebraska	(5)	5	-	-
Alaska	(3)	3	-	-	Nevada	(3)	3	-	-
Arizona	(5)	5	-	-	New Hampshire	(4)	4	-	-
Arkansas	(6)	-	-	6	New Jersey	(17)	17	-	-
California	(40)	40	-	-	New Mexico	(4)	4	-	-
Colorado	(6)	6	-	-	New York	(43)	-	43	-
Connecticut	(8)	-	8	-	North Carolina[1]	(13)	12	-	1
Delaware	(3)	3	-	-	North Dakota	(4)	4	-	-
District of Columbia	(3)	-	3	-	Ohio	(26)	26	-	-
Florida	(14)	14	-	-	Oklahoma	(8)	8	-	-
Georgia	(12)	-	-	12	Oregon	(6)	6	-	-
Hawaii	(4)	-	4	-	Pennsylvania	(29)	-	29	-
Idaho	(4)	4	-	-	Rhode Island	(4)	-	4	-
Illinois	(26)	26	-	-	South Carolina	(8)	8	-	-
Indiana	(13)	13	-	-	South Dakota	(4)	4	-	-
Iowa	(9)	9	-	-	Tennessee	(11)	11	-	-
Kansas	(7)	7	-	-	Texas	(25)	-	25	-
Kentucky	(9)	9	-	-	Utah	(4)	4	-	-
Louisiana	(10)	-	-	10	Vermont	(3)	3	-	-
Maine	(4)	-	4	-	Virginia	(12)	12	-	-
Maryland	(10)	-	10	-	Washington	(9)	-	9	-
Massachusetts	(14)	-	14	-	West Virginia	(7)	-	7	-
Michigan	(21)	-	21	-	Wisconsin	(12)	12	-	-
Minnesota	(10)	-	10	-	Wyoming	(3)	3	-	-
Mississippi	(7)	-	-	7					
Missouri	(12)	12	-	-	Totals	(538)	301	191	46
Montana	(4)	4	-	-					

1. For explanation of split electoral votes, see p. 158.

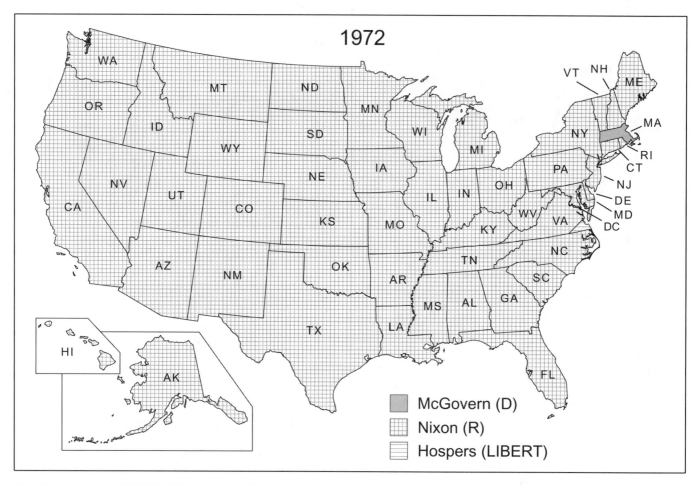

1972

McGovern (D)
Nixon (R)
Hospers (LIBERT)

Key: D—Democrat; LIBERT—Libertarian; R—Republican

States	Electoral votes	Nixon	McGovern	Hospers	States	Electoral votes	Nixon	McGovern	Hospers
Alabama	(9)	9	–	–	Nebraska	(5)	5	–	–
Alaska	(3)	3	–	–	Nevada	(3)	3	–	–
Arizona	(6)	6	–	–	New Hampshire	(4)	4	–	–
Arkansas	(6)	6	–	–	New Jersey	(17)	17	–	–
California	(45)	45	–	–	New Mexico	(4)	4	–	–
Colorado	(7)	7	–	–	New York	(41)	41	–	–
Connecticut	(8)	8	–	–	North Carolina	(13)	13	–	–
Delaware	(3)	3	–	–	North Dakota	(3)	3	–	–
District of Columbia	(3)	–	3	–	Ohio	(25)	25	–	–
Florida	(17)	17	–	–	Oklahoma	(8)	8	–	–
Georgia	(12)	12	–	–	Oregon	(6)	6	–	–
Hawaii	(4)	4	–	–	Pennsylvania	(27)	27	–	–
Idaho	(4)	4	–	–	Rhode Island	(4)	4	–	–
Illinois	(26)	26	–	–	South Carolina	(8)	8	–	–
Indiana	(13)	13	–	–	South Dakota	(4)	4	–	–
Iowa	(8)	8	–	–	Tennessee	(10)	10	–	–
Kansas	(7)	7	–	–	Texas	(26)	26	–	–
Kentucky	(9)	9	–	–	Utah	(4)	4	–	–
Louisiana	(10)	10	–	–	Vermont	(3)	3	–	–
Maine	(4)	4	–	–	Virginia[1]	(12)	11	–	1
Maryland	(10)	10	–	–	Washington	(9)	9	–	–
Massachusetts	(14)	–	14	–	West Virginia	(6)	6	–	–
Michigan	(21)	21	–	–	Wisconsin	(11)	11	–	–
Minnesota	(10)	10	–	–	Wyoming	(3)	3	–	–
Mississippi	(7)	7	–						
Missouri	(12)	12	–	–	Totals	(538)	520	17	1
Montana	(4)	4	–	–					

1. For explanation of split electoral votes, see p. 158.

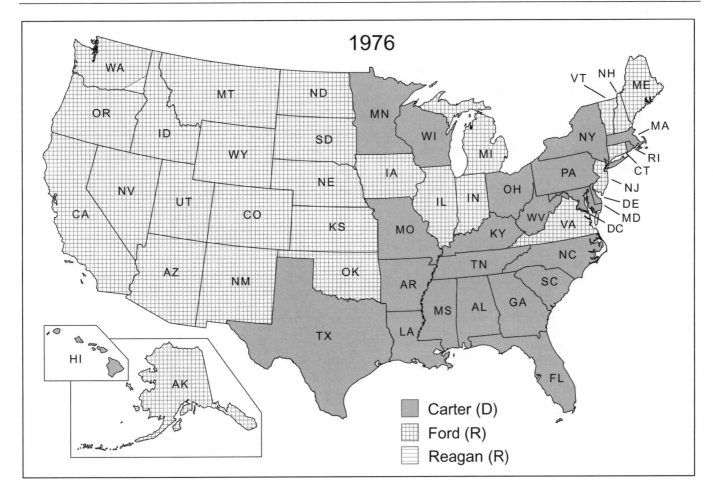

1976

Carter (D)
Ford (R)
Reagan (R)

Key: D—Democrat; R—Republican

States	Electoral votes	Carter	Ford	Reagan	States	Electoral votes	Carter	Ford	Reagan
Alabama	(9)	9	–	–	Nebraska	(5)	–	5	–
Alaska	(3)	–	3	–	Nevada	(3)	–	3	–
Arizona	(6)	–	6	–	New Hampshire	(4)	–	4	–
Arkansas	(6)	6	–	–	New Jersey	(17)	–	17	–
California	(45)	–	45	–	New Mexico	(4)	–	4	–
Colorado	(7)	–	7	–	New York	(41)	41	–	–
Connecticut	(8)	–	8	–	North Carolina	(13)	13	–	–
Delaware	(3)	3	–	–	North Dakota	(3)	–	3	–
District of Columbia	(3)	3	–	–	Ohio	(25)	25	–	–
Florida	(17)	17	–	–	Oklahoma	(8)	–	8	–
Georgia	(12)	12	–	–	Oregon	(6)	–	6	–
Hawaii	(4)	4	–	–	Pennsylvania	(27)	27	–	–
Idaho	(4)	–	4	–	Rhode Island	(4)	4	–	–
Illinois	(26)	–	26	–	South Carolina	(8)	8	–	–
Indiana	(13)	–	13	–	South Dakota	(4)	–	4	–
Iowa	(8)	–	8	–	Tennessee	(10)	10	–	–
Kansas	(7)	–	7	–	Texas	(26)	26	–	–
Kentucky	(9)	9	–	–	Utah	(4)	–	4	–
Louisiana	(10)	10	–	–	Vermont	(3)	–	3	–
Maine	(4)	–	4	–	Virginia	(12)	–	12	–
Maryland	(10)	10	–	–	Washington[1]	(9)	–	8	1
Massachusetts	(14)	14	–	–	West Virginia	(6)	6	–	–
Michigan	(21)	–	21	–	Wisconsin	(11)	11	–	–
Minnesota	(10)	10	–	–	Wyoming	(3)	–	3	–
Mississippi	(7)	7	–	–					
Missouri	(12)	12	–	–	Totals	(538)	297	240	1
Montana	(4)	–	4	–					

1. For explanation of split electoral votes, see p. 158.

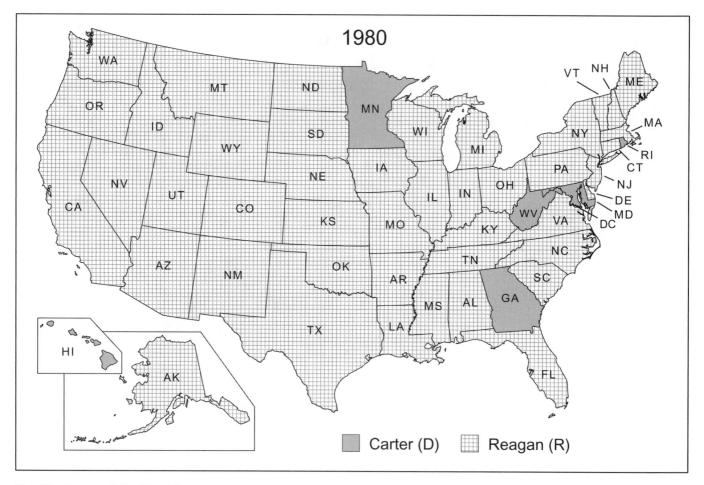

Key: D—Democrat; R—Republican

States	Electoral votes	Reagan	Carter	States	Electoral votes	Reagan	Carter
Alabama	(9)	9	–	Nebraska	(5)	5	–
Alaska	(3)	3	–	Nevada	(3)	3	–
Arizona	(6)	6	–	New Hampshire	(4)	4	–
Arkansas	(6)	6	–	New Jersey	(17)	17	–
California	(45)	45	–	New Mexico	(4)	4	–
Colorado	(7)	7	–	New York	(41)	41	–
Connecticut	(8)	8	–	North Carolina	(13)	13	–
Delaware	(3)	3	–	North Dakota	(3)	3	–
District of Columbia	(3)	–	3	Ohio	(25)	25	–
Florida	(17)	17	–	Oklahoma	(8)	8	–
Georgia	(12)	–	12	Oregon	(6)	6	–
Hawaii	(4)	–	4	Pennsylvania	(27)	27	–
Idaho	(4)	4	–	Rhode Island	(4)	–	4
Illinois	(26)	26	–	South Carolina	(8)	8	–
Indiana	(13)	13	–	South Dakota	(4)	4	–
Iowa	(8)	8	–	Tennessee	(10)	10	–
Kansas	(7)	7	–	Texas	(26)	26	–
Kentucky	(9)	9	–	Utah	(4)	4	–
Louisiana	(10)	10	–	Vermont	(3)	3	–
Maine	(4)	4	–	Virginia	(12)	12	–
Maryland	(10)	–	10	Washington	(9)	9	–
Massachusetts	(14)	14	–	West Virginia	(6)	–	6
Michigan	(21)	21	–	Wisconsin	(11)	11	–
Minnesota	(10)	–	10	Wyoming	(3)	3	–
Mississippi	(7)	7	–				
Missouri	(12)	12	–	Totals	(538)	489	49
Montana	(4)	4	–				

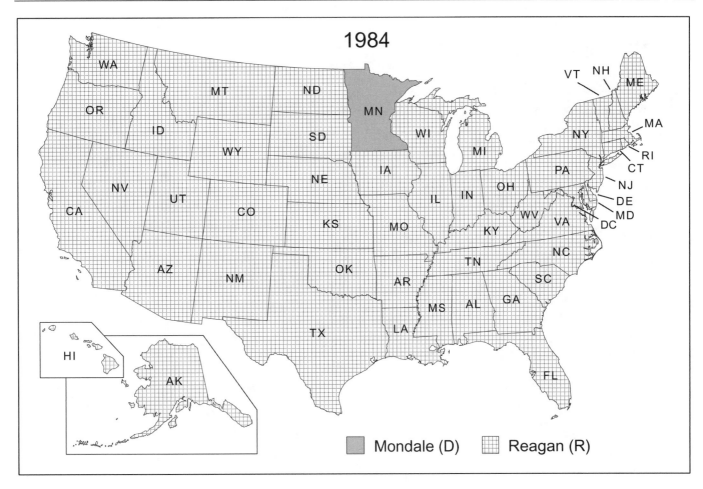

1984

Mondale (D)   Reagan (R)

Key: D—Democrat; R—Republican

States	Electoral votes	Reagan	Mondale	States	Electoral votes	Reagan	Mondale
Alabama	(9)	9	–	Nebraska	(5)	5	–
Alaska	(3)	3	–	Nevada	(4)	4	–
Arizona	(7)	7	–	New Hampshire	(4)	4	–
Arkansas	(6)	6	–	New Jersey	(16)	16	–
California	(47)	47	–	New Mexico	(5)	5	–
Colorado	(8)	8	–	New York	(36)	36	–
Connecticut	(8)	8	–	North Carolina	(13)	13	–
Delaware	(3)	3	–	North Dakota	(3)	3	–
District of Columbia	(3)	–	3	Ohio	(23)	23	–
Florida	(21)	21	–	Oklahoma	(8)	8	–
Georgia	(12)	12	–	Oregon	(7)	7	–
Hawaii	(4)	4	–	Pennsylvania	(25)	25	–
Idaho	(4)	4	–	Rhode Island	(4)	4	–
Illinois	(24)	24	–	South Carolina	(8)	8	–
Indiana	(12)	12	–	South Dakota	(3)	3	–
Iowa	(8)	8	–	Tennessee	(11)	11	–
Kansas	(7)	7	–	Texas	(29)	29	–
Kentucky	(9)	9	–	Utah	(5)	5	–
Louisiana	(10)	10	–	Vermont	(3)	3	–
Maine	(4)	4	–	Virginia	(12)	12	–
Maryland	(10)	10	–	Washington	(10)	10	–
Massachusetts	(13)	13	–	West Virginia	(6)	6	–
Michigan	(20)	20	–	Wisconsin	(11)	11	–
Minnesota	(10)	–	10	Wyoming	(3)	3	–
Mississippi	(7)	7	–				
Missouri	(11)	11	–	Totals	(538)	525	13
Montana	(4)	4	–				

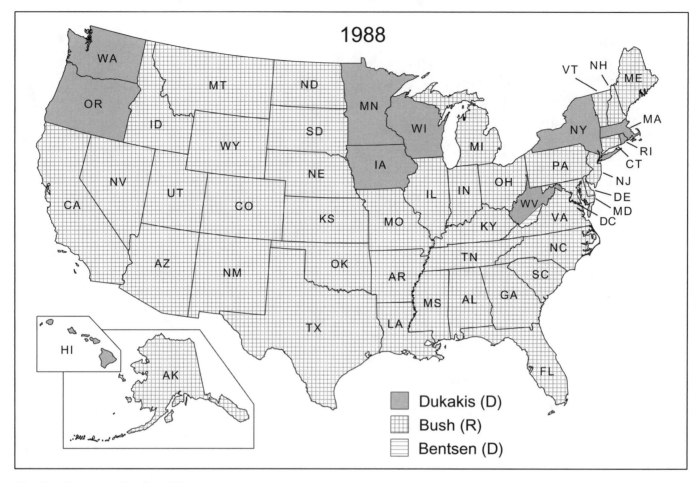

1988

Key: D—Democrat; R—Republican

States	Electoral votes	Bush	Dukakis	Bentsen	States	Electoral votes	Bush	Dukakis	Bentsen
Alabama	(9)	9	–	–	Nebraska	(5)	5	–	–
Alaska	(3)	3	–	–	Nevada	(4)	4	–	–
Arizona	(7)	7	–	–	New Hampshire	(4)	4	–	–
Arkansas	(6)	6	–	–	New Jersey	(16)	16	–	–
California	(47)	47	–	–	New Mexico	(5)	5	–	–
Colorado	(8)	8	–	–	New York	(36)	–	36	–
Connecticut	(8)	8	–	–	North Carolina	(13)	13	–	–
Delaware	(3)	3	–	–	North Dakota	(3)	3	–	–
District of Columbia	(3)	–	3	–	Ohio	(23)	23	–	–
Florida	(21)	21	–	–	Oklahoma	(8)	8	–	–
Georgia	(12)	12	–	–	Oregon	(7)	–	7	–
Hawaii	(4)	–	4	–	Pennsylvania	(25)	25	–	–
Idaho	(4)	4	–	–	Rhode Island	(4)	–	4	–
Illinois	(24)	24	–	–	South Carolina	(8)	8	–	–
Indiana	(12)	12	–	–	South Dakota	(3)	3	–	–
Iowa	(8)	–	8	–	Tennessee	(11)	11	–	–
Kansas	(7)	7	–	–	Texas	(29)	29	–	–
Kentucky	(9)	9	–	–	Utah	(5)	5	–	–
Louisiana	(10)	10	–	–	Vermont	(3)	3	–	–
Maine	(4)	4	–	–	Virginia	(12)	12	–	–
Maryland	(10)	10	–	–	Washington	(10)	–	10	–
Massachusetts	(13)	–	13	–	West Virginia[1]	(6)	–	5	1
Michigan	(20)	20	–	–	Wisconsin	(11)	–	11	–
Minnesota	(10)	–	10	–	Wyoming	(3)	3	–	–
Mississippi	(7)	7	–	–					
Missouri	(11)	11	–	–	Totals	(538)	426	111	1
Montana	(4)	4	–	–					

1. For explanation of split electoral vote, see p. 158.

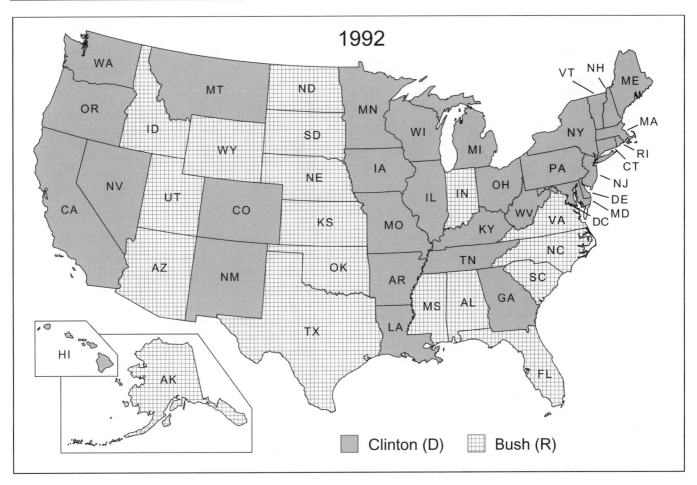

1992

Clinton (D)   Bush (R)

Key: D—Democrat; R—Republican

States	Electoral votes	Clinton	Bush	States	Electoral votes	Clinton	Bush
Alabama	(9)	–	9	Nebraska	(5)	–	5
Alaska	(3)	–	3	Nevada	(4)	4	–
Arizona	(8)	–	8	New Hampshire	(4)	4	–
Arkansas	(6)	6	–	New Jersey	(15)	15	–
California	(54)	54	–	New Mexico	(5)	5	–
Colorado	(8)	8	–	New York	(33)	33	–
Connecticut	(8)	8	–	North Carolina	(14)	–	14
Delaware	(3)	3	–	North Dakota	(3)	–	3
District of Columbia	(3)	3	–	Ohio	(21)	21	–
Florida	(25)	–	25	Oklahoma	(8)	–	8
Georgia	(13)	13	–	Oregon	(7)	7	–
Hawaii	(4)	4	–	Pennsylvania	(23)	23	–
Idaho	(4)	–	4	Rhode Island	(4)	4	–
Illinois	(22)	22	–	South Carolina	(8)	–	8
Indiana	(12)	–	12	South Dakota	(3)	–	3
Iowa	(7)	7	–	Tennessee	(11)	11	–
Kansas	(6)	–	6	Texas	(32)	–	32
Kentucky	(8)	8	–	Utah	(5)	–	5
Louisiana	(9)	9	–	Vermont	(3)	3	–
Maine	(4)	4	–	Virginia	(13)	–	13
Maryland	(10)	10	–	Washington	(11)	11	–
Massachusetts	(12)	12	–	West Virginia	(5)	5	–
Michigan	(18)	18	–	Wisconsin	(11)	11	–
Minnesota	(10)	10	–	Wyoming	(3)	–	3
Mississippi	(7)	–	7				
Missouri	(11)	11	–	Totals	(538)	370	168
Montana	(3)	3	–				

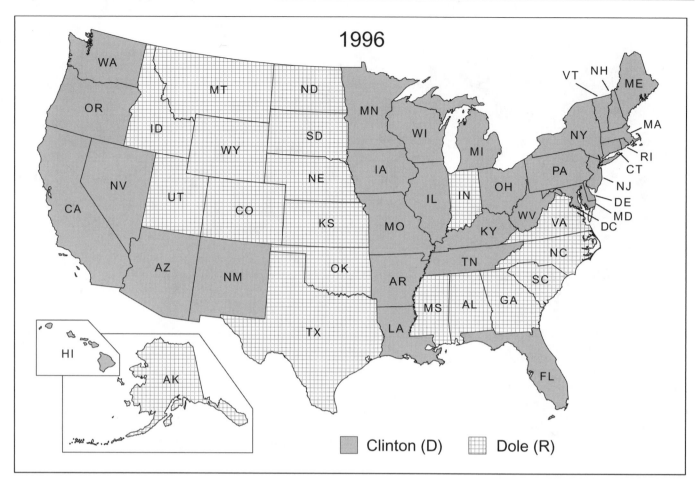

1996

Key: D—Democrat; R—Republican

States	Electoral votes	Clinton	Dole	States	Electoral votes	Clinton	Dole
Alabama	(9)	–	9	Nebraska	(5)	–	5
Alaska	(3)	–	3	Nevada	(4)	4	–
Arizona	(8)	8	–	New Hampshire	(4)	4	–
Arkansas	(6)	6	–	New Jersey	(15)	15	–
California	(54)	54	–	New Mexico	(5)	5	–
Colorado	(8)	–	8	New York	(33)	33	–
Connecticut	(8)	8	–	North Carolina	(14)	–	14
Delaware	(3)	3	–	North Dakota	(3)	–	3
District of Columbia	(3)	3	–	Ohio	(21)	21	–
Florida	(25)	25	–	Oklahoma	(8)	–	8
Georgia	(13)	–	13	Oregon	(7)	7	–
Hawaii	(4)	4	–	Pennsylvania	(23)	23	–
Idaho	(4)	–	4	Rhode Island	(4)	4	–
Illinois	(22)	22	–	South Carolina	(8)	–	8
Indiana	(12)	–	12	South Dakota	(3)	–	3
Iowa	(7)	7	–	Tennessee	(11)	11	–
Kansas	(6)	–	6	Texas	(32)	–	32
Kentucky	(8)	8	–	Utah	(5)	–	5
Louisiana	(9)	9	–	Vermont	(3)	3	–
Maine	(4)	4	–	Virginia	(13)	–	13
Maryland	(10)	10	–	Washington	(11)	11	–
Massachusetts	(12)	12	–	West Virginia	(5)	5	–
Michigan	(18)	18	–	Wisconsin	(11)	11	–
Minnesota	(10)	10	–	Wyoming	(3)	–	3
Mississippi	(7)	–	7				
Missouri	(11)	11	–	Totals	(538)	379	159
Montana	(3)	–	3				

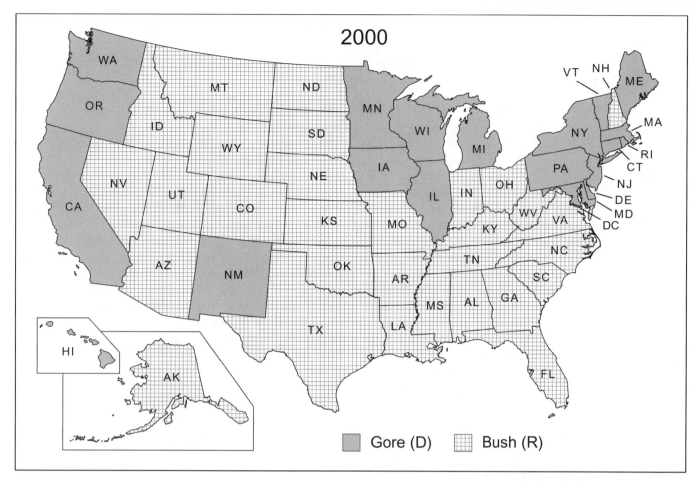

Key: D—Democrat; R—Republican

States	Electoral votes	Bush	Gore	States	Electoral votes	Bush	Gore
Alabama	(9)	9	–	Nebraska	(5)	5	–
Alaska	(3)	3	–	Nevada	(4)	4	–
Arizona	(8)	8	–	New Hampshire	(4)	4	–
Arkansas	(6)	6	–	New Jersey	(15)	–	15
California	(54)	–	54	New Mexico	(5)	–	5
Colorado	(8)	8	–	New York	(33)	–	33
Connecticut	(8)	–	8	North Carolina	(14)	14	–
Delaware	(3)	–	3	North Dakota	(3)	3	–
District of Columbia[1]	(3)	–	2	Ohio	(21)	21	–
Florida	(25)	25	–	Oklahoma	(8)	8	–
Georgia	(13)	13	–	Oregon	(7)	–	7
Hawaii	(4)	–	4	Pennsylvania	(23)	–	23
Idaho	(4)	4	–	Rhode Island	(4)	–	4
Illinois	(22)	–	22	South Carolina	(8)	8	–
Indiana	(12)	12	–	South Dakota	(3)	3	–
Iowa	(7)	–	7	Tennessee	(11)	11	–
Kansas	(6)	6	–	Texas	(32)	32	–
Kentucky	(8)	8	–	Utah	(5)	5	–
Louisiana	(9)	9	–	Vermont	(3)	–	3
Maine	(4)	–	4	Virginia	(13)	13	–
Maryland	(10)	–	10	Washington	(11)	–	11
Massachusetts	(12)	–	12	West Virginia	(5)	5	–
Michigan	(18)	–	18	Wisconsin	(11)	–	11
Minnesota	(10)	–	10	Wyoming	(3)	3	–
Mississippi	(7)	7	–				
Missouri	(11)	11	–	Totals	(538)	271	266
Montana	(3)	3	–				

1. For explanation of split electoral votes, see p. 158.

Electoral Votes for Vice President, 1804–2000

The following list gives the electoral votes for vice president from 1804 to 2000. Unless indicated by a note, the state-by-state breakdown of electoral votes for each vice-presidential candidate was the same as for his or her party's presidential candidate.

Prior to 1804, under Article II, Section 1 of the Constitution, each elector cast two votes—each vote for a different person. The electors did not distinguish between votes for president and vice president. The candidate receiving the second highest total became vice president. The Twelfth Amendment, ratified in 1804, required electors to vote separately for president and vice president.

In some cases, persons had received electoral votes although they had never been formally nominated. The word *candidate* is used in this section to designate persons receiving electoral votes.

The *Senate Manual* (Washington, D.C.: Government Printing Office, 1997) was the source used for vice-presidential elec-

toral votes for all elections up to 1996. The source for 2000 was the *CQ Weekly*.

For political party designation, the basic source was Svend Petersen, *A Statistical History of the American Presidential Elections* (Westport, Conn.: Greenwood Press, 1981). Petersen gives the party designation of *presidential candidates only*. Congressional Quarterly adopted Petersen's party designations for the running mates of presidential candidates.

To supplement Petersen, Congressional Quarterly consulted the *Biographical Directory of the American Congress, 1774–1996* (Washington, D.C.: CQ Staff Directories, 1997); the *Dictionary of American Biography* (New York: Charles Scribner's Sons, 1928–1936); the *Encyclopedia of American Biography* (New York: Harper and Row, 1974); and *Who Was Who in America, 1607–1968* (Chicago: Marquis Co., 1943–1968).

Year	Candidate	Electoral Votes
1804	George Clinton (Democratic-Republican)	162
	Rufus King (Federalist)	14
1808	George Clinton (Democratic-Republican)[1]	113
	John Langdon (Democratic-Republican)	9
	James Madison (Democratic-Republican)	3
	James Monroe (Democratic-Republican)	3
	Rufus King (Federalist)	47
1812	Elbridge Gerry (Democratic-Republican)[2]	131
	Jared Ingersoll (Federalist)	86
1816	Daniel D. Tompkins (Democratic-Republican)	183
	John E. Howard (Federalist)[3]	22
	James Ross (Federalist)	5
	John Marshall (Federalist)	4
	Robert G. Harper (Federalist)	3
1820	Daniel D. Tompkins (Democratic-Republican)[4]	218
	Richard Rush (Democratic-Republican)	1
	Richard Stockton (Federalist)	8
	Daniel Rodney (Federalist)	4
	Robert G. Harper (Federalist)	1
1824	John C. Calhoun (Democratic-Republican)[5]	182
	Nathan Sanford (Democratic-Republican)	30
	Nathaniel Macon (Democratic-Republican)	24
	Andrew Jackson (Democratic-Republican)	13
	Martin Van Buren (Democratic-Republican)	9
	Henry Clay (Democratic-Republican)	2
1828	John C. Calhoun (Democratic-Republican)[6]	171
	William Smith (Independent Democratic-Republican)	7
	Richard Rush (National Republican)	83
1832	Martin Van Buren (Democrat)[7]	189
	William Wilkins (Democrat)	30
	Henry Lee (Independent Democrat)	11
	John Sergeant (National Republican)	49
	Amos Ellmaker (Anti-Mason)	7
1836	Richard M. Johnson (Democrat)[8]	147
	William Smith (Independent Democrat)	23

Year	Candidate	Electoral Votes
	Francis Granger (Whig)	77
	John Tyler (Whig)	47
1840	John Tyler (Whig)	234
	Richard M. Johnson (Democrat)[9]	48
	L. W. Tazewell (Democrat)	11
	James K. Polk (Democrat)	1
1844	George M. Dallas (Democrat)	170
	Theodore Frelinghuysen (Whig)	105
1848	Millard Fillmore (Whig)	163
	William Orlando Butler (Democrat)	127
1852	William R. King (Democrat)	254
	William Alexander Graham (Whig)	42
1856	John C. Breckinridge (Democrat)	174
	William L. Dayton (Republican)	114
	Andrew Jackson Donelson (Whig-American)	8
1860	Hannibal Hamlin (Republican)	180
	Joseph Lane (Southern Democrat)	72
	Edward Everett (Constitutional Union)	39
	Herschel V. Johnson (Democrat)	12
1864	Andrew Johnson (Republican)	212
	George H. Pendleton (Democrat)	21
1868	Schuyler Colfax (Republican)	214
	Francis P. Blair (Democrat)	80
1872	Henry Wilson (Republican)	286
	Benjamin Gratz Brown (Democrat)[10]	47
	Alfred H. Colquitt (Democrat)	5
	John M. Palmer (Democrat)	3
	Thomas E. Bramlette (Democrat)	3
	William S. Groesbeck (Democrat)	1
	Willis B. Machen (Democrat)	1
	George W. Julian (Liberal Republican)	5
	Nathaniel P. Banks (Liberal Republican)	1
1876	William A. Wheeler (Republican)	185
	Thomas A. Hendricks (Democrat)	184
1880	Chester A. Arthur (Republican)	214
	William H. English (Democrat)	155

Year	Candidate	Electoral Votes
1884	Thomas A. Hendricks (Democrat)	219
	John A. Logan (Republican)	182
1888	Levi P. Morton (Republican)	233
	Allen G. Thurman (Democrat)	168
1892	Adlai E. Stevenson (Democrat)	277
	Whitelaw Reid (Republican)	145
	James G. Field (Populist)	22
1896	Garret A. Hobart (Republican)	271
	Arthur Sewall (Democrat)[11]	149
	Thomas E. Watson (Populist)	27
1900	Theodore Roosevelt (Republican)	292
	Adlai E. Stevenson (Democrat)	155
1904	Charles W. Fairbanks (Republican)	336
	Henry G. Davis (Democrat)	140
1908	James S. Sherman (Republican)	321
	John W. Kern (Democrat)	162
1912	Thomas R. Marshall (Democrat)	435
	Hiram W. Johnson (Progressive)	88
	Nicholas Murray Butler (Republican)[12]	8
1916	Thomas R. Marshall (Democrat)	277
	Charles W. Fairbanks (Republican)	254
1920	Calvin Coolidge (Republican)	404
	Franklin D. Roosevelt (Democrat)	127
1924	Charles G. Dawes (Republican)	382
	Charles W. Bryan (Democrat)	136
	Burton K. Wheeler (Progressive)	13
1928	Charles Curtis (Republican)	444
	Joseph T. Robinson (Democrat)	87
1932	John N. Garner (Democrat)	472
	Charles Curtis (Republican)	59
1936	John N. Garner (Democrat)	523
	Frank Knox (Republican)	8
1940	Henry A. Wallace (Democrat)	449
	Charles L. McNary (Republican)	82
1944	Harry S. Truman (Democrat)	432
	John W. Bricker (Republican)	99
1948	Alben W. Barkley (Democrat)	303
	Earl Warren (Republican)	189
	Fielding L. Wright (States' Rights Democrat)	39
1952	Richard Nixon (Republican)	442
	John J. Sparkman (Democrat)	89
1956	Richard Nixon (Republican)	457
	Estes Kefauver (Democrat)	73
	Herman Talmadge (Democrat)	1
1960	Lyndon B. Johnson (Democrat)	303
	Strom Thurmond (Democrat)[13]	14
	Henry Cabot Lodge Jr. (Republican)	219
	Barry Goldwater (Republican)	1
1964	Hubert H. Humphrey (Democrat)	486
	William E. Miller (Republican)	52
1968	Spiro T. Agnew (Republican)	301
	Edmund S. Muskie (Democrat)	191
	Curtis E. LeMay (American Independent)	46
1972	Spiro T. Agnew (Republican)	520
	R. Sargent Shriver (Democrat)	17
	Theodora Nathan (Libertarian)	1
1976	Walter F. Mondale (Democrat)	297
	Robert Dole (Republican)[14]	241
1980	George Bush (Republican)	489
	Walter F. Mondale (Democrat)	49
1984	George Bush (Republican)	525
	Geraldine A. Ferraro (Democrat)	13
1988	Dan Quayle (Republican)	426
	Lloyd Bentsen (Democrat)[15]	111
	Michael S. Dukakis (Democrat)	1
1992	Al Gore (Democrat)	370
	Dan Quayle (Republican)	168
1996	Al Gore (Democrat)	379
	Jack Kemp (Republican)	159
2000	Richard Cheney (Republican)	271
	Joseph Lieberman (Democrat)[16]	266

1. New York cast 13 presidential electoral votes for Democratic-Republican James Madison and 6 votes for Clinton; for vice president, New York cast 13 votes for Clinton, 3 votes for Madison, and 3 votes for Monroe. Langdon received Ohio's 3 votes and Vermont's 6 votes.

2. The state-by-state vote for Gerry was the same as for Democratic-Republican presidential candidate Madison, except for Massachusetts and New Hampshire. Massachusetts cast 2 votes for Gerry and 20 votes for Ingersoll; New Hampshire cast 1 vote for Gerry and 7 votes for Ingersoll.

3. Four Federalists received vice-presidential electoral votes: Howard—Massachusetts, 22 votes; Ross—Connecticut, 5 votes; Marshall—Connecticut, 4 votes; Harper—Delaware, 3 votes

4. The state-by-state vote for Tompkins was the same as for Democratic-Republican presidential candidate Monroe, except for Delaware, Maryland, and Massachusetts. Delaware cast 4 votes for Rodney; Maryland cast 10 votes for Tompkins and 1 for Harper; Massachusetts cast 7 votes for Tompkins and 8 for Stockton.

New Hampshire, which cast 7 presidential electoral votes for Monroe and 1 vote for John Quincy Adams, cast 7 vice-presidential electoral votes for Tompkins and 1 vote for Rush.

5. The state-by-state vice-presidential electoral vote was as follows:

Calhoun—Alabama, 5 votes; Delaware, 1 vote; Illinois, 3 votes; Indiana, 5 votes; Kentucky, 7 votes; Louisiana, 5 votes; Maine, 9 votes; Maryland, 10 votes; Massachusetts, 15 votes; Mississippi, 3 votes; New Hampshire, 7 votes; New Jersey, 8 votes; New York, 29 votes; North Carolina, 15 votes; Pennsylvania, 28 votes; Rhode Island, 3 votes; South Carolina, 11 votes; Tennessee, 11 votes; Vermont, 7 votes.

Sanford—Kentucky, 7 votes; New York, 7 votes; Ohio, 16 votes.

Macon—Virginia, 24 votes.

Jackson—Connecticut, 8 votes; Maryland, 1 vote; Missouri, 3 votes; New Hampshire, 1 vote.

Van Buren—Georgia, 9 votes.

Clay—Delaware, 2 votes.

6. The state-by-state vote for Calhoun was the same as for Democratic-Republican presidential candidate Jackson, except for Georgia, which cast 2 votes for Calhoun and 7 votes for Smith.

7. The state-by-state vote for Van Buren was the same as for Democratic-Republican presidential candidate Jackson, except for Pennsylvania, which cast 30 votes for Wilkins.

South Carolina cast 11 presidential electoral votes for Independent Democratic presidential candidate Floyd and 11 votes for Independent Democratic vice-presidential candidate Lee.

Vermont cast 7 presidential electoral votes for Anti-Masonic candidate Wirt and 7 vice-presidential electoral votes for Wirt's running mate, Ellmaker.

8. The state-by-state vote for Johnson was the same as for Democratic presidential candidate Van Buren, except for Virginia, which cast 23 votes for Smith.

Granger's state-by-state vote was the same as for Whig presidential candidate Harrison, except for Maryland and Massachusetts. Maryland cast 10 presidential electoral votes for Harrison and 10 vice-presidential votes for Tyler; Massachusetts cast 14 presidential electoral votes for Whig candidate Webster and 14 vice-presidential votes over Granger.

Tyler received 11 votes from Georgia, 10 from Maryland, 11 from South Carolina, and 15 from Tennessee.

No vice-presidential candidate received a majority of the electoral vote. As a result the Senate, for the only time in history, selected the vice president under the provisions of the Twelfth Amendment. Johnson was elected vice president by a vote of 33 to 16 over Granger.

9. The Democratic party did not nominate a vice-presidential candidate in 1840. Johnson's state-by-state vote was the same as for presidential candidate Van Buren, except for South Carolina and Virginia. South Carolina cast 11 votes for Tazewell. Virginia cast 23 presidential electoral votes for Van Buren, 22 vice-presidential votes for Johnson, and 1 vice-presidential vote for Polk.

10. Liberal Republican and Democratic presidential candidate Horace Greeley died November 29, 1872. As a result eighteen electors pledged to Greeley cast their presidential electoral votes for Brown, Greeley's running mate.

The vice-presidential vote was as follows:

Brown—Georgia, 5 votes; Kentucky, 8 votes; Maryland, 8 votes; Missouri, 6 votes; Tennessee, 12 votes; Texas, 8 votes.

Colquitt—Georgia, 5 votes.
Palmer—Missouri, 3 votes.
Bramlette—Kentucky, 3 votes.
Groesbeck—Missouri, 1 vote.
Machen—Kentucky, 1 vote.
Julian—Missouri, 5 votes.
Banks—Georgia, 1 vote.

11. The state-by-state vote for Sewall was the same as for Democratic-Populist candidate William Jennings Bryan, except for the following states, which cast electoral votes for Watson: Arkansas, 3 votes; Louisiana, 4; Missouri, 4; Montana, 1; Nebraska, 4; North Carolina, 5; South Dakota, 2; Utah, 1; Washington, 2; Wyoming, 1.

12. Butler received the 8 electoral votes of Vice President James Sherman, who died Oct. 30, 1912, after being renominated on the Republican ticket. Butler was named as the substitute candidate.

13. Democratic electors carried Alabama's 11 electoral votes. Five of the electors were pledged to the national Democratic ticket of Kennedy and Johnson. Six electors ran unpledged and voted for Harry F. Byrd for president and Strom Thurmond for vice president.

Mississippi's eight electors voted for Byrd and Thurmond.

In Oklahoma the Republican ticket of Nixon and Lodge carried the state, but Henry D. Irwin, 1 of the state's 8 electors voted for Byrd for president and Goldwater for vice president.

14. Mike Padden, a Republican elector from the state of Washington cast his presidential electoral vote for Reagan instead of the Republican nominee, Ford. But he voted for Dole, Ford's running mate, for vice president. Dole thus received one more electoral vote than Ford.

15. Margaret Leach, a Democratic elector from West Virginia, cast her vice-presidential electoral vote for Dukakis, the Democratic nominee for president, and her presidential vote for his running mate, Bentsen.

16. Barbara Lett-Simmons, a Democratic elector from the District of Columbia, withheld her vice-presidential electoral vote for Lieberman (and presidential electoral vote for Gore).

Biographical Directory of Presidential and Vice-Presidential Candidates

THE NAMES in the directory include all persons who have received electoral votes for president or vice president since 1789. Also included are prominent third-party candidates who received popular votes but no electoral votes, and Nelson A. Rockefeller, appointed vice president by Gerald R. Ford, who became president following the resignation of Richard Nixon. For the 2000 election, only the presidential and vice-presidential candidates for the Democratic and Republican parties are included.

The material is organized as follows: name, state of residence in the year(s) the individual received electoral votes, party or parties with which the individual identified when he or she received electoral votes, date of birth, date of death (where applicable), major offices held, and the year(s) of candidacy.

For the elections of 1789 through 1800, presidential electors did not vote separately for president or vice president. It was, therefore, difficult in many cases to determine if an individual receiving electoral votes in these elections was a candidate for the office of president or vice president. Where no determination could be made from the sources consulted by Congressional Quarterly, the year in which the individual received electoral votes is given with no specification as to

whether the individual was a candidate for president or vice president.

The following sources were used: *American Political Leaders, 1789–2000,* (Washington, D.C.: Congressional Quarterly, 2000); *Biographical Directory of the United States Congress, 1774–1989,* (Washington, D.C.: Government Printing Office, 1989); *Dictionary of American Biography,* (New York: Scribner's, 1928–36); John A. Garraty, ed., *Encyclopedia of American Biography,* (New York: Harper and Row, 1974); Jaques Cattell Press, ed., *Who's Who in American Politics, 1977–78,* 6th ed. (New York: R. R. Bowker, 1977); *Who Was Who in America, 1607–1968,* (Chicago: Marquis, 1943–68); Svend Petersen, *A Statistical History of the American Presidential Elections,* (Westport, Conn.: Greenwood Press, 1981); Richard M. Scammon, *America Votes 10* (Washington, D.C.: Congressional Quarterly, 1973); Richard M. Scammon and Alice V. McGillivray, *America Votes 12* (Washington, D.C.: Congressional Quarterly, 1977); *America Votes 14* (Washington, D.C.: Congressional Quarterly, *America Votes 18* (Washington, D.C.: Congressional Quarterly, *America Votes 20* (Washington, D.C.: Congressional Quarterly, 1993); Rhodes Cook, *America Votes 22* (Washington, D.C.: Congressional Quarterly, 1997); Rhodes Cook, *America Votes 24* (Washington, D.C.: CQ Press, 2001).

Adams, Charles Francis - Mass. (Free Soil) Aug. 18, 1807–Nov. 21, 1886; House, 1859–1861; minister to Great Britain, 1861–1868. Candidacy: VP - 1848.

Adams, John - Mass. (Federalist) Oct. 30, 1735–July 4, 1826; Continental Congress, 1774; signer of Declaration of Independence, 1776; minister to Great Britain, 1785; U.S. vice president, 1789–1797; U.S. president, 1797–1801. Candidacies: VP - 1789, 1792; P - 1796, 1800.

Adams, John Quincy - Mass. (Democratic-Republican, National Republican) July 11, 1767–Feb. 23, 1848; Senate, 1803–1808; minister to Russia, 1809–1814; minister to Great Britain, 1815–1817; secretary of state, 1817–1825; U.S. president, 1825–1829; House, 1831–1848. Candidacies: P - 1820, 1824, 1828.

Adams, Samuel - Mass. (Federalist) Sept. 27, 1722–Oct. 2, 1803; Continental Congress, 1774–1781; signer of Declaration of Independence; governor, 1793–1797. Candidacy: 1796.

Agnew, Spiro Theodore - Md. (Republican) Nov. 9, 1918–Sept. 17, 1996; governor, 1967–1969; U.S. vice president, 1969–1973 (resigned Oct. 10, 1973). Candidacies: VP - 1968, 1972.

Anderson, John B. - Ill. (Republican, Independent) Feb. 15, 1922– ; state's attorney, 1956–1960; House, 1961–1981. Candidacy: P - 1980.

Armstrong, James - Pa. (Federalist) Aug. 29, 1748–May 6, 1828; House, 1793–1795. Candidacy: 1789.

Arthur, Chester Alan - N.Y. (Republican) Oct. 5, 1830–Nov. 18, 1886; collector, Port of N.Y., 1871–1878; U.S. vice president, 1881; U.S. president, 1881–1885. Candidacy: VP - 1880.

Banks, Nathaniel Prentice - Mass. (Liberal Republican) Jan. 30, 1816–Sept. 1, 1894; House, 1853–1857, 1865–1873, 1875–1879, 1889–1891; governor, 1858–1861. Candidacy: VP - 1872.

Barkley, Alben William - Ky. (Democratic) Nov. 24, 1877–April 30, 1956; House, 1913–1927; Senate, 1927–1949, 1955–1956; Senate majority leader, 1937–1947; Senate minority leader, 1947–1949; U.S. vice president, 1949–1953. Candidacy: VP - 1948.

Bell, John - Tenn. (Constitutional Union) Feb. 15, 1797–Sept. 10, 1869; House, 1827–1841; Speaker of the House, 1834–1835; secretary of war, 1841; Senate, 1847–1859. Candidacy: P - 1860.

Benson, Allan Louis - N.Y. (Socialist) Nov. 6, 1871–Aug. 19, 1940; writer, editor; founder of *Reconstruction Magazine,* 1918. Candidacy: P - 1916.

Bentsen, Lloyd Millard Jr. - Texas (Democratic) Feb. 11, 1921– ; House 1948–1955; Senate 1971–1993; secretary of Treasury, 1993–1994. Candidacy: VP - 1988.

Bidwell, John - Calif. (Prohibition) Aug. 5, 1819–April 4, 1900; California pioneer; major in Mexican War; House, 1865–1867. Candidacy: P - 1892.

Birney, James Gillespie - N.Y. (Liberty) Feb. 4, 1792–Nov. 25, 1857; Kentucky Legislature, 1816–1817; Alabama Legislature, 1819–1820. Candidacies: P - 1840, 1844.

Blaine, James Gillespie - Maine (Republican) Jan. 31, 1830–Jan. 27, 1893; House, 1863–1876; Speaker of the House, 1869–1875; Senate, 1876–1881; secretary of state, 1881, 1889–1892; president, first Pan American Congress, 1889. Candidacy: P - 1884.

Blair, Francis Preston Jr. - Mo. (Democratic) Feb. 19, 1821–July 8, 1875; House, 1857–1859, 1860, 1861–1862, 1863–1864; Senate, 1871–1873. Candidacy: VP - 1868.

Bramlette, Thomas E. - Ky. (Democratic) Jan. 3, 1817–Jan. 12, 1875; governor, 1863–1867. Candidacy: VP - 1872.

Breckinridge, John Cabell - Ky. (Democratic, Southern Democratic) Jan. 21, 1821–May 17, 1875; House, 1851–1855; U.S. vice president, 1857–1861; Senate, 1861; major general, Confederacy, 1861–1865; secretary of war, Confederacy, 1865. Candidacies: VP - 1856; P - 1860.

Bricker, John William - Ohio (Republican) Sept. 6, 1893–March 22, 1986; attorney general of Ohio, 1933–1937; governor, 1939–1945; Senate, 1947–1959. Candidacy: VP - 1944.

Brown, Benjamin Gratz - Mo. (Democratic) May 28, 1826–Dec. 13, 1885; Senate, 1863–1867; governor, 1871–1873. Candidacy: VP - 1872.

Bryan, Charles Wayland - Neb. (Democratic) Feb. 10, 1867–March 4, 1945; governor, 1923–1925, 1931–1935; Candidacy: VP - 1924.

Bryan, William Jennings - Neb. (Democratic, Populist) March 19, 1860–July 26, 1925; House, 1891–1895; secretary of state, 1913–1915. Candidacies: P - 1896, 1900, 1908.

Buchanan, James - Pa. (Democratic) April 23, 1791–June 1, 1868; House, 1821–1831; minister to Russia, 1832–1834; Senate, 1834–1845; secretary of state, 1845–1849; minister to Great Britain, 1853–1856; U.S. president, 1857–1861. Candidacy: P - 1856.

Burr, Aaron - N.Y. (Democratic-Republican) Feb. 6, 1756–Sept. 14, 1836; attorney general of N.Y., 1789–1790; Senate, 1791–1797; U.S. vice president, 1801–1805. Candidacies: 1792, 1796, 1800.

Bush, George - Texas (Republican) June 12, 1924– ; House, 1967–1970; ambassador to the United Nations, 1971–1973; chairman of the Republican National Committee, 1973–1974; head of the U.S. liaison office in Peking, 1974–1975; director of the Central Intelligence Agency, 1976–1977; U.S. vice president, 1981–1989; U.S. president, 1989–1993. Candidacies: VP - 1980, 1984; P - 1988, 1992.

Bush, George W. - Texas (Republican) July, 6, 1946– ; governor, 1995–2000; U.S. president, 2001– . Candidacy: P - 2000.

Butler, Benjamin Franklin - Mass. (Greenback, Anti-Monopoly) Nov. 5, 1818–Jan. 11, 1893; House, 1867–1875, 1877–1879; governor, 1883–1884. Candidacy: P - 1884.

Butler, Nicholas Murray - N.Y. (Republican) April 2, 1862–Dec. 7, 1947; president, Columbia University, 1901–1945; president, Carnegie Endowment for International Peace, 1925–1945. Candidacy: VP - 1912. (Substituted as candidate after Oct. 30 death of nominee James S. Sherman.)

Butler, William Orlando - Ky. (Democratic) April 19, 1791–Aug. 6, 1880; House, 1939–1943. Candidacy: VP - 1848.

Byrd, Harry Flood - Va. (States' Rights Democratic, Independent Democratic) June 10, 1887–Oct. 20, 1966; governor, 1926–1930; Senate, 1933–1965. Candidacies: P - 1956, 1960.

Calhoun, John Caldwell - S.C. (Democratic-Republican, Democratic) March 18, 1782–March 31, 1850; House, 1811–1817; secretary of war, 1817–1825; U.S. vice president, 1825–1832; Senate, 1832–1843, 1845–1850; secretary of state, 1844–1845. Candidacies: VP - 1824, 1828.

Carter, James Earl Jr. - Ga. (Democratic) Oct. 1, 1924– ; Georgia Legislature, 1963–1967; governor, 1971–1975; U.S. president, 1977–1981. Candidacies: P - 1976, 1980.

Cass, Lewis - Mich. (Democratic) Oct. 9, 1782–June 17, 1866; military and civil governor of Michigan Territory, 1813–1831; secretary of war, 1831–1836; minister to France, 1836–1842; Senate, 1845–1848, 1849–1857; secretary of state, 1857–1860. Candidacy: P - 1848.

Cheney, Richard - Wyo. (Republican) Jan. 30, 1941– ; House 1979–1989; secretary of defense, 1989–1993; U.S. vice president, 2001– . Candidacy: VP - 2000.

Clay, Henry - Ky. (Democratic-Republican, National Republican, Whig) April 12, 1777–June 29, 1852; Senate, 1806–1807, 1810–1811, 1831–1842, 1849–1852; House, 1811–1814, 1815–1821, 1823–1825; Speaker of the House, 1811–1814, 1815–1820, 1823–1825; secretary of state, 1825–1829. Candidacies: P - 1824, 1832, 1844.

Cleveland, Stephen Grover - N.Y. (Democratic) March 18, 1837–June 24, 1908; mayor of Buffalo, 1882; governor, 1883–1885; U.S. president, 1885–1889, 1893–1897. Candidacies: P - 1884, 1888, 1892.

Clinton, Bill - Ark. (Democrat) Aug. 19, 1946– ; attorney general of Arkansas, 1977–1979; governor, 1979–1981, 1983–1992; U.S. president, 1993–2001. Candidacies: P - 1992, 1996.

Clinton, De Witt - N.Y. (Independent Democratic-Republican, Federalist) March 2, 1769–Feb. 11, 1828; Senate, 1802–1803; mayor of New York, 1803–1807, 1810, 1811, 1813, 1814; governor, 1817–1823, 1825–1828. Candidacy: P - 1812.

Clinton, George - N.Y. (Democratic-Republican) July 26, 1739–April 20, 1812; Continental Congress, 1775–1776; governor, 1777–1795, 1801–1804; U.S. vice president, 1805–1812. Candidacies: VP - 1789, 1792, 1796, 1804, 1808.

Colfax, Schuyler - Ind. (Republican) March 23, 1823–Jan. 13, 1885; House, 1855–1869; Speaker of the House, 1863–1869; U.S. vice president, 1869–1873. Candidacy: VP - 1868.

Colquitt, Alfred Holt - Ga. (Democratic) April 20, 1824–March 26, 1894; House, 1853–1855; governor, 1877–1882; Senate, 1883–1894. Candidacy: VP - 1872.

Coolidge, Calvin - Mass. (Republican) July 4, 1872–Jan. 5, 1933; governor, 1919–1921; U.S. vice president, 1921–1923; U.S. president, 1923–1929. Candidacies: VP - 1920; P - 1924.

Cox, James Middleton - Ohio (Democratic) March 31, 1870–July 15, 1957; House, 1909–1913; governor, 1913–1915, 1917–1921. Candidacy: P - 1920.

Crawford, William Harris - Ga. (Democratic-Republican) Feb. 24, 1772–Sept. 15, 1834; Senate, 1807–1813; president pro tempore of the Senate, 1812–1813; secretary of war, 1815–1816; secretary of Treasury, 1816–1825. Candidacy: P - 1824.

Curtis, Charles - Kan. (Republican) Jan. 25, 1860–Feb. 8, 1936; House, 1893–1907; Senate, 1907–1913, 1915–1929; president pro tempore of the Senate, 1911; Senate majority leader, 1925–1929; U.S. vice president, 1929–1933. Candidacies: VP - 1928, 1932.

Dallas, George Mifflin - Pa. (Democratic) July 10, 1792–Dec. 31, 1864; Senate, 1831–1833; minister to Russia, 1837–1839; U.S. vice president, 1845–1849; minister to Great Britain, 1856–1861. Candidacy: VP - 1844.

Davis, David - Ill. (Democratic) March 9, 1815–June 26, 1886; associate justice of U.S. Supreme Court, 1862–1877; Senate, 1877–1883; president pro tempore of the Senate, 1881. Candidacy: P - 1872.

Davis, Henry Gassaway - W.Va. (Democratic) Nov. 16, 1823–March 11, 1916; Senate, 1871–1883; chairman of Pan American Railway Committee, 1901–1916. Candidacy: VP - 1904.

Davis, John William - W.Va., N.Y. (Democratic) April 13, 1873–March 24, 1955; House, 1911–1913; solicitor general, 1913–1918; ambassador to Great Britain, 1918–1921. Candidacy: P - 1924.

Dawes, Charles Gates - Ill. (Republican) Aug. 27, 1865–April 3, 1951; U.S. comptroller of the currency, 1898–1901; first director of Bureau of the Budget, 1921–1922; U.S. vice president, 1925–1929; ambassador to Great Britain, 1929–1932. Candidacy: VP - 1924.

Dayton, William Lewis - N.J. (Republican) Feb. 17, 1807–Dec. 1, 1864; Senate, 1842–1851; minister to France, 1861–1864. Candidacy: VP - 1856.

Debs, Eugene Victor - Ind. (Socialist) Nov. 5, 1855–Oct. 20, 1926; Indiana Legislature, 1885; president, American Railway Union, 1893–1897. Candidacies: P - 1900, 1904, 1908, 1912, 1920.

Dewey, Thomas Edmund - N.Y. (Republican) March 24, 1902–March 16, 1971; district attorney, New York County, 1937–1941; governor, 1943–1955. Candidacies: P - 1944, 1948.

Dole, Robert Joseph - Kan. (Republican) July 22, 1923– ; House, 1961–1969; Senate, 1969–1996; Senate majority leader, 1985–1987, 1995–1996; Senate minority leader, 1987–1995; chairman of the Republican National Committee, 1971–1973. Candidacies: VP - 1976; P - 1996.

Donelson, Andrew Jackson - Tenn. (American "Know-Nothing") Aug. 25, 1799–June 26, 1871; minister to Prussia, 1846–1848; minister to Germany, 1848–1849. Candidacy: VP - 1856.

Douglas, Stephen Arnold - Ill. (Democratic) April 23, 1813–June 3, 1861; House, 1843–1847; Senate, 1847–1861. Candidacy: P - 1860.

Dukakis, Michael Stanley - Mass. (Democratic) Nov. 3, 1933– ; governor, 1975–1979, 1983–1991. Candidacy: P - 1988.

Eagleton, Thomas Francis - Mo. (Democratic) Sept. 4, 1929– ; attorney general of Missouri, 1961–1965; lieutenant governor, 1965–1968; Senate, 1968–1987. Candidacy: VP - 1972. (Resigned from Democratic ticket July 31; replaced by R. Sargent Shriver Jr.)

Eisenhower, Dwight David - N.Y., Pa. (Republican) Oct. 14, 1890–March 28, 1969; general of U.S. Army, 1943–1948; Army chief of staff, 1945–1948; president of Columbia University, 1948–1951; commander of North Atlantic Treaty Organization, 1951–1952; U.S. president, 1953–1961. Candidacies: P - 1952, 1956.

Ellmaker, Amos - Pa. (Anti-Masonic) Feb. 2, 1787–Nov. 28, 1851; elected to the House for the term beginning in 1815 but did not qualify; attorney general of Pennsylvania, 1816–1819, 1828–1829. Candidacy: VP - 1832.

Ellsworth, Oliver - Conn. (Federalist) April 29, 1745–Nov. 26, 1807; Continental Congress, 1778–1783; Senate, 1789–1796; chief justice of United States, 1796–1800; minister to France, 1799. Candidacy: 1796.

English, William Hayden - Ind. (Democratic) Aug. 27, 1822–Feb. 7, 1896; House, 1853–1861. Candidacy: VP - 1880.

Everett, Edward - Mass. (Constitutional Union) April 11, 1794–Jan. 15, 1865; House, 1825–1835; governor, 1836–1840; minister to Great Britain, 1841–1845; president of Harvard University, 1846–1849; secretary of state, 1852–1853; Senate, 1853–1854. Candidacy: VP - 1860.

Fairbanks, Charles Warren - Ind. (Republican) May 11, 1852–June 4, 1918; Senate, 1897–1905; U.S. vice president, 1905–1909. Candidacies: VP - 1904, 1916.

Ferraro, Geraldine Anne - N.Y. (Democratic) Aug. 26, 1935– ; assistant district attorney, Queens County, 1974–1978; House, 1979–1985. Candidacy: VP - 1984.

Field, James Gaven - Va. (Populist) Feb. 24, 1826–Oct. 12, 1901; major in the Confederate Army, 1861–1865; attorney general of Virginia, 1877–1882. Candidacy: VP - 1892.

Fillmore, Millard - N.Y. (Whig, American "Know-Nothing") Jan. 7, 1800–March 8, 1874; House, 1833–1835, 1837–1843; N.Y. comptroller, 1847–1849; U.S. vice president, 1849–1850; U.S. president, 1850–1853. Candidacies: VP - 1848; P - 1856.

Fisk, Clinton Bowen - N.J. (Prohibition) Dec. 8, 1828–July 9, 1890; Civil War brevet major general; founder of Fisk University, 1866; member, Board of Indian Commissioners, 1874, president, 1881–1890. Candidacy: P - 1888.

Floyd, John - Va. (Independent Democratic) April 24, 1783–Aug. 17, 1837; House, 1817–1829; governor, 1830–1834. Candidacy: P - 1832.

Ford, Gerald Rudolph Jr. - Mich. (Republican) July 14, 1913– ; House, 1949–1973; House minority leader, 1965–1973; U.S. vice president, 1973–1974; U.S. president, 1974–1977. Candidacy: P - 1976.

Frelinghuysen, Theodore - N.J. (Whig) March 28, 1787–April 12, 1862; attorney general of New Jersey, 1817–1829; Senate, 1829–1835; president of Rutgers College, 1850–1862. Candidacy: VP - 1844.

Fremont, John Charles - Calif. (Republican) Jan. 21, 1813–July 13, 1890; explorer and Army officer in West before 1847; Senate, 1850–1851; governor of Arizona Territory, 1878–1881. Candidacy: P - 1856.

Garfield, James Abram - Ohio (Republican) Nov. 19, 1831–Sept. 19, 1881; major general in Union Army during Civil War; House, 1863–1880; U.S. president, 1881. Candidacy: P - 1880.

Garner, John Nance - Texas (Democratic) Nov. 22, 1868–Nov. 7, 1967; House, 1903–1933; House minority leader, 1929–1931; Speaker of the House, 1931–1933; U.S. vice president, 1933–1941. Candidacies: VP - 1932, 1936.

Gerry, Elbridge - Mass. (Democratic-Republican) July 17, 1744–Nov. 23, 1814; Continental Congress, 1776–1780, 1783–1785; signer of Declaration of Independence; Constitutional Convention, 1787; House, 1789–1793; governor, 1810–1812; U.S. vice president, 1813–1814. Candidacy: VP - 1812.

Goldwater, Barry Morris - Ariz. (Republican) Jan. 1, 1909–May 29, 1998; Senate, 1953–1965, 1969–1987. Candidacies: VP - 1960; P - 1964.

Gore, Albert Jr. - Tenn. (Democrat) March 31, 1948– ; House, 1977–1985; Senate, 1985–1993; U.S. vice president, 1993–2001. Candidacies: VP - 1992, 1996; P - 2000.

Graham, William Alexander - N.C. (Whig) Sept. 5, 1804–Aug. 11, 1875; Senate, 1840–1843; governor, 1845–1849; secretary of the Navy, 1850–1852; Confederate Senate, 1864. Candidacy: VP - 1852.

Granger, Francis - N.Y. (Whig) Dec. 1, 1792–Aug. 31, 1868; House, 1835–1837, 1839–1841, 1841–1843; postmaster general, 1841. Candidacy: VP - 1836.

Grant, Ulysses Simpson - Ill. (Republican) April 27, 1822–July 23, 1885; commander-in-chief, Union Army during Civil War; U.S. president, 1869–1877. Candidacies: P - 1868, 1872.

Greeley, Horace - N.Y. (Liberal Republican, Democratic) Feb. 3, 1811–Nov. 29, 1872; founder and editor, *New York Tribune,* 1841–1872; House, 1848–1849. Candidacy: P - 1872.

Griffin, S. Marvin - Ga. (American Independent) Sept. 4, 1907–June 13, 1982; governor, 1955–1959. Candidacy: VP - 1968. (Substituted as candidate until permanent candidate Curtis LeMay was chosen.)

Groesbeck, William Slocum - Ohio (Democratic) July 24, 1815–July 7, 1897; House, 1857–1859; delegate to International Monetary Conference in Paris, 1878. Candidacy: VP - 1872.

Hale, John Parker - N.H. (Free Soil) March 31, 1806–Nov. 19, 1873; House, 1843–1845; Senate, 1847–1853, 1855–1865; minister to Spain, 1865–1869. Candidacy: P - 1852.

Hamlin, Hannibal - Maine (Republican) Aug. 27, 1809–July 4, 1891; House, 1843–1847; Senate, 1848–1857, 1857–1861, 1869–1881; governor, 1857; U.S. vice president, 1861–1865. Candidacy: VP - 1860.

Hancock, John - Mass. (Federalist) Jan. 23, 1737–Oct. 8, 1793; Continental Congress, 1775–1778, 1785–1786; president of Continental Congress, 1775–1777; governor, 1780–1785, 1787–1793. Candidacy: 1789.

Hancock, Winfield Scott - Pa. (Democratic) Feb. 14, 1824 - Feb. 9, 1886; brigadier general, commander of II Army Corps, Civil War. Candidacy: P - 1880.

Harding, Warren Gamaliel - Ohio (Republican) Nov. 2, 1865–Aug. 2, 1923; lieutenant governor, 1904–1905; Senate, 1915–1921; U.S. president, 1921–1923. Candidacy: P - 1920.

Harper, Robert Goodloe - Md. (Federalist) January 1765–Jan. 14, 1825; House, 1795–1801; Senate, 1816. Candidacies: VP - 1816, 1820.

Harrison, Benjamin - Ind. (Republican) Aug. 20, 1833–March 13, 1901; Union officer in Civil War; Senate, 1881–1887; U.S. president, 1889–1893. Candidacies: P - 1888, 1892.

Harrison, Robert H. - Md. 1745–1790; chief justice, General Court of Maryland, 1781. Candidacy: 1789.

Harrison, William Henry - Ohio (Whig) Feb. 9, 1773–April 4, 1841; delegate to Congress from the Northwest Territory, 1799–1800; territorial governor of Indiana, 1801–1813; House, 1816–1819; Senate, 1825–1828; U.S. president, 1841. Candidacies: P - 1836, 1840.

Hayes, Rutherford Birchard - Ohio (Republican) Oct. 4, 1822–Jan. 17, 1893; major general in Union Army during Civil War; House, 1865–1867; governor, 1868–1872, 1876–1877; U.S. president, 1877–1881. Candidacy: P - 1876.

Hendricks, Thomas Andrews - Ind. (Democratic) Sept. 7, 1819–Nov. 25, 1885; House, 1851–1855; Senate, 1863–1869; governor, 1873–1877; U.S. vice president, 1885. Candidacies: P - 1872; VP - 1876, 1884.

Henry, John - Md. (Democratic-Republican) Nov. 1750–Dec. 16, 1798; Continental Congress, 1778–1780, 1785–1786; Senate, 1789–1797; governor, 1797–1798. Candidacy: - 1796.

Hobart, Garret Augustus - N.J. (Republican) June 3, 1844–Nov. 21, 1899; New Jersey Senate, 1876–1882; president of New Jersey Senate, 1881–1882; Republican National Committee, 1884–1896; U.S. vice president, 1897–1899. Candidacy: VP - 1896.

Hoover, Herbert Clark - Calif. (Republican) Aug. 10, 1874–Oct. 20, 1964; U.S. food administrator, 1917–1919; secretary of commerce, 1921–1928; U.S. president, 1929–1933; chairman, Commission on Organization of the Executive Branch of Government, 1947–1949, 1953–1955. Candidacies: P - 1928, 1932.

Hospers, John - Calif. (Libertarian) June 9, 1918– ; director of school of philosophy at University of Southern California. Candidacy: P - 1972.

Howard, John Eager - Md. (Federalist) June 4, 1752–Oct. 12, 1827; Continental Congress, 1788; governor, 1788–1791; Senate, 1796–1803. Candidacy: VP - 1816.

Hughes, Charles Evans - N.Y. (Republican) April 11, 1862–Aug. 27, 1948; governor, 1907–1910; associate justice of U.S. Supreme Court, 1910–1916; secretary of state, 1921–1925; chief justice of United States, 1930–1941. Candidacy: P - 1916.

Humphrey, Hubert Horatio Jr. - Minn. (Democratic) May 27, 1911–Jan. 13, 1978; mayor of Minneapolis, 1945–1948; Senate, 1949–1964, 1971–1978; U.S. vice president, 1965–1969. Candidacies: VP - 1964; P - 1968.

Huntington, Samuel - Conn., July 3, 1731–Jan. 5, 1796; Continental Congress, 1776, 1778–1781, 1783; president of the Continental Congress, 1779–1781; governor, 1786–1796. Candidacy: - 1789.

Ingersoll, Jared - Pa. (Federalist) Oct. 24, 1749–Oct. 31, 1822; Continental Congress, 1780–1781; Constitutional Convention, 1787. Candidacy: VP - 1812.

Iredell, James - N.C. (Federalist) Oct. 5, 1751–Oct. 20, 1799; associate justice of U.S. Supreme Court, 1790–1799. Candidacy: - 1796.

Jackson, Andrew - Tenn. (Democratic-Republican, Democratic) March 15, 1767–June 8, 1845; House, 1796–1797; Senate, 1797–1798, 1823–1825; territorial governor of Florida, 1821; U.S. president, 1829–1837. Candidacies: P - 1824, 1828, 1832.

Jay, John - N.Y. (Federalist) Dec. 12, 1745–May 17, 1829; Continental Congress, 1774–1776, 1778–1779; president of Continental Congress, 1778–1779; minister to Spain, 1779; chief justice of United States, 1789–1795; governor, 1795–1801. Candidacies: - 1789, 1796, 1800.

Jefferson, Thomas - Va. (Democratic-Republican) April 13, 1743–July 4, 1826; Continental Congress, 1775–1776, 1783–1784; author and signer of Declaration of Independence, 1776; governor, 1779–1781; minister to France, 1784–1789; secretary of state, 1790–1793; U.S. vice president, 1797–1801; U.S. president, 1801–1809. Candidacies: VP - 1792; P - 1796, 1800, 1804.

Jenkins, Charles Jones - Ga. (Democratic) Jan. 6, 1805–June 14, 1883; governor, 1865–1868. Candidacy: P - 1872.

Johnson, Andrew - Tenn. (Republican) Dec. 29, 1808–July 31, 1875; House, 1843–1853; governor, 1853–1857; Senate, 1857–1862, 1875; U.S. vice president, 1865; U.S. president, 1865–1869. Candidacy: VP - 1864.

Johnson, Herschel Vespasian - Ga. (Democratic) Sept. 18, 1812–Aug. 16, 1880; Senate, 1848–1849; governor, 1853–1857; senator, Confederate Congress, 1862–1865. Candidacy: VP - 1860.

Johnson, Hiram Warren - Calif. (Progressive) Sept. 2, 1866–Aug. 6, 1945; governor, 1911–1917; Senate, 1917–1945. Candidacy: VP - 1912.

Johnson, Lyndon Baines - Texas (Democratic) Aug. 27, 1908–Jan. 22, 1973; House, 1937–1949; Senate, 1949–1961; Senate minority leader, 1953–1955; Senate majority leader, 1955–1961; U.S. vice president, 1961–1963; U.S. president, 1963–1969. Candidacies: VP - 1960; P - 1964.

Johnson, Richard Mentor - Ky. (Democratic) Oct. 17, 1780–Nov. 19, 1850; House, 1807–1819, 1829–1837; Senate, 1819–1829; U.S. vice president, 1837–1841. Candidacies: VP - 1836, 1840.

Johnston, Samuel - N.C. (Federalist) Dec. 15, 1733–Aug. 17, 1816; Continental Congress, 1780–1781; governor, 1787–1789; Senate, 1789–1793. Candidacy: - 1796.

Jones, Walter Burgwyn - Ala. (Independent Democratic) Oct. 16, 1888–Aug. 1, 1963; Alabama Legislature, 1919–1920; Alabama circuit court judge, 1920–1935; presiding judge, 1935–1963. Candidacy: P - 1956.

Julian, George Washington - Ind. (Free Soil, Liberal Republican) May 5, 1817–July 7, 1899; House, 1849–1851, 1861–1871. Candidacies: VP - 1852, 1872.

Kefauver, Estes - Tenn. (Democratic) July 26, 1903–Aug. 10, 1963; House, 1939–1949; Senate, 1949–1963. Candidacy: VP - 1956.

Kemp, Jack F. - N.Y. (Republican) July 13, 1935– ; House, 1971–1989; secretary of Housing and Urban Development, 1989–1993. Candidacy: VP - 1996.

Kennedy, John Fitzgerald - Mass. (Democratic) May 29, 1917–Nov. 22, 1963; House, 1947–1953; Senate, 1953–1960; U.S. president, 1961–1963. Candidacy: P - 1960.

Kern, John Worth - Ind. (Democratic) Dec. 20, 1849–Aug. 17, 1917; Senate, 1911–1917; Senate majority leader, 1913–1917. Candidacy: VP - 1908.

King, Rufus - N.Y. (Federalist) March 24, 1755–April 29, 1827; Continental Congress, 1784–1787; Constitutional Convention, 1787; Senate, 1789–1796, 1813–1825; minister to Great Britain, 1796–1803, 1825–1826. Candidacies: VP - 1804, 1808; P - 1816.

King, William Rufus de Vane - Ala. (Democratic) April 7, 1786–April 18, 1853; House, 1811–1816; Senate, 1819–1844, 1848–1852; president pro tempore of the Senate, 1836, 1837, 1838, 1839, 1840, 1841, 1850; minister to France, 1844–1846; U.S. vice president, 1853. Candidacy: VP - 1852.

Knox, Franklin - Ill. (Republican) Jan. 1, 1874–April 28, 1944; secretary of the Navy, 1940–1944. Candidacy: VP - 1936.

La Follette, Robert Marion - Wis. (Progressive) June 14, 1855–June 18, 1925; House, 1885–1891; governor, 1901–1906; Senate, 1906–1925. Candidacy: P - 1924.

Landon, Alfred Mossman - Kan. (Republican) Sept. 9, 1887–Oct. 12, 1987; governor, 1933–1937. Candidacy: P - 1936.

Lane, Joseph - Ore. (Southern Democratic) Dec. 14, 1801–April 19, 1881; governor of Oregon Territory, 1849–1850, 1853; House (territorial delegate), 1851–1859; Senate, 1859–1861. Candidacy: VP - 1860.

Langdon, John - N.H. (Democratic-Republican) June 26, 1741–Sept. 18, 1819; Continental Congress, 1775–1776, 1787; governor, 1805–1809, 1810–1812; Senate, 1789–1801; first president pro tempore of the Senate, 1789. Candidacy: VP - 1808.

Lee, Henry - Mass. (Independent Democratic) Feb. 4, 1782–Feb. 6, 1867; merchant and publicist. Candidacy: VP - 1832.

LeMay, Curtis Emerson - Ohio (American Independent) Nov. 15, 1906–Oct. 1, 1990; Air Force chief of staff, 1961–1965. Candidacy: VP - 1968.

Lemke, William - N.D. (Union) Aug. 13, 1878–May 30, 1950; House, 1933–1941, 1943–1950. Candidacy: P - 1936.

Lieberman, Joseph I. - Conn. (Democratic) Feb. 24, 1942– ; Connecticut Legislature, 1971–1981; attorney general of Connecticut, 1983–1989; Senate 1989– . Candidacy: VP - 2000.

Lincoln, Abraham - Ill. (Republican) Feb. 12, 1809–April 15, 1865; House, 1847–1849; U.S. president, 1861–1865. Candidacies: P - 1860, 1864.

Lincoln, Benjamin - Mass. (Federalist) Jan. 24, 1733–May 9, 1810; major general in Continental Army, 1777–1781. Candidacy: - 1789.

Lodge, Henry Cabot Jr. - Mass. (Republican) July 5, 1902–Feb. 27, 1985; Senate, 1937–1944, 1947–1953; ambassador to United Nations, 1953–1960; ambassador to Republic of Vietnam, 1963–1964, 1965–1967. Candidacy: VP - 1960.

Logan, John Alexander - Ill. (Republican) Feb. 9, 1826–Dec. 26, 1886; House, 1859–1862, 1867–1871; Senate, 1871–1877, 1879–1886. Candidacy: VP - 1884.

Machen, Willis Benson - Ky. (Democratic) April 10, 1810–Sept. 29, 1893; Confederate Congress, 1861–1865; Senate, 1872–1873. Candidacy: VP - 1872.

Macon, Nathaniel - N.C. (Democratic-Republican) Dec. 17, 1757–June 29, 1837; House, 1791–1815; Speaker of the House, 1801–1807; Senate, 1815–1828; president pro tempore of the Senate, 1826, 1827. Candidacy: VP - 1824.

Madison, James - Va. (Democratic-Republican) March 16, 1751–June 28, 1836; Continental Congress, 1780–1783, 1787–1788; Constitutional Convention, 1787; House, 1789–1797; secretary of state, 1801–1809; U.S. president, 1809–1817. Candidacies: P - 1808, 1812.

Mangum, Willie Person - N.C. (Independent Democrat) May 10, 1792–Sept. 7, 1861; House, 1823–1826; Senate, 1831–1836, 1840–1853. Candidacy: P - 1836.

Marshall, John - Va. (Federalist) Sept. 24, 1755–July 6, 1835; House, 1799–1800; secretary of state, 1800–1801; chief justice of United States, 1801–1835. Candidacy: VP - 1816.

Marshall, Thomas Riley - Ind. (Democratic) March 14, 1854–June 1, 1925; governor, 1909–1913; U.S. vice president, 1913–1921. Candidacies: VP - 1912, 1916.

McCarthy, Eugene Joseph - Minn. (Independent) March 29, 1916– ; House, 1949–1959; Senate, 1959–1971. Candidacy: P - 1976.

McClellan, George Brinton - N.J. (Democratic) Dec. 3, 1826–Oct. 29, 1885; general-in-chief of Army of the Potomac, 1861; governor, 1878–1881. Candidacy: P - 1864.

McGovern, George Stanley - S.D. (Democratic) July 19, 1922– ; House, 1957–1961; Senate, 1963–1981. Candidacy: P - 1972.

McKinley, William Jr. - Ohio (Republican) Jan. 29, 1843–Sept. 14, 1901; House, 1877, 1885–1891; governor, 1892–1896; U.S. president, 1897–1901. Candidacies: P - 1896, 1900.

McNary, Charles Linza - Ore. (Republican) June 12, 1874–Feb. 25, 1944; state Supreme Court judge, 1913–1915; Senate, 1917–1918, 1918–1944; Senate minority leader, 1933–1944. Candidacy: VP - 1940.

Miller, William Edward - N.Y. (Republican) March 22, 1914–June 24, 1983; House, 1951–1965; chairman of Republican National Committee, 1960–1964. Candidacy: VP - 1964.

Milton, John - Ga. circa 1740–circa 1804; secretary of state, Georgia, circa 1778, 1781, 1783. Candidacy: - 1789.

Mondale, Walter Frederick - Minn. (Democratic) Jan. 5, 1928– ; Senate, 1964–1976; U.S. vice president, 1977–1981; ambassador to Japan, 1993–1996. Candidacies: VP - 1976, 1980; P - 1984.

Monroe, James - Va. (Democratic-Republican) April 28, 1758–July 4, 1831; Continental Congress, 1783–1786; Senate, 1790–1794; minister to France, 1794–1796, 1803; minister to England, 1803–1807; governor, 1799–1802, 1811; secretary of state, 1811–1814, 1815–1817; U.S. president, 1817–1825. Candidacies: VP - 1808; P - 1816, 1820.

Morton, Levi Parsons - N.Y. (Republican) May 16, 1824–May 16, 1920; House, 1879–1881; minister to France, 1881–1885; U.S. vice president, 1889–1893; governor, 1895–1897. Candidacy: VP - 1888.

Muskie, Edmund Sixtus - Maine (Democratic) March 28, 1914–March 26, 1996; governor, 1955–1959; Senate, 1959–1980; secretary of state, 1980–1981. Candidacy: VP - 1968.

Nathan, Theodora Nathalia - Ore. (Libertarian) Feb. 9, 1923– ; broadcast journalist; National Judiciary Committee, Libertarian Party, 1972–1975; vice chairperson, Oregon Libertarian Party, 1974–1975. Candidacy: VP - 1972.

Nixon, Richard Milhous - Calif., N.Y. (Republican) Jan. 9, 1913–April 22, 1994; House, 1947–1950; Senate, 1950–1953; U.S. vice president, 1953–1961; U.S. president, 1969–1974. Candidacies: VP - 1952, 1956; P - 1960, 1968, 1972.

Palmer, John McAuley - Ill. (Democratic, National Democratic) Sept. 13, 1817–Sept. 25, 1900; governor, 1869–1873; Senate, 1891–1897. Candidacies: VP - 1872; P - 1896.

Parker, Alton Brooks - N.Y. (Democratic) May 14, 1852–May 10, 1926; chief justice of N.Y. Court of Appeals, 1898–1904. Candidacy: P - 1904.

Pendleton, George Hunt - Ohio (Democratic) July 19, 1825–Nov. 24, 1889; House, 1857–1865; Senate, 1879–1885; minister to Germany, 1885–1889. Candidacy: VP - 1864.

Perot, H. Ross - Texas (Independent, Reform) June 27, 1930– ; business executive and owner. Candidacies: P - 1992, 1996.

Pierce, Franklin - N.H. (Democratic) Nov. 23, 1804–Oct. 8, 1869; House, 1833–1837; Senate, 1837–1842; U.S. president, 1853–1857. Candidacy: P - 1852.

Pinckney, Charles Cotesworth - S.C. (Federalist) Feb. 25, 1746–Aug. 16, 1825; president, state senate, 1779; minister to France, 1796. Candidacies: VP - 1800; P - 1804, 1808.

Pinckney, Thomas - S.C. (Federalist) Oct. 23, 1750–Nov. 2, 1828; governor, 1787–1789; minister to Great Britain, 1792–1796; envoy to Spain, 1794–1795; House, 1797–1801. Candidacy: - 1796.

Polk, James Knox - Tenn. (Democratic) Nov. 2, 1795–June 15, 1849; House, 1825–1839; Speaker of the House, 1835–1839; governor, 1839–1841; U.S. president, 1845–1849. Candidacies: VP - 1840; P - 1844.

Quayle, Dan - Ind. (Republican) Feb. 4, 1947– ; House, 1977–1981; Senate, 1981–1989; U.S. vice president, 1989–1993. Candidacies: VP - 1988, 1992.

Reagan, Ronald Wilson - Calif. (Republican) Feb. 6, 1911– ; governor, 1967–1975; U.S. president, 1981–1989. Candidacies: P - 1980, 1984.

Reid, Whitelaw - N.Y. (Republican) Oct. 27, 1837–Dec. 15, 1912; minister to France, 1889–1892; editor-in-chief, *New York Tribune*, 1872–1905. Candidacy: VP - 1892.

Robinson, Joseph Taylor - Ark. (Democratic) Aug. 26, 1872–July 14, 1937; House, 1903–1913; governor, 1913; Senate, 1913–1937; Senate minority leader, 1923–1933; Senate majority leader, 1933–1937. Candidacy: VP - 1928.

Rockefeller, Nelson Aldrich - N.Y. (Republican) July 8, 1908–Jan. 26, 1979; governor, 1959–1973; U.S. vice president, 1974–1977 (nominated under the provisions of the 25th Amendment).

Rodney, Daniel - Del. (Federalist) Sept. 10, 1764–Sept. 2, 1846; governor, 1814–1817; House, 1822–1823; Senate, 1826–1827. Candidacy: VP - 1820.

Roosevelt, Franklin Delano - N.Y. (Democratic) Jan. 30, 1882–April 12, 1945; assistant secretary of the Navy, 1913–1920; governor, 1929–1933; U.S. president, 1933–1945. Candidacies: VP - 1920; P - 1932, 1936, 1940, 1944.

Roosevelt, Theodore - N.Y. (Republican, Progressive) Oct. 27, 1858–Jan. 6, 1919; assistant secretary of the Navy, 1897–1898; governor, 1899–1901; U.S. vice president, 1901; U.S. president, 1901–1909. Candidacies: VP - 1900; P - 1904, 1912.

Ross, James - Pa. (Federalist) July 12, 1762–Nov. 27, 1847; Senate, 1794–1803. Candidacy: VP - 1816.

Rush, Richard - Pa. (Democratic-Republican, National-Republican) Aug. 29, 1780–July 30, 1859; attorney general, 1814–1817; minister to Great Britain, 1817–1824; secretary of Treasury, 1825–1829. Candidacies: VP - 1820, 1828.

Rutledge, John - S.C. (Federalist) Sept. 1739–July 23, 1800; Continental Congress, 1774–1775, 1782–1783; governor, 1779–1782; Constitutional Convention, 1787; associate justice of U.S. Supreme Court, 1789–1791; chief justice of United States, 1795. Candidacy: - 1789.

Sanford, Nathan - N.Y. (Democratic-Republican) Nov. 5, 1777–Oct. 17, 1838; Senate, 1815–1821, 1826–1831. Candidacy: VP - 1824.

Schmitz, John George - Calif. (American Independent) Aug. 12, 1930– ; House, 1970–1973. Candidacy: P - 1972.

Scott, Winfield - N.J. (Whig) June 13, 1786–May 29, 1866; general-in-chief of U.S. Army, 1841–1861. Candidacy: P - 1852.

Sergeant, John - Pa. (National-Republican) Dec. 5, 1779–Nov. 23, 1852; House, 1815–1823, 1827–1829, 1837–1841. Candidacy: VP - 1832.

Sewall, Arthur - Maine (Democratic) Nov. 25, 1835–Sept. 5, 1900; Democratic National Committee member, 1888–1896. Candidacy: VP - 1896.

Seymour, Horatio - N.Y. (Democratic) May 31, 1810–Feb. 12, 1886; governor, 1853–1855, 1863–1865. Candidacy: P - 1868.

Sherman, James Schoolcraft - N.Y. (Republican) Oct. 24, 1855–Oct. 30, 1912; House, 1887–1891, 1893–1909; U.S. vice president, 1909–1912. Candidacies: VP - 1908, 1912. (Died during 1912 campaign; Nicholas Murray Butler replaced Sherman on the Republican ticket.)

Shriver, Robert Sargent Jr. - Md. (Democratic) Nov. 9, 1915– ; director, Peace Corps, 1961–1966; director, Office of Economic Opportunity, 1964–1968; ambassador to France, 1968–1970. Candidacy: VP - 1972. (Replaced Thomas F. Eagleton on Democratic ticket Aug. 8.)

Smith, Alfred Emanuel - N.Y. (Democratic) Dec. 30, 1873–Oct. 4, 1944; governor, 1919–1921, 1923–1929. Candidacy: P - 1928.

Smith, William - S.C., Ala. (Independent Democratic-Republican) Sept. 6, 1762–June 26, 1840; Senate, 1816–1823, 1826–1831. Candidacies: VP - 1828, 1836.

Sparkman, John Jackson - Ala. (Democratic) Dec. 20, 1899–Nov. 16, 1985; House, 1937–1946; Senate, 1946–1979. Candidacy: VP - 1952.

Stevenson, Adlai Ewing - Ill. (Democratic) Oct. 23, 1835–June 14, 1914; House, 1875–1877, 1879–1881; assistant postmaster general, 1885–1889; U.S. vice president, 1893–1897. Candidacies: VP - 1892, 1900.

Stevenson, Adlai Ewing II - Ill. (Democratic) Feb. 5, 1900–July 14, 1965; assistant to the secretary of Navy, 1941–1944; assistant to the secretary of state, 1945; governor, 1949–1953; ambassador to United Nations, 1961–1965. Candidacies: P - 1952, 1956.

Stockton, Richard - N.J. (Federalist) April 17, 1764–March 7, 1828; Senate, 1796–1799; House, 1813–1815. Candidacy: VP - 1820.

Taft, William Howard - Ohio (Republican) Sept. 15, 1857–March 8, 1930; secretary of war, 1904–1908; U.S. president, 1909–1913; chief justice of United States, 1921–1930. Candidacies: P - 1908, 1912.

Talmadge, Herman Eugene - Ga. (Independent Democratic) Aug. 9, 1913– ; governor, 1947, 1948–1955; Senate, 1957–1981. Candidacy: VP - 1956.

Taylor, Glen Hearst - Idaho (Progressive) April 12, 1904–April 28, 1984; Senate, 1945–1951. Candidacy: VP - 1948.

Taylor, Zachary - La. (Whig) Nov. 24, 1784–July 9, 1850; major general, U.S. Army; U.S. president, 1849–1850. Candidacy: P - 1848.

Tazewell, Littleton Waller - Va. (Democratic) Dec. 17, 1774–May 6, 1860; House, 1800–1801; Senate, 1824–1832; president pro tempore of the Senate, 1832; governor, 1834–1836. Candidacy: VP - 1840.

Telfair, Edward - Ga. (Democratic-Republican) 1735–Sept. 17, 1807; Continental Congress, 1778, 1780–1782; governor, 1789–1793. Candidacy: - 1789.

Thomas, Norman Mattoon - N.Y. (Socialist) Nov. 20, 1884–Dec. 19, 1968; Presbyterian minister, 1911–1931; author and editor. Candidacies: P - 1928, 1932, 1936, 1940, 1944, 1948.

Thurman, Allen Granberry - Ohio (Democratic) Nov. 13, 1813–Dec. 12, 1895; House, 1845–1847; Ohio Supreme Court, 1851–1856; Senate, 1869–1881; president pro tempore of the Senate, 1879, 1880. Candidacy: VP - 1888.

Thurmond, James Strom - S.C. (States' Rights Democrat) Dec. 5, 1902– ; governor, 1947–1951; Senate, 1954–1956, 1956– ; president pro tempore of the Senate, 1981–1987; 1995– . Candidacies: P - 1948.

Tilden, Samuel Jones - N.Y. (Democratic) Feb. 9, 1814–Aug. 4, 1886; governor, 1875–1877. Candidacy: P - 1876.

Tompkins, Daniel D. - N.Y. (Democratic-Republican) June 21, 1774–June 11, 1825; elected to the House for the term beginning in 1805 but resigned before taking seat; governor, 1807–1817; U.S. vice president, 1817–1825. Candidacies: VP - 1816, 1820.

Truman, Harry S. - Mo. (Democratic) May 8, 1884–Dec. 26, 1972; Senate, 1935–1945; U.S. vice president, 1945; U.S. president, 1945–1953. Candidacies: VP - 1944; P - 1948.

Tyler, John - Va. (Whig) March 29, 1790–Jan. 18, 1862; governor, 1825–1827; Senate, 1827–1836; U.S. vice president, 1841; U.S. president, 1841–1845. Candidacies: VP - 1836, 1840.

Van Buren, Martin - N.Y. (Democratic, Free Soil) Dec. 5, 1782–July 24, 1862; Senate, 1821–1828; governor, 1829; secretary of state, 1829–1831; U.S. vice president, 1833–1837; U.S. president, 1837–1841. Candidacies: VP - 1824, 1832; P - 1836, 1840, 1848.

Wallace, George Corley - Ala. (American Independent) Aug. 25, 1919–Sept. 13, 1998; governor, 1963–1967, 1971–1979, 1983–1989. Candidacy: P - 1968.

Wallace, Henry Agard - Iowa (Democratic, Progressive) Oct. 7, 1888–Nov. 18, 1965; secretary of agriculture, 1933–1940; U.S. vice president, 1941–1945; secretary of commerce, 1945–1946. Candidacies: VP - 1940; P - 1948.

Warren, Earl - Calif. (Republican) March 19, 1891–July 9, 1974; governor, 1943–1953; chief justice of United States, 1953–1969. Candidacy: VP - 1948.

Washington, George - Va. (Federalist) Feb. 22, 1732–Dec. 14, 1799; First and Second Continental Congresses, 1774, 1775; commander-in-chief of armed forces, 1775–1783; president of Constitutional Convention, 1787; U.S. president, 1789–1797. Candidacies: P - 1789, 1792, 1796.

Watson, Thomas Edward - Ga. (Populist) Sept. 5, 1856–Sept. 26, 1922; House, 1891–1993; Senate, 1921–1922. Candidacies: VP - 1896; P - 1904, 1908.

Weaver, James Baird - Iowa (Greenback, Populist) June 12, 1833–Feb. 6, 1912; House, 1879–1881, 1885–1889; Candidacies: P - 1880, 1892.

Webster, Daniel - Mass. (Whig) Jan. 18, 1782–Oct. 24, 1852; House, 1813–1817, 1823–1827; Senate, 1827–1841, 1845–1850; secretary of state, 1841–1843, 1850–1852. Candidacy: P - 1836.

Wheeler, Burton Kendall - Mont. (Progressive) Feb. 27, 1882–Jan. 6, 1975; Senate, 1923–1947. Candidacy: VP - 1924.

Wheeler, William Almon - N.Y. (Republican) June 30, 1819–June 4, 1887; House, 1861–1863, 1869–1877; U.S. vice president, 1877–1881. Candidacy: VP - 1876.

White, Hugh Lawson - Tenn. (Whig) Oct. 30, 1773–April 10, 1840; Senate, 1825–1835, 1835–1840. Candidacy: P - 1836.

Wilkins, William - Pa. (Democratic) Dec. 20, 1779–June 23, 1865; Senate, 1831–1834; minister to Russia, 1834–1835; House, 1843–1844; secretary of war, 1844–1845. Candidacy: VP - 1832.

Willkie, Wendell Lewis - N.Y. (Republican) Feb. 18, 1892–Oct. 8, 1944; utility executive, 1933–1940. Candidacy: P - 1940.

Wilson, Henry - Mass. (Republican) Feb. 16, 1812–Nov. 22, 1875; Senate, 1855–1873; U.S. vice president, 1873–1875. Candidacy: VP - 1872.

Wilson, Woodrow - N.J. (Democratic) Dec. 28, 1856–Feb. 3, 1924; governor, 1911–1913; U.S. president, 1913–1921. Candidacies: P - 1912, 1916.

Wirt, William - Md. (Anti-Masonic) Nov. 8, 1772–Feb. 18, 1834; attorney general, 1817–1829. Candidacy: P - 1832.

Wright, Fielding Lewis - Miss. (States' Rights Democratic) May 16, 1895–May 4, 1956; governor, 1946–1952. Candidacy: VP - 1948.

Selected Bibliography

Presidential Elections

Abbott, David W., and James P. Levine. *Wrong Winner: The Coming Debacle in the Electoral College.* New York: Praeger, 1991.

Abramson, Paul R., John H. Aldrich, and David W. Rohde. *Change and Continuity in the 2000 Elections.* Washington, D.C.: CQ Press, 2002.

Aldrich, John H. *Before the Convention: Strategies and Choices in Presidential Nomination Campaigns.* Chicago: University of Chicago Press, 1980.

American Enterprise Institute. *Direct Election of the President.* Washington, D.C.: AEI Press, 1977.

Ansolabehere, Stephen, and Shanto Iyengar. *Going Negative: How Political Ads Shrink and Polarize the Electorate.* New York: Free Press, 1995.

Asher, Herbert. *Presidential Elections and American Politics: Votes, Candidates, and Campaigns since 1952.* 5th ed. Pacific Grove, Calif.: Brooks-Cole, 1992.

Barber, James D. *The Presidential Character: Predicting Performance in the White House.* 4th ed. Englewood Cliffs, N.J.: Prentice-Hall, 1992.

Bartels, Larry M. *Presidential Primaries and the Dynamics of Public Choice.* Princeton, N.J.: Princeton University Press, 1988.

Berns, Walter, ed. *After the People Vote: A Guide to the Electoral College.* Rev. ed. Washington, D.C.: AEI Press, 1992.

Best, Judith. *The Choice of the People? Debating the Electoral College.* Lanham, Md.: Rowman and Littlefield, 1996.

Bickel, Alexander M. *Reform and Continuity: The Electoral College, the Convention, and the Party System.* New York: Harper and Row, 1971.

Black, Earl, and Merle Black. *The Vital South: How Presidential Elections Are Won.* Cambridge, Mass.: Harvard University Press, 1992.

Blumenthal, Sidney. *The Permanent Campaign.* Rev. ed. New York: Simon and Schuster, 1982.

Boller, Paul F., Jr. *Presidential Campaigns.* Rev. ed. New York: Oxford University Press, 1996.

Buell, Emmett H., Jr., and Lee Sigelman. *Nominating the President.* Knoxville: University of Tennessee Press, 1991.

Burnham, Walter D. *Critical Elections and the Mainsprings of American Politics.* New York: Norton, 1971.

Byrne, Gary C., and Paul Marx. *The Great American Convention: A Political History of Presidential Elections.* Palo Alto, Calif.: Pacific Books, 1977.

Ceaser, James W. *Presidential Selection: Theory and Development.* Princeton, N.J.: Princeton University Press, 1979.

Ceaser, James W., and Andrew Busch. *Upside Down and Inside Out: The 1992 Elections and American Politics.* Lanham, Md.: Rowman and Littlefield, 1993.

Chase, James S. *Emergence of the Presidential Nominating Convention: 1789–1832.* Urbana: University of Illinois Press, 1973.

Congressional Quarterly. *National Party Conventions: 1831–2000.* Washington, D.C.: CQ Press, 2000.

Congressional Quarterly. *Presidential Elections: 1789–1996.* Washington, D.C.: Congressional Quarterly, 1997.

Congressional Quarterly. *Selecting the President: From 1789–1996.* Washington, D.C.: Congressional Quarterly, 1997.

Cook, Rhodes. *Race for the Presidency: Winning the 2000 Nomination.* Washington, D.C.: CQ Press, 2000.

___. *U.S. Presidential Primary Elections, 1968–1996.* Washington, D.C.: CQ Press, 2000.

Cravit, Lawrence. *The Forty-Year Parallel in Presidential Elections.* New York: Vantage Press, 1980.

Davis, James W. *National Conventions in an Age of Party Reform.* Westport, Conn.: Greenwood, 1983.

___. *U.S. Presidential Primaries and the Convention System: A Sourcebook.* Westport, Conn.: Greenwood, 1997.

Davis, James W., and Robert E. DiClerico. *Choosing Our Choices: Debating the Presidential Nominating Process.* Lanham, Md.: Rowman and Littlefield, 2000.

Denton, Robert E., Jr., ed. *The 1996 Presidential Campaign: A Communication Perspective.* Westport, Conn.: Praeger, 1998.

DiClerico, Robert E. *The American President.* 4th ed. Englewood Cliffs, N.J.: Prentice Hall, 1995.

___. *Political Parties, Campaigns and Elections.* Upper Saddle River, N.J.: Prentice Hall, 2000.

DiClerico, Robert E., and James W. Davis. *Choosing our Choices: Debating the Presidential Nominating Process.* Lanham, Md.: Rowman & Littlefield, 2000.

Eaton, Herbert. *Presidential Timber: A History of Nominating Conventions, 1868–1960.* New York: Free Press, 1964.

Ewing, Cortez A. M. *Presidential Elections from Abraham Lincoln to Franklin Roosevelt.* Westport, Conn.: Greenwood Press, 1972.

Fenno, Richard F., Jr. *The Presidential Odyssey of John Glenn.* Washington, D.C.: CQ Press, 1990.

Friedenberg, Robert V. *Communication Consultants in Political Campaigns: Ballot Box Warriors.* Westport, Conn.: Praeger, 1997.

Geer, John G. *Nominating Presidents: An Evaluation of Voters and Primaries.* Westport, Conn.: Greenwood, 1989.

Glennon, Michael J. *When No Majority Rules: The Electoral College and Presidential Succession.* Washington, D.C.: Congressional Quarterly, 1992.

Goldstein, Michael L. *Guide to the 2000 Presidential Election.* Washington, D.C.: CQ Press, 1999.

Hacker, Kenneth L., ed. *Candidate Images in Presidential Elections.* Westport, Conn.: Praeger, 1995.

Haskell, John. *Fundamentally Flawed: Understanding and Reforming Presidential Primaries.* Lanham, Md.: Rowman and Littlefield, 1996.

Havel, James T. *U.S. Presidential Candidates and the Elections: A Biographical and Historical Guide.* New York: Macmillan Library Reference, 1996.

Haworth, Paul L. *The Hayes-Tilden Disputed Presidential Election of 1876.* 1906. Reprint, New York: AMS Press, 1979.

Heale, M. J. *The Presidential Quest: Candidates and Images in American Political Culture, 1787–1852.* New York: Longman, 1982.

Hertzke, Allen D. *Echoes of Discontent: Jesse Jackson, Pat Robertson, and the Resurgence of Populism.* Washington, D.C.: CQ Press, 1993.

Huckfeldt, Robert, and John Sprague. *Citizens, Politics, and Social Communication: Information and Influence in an Election Campaign.* New York: Cambridge University Press, 1995.

Jackson, John S., and William Crotty. *The Politics of Presidential Selection.* New York: HarperCollins, 1996.

Jamieson, Kathleen Hall. *Packaging the Presidency: A History and Criticism of Presidential Campaign Advertising.* 3rd ed. New York: Oxford University Press, 1996.

Jensen, Merrill, ed. *The Documentary History of the First Federal Elections, 1788–1790.* Madison, Wis.: Madison House, 1991.

Johnson, Donald B. *National Party Platforms.* Rev. ed. Urbana: University of Illinois Press, 1978.

Just, Marion R., et al. *Crosstalk: Citizens, Candidates, and the Media in a Presidential Campaign.* Chicago: University of Chicago Press, 1996.

Keech, William R., and Donald R. Matthews. *The Party's Choice.* Washington, D.C.: Brookings Institution Press, 1976.

Kessel, John H. *Presidential Campaign Politics.* 4th ed. Pacific Grove, Calif.: Brooks-Cole, 1992.

Key, V. O., Jr. *The Responsible Electorate: Rationality in Presidential Voting, 1936–1960.* Cambridge, Mass.: Harvard University Press, 1966.

Kleppner, Paul. *Who Voted? The Dynamics of Electoral Turnout, 1870–1980.* New York: Praeger, 1982.

Kleppner, Paul, and Walter D. Burnham. *The Evolution of American Electoral Systems.* Westport, Conn.: Greenwood Press, 1982.

Kraus, Sidney. *Televised Presidential Debates and Public Policy.* 2nd ed. Mahwah, N.J.: Lawrence Erlbaum Associates, 2000.

League of Women Voters of the United States. *Choosing the President: A Citizen's Guide to the 2000 Election.* Washington, D.C.: Lyons Press, 1999.

Longley, Lawrence D. *The Politics of Electoral College Reform.* New Haven, Conn.: Yale University Press, 1972.

Longley, Lawrence D., and Neal R. Peirce. *The Electoral Primer.* New Haven, Conn.: Yale University Press, 1996.

Maisel, L. Sandy. *Parties and Elections in America: The Electoral Process.* 3rd ed. Lanham, Md.: Rowman and Littlefield, 1999.

Mayer, William G., ed. *In Pursuit of the White House 2000: How We Choose Our Presidential Nominees.* Chatham, N.J.: Chatham House, 1999.

Mayhew, David R. *Divided We Govern: Party Control, Lawmaking & Investigations.* New Haven, Conn.: Yale University Press, 1991.

McCubbins, Matthew D., ed. *Under the Watchful Eye: Managing Presidential Campaigns in the Television Era.* Washington, D.C.: CQ Press, 1992.

McGillivray, Alice V. *Presidential Primaries and Caucuses: 1992, A Handbook of Election Statistics.* Washington, D.C.: Congressional Quarterly, 1992.

McKee, Thomas H. *The National Conventions and Platforms of All Political Parties, 1789–1905: Convention, Popular and Electoral Vote.* New York: AMS Press, 1971.

Menefee-Libey, David. *The Triumph of Campaign-Centered Politics.* New York: Chatham House, 2000.

Miller, Arthur H., and Bruce E. Gronbeck, eds. *Presidential Campaigns and American Self Images.* Boulder, Colo.: Westview, 1994.

Miller, Warren E., and Teresa E. Levitin. *Leadership and Change: Presidential Elections from 1952 to 1976.* Cambridge, Mass.: Winthrop, 1976.

Moore, John L. *Elections A to Z.* Washington, D.C.: CQ Press, 1999.

Nelson, Michael, ed. *Historical Documents on Presidential Elections, 1787–1988.* Washington, D.C.: Congressional Quarterly, 1991.

___. *The Presidency and the Political System.* 7th ed. Washington, D.C.: CQ Press, 2003.

——, ed. *The Elections of 2000.* Washington, D.C.: CQ Press, 2001.

Newman, Bruce I. *The Marketing of the President: Political Marketing as a Campaign Strategy.* Thousand Oaks, Calif.: Sage, 1994.

Nimmo, Dan. *The Political Persuaders: The Technique of Modern Election Campaigns.* Englewood Cliffs, N.J.: Transaction Publishers, 1999.

Norrander, Barbara. *Super Tuesday: Regional Politics and Presidential Primaries.* Lexington: University Press of Kentucky, 1992.

Peirce, Neal, and Lawrence D. Longley. *The People's President: The Electoral College and the Emerging Consensus for a Direct Vote Alternative.* Rev. ed. New Haven, Conn.: Yale University Press, 1981.

Pika, Joseph H., and Richard Watson. *The Presidential Contest.* 5th ed. Washington, D.C.: CQ Press, 1995.

Polsby, Nelson W., and Aaron Wildavsky. *Presidential Elections: Strategies and Structures of American Politics.* 10th ed. New York: Chatham House, 2000.

Pomper, Gerald M., et al. *The Election of 1996: Reports and Interpretations.* Chatham, N.J.: Chatham House, 1997.

Robinson, Edgar E. *The Presidential Vote, 1896–1932.* Stanford, Calif.: Stanford University Press, 1947.

___. *They Voted for Roosevelt: The Presidential Vote, 1932–1944.* Stanford, Calif.: Stanford University Press, 1947.

Roseboom, Eugene H. *A History of Presidential Elections: From George Washington to Jimmy Carter.* 4th ed. New York: Macmillan, 1979.

Rosenstone, Steven J., Roy L. Behr, and Edward Lazarus. *Third Parties in America: Citizen Response to Major Party Failure.* Princeton, N.J.: Princeton University Press, 1984.

Runyon, John H. *Source Book of American Presidential Campaign and Election Statistics, 1948–1968.* New York: Ungar, 1971.

Scammon, Richard M. *America Votes: A Handbook of Contemporary Election Statistics.* Vols. 1–2. New York: Macmillan, 1956–58. *America Votes.* Vols. 3–5. Pittsburgh: University of Pittsburgh, 1959–64. *America Votes.* Vols. 6–11. Washington, D.C.: Congressional Quarterly, 1966–1975.

Scammon, Richard M., and Alice V. McGillivray. *America Votes.* Vols. 12–21. Washington, D.C.: Congressional Quarterly, 1977–1995.

Scammon, Richard M., Alice V. McGillivray, and Rhodes Cook. *America Votes.* Vols. 22–24. Washington, D.C.: CQ Press, 1997–2001.

Schantz, Harvey L., ed. *American Presidential Elections: Process, Policy, and Political Change.* Albany: State University of New York Press, 1996.

Scher, Richard K. *The Modern Political Campaign: Mudslinging, Bombast, and the Vitality of American Politics.* Armonk, N.Y.: Sharpe, 1997.

Schlesinger, Arthur M., Jr., *The Coming to Power: Critical Presidential Elections in American History.* New York: Chelsea House, 1981.

___, ed. *History of American Presidential Elections.* 4 vols. New York: McGraw Hill, 1971.

___, ed. *Running for President: The Candidates and Their Images.* New York: Simon and Schuster, 1994.

Shafer, Byron. *Bifurcated Politics: Evolution and Reform in the National Party Convention.* Cambridge, Mass.: Harvard University Press, 1988.

Shields-West, Eileen. *World Almanac of Presidential Campaigns.* New York: World Almanac, 1992.

Singer, Aaron, ed. *Campaign Speeches of American Presidential Candidates, 1928–1972.* New York: Ungar, 1976.

___. *Campaign Speeches of American Presidential Candidates, 1948–1984.* New York: Ungar, 1985.

Squire, Peverill, ed. *The Iowa Caucuses and the Presidential Nominating Process.* Boulder, Colo.: Westview, 1989.

Stephenson, D. Grier, Jr. *Campaigns and the Court: The U.S. Supreme Court in Presidential Elections.* New York: Columbia University Press, 1999.

Sullivan, Denis G., Jeffrey L. Pressman, and F. Christopher Arterton. *Explorations in Convention Decision-Making: The Democratic Party in the 1970s.* San Francisco: Freeman, 1974.

Tenpas, Kathryn D. *Presidents as Candidates: Inside the White House for the Presidential Campaign.* New York: Garland, 1997.

Thurber, James A., and Candice J. Nelson, eds. *Campaigns and Elections American Style.* Boulder, Colo.: Westview, 1995.

Troy, Gil. *See How They Ran: The Changing Role of the Presidential Candidate.* Rev. ed. Cambridge, Mass.: Harvard University Press, 1996.

Tugwell, Rexford G. *How They Became President: Thirty-Five Ways to the White House.* New York: Simon and Schuster, 1965.

Wattenberg, Martin P. *The Rise of Candidate-Centered Politics: Presidential Elections of the 1980s.* Cambridge, Mass.: Harvard University Press, 1991.

Wayne, Stephen J. *The Road to the White House 2000: The Politics of Presidential Elections.* New York: St. Martin's, 1999.

West, Darrell M. *Air Wars: Television Advertising in Election Campaigns, 1952–2000.* 3d ed. Washington, D.C.: CQ Press, 2001.

White, Theodore H. *America in Search of Itself: The Making of the President, 1956–1980.* New York: Harper and Row, 1982.

Witcover, Jules. *No Way to Pick a President.* New York: Farrar, Straus, and Giroux, 1999.

Illustration Credits

1 Introduction
2 AP/Wide World Photos   5 AP/Wide World Photos
13 Library of Congress

2 Chronology of Presidential Elections
18 John Frost, *History of the United States, 1836,* The New York Public Library   19 Library of Congress   21 Courtesy of the New-York Historical Society, New York City   25 Library of Congress   34 Bettmann/Corbis Archive   35 Library of Congress   36 Library of Congress   37 Library of Congress   41 Library of Congress   43 Library of Congress   44 Library of Congress   47 (left) Library of Congress (right) Library of Congress 49 Library of Congress   51 Franklin D. Roosevelt Library   52 Smithsonian Institute   54 AP/Wide World Photos   55 Franklin D. Roosevelt Library   58 (left) Library of Congress, (center) Library of Congress, (right) courtesy of the New-York Historical Society, New York City 62 From the collection of the St. Louis Mercantile Library Association 66 *Charleston Gazette* 69 Library of Congress   71 AP/Wide World Photos   74 Corbis Sygma 77 AP/Wide World Photos   79 David Valdez, White House   83 AP/Wide World Photos   85 MTV   87 Reuters 89 Reuters   92 AP/Wide World Photos

3 Presidential Primaries
100 No credit   107 No credit

5 The Electoral College
171 AP/Wide World Photos

Index